Introduction to

Guatemala

Spanning the narrow Central American isthmus,
Guatemala is a physical and cultural microcosm of Latin
America, incorporating an astonishing array of contradictions in a country roughly the size of Ireland. Uniquely,
it still has a population which is at least half native
American, and the strength of indigenous culture is
greater here than perhaps anywhere else in the hemisphere. More than anywhere, Guatemala is the product of
the merger of sophisticated pre-Columbian cultures with
Spanish colonialism and the consumerist influences of
modern America.

Today, its **Maya** society is a hybrid of ancient traditions and more recent cultural and religious
influences, which combine – above all in the
highlands – to form perhaps the most distinctive
culture in all of Latin America. Countering this is
a powerful **ladino** society of equal strength, a
blend of Latin machismo that is decidedly urban and commercial in its
outlook. At the edges there is a certain blurring between the two cultures,
but the contrast between the hustle of Guatemala City and the murmur of
indigenous village markets could hardly be more extreme.

Both cultures have left Guatemala with an exceptional wealth of **architectural** and **archeological remains**, and it is this outstanding legacy
that makes the country so compelling for the traveller. The Maya civilization, which dominated the entire region from 2000 BC until the arrival
of the Spanish, has left its traces everywhere, and Guatemala is scattered

iii

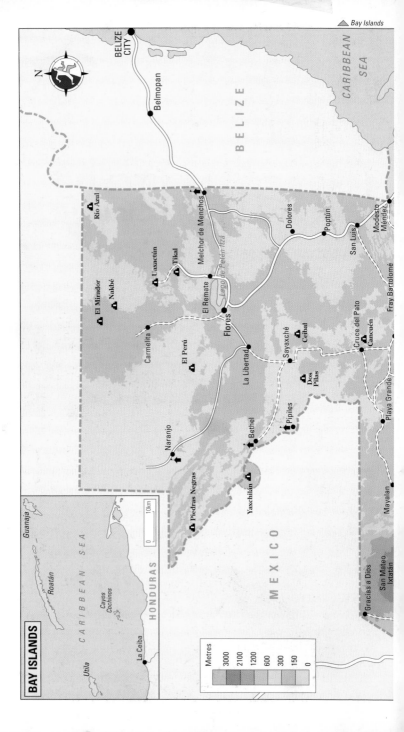

▲ Bay Islands

BAY ISLANDS

iv

Guatemala

written and researched by

Iain Stewart

with additional contributions by

Peter Eltringham and Mark Whatmore

ROUGH
GUIDES

www.roughguides.com

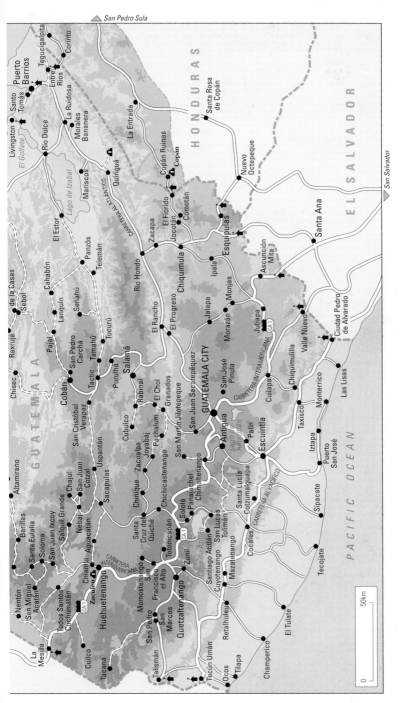

v

Fact file

● The republic of Guatemala is situated at the northern end of the Central American isthmus, bordered by Mexico to the north and west, Belize to the northeast, and Honduras and El Salvador to the south and east. Its 108,890 square kilometres include 328km of Pacific coastline and 74km of Caribbean coast.

● By October 2001, Guatemala's population had reached over 13.5 million, and with one of the highest birth rates in the hemisphere, this figure is set to double by 2022. Eighty percent of *Guatemaltecos* live in the south of the country, in a swathe of mountainous land between the Mexican and Salvadorean borders; the northern and eastern departments are very thinly populated.

● Ethnically, the population is almost equally divided between indigenous Maya and ladinos (who are mainly of mixed race) though there are also tiny numbers of black Caribs or Garífuna (around 6000), ethnic Chinese and non-Maya Xinca, as well as several thousand resident European and North Americans. Though Spanish is the official language, there are 23 other languages spoken, including K'iche', Mam, Kaqchikel, and Q'eqchi'.

● Guatemala draws almost a million tourists a year, up from around 700,000 in 1995, with the sector overtaking coffee as the nation's largest income-earner in 2001. Sugar, bananas and textiles are the other main exports. There is little domestic industry.

● Around 63 percent of Guatemalans are nominally Roman Catholic – the lowest figure in Latin America – though many highland Maya practise a unique mix of religion that's heavily dependent on ancient religious ritual. Most others worship at US-based evangelical Protestant churches.

with ruins, rising mysteriously out of the rainforest and marking out the more fertile of the highland valleys. These ancient cities, such as the magnificent Tikal, surrounded by pristine jungle, are a fascinating testament to a civilization of great complexity and with a tremendous enthusiasm for architectural grandeur. In contrast, the country's ladino heritage is typified by the colonial grace and beauty of the

Physically, Guatemala offers an astonishing range of landscape, defined by extremes, and shaken by regular earthquakes and volcanic eruptions

former capital, Antigua, with almost every town or large village in the country boasting a whitewashed church, belltower and a classic Spanish-style plaza.

Physically, Guatemala offers an astonishing range of **landscape**, defined by extremes, and shaken by regular earthquakes and volcanic eruptions (though you're unlikely to encounter either of these). In the south, the steamy ladino-dominated Pacific coastal plain rises towards a string of magnificent **volcanic cones** that mark the southern limit of the central highlands. Beyond them lies a series of rolling hills and larger granite peaks, forming the country's heartland, and home to the vast majority of the indigenous population. The scenery here is astonishingly beautiful with unfeasibly picturesque lakes, forests and lush pine-clad hills, dotted with sleepy traditional villages. Further east towards the Caribbean coast, the landscape is more **tropical**, replete with mangrove swamps, banana plantations and coconut palms. In the north of the country the peaks of the last great **mountain** range, the Cuchumatanes, drop off into the lowlands of Petén – a huge, sparsely populated area of virgin **rainforest**, among the best preserved in Latin America, which harbours a tremendous array of **wildlife**, including jaguar,

Maya fiestas

Guatemala's indigenous fiestas are some of the most compelling in Latin America: riotous, often deeply poignant and very drunken celebrations of Maya identity. Though there's often a central religious element, usually focusing on a patron saint's day, most tend to follow a familiar, tried-and-tested formula. Count on seeing a series of almost comical-looking, traditional costumed dances like the Dance of the Conquistadors, the performances charged with bitter historical sentiment and heavy symbolism. Obligatory barrages of eardrum-threatening firecrackers, wobbly-looking fairground rides, endless marimba music and lashings of liquor complete the scene. The most spectacular events also include an additional element: the wild horse race at Todos Santos Cuchumatán (see p.216), the kite-flying extravaganzas at Santiago Sacatépequez and Sumpango (see p.93 and p.94) or the Palo Volador (see p.144), a Maya-style bungy jump (see pp.137 and 300).

vii

An archeological hotbed

The remote jungles of Petén are currently one of the most exciting archeological zones in the world, the target of more than a dozen ongoing digs which have unearthed several revelatory findings. Major progress in the reading of Maya glyphs has meant that the history of the core region, and the nature of Maya society, is becoming increasingly clear. Ruling family lineages, dates of accessions and wars and the key political alliances are all being steadily chronicled, while it's now known that bloodletting and human sacrifice were pivotal to Maya religious life. Yet the events that have grabbed the recent international headlines have been the unearthing of the remains of three buried Maya cities – Wakná (see p.358), El Pajaral and Cancuén (see p.364) in the Petén. Only one (Wakná, located near El Mirador, which was found using satellite imagery) was actually a genuine "lost city", though El Pajaral and Cancuén were revealed to be much larger than originally thought. Nevertheless, there are hundreds more huge jungle-clad mounds in the region, and, such is the nature of the terrain, few archeologists would contest that there are almost certainly more ruined cities to be discovered.

> **All this natural beauty exists against the nagging background of Guatemala's turbulent and bloody history**

ocelot, tapir, spider and howler monkeys, storks and scarlet macaws. Further south, in the **cloudforests** near Cobán, you may glimpse the elusive quetzal, Guatemala's national symbol, or spot a manatee in the Río Dulce.

All this natural beauty exists against the nagging background of Guatemala's turbulent and bloody **history**. Over the years the huge gulf between the rich and the poor, and between indigenous and ladino culture has produced bitter conflict. With the signing of the 1996 Peace Accords between the government and the former guerrillas, however, the armed confrontation has ceased and things have calmed down considerably, though many of the country's deep-rooted inequalities remain. Despite the country's considerable difficulties, most travellers find Guatemalans to be extraordinarily courteous and helpful. Though more reserved than neighbouring Mexicans or Salvadoreans and often formal in social situations, they are an incredibly hospitable nation, and you'll find most people only too eager to help you make the right bus connection or practise your Spanish.

Where to go

Whilst each region has its own particular attractions, it is to the Maya-dominated **western highlands** that most travellers head first, and rightly so. The colour, the markets, the fiestas, the culture, and above all the people make it a wholly unique experience. And it seems almost an unfair bonus that all this is set in countryside of such mesmerizing beauty: for photographers, it's exceptional. **Antigua**, the delightful colonial capital is another huge draw, its refined atmosphere and café society contrasting with the hectic, fume-filled bustle of the current capital **Guatemala City**. To the west is **Lago de Atitlán**, an astonishingly beautiful highland lake, ringed by sentinel-like volcanoes. The shores of the lake are dotted with traditional indigenous villages, as well as a few tranquil low-key settlements such as **Santa Cruz la Laguna**, **San Marcos la Laguna** and **Jaibalito**, where there are some idyllic hotels and breathtaking shoreline hikes. The booming lakeside resort of **Panajachel** is much more lively, with excellent restaurants, cafés and textile stores, while the bohemian scene and rock-bottom prices in **San Pedro la Laguna** attract travellers from all over the world. High up above the lake, the traditional Maya town of **Sololá** has one of the country's best (and least-touristy) markets, a complete contrast to the vast twice-weekly affair at **Chichicastenango**, with

its incredible selection of weavings and handicrafts. Further west, the proud provincial city of **Quetzaltenango (Xela)**, an increasingly important language-school centre, makes a good base for exploring the amazing natural spa at Fuentes Georginas and the forest-fringed crater lake of Volcán Chicabal. North of Quetzaltenango are the market towns of **Momostenango**, famed for its wool production, and **San Francisco el Alto**, while **Huehuetenango**, the gateway to Guatemala's greatest mountain range, the **Cuchumatanes**, is a little further distant. In these granite peaks you'll find superb scenery and some of the most isolated and traditional villages in the Maya world, with **Nebaj**, in the Ixil triangle, and **Todos Santos Cuchumatán** both making good bases for some serious hiking and adventure.

> In these granite peaks you'll find superb scenery and some of the most isolated and traditional villages in the Maya world

The **Pacific coast** (usually taken to mean the entire coastal plain) is generally hot and dull, with scrubby, desolate **beaches** backed by a smattering of mangrove swamps. The sole exception is the relaxed seaside village of **Monterrico**, part of a wildlife reserve where you can watch sea turtles coming ashore to lay their eggs. Inland, the region includes some of the country's most productive farmland, devoted purely to commercial agriculture, and dotted with bustling urban centres such as **Escuintla** and **Retalhuleu**. Points of interest are thin on the ground, confined mainly to the pre-Columbian ruins of **Abaj Takalik** and the three minor sites around the town of **Santa Lucía Cotzumalguapa**.

None of these, however, can compete with the archeological wonders of **Petén**. This unique lowland area, which makes up about a third of the country, is covered with dense tropical forest and savannah. Though loggers and ranchers have laid waste to large chunks of the terrain, much still remains to be seen, with reserves alive with wildlife and dotted with outstanding Maya ruins. The only places of any size are the twin towns of **Flores**, superbly situated on an islet on Lago de Petén Itzá, and neighbouring Santa Elena, which is much scruffier and less appealing. It's easy to reach **Tikal**, the most impressive of all the Maya sites and rivalling any ruin in Latin America, from either of these towns, or the pleasant, low-key village of **El Remate**, set on the eastern shores of Lago de Petén Itzá. The region's forest also hides numerous smaller sites, including **Yaxhá**, **Ceibal**, **Yaxchilán** (just across the border in Mexico) and **Uaxactún**, while adventurous travellers may seek out Petén's more remote ruins, such as the dramatic, pre-Classic sites of **El Mirador** (possibly even larger than Tikal) and **Nakbé**, which require days of tough travel to reach.

Finally, the **east** of the country includes another highland area, this time with little to offer the visitor, though in the Motagua valley you'll find the superb Maya site of **Quiriguá**, while just over the border in Honduras are the first-class ruins of **Copán**. Further into Honduras are the idyllic **Bay Islands**, whose pristine coral reefs

Men of maize

Sacred to the ancient Maya, who believed that the gods fashioned man from maize dough, corn is Guatemala's staple food. A central part of almost every meal, it's usually consumed as a *tortilla*, a flat, hand-shaped corn pancake which is toasted over a fire on a metal hot plate called a *comal*, though *tamales* (steamed corn dumplings stuffed with meat) are also eaten. Maize is deeply entwined with the national identity: the original magical realist novel, *Men of Maize*, was written by a Guatemalan, Miguel Ángel Asturias, the first Latin American to win the Nobel prize for literature.

offer some of the finest scuba-diving and snorkelling in the Caribbean. You can also travel up into the rain-soaked highlands of the **Verapaces**, similar in many ways to the central highlands, though fresher and greener. Just south of here is **Lago de Izabal**, Guatemala's largest inland lake, around whose shores there's plenty of interest including an amazing hot spring waterfall, the Boquerón canyon and the bird-rich wetlands of the Reserva Bocas del Polochic. The lake drains into the Caribbean via the **Río Dulce**, a series of remarkable jungle-clad gorges just to the east. At the mouth of the river is the funky town of **Lívingston**, an outpost of Caribbean culture and home to Guatemala's only black community, the Garífuna.

When to go

Guatemala enjoys one of the most pleasant climates on earth, with the bulk of the country enjoying warm or hot days with mild or cool evenings year-round. The immediate climate is largely determined by **altitude**. In those areas between 1300 and 1600 metres, which includes Guatemala City, Antigua, Lago de Atitlán and Cobán, the air is almost always fresh and the nights cool and, despite the heat of the midday sun, humidity is never a problem. However, parts of the departments of Quetzaltenango, Huehuetenango and El Quiché are above this height, so have a cool, damp climate with distinctly chilly nights between early December and late February. Low-lying Petén suffers from sticky, steamy conditions most of the year, as do the Pacific and Caribbean coasts, though here at least you can usually rely on the welcome relief of a sea breeze.

The **rainy season** runs roughly from May to October, with the worst of the rain falling in September and October. In Petén, however, the season can extend into December, whilst around Cobán and on the Caribbean coast it can rain at any time of the year. Even at the height of the wet season, though, the rain is usually confined to late afternoon downpours with most of the rest of the day being warm and pleasant. In many parts of the country you can travel without disruption throughout the rainy season, although in the more out-of-the-way places, like the Cuchumatanes, flooding may slow you down by converting the roads into a sea of mud. Also, if you intend visiting Petén's more remote ruins, you'd be well advised to wait until February, as the mud can be thigh deep at the height of the rains. The **Bay Islands' climate** is distinctly different, with clear skies between March and September, and rains starting in October and continuing until late February – Christmas and New Year are often very wet.

The **busiest time** for tourists is between December and March, though plenty of people take their summer vacations here in July and August. This is also the period when the language schools and hotels are at their fullest, and many of them hike their prices correspondingly.

Average temperatures (°F)

	Jan/Feb		Mar/Apr		May/Jun		July/Aug		Sept/Oct		Nov/Dec	
Puerto Barrios												
Avg daily temp	27	28	29	31	32	31	30	30	30	30	29	28
Huehuetenango												
Avg daily temp	22	24	27	30	31	28	26	25	26	25	23	22
Guatemala City												
Avg daily temp	23	25	27	28	29	27	26	26	26	24	23	22

33

things not to miss

It's not possible to see everything that Guatemala has to offer in one trip – and we don't suggest you try. What follows is a selective taste of the country's highlights: amazing ruined cities, outstanding national parks, spectacular wildlife – and even good things to eat and drink. It's arranged in five colour-coded categories, so that you can browse through to find the very best things to see, do and experience. All highlights have a page reference to take you straight into the guide, where you can find out more.

02 National Archeological Museum Page **180** • Guatemala City's Museo Nacional de Arqueología y Etnología contains a wonderful collection of Maya artwork and jewellery, plus carved stone stelae and altars from many of the major Petén sites.

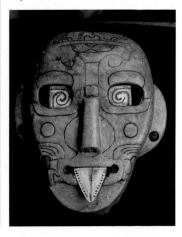

01 Semana Santa Page **100** • During Easter Week, head for either Antigua for its epic Catholic processions, or Santiago Atitlán to witness the symbolic confrontation between Maximón and Christ.

03 Chichicastenango Page **138** • Go textile- and souvenir-hunting at the legendary twice-weekly market of Chichicastenango.

04 Caribbean architecture Page **264** • The quirky clapped-out timber buildings of Puerto Barrios, a faded port with little else going for it.

05 Río Dulce Page **271** • Explore the soaring jungle-clad gorges and estuaries of Guatemala's "sweet river" by boat, and marvel at the many water lilies.

XV

06 Scuba diving Page **401** • Glide along the pristine coral-reef walls of Roatán and Guanaja in the idyllic Honduran Bay Islands.

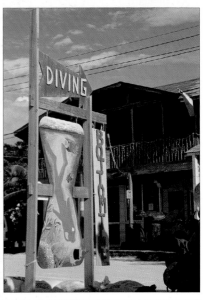

07 Lívingston Page **268** • Shake your booty to the hypnotic drum-driven punta beat in the swinging Garífuna village of Lívingston.

08 Copán ruins Page **383** • A towering hieroglyphic stairway, an outstanding site museum and a plethora of exquisitely carved stelae and altars to admire at the remains of the city dubbed the "Athens of the Maya World".

09 Highland hiking Page **217** • Explore the beguiling highland paths in the Cuchumatanes mountains around San Juan Atitán and Todos Santos Cuchumatán.

10 **Volcán de Pacaya** Page **90** • Hike for a glimpse of the lava-spewing cone of Pacaya, Central America's most spectacular sound and light show.

11 **Quetzal** Page **303** • Guatemala's emblematic national symbol inhabits the cloudforests of the Verapaces.

12 **Kite-flying fiestas** Pages **93 & 94** • Head for Santiago Sacatépequez and Sumpango and watch some dazzling aerial displays.

13 Monterrico Page **246** • A rich reserve and village on the Pacific coast, with a sweeping beach where three species of sea turtle nest, including the giant leatherback.

14 Río Cahabón Page **313** • The emerald ribbon that cuts through pristine lowland jungle to Lago de Izabal is perfect for white-water rafting.

15 Maximón Page **167 & 192** • Visit the pagan temple of this liquor-swilling, cigar-smoking evil saint.

16 Eastern highlands Page **280** • Ancient eroded volcanoes, cacti-spiked hills, a sparkling crater lake and virtually no other tourists.

17 Fuentes Georginas Page **192** • A stunning natural spa, with open-air pools fringed by a dense foliage of ferns, perched halfway up a volcano near Quetzaltenango.

18 Esquipulas Page **287** • The vast basilica of Esquipulas is home to an ancient carved image of a black Christ, and the focus for Central America's largest pilgrimage.

19 Baroque churches Page **104** • Built in a unique Iberian-American "squat-Baroque" style – to resist the ever-present threat of earthquakes – Guatemala's churches boast fabulously decorative and theatrically embellished facades.

20 San Francisco el Alto Page **195** • One of the wildest markets in Central America, a seething mass of highland Maya humanity – though not the place to buy souvenirs, unless you want to take home a pig.

21 **Finca el Paraíso** Page **277** • Soak away an afternoon or more at the blissful hot spring waterfall and natural pools near the Finca el Paraíso.

22 **The Ixil Triangle** Page **146** • Bewitching scenery and the colour, costume and traditions of three remote highland villages: Nebaj, Cotzal and Chajul.

23 **Semuc Champey** Page **312** • Swim in the exquisite turquoise pools of Semuc Champey, a natural limestone bridge over the Río Cahabón.

24 **Punta de Manabique** Page **267** • Protected Caribbean nature reserve, rich in wildlife and boasting breathtaking beaches.

25 **Todos Santos Cuchumatán** Page **215** • This normally sleepy town hosts a legendary fiesta, featuring a rip-roaring horse race, in a stunning highland valley setting.

26 **Antigua** Page **94** • The serene, cultured former capital, with an incredible legacy of colonial architecture, is a UNESCO World Heritage site and one of the most elegant cities in the Americas.

27 **Tikal** Page **340** • Monumental Maya temples set in a tropical forest reserve alive with screaming howler monkeys and chattering parakeets.

28 **Chicken buses** Page **31** • Garishly painted, outrageously uncomfortable, there's never a dull journey aboard Guatemala's iconic fume-belching camionetas.

29 Cobán Page **305** • Some of the world's finest coffee is grown in the easy-going environs of the capital of Alta Verapaz.

30 Quiriguá Page **259** • Diminutive Maya site, where the central plaza is dotted with colossal sandstone stelae embellished with glyphs and images of the ruler, Cauac Sky.

31 Whale shark Page **394** • Search for the world's largest fish, a year-round resident in the seas around Utila.

32 **Jungle trekking** Page **356** • Tramp through the Maya Biosphere Reserve to the jungle-choked remains of the cities of El Mirador and Nakbé in the Petén.

33 **Lago de Atitlán** Page **154** • Encircled by three volcanoes, the awesome crater lake of Lago de Atitlán was famously described by Aldous Huxley as "the most beautiful lake in the world".

contents

using the Rough Guide

We've tried to make this Rough Guide a good read and easy to use. The book is divided into six main sections, and you should be able to find whatever you want in one of them.

colour section

The front colour section offers a quick tour of Guatemala. The **introduction** aims to give you a feel for the place, with suggestions on where to go. We also tell you what the weather is like and include a basic country fact file. Next, our authors round up their favourite aspects of Guatemala in the **things not to miss** section – whether it's great food, amazing sights or a special hotel. Right after this comes a full **contents** list.

basics

The Basics section covers all the **pre-departure** nitty-gritty to help you plan your trip. This is where to find out which airlines fly to your destination, what paperwork you'll need, what to do about money and insurance, about internet access, food, security, public transport, car rental – in fact just about every piece of **general practical information** you might need.

guide

This is the heart of the Rough Guide, divided into user-friendly chapters, each of which covers a specific region. Every chapter starts with a list of **highlights** and an **introduction** that helps you decide where to go, depending on your time and budget. Likewise, introductions to the various towns and smaller regions within each chapter should help you plan your

itinerary. We start most town accounts with information on arrival and accommodation, followed by a tour of the sights, and finally reviews of places to eat and drink, and details of nightlife. Longer accounts also have a directory of practical listings. Each chapter concludes with **public transport** details for that region.

contexts

Read Contexts to get a deeper understanding of what makes Guatemala tick. We include a brief history, articles about **the Maya** and **human rights**, and a detailed further reading section that reviews dozens of **books** relating to the country.

language

The **language** section gives useful guidance for speaking Spanish and pulls together all the vocabulary you might need on your trip, including a comprehensive menu reader. Here you'll also find a glossary of words and terms peculiar to the country.

index + small print

Apart from a **full index**, which includes maps as well as places, this section covers publishing information, credits and acknowledgements, and also has our contact details in case you want to send in updates and corrections to the book – or suggestions as to how we might improve it in future editions.

chapter map of **Guatemala**

contents

contexts

language

index and small print

map symbols

maps are listed in the full index using coloured text

-------	International border	†	Immigration post
- - - -	Chapter division boundary	✈	Airport
CA 1	Carretera Interamericana	★	Bus stop
======	Other major highways	P	Parking
======	Minor highways & roads (paved)	⛽	Gas station
= = = =	Unpaved highways & roads	⚠	Campground
------	Seasonal track	◉	Accommodation
- - - - -	Footpath	(i)	Information office
━━━━	Railway	(C)	Telephone
— — -	Ferry route	✉	Post office
〽	Mountain range	@	Internet access
🌊	Waterfall	■	Building
🌋	Volcano	✚	Church
🕳	Cave	✝	Cemetery
⚓	Ruin	▨	Park
♜	Castle	⋯	Beach
⊙	Statue		

basics

basics

Getting there

Most people **get to** Guatemala by plane, arriving in the capital Guatemala City. There's another international airport at Flores, which is handy for the ruins of Tikal, but this is only served by a few international flights, all from neighbouring Mexico and Belize. If you're already in Central America or Mexico, all Guatemalan land and sea entry points are relatively hassle-free, unless you're bringing your own transport, in which case you can expect plenty of red tape and delays.

Airfares always depend on the **season**, with the highest being from Christmas to February, around Easter and in July and August; fares drop at all other times of year. You can often cut costs by going through a **specialist flight agent** – either a consolidator, who buys up blocks of tickets from the airlines and sells them at a discount, or a **discount agent**, who in addition to dealing with reduced-price flights may also offer special student and youth fares as well as travel insurance, rail passes, car rentals, tours and the like. Another possibility is to see if you can arrange a **courier flight**, although you'll need a flexible schedule, and preferably be travelling alone with very little luggage. In return for shepherding a parcel through customs, you can expect to get a deeply discounted ticket. You'll probably also be restricted in the duration of your stay.

If Guatemala is only one stop on a longer journey, you might want to consider buying a **Round-the-World (RTW) ticket**. Guatemala City is very rarely included on standard itineraries, however, so it's best to get an agent to assemble one for you, which will inevitably work out to be more expensive than many standard RTW tickets. Figure on around US$2400/£1450 for a RTW ticket including Guatemala.

Booking flights online

Many airlines and discount travel websites offer you the opportunity to book your tickets online, cutting out the costs of agents and middlemen. Good deals can often be found through discount or auction sites, as well as through the airlines' own websites.

Online booking agents and general travel sites

ⓦ**www.cheapflights.com** Flight deals, travel agents, plus links to other travel sites.

ⓦ**www.cheaptickets.com** Discount flight specialist.

ⓦ**www.deckchair.com** Extensive choice of tickets, drawing on a wide range of airlines.

ⓦ**www.etn.nl/discount.htm** A hub of consolidator and discount agent web links, maintained by the nonprofit European Travel Network.

ⓦ**www.expedia.com** Discount airfares, all-airline search engine and daily deals.

ⓦ**www.flyaow.com** Online air travel info and reservations site.

ⓦ**www.hotwire.com** Bookings from the US only. Last-minute savings of up to forty percent on regular published fares. Travellers must be at least eighteen and there are no refunds, transfers or changes allowed. Log-in required.

ⓦ**www.lastminute.com** Offers good last-minute holiday package and flight-only deals.

ⓦ**www.priceline.com** Bookings from the US only. Name-your-own-price website that has deals at around forty percent off standard fares. You cannot specify flight times (although you do specify dates) and the tickets are non-refundable, non-transferable and non-changeable.

ⓦ**www.princeton.edu/Main/air800.html** Has an extensive list of airline toll-free numbers and websites.

ⓦ**www.skyauction.com** Bookings from the US only. Auctions tickets and travel packages using a "second bid" scheme. The best strategy is to offer the maximum you're willing to pay, since if you win you'll pay just enough to beat the runner-up regardless of your maximum bid.

ⓦ**www.smilinjack.com/airlines.htm** Lists an up-to-date compilation of airline website addresses.

ⓦ**travelocity.com** Destination guides, hot web fares and best deals for car rental and accommodation. Provides access to SABRE, the most comprehensive central travel reservations system in the US.

🖰 www.travelshop.com.au Australian website offering discounted flights, packages, insurance and online bookings.

🖰 http://travel.yahoo.com Incorporates a lot of Rough Guide material in its coverage of destination countries and cities across the world, with information about places to eat and sleep.

🖰 www.uniquetravel.com.au Australian site with a good range of packages and good-value flights.

Flights from the USA and Canada

Only a small number of North American airlines fly to Guatemala and most flights to the country are routed through a few US hub cities. Flights from the southern US cities of **Miami, Houston** and **New Orleans** are non-stop and usually cost between US$350 and US$550 return. Flights from **Atlanta, Dallas** or **LA** are also non-stop, but tend to cost an extra US$50–100. There are some non-stop flights available from **New York** and **San Francisco**, though most flights require a change of plane in either the US or Mexico; expect to pay between US$500 and US$700.

From Canada

There are no non-stop flights **from Canada** to Guatemala, so your best bet is to fly to Miami or Houston and change there. Non-stop flights from Toronto to Miami can go as low as C$250, while flights from Vancouver to Houston can drop to around C$450.

Airlines

Aeroméxico ☎1-800/237-6639, 🖰 www .aeromexico.com. Direct flights from many US gateway cities to Mexico City, for connections on Méxicana Airlines to Guatemala City.
American Airlines ☎1-800/433-7300, 🖰 www.aa.com. Three daily flights from Miami; two daily flights from Los Angeles (one via Dallas).
Continental Airlines ☎1-800/231-0856, 🖰 www.continental.com. Two daily flights from Houston, and two flights weekly from Newark. Route-sharing with Air Canada means good connections from Canada.
Delta Air Lines ☎1-800/241-4141, 🖰 www.delta .com. Daily flights from Atlanta and New York.

Iberia ☎1-800/772-4642, 🖰 www.iberia.com. One daily flight from Miami to Guatemala City.
Méxicana ☎1-800/531-7921, 🖰 www.mexicana.com. Frequent flights from Chicago, Denver, LA, Newark, San Francisco, Montréal and Toronto to Mexico City, with connections to Guatemala City. Tickets can be linked to flights on subsidiary airline Aerocaribe to Flores airport in Petén.
Northwest ☎1-800/447-4747, in Canada ☎514 /397-0775, 🖰 www.nwa.com. One daily flight from Houston.
Taca ☎1-888/477-8222, 🖰 www.grupotaca.com. Reservations for four of the national airlines of Central America (including Aviateca of Guatemala). Two daily flights from Los Angeles and Miami, one daily flight from New York, Washington and Dallas, and thrice-weekly flights from Atlanta, all to Guatemala City.
United Airlines ☎1-800/538–2929, 🖰 www.ual .com. One daily flight from Los Angeles and three flights weekly from San Francisco.

Courier flights

Air Courier Association ☎1-800/282-1202, 🖰 www.aircourier.org. Courier flight broker. Membership (1 year US$49, 3 years US$98) also entitles you to a twenty percent discount on travel insurance and name-your-own-price non-courier flights.
Airtech see "Discount travel companies", below.
International Association of Air Travel Couriers ☎561/582-8320, 🖰 www.courier.org. Courier flight broker with membership fee of US$45 a year.
Now Voyager ☎212/431-1616, 🖰 www .nowvoyagertravel.com. Courier flight broker and consolidator, with an annual membership fee of US$50.

Discount travel companies

Airtech ☎212/219-7000, 🖰 www.airtech.com. Standby seat broker; also deals in consolidator fares and courier flights. Very good deals on their website, if you're prepared to be flexible.
Council Travel ☎1-800 226 8624 or 617/528-2091, 🖰 www.counciltravel.com. Nationwide organization that mostly, but by no means exclusively, specializes in student/budget travel.
Educational Travel Center ☎1-800/747-5551 or 608/256 5551, 🖰 www.edtrav.com. Student/ youth discount agent.
Exito ☎1-800/655-4053, 🖰 www.exitotravel.com. North America's top specialist for travel to Latin

America. Website has a particularly useful airfare finder, with a comparison of the merits of various airpasses in addition to masses of invaluable travel information.

High Adventure Travel ☎1-800/350-0612 or 415/912-5600, ✉www.airtreks.com. Round-the-World tickets; the website features an interactive database that lets you build and price your own RTW itinerary.

Now Voyager ☎212/431-1616, ✉www.nowvoyager-travel.com. Courier flight broker with an excellent website. Excellent deals to Mexico and Central America.

Skylink US ☎1-800/AIR-ONLY or 212/573-8980, Canada ☎1-800/SKY-LINK. Consolidator.

STA Travel ☎1-800/777-0112 or 1-800/781-4040, ✉www.sta-travel.com. Worldwide specialists in independent travel; also travel insurance and car rental.

Travac ☎1-800/872-8800, ✉www.thetravelsite.com. Consolidator and charter broker.

Travelers Advantage Cendant Membership Services Inc ☎1-877/259-2691, ✉www.travelersadvantage.com. Discount travel club; annual membership fee required (currently US$1 for 3-month trial).

Travel Avenue ☎1-800/333-3335, ✉www.travelavenue.com. Full-service travel agent that offers discounts in the form of rebates.

Travel Cuts in Canada ☎1-800/667 2887, in US ☎416/979 2406. Foremost Canadian specialists in student fares, insurance and other travel services.

Dozens of branches throughout Canada, often on college campuses.

Worldtek Travel, ☎1/800-243-1723, ✉www.worldtek.com. Discount travel agency for worldwide travel.

Worldwide Discount Travel Club ☎305/534-2642. Discount travel club.

Organized tours

The range of **organized tours** to Guatemala and the Maya region increases every year. Specialist companies take escorted groups on tours to Maya ruins, colonial towns, markets and beaches, often crossing several borders, and with options including biking, diving, rafting and bird-watching. If time is short, these can be very good value.

Budget tour groups usually travel by van, staying at comfortable, family-run hotels or camping, and calling at the main tourist attractions as well as some lesser-known places. More expensive tours stay at some luxury hotels and lodges, and can offer caving, rafting and sea-kayaking, or take you on expeditions with archeologists and scientists to remote sites and nature reserves.

Though in most cases you could organize the same or very similar itineraries yourself for a little less money, you'll need good Spanish and plenty of patience. If you're

Airpasses

If you want to visit other countries in the region you can cut costs by taking advantage of a couple of airpasses linking gateways in North America with Guatemala and other cities in Mexico and Central America (and even onwards to South America). The conditions and costs of airpasses change frequently (and the price you pay will not include internal departure taxes), though you can expect savings of between thirty and fifty percent on the same flights bought separately. The best way to find out if you'll benefit from an airpass is to call a recommended flight specialist and book as far ahead as possible (see p.10 & 14).

The **"Latin AirFlex"** programme offered by Grupo Taca consists of pre-booked, pre-paid coupons (minimum 3, maximum 16), valid for 180 days. You'll need to book outside Central America and there's a US$75 surcharge if you fly into the region on an airline not a member of Grupo Taca; once booked, a reservation change costs US$50. For example, flying from Guatemala City to Belize City, then from there to Roatán and back to Guatemala City (3 coupons) costs US$195. If you fly to Guatemala City from Toronto, San Francisco or Montréal, for instance, using Grupo Taca, a return flight will add roughly US$530 to the above itinerary, a total of around US$725.

The **"Mexipass International"** offered by Aeroméxico and Méxicana, both of which have an extensive network throughout the US, Canada and Mexico, can be linked with flights from North America, within Mexico and on to Central America. This pass also consists of pre-booked, pre-paid coupons (minimum purchase of 3) at discount prices for travellers from outside Mexico, and is particularly good value if you're flying from Canada or Europe. The airpass is valid for ninety days and offers real savings on longer, multi-stop routes: you need to book routes and dates in advance.

considering an **upmarket package** it may be impossible to negotiate a better deal on your own anyway – tour operators are able to secure reduced rates in hotels that are not normally available to independent travellers. You'll also get at least one guide for the entire trip.

Adventure trips (sea-kayaking, caving and expeditions to remote jungle ruins) are even more difficult to organize on your own, and are best done in an organized group, with expert leaders and emergency back-up.

The tour prices below do not include airfares to the region, unless stated.

US tour operators

Adventure Center ☎1-800/228-8747 or 510/654-1879, ⊛www.adventure-center.com. Hiking and "soft adventure" specialists. The fifteen-day "Ancient Land of the Maya" trip costs US$1150 and includes highland Guatemalan market towns and the lowland ruins of Quiriguá and Tikal.

Ceiba Adventures ☎928/527-0171 or 1-800/217-1060, ⊛www.ceibaadventures.com. Multi-sport adventures, including rafting, kayaking and caving, and archeological tours throughout the Maya region. The ten-day "River of Ruins" (US$2450) tour includes many of the Usumacinta sites, plus Tikal and Ceibal.

Elderhostel ☎1-877/426-8056 or 978/323-4141, ⊛www.elderhostel.org. A nonprofit organization offering upmarket educational programmes for over-55s. Their "Maya and More" fifteen-day tour includes visits to Lago de Atitlán, Tikal and Copán and costs around US$2900 including airfare.

Far Horizons ☎1-800/552-4575, ⊛www.farhorizon.com. Some of the very best archeological trips in the region, including remote Maya sites where the latest discoveries are being unearthed like Nakbé and El Mirador in Petén. About US$3000 for a nine-day expedition.

Green Tortoise Adventure Travel ⊛www.greentortoise.com. Tours to "cool places off the beaten path" on converted buses with sleeping space. The "Southern Migration" is a very popular 23-day journey from San Francisco to Antigua in Guatemala via Baja California and Chiapas. Leaves in December and costs US$900 including food.

Guatemala Unlimited ☎1-800-733-3350 or 510/496-0631, ⊛www.guatemalaunlimited.com. Experienced company with an extensive array of custom-arranged tours to obscure and better-known Maya ruins, as well as jungle trekking, sportfishing, river-rafting, mountain-biking and volcano tours; also a good source of discount flights to Guatemala.

International Expeditions ☎1-800/633-4377, ⊛www.ietravel.com. Superbly led, very comfortable natural history tours throughout Guatemala and Belize. A nine-day "Naturalist's Quest" trip costs US$2500, while it's US$3195 for a ten-day tour of the Guatemalan highlands; both include airfare from Miami, Dallas or Houston.

Lost World Adventures ☎1-800/999-0558, ⊛www.lostworldadventures.com. Well-priced tours with accommodation in four- and five-star hotels. The "Highlands of Guatemala" trip (US$1195) also includes a night in the Petén.

Toucan Adventure Tours ☎805/927-5885, ⊛www.toucanadventures.com. Inexpensive, sociable camping tours through the Maya region of Yucatán, Belize, Guatemala and Copán in Honduras. The three-week "Ruta Maya" trip costs US$1250.

Tread Lightly Limited ☎1-800/643-0060 or 860/868-1710, ⊛www.treadlightly.com. Wide selection of top-notch "low impact" natural history, archeological and cultural trips to Guatemala, often including kayaking, rafting and hiking and reaching the less visited Maya sites. The five-day "El Petén" trip (US$595) includes the ruins of Tikal, Uaxactún, Ceibal and Aguateca while the seven-day "Guatemala Discovery" tour (US$995) explores the Western Highlands.

Victor Emanuel Nature Tours ☎1-800/328-VENT or 512/328-5221, ⊛www.ventbird.com. The best small-group bird-watching tours you can get, led by dedicated professionals. US$2795 for ten days at Chan Chich, Belize, with a side trip to Tikal.

Wilderness Travel ☎1-800/368-2794, ⊛www.wildernesstravel.com. Specialized, well-organized cultural and wildlife adventures trips. There's a twelve-day "La Ruta Maya" tour to Copán, the Guatemalan highlands and along the Usumacinta site for around US$2750, and a nine-day, marine biologist-led "Roatán Snorkelling Adventure" (around US$2600), which includes two days at Copán.

Canadian tour operators

Adventures Abroad ☎1-800/665-3998 or 604/303-1099, ⊛www.adventures-abroad.com. Adventure specialists with a selection of comfortable small group tours in Guatemala and the Maya region; the eleven-day Guatemala tour (C$1400) includes Copán, Tikal and Lago de Atitlán, while eight days in Honduras including Roatán and Copán is C$1231.

Gap Adventures ☎1-800/465-5600 or 416/260-0999, ⊛www.gap.ca. Wide range of budget group trips (some camping) with diving and kayaking; C$2370 for a 32-day "Central American Journey".

Offbeat Adventures ☎905/509-4494, ⊛www.offbeatadventures.ca. Dutch-Canadian tour company with several trips to Central America including a Guatamala and Honduras excursion (C\$2150) that includes hikes, ruins and PADI open-water scuba-diving certification.

Flights from the UK and Ireland

There are no scheduled flights from the UK (or Ireland) to Guatemala. Flying there involves changing aircraft (and sometimes airline), usually in the US cities of Miami, Atlanta or Houston; the best connections are with American, Continental and Iberia.

London airports offer the greatest variety of flights to the US and onwards to Mexico or Central America, though you can often travel from other UK airports for the same or only a slightly higher price. A scheduled return flight to Guatemala City on American (via Miami) or Continental (via Newark or Houston) will cost around £484 low season/£605 high season.

From Ireland, Delta has the widest range of direct flights from Dublin (and several from Shannon) to New York (JFK) and Atlanta, with daily connections to Mexico City and Guatemala – expect to pay around IR£535 low season/IR£674 high season. American Airlines also has competitive prices.

The only **European** airline to fly to Guatemala is Iberia (£495/625, from London via Madrid and Miami); note that Iberia flights from Manchester require an overnight stop in Madrid. KLM (via Amsterdam and Mexico City) has very similar fares.

Many travellers opt to get to Guatemala via Mexico (see p.17). British Airways flies from London non-stop to Mexico City from around £455 low/£585 high – though promotional offers can make this as little as £299 return. Continental's fares to Mexico City are similar, and their fares to Cancún are usually very competitive, at around £378/598. The very cheapest way to get to Guatemala from the UK is to book a charter flight to Cancún (as low as £220 return, though tickets are very rarely valid for more than one month) and then travel overland through Belize to the northern department of Petén – though this route entails around fourteen hours of bus travel just to get to the city of Flores.

If you want to travel through several countries in Central America, or even continue into South America, then it's worth considering an **open-jaw ticket** (which lets you fly into one city and out of another). The low-season price for an open-jaw flying London–Cancún and returning Guatemala City–London can be as little as around £500, and lots of other options are available. For details of the Mexipass International from Aeroméxico/Méxicana and the Latin AirFlex **airpasses**, see box on p.11.

On the **internet** ⊚ www.cheapflights.co.uk has one of the best and fastest farefinders, allowing rapid comparisons and best-buy deals on fares to Guatemala (and Mexico and other Central American cities) from various UK airports; the site provides a link to the travel agent offering the best price. Frequently, however, no single general travel website is consistently going to give you the best deal, so it's worth shopping around on ⊚ www.travelocity.co.uk and ⊚ www.expedia .co.uk. Despite the rapid advances of the giant internet travel sites, however, you'll find the **specialist flight agents** (see, p.14) usually offer the best fares, backed by expert first-hand travel advice. Journey Latin America's website leads the field, closely followed by those of USIT Campus, Trailfinders and South American Experience.

Airlines

If no separate Northern Ireland number is given, call the general UK number.
American Airlines ☎ 0845/778 9789, ⊚ www.aa .com. Flies daily from London Heathrow to Miami, with frequent flights on to Guatemala City (some with partner Grupo Taca).
British Airways ☎ 0845/773 3377, in Republic of Ireland ☎ 0141/2222345, ⊚ www.britishairways.com. Codeshares with American Airlines.
Continental ☎ 0800/776464, in Republic of Ireland ☎ 01/814 5311, ⊚ www.flycontinental.com. Daily flights to Houston from London, with good connections on to Guatemala City.
Delta ☎ 0800/414767, in Northern Ireland ☎ 028/9048 0526, in Republic of Ireland ☎ 1800 /414767, ⊚ www.delta.co.uk. Daily flights from London to Atlanta, with connections to Guatemala.
Grupo Taca ☎ 0870/241 0340, ⊚ www.grupotaca .com. Agents for several Central American airlines but no flights from Europe.
Iberia Airlines ☎ 020/7830 0011, in Republic of Ireland ☎ 01/677 9846, ⊚ www.iberia.com. Daily flights from Madrid to Guatemala City.
KLM ☎ 08705/074074, in Northern Ireland ☎ 0990 /074074, in Republic of Ireland ☎ 0345/445588, ⊚ www.klmuk.com. Daily flights from Heathrow and

London City (via Amsterdam) to Mexico City; from where partners fly daily to Guatemala City.

Méxicana ☎020/8492 0000, ⊛www.mextours.co.uk. Information and reservations only; no Méxicana flights between UK and Mexico, but they do sell the "Mexipass International" airpass (see box on p.11).

Courier flights

Ben's Travel ☎020/7462 0022, ⊛www.benstravel.co.uk.

International Association of Air Travel Couriers ☎0800 0746 481 or 01305/216 920, ⊛www.aircourier.co.uk. Agent for lots of companies.

Flight and travel agents

Apex Travel in Ireland ☎01/671 5933, ⊛www.apextravel.ie. Long-haul specialists.

Bridge the World ☎020/7911 0900, ⊛www.bridgetheworld.com. Specializing in Round-the-World tickets, with good deals aimed at the backpacker market.

Journey Latin America ☎020/8747 3108 or 0161/832 1441, ⊛www.journeylatinamerica.co.uk. The acknowledged leaders for airfares to Guatemala and the region, with some of the best prices on high-season flights. Also run some excellent tours (see below).

Maxwell's Travel in Ireland ☎01/677-9479. Experienced in travel to Latin America and Ireland's representatives for many of the specialist tour operators in the UK.

North South Travel ☎01245/608291, ⊛www.northsouthtravel.co.uk. Small, friendly and competitive agency offering worldwide discounted fares. Profits are used to support development projects in Africa, Asia and Latin America.

South American Experience ☎020/7976 5511, ⊛www.southamericanexperience.co.uk. Flights and tailor-made itinerary specialists, with very good airfare prices on their website and high-quality tours to the Maya region.

STA Travel ☎0870/160 6070, ⊛www.statravel.co.uk. Student/youth travel specialists with 250 branches worldwide, offering flights, tours, accommodation and many travel-related services, including a help desk if you have problems while abroad.

Trailfinders long-haul flights ☎020/7938 3939, in Ireland ☎01/677 7888, ⊛www.trailfinders.co.uk. Independent travel company with a wide range of deals on flights to Central America and specializing in tailor-made travel, hotels and car rental; there's also an excellent travel health clinic in the Kensington High St branch.

Usit Campus ☎0870/240 1010, in Ireland ☎01/602-1700, ⊛www.usitcampus.co.uk. Student/youth travel specialists, with 57 branches on university campuses, in YHA shops and in cities all over Britain and Ireland, and dozens worldwide.

Tour operators in the UK

There's a wide choice of UK-based companies offering guided **package tours** in Guatemala. Many represent very good value, with accommodation booked in quality hotels, and can be ideal if you're short of time. Most of these trips also include several stops at other sights in Mexico Belize, and Copán in Honduras, while there are also overland options that continue down as far as Panamá. They're usually led by someone from the UK who knows the area and in many cases you'll have a local guide too. The itineraries are usually very popular, so you should book well ahead. Transport varies from local "chicken" buses to comfortable a/c minibuses, fast launches to light aircraft. The list below covers the best and most experienced UK operators going to Guatemala and the Maya area; all can provide detailed information sheets on each trip. Prices given are a guide only; several tours also require local payment for some meals. Some tours operate only through the winter period but many run year-round.

Tour prices do not include airfare unless stated.

Adventure Bound ☎020/8742 8612, ⊛www.adventurebound.co.uk. A range of good budget trips through the Maya region, staying at hotels and using public transport; the nine-day "Quetzal Highway" including Tikal and Belize is £590; the 22-day "Mayan Circle" is £1150.

Cox and Kings ☎020/7873 5000, ⊛www.coxandkings.co.uk. Offers a fifteen-day "Mexico and Guatemala Grand Tour" (£2245) which visits many of the main Maya ruins, plus Lago de Atitlán and Antigua.

Dragoman ☎01728/861133, ⊛www.dragoman.com. Eight-week overland camping/hotel expeditions through Mexico and Central America to Panamá; around £1600, plus US$750 food/hotel kitty; four weeks for around £900 plus US$385 kitty.

Exodus ☎020/8675 5550, ⊛www.exodus.co.uk. Sixteen-day escorted hotel-based tours through Guatemala and the Maya region for around £1450, including airfare from London.

Explore Worldwide ☎01252/760000, ⊛www.exploreworldwide.com. Wide range of two- to three-week hotel-based tours; around £1250 for fifteen days in Mexico, Guatemala and Belize, including airfare.

Global Travel Club ☎01268/541732, ⊛www .global-travel.co.uk. Small company specializing in individually arranged diving and cultural tours to Guatemala, Mexico and Belize.

Journey Latin America ☎020/8747 8315, ⊛www.journeylatinamerica.co.uk. Wide range of high-standard group tours and tailor-made itineraries from the acknowledged experts. The three-week "Quetzal Journey" through Guatemala, Chiapas, Yucatán and Belize costs around £1820 including airfare and good-quality accommodation, but not meals.

Kumuka ☎020/7397 6664 ⊛www.kumuka.co.uk. Hotel-based group trips (maximum 15) through Mexico and Central America. The seven-week "Central American Explorer" (around £1600, excluding airfare and meals) takes in Guatemala, Chiapas and Yucatán in Mexico before visiting Belize then Honduras, Nicaragua and Costa Rica. A similar five-week trip is around £1250.

Reef and Rainforest Tours ☎01803/866965, ⊛www.reefrainforest.co.uk. Individual itineraries from a very experienced company, focusing on nature reserves, research projects and diving in the Honduran Bay Islands (and Belize).

Scuba Safaris ☎01342/851196, ⊛www.scuba -safaris.com. A knowledgeable, well-organized company, specializing in fully inclusive dive packages. Around £2000 for a week on a live-aboard boat in the Bay Islands; £200 less for a week in a luxury dive resort. Prices include airfare, overnight accommodation in Houston and six days' diving (tuition about US$200 extra).

Travelbag Adventures ☎01420/541007, ⊛www .travelbag-adventures.com. Small-group hotel-based tours through Yucatán and Central America; sixteen-day "Realm of the Maya" trip, from Cancún through Belize and Guatemala for around £1300 including airfare but not meals.

Trips ☎0117/987 2626, ⊛www.tripsworldwide .co.uk. Friendly, experienced company with an inspired range of high-quality tailor-made itineraries and tours to Guatemala, Mexico and the rest of Central America. A fifteen-day "Ruins and Rainforest" trip taking in Guatemala's Western Highlands, Tikal and parts of Belize is £1920. Also agents for many other recommended tour operators.

Wildlife Worldwide ☎020/8667 9158, ⊛www .wildlifeworldwide.com. Superb bird-watching trips in Guatemala and Belize led by expert naturalists, visiting some remote protected areas and staying at very comfortable jungle lodges. Around £2500 for sixteen days.

Flights from Australia and New Zealand

There are no direct flights from Australasia to Guatemala (or any other city in Central America), so consequently you've little choice but to fly via the US or Mexico City.

Flight Centres, STA and Trailfinders generally offer the lowest **fares**; in New Zealand also try USIT Beyond. You might also want to have a look on the **internet**: ⊛www.travel .com.au and ⊛www.travelforless.co.nz offer discounted fares.

While few Round-the-World tickets include Central America, it is possible to visit as a side trip (sometimes at extra cost) with the more flexible mileage-based tickets, such as the "Star Alliance 1" offered by Ansett Australia/Air New Zealand/United/Thai, starting at AUS$2499/NZ$3289, and "One World Explorer" by Qantas/British Airways/American Airlines/Cathay, which starts at AUS$2599 /NZ$3799, both of which allow side trips, backtracking and open-jaw travel. If you intend to see something of Mexico or other Central American countries you may want to check out the various **airpasses** on offer (see box on p.11 for details); most of the discount agents listed below can help you choose the most suitable one.

From **Australia** (Sydney), the cheapest fares **to LA** are direct on United Airlines, Qantas and Air New Zealand at AUS$1179 (low season) to AUS$1759 (high season). Via Asia, fares are higher but include an overnight stop in the carrier's home city, with the best deals on All Nippon Airways (ANA) via Osaka, and Korean Airlines via Seoul, for AUS$1429/1899. The best-value flights **to Mexico City** are with JAL (via an overnight in Tokyo) for AUS$1629/1979, however, if you're after a more direct route Air New Zealand can get you there for AUS$2429 /2802, while Qantas' and United Airlines' fares are more expensive at AUS$2669 /2857. Fares from all eastern Australian state capitals are generally the same (with Ansett and Qantas providing a free connecting service between these cities), whereas fares from Perth and Darwin are about AUS$200 more.

From Australia **to Guatemala City** (via LA on Air New Zealand continuing on Taca or Méxicana) are from AUS$2299/2899, while United have similar prices. Also for roughly the same price, both Qantas and Air New

Zealand team up with Continental to provide a through-service via LA and Houston to all the Central American capitals. American Airlines' fares via LA are higher at AUS$2699/3059, but still competitive.

From **New Zealand** (Auckland) some of the cheapest fares **to LA** are NZ$1729 (low season) and NZ$1966 (high season) on Air Tahiti Nui. Qantas Air Pacific flights (either direct or via Pacific island stopovers) are around NZ$1799/2071 and United fares are around NZ$1825/2095. If you want to fly right into Guatemala City, you'll have at least one stopover and another change of flight in the US. Air Tahiti Nui/Continental fares begin at NZ$2440/2845, with United and American working out slightly higher.

Airlines

Air New Zealand Australia ☎13 2476, New Zealand ☎0800 737000 or 09/357 3000, ⓦwww.airnz.com. Daily to LA from Sydney, Brisbane, Melbourne, Adelaide and Auckland, either direct or via Honolulu/Tonga/Fiji/Papeete.
Continental Airlines Australia ☎02/9321 9242, New Zealand ☎09/308 3350, ⓦwww.continental.com. Teams up with Qantas and Air New Zealand to offer a through-service to Guatemala via LA and Houston.
Grupo Taca Australia ☎02/9221 8200, ⓦwww.grupotaca.com. No NZ office. Alliance of four main Central American airlines, with a useful airpass connecting cities in USA, Mexico and Central America.
JAL Australia ☎02/9272 1111, New Zealand ☎09/379 9906, wwww.japanair.com. Several flights a week to LA and Mexico City from Sydney, Brisbane, Cairns and Auckland with an overnight stopover in Tokyo.
Korean Airlines Australia ☎02/9262 6000, New Zealand ☎09/307 3687, ⓦwww.koreanair.com. Several flights a week from Sydney, Brisbane and Auckland to LA with an overnight stopover in Seoul.
Qantas Australia ☎13 1313, New Zealand ☎09/357 8900 or 0800/808767, ⓦwww.qantas.com.au. Daily to LA from major Australian cities, either non-stop or via Honolulu, and daily from Auckland via Sydney.
United Airlines Australia ☎13 1777, New Zealand ☎09/379 3800, ⓦwww.ual.com. Daily to LA and San Francisco from Sydney, Melbourne and Auckland (either direct or via Honolulu) with direct connections to Guatemala City.

Travel agents

Flight Centre Australia ☎1300/733, New Zealand 09/358 4310, ⓦwww.flightcentre.com.au.
STA Travel Australia ☎1300/360960, New Zealand ☎0800/ 874773, ⓦwww.statravel.com.au.
Student Uni Travel Australia ☎02/9232 8444, ⓦwww.sut.com.au.
Thomas Cook Australia ☎131771 or 1800 /801002, New Zealand: 96 ☎09/379 3920, ⓦwww.thomascook.com.au.
Trailfinders Australia ☎02/9247 7666, ⓦwww.trailfinders.com.au. Agents for many adventure travel specialists to Mexico and Central America.
Travel.com Australia ☎02/9249 5232 or 1300 /130482, ⓦwww.travel.com.au. Excellent fare-finder on website and superb links to tours and voluntary work contacts in Guatemala.
Usit Beyond New Zealand ☎09/379 4224 or 0800/874823, ⓦwww.usitbeyond.co.nz.

Tour operators

There are a number of **tour operators** and **specialist agents** who can help co-ordinate a trip to Guatemala and Central America. Most can do anything from booking a few nights' accommodation to arranging fully escorted archeological–cultural tours. Some of the "adventure" specialists can also help organize activities such as diving, rafting and jungle treks. Note that few of the tour prices include air fares, but the same agents can usually assist with flight arrangements. Many of the US and UK specialist agents (on pp.12 & 14) will also accept bookings from Australasia and some below are agents for those companies.
Adventure Associates ☎02/9389 7466 or 1800/222141, ⓦwww.adventureassociates.com. Escorted tours and tailor-made archeological and cultural expeditions to Guatemala and the Maya region from a top company.
Adventure Specialists ☎02/9261 2927 or 1800/634465. Variety of adventure-travel options to Central America, specializing in Guatemala and Belize.
The Adventure Travel Company ☎09/3799755, ⓦwww.advakl@hot.co.nz. Agents for many of the UK and US adventure travel specialists organizing tours to Mexico and Central America.
Adventure World Australia ☎02/9567766 or 1800/221931, New Zealand ☎09/524 5118. Variety of Guatemala tours, including trips to Tikal and Chichicastenango.

Contours ☎03/9670 6900 or 1300/135391, ⓦwww.contourstravel.com.au. Specialists in cultural and archeological tours to Central America ranging from short stays to a 27-day expedition including Mexico, Guatemala, Belize and Honduras. Geckos ☎02/9290 2770, ⓦwww.geckos.com.au. Extended overland adventures from southern Mexico through Guatemala and the rest of Central America; agents for Exodus in the UK.

Overland from Mexico

It's a long haul **overland** to Guatemala from the US and Canada, with several possible routes through Mexico. For those needing a **visa** to visit any of the Central American countries, there are Guatemalan consulates in Tapachula and Comitán and a Belize consulate in Chetumal; for more on entry requirements, see p.18.

Greyhound (☎1-800/229-9424, ⓦwww.greyhound.com) runs regularly to all the major US border crossings, and some buses even take you over the frontier and into the Mexican bus station, and in many cases you can reserve tickets with their Mexican counterparts. Mexican buses similarly cross the border into US bus stations. Green Tortoise (see p.12) runs cheap and cheerful long-haul trips through Mexico to Guatemala. You can buy all these tickets and the **"Ameripass"** buspass online.

There are constant buses to Mexico City from every Mexican border crossing (roughly 18–22hr), and beyond Mexico City there are good bus connections to the main Guatemala border crossings. The best route **into Guatemala** takes you along the Carretera Interamericana (Pan-American Highway) through Oaxaca and San Cristóbal de las Casas, over the border at La Mesilla (see p.220) and then on to Huehuetenango. There's another route along Mexico's Pacific coast to Tapachula, from where you can take direct buses to Guatemala City. Alternatively, there are several border crossings (see p.364) into Guatemala's northern department of Petén: the routes via Tenosique and El Naranjo, and Frontera Corozal and Bethel are the most popular points of entry.

Driving south may give you a lot of freedom, but it does entail a great deal of bureaucracy. You need a separate insurance policy for Central America (sold at the border). Sanborn's (in US ☎1-800/222-0158) arranges insurance for Mexico and Central America, and also offers legal assistance, road maps and guides, and a 24-hour emergency hotline. The car will also require an entry permit, for which you'll need to show the registration and licence. US, Canadian, EU, Australian and New Zealand driving licences are valid in Mexico and throughout Central America, but it's a good idea to arm yourself with an **International Driving Licence** as well. If you belong to a motoring organization at home you may find they'll offer advice, maps and even help from reciprocal organizations in Mexico. Unleaded petrol/gasoline is widely available in the region.

Red tape and visas

Citizens of the EU, the US, Canada, Japan, Switzerland, Norway, Mexico, Israel, Brazil, Australia and New Zealand need only a **valid passport** to enter Guatemala. Passport-holders from some countries (including the Czech Republic and South Africa) also need a **tourist card**, available at the point of entry and costing US$5; these are valid for up to ninety days. Finally, citizens from a number of countries including most of Africa and Asia need **visas** (US$10), which must be obtained in advance from a Guatemalan consulate and may take up to a month to process. If you're in any doubt about whether you need a visa for Guatemala it's always worth phoning an embassy or consulate to check on the latest entry requirements; there are embassies in all the region's capitals.

When you arrive at immigration you may be asked by the official how long you plan to stay, and offered thirty, sixty or ninety days. If you want ninety days make sure you get it. There is no charge to enter Guatemala, though it's common for border officials at land crossings to ask for a fee (typically Q10/US$1.25), which is destined straight for their back pockets; travellers often avoid payment of this by asking for *un recibo* (a receipt), but be prepared for a lengthy delay before being waved through.

If you want to **extend your visit** for an additional 90 days, go to the immigration department (*migración*) in the Inguat (tourist information) building at 7 Av 1–17, Zona 4 in Guatemala City, or simply cross a border and re-enter. There's also a new Antigua immigration office opening at 4 Av and 5 C in late 2001; and plans to open other offices in Panajachel and Quetzaltenango – check with the Inguat tourist information offices in those towns to see if they're open yet.

Travelling over the border **to Honduras** is very straightforward for most nationalities. Citizens of the US, EU, Canada, Switzerland, Norway, Japan, Australia and New Zealand with a valid passport get a thirty-day stamp at the border on arrival, which can be extended to a maximum of ninety days at immigration offices throughout the country. There is an semi-official charge of US$0.50 to enter the country, though border officials usually demand a dollar or more. Citizens of South Africa and many Eastern European, Asian and African countries will need a **visa** to enter Honduras, best obtained at the embassy in Guatemala City (see p.88) or at the consulate in Esquipulas (see p.290), close to the border with Copán. A search on the Honduran government website @www.sre.hn (in Spanish only) will reveal a list of **Honduran embassies**.

Note that if you plan to go over the border **into Mexico**, to Yaxchilán (see p.367) or Palenque for a few days, travellers entering from Guatemala are currently only receiving **fifteen-day visas** due to the unstable political situation in the state of Chiapas.

Useful websites

US State Department Travel Advisories @ http://travel.state.gov/travel_warnings.html. Website providing "consular information sheets" detailing the dangers of travelling in most countries of the world.
British Foreign and Commonwealth Office @ www.fco.gov.uk. Constantly updated advice for travellers on circumstances affecting safety in over 130 countries.
Australian Department of Foreign Affairs @ www.dfat.gov.au. Advice and reports on unstable countries and regions.

Guatemalan embassies and consulates abroad

Australia 4/118 Hewlett St, Bronte 2024, NSW ☏02/9389 4181, ℻938 9023.
Belize 8 A St, King's Park ☏02/33150, ℻35140.
Canada 130 Albert St, Suite 1010, Ottawa ON K1P 5G4 ☏613/233-7188, ℻233-0135.
Honduras 8 C 5–38, Barrio Guamilito, San Pedro Sula ☏533560, ℻331242.

Mexico Embassy: Av Explanada 1025, Lomas de Chapultepec 11000, Mexico D.F. 4 ☎05/540 7520, ⓕ202 1142. Consulates: C Héroes de Chapultepec 354, Chetumal Q.R. ☎983 28585; 2 Av Pte Nte 28, Comitán, Chiapas ☎963 22669; 2 C Orte 33, Tapachula, Chiapas ☎962 61252.
New Zealand no representative; contact Australian embassy.

UK 13 Fawcett St, London SW10 9HN ☎020/7351 3042, ⓕ7376 5708, ⓔembaguatelondon @btinternet.com.
US 2220 R St NW, Washington DC 20008 ☎202 /745-4952, ⓔembaguat@sysnet.net. There are also consulates in Chicago, Houston, LA, Miami, New York and San Diego.

Information, websites and maps

Information about Guatemala is relatively easy to come by both inside and outside the country. There are several excellent websites dedicated to it, and the material produced by Inguat (see below), the tourist board, is also improving, though much of it is of limited practical use. When digging out information on Guatemala, don't forget the specialist travel agents (see pp.9–16) and the embassies (see p.88).

The Guatemalan tourist board, **Inguat**, at 7 Av 1–17, Centro Cívico, Zona 4 Guatemala City (☎331 1333, ⓕ331 8893, ⓦwww .guatemala.travel.com.gt) is usually very helpful, with a friendly team of English-speaking staff; there are smaller branches at Guatemala City airport, Antigua, Quetzal-tenango, Chichicastenango, Panajachel, Flores and Flores airport. The quality of information varies, though generally the main office and the Antigua and Panajachel branches are the most reliable: these should all have bus timetables, hotel listings and dozens of brochures and leaflets. All offices should have copies of a free, Inguat-published

guide for tourists, *Guatemala Bits and Tips*, which is worth picking up though rather generic in its scope, and reasonable **maps** of the country (US$1).

Current political analysis and an interesting and informative overview of the society, economy and environment of each country is provided by two specialist publishers: the **Resource Center** in the US (ⓦwww.lrc-online .org), which produces the *Inside* series covering each country, and the Latin America Bureau in the UK (ⓦwww.lab.org.uk), an independent, non-profit research organization, whose *Guatemala In Focus* booklet is a good general introduction to the nation.

Also in the UK are two highly useful resources. **Maya – The Guatemalan Indian Centre**, 94A Wandsworth Bridge Rd, London SW6 2TF (☎ & ⓕ020/7371 5291, ⓦwww .maya.org.uk; closed Jan, Easter & Aug) is one of the finest Guatemalan resource centres in the world. Membership (£5 annually) gives you access to a library (reference only) stocked with over 2000 books on Guatemala, along with several hundred videos and all the main periodicals. The centre also hosts monthly cultural events, film shows and exhibitions on all things Guatemalan. There is an outstanding textile collection, and the centre's director, Krystyna Deuss, is the acknowledged British authority on historic and contemporary Maya dress and ritual. Also in

Resource centre outlets

US Interlink Publishing Group, ☏413/582-7054, ⓦ www.interlinkbooks.com, ⓔ interpg@aol.com; Monthly Review Press ☏212/691-2555, ⓔ mreview@igc.apc.org. **Canada** Fernwood Books, ☏902/422-3302, ⓦ www.fernwoodbooks.ca, ⓔ fernwood @istar.ca. **UK** Latin America Bureau, ☏020/7278 2829, ⓔ lab@gn.apc.org, ⓦ www.lab.org.uk. **Ireland** Trocaire Resource Centre, ☏01/874-3875, ⓦ www.trocaire.org. **Australia** Bushbooks, ☏02/4323-3274.

London, **Canning House Library**, 2 Belgrave Square, SW1X 8PJ (☏020/7235 2303, ⓦ www.canninghouse.com), has the UK's largest publicly accessible collection of books and periodicals on Latin America, with numerous shelves devoted to Guatemala and Maya issues. It's free to use, though you have to be a member to take books out and receive the twice-yearly *Bulletin*, a review of recently published books on Latin America.

The internet

The number of pages on the **internet** devoted to Guatemala and the region is growing daily. The first place to check out is the very comprehensive homepage of the **Guatemalan Web Page Directory** ⓦhttp://mars.cropsoil.uga.edu/tropag/guatem.htm, which, despite the misleading domain name, has a seemingly never-ending series of superb links about all things Guatemalan. The **Latin American Information Center** (LANIC; ⓦwww.lanic.utexas.edu) is another good place to begin a search, while the best portal for **Central America** is undoubtedly ⓦwww.centramerica.com. **Planeta** (ⓦwww.planeta.com) is an excellent resource for ecotourism and independent travel in the region, run by the prolific author and journalist Ron Mader. Finally, the ever-helpful members of the **newsgroup** ⓦwww.rec.travel.latin-america have a huge (and generally accurate) information base and will answer any query about travel in the region.

Useful websites

ⓦ**www.atitlan.com** Well-designed site with encyclopedic coverage of the Atitlán region, rich with cultural content and hotel and restaurant listings.

ⓦ**www.bayislands.com** Roatán articles and listings on the Coconut Telegraph's website.

ⓦ**www.copanruinas.com** News, reviews, hotels and restaurants in the Copán region.

ⓦ**www.famsi.org** The web pages of The Foundation for the Advancement of Mesoamerican Studies Inc includes all the latest reports from Mayanist archeologists, epigraphers and ethnographers.

ⓦ**http://fhrg.org** Website of the Foundation for Human Rights in Guatemala, with a superb overview of the current situation and detailed reports and analysis.

ⓦ**www.ghrc-usa.org** Extensive monitoring of Guatemalan human rights issues, with bimonthly updates and analysis.

ⓦ**www.guatemalantravelmall.com** Comprehensive site with on-line hotel, restaurant, and Spanish school bookings and some interesting ecotours.

ⓦ**www.guatemala365.com** An excellent, independent and very well-researched place to begin the search for a Spanish school, with a list of professional schools and tips about the relative advantages of different study centres.

ⓦ**www.guatemaladaily.com** All the latest Guatemalan news stories, in English.

ⓦ**www.guatemalaweb.com** Very comprehensive site, content includes everything from ATM locations to the latest visa information.

ⓦ**www.iloveutila.com** Some island news, but mainly deals with real estate and property.

ⓦ**www.interhuehue.com** Informative site with good links and listings of the Huehue area.

ⓦ**www.larutamaya.net** Guatemalan travel and cultural information and links to some good tour operators.

ⓦ**www.marrder.com/htw** This is the superb, regularly updated site of Honduras This Week, the best English-language information source about the country. Reliable news reports plus interesting content from regions including Copán and the Bay Islands.

ⓦ**http://mars.cropsoil.uga.edu/tropag/guatem.htm** The homepages of the Guatemalan Web Page Directory form undoubtedly the finest Guatemalan portal, and are the best place to start a search on virtually any topic concerning the country.

ⓦ**www.maya.org.uk** London-based Maya–Guatemalan Indian Centre's effective site has news of forthcoming UK cultural events and good links.

ⓦ**www.mayadiscovery.com** Focuses upon the architecture and art of the ancient Maya, though there are also cultural essays about contemporary issues.

ⓦ**www.mayaparadise.com** Useful listings and information about the Río Dulce and Lago de Izabal area.

ⓦ **www.mesoweb.com** Round-up of all the latest Mayanist developments, plus news stories about the region.

ⓦ **www.pmg.dk** Project Mosaic Guatemala's voluntary work website has dozens of opportunities and links to over sixty local organizations.

ⓦ **www.revuemag.com** Tourism and travel issues, mainly dealing with Guatemala.

ⓦ **www.rigobertamenchu.org** Nobel Peace Prize winner Rigoberta Menchú's site, concentrating on development and human rights matters.

ⓦ **www.roatanet.com** Excellent, well-designed site with hotels, music, and a superb, very quirky news archive.

ⓦ **www.sigloxxi.com** Leading Guatemalan newspaper Siglo XX's Spanish-only website.

ⓦ **www.stetson.edu/~rsitter/TodosSantos** Useful cultural content and practical coverage of the Todos Santos Cuchumatán region.

ⓦ **www.theantiguajournal.com** Plenteous facts and links in this city-specific site.

ⓦ **www.xelapages.com** Excellent, well-structured site covering the Quetzaltenango area, with comprehensive language school and business listings, plus a decent message board.

Maps

The **best map of Guatemala** (1:500,000) is produced by International Travel Map Productions (736A Granville St, Vancouver, BC, V62 1G3, Canada; ⓦ www.nas.com), and is available in the US and the UK and from online bookshops such as Amazon (ⓦ www.amazon.com). In Guatemala, you can usually get a copy from bookshops in Guatemala City (see p.86) and Antigua, including Casa Andinista (see p.109) in the latter. Inguat also publishes a "tourist map" (1:1,000,000), which although now rather outdated, gives reasonable coverage of Guatemala (and Belize), with a detailed map of the central area and plans of all the main towns. It's sold for US$1 at Inguat offices and some shops in Guatemala. Another reasonable map is the freebie given away by the car rental outlet Hertz, though again it's out of date and many of the newer roads aren't featured. The only **large-scale maps** of Guatemala (1:50,000) are produced by the Instituto Geográfico Militar, Av de las Américas 5–76, Zona 13, Guatemala City (Mon–Fri 8am–4pm; ☏332 2611). These cover the country in 250 sections and are accurately contoured, although many aspects are now out of date. You can consult these at the Instituto's

offices, and most can be bought for around US$4.50. A cheaper option, however, is to buy photocopies of these maps – many are available at Casa Andinista in Antigua.

Map outlets

In the US and Canada

Adventurous Traveler Bookstore PO Box 64769, Burlington, VT 05406 ☏ 1-800/282-3963, ⓦ www.AdventurousTraveler.com.

Book Passage 51 Tamal Vista Blvd, Corte Madera, CA 94925 ☏ 415/927-0960, ⓦ www.bookpassage.com.

Elliot Bay Book Company 101 S Main St, Seattle, WA 98104 ☏ 1-800/962-5311 or 206/624-6600, ⓦ www.elliotbaybook.com.

Forsyth Travel Library 226 Westchester Ave, White Plains, NY 10604 ☏ 1-800/367-7984, ⓦ www.forsyth.com.

Globe Corner Bookstore 28 Church St, Cambridge, MA 02138 ☏ 1-800/358-6013, ⓦ www.globercorner.com.

GORP Adventure Library online only ☏ 1-800/754-8229, ⓦ www2.gorp.com.

Map Link Inc 30 S La Patera Lane, Unit 5, Santa Barbara, CA 93117 ☏ 805/692-6777, ⓦ www.maplink.com.

Phileas Fogg's Travel Center #87 Stanford Shopping Center, Palo Alto, CA 94304 ☏ 1-800/533-3644, ⓦ www.foggs.com.

Rand McNally 444 N Michigan Ave, Chicago, IL 60611 ☏ 312/321-1751, ⓦ www.randmcnally.com; 150 E 52nd St, New York, NY 10022 ☏ 212/758-7488; 595 Market St, San Francisco, CA 94105 ☏ 415/777-3131; around thirty stores across the US – call ☏ 1-800/333-0136 ext 2111 or check the website for the nearest store.

Travel Books & Language Center 4437 Wisconsin Ave, Washington, DC 20016 ☏ 1-800 /220-2665, ⓦ www.bookweb.org/bookstore /travellers.

The Travel Bug Bookstore 2667 W Broadway, Vancouver V6K 2G2 ☏ 604/737-1122, ⓦ www.swifty .com/tbug.

World of Maps 118 Holland Ave, Ottawa, Ontario K1Y 0X6 ☏ 613/724-6776, ⓦ www.itmb.com.

World Wide Books and Maps 1247 Granville St, Vancouver V6Z 1G3 ☏ 604/687-3320, ⓦ www .worldofmaps.com.

In the UK and Ireland

Blackwell's Map and Travel Shop 53 Broad St, Oxford OX1 3BQ ☏ 01865/792792, ⓦ www.bookshop .blackwell.co.uk.

Easons Bookshop 40 O'Connell St, Dublin 1 ☎01/873 3811, ⊛www.eason.ie.

Heffers Map and Travel 20 Trinity St, Cambridge CB2 1TJ ☎01223/568568, ⊛www.heffers.co.uk.

Hodges Figgis Bookshop 56–58 Dawson St, Dublin 2 ☎01/677 4754, ⊛www.hodgesfiggis.com.

James Thin Melven's Bookshop 29 Union St, Inverness IV1 1QA ☎01463/233500, ⊛www.jthin.co.uk.

John Smith and Sons 26 Colquhoun Ave, Glasgow G52 4PJ ☎0141/552 3377, ⊛www.johnsmith.co.uk.

The Map Shop 30a Belvoir St, Leicester LE1 6QH ☎0116/2471400.

National Map Centre 22–24 Caxton St, London SW1H 0QU ☎020/7222 2466, ⊛www.mapsnmc.co.uk.

Newcastle Map Centre 55 Grey St, Newcastle upon Tyne NE1 6EF ☎0191/261 5622, ⊛www.traveller.ltd.uk.

Stanfords 12–14 Long Acre, London WC2E 9LP ☎020/7836 1321, ⊛www.stanfords.co.uk; maps by mail or phone order are available on this number and via ℮ sales@stanfords.co.uk. Other branches within British Airways offices at 156 Regent St, London W1R 5TA (☎020/7434 4744), and 29 Corn St, Bristol BS1 1HT (☎0117/929 9966).

The Travel Bookshop 13–15 Blenheim Crescent W11 2EE ☎020/7229 5260, ⊛www.thetravelbookshop.co.uk.

In Australia and New Zealand

Mapland 372 Little Bourke St, Melbourne ☎03/9670 4383, ⊛www.mapland.com.au.

The Map Shop 6 Peel St, Adelaide ☎08/8231 2033, ⊛www.mapshop.net.au.

Mapworld 173 Gloucester St, Christchurch ☎03/374 5399, ℻03/374 5633, ⊛www.mapworld.co.nz.

Perth Map Centre 1/884 Hay St, Perth ☎08/9322 5733, ⊛www.perthmap.com.au.

Specialty Maps 46 Albert St, Auckland ☎09/307 2217, ⊛www.ubd-online.co.nz/maps.

Insurance

A comprehensive travel insurance policy is essential for visitors to Guatemala. Medical insurance (you want coverage of US$2,000,000) should include provision for repatriation by air ambulance, and your policy should also cover you for illness or injury, and against theft. Before paying for a new policy, however, it's worth checking whether you are already covered: some all-risks home insurance policies may cover your possessions when overseas, and many private medical schemes include cover when abroad. In Canada, provincial health plans usually provide partial cover for medical mishaps overseas, while holders of official student/teacher/youth cards in Canada and the US are entitled to meagre accident coverage and hospital in-patient benefits. Students will often find that their student health coverage extends during the vacations and for one term beyond the date of last enrolment.

After exhausting the possibilities above, you might want to contact a specialist travel insurance company, or consider the travel insurance deal we offer (see box). A typical travel insurance policy usually provides cover for the loss of baggage, tickets and – up to a certain limit – cash or cheques, as well as cancellation or curtailment of your journey. Most of them exclude so-called dangerous sports unless an extra premium is paid: this can mean scuba-diving, white-water rafting, windsurfing and trekking, though probably not kayaking or jeep safaris. Many policies can be chopped and changed to exclude coverage you don't need – for example, sickness and accident benefits can often be excluded or included at will. If you do take medical coverage, ascertain whether benefits will be paid as treatment proceeds or only after return home, and whether there is a 24-hour medical emergency number. When securing

Rough Guide travel insurance

Rough Guides offers its own travel insurance, customized for our readers by a leading UK broker and backed by a Lloyds underwriter. It's available for anyone, of any nationality, travelling anywhere in the world.

There are two main Rough Guide insurance plans: **Essential**, for basic, no-frills cover; and **Premier** – with more generous and extensive benefits. Alternatively, you can take out **annual multi-trip insurance**, which covers you for any number of trips throughout the year (with a maximum of 60 days for any one trip). Unlike many policies, the Rough Guides schemes are calculated by the day, so if you're travelling for 27 days rather than a month, that's all you pay for. If you intend to be away for the whole year, the Adventurer policy will cover you for 365 days. Each plan can be supplemented with a "Hazardous Activities Premium" if you plan to indulge in sports considered dangerous, such as skiing, scuba-diving or trekking. Rough Guides also does good deals for older travellers, and will insure you up to any age, at prices comparable to SAGA's.

For a policy quote, call the Rough Guide Insurance Line on US freefone ☏1-866/220 5588, UK freefone ☏0800/015 09 06, or, if you're calling from elsewhere, ☏+44 1243/621 046. Alternatively, get an online quote at ⊛www.roughguides.com/insurance.

baggage cover, make sure that the per-article limit – typically under £500 – will cover your most valuable possession. If you need to make a claim, you should keep receipts for medicines and medical treatment, and in the event you have anything stolen, you must obtain an official statement (*una afirmación*) from the police.

Health

Most visitors get home from Guatemala without experiencing any significant health problems at all. However it's always easier to become ill in a country with a different climate, different food and different germs – still more so in a poor country with lower standards of sanitation than you might be used to.

It's vital to get the best health advice you can before you set off. Pay a visit to your doctor or a travel clinic (see p.26–27) as far in advance of travel as possible (at least eight weeks) and if you're pregnant or likely to become so mention this at the outset. Many clinics also sell the latest travel health products, including mosquito nets, water filters, medical kits and so on. In addition to the websites mentioned on p.20 there are a number of books advising on health precautions and disease prevention; the best and most up to date is *The Rough Guide to Travel Health*, a pocket-size volume packed with accurate information for all parts of the world. Finally, regardless of how well prepared you are medically, you will still want the security of health insurance (see "Insurance" opposite).

Once you're there, what you **eat and drink** is crucial. In addition to the hazards mentioned under "Intestinal troubles" below, contaminated food and water can transmit the hepatitis A virus, which can lay a victim low for several months with exhaustion, fever and diarrhoea, and can even cause liver damage.

Vaccinations, inoculations and malaria precautions

There are no obligatory inoculations for Guatemala (unless you're arriving from a "high-risk" area of yellow fever – northern South America and equatorial Africa – in which case you need to carry your vaccination certificate). Nevertheless, there are several you should have anyway. Make sure you're up to date with polio, tetanus and typhoid vaccinations and consider having diphtheria, hepatitis A and tuberculosis (TB) jabs. Long-term travellers or anyone spending time in rural areas should think about having the combined hepatitis A and B and the rabies vaccines (though see opposite for a caveat on that).

Malaria is a danger in some parts of the country (particularly in the rural lowlands). It's not a problem in the big cities, or anywhere over 1500m – which includes Guatemala City, Antigua, Chichicastenango, Lago de Atitlán, Quetzaltenango and virtually all of the Western Highlands. However, if you plan to visit any lowland areas, including Petén and the Pacific coast, you should consider taking a course of tablets.

The recommended prophylactic is **chloroquine** (inexpensive, available without prescription, and safe in pregnancy); you'll need to begin taking the pills a week before you enter an area where there's a risk of malaria and continue for four weeks after you return. An alternative (especially if you're only going for a short time) is **malarone**, which you need start only two days before you go and continue for a week after you return. Although it's a very effective drug, there are some drawbacks – it's much more expensive than chloroquine, it's available on prescription only, you can only take it for up to 28 days, and it's not suitable for pregnant women or babies. Whichever antimalarial you choose, you should still take **precautions** to avoid getting bitten by insects: sleep in screened rooms or under nets, burn mosquito coils containing permethrin (available everywhere), cover up arms and legs, especially around dawn and dusk when mosquitoes are most active, and use insect repellent containing fifty percent DEET on your skin and up to one hundred percent on clothing.

Also prevalent in some lowland areas (usually occurring in epidemic outbreaks), **dengue fever** is a viral infection transmitted by mosquitoes which are active during the day. There is no vaccine or specific treatment, so you need to pay great attention to avoiding bites.

North Americans can get inoculations at any immunization centre or at most local clinics, and will have to pay a fee. Many GPs in the UK have a travel surgery where you can get advice and certain vaccines on prescription, though they may not administer some of the less common immunizations. Note too that though some jabs (diphtheria, typhoid) are free, others will incur quite a hefty charge; it can be worth checking out a travel clinic where you can receive vaccinations almost immediately, often at lower cost. In Australasia, vaccination centres are always less expensive than doctors' surgeries.

Intestinal troubles

Despite all the dire warnings given here, a bout of **diarrhoea** is the medical problem you're most likely to encounter. Even following all the usual precautions – drinking clean water (any bottled drinks, including beer and soft drinks, are already purified; see box on p.26 for more), avoiding food that has been on display for a while and steering clear of salads and raw shellfish – no one seems to avoid it altogether. Its main cause is simply the change of diet: the food in the region contains a whole new set of bacteria, and perhaps rather more of them than you're used to. If you're struck down, the best cure is the simplest one; take it easy for a day or two, drink lots of bottled water and eat only the blandest of foods – papaya is good for soothing the stomach and is also crammed with vitamins. Only if the symptoms last more than four or five days do you need to worry. Finally, if you're taking oral contraception or any other orally administered drugs, bear in mind that severe diarrhoea can reduce their efficacy.

Cholera is an acute bacterial infection, recognizable by watery diarrhoea and vomiting. However, risk of infection is considered low, particularly if you're following the health advice above, and symptoms are rapidly relieved by prompt medical attention and clean water. If you're spending any time in rural areas you also run the risk of picking up various **parasitic infections**: protozoa – amoeba and giardia – and intestinal worms. These sound (and can be) hideous, but they're easily treated once detected. If you suspect you may have an infestation, take a stool sample to a good **pathology lab** and go to a doctor or pharmacist with the test results (see "Getting Medical Help" on p.26). More serious is **amoebic dysentery**, which is endemic in many parts of the region. The symptoms are similar to a bad dose of diarrhoea but include bleeding too. On the whole, a course of flagyl (metronidazole or tinidazole) will cure it. If you plan to visit farflung corners then it's worth getting hold of this before you go, and some advice from a doctor on its use.

Bites and stings

Taking steps to avoid getting bitten by **insects**, particularly mosquitoes, is always good practice. **Sandflies**, which are very common in the Bay Islands, are tiny, but their bites, usually on feet and ankles, itch like hell and last for days. **Ticks**, which you're likely to pick up if you're walking or riding in areas with domestic livestock (and sometimes in the forests generally), need careful removal with tweezers – those in a Swiss Army knife are ideal. Head or body **lice** can be picked up from people or bedding, and are best treated with medicated soap or shampoo; very occasionally, they may spread typhus, characterized by fever, muscle aches, headaches and eventually a measles-like rash. If you think you have it, seek treatment from a doctor.

Scorpions are common; mostly nocturnal, they hide during the heat of the day – often in thatched roofs. If you're camping, or sleeping under a thatched roof, shake your shoes out before putting them on and try not to wander round barefoot. Their sting is painful (rarely fatal) and can become infected, so you should seek medical treatment if the pain seems significantly worse than a bee sting. You're less likely to be bitten by a **spider**, but the advice is the same as for scorpions and insects: seek medical treatment if the pain persists or increases.

You're unlikely to see a **snake**, and most are harmless in any case. Wearing boots and long pants will go a long way towards preventing a bite – tread heavily and they will usually slither away. If you do get bitten, remember what the snake looked like (kill it if you can), immobilize the bitten limb as far as possible and seek medical help immediately: antivenins are available in most main hospitals.

Swimming and snorkelling might bring you into contact with potentially dangerous or venomous **sea creatures**. You're extremely unlikely to be a victim of a shark attack (though the dubious practice of shark-feeding as a tourist attraction is growing, and could lead to an accidental bite), but **jellyfish** are common and most corals will sting, especially fire coral. Some jellyfish, like the Portuguese man-o'-war, with its distinctive purple, bag-like sail, have very long tentacles with stinging cells, and an encounter will result in raw, red weals. If you are stung, clean the wound with vinegar or iodine and seek medical help if the pain persists or infection develops. The spines of sting rays and scorpion fish are all extremely poisonous, so be careful where you put your feet.

Finally, **rabies** is present, but not common in Guatemala. The best advice is to give dogs a wide berth and not to play with animals at all, no matter how cuddly they may look. Treat any bite as suspect: wash any wound immediately with soap or detergent and apply alcohol or iodine if possible. Act immediately to get treatment – rabies can be fatal once symptoms appear. There is a **vaccine**, but it is expensive, serves only to shorten the course of treatment you need anyway and is effective for no more than three months.

Heat and altitude problems

Two other common causes of illness are **altitude** and the **sun**. The best advice in both cases is to take it easy; allow yourself time to acclimatize before you race up a volcano, and build up exposure to the sun gradually. If going to higher altitudes, you may develop symptoms of Acute Mountain Sickness (AMS), such as breathlessness, headaches, dizziness, nausea and appetite loss. More extreme cases might cause vomiting, disorientation, loss of balance and coughing up of pink frothy phlegm. The simple cure – a slow descent – almost always brings immediate recovery.

Tolerance to the sun, too, takes a while to build up: use a strong sunscreen and, if you're walking during the day, wear a hat and try to keep in the shade. Avoid dehydration by drinking plenty of water or fruit juice. The most serious result of overheating is heatstroke, which can be potentially fatal. Lowering the body temperature (by taking a tepid shower, for example) is the first step in treatment.

Getting medical help

For minor medical problems, head for a **farmacia** – look for the green cross – there's one in every town and most villages. Pharmacists are knowledgeable and helpful, and many speak some English. They can also sell drugs over the counter (if necessary) which are only available on prescription at home. Every capital city has **doctors** and dentists, many trained in the US, who are experienced in treating visitors and speak good English. Your embassy will always have a list of recommended doctors, and we've included some in our "Listings" for the main towns. Health insurance (see p.22) is essential and for anything serious you should to go to the best **private hospital** you can reach; again, these are located mainly in the capital cities. If you suspect something is amiss with your insides, it might be worth heading straight for the local **pathology lab** (all the main towns have them), before seeing a doctor, as the doctor will send you there anyway. Many rural communities have a **health centre** (*centro de salud* or *puesto de salud*), where health care is free, although there may only be a nurse or health worker available and you can't rely on finding anyone who speaks English. Should you need an injection or transfusion, make sure that the equipment is **sterile** (it might be worth bringing a sterile kit from home) and ensure any blood you receive is screened.

Medical resources for travellers

Websites

⊛ http://health.yahoo.com Information on specific diseases and conditions, drugs and herbal remedies, as well as advice from health experts.
⊛ www.tmvc.com.au Contains a list of all Travellers Medical and Vaccination Centres throughout Australia, New Zealand and Southeast Asia, plus general information on travel health.
⊛ www.istm.org The website of the International Society for Travel Medicine, with a full list of clinics specializing in international travel health.
⊛ www.tripprep.com Travel Health Online provides an online only comprehensive database of necessary vaccinations for most countries, as well as destination and medical service provider information.
⊛ www.fitfortravel.scot.nhs.uk UK NHS website carrying information about travel-related diseases and how to avoid them.

In the US and Canada

Canadian Society for International Health 1 Nicholas St., Suite 1105, Ottawa, ON K1N 7B7 (☎613/241-5785, ⊛www.csih.org). Distributes a free pamphlet, "Health Information for Canadian Travellers", containing an extensive list of travel health centres in Canada.
Centers for Disease Control 1600 Clifton Rd NE, Atlanta, GA 30333 (☎1-800/311-3435 or 404/639-3534, ☎1-888/232-3299, ⊛www.cdc.gov). Publishes outbreak warnings, suggested inoculations,

What about the water?

Contaminated water is a major cause of sickness in Guatemala and, even if it looks clean, all tap water should be regarded with caution. In most big cities and resorts tap water will be filtered and treated, often using a heavy dose of chlorine. Purified bottled water (check the seal is intact) is widely available in shops, many restaurants use purified water (*agua purificada*) and hotels frequently provide bottles in your room; you'll only need to consider treating your own water if you plan to travel to very remote areas. Any good outdoor equipment shop will stock a range of water treatment products.

While boiling water for ten minutes kills most micro-organisms, it's not the most convenient method. Water filters remove visible impurities and larger pathogenic organisms (most bacteria and cysts). Chemical sterilization with either chlorine or iodine tablets (or a tincture of iodine liquid) is effective (except in preventing amoebic dysentery or giardiasis), but the resulting liquid doesn't taste very pleasant – though it can be masked with lemon or lime juice. Iodine is unsafe for pregnant women, babies and people with thyroid complaints. Purification, involving both filtration and sterilization, gives the most complete treatment, and travel clinics and good outdoor equipment shops will stock a wide range of portable water purifiers. In the UK the "Aqua Pure Traveller" is the best-value portable water filter and purifier, costing under £30 and capable of treating 350 litres of water; it's available from all the UK travel health specialists listed opposite, branches of Boots or from the manufacturer's website, ⊛www.thirstpoint.com. The Swiss-made Katadyn filters are expensive but extremely useful.

precautions and other background information for travellers. Useful website plus International Travelers Hotline on ☎1-877/FYI-TRIP.

International Association for Medical Assistance to Travellers (IAMAT) 417 Center St, Lewiston NY 14092 (☎716/754-4883, ⊛www.sentex.net/~iamat) and 40 Regal Rd, Guelph, ON N1K 1B5 (☎519/836-0102). A non-profit organization supported by donations, it can provide a list of English-speaking doctors in Guatemala, climate charts and leaflets on various diseases and inoculations.

International SOS Assistance Eight Neshaminy Interplex Suite 207,Trevose, USA 19053-6956 (☎1-800/523-8930, ⊛www.intsos.com). Members receive pre-trip medical referral info, as well as overseas emergency services designed to complement travel insurance coverage.

Travel Medicine ☎1-800/872-8633 ℻1-413 /584-6656, ⊛www.travmed.com. Sells first-aid kits, mosquito netting, water filters, reference books and other health-related travel products.

Travelers Medical Center 31 Washington Square West, New York, NY 10011 (☎212/982-1600). Consultation service on immunizations and treatment of diseases for people travelling to developing countries.

In the UK and Ireland

British Airways Travel Clinics 28 regional clinics (call ☎01276/685040 for the nearest, or consult ⊛www.britishairways.com), with several in London (Mon–Fri 9.30am–5.15pm, Sat 10am–4pm), including 156 Regent St, London W1 (☎020/7439 9584, no appointment necessary). There are appointment-only branches at 101 Cheapside, London EC2 (☎020/7606 2977); and at the BA terminal in London's Victoria Station (☎020/7233 6661). All clinics offer vaccinations, tailored advice from an online database and a complete range of travel healthcare products.

Dun Laoghaire Medical Centre 5 Northumberland Ave, Dun Laoghaire, Co. Dublin (☎01/280 4996, ℻280 5603). Advice on medical matters abroad.

Hospital for Tropical Diseases Travel Clinic second floor, Mortimer Market Centre, off Capper St, London WC1E 6AU (Mon–Fri 9am–5pm by appointment only; ☎020/7388 9600; a consultation costs £15 which is waived if you have your injections here). A recorded Health Line (☎09061/337733, 50p per min) gives hints on

hygiene and illness prevention as well as listing appropriate immunizations.

Malaria Helpline 24-hour recorded message (☎0891/600350, 60p per minute).

MASTA (Medical Advisory Service for Travellers Abroad) London School of Hygiene and Tropical Medicine. Operates a prerecorded 24-hour Travellers' Health Line (☎0906/822 4100, 60p per min; Republic of Ireland ☎01560/147000, 75p per minute), giving written information tailored to your journey by return of post.

Nomad Pharmacy surgeries 40 Bernard St, London, WC1; and 3–4 Wellington Terrace, Turnpike Lane, London N8 (Mon–Fri 9.30am–6pm, ☎020 /7833 4114 to book vaccination appointment). They give advice free if you go in person, or their telephone helpline is ☎09068/633414 (60p per minute). They can give information tailored to your travel needs.

Trailfinders Immunization clinics (no appointments necessary) at 194 Kensington High St, London (Mon–Fri 9am–5pm except Thurs to 6pm, Sat 9.30am–4pm; ☎020/7938 3999).

Travel Health Centre Dept of International Health and Tropical Medicine, Royal College of Surgeons in Ireland, Mercers Medical Centre, Stephen's St Lower, Dublin (☎01/402 2337). Expert pre-trip advice and inoculations.

Travel Medicine Services PO Box 254, 16 College St, Belfast 1(☎028/9031 5220). Offers medical advice before a trip and help afterwards in the event of a tropical disease.

Tropical Medical Bureau Grafton Buildings, 34 Grafton St, Dublin 2 (☎01/671 9200, ⊛www.iol.ie/-tmb).

In Australia and New Zealand

Travellers' Medical and Vaccination Centres: 27–29 Gilbert Place, Adelaide (☎08/8212 7522). 1/170 Queen St, Auckland (☎09/373 3531). 5/247 Adelaide St, Brisbane (☎07/3221 9066). 5/8–10 Hobart Place, Canberra (☎02/6257 7156). 147 Armagh St, Christchurch (☎03/379 4000). 5 Westralia St, Darwin (☎08/8981 2907). 270 Sandy Bay Rd, Sandy Bay, Hobart (☎03/6223 7577). 2/393 Little Bourke St, Melbourne (☎03/9602 5788). 5 Mill St, Perth (☎08/9321 1977), plus branch in Fremantle. 7/428 George St, Sydney (☎02/9221 7133), plus branches in Chatswood and Parramatta. Shop 15, Grand Arcade, 14–16 Willis St, Wellington (☎04/473 0991).

Costs, money and banks

By European or North American standards the cost of living in Guatemala is very low, and by Latin American standards the currency, the Quetzal (Q), is relatively stable. However, fluctuations can and do take place, so we have quoted all prices in the guide in US dollars. Legal tender since May 2001, the US dollar is by far the most widely accepted foreign currency in Guatemala. It continues to float against the quetzal; in September 2001 the rate was Q7.90 to US$1.

Credit cards are very useful for withdrawing currency from bank ATMs, but don't count on paying with them except in upmarket hotels and restaurants. It's always a good idea to have some **travellers' cheques**, which you can cash in most towns, and some US dollar bills wherever you are, in case you run short of local currency a long way from the nearest bank. All the international airports have banks for currency exchange, while at all the main land border crossings there are usually banks and a swarm of moneychangers who generally give fair rates for cash (and sometimes travellers' cheques). Even at the most remote border crossings, you'll usually find a wad-wielding local from whom you can get some local currency.

Costs

Guatemala is one of the cheapest countries in the Americas for travellers, though there are plenty of opportunities for a modest (or serious) splurge if you feel like it. The extremely frugal may be able to get by on around US$90 a week. However, if you allow yourself the odd treat, you can expect to spend around US$120 per person per week if you're travelling as a couple, while solo travellers should reckon on US$140 a week. On the other hand, for US$30 a day you can expect to live quite well. Things are more expensive in regions where the local economy is tourist-driven (Antigua, Guanaja and Roatán especially), though even in these places there are some cheap places to stay, and it's possible to keep to a reasonable budget if you can exercise some sense of thrift.

Prices

The following prices should give you a rough idea of what you might end up paying. Basic **rooms** cost anything from US$2 to US$8 for a single, US$3.50 to US$10 a double, while you can pay up to US$200 a night for a suite in the most luxurious establishments. **Food** prices don't vary quite as much as you might expect; eating a filling meal in a simple comedor will cost around US$2 anywhere in the country, while in a smarter restaurant you can expect to pay a little over double that. Anything that is imported will be expensive, so if you have a taste for fancy cheeses, wine or ice cream you'll have to pay for your indulgences. Fresh produce from the market is very good value – although to get anywhere near the price that locals pay you'll have to bargain in Spanish. Check the fixed-price goods in supermarkets first.

A bottle of Guatemalan **beer** costs a little over US$1 in most bars, and half that in a supermarket. Rum starts at around US$3.50 a bottle while local fire-water, such as the ubiquitous *Quezalteca*, is even cheaper. **Cigarettes** cost less than US$1 a pack for local brands, and US$1.50 for North American imports; **cigar** smokers will be pleased to find excellent Honduran cigars at bargain rates. If you roll your own, bring a supply of cigarette papers as they are expensive and difficult to obtain in Guatemala.

Travel is probably the greatest bargain, providing you stick to the "chicken buses", which charge around US$0.60 an hour. To a certain extent you get what you pay for – these buses are always crowded, slow and rudimentary in the extreme – though they can be a lot of fun. There are also better quality "pullman" buses, some are excellent, though these only serve the main highways. Travelling by car is expensive, and the cost of **renting a car** (from US$45 a day) is higher in Guatemala than it is in the USA, as is the cost of fuel – although both are still cheaper than in Europe.

Generally anything produced in Central America is cheap, anything imported expensive. This applies to most tinned food, American clothing – although plenty of imitations are produced inside Guatemala – and many high-tech goods such as cameras, film and radios. However, almost everything is available at a price, from French wine to canned baby food. A **student card** is not very useful but may occasionally come in handy as a bargaining tool.

Credit/debit cards and travellers' cheques

Credit cards are becoming increasingly useful in Guatemala, though you shouldn't expect to be able to use them as you would in North America or Europe. They are accepted in most upmarket shops, hotels and restaurants, but you won't be able to pay for your comedor meal or pensión bill with plastic.

Visa is by far the most useful brand, with Mastercard a distant second best. You can use your card to get cash over the counter at banks and from **ATM**s – there's a least one in most towns and at many petrol garages – for a comprehensive ATM list check the website ⊛www.guatemalatravel .com/1/cashiers.htm. Although most ATMs are in service 24 hours, it's wiser to use them when the bank is open: firstly you can see a bank employee if something goes wrong and the machine keeps your card (though this is very rare), and secondly you benefit from the security of daylight. Using your **debit card** means you don't have to buy and countersign travellers' cheques and, though you pay a handling charge each time you use it, the amount may be less than the commission on cheques and you may benefit from a better exchange rate.

Note that Plus and Visa debit cards (see box) are much more widely accepted than the Cirrus brand in Guatemala and throughout Central America.

Remember that all cash advances are treated as loans, with interest accruing daily from the date of withdrawal. Make sure you have a four-digit personal identification number (PIN) that's designed to work overseas.

Travellers' cheques

Travellers' cheques are a safe way to bring money, as they offer the security of a refund if they're stolen. It's essential to purchase US dollar cheques – other currencies including sterling- and even Euro-issued cheques are almost impossible to cash. Make sure that you have your travellers' cheques issued by one of the big names (such as American Express, Visa, Thomas Cook or Citibank), which are more readily accepted. You should also always carry your proof of purchase when trying to change travellers' cheques, as some places will refuse to deal with you otherwise. The usual fee for travellers' cheque sales is one or two percent, though this fee may be waived if you buy the cheques through a bank where you have an account. It pays to get a selection of denominations. Make sure to keep the purchase agreement and a record of cheque serial numbers safe and separate from the cheques themselves. In the event that cheques are lost or stolen, the issuing company will expect you to report the loss forthwith to their office in Guatemala most companies claim to replace lost or stolen cheques within 24 hours.

Wiring money

Having money wired from home using one of the companies listed below is never convenient or cheap, and should be considered a

---

Visa Travel Money (www.visa.com)

This is a disposable debit card prepaid with dedicated travel funds which you can access from over 457,000 Visa ATMs in 120 countries with a PIN that you select yourself. When your funds are depleted, you simply throw the card away. Since you can buy up to nine cards to access the same funds – useful for couples or families travelling together – it's recommended that you buy at least one extra as a back-up in case your first is lost or stolen. There is a 24-hour Visa global customer assistance services centre which you can call from any of the 120 countries toll-free. **If you lose your Visa debit card in Guatemala, call 1-800-999-0115**. In the UK, many Thomas Cook outlets sell the card.

last resort. It's also possible to have money wired directly from a bank in your home country to a bank in Guatemala, although this is somewhat less reliable because it involves two separate institutions. If you go this route, your home bank will need the address of the branch bank where you want to pick up the money and the address and telex number of the Guatemala City head office, which will act as the clearing house; money wired this way normally takes two working days to arrive, and costs around £25/US$40 per transaction.

Money-wiring companies

In the US and Canada

American Express Moneygram ☏1-800/926-9400, ⊛www.moneygram.com.
Thomas Cook US ☏1-800/287-7362, Canada ☏1-888 /8234-7328, ⊛www.us.thomascook.com.
Western Union ☏1-800/325-6000, ⊛www.westernunion.com.

In the UK and Ireland

Moneygram ☏0800/018 0104, ⊛www.moneygram.com.
Thomas Cook ☏01733/318922, Belfast ☏028/9055 0030, Dublin ☏01/677 1721.

Western Union Money Transfer ☏0800/833833, ⊛www.westernunion.com.

In Australia

American Express Moneygram ☏1800/230100, NZ ☏09/379 8243 or 0800/262263, ⊛www.moneygram.com.
Western Union ☏1800/649565, NZ ☏09/2700050, ⊛www.westernunion.com.

Youth and student discounts

There are very few **discounts** for youth and student ID card holders in Guatemala. No museums (except the Museo Ixchel in Guatemala City) offer discounts to students, and there are no reduced prices for transportation on internal airlines or bus companies. Some of the Antigua travel agents (see p.112) do offer discounted international airfares for students, though it's not so hard to get these rates if you're prepared to bargain anyway. Some language schools, including La Unión in Antigua, are now issuing their own student cards which qualify holders to discounts (typically ten percent) with selected internal tour operators, restaurants and cybercafés.

Getting around

With no passenger trains and only the privileged few being able to afford cars, virtually everyone travels by "chicken bus" in Guatemala. These buses may be decrepit, uncomfortable, fume-filled and overcrowded, but they give you a unique opportunity to mix with ordinary Guatemalans, and by sticking to flights or the sanitized tourist shuttles, you'll be missing out on one of the country's most essential experiences. Along the main highways there are more comfortable buses – some of them quite fast and luxurious – but once you leave the central routes and head off on the byways, there's usually no alternative to a bumpy ride inside a bus or a pick-up truck.

Though recent governments have upgraded the country's road system, Guatemala's road network is still alarmingly inadequate, and suffers by comparison with neighbouring Mexico, or even Honduras. You'll often find yourself stuck behind smoking trucks, even on the main highways, while large swathes

of the country are still only served with rutted dirt roads where the going can be painfully pedestrian. Fortunately, whatever the pace of your journey, you always have the spectacular Guatemalan countryside outside to wonder at.

By bus

Buses are cheap, convenient and can be wildly entertaining. For the most part the service is extremely comprehensive, reaching even the smallest of villages, and the driver will usually stop to pick up passengers anywhere, regardless of how many people are already on board. Though in remote areas many buses leave in the dead of night and travel through the early hours to reach the morning markets, try to avoid travelling after dark, as the risk of robbery is much higher.

There are two classes of bus. **Second-class** or **"chicken buses"**, known as *camionetas* in Guatemala, are the most common and easily distinguished by their trademark clouds of thick black noxious fumes and rasping exhausts. These are all old North American school buses, their seats designed for the under-fives, so you're liable to have bruised knees after a day or two's travel. They are open to all and cram their seats, aisles and occasionally even roofs with passengers. The driver always seems to be a moustachioed ladino with an eye for the ladies and his helper (*ayudante*) always overworked and underage. It's the *ayudante*'s job to scramble up to the roof to retrieve your rucksack, collect the fares and bellow out the destination to all and sundry. While travel by second-class bus may be uncomfortable and frustratingly slow, it is never dull, with chickens clucking, music assaulting your eardrums, and snack vendors touting for business.

Guatemala has hundreds of small bus companies, each determined to outdo the next in the garishness of their vehicles' paint jobs. Almost all chicken buses operate out of **bus terminals**, usually on the edge of town, and often adjacent to the market; between towns you can hail buses and they'll almost always stop for you. **Tickets** are bought on the bus, and whilst they are always very cheap, gringos do sometimes get ripped off – look and listen to what the locals are paying. **Fares** vary a little throughout the country, but average out at around US$0.60 an hour.

The so-called **pullman** is usually an old Greyhound bus, and is rated as first-class: each passenger will be sure of a seat to him- or herself, and tickets can be bought in advance. These "express" buses are about forty percent more expensive than the regular buses – around US$1 an hour, though

there are some very pricey services to Petén. Pullmans are quicker than chicken buses, not only because the buses themselves are better, but also because they make fewer stops. Services vary tremendously, with some companies' buses being comfortable and pleasant, while other operators use decrepit buses with cracked windows and bald tyres, and pack in extra passengers standing in the aisles. However, all pullmans have two things in common – speed and, unlikely though it may seem, punctuality.

Pullmans usually leave from the offices of the bus company – addresses are listed in the text – and on the whole they serve only the main routes, connecting the capital with Río Dulce and Flores/Santa Elena, Quetzaltenango and San Marcos, Huehuetenango, the Mexican border, Chiquimula and Esquipulas, Puerto Barrios, Cobán and San Salvador. This means that most long journeys can be done at least part of the way by pullman. Note that tickets are sometimes (always in Petén) collected by conductors at the end of the journey, so make sure you don't lose yours.

Providing fast, non-stop links between the main tourist centres, **shuttle buses** are becoming increasingly common in Guatemala. Conveniently, passengers are picked up from their hotels, so you won't have to lug any heavy bags around. Services are expanding rapidly, but the main routes run from Antigua and Guatemala City to Chichicastenango, Panajachel, Monterrico and Copán. There are also connections from Panajachel to Chichicastenago and Quetzaltenango, and between Tikal and Flores/Santa Elena. Shuttles are expensive at around US$5 an hour, though they can be very useful if you're short of time. An innovative new shuttle bus service called **La Vía Maya** (☎339 3601, ⊛www.laviamaya.com) now links all the main tourist destinations in a circuitous loop around Guatemala, providing a comfortable way to get around the country.

By air

The internal **flight** you're most likely to take in Guatemala is from the capital to Flores. It costs between US$70 and US$120 return and takes only fifty minutes (as opposed to some 8–10 hours on the bus), with four rival airlines offering daily flights. Their addresses and other details can be found in the Petén chapter; tickets can be bought from virtually any travel agent in the country. A domestic airline, Inter, operated by the Taca Group, flies to numerous other destinations within Guatemala, but as distances are not that great (and cancellations are frequent) few people choose to fly with them. Nevertheless you can fly from Guatemala City to Huehuetenango via Santa Cruz de Quiché, Quetzaltenango, Retalhuleu, Cobán, Río Dulce and Puerto Barrios. Prices on all flights cost between US$45 and US$60 one way. It's also possible to fly to a number of other airstrips including Copán, Poptún, Playa Grande and Sayaxché by tiny charter airlines when there's sufficient demand; details are given in the relevant chapters.

By train

There are currently no **passenger trains** in Guatemala except for a tourist steam train. This chuffs from Guatemala City to the little spa settlement of Agua Caliente, just 25km away in the Motagua valley – a delightful, if costly, day-trip at US$35 return. For more details and bookings contact any of the travel agents in Guatemala City or Flores, or contact the operators' website ⊛www .go2guatemala.com.

By car

On the whole, **driving** in Guatemala is pretty straightforward and it certainly offers unrivalled freedom – traffic is rarely heavy other than in the capital and along the major highways, although local driving practices can be alarming at times.

Parking and security constitute the main problems, particularly in the cities where theft and vandalism are common. You should always put your car in a guarded car park and choose a hotel with protected parking space. Even budget hotels often have this facility, and there are appropriate recommendations throughout the Guide.

Most of the main routes are paved, but beyond this the roads are often extremely rough. **Filling stations** (*gasolineras*) are quite scarce once you venture away from the main roads, while **fuel** is extremely cheap by European standards, though about double the US price. Should you break down there'll usually be an enthusiastic local mechanic,

but **spare parts** can be a problem, especially for anything beyond the most basic of models. For obscure makes you'd be sensible to bring a basic spares kit. Tyres in particular suffer badly on the burning hot roads and rough dirt tracks. If you plan to head up into the mountains or along any of the smaller roads in Petén then you'll need high clearance and four-wheel drive.

Local **warning signs** are also worth getting to know. The most common is placing a branch in the road, which indicates the presence of a broken-down car. Most other important road signs should be fairly recognizable: you'll see many *Alto* ("stop") signs marking the military checkpoints from more troubled times. Locals usually know which to ignore, but if in doubt it's safest to stop anyway. *Derrumbes* means "landslides", *frene con motor* "brake with motor" (meaning a steep descent) and *tumulos* "bumps in the road", a favourite technique for slowing down traffic.

Renting a car takes some of the worries out of driving but is expensive, costing at least US$45 a day (or around US$230 a week) by the time you've added the extras. Nonetheless, it can be worth doing if you can get a few people together – even better value if you get a larger group and rent a minibus. If you do rent, make sure you check the details of the insurance, which often does not cover damage to your vehicle at all. Always take full-cover insurance and beware that many companies will make you sign a "waiver" document so you are responsible for the first US$1000 of damage in the event of an accident or damage.

Local rental companies are in the "Listings" sections for all the main towns. There's little to be gained financially by organizing a rental in advance from home.

Car rental operators abroad

In North America

Avis US ☎1-800/331-1084, Canada ☎1-800 /272-5871, ⊛www.avis.com.
Budget ☎1-800/527-0700, ⊛www.budgetrentacar .com.
Dollar ☎1-800/800-6000, ⊛www.dollar.com.
Hertz US ☎1-800/654-3001, Canada ☎1-800 /263-0600, ⊛www.hertz.com.
National ☎1-800/227-7368, ⊛www.nationalcar .com.
Thrifty ☎1-800/367-2277, ⊛www.thrifty.com.

In the UK

Avis ☎0870/606 0100, ⊛www.avisworld.com.
Budget ☎0800/181181, ⊛www.go-budget.co.uk.
National ☎0870/536 5365, ⊛www.nationalcar
.com.
Hertz ☎0870/844 8844, ⊛www.hertz.co.uk.
Thrifty ☎01494/751600, ⊛www.thrifty.co.uk.

In Ireland

Avis Northern Ireland ☎028/9442 3333, Republic
of Ireland ☎01/605 7555, ⊛www.avis.co.uk.
Budget Northern Ireland ☎028/9442 3332,
Republic of Ireland ☎01/878 7814, ⊛www
.budgetcarrental.ie or ⊛www.budgetireland.co.uk.
Cosmo Thrifty ☎028/9445 2565, ⊛www.thrifty
.co.uk.
Hertz Northern Ireland ☎028/9442 2533, Republic
of Ireland 0903/27711, ⊛www.hertz.co.uk.

In Australia

Avis ☎13 6333, ⊛www.avis.com.
Budget, ☎1300/362848, ⊛www.budget.com.
Dollar ☎02/9223 1444 or 1800/358008, ⊛www
.dollarcar.com.au.
Hertz ☎1800/550067, ⊛www.hertz.com.
National ☎13/1908. ⊛www.nationalcar.com.
Thrifty ☎1300/367227, ⊛www.thrifty.com.au.

In New Zealand

Avis ☎09/526 5231 or 0800 655111, ⊛www
.avis.com.
Budget, ☎0800/652227 or 09/375 2270,
⊛www.budget.com.
Hertz ☎09/309 0989 or 0800 655955, ⊛www
.hertz.com.
National ☎09/537 2582.
Thrifty ☎09/309 0111, ⊛www.thrifty.com.nz.

Pick-ups

If you plan to visit the more remote parts of
the country then it is almost inevitable that
you'll be hitching a ride in a **pick-up** from
time to time. Increasingly, pick-ups are
supplementing bus services in the mountains and backroads – they are quicker,
and you can't beat the open-air views
(unless it's raining). In remote areas such
as the Ixil triangle and northern Alta
Verapaz, trucks and pick-ups are an
essential form of transport for the locals.
Off the main highways, many pick-ups run
as a bus service, charging passengers
about the same rate as chicken buses
(around US$0.60 per hour).

By taxi

Taxis are available in all the main towns and
their rates are fairly low. Outside Guatemala
City, metered cabs are non-existent so it's
essential to fix a price before you set off.
Local taxi drivers will almost always be prepared to negotiate a price for a half-day or
day's excursion to nearby villages or sites,
and if time is short this can be a good way
of seeing places where the bus service is
awkwardly timed. If you can organize a
group this need not be an expensive option,
possibly even cheaper than renting a car for
the day.

In the Pacific seaside resort of Puerto San
José, three-wheeled Thai **tuk tuks** operate
as taxis, buzzing around the streets
Bangkok style.

By bike and motorbike

Bicycles are quite common in Guatemala,
and cycling has to be one of the most popular sports. You'll be well received almost anywhere if you travel by bike, and if you've got
the energy to make your way through the
highlands it's a great way to see the country.
Most towns will have a repair shop where
you can get hold of spare parts, although
you still need to carry the basics for emergencies on the road. Mountain bikes make
the going easier, as even the main roads
include plenty of formidable potholes, and
it's a rare ride that doesn't involve at least
one steep climb. Chicken buses will carry
bikes on the roof, so if you can't face the
hills then there's always an easy option. In
case you didn't bring your own bike, you can
rent them in Antigua or Panajachel: mountain bikes can be rented by the day (about
US$7–10), week (US$25–35) or month
(US$75–$90).

For real two-wheeled enthusiasts, an excellent contact in Guatemala is Beat at Maya
Mountain Bike Tours in Antigua (see p.110).
Membership of the UK's Cyclists' Touring
Club (☎01483/417217, ⓔcycling@ctc.org.uk,
⊛www.ctc.org.uk) is also useful, as you can
access trip reports from cyclists who have
taken bikes to Central America.

Motorbikes are not that common in
Guatemala, and locating parts and mechani-
cal expertise can be tricky. There are rental
outlets in Guatemala City, Panajachel, Antigua
(see relevant "Listings") and Roatán, typically

charging around US$28 a day for a 200cc machine or US$160 for a weekly rental.

By ferry and boat

Ferries operate between Puerto Barrios and Lívingston on the Caribbean coast of Guatemala; between Puerto Barrios and Punta Gorda in Belize, and connect La Ceiba on the north coast of Honduras with the Bay Islands of Utila and Roatán.

In Petén, there are a number of regular boat services, including the journey along the Río San Pedro from El Naranjo to the Mexican border and beyond; along the Río Salinas from Sayaxché to Benemerito; on the Río Usumacinta from Bethel and La Técnica to Frontera Corozal; and on Lago de Petén Itzá between Flores and the villages of

San Andrés and San José. Once again, precise details of schedules are given in the relevant chapters of the guide.

Along the **Pacific coast** the Chiquimulilla canal separates much of the shoreline from the mainland. If you're heading for a beach you'll find a regular shuttle of small boats to take you across the canal, including services from La Avellena to Monterrico.

Two of Guatemala's most unmissable **boat trips** are up through the spectacular Río Dulce gorge starting in either Lívingston or the town of Río Dulce, and across volcano-framed Lago de Atitlán, usually starting in Panajachel. On almost any of the other navigable waterways you should be able to rent a boat somewhere, though be prepared for hours of patient bargaining, as the boat owners ask serious money for any excursions.

Accommodation

Guatemalan hotels come in all shapes and sizes, and unless you're really off the beaten track there's usually a good range of accommodation to choose from. Though Inguat fixes a maximum price for every hotel room in the country, there are bargains and rip-offs at every level. At the top end of the scale, you can stay in some magnificent colonial hotels decorated with taste and period detail. In the mid-price bracket, you'll also find some brilliant deals – you can still expect character and comfort, but perhaps without the service and facilities. But Guatemala really is a budget travellers' dream, and you should be able to find a clean double room for under US$10 a night in any town in the country, except the capital.

Accommodation comes under a bewildering assortment of names: *hoteles*, pensiones, *posadas*, hospedajes and *huespedes*. The names don't always mean a great deal: in theory a hospedaje is less formal than a *hotel*, but in practice the reverse is almost as common. There are no official youth hostels in Guatemala, but you will find the odd dormitory.

Prices for rooms vary as much as anything else. On the whole you can expect the cheapest places to charge US$2–5 per person, and to get a reasonable but basic room with its own bathroom for around US$10 (a little more in the capital). But price and quality are not always as closely linked as you might expect and, despite rates being officially

regulated, it's well worth trying to **haggle** a little, or asking if there are any cheaper rooms. The official prices are meant to be displayed in the room. If travelling in a group you can often save money by **sharing** a larger room, which almost all the cheaper hotels offer.

Prices are at their highest in Guatemala City, where you'll be well advised to budget for more than you'd normally pay (around US$20 a double) as the very cheapest rooms can be very grim. Costs are also higher than average in Antigua and Flores, but extremely cheap in the Western highlands. At fiesta and holiday times, particularly Holy Week and Christmas, rooms tend to be more expensive and harder to find, and the summer tourist season can also be crowded.

Accommodation price codes

All accommodation listed in this guide has been graded according to the following price scales. These refer to the price in US dollars of the cheapest double room in high season. Many places, however, will offer reductions at quieter times of the year, particularly those in the more popular tourist centres, where there is plenty of competition. It is always worth negotiating if you think the hotel is not very full.

❶ Under US$5
❷ US$5–10
❸ US$10–15

❹ US$15–25
❺ US$25–40
❻ US$40–60

❼ US$60–80
❽ US$80–100
❾ Over US$100

At these times, particularly if you're going to arrive in Guatemala City at night, it's worth booking a room, but in other parts of the country it's hardly worth it. Wherever you are, you'll find that most mid- and top-range hotels insist on charging solo travellers around eighty percent of the cost of a double. When you arrive at a hotel you should always insist on seeing the room before any money changes hands, otherwise they may dump you in the noisiest part of the building and save the good rooms for more discerning customers. In general the cheaper hotels (❶–❷) recommended in this book are not the very cheapest – which are often genuinely squalid, although we do list some notable bargains – but one step up. Rooms in these places will be simple, with a shared toilet and bathroom usually at the end of the corridor. In the brackets above this (❸ and ❹), you can expect a private bathroom with hot water. Rooms in the ❺ and ❻ categories should be very comfortable and attractive, while for US$60 upwards (❼, ❽ and ❾), you can expect international standards of comfort and luxury, with facilities such as swimming pools, gyms and a good restaurant.

It's only in the Petén, Eastern Highlands and on the Pacific and Caribbean coasts that you'll need a **fan** or **air conditioning**. In the highlands, even the luxury hotels rarely have a/c – many have lovely logwood fires to keep out the winter chill instead. **Mosquito nets** are rarely provided, even in the lowland areas, so if you plan to spend some time in Petén or by the coast it's well worth investing in one, and it's an essential purchase if you plan to so some jungle trekking.

Camping

Campsites are extremely thin on the ground in Guatemala. The main cities certainly don't

have them and the only places with any decent formal provision for camping are around Lago de Atitlán, and in the Petén. However if you decide to set off into the wilds, then a tent can be useful, although even here it's by no means essential.

Hiking in the highlands usually takes you from village to village, and wherever you go it's possible to find somewhere to bed down for the night. In villages that don't have hotels you should track down the mayor (*alcalde*) and ask if you can stay in the town hall (*municipalidad*) or local school. If that isn't possible then you'll almost certainly be found somewhere else. If you do take a tent along, the Guatemalan countryside offers plenty of superb spots, although you should always take care where you camp and also try to ask the landowner. In some places, such as Semuc Champey and the ruins of Mixco Viejo, there are thatched shelters where you can sling a hammock or bed down out of the rain.

When it comes to hiking in the jungle you'll need to hire a guide. They usually sleep out in the open, protected only by a mosquito net, so you can either follow suit or use a tent. At most of the smaller Maya sites there are guards who will usually let you sleep in their shelters and cook on their fires. If you plan to use their facilities then bring along some food to share with them.

The other occasion for which a tent is useful is climbing **volcanoes**, which often entails a night under the stars. On the lower cone of Acatenango there's a small hut that provides shelter for sleeping out, but it sometimes fills up at weekends. For renting tents, sleeping bags, stoves and rucksacks, contact Maya Mountain Bike Tours in Antigua or Quetzaltrekkers inside the *Casa Argentina* hotel in Quetzaltenango (see "Listings").

Communications

Guatemala's mail and telecommunication services were both recently privatized and are steadily becoming more efficient. Generally, postal services are cheap though still pretty unreliable, and many locals use courier companies to send important packages and documents overseas. Telgua, the former state phone company, has branches throughout the country; its national telephone and fax rates are low, but its international calls are extremely pricey. If at all possible try to use a private communications office to call abroad – there are plenty in the main tourist centres. Cybercafés and email facilities are mushrooming throughout Guatemala, especially wherever foreigners gather, and though rates are generally inexpensive, connection can be slow.

Mail

When sending mail home, the best way to ensure speedy delivery is to use the **main post office** in a capital city; this will also be the best place to send parcels. **Post boxes** are rare – you'll find them in the lobbies of big hotels and some tourist shops, but the best bet is to take mail to a post office. Generally, an airmail letter to the US takes about a week and to Europe from ten days to two weeks. **Receiving mail** is less certain; and, as the Poste Restante (Lista de Correos) system has recently been suspended, it's essential to get your mail sent to a reliable address – many language schools and tour operators will hold mail for you. American Express in Guatemala City (see p.86) will also keep mail if you are a card holder or have Amex travellers' cheques.

Always use some type of registration when sending **parcels**; it won't cost much more than the postage and you'll get a certificate to give you peace of mind. You can send parcels via surface mail but this takes months. Be prepared for the parcel to undergo some form of inspection, and there may also be some quirky labelling and wrapping regulations to observe. You may want to use a **specialized shipping agency** instead: see the Antigua and Panajachel "Listings" (p.109 and p.163) for recommended companies.

Courier companies (DHL, Federal Express etc) are establishing more and more offices throughout the region and even small towns now have offices. Obviously the charges involved are way above the standard postal rates, but they do represent the safest method of sending packages or documents home.

Phones

Although telephone systems are gradually improving, Guatemala's telecommunications technology is still pretty basic and connections are not always what they should be. Local calls are very cheap (around US$0.15 per minute) and long-distance domestic calls are not too expensive either (around US$0.30 per minute). Call boxes (operated by a number of companies) are becoming more widespread in urban areas; if you're going to be in Guatemala for a long stay, it's probably worth getting a **local calling card** (Telgua's is the most useful) as many call boxes don't accept cash.

For **international calls**, only use Telgua's phone offices in an emergency. The former state telecom company rates are prohibitively expensive at US$7 to North America, US$11 to the EU, and US$13 to Australasia for a three-minute call (the minimum length). By far the best international call rates are offered by a growing number of private communication businesses (and cybercafés) in most of the main tourist centres. Rates start from US$0.20 to the USA and Canada, US$0.40 to the EU and US$0.60 per minute to Australia and New Zealand at Kall Shop, who have branches in Antigua and Quetzaltenango. Even cheaper still, **webcall** internet phone connections are offered in some cybercafés, cutting costs as low as US$0.80 for a thirty-minute call, though the quality of the line can be appalling.

Calling home from overseas

USA and Canada: international access code + 1 + city code
UK and Northern Ireland: international access code + 44 + city code
Republic of Ireland: international access code + 353 + city code
Australia: international access code + 61 + city code
New Zealand: international access code + 64 + city code

Taking a **telephone charge card** or calling card with you is a good idea. Most North American cards work in Guatemala: AT&T, MCI, Sprint, Canada Direct and long-distance companies all enable their customers to make credit-card calls while overseas. Call your company's customer service line to find out if they provide service from Guatemala and, if so, what the toll-free access code is. Calls made from overseas will automatically be billed to your home number. At present UK-, Australian- and New Zealand-issued charge cards do not function in Central America.

Calling home collect (*llamar por cobrar*) to North America is fairly simple from Guatemala, though it's not possible to call Australia, New Zealand, the UK or any other EU countries (except Spain and Italy) collect. You can call collect from any Telgua phone by dialling ☎1671. You should be able to send (and receive) a **fax** from any (largish) Telgua or private telecom office, and it's often easier than making a phone call abroad.

Mobile phones

If you want to use your mobile phone on your travels, you'll need to check with your phone provider whether it will work abroad, and what the call charges are. However Guatemala is something of an international telecoms black hole – virtually no North American or UK tri-band phone functions here. If you need a mobile in Guatemala, you'll probably be forced to rent one in the country. Try Cellular Rent, 6 Av 6–45, Zona 10 in Guatemala City (☎ & ℻ 331 6251).

Email and the internet

Online services are now very established in Guatemala. You'll find **cybercafés** in all the major tourist centres (and many minor ones) so if you have a service provider which allows you to pick up email anywhere, like ⊛www.yahoo.com or ⊛www.hotmail.com, you can easily stay in touch. Rates vary considerably throughout the country: as little as US$1.50 per hour in Antigua, Quetzaltengango and Panajachel (which each have over a dozen cybercafés); around US$3–4 per hour in Flores, Huehuetenango, Puerto Barrios and Cobán; around US$6 in Lívingston and Copán; and an extortionate US$12 an hour in the Bay Islands, where all calls are classified as long-distance because they have to be routed via the mainland. Virtually all language schools are online, and many offer their students discount internet rates upon enrolment.

It's also becoming increasingly easy to reserve hotels, tours and services via email, though few budget places are yet online. Additionally many towns and regions now boast superb community **websites** (see p.20), replete with accommodation, restaurant, cultural and entertainment information.

Finally, ⊛www.kropka.com is a useful website giving details of how to plug your lap-top in when abroad, phone country codes around the world, and information about electrical systems in different countries.

The media

After a couple of decades when being a journalist in Guatemala was one of the most dangerous professions on the entire continent, things have cooled down somewhat. The nation's newspapers have expanded in both volume and coverage and, in theory, there is little restriction on their freedom, although pressures are still exerted by criminal gangs, the military and those in authority.

Guatemala has a number of daily newspapers with extensive national coverage and a more limited international perspective. Best of the **dailies** are the forthright and outspoken *El Periódico*, which is often tricky to find, and the more widely distributed *Siglo Veintiuno*. The most popular paper is the *Prensa Libre*, a conservative business-driven institution, though it does have a reasonable sports section. *El Gráfico* is also to the right of centre and broadly supportive of the economic, military and big business elite. Look out for a good **weekly** paper called *El Regional*, which is published in both Spanish and Maya languages. As for the **periodicals**, *La Crónica* is usually a decent read, concentrating on Guatemalan current political affairs and business news with a smattering of foreign coverage.

Not surprisingly for a country so dependent on tourism, there is a substantial **English-language** press in Guatemala. Well worth picking up, both for their features and to keep up with the current security situation, are two publications widely available in hotels, bookstores and cafés. The free monthly *Revue* magazine, published in Antigua, always has interesting articles about Guatemala, and has expanded in recent years to cover Belize, El Salvador and Honduras. It doesn't seek to cover much

political stuff but there's often a good cultural or historical feature, plus comprehensive accommodation, restaurant and shopping listings. Alternatively, the *Guatemala Post* (US$0.40) is an essential aid to the independent traveller, offering concise, independent coverage of the main Guatemalan news stories.

For really reliable, in-depth reporting, *Central America Report* excels, with proper journalistic investigation of controversial news stories like the plight of street children in Guatemala City. It's published by Inforpress Centroamericana and available from their offices at 7 Av 2–05, Zona 1, Guatemala City (☎ & ⓕ 232 9034, ⓦ www .inforpressca.com).

As for **foreign publications**, *Newsweek*, *Time* and *The Economist* are all sold in the streets of Guatemala City, particularly on the south side of the main plaza. Some American newspapers are also available: check in the *Camino Real Hotel* bookstore in Guatemala City and the bookshops in Antigua.

Radio and television

Guatemala has an abundance of **radio stations**, though variety is not their strong point. Most transmit a turgid stream of Latin pop and cheesy merengue, which you're sure to hear plenty of on the buses. There is a host of religious stations, too, broadcasting an onslaught of rabid evangelical lectures, services, "miracles", and so on. Try Radio Fama on 102.5FM for jazz and Western music. If you're visiting Guatemala City, it's worth twiddling your FM dial – there can be some interesting stuff broadcast over the capital's airwaves at weekends, including European techno.

Television stations are also in plentiful supply. Viewers can choose from five local

In Honduras, the most useful publications for travellers are *Honduras This Week* (ⓦ www.marrder.com/htw), an excellent weekly English-language newspaper with in-depth coverage of events in Honduras, plus tourist and business information, and *Honduras Tips*, a free tourism magazine with plenty of valuable information and features, plus hotel and restaurant listings. Both are widely available in Copán and the Bay Islands.

channels and over a dozen cable stations, all of them dominated by American programmes, either subtitled or dubbed into Spanish. Many upmarket hotels and some bars in tourist areas also have direct satellite links to US stations, which can be handy for catching up with the news on CNN.

The **BBC World Service** in English can be picked up by radios with short wave on 5975KHz in the 49m band, especially in the evening, on 15,220KHz in the 25m band, especially in the morning, and on 17,840KHz, especially in the afternoon. Other possible frequencies include: 6175KHz, 6195KHz, 9590KHz and 9895KHz. **The Voice of America** broadcasts on 15,210KHz, 11,740KHz, 9815KHz and 6030KHz.

Eating and drinking

Food doesn't come high in the list of reasons to visit Guatemala, with many Guatemalans surviving on a strict diet of eggs, beans and tortillas. However, in all the main tourist centres there's more choice, and in Antigua you can feast on numerous different European cuisines, several Asian ones, and even sample Middle Eastern dishes.

Where to eat

The most important distinction in Guatemala is between the **restaurant** and the comedor. The latter translates as an "eatery", and in general these are simple local cafés serving the food of the poor at rock-bottom prices. In a comedor there is often no menu, and you simply ask what's on offer, or look into the bubbling pots. Restaurants, in general, are slightly more formal and expensive. As usual, however, there are plenty of exceptions to this rule: many a restaurant has a very comedor-like menu, and vice versa. On the whole you'll find restaurants in the towns, while in small villages there are usually just one or two comedores, clustered around the market area. Comedores generally look scruffier, but the food is almost always fresh and the turnover is fast.

In the cities you'll also find **fast-food** joints, modelled on the American originals and often owned by the same companies. When you're travelling you'll also come across the local version of fast food: when buses pause they're besieged by vendors offering a huge selection of drinks, sweets, local specialities and complete meals. Many of these are delicious, but you do need to treat this kind of food with a degree of caution, and bear in mind the general lack of hygiene.

Traditionally, Guatemalans eat a **breakfast** of tortillas and eggs, accompanied by the inevitable beans – and sometimes also a sauce of sour cream. **Lunch** is the main meal of the day, and this is the best time to fill up as restaurants often offer comidas corridas, a set two- or three-course meal that sometimes costs as little as a dollar. It's always filling and occasionally delicious. Sometimes the same deal is on offer in the evenings, but usually not, so **evening meals** are likely to be more expensive.

Vegetarians are rarely catered for specifically, except in the tourist restaurants of Antigua and Panajachel and at a handful of places in Guatemala City. It is, however, fairly easy to get by eating plenty of beans and eggs which are always on the menu (although you should check, as beans, especially, are often fried in lard). The markets also offer plenty of superb fruit, and snacks like *tostadas* and *pupusas*.

There are three distinct **types of cooking** in Guatemala, and although they overlap to an extent it's still clear enough which one it is that you're eating.

See p.496 of Contexts for a list of food and dishes you'll find on a menu.

Maya cuisine

The oldest style of cuisine is **Maya cooking**, in which the basic staples of beans and maize dominate. **Beans** (*frijoles*) are the black kidney-shaped variety and are served in two ways: either *volteados*, which are boiled up, mashed, and then refried in a great dollop; or *parados*, which are boiled up whole, with a few slices of onion, and served in their own black juice. For breakfast, beans are usually served with eggs and cream, and at other times of the day they're offered up on a separate plate from the main dish. Almost all truly Guatemalan meals include a portion of beans, and for many highland Maya, beans are the only regular source of protein.

Maize is the other essential, a food which for the Maya (and many other native Americans) is almost as nourishing spiritually as it is physically – in Maya legend, humankind was originally formed from maize. It appears most commonly as the **tortilla**, a thin pancake. The maize is traditionally ground by hand and shaped by clapping it between two hands, a method still in widespread use. The tortilla is cooked on a **comal**, which is a flat pan of clay placed over the fire, and the very best tortillas are eaten while warm, usually brought to the table wrapped in cloth. For the Maya, the tortilla forms the hub of a meal, with beans or the odd piece of meat to spice it up. The very best warm tortillas have a lovely pliable texture, with a delicate, slightly burnt, smoky taste which will become very much a part of your trip – the smell of them is enough to revive memories years later. Where there's an option local people often serve gringos with bread, assuming they won't want tortillas.

Maize is also used to make a number of traditional **snacks**, which are sold on buses, at markets and during fiestas. The most common of these is the *tamal*, a pudding-like cornmeal package sometimes stuffed with chicken. It's wrapped in a banana leaf and then boiled. Slightly more exciting is the *chuchito*, which is similar but tends to include a bit of tomato and a pinch of hot chilli. Other popular snacks are *chiles rellenos*, stuffed peppers, and *pacaya*, which is a rather stodgy local vegetable.

Chillies are the final essential ingredient of the Maya diet (especially for the Kekchi). They are sometimes placed raw or pickled in the middle of the table in a jar, but also served as a sauce – *salsa picante*. The strength of these can vary tremendously, so treat them with caution until you know what you're dealing with.

Other traditional Maya dishes include a superb range of **stews** – known as *caldos* – made with duck, beef, chicken or turkey; and *fiambre*, which is the world's largest salad, a delicious mix of meat and vegetables traditionally served on the Day of the Dead (November 1), when you can usually find it in restaurants. The best chance to sample traditional food is at a market or fiesta, when makeshift comedores serve freshly cooked dishes. A highland breakfast often includes a plate of *mosh*, which is made with milk and oats and tastes rather like porridge. It's the ideal antidote to the early morning chill.

Ladino cuisine

Guatemala's second culinary style is **ladino food**, which is indebted to the range of cultures that go to make up the ladino population. Most of the food has a mild Latin American bias, incorporating a lot of Mexican ideas, but the influence of the United States and Europe is also strongly felt. At its most obvious, ladino food includes *bistek* (steak), *hamburguesa* and *chao mein*, all of which are readily available in most Guatemalan towns, with rice and fries (chips) usually providing the carbohydrate. Guatemalan-style *ceviche* (raw fish with spicy salad) is also popular on the coasts. In addition, you'll find a mild **German** influence in the widespread availability of frankfurter-type sausages, and plenty of **Italian**-influenced restaurants offering pasta and pizza. Ladino-style cakes and pastries are widely available, but tend to be pretty dull and dry.

Creole cuisine

The final element is the **Creole cooking** found on Guatemala's Caribbean coast. Here, **bananas**, **coconuts** and **seafood** dominate the scene, all of them, if you're lucky, cooked superbly. You have to hunt around to find true Creole cooking, which incorporates the influences of the Caribbean with those of Africa, but it's well worth the effort. Some of the more obvious elements have also penetrated the mainstream; for example, you can get fried plantains (*plátanos fritos*) just about anywhere in the country.

Drink

To start off the day most Guatemalans drink a cup of hot **coffee**, **chocolate** or **tea** (all of which are usually served with plenty of sugar), but in the highlands you'll also be offered *atol*, a warm, sweet drink made with either rice or maize and sugar. At other times of day, **soft drinks** and beer are usually drunk with meals. Coca-Cola, Pepsi, Sprite and Fanta (all called *aguas*) are common, as are *refrescos*, thirst-quenching water-based drinks with a little fruit flavour added. In many places, you can also get *licuado*, a delicious, thick fruit-based drink with either milk or water added (milk is safer).

Tap water in the main towns is purified and you can usually taste the chlorine. However, this doesn't mean that it won't give you stomach trouble, and it's always safest to stick to **bottled water** (*agua mineral or agua pura*), which is almost always available.

Guatemalan **beers** tend to be bland, unexciting and rarely on draught. One characterless brew has a near monopoly, the ubiquitous *Gallo*, a medium-strength lager-style beer that comes in 33cl- (around US$0.80) or litre- (around US$2) bottles.

More interesting, but not so widely available, is *Moza*, a dark brew with a slight caramel flavour. The best of the lagers is *Montecarlo*, an expensive premium beer that is worth the extra quetzal or two, if you can get it. You may also come across *Dorada Draft*, another dull lager brew, and occasionally *Cabra*, which has a little more flavour. Imported beers are rare, though Mexican brands can be found in places like Huehuetenango.

As for **spirits**, rum (*ron*) and *aguardiente*, a clear and lethal sugar cane spirit, are very popular and cheap. *Ron Botran Añejo* is a good rum (around US$4 a bottle), while *Ron Zacapa Centenario*, which regularly wins international prizes, is fabulously smooth. Hard drinkers will soon get to know *Quezalteca* and *Venado*, two local *aguardientes* available everywhere. If you're after a real bargain, then try locally brewed alcohol (*chicha*), which is practically given away. Its main ingredient can be anything: apple, cherry, sugar cane, peach, apricot and quince are just some of the more common varieties.

Wine is also made in Guatemala, from local fruits or imported concentrates. It's interesting to try, but for something really drinkable stick to the more expensive imports. Chilean wines are the best value with decent bottles available from around US$5 in supermarkets, and from double that in restaurants.

Opening hours and public holidays

Guatemalan opening hours are subject to considerable local variations, but in general most offices, shops, post offices and museums open between around 8.30am and 5pm, though some take an hour or so break for lunch. Banking hours are extremely convenient, with many staying open until 7pm (and some as late as 8pm) from Monday to Friday, but closing at 1pm on Saturdays. You may not always be able to exchange money after 5.30pm in some places, however, even though the bank is open.

Archeological sites open every day, usually from 8am to 5pm, though Tikal is open from 6am to 6pm (until 8pm with permission). Principal public holidays, when almost all businesses close down, are listed below, but each village or town will also have its own fiestas or saints' days when everything will be shut. These can last anything from one day to two weeks.

Public holidays

January 1 New Year's Day
Semana Santa The four days of Holy Week leading up to Easter
May 1 Labour Day
June 30 Army Day, anniversary of the 1871 revolution
August 15 Guatemala City fiesta (Guatemala City only)

September 15 Independence Day
October 12 Discovery of America (only banks close)
October 20 Revolution Day
November 1 All Saints' Day
December 24 From noon
December 25 Christmas
December 31 From noon

Fiestas

Traditional fiestas are one of the great excitements of a trip to Guatemala, and every town and village, however small, devotes at least one day a year to celebration. The main day is normally prescribed by the local saint's day, though the celebrations often extend to a week or two around that date. On almost every day of the year there's a fiesta in some forgotten corner of the country, and with a bit of planning you should be able to witness at least one. Most of them are well worth going out of your way for. A list of all the regional fiestas appears at the end of each chapter in the Guide.

The **format** of fiestas varies between two basic models (except on the Caribbean coast – see box below). In towns with a largely ladino population, fairs are usually set up and the days are filled with processions, beauty contests and perhaps the odd marching band, while the nights are dominated by dancing to merengue and salsa. In the highlands, where the bulk of the population is Maya, you'll see traditional dances, costumes and musicians, and a blend of religious and secular celebration that incorporates pre-Columbian elements. What they all share is an astonishing energy and an unbounded enthusiasm for drink, dance and fireworks, all of which are virtually impossible to escape during the days of fiesta.

One thing you shouldn't expect is anything too dainty or organized: fiestas are above all chaotic, and the measured rhythms of traditional dance and music are usually obscured by the crush of the crowd and the huge volumes of alcohol consumed by participants. If you can join in the mood there's no doubt that fiestas are wonderfully entertaining and that they offer a real insight into Guatemalan culture, ladino or indigenous.

Many of the **best fiestas** include some

specifically local element, such as the giant kites at Santiago Sacatepéquez, the religious processions in Antigua, the horse race in Todos Santos Cuchumatán or the skull bearers of San José. The dates of most fiestas, along with their main features, are listed at the end of each chapter. At certain times virtually the whole country erupts simultaneously: Easter Week is perhaps the most important, particularly in Antigua, but both All Saints' Day (November 1) and Christmas are also marked by partying across the land.

Fiesta dances

In Guatemala's Maya villages **traditional dances** – heavily imbued with history and symbolism – form a pivotal part in the fiesta celebrations. The drunken dancers may look out of control, but the process is taken very seriously and involves great expense on the part of the participants, who have to rent their ornate costumes. The most common dance is the **Baile de la Conquista**, which re-enacts the victory of the Spanish over the Maya, while at the same time managing to ridicule the conquistadors. According to some studies, the dance is based in pre-

Carribbean fiestas and music

Fiestas in Lívingston and the Honduran Bay Islands have different traditions from those in Guatemala and swing to other rhythms. In the Bay Islands, the Creole festivals are unabashedly hedonistic affairs, much more like a Caribbean carnival than a Latin fiesta, with floats, lashings of rum punch and plenty of heavy sexual innuendo. Reggae basslines boom from giant stacks of speakers and the streets and dancehalls are crammed with hip-grinding groovers. Much of the music comes from Jamaica and is sung in English, although there are popular tunes from Central America, with the most important reggae bands coming from Belize, Costa Rica and Panamá. In Lívingston on Guatemala's Caribbean coast, some of the best dancing you'll ever see is to the hypnotic drum patterns of punta, the music of the Garífuna (see p.272) which betrays a distinctive West African heritage. The Garífuna really know how to party, and if you get the chance to attend a fiesta, be prepared for some explosively athletic shimmying and provocative hip movements – nineteenth-century Methodists were so outraged they called it "devil dancing". Garífuna day (November 26) is the ideal time to see Lívingston really celebrate, though there seems to be a punta party going on most weekends.

Columbian traditions. Other popular dances are the **Baile de los Gracejos**, the dance of the jesters; the **Baile del Venado**, the dance of the deer; and the **Baile de la Culebra**, the dance of the snake; all of them again rooted in pre-Columbian traditions. One of the most impressive is the **Palo Volador**, in which men swing by ropes from a thirty-metre pole. Today this Maya-style bungy jump is only performed in Chichicastenango, Joyabaj and Cubulco.

Fiesta music

Guatemalan **music** combines many different influences, but yet again it can be broadly divided between ladino and Maya. For fiestas, bands are always shipped in, complete with a crackling PA system and a strutting lead singer.

Traditional Guatemalan music is dominated by the **marimba**, a type of wooden xylophone that originated in Africa. The oldest versions use gourds beneath the sounding board and can be played by a single musician, while modern models, using hollow tubes to generate the sound, can need as many as seven players. The marimba is at the heart of traditional music, and marimba orchestras play at every occasion, for both ladino and indigenous communities. In the remotest of villages you sometimes hear them practising well into the night, particularly around market day. Other important instruments, especially in Maya bands, are the *tun*, a drum made from a hollow log; the *tambor*, another drum traditionally covered with the skin of a deer; *los chichines*, a type of maracas made from hollow gourds; the *tzijolaj*, a kind of piccolo; and the *chirimia*, a flute.

Ladino music is a blend of North American and Latin sounds, much of it originating in Miami, Colombia, the Dominican Republic and Puerto Rico, although there are plenty of local bands producing their own version of the sound. It's fast-moving, easy-going and very rhythmic, and on any bus you'll hear many of the most popular tracks. It draws on merengue, a rhythm that originally came from the Dominican Republic, and includes elements of Mexican music and the cumbia and salsa of Colombia and Cuba.

Sports and outdoor pursuits

Guatemalans have a furious appetite for spectator sports and the daily papers always devote four or five pages to the subject. Fútbol (soccer) tops the bill, and if you get the chance to see a major game it's a thrilling experience, if only to watch the crowd. There's a great website (®www.futbol.guatemala.org) dedicated to the national sport. Otherwise North American sport predominates – baseball, American football, boxing and basketball are all popular.

Hiking is perhaps the most popular sport among visitors, particularly volcano climbing, which is certainly hard work but almost always worth the effort – unless you end up wrapped in cloud. Guatemala has some 37 volcanic peaks; the tallest is Tajumulco in the west, which at 4220m is a serious undertaking, and should only be tackled when you're been acclimatized to an altitude of over 2000m for a few days. Among the active peaks Pacaya is a fairly easy climb and a dramatic sight, although as it has been the scene of violent attacks it should not be attempted alone. Volcano climbing trips are organized by a number of tour groups in Antigua and Quetzaltenango (see p.105 and p.188).

As a participatory sport, **fishing** is also popular, with good sea fishing available on both coasts. On the Pacific side the coastal waters offer sierra mackerel, jack cravelle, yellow and black tuna, snappers, bonito and dorado, with marlin and sailfish further offshore, while the Caribbean side also offers excellent opportunities. In Petén the rivers and lakes are packed with sport fish, including snook, tarpon and peacock bass, and lakes Petexbatún, Izabal and Yaxjá all offer superb fishing, as do the Usumacinta and Dulce rivers. Fishing trips to both coasts and on the inland waterways are organized by Tropical Tours 4 C, 2–51, Zona 10, Guatemala City (☎339 3662 ®tropicaltour @guate.net) and Guatemala Unlimited (®www.guatemalaunlimited.com), though these trips are expensive, and if you just want

to dabble around then you should be able to sort something out with local fishermen in the coastal villages or in Sayaxché or El Estor.

Guatemala's dramatic highland landscape and tumbling rivers also provide some excellent opportunities for **whitewater rafting**. Three-day trips down the Río Cahabón are organized by Maya Expeditions (see p.89) who also run trips on the Usumacinta, Naranjo and Motagua, giving you the chance to see some really remote areas and visit some of the country's most inaccessible Maya sites.

Scuba diving is another up-and-coming sport in this part of the world, although Guatemala has little to offer compared with the splendours of the neighbouring Belizean or Honduran coastal waters. Nevertheless, there are some diving possibilities here, including Lago de Atitlán and Lago de Izabal, as well as some reasonable Pacific and Caribbean dive sites. Highly recommended for freshwater, high-altitude dives, and excellent instruction are ATI Divers, based in the *Iguana Perdida* hotel in Santa Cruz, Lake Atitlán (see p.175) – they also have a spectacular dive excursion through the Río Dulce to the Belize cayes (see p.276). Dive trips and courses are also offered by Prodiver, 6 Av 9–85, Zona 9, Guatemala City (☎331 2738, ®478 2286).

There is also some **surfing** in Guatemala, on the Pacific coast, although if you've come all this way for the waves you may be disappointed; you'll certainly find better breaks in El Salvador or Costa Rica.

Trouble and the police

Personal safety is a serious problem in Guatemala, partly owing to a recent nationwide rise in crime that has also affected tourists. There is little pattern to these attacks, but some areas can be considered safer than others. It's wise to register with your embassy on arrival, try to keep informed of events by reading newspapers, and avoid travelling at night.

Crime

Though Guatemala attracts around 900,000 tourists a year and relatively few have any trouble, it's essential that you try to minimize the chance of becoming a victim. **Petty theft** and **pickpockets** are likely to be your biggest worry. Theft is most common in Zona 1 and the bus stations of Guatemala City, but you should also take extra care when visiting markets popular with tourists (like Sololá and Chichicastenango) and during fiestas. Avoid wearing flashy jewellery or waving your money around. When **travelling**, there is actually little danger to your pack when it's on top of a bus; it's the conductor's responsibility alone to go up the roof and collect luggage.

Muggings and **violent crime** are on the increase in Guatemala City. There's not too much danger in the daylight hours but don't amble about at night, especially if you don't know your way about. Stick to the main streets and use buses and taxis. There have also been a few cases of armed robbery in Antigua and attacks on tourists in many of the volcanoes, including Volcanes Pacaya, San Pedro and Santa María.

If you are robbed you'll have to report it to the police, which can be a very long process and may seem like little more than a symbolic gesture; however, most insurance companies will only pay up if you can produce a police statement.

Drugs

Drugs are increasingly available as Guatemala is becoming a centre for both shipment and production. Marijuana and cocaine are both readily available and cheap heroin is also to be found on the streets. However, be aware that **drug offences** are dealt with severely. Even the possession of marijuana could land you in jail – a sobering experience in Guatemala. If you do get into a problem with drugs, it may be worth enquiring with the first policeman if there is a "fine" (*multa*) to pay, to save expensive arbitration later. At the first possible opportunity, get in touch with your embassy and negotiate through them: they will understand the situation better than you. The addresses of embassies and consulates in Guatemala City are listed on p.88. Officially you should **carry your passport** (or a photocopy) at all times.

Sexual harassment

Machismo is very much a part of Latin American culture, and many Guatemalan men consider it their duty to put on a bit of a show to impress the Western *gringas*. It's usually best to ignore any such hassle. Ladino towns and *cantinas* are the worst places. Indigenous society is more deferential so you're unlikely to experience any trouble in the western highlands.

Homosexuality is publicly frowned upon – although not theoretically illegal – so it's sensible to be discreet. (See "Directory for more.)

The police

For Europeans and North Americans expecting to enter a police state, Guatemala may come as something of a surprise. Though there are a lot of police, soldiers and armed security guards on the streets, there's rarely anything intimidating about their presence.

Useful numbers

Police ☎ 120
Tourism Police ☎ 110
Red Cross ambulance ☎ 125

Guatemala's civilian **police force**, introduced in 1997, was trained by experts from Spain, the USA, France and Chile in an effort to improve working practices. Despite these efforts, the force still suffers from an appalling reputation for corruption and inefficiency, so don't expect much help if you experience any trouble. Things are a little better in Antigua, where a **tourist police force** (see p.97) has been set up. Officers patrol the streets at night and will escort groups up to the Cross overlooking Antigua for a view of the city.

If for any reason you do find yourself in **trouble with the law**, be as polite as possible – and remember that bribery is a way of life here.

Shopping

Guatemalan craft traditions, locally known as artesanía, are very much a part of modern Maya culture, stemming from practices that in most cases predate the arrival of the Spanish. Many of these traditions are highly localized, with different regions and even different villages specializing in particular crafts. It makes sense to visit as many markets as possible, particularly in the highland villages, where the colour and spectacular settings are like nowhere else in Central America.

As for **everyday goods**, you'll find that both slide and print film is available in most towns in the country, though monochrome is much less common. Camcorder videotapes are also widely on sale though DV tapes are difficult to find.

Artesanía

The best place to buy Guatemalan **crafts** is in their place of origin, where prices are reasonable and the craftsmen and women get a greater share of the profit. If you haven't the time to travel to remote highland villages, the best places to head for are Chichicastenango on market days (Thurs and Sun) and the shops and street hawkers in Antigua and Panajachel.

The greatest craft in Guatemala has to be **textile weaving**. Each Maya village has its own traditional designs, woven in fantastic patterns and with superbly vivid colours. All the finest weaving is done on the **backstrap loom**, using complex weft float and wrapping techniques. Chemical dyes have been dominant in Guatemala for over a century now and virtually no natural colourings are used.

One of the best places to start looking at textiles is in Antigua's Nim Po't, 5 Av Nte 29 (daily 9am–9pm; ☎ & ℻832 2681), a large store with an excellent collection of styles and designs. Guatemala City's Museo Ixchel (see p.77) is another essential visit.

You should bear in mind that while most Maya are proud that foreigners find their textiles attractive, for them clothing has a spiritual significance – so it's not wise for women travellers to wear men's shirts or men to wear *huipiles*.

Alongside Guatemalan weaving most **other crafts** suffer by comparison. However, if you hunt around you'll also find good ceramics, baskets, mats, silver and jade. Antigua has the most comprehensive collection of shops. For anything woollen, particularly blankets, head for Momostenango Sunday market (see p.196).

Markets

For shopping – or simply sightseeing – the **markets** of Guatemala are some of the finest anywhere in the world. The large markets of Chichicastenango, Sololá and San Francisco el Alto are all well worth a visit, but equally fascinating are the tiny weekly gatherings in remote villages like San Juan Atitán and Chajul, where the atmosphere is hushed and unhurried. In these isolated settlements market day is as much a social event as a commercial affair, providing the chance for villagers to catch up on local news, and perhaps enjoy a tipple or two, as well as selling some vegetables and buying a few provisions. Most towns and villages have at least one weekly event; for a comprehensive list, see p.128.

Work and study

Guatemala is one of the best – and most popular – places in Latin America to study Spanish. The language school industry is big business, with around sixty well-established schools and many more less reliable set-ups. Thousands of foreigners from all over the world study each year in Guatemala – mainly travellers, but also college students, airline crew and business people. As for work, there's little paid employment apart from teaching English, though there are always opportunities for committed volunteers.

Studying Spanish

Most schools offer a weekly deal that includes four or five hours' one-on-one tuition a day, plus full board with a local family, at an inclusive **cost** of around US$130 a week. It's important to bear in mind that the success of the exercise is dependent both on your personal commitment to study and on the enthusiasm and aptitude of your **teacher** – if you are not happy with the teacher you've been allocated, ask for another. Insist on knowing the number of other students that will be sharing your family house; some schools pack as many as ten foreigners in with one family. Virtually all schools have a student liaison officer, usually an English-speaking foreigner who acts as a go-between for students and teachers, so if you're a complete beginner there will usually be someone around who you can communicate with.

The first decision to make is to choose where you want to study. By far the most popular choices are the towns of Antigua and Quetzaltenango. **Antigua** is undoubtedly an excellent place to study Spanish: a beautiful, relaxed town with several superb schools, a vibrant social scene and plenty of cultural activities. The major drawback is that there are so many other students and tourists here that you'll probably end up spending your evenings speaking English. **Quetzaltenango** (Xela) has a very different atmosphere, with a much stronger "Guatemalan" character and far fewer tourists; despite its popularity with language students, it's still possible to really immerse yourself in the language and local culture here. Several new language schools have recently been set up in the **Lago de Atitlán** area, in Panajachel and San Pedro La Laguna, with more planned in other lakeside villages. As yet, tuition standards in the Atitlán area are only average, but, such is the draw of the lake, the schools have nevertheless quickly become popular with international travellers. If you already speak some basic Spanish and really want to accelerate your learning, you could study somewhere where you're unlikely to be able to speak any English at all, such as **Huehuetenango**, **Cobán** or the "eco-schools" based in San Andrés and San José in **Petén**. Finally, **Copán** in Honduras, where there are two language schools, is a delightful place to study, though rates are slightly higher than Guatemala at around US$185 for tuition and full board. It's also rumoured that a new school is soon to be set up in **Utila**, though as most people in the island speak English, it's hardly an ideal base.

Recommended language schools

Many of the schools listed overleaf have academic accreditation agreements with North American and European universities. Some also have US offices, consult the schools' websites for more information. The **website** ⓦ www.guatemala365.com is a reliable place to begin the search for a school in Guatemala, with a good list of professional schools and tips about the relative advantages of different study centres. Details of schools are also given at relevant places in the Guide.

Antigua

APPE 6 C Pte 40 ☎832 0720, ⊕www.guacalling .com/appe.

Centro America Spanish Academy inside La Fuente, 4 C Ote 14 ☎ & ℗832 6268, ⊕www.quik .guate.com/spanishacademy.

Centro Lingüístico de la Fuente 1 C Pte 27 ☎ & ℗832 2711, ⊕www.delafuenteschool.com.

Centro Lingüístico Maya 5 C Pte 20 ☎ & ℗ 832 0656, ⊕www.travellog.com/guatemala /antigua/clmaya/school.html.

Christian Spanish Academy 6 Av Nte 15 ☎832 3922, ℗832 3760, ⊕www.learncsa.com.

Probigua 6 Av Nte 41B ☎ & ℗832 0860, http: //probigua.conexion.com.

Projecto Linguístico Francisco Marroquín 7 C Pte 31 ☎832 2886, ⊕www.plfm-antigua.org. Also offers classes in Maya languages.

San José El Viejo 5 Av Sur 34 ☎832 3028, ℗832 3029, ⊕www.guate.net/spanish.

Sevilla 1 Av Sur 8 ☎ & ℗832 0442, ⊕www .sevillantigua.com.

Tecún Umán Linguistic School 6 C Pte 34 A ☎ & ℗ 831 2792, ⊕www.tecunuman.centramerica.com.

La Unión 1 Av Sur 21 ☎ & ℗832 7337, ⊕www .launion.conexion.com.

Quetzaltenango

ALM 15 Av 6–75, Zona 1 ☎761 2877, ℗763 2176, ⊕http://travel.to/alm. Also has branches in Antigua and Monterrico.

Casa de Español Xelajú Callejón 15, Diagonal 13-02, Zona 1 ☎761 5954, ℗761 5953, ⊕www .casaxelaju.com.

Centro Bilingüe Amerindia (CBA) 7 Av 9–05, Zona 1 ☎761 1613, ⊕www.xelapages.com/cba.

Centro Maya de Idiomas 21 Av 5–69, Zona 3 ☎767 0352, ⊕www.centromaya.org. Also offers classes in six Maya languages.

Educación para Todos 12 Av 1–78, Zona 3 ☎ & ℗765 0715, ⊕www.xelapages.com/paratodos.

English Club International Language School Diagonal 4 9–71, Zona 9 ☎763 2198. Also classes in K'iche' and Mam.

Escuela Juan Sisay 15 Av 8–38, Zona 1 ☎ & ℗ 763 1318, ⊕www.juansisay.com.

Guatemalensis 19 Av 2–14, Zona 1 ☎ & ℗765 1384, ⊕www.infovia.com.gt/gssxela.

Kie–Balam Diagonal 12 4–46 ☎761 1636 ℗761 0391, ⊕www.super-highway.net/users/moebius.

La Paz 2 C 19–30, Zona 1 ☎761 4243, ⊕www .xelapages.com/lapaz.

Pop Wuj 1 C 17–72, Zona 1 ☎761 8286; ⊕www .popwuj.org.

Proyecto Lingüístico Quetzalteco de Español 5 C 2–40, Zona 1 ☎761 2620, ⊕www.inforserve .net/hermandad/montana.html. Also has sister schools on the Pacific coast and in Todos Santos Cuchumatán.

Sakribal 10C 7–17, Zona 1 ☎ & ℗761 5211, ⊕http://kcyb.com/sakribal.

Lago de Atitlán

Casa Rosario south of Santiago Atitlán dock, San Pedro La Laguna, ⊕www.worldwide.edu/ci /guatemala/schools/34451.html.

Centro Maya de Idiomas 21 Av 5–69 Zona 3 ☎767 0352 ⊕www.centromaya.org. Also offers classes in six Maya languages.

Escuela Jabel Tinamit off C Santander, Panajachel ☎762 0238, ⊕http://members.nbci.com /learnspanish.

Jardín de América C 14 de Febrero, Panajachel ☎ & ℗762 2637, ⊕www.atitlan.com/jardin.htm.

San Pedro Spanish School between the piers, San Pedro La Laguna ☎703 1100, ⊕www.spanish -schools.com.

Huehuetenango

Casa Xelajú contact its Quetzaltenango school (see above) for more information.

Fundación XXIII 6 Av 6–126, Zona 1 ☎764 1478, ⊕www.worldwide.edu/ci/guatemala/schools /10024.html.

Insituto El Portal 1 C 1–64, Zona 3 ☎ & ℗764 1987, ⊕www.guatemala365.com/english/schools /schu003.htm.

Xinabajul 6 Av 0–69 ☎ & ℗764 1518, ⊕www .spanish-schools.com/huehue/inf/infoe.htm.

Petén

Eco-Escuela San Andrés, Lago de Petén Itzá ☎928 8106, ⊕www.conservation.org/ecoescuela /about.htm.

Escuela Bio–Itzá San José, Lago de Petén Itzá ☎928 8142, ⊕www.conservation.org/ecoescuela /bioitza.htm.

Cobán

Active Spanish School 3 C 6–12, Zona 1 ☎ & ℗952 1432, ⊕www.spanish-schools.com/coban /city/ce.htm.

Instituto Cobán Internacional (INCO Int) 6 Av 5–39, Zona 3 ☎ & ℗951 2459, ⊕www.worldwide .edu/ci/guatemala/schools/15017.html.

Muq'b'ilbe 6 Av 5–39, Zona 3 ☎951 2459,

@ www.guatemala365.com/english/schools /schu005.htm. Also offers Q'eqchi' language study.

Todos Santos Cuchumatán

Hispano Maya @ www.personal.umich.edu/ ~kakenned.
Nuevo Amanacer contact Centro Maya de Idiomas (see above).
Proyecto Lingüístico Mam contact Proyecto Lingüístico Quetzalteco de Español (see above).

Copán, Honduras

Guacamaya three blocks north of the Parque, ☎ & ⓕ651 4360, @ www.guacamaya.com.
Ixbalanque ☎ & ⓕ651 4432, @ ixbalan@hn2.com.

Volunteer and paid work

There are dozens of excellent organizations offering **voluntary work** placements in Guatemala. Medical and health specialists are always desperately needed, though there are always openings in other areas, from work helping to improve the lives of street children to environmental projects and wildlife conservation. The best place to start a search for organizations is on the web (see below) though there are also useful publications you can consult before you go. In the US *Work Abroad* is an informative book produced by the US-based Transitions Abroad, PO Box 1300, Amherst, MA 01004 (☎413 /256-3414, @ www.transabroad.com) while in the UK, the **Central Bureau for Educational Visits**, 10 Spring Gardens, London SW1A 2BN (☎020/7389 4880, @ www.centralbureau.org.uk), publishes *A Year Between* with excellent sections on voluntary work placements in Central America.

In Guatemala, the **Project Mosaic Guatemala** 1 Av Sur 21, Antigua (☎813 5758, ⓕ832 7337, @ www.pmg.dk, @ promigua @yahoo.com) has links to over sixty groups. There's a second good drop-in resource centre in Antigua called **El Arco** at 5 Av Nte 25B (☎832 0162, ⓕ832 1540, @ www .adventravelguatemala.com, @ elarco@guate .net). The best places to head for in Quetzaltenango are the language school **Casa Xelajú** (see above) and **Entremundos** at 6 C 7–31, Zona 1 (☎761 2179, @ www. entremundos.org); both have links to dozens of local development projects.

As for **paid work**, teaching English is your best bet, particularly if you have an ELT (English Language Teaching) or TEFL (Teaching English as a Foreign Language) qualification. Check the English schools in Guatemala City and Quetzaltenango (listed in the phone books). All language schools (see opposite) employ student coordinators to liaise between staff and pupils – though you'll need near-fluent Spanish. In Antigua there are always a few vacancies for staff in the gringo bars and sales positions in jade showrooms. The English language press (the *Revue* and the *Guatemala Post*) and noticeboards in the popular bars and restaurants in Antigua and Quetzaltenango also occasionally advertise vacancies. To work anywhere in Guatemala you'll need to speak some Spanish.

Project websites and email addresses

Ak'Tenamit @ www.aktenamit.org. Health, education and agriculture volunteer positions in a large established project, working with Q'eqchi' Maya in the Río Dulce region of Guatemala.
Alternatives @ www.alternatives.ca. Canadian organization with numerous development projects in Central America.
Arcas @ arcaspeten@intelnet.net.gt. Volunteers needed in the Petén to help rehabilitate animals illegally kept as pets for release back into the wild, and opportunities to help out in a sea turtle reserve at Hawaii on the Pacific coast.
Casa Alianza @ www.casa-alianza.org. Charity helping street children in Guatemala and throughout Central America; the work is extremely demanding and volunteers need to give a minimum six-month commitment. See box on p.65.
Casa Guatemala @ http://mayaparadise.com /casaguae.htm. Teachers, doctors, nurses and helpers needed to work with street children and orphans in the Río Dulce region.
Casa Xelajú @ www.casaxelaju.com/volunteer. Language school with myriad opportunities and links to projects – including women's co-operatives and journalism – in the Quetzaltenango region.
Council on International Educational Exchange @ www.ciee.org. Large US-based organization with many voluntary programmes.
Gap Year @ www.gap-year.com. Lots of volunteer and work placements, including links to Quetzaltrekkers in Xela where trekking guides are needed. Also publish the *Gap-Year Guidebook*.
Guatemala Accompaniment Project @ nisguap @igc.org. Monitoring the human rights and resettlement of returned refugees in Guatemala; minimum commitment of one year.
Habitat for Humanity @ www.habitat.org/intl.

One-to-three-week house building projects in Guatemala and elsewhere in Central America.
Hospital ⊛ www.hospitaldelafamilia.org. Doctors, nurses and medical staff needed to help out in the San Marcos region of Guatemala's Western Highlands.
Idealist ⊛ www.idealist.org. Excellent place to start a search, with a massive database of links to a wide range of projects in the region; from ecotourism to human rights work and both voluntary and paid work opportunities.
International Voluntary Programs Association ⊛ www.volunteerinternational.org. Dozens of voluntary opportunities throughout Central America in all fields.
Peace Corps ⊛ www.peacecorps.gov. Community-based development work throughout Guatemala.

Project Honduras ⊛ www.projecthonduras.com /projectspage.htm. Voluntary work opportunities for medical, teachers, architects, builders in Honduras.
Proyecto eco-Quetzal ⊜ bidaspeg@guate.net. Placements in the Verapaz region, working on ecotourism projects. A six-month commitment is required.
Quetzaltrekkers ⊛ www.quetzalventures.com.
Remote Area Medical Corp ⊛ www.ramusa.org. Voluntary physicians, eye specialists, surgeons, dentists, nurses, and veterinarians needed to work in poor areas of Central America.
Volunteers for Peace ⊛ www.vfp.org. Large US-based nonprofit group that organizes work camps in the region.

Travellers with specific needs

Whether you're trying to placate a sobbing child or struggling to steer a wheelchair around a crowded market, you'll find that most Guatemalans are extremely helpful and courteous.

Travellers with disabilities

Disabled travellers are faced with many obstacles when travelling in Guatemala. **Wheelchair users** will have to manoeuvre their way over cobbled streets, cracked (or non-existent) pavements, and pot-holed roads in cities, towns and villages throughout the country. Getting around Guatemala by public transport can be exhausting enough for able-bodied travellers, but trying to clamber aboard a packed chicken bus with a wheelchair or walking sticks, even with a friend to help, presents a whole set of other challenges. Nevertheless, plenty of disabled travellers do successfully negotiate their way around the country. Most of the main sites are connected by tourist shuttle minibuses, which pick you up from your hotel, and have a driver whose job it is to assist passengers with their luggage. Many Guatemalan hotels are low rise (and larger, upmarket places often have lifts and ramps) so it shouldn't be too difficult to find an easily accessible room. You'll only find disabled toilets in the most expensive hotels however.

Contacts for travellers with disabilities

In the US and Canada

Access-Able ⊛ www.access-able.com. Online resource for travellers with disabilities.
Directions Unlimited 123 Green Lane, Bedford Hills, NY 10507 ☏ 1-800/533-5343 or 914/241-1700. Tour operator specializing in custom tours for people with disabilities.
Mobility International USA 451 Broadway, Eugene, OR 97401 Voice and TDD ☏ 541/343-1284, ⊛ www.miusa.org. Information and referral services, access guides, tours and exchange programmes. Annual membership US$35 (includes quarterly newsletter).
Society for the Advancement of Travelers with Handicaps (SATH) 347 Fifth Ave, New York, NY 10016 ☏ 212/447-7284, ⊛ www.sath.org. Nonprofit educational organization that has actively represented travellers with disabilities since 1976.
Travel Information Service ☏ 215/456-9600. Telephone-only information and referral service.
Twin Peaks Press Box 129, Vancouver, WA 98661 ☏ 1-800/637-2256 or 360/694-2462, ⊛ www.twinpeak.virtualave.net. Publisher of the *Directory of Travel Agencies for the Disabled*

(US$19.95), listing more than 370 agencies worldwide; *Travel for the Disabled* ($19.95); the *Directory of Accessible Van Rentals* (US$12.95) and *Wheelchair Vagabond* (US$19.95), loaded with personal tips.

Wheels Up! ☎1-888/389-4335, ⊛www.wheelsup .com. Provides discounted airfare, tour and cruise prices for disabled travellers, also publishes a free monthly newsletter and has a comprehensive website.

In the UK and Ireland

Disability Action Group 2 Annadale Ave, Belfast BT7 3JH ☎028/9049 1011. Provides information about access for disabled travellers abroad.

Irish Wheelchair Association Blackheath Drive, Clontarf, Dublin 3 ☎01/833 8241, ⊕833 3873, ⊛iwa@iol.ie. Useful information provided about travelling abroad with a wheelchair.

Tripscope Alexandra House, Albany Rd, Brentford, Middlesex TW8 0NE ☎08457/585 641, ⊛www .justmobility.co.uk/tripscope, ⊛tripscope@cableinet .co.uk. This registered charity provides a national telephone information service offering free advice on international transport for those with a mobility problem.

In Australia and New Zealand

ACROD (Australian Council for Rehabilitation of the Disabled) PO Box 60, Curtin ACT 2605 ☎02 6282 4333; 24 Cabarita Rd, Cabarita NSW 2137 ☎02 9743 2699. Provides lists of travel agencies and tour operators for people with disabilities.

Disabled Persons Assembly 4/173–175 Victoria St, Wellington, New Zealand ☎04/801 9100. Resource centre with lists of travel agencies and tour operators for people with disabilities.

Travelling with children

It can be exceptionally rewarding to travel with children in Guatemala. Most locals have children at an early age, and as families are much larger than in the west, your kids will always have some company. By bringing your children along to Guatemala, you'll instantly dismantle one of the main barriers between cultures, and families can expect an extra warm welcome. Hotels, too, are usually extremely accommodating and are well used to putting up big Guatemalan families.

Obviously you'll have to take a few extra precautions with your **children's health** (see p.23) paying particular care to hygiene and religiously applying sunscreen. Dealing with the sticky tropical heat of the Petén is likely to be one of the biggest difficulties, but elsewhere humidity is much less of a problem. As young children are rarely enthralled by either modern highland or ancient Maya culture, you may want to plan some excursions: the giant Xocomil water park (see p.236) and Auto Safari Chapín (see p.251) make great days out for kids. Take extra care if you head for the Pacific coast beaches, as every year several children (and adults) drown in the strong undertow.

If you're planning to bring a **baby** to Guatemala, you'll find disposable nappies are widely available in supermarkets and pharmacies in major towns; you'll need to take an extra stock if you're visiting remote areas.

Directory

ADDRESSES Almost all addresses are based on the grid system that's used in most towns, with avenidas running in one direction (north to south) and calles in the other. All addresses specify the street first, then the block, and end with the zone. For example, the address Av la Reforma 3–55, Zona 1 means that house is on Avenida la Reforma, between 3 and 4 calles, at no. 55, in Zona 1. Almost all towns have numbered streets, but in some places the old names are also used. In Antigua calles and avenidas are also divided according to their direction from the central plaza – north, south, east or west (*norte*, *sur*, *oriente* and *poniente*). *Diagonales* (diagonals) are what you'd expect – a street that runs in an oblique direction.

AIRPORT TAX Has to be paid before departure on all international flights. It's currently set at US$30, only payable in cash, either in quetzals or dollars.

BAGS If you're planning to travel around by bus – and certainly if you're going to do some walking with your gear as well – then a backpack is by far the best option. Guatemalans have a word for backpackers, "*mochileros*", and consider them to be slightly quirky because they're always running around with huge bags (*mochilas*) on their backs. Whatever you pack your stuff in, make sure it's tough enough to handle being thrown on and off the top of buses. It's a good idea to buy an old sack and string net in a local market, to enclose your bags and make them less of a target for thieves. Better still carry something small enough to fit inside a bus, on the luggage rack, which is both more convenient and safer.

CONTRACEPTION Condoms are available from pharmacies (*farmacias*) in all the main towns, though they are so expensive that many Guatemalans can't afford to use them. Some makes of the Pill are available, mostly those manufactured in the States, but these are also pricey, so it's more sensible to bring

enough to last for your entire stay. Bear in mind that diarrhoea can reduce the reliability of the Pill (or any other drug) as it may not be in your system long enough to be fully absorbed.

DRUGS Increasingly available as the country is becoming a centre for both shipment and production. Marijuana is readily available and cheap – especially as in recent years Petén has become an area of production, and there is a plentiful supply across the border in Belize. Cocaine is also extremely cheap as it is shipped to the States through Guatemala, and heroin, now produced here, is also to be found on the streets. The drugs problem is viewed increasingly seriously by the government and users will be dealt with harshly. If you're caught, expect to go to jail, or at least pay a hefty fine or bribe in order to avoid it.

ELECTRICITY 110 volts AC in most places, although in isolated spots the current is 220 volts, so ask before you plug in any vital equipment. Anything from Britain will need a transformer and a plug adapter, as may some US appliances. Cuts in the supply and wild fluctuations in the current are fairly common, and in some isolated villages, where they have their own generator, the supply only operates for part of the day (usually the early evening and morning).

EMBASSIES AND CONSULATES Listed on p.88 in the Guatemala City section, where almost every country is represented. In addition there are Mexican consulates in Quetzaltenango and Retalhuleu, and Honduran consulates in Esquipulas and Puerto Barrios.

GAY TRAVELLERS Homosexuality is legal for consenting adults aged eighteen or over. However, though Guatemalan society is not as overtly machismo as many Latin American countries, it's wise to be discreet and avoid canoodling in public. There's a small, almost entirely male, scene in Guatemala City (see box on p.85) and

Metric weights and measures

1 ounce = 28.3 grams	1 inch = 2.54 centimetres
1 pound = 454 grams	1 foot = 0.3 metre
2.2 pounds = 1 kilogram	1 yard = 0.91 metre
1 pint = 0.47 litre	1.09 yards = 1 metre
1 quart = 0.94 litre	1 mile = 1.61 kilometres
1 gallon = 3.78 litres	0.62 miles = 1 kilometre

Guatemalan Maya also use the *legua*, a distance of about four miles, which is roughly the distance a person can walk in an hour. *Yardas* are yards, *pies* are feet.

Indigenous fabrics are often sold by the *vara*, an old Spanish measure of about 33 inches, while land is sometimes measured by the *cuerda*, a square with sides of 32 *varas*. The larger local units are the *manzana*, equivalent to three-quarters of a hectare or 1.73 acres, and the *caballeria* (45.12 hectares).

Antigua, where the club La Casbah has a gay night every Thursday.

LAUNDRY Hotels occasionally offer a laundry service, and most inexpensive places will have somewhere where you can wash and dry your own clothes. In Guatemala City, Quetzaltenango, Panajachel, Huehuetenango and Antigua there are self-service laundries, as well as several places that will do your washing for you – on the whole these are much easier and cost about the same.

METRIC WEIGHTS AND MEASURES See box above.

RELIGION Guatemala is the least Catholic of all Latin American countries. It's estimated that between 35 and 40 percent of the population now belong one of several dozen US-based Protestant churches – for more about this evangelical movement see p.454. Many of Guatemala's Catholics also continue to practise ancient Maya religious customs in the indigenous villages of the highlands. There has been a resurgence of interest in Maya spiritualism amongst young educated Guatemalans since the end of the civil war, and attending "shamanic colleges" has become fashionable. Guatemala City also has tiny Jewish and Muslim communities.

TIME ZONES Guatemala is on the equivalent of Central Standard Time, six hours earlier than GMT. There is very little seasonal change – it gets light around 6am, with sunset at around 6.30pm all year round.

TIPS In upmarket restaurants a ten percent tip is appropriate, but in most places, especially the cheaper ones, tipping is the exception rather than the rule. Taxi drivers are not normally tipped.

TOILETS These are nearly always Western-style (the squat-toilet is rare), with a bucket beside the bowl for your toilet paper. Standards vary greatly throughout the country, but in general the further you are from a city the worse the condition. Public toilets are few and far between; some are filthy, while others are well looked after by an attendant who usually sells toilet paper. The most common name is *baños*, and the signs are *damas* (women) and *caballeros* (men).

guide

guide

Guatemala City, Antigua and around

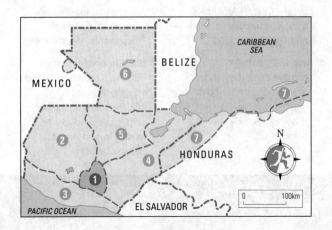

CHAPTER 1 # Highlights

✳ **Museo Nacional de Arqueología y Etnología** Guatemala's greatest Maya sculptures and artefacts, under one roof. **p.80**

✳ **Volcán de Pacaya** Hike up for a peek of the fume- and lava-belching cone of this active volcano – Central America's most spectacular sound-and-light show. **p.90**

✳ **Semana Santa** The sombre ceremony and processions of the continent's most fervent Easter-week celebrations. **p.100**

✳ **Antigua's colonial architecture** A stunning UNESCO-listed legacy of Baroque churches, elegant municipal buildings and graceful plazas. **pp.100–105**

✳ **Gourmet dining** Feast on a cornucopia of global cuisine, in sumptuous surrounds, in Antigua's remarkable array of restaurants. **pp.106–108**

✳ **San Simón (Maximón)** Soak up the scene at the pagan temple of Guatemala's liquor-swilling, cigar-smoking "evil saint" in San Andrés Itzapa. **p.118**

Guatemala City, Antigua and around

Situated just forty kilometres apart in Guatemala's highlands, the two cities of Guatemala City and Antigua could hardly be more different. The capital, Guatemala City, fume-filled and concrete-clad, is a maelstrom of industry and commerce. There are few attractions or sights here to detain the traveller, though a day or two spent visiting the museums and exploring the markets and shops won't be wasted. Antigua is everything the capital is not: tranquil, urbane and resplendent with spectacular colonial buildings and myriad cosmopolitan cafés, restaurants and hotels. Unsurprisingly, it is the town where most travellers choose to base themselves, finding the relaxed atmosphere a welcome break after the frenzied pace of life in Guatemala City.

Guatemala City sprawls across a huge upland basin, surrounded on three sides by low hills and volcanic cones. The capital was moved here in 1776 after the seismic destruction of Antigua, but the site had been of importance long before the arrival of the Spanish. These days, its shapeless and swelling mass, ringed by shanty towns, ranks as the largest city in Central America. It is home to more than three million people, almost a quarter of Guatemala's population, and is the undisputed centre of politics, power and wealth.

The capital has an intensity and vibrancy that are both its fascination and its horror, and for many travellers a trip to the capital is an exercise in damage limitation, as they struggle through a swirling mass of bus fumes and crowds. For decades, the city has been run-down and polluted, abandoned by the affluent middle classes and blue-chip businesses who long ago fled to the suburbs. However, after all these years of neglect and decay, efforts are being made by a small group of conservationists to preserve what's left of the **centro histórico** in Zona 1, and a smattering of fashionable new cafés and bars, popular with students, have opened in restored buildings in the heart of the city. These initiatives hardly amount to a significant renaissance as yet, however, and most travellers still choose to spend as little time as possible in the place. Nevertheless the city is the crossroads of the country, and you'll certainly end up here at some time, if only to hurry between bus terminals or catch a plane to Petén.

Antigua, conversely, is the most impressive colonial city in Central America, and its tremendous wealth of architectural riches has ensured that it has become one of Guatemala's premier tourist attractions. With just 30,000

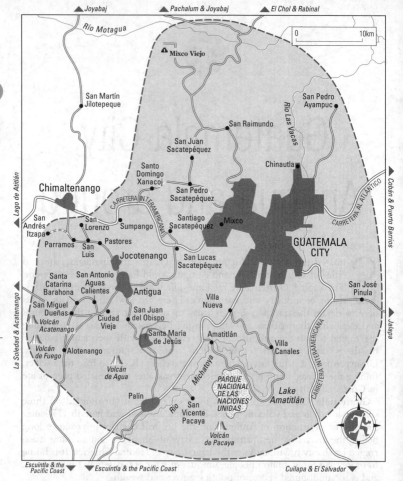

inhabitants, and a small central zone, the city's graceful cobbled streets are ideal to explore on foot. Spanish architects and Maya labourers constructed a classically designed city of elegant squares, churches, monasteries and grand houses, and it's this magnificent historical legacy that ensures Antigua's continuing appeal. Affluent and self-confident, Antigua's reknowned **language schools** also attract students from all over the world, and the education and tourism industries form the city's prime source of wealth.

The countryside around Antigua and Guatemala City – an astonishing landscape of volcanoes, pine forests, meadows, *milpas* and coffee farms, punctuated with villages – also begs to be explored. Looming over the capital is the **Volcán de Pacaya**, one of the most active volcanoes in Latin America. In recent years it has been spewing a spectacular fountain of sulphurous gas and molten rock and every year or so an eruption douses Guatemala City in ash, closing the airport for a day or two. However, it's usually possible to climb a secondary peak that overlooks the main cone of Pacaya, as well as the volcanoes of **Agua** and **Acatenango**, close to Antigua.

There are countless interesting villages to visit in this area, including **San Andrés Itzapa**, where there is a pagan shrine to the "evil saint" Maximón, **Jocotenango**, which boasts two new museums dedicated to coffee and Maya music, and **Santa María de Jesús**, a Maya village where the trail to the Volcán de Agua begins. The one **Maya ruin** in the region that can compete with the lowland sites further north is **Mixco Viejo**; it's tricky to get to unless you have your own transport, but its setting, in splendid isolation, is tremendous. Little evidence remains of the ancient capital of **Kaminaljuyú**, today almost buried in the capital's suburbs, but this was once one of the largest and most important cities of the Maya World.

Guatemala City and around

Guatemala City, an extremely horizontal place, is like a city on its back. Its ugliness, which is a threatened look (the low morose houses have earthquake cracks in their facades; the buildings wince at you with fright lines), is ugliest on those streets where, just past the toppling houses, a blue volcano's cone bulges. I could see the volcanoes from the window of my hotel room. I was on the third floor, which was also the top floor. They were tall volcanoes and looked capable of spewing lava. Their beauty was undeniable; but it was the beauty of witches. The rumbles from their fires had heaved this city down.

Paul Theroux, The Old Patagonian Express

Though Theroux's dark impressions remain relevant for much of the city most of the time, Guatemala City is by no means always as black as he implies. It is certainly not somewhere you visit for its beauty or architectural charm, with a few notable exceptions, but a near idyllic climate and the lush greenery of the suburbs give it a certain appeal. Its setting is also dramatic, positioned in a massive highland bowl on a site that was a centre of population and political power long before the arrival of the Spanish.

Some history

The pre-conquest city of **Kaminaljuyú**, with its ruins still scattered amongst the western suburbs, was well established here two thousand years ago. In early Classic times (250–550 AD), as a result of an alliance with the great northern power of Teotihuacán (near present-day Mexico City), Kaminaljuyú came to dominate the highlands, and eventually provided the political and commercial

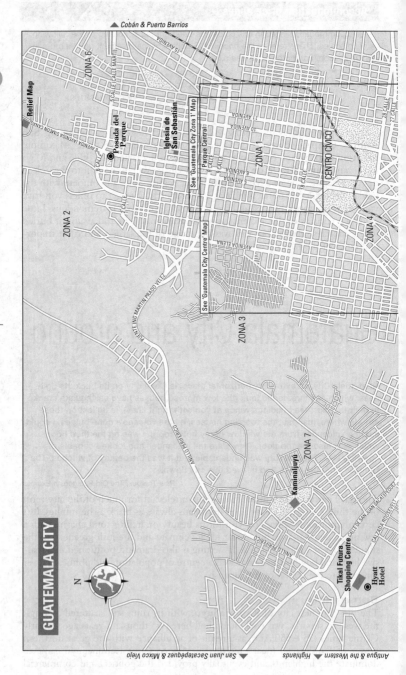

GUATEMALA CITY

N

▲ Cobán & Puerto Barrios

Relief Map

ZONA 6

5 AVENIDA

6 CALLE (CALLE MARTI)

ZONA 2

6 CALLE

2 AVENIDA (AVENIDA SIMEON CAÑAS)

Posada del Parque

Iglesia de San Sebastián

See 'Guatemala City Zona 1' Map

Parque Central

2 CALLE
3 CALLE
5 CALLE

5 AVENIDA
6 AVENIDA

11 AVENIDA
10 AVENIDA
11 AVENIDA

ZONA 1

18 CALLE

CENTRO CÍVICO

28 CALLE
27 CALLE

ZONA 4

AVENIDA ELENA

See 'Guatemala City Centre' Map

ZONA 3

PUENTE ING MARTIN PRADO VELEZ

ANILLO PERIFERICO

ZONA 7

Kaminaljuyú

ANILLO PERIFERICO

Tikal Futura
Shopping Centre

CALLE DE SAN JUAN SACATEPÉQUEZ

CALZADA ROOSEVELT

Hyatt
Hotel

San Juan Sacatepéquez & Mixco Viejo ▼   Highlands ▼   Antigua & the Western ▼

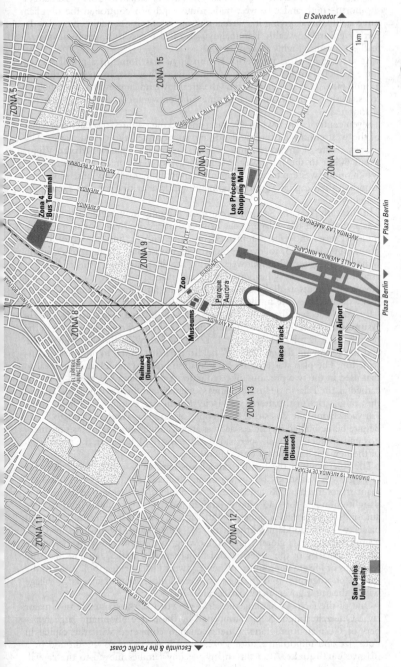

1

El Salvador ▲

ZONA 5

ZONA 15

7 CALLE

DIAGONAL 6 CALLE REAL DE LA VILLA DE GUADALUPE

Zona 4
Bus Terminal

AVENIDA LA REFORMA

6 AVENIDA

9 AVENIDA

0 CALLE

6 CALLE

ZONA 10

ZONA 9

12 CALLE

Los Proceres
Shopping Mall

DIAGONAL 12

ZONA 14

AVENIDA LAS AMERICAS

14 CALLE AVENIDA HINCAPIE

▼ Plaza Berlin

▼ Plaza Berlin

Zoo

Parque
Aurora

7 AVENIDA

Museums

Race Track

Aurora Airport

CALZADA ROOSEVELT

ZONA 8

EL TREBOL JUNCTION

Railtrack
(Disused)

ZONA 13

Railtrack
(Disused)

DIAGONAL 19 AVENIDA DE PETAPA

ZONA 11

ZONA 12

ANILLO PERIFERICO

San Carlos
University

CALZADA AGUILAR BATRES

0   1km

▲ Escuintla & the Pacific Coast

backing that fostered the rise of Tikal. The city was situated at the crossroads of the north–south and east–west trade routes, and also controlled the obsidian mine at El Chayal, giving it a virtual monopoly of this essential commodity. To further ensure its wealth, Kaminaljuyú also had access to a supply of quetzal feathers, another highly valued item.

At the height of its prosperity Kaminaljuyú was home to a population of some 50,000. However, following the decline of Teotihuacán and its influence, around 600 AD, it was surpassed by the great lowland centres that it had helped to establish. Soon after their rise, some time between 600 and 900 AD, it was abandoned.

Seven centuries later, when Alvarado entered the country, the fractured tribes of the west controlled the highlands and preoccupied the conquistadors. The nearest centre of any importance was the Poqomam capital of **Mixco Viejo**, about 60km to the northwest. Mainly because of the need to keep a close watch on the western tribes, the Spanish ignored the possibility of settling here, founding their capital instead at Iximché, and later at two separate sites in the Panchoy valley.

In the early years of Spanish occupation the only new building in this area was a church in the village of La Ermita, founded in 1620. For more than a hundred years the village remained no more than a tiny cluster of Indian homes, but in 1773, following months of devastating earthquakes, Captain Mayorga and some 4200 followers, fleeing the disease-ridden ruins of Antigua, established a temporary headquarters in the village. From here they despatched envoys and scouts in all directions, seeking a site for the new capital, and eventually decided to settle in the neighbouring Valley of the Virgin.

By royal decree the new city was named **Nueva Guatemala de la Asunción**, in honour of the Virgin of the Ascension, whose image stood in the church at La Ermita. On January 1, 1776, the city was officially inaugurated, and the following day its "fathers" held their first council to administer construction. The plan was typical of the Spanish colonial model, and identical to that used in the two previous, ill-fated cities. A main plaza was boxed in by the cathedral, the Palacio de los Capitanes Generales and the town hall, and around this, on a strict grid pattern, was a city fifteen streets long and fifteen wide. Early development was slow: the people of Antigua were reluctant to leave, despite being bullied by endless decrees and deadlines, although waves of smallpox and cholera eventually persuaded some. By 1800, however, the population of the new capital was still only 25,000.

The splendour of the former capital was hard to re-establish and the new city's growth was steady but by no means dramatic. An 1863 census listed the main structures as 1206 residences, 7 warehouses, 130 shops, 28 churches, 1 slaughterhouse, 2 forts, 12 schools, and 25 fountains and public laundries. The author, Enrique Palacios, concluded that it was "a delightful city and a pleasant place to live". Boddam-Wetham, on the other hand, living here in 1877, claimed that it was "gloomy and dull; owing to the uniformity of the houses ... the regularity of the streets ... and the absence of traffic", adding that "the few signs of life are depressing". When Eadweard Muybridge took some of the earliest photographs in 1875, the city was still little more than a large village with a theatre, a government palace and a fort.

One of the factors retarding the city's growth was the existence of a major rival, Quetzaltenango (Xela). Stimulated by the coffee boom and large numbers of German immigrants, Quetzaltenango competed with the capital in both size and importance, until 1902, when it was razed to the ground by a massive **earthquake**. After this, many wealthy families moved to the capital, finally establishing it as the country's primary city. By then, Guatemala City's population had already been boosted by the exodus from another major earthquake, this time in Antigua. Inevitably, the capital's turn came. On Christmas Eve 1917 Guatemala City was shaken by the first in a series of devastating tremors, and not until early February, after six long weeks of destruction, did the ground stabilize and the dust settle. This time, however, there was nowhere to run; spurred on by the celebrations of a century of independence, and the impetus of the eccentric President Ubico, reconstruction began.

Street children and social cleansing in Guatemela City

One of the most disturbing manifestations of the city's poverty is the number of **street children** – as many as 5000 – living on the streets of the capital. Most scratch a living from begging, prostitution and petty crime, and many sniff glue to numb the boredom, hunger, cold and depression. The city's police have directed much of the blame for the capital's perennially high crime rate towards these children, on whom violent attacks and beatings are common. Homelessness became a serious issue in the early 1980s when hundreds of children began arriving in the capital, many orphans fleeing the civil war, others escaping family abuse. For almost two decades the police, private security guards and military enjoyed a virtual impunity against prosecution for crimes committed against street children, and dozens of cases of "**social cleansing**" (disappearances and murders) went unpunished. In one week in September 1997, forty people, including seven children, were "cleansed" from the streets of Guatemala City.

Fighting against these injustices is **Casa Alianza**, a project set up in Guatemala in 1981 by the British-born Bruce Harris, who, despite a drive-by shooting of the crisis centre and countless death threats, has personally led the campaign to curb violence against street children, with more than 500 judicial cases against police officers and others in Guatemala logged by 2001. "One of the greatest favours the perpetrators of this violence did for us was to spray our building with machine-gun fire because it was tangible evidence that we were doing something that affected interests. We were challenging the status quo, the way Guatemala had for decades operated, challenging the assumption that if a man had the gun and the uniform, he could get away with murder – literally," he said. The charity provides shelter, food and emotional support for street children and attempts to reunite families where possible. Through dogged perseverance, meticulous documentation and globally based support, Casa Alianza has steadily eroded this long-standing impunity and, after years of set backs, the tide seems to be turning, as the charity has scored a series of high profile victories on behalf of the victims. In June 2001, another coup saw the Inter American Court of Human Rights order the state of Guatemala to pay over US$500,000 to the families of five street children who were brutally tortured and murdered by two National Policemen in June 1990. Yet despite these legal successes, obtaining prosecution for extra-judicial killing in Guatemala is fraught with difficulties and the violence continues.

Casa Alianza now operates across Central America and Mexico, and has set up crisis centres, transition and group homes, legal aid offices, hospices for street children in the final stages of AIDS, a program for street girls and their babies, and drug rehabilitation centres. By 2001 around 10,000 street children were being served each year. The organization has been bestowed a clutch of prestigious awards, including US$1 million from the **Hilton Humanitarian Prize** in October 2000.

Several children's refuges are well established in Guatemala, and the projects are always on the look out for **volunteers**. You can contact them at Casa Alianza, Apartado Postal, 2704 Guatemala (℡253 2965, ℻253 3003, ✉bruce@casa-alianza .org); or at SJO 1039, PO Box 025216, Miami, FL 33102–5216, in the US; or The Coach House, Grafton Underwood, Northants NN14 3AA in the UK. More information is available on their website, ⓦwww.casa-alianza.org.

Since 1918 Guatemala City has grown at an incredible rate, tearing ahead of the rest of the country at a pace that still shows little sign of letting up. The flight from the fields, characteristic of all developing countries, is caused by a chronic shortage of land and employment in the countryside, and was exacerbated during the civil war by the army's scorched-earth tactics to combat guerrilla groups. According to some estimates, six hundred new campesinos arrive in the city every day, economic migrants high on hope and dreams of wealth. In some ways the capital is becoming a city of refugees, filled with displaced people, many of them Mayan, who struggle to settle here. The deep ravines that surround the city, thought by the original Spanish planners to offer protection from the force of earthquakes, are now filling rapidly with rubbish and shanty towns, while street crime increases daily.

The divisions that cleave Guatemalan society are at their most acute in the capital's crumbling streets. While the wealthy elite sip coffee in air-conditioned shopping malls and plan their next visit to Miami, swathes of the city have been left to disintegrate into a threatening tangle of fume-choked streets, largely devoid of any kind of life after dark. A small army of **street children** lives rough, and gang violence is growing. The disparities of life in the city are glaringly extreme, as glass skyscrapers tower over sprawling shanty towns, and shoeless widows peddle cigarettes and chewing gum to designer-clad nightclubbers.

Orientation, arrival and information

Although the scale of Guatemala City, with its suburbs sprawled across some 21 **zones**, can seem overwhelming at first glance, the layout is straightforward and the central area, which is all that you need to worry about, is really quite small. Like almost all Guatemalan towns it's arranged on a strict grid pattern, with **avenidas** running north–south and **calles** east–west.

Broadly speaking, the city divides into two distinct halves. The northern section, centred on **Zona 1**, is the old part of town, containing the central plaza or **Parque Central**, most of the budget hotels, shops, restaurants, cinemas, the post office, and many of the bus companies. This part of the city is cramped, congested and polluted but bustling with activity. The two main streets are 5 and 6 avenidas, both thick with street traders, fast-food joints and neon lights. Directly north of the parque central is **Zona 2**, a largely residential suburb, with the sole attraction of the **Parque Minerva**, where there is a relief map of the country, a popular local attraction.

To the south, acting as a buffer between the two halves of town, is **Zona 4**, home of the city's main **bus terminal** and the **Centro Cívico**, where you'll find all the main administrative buildings, the tourist office, the central market, and the National Theatre. Further south still, the modern half of the city comprises wealthy **Zonas 9** and **10**, which are separated by the main artery the **Avenida La Reforma**. Here, you'll find exclusive offices, apartment blocks, hotels and shops as well as Guatemala's most expensive nightclubs, restaurants and cafés. Many of the embassies and two of the country's finest museums are also here. Continuing south, the neighbouring **Zonas 13** and **14** hold rich, leafy suburbs, and are home to the airport, zoo, a cluster of guest houses and more museums and cinemas.

Arrival

Arriving in Guatemala City is always a bit disconcerting. If you're laden with luggage, it's probably not a good idea to take on the bus system, and a taxi is

Addresses in Guatemala City

The system of **street numbering** in the capital may seem a little confusing at first, as the same numbers and street names are given to different streets in different zones. However, once learnt, the system is remarkably logical and simple to use.

When it comes to finding an address, always check for the **zone** first and then the street. For example "4 Av 9–14, Zona 1" is in Zona 1, on 4 Avenida between 9 and 10 Calle, house number 14.

You may see street numbers written as 1a, 7a, etc, rather than simply 1, 7. This is technically more correct, since the names of the streets are not One Avenue and Seven Street, but First (*primera*), Seventh (*séptima*) and so on. A capital "A" used as a suffix indicates a smaller street between two large ones: 1 Calle A is a short street between 1 and 2 calles.

well worth the extra cost (see p.68 for details). For details on using the transport terminals to **move on** from the capital, see p.86. Note that there is only one passenger **train** running in Guatemala, taking people on day-trips away from the capital; see p.120 for details.

By air

Aurora airport (☎334 7680 or 334 7689) is on the edge of the city in Zona 13, some way from the centre, but close to Zona 10. The domestic terminal, though in the same complex, is separate, and entered by Avenida Hincapié. Much the easiest way to get to and from the airport is by **taxi**: you'll find plenty of them waiting outside the terminal. The fare to Zona 10 costs around US$6, to Zona 1 around US$10. **Buses** also leave from directly outside the terminal, across the concrete plaza – take #83 for Zonas 10 and 11. It's well worth remembering that virtually all Guatemala City's four- and five-star hotels, and the Zona 13 guest houses, offer free pick-ups from the airport if you inform them first.

If, like many travellers, you're **heading for Antigua**, there are regular shuttle bus services from the airport (US$8–10 per person) though they don't run to a fixed schedule and only leave when there's a minimum of three passengers. A taxi from the airport is US$25. In daylight hours, you can also get to Antigua cheaply and fairly conveniently by taking a taxi to the Tikal Futura shopping mall on the Calzada Roosevelt highway (US$5), crossing the road via the pedestrian bridge and catching an Antigua-bound bus (US$0.60) from the bus stop beside the bridge.

At the airport, the Banco del Quetzal (Mon–Fri 6am–8pm, Sat & Sun 6am–6pm) gives a better **exchange** rate than you'll get outside the country, and takes most European currencies as well as dollars. There are also several 24-hour **cashpoints** which accept Visa, Mastercard, Cirrus and Plus cards; and though virtually all foreign cards are accepted it's also useful to have a supply of dollar bills in case of any difficulties. On the upper (departures) floor you'll find the **tourist information** office (daily 6am–9pm; ☎331 4256), a Telgua phone office and a post office (both Mon–Sat 7am–9pm).

By bus

If you arrive in the city by second-class bus prepare yourself for the jungle of the **Zona 4 bus terminal**, which has to rate as Guatemala City's most chaotic, fume-filled corner. On the whole, it's only second-class buses from the western and eastern highlands that arrive here, so if you're coming in from the Pacific coast or from Petén you'll be spared, arriving instead at the Zona 1 terminal (see below). However, if you do end up in Zona 4, and decide not to take a taxi – there are always plenty around at the entrance to the terminal – you'll need to walk a couple of blocks to the corner of 2 C and 4 Av, from where local buses go to the centre of town (#17 is one, but always doublecheck that the driver is going to *Zona Uno*).

Most of the arriving buses that don't drop off at the Zona 4 terminal will end up somewhere in Zona 1, close enough to walk to a hotel, or at least an inexpensive taxi ride away. The Zona 1 bus terminal is centred around 18 C and 9 Av, where many companies, especially first-class ones, have their own offices. All the main bus companies, their addresses and bus departure times, are given in "Moving on from Guatemala City" on p.86.

Information and maps

The main **tourist office**, Inguat, at 7 Av 1–17, Zona 4 (Mon–Fri 8am–4pm; ☎331 1333, ℻331-8893, ✉inguat@guate.net), has an information desk on the ground floor where you can buy a half-decent **map** of the country and city, or put your questions to the helpful staff – there's always someone available who speaks English. There's also an Inguat office at the airport (see above). For detailed maps of Guatemala suitable for trekking and exploration, try the Instituto Geográfico Militar, Av las Américas 5–76, Zona 13 (Mon–Fri 8am–4pm); bus #65 from the Centro Cívico gets you nearest, or take a taxi. Selected photocopies of these maps are also sold in Antigua at the Casa Andinista bookshop (see p.109 for details).

City transport

In any big city, coping with the public transport system takes time, and Guatemala City is no different; even locals are often baffled by its anarchic web of **bus routes**. To complicate matters further, the city authorities regularly re-route buses in an attempt to control traffic congestion, and most of Zona 1's streets are one-way so buses return along different roads. Add to this the fact that some buses with the same numbers operate along different routes, and confusion reigns. The easiest way to handle it is to accept that getting on the wrong bus isn't the end of the world, and that you can always get off and catch another, or cross the road and go back to where you started. Above all else the buses are cheap (US$0.10) so you'll need some small change to hand. In Zona 1, the most useful streets are **4 Avenida**, where buses leave for many different parts of the city (destinations are posted on the front of the bus), and **10 Avenida** for buses #82 and #83. Buses **run** from around 6 or 7am until about 9.30pm, but try and avoid travelling during the ferocious rush hour (7.30–9am and 4.30–7pm), when many roads throughout the city are jammed solid.

Some routes are covered by a number of slightly newer buses called *preferenciales*, which are a little cleaner, more modern and a touch more expensive (US$0.15) than the ordinary buses. In addition, minibuses serve similar routes to the ordinary buses, but tend to be a little more expensive. After 10pm, the pick-ups known as *ruteleros* effectively operate as buses, running along vaguely defined routes all night.

Taxis

If you can't face the complexities of the bus system, or it's late at night, then taxis are a good option and not necessarily that expensive. The excellent new

Useful bus routes

#35 From 4 Avenida in Zona 1 will take you to the ruins, alternatively, any bus with a small "Kaminaljuyú" sign in the windscreen passes within a block or two.

#82 Starts in Zona 2, then heads along 10 Av, through Zona 1 and the Centro Cívico in Zona 4, then continues down Avenida La Reforma before turning left at the Obelisco. Ideal for getting between Zonas 1 and 10, this route takes you past many of the embassies, the Popol Vuh and Ixchel museums (see p.77) and the Los Próceres shopping centre.

#83 Starts on 10 Avenida Zona 1, and goes via the Centro Cívico to the airport.

Terminal Any bus marked *terminal*, and there are plenty of these on 4 Avenida in Zona 1, will take you to the main bus terminal in Zona 4.

Bolívar or Trébol Any bus with either of these written on will take you along the western side of the city, down Avenida Bolívar to the Trébol junction.

metered taxis are comfortable and cheap – *Amarillo* cabs (☎332 1515; 24hr) are highly recommended; all cabs are equipped with state-of-the-art navigation systems and will pick you up from anywhere in the city; the fare from Zona 1 to Zona 10 is US$4–5. There are also plenty of **unmetered** taxis around, though you'll have to use your bargaining skills with these. They invariably ask for more than their metered cousins, so always fix the price beforehand.

Accommodation

Accommodation in Guatemala City comes in all shapes and sizes and to suit all pockets, though you'll almost certainly pay more here than in the rest of the country. The majority of the budget and mid-range hotels are grouped in noisy central and eastern **Zona 1**; it's not the safest neighbourhood at night and not a great place for wandering around in search of a room. Many travellers are now choosing to stay close to the airport, in **Zona 13**, where there are a number of good new options – all offer free airport pick-ups and drop-offs, though be sure to book ahead. The disadvantage with this quiet, suburban location is that there are very few restaurants and cafés close by, and the bus service is infrequent. Guatemala City's luxury hotels are clustered in a relatively safe part of town, **Zonas 9 and 10**, where there's a glut of dining options, bars and nightclubs in the Zona Viva.

All Zona 1 accommodation reviewed below is marked on the map on p.73, the accommodation in Zona 2 is marked on the map on pp.62–63, and all accommodation in Zonas 9 and 10 is marked on pp.70–71. The Zona 13 guest houses are grouped around the airport 2–3km from Zona 10.

Zonas 1 and 2

Chalet Suizo 14 C 6–82, Zona 1 ☎251 3786, ☎232 0429. Friendly, comfortable and, as it's right opposite the police headquarters, very safe. Nicely designed, spotlessly clean and all very Swiss and organized, with left luggage and a new café that's open all day. Private or shared bath. No double beds. ❹/❺

Hotel Casa Lessing 12 C 4–35, Zona 1 ☎238 1881. Simple budget hotel: the small rooms aren't very exiting, but it's central, clean and friendly. ❸

Hotel Colonial 7 Av 14–19, Zona 1 ☎232 6722, ☎232 8671, ✉colonial@infovia.com.gt. Well-situated colonial-style hotel with dark wood, wrought iron and an attractive tiled lobby. Tasteful and comfortable, but slightly old-fashioned; the rooms come with or without private bathroom. ❹

Hotel Fénix 7 Av 15–81, Zona 1 ☎251 6625. Safe, friendly and vaguely atmospheric, set in an old, warped, wooden building. There's a quirky café downstairs and some rooms have private bath, though it can be noisy early in the morning. ❷

Hotel Fortuna Real 12 C 8–42, Zona 1 ☎230 3378; ☞251 2215. Spotless, Chinese-owned hotel in a safe location at the heart of Zona 1. All rooms boast rather bizarre decor, but have TV and private bath, and there's a restaurant downstairs. ❺

Hotel Hernani corner 15 C and 6 Av A, Zona 1 ☎232 2839. Comfortable old building with good, clean rooms, all with their own shower. One of the better budget deals in town. ❷

Hotel Monteleone 18 C 4–63, Zona 1 ☎238 2600, ☞238 2509. Rooms are attractively decorated, with quality mattresses and bedside lamps, and some have private bath. Very decent value – clean, safe and right by the Antigua terminal – but not the best area to be in after dark. ❷/❸

Hotel PanAmerican 9 C 5–63, Zona 1 ☎232 6807, ☞251 8749, ⓦwww.hotelpanamerican .com. The city's oldest smart hotel, very formal and civilized, with a strong emphasis on Guatemalan tradition. Cable TV, continental breakfast and air-port transfer included. Even if you don't stay here, the hotel's restaurant is brilliant for Sunday breakfast. ❻

Hotel Posada Belén 13 C A 10–30, Zona 1 ☎253 4530, ☞251 3478, ⓦwww.guateweb .com. Tucked down a side street in a beautiful old building. Supremely quiet, safe and very homely, with its own restaurant. The owners are a mine of information about the city. No children under five, however. ❻

Hotel Royal Palace 6 Av 12–66, Zona 1 ☎ & ☞332 4036. Very comfortable, Best Westin-owned landmark right in the heart of Zona 1 with well-appointed, spacious rooms and good service, but be sure to avoid the noisy streetside rooms. Seasonal bargain rates. ❼

Hotel San Martín 16 C 7–65, Zona 1 ☎238 0319. Very cheap, clean and friendly, this is among the best deals at the lower end of the scale. Some rooms with private bath. ❷

Hotel Spring 8 Av 12–65, Zona 1 ☎232 2858, ☞232 0107. An excellent deal and a safe location, though it's often full, popular as it is with Peace Corps volunteers. The fairly spacious rooms, with or without private bath, are set around a pretty colonial courtyard and some have private bath; there's also a new block where all rooms have

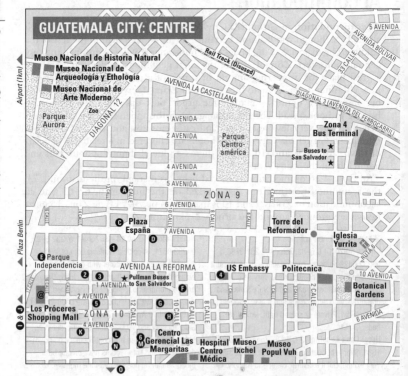

cable TV. Breakfast available and free mineral water. ❷/❸

Pensión Meza 10 C 10–17, Zona 1 ☎ 232 3177 or 253 4576. Infamous budget travellers' hangout; cheap and laid-back, with plenty of 1960s-style decadence. Fidel Castro and Che Guevara stayed here – the latter in room 21. Pretty dilapidated dorms and doubles, some with private shower. Noticeboard, ping pong, music all day, and the helpful owner, Mario, speaks good English. ❷

Posada del Parque 6 Av 4–12, Zona 2 ☎ & ℱ 232 1146, ⓦ www.posadadelparque.com. Set 400m north of the parque central in a quiet plaza, this is an excellent new hotel occupying an atmospheric colonial house. The attractively presented singles, doubles and triples, all with TV and private bath, represent very good value and there's a small dining room, laundry facilities and a pretty little patio. ❹

Zona 13

El Aeropuerto Guest House 15 C A 7–32 ☎ 332 3086, ℱ 362 1264, ⓔ hotairpt@guate.net. Five minutes' walk from the international airport. Call for a free pick-up from the airport, or walk across the grass outside and follow the road to the left. A pleasant, convenient and comfortable place: rooms have cable TV, private showers and fluffy towels. Continental breakfast is included and there are email and fax facilities for guests. ❺

Dos Lunas 21 C 10-92 ☎ & ℱ 334 5264, ⓦ wwwxelapages.com/doslunas. Clean, secure and friendly guest house set in quiet suburban surrounds a short drive from the airport. Free pick-up, drop-off and breakfast, plus excellent travel information and tips from the dynamic Guatemalan owner. Very popular, so essential to book well ahead. ❹

Economy Dorms 8 Av 17–74, Col Aurora I ☎ 331 8029. Basic dormitory accommodation with free continental breakfast and transfers from the airport. ❹

Hotel Hincapié Av Hincapié 18–77 ☎ 332 7771, ℱ 337 4469, ⓔ aruedap@infovia.com.gt. Under the same management as the *El Aeropuerto* and conveniently located for the domestic terminal. Rates include local calls, continental breakfast, and transport to and from the airport. ❹

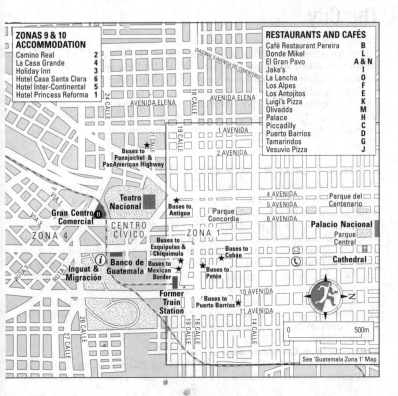

ZONAS 9 & 10
ACCOMMODATION
Camino Real   2
La Casa Grande   4
Holiday Inn   3
Hotel Casa Santa Clara   6
Hotel Inter-Continental 5
Hotel Princess Reforma   1

RESTAURANTS AND CAFÉS
Café Restaurant Pereira   B
Donde Mikel   L
El Gran Pavo   A & N
Jake's   I
La Lancha   O
Los Alpes   F
Los Antojitos   E
Luigi's Pizza   K
Olivadda   M
Palace   H
Piccadilly   C
Puerto Barrios   D
Tamarindos   G
Vesuvio Pizza   J

See 'Guatemala Zona 1' Map

Patricia's Bed and Breakfast 19 C 10–65, Col Aurora II ☎ 331 0470; ⊛ wwwgeocites.com /xelaju2001. Small, family-run guest house with pleasant rooms and friendly atmosphere a short distance from the airport. ❹

Zonas 9 and 10

Camino Real Av la Reforma and 14 C, Zona 10 ☎ 333 4633, ℉ 337 4313, ⊛ www.quetzalnet .com/caminoreal. Landmark hotel, now run by the Best Westin group, long favoured by visiting heads of state and anyone on expenses, though the chintz-heavy decor is beginning to look rather dated. Excellent location in the heart of the Zona Viva, plus bars, shops and sports facilities – including two pools. Rooms from US$167. ❾

La Casa Grande Av La Reforma 7–67, Zona 10 ☎ & ℉ 332 0914. Elegant villa set slightly back from the road, right next to the US embassy. ❼

Holiday Inn 1 Av 13–22, Zona 10 ☎ 332 2555, ℉ 332 2584, ⊛ wwwguatered.com/holidayinn. First-class hotel, within walking distance of the city's best upmarket shops, bars and restaurants.

Commodious rooms and suites, plus a fully equipped business centre and an in-house internet café. Rooms from US$140. ❾

Hotel Casa Santa Clara 12 C 4–51, Zona 10 ☎ 339 1811, ℉ 332 0775, ⊛ www .hotelcasasantaclara.com. Small, beautifully appointed hotel in the Zona Viva, with tastefully decorated modern rooms. Also boasts a quality in-house Mediterranean restaurant. ❼

Hotel Inter-Continental 14 C 2–51 Zona 10 ☎ 379 4444, ℉ 379 4447, ⊛ www.interconti.com. This spectacular new Zona Viva hotel is now the city's most stylish five-star address. Among its many charms are a monumental lobby featuring fine art, modern sculpture and a modish bar, sumptuous bedrooms, a fine French restaurant and a wonderful outdoor pool. Rooms from US$145. ❾

Hotel Princess Reforma 13 C 7–65, Zona 9 ☎ 334 4545, ℉ 334 4546, ⊛ www .hotelesprincess.com. Pleasant mid-sized hotel with very comfortable rooms, and high standards of service. There's a small pool, sauna, gym and tennis courts. Rooms from US$134. ❾

The City

Though few people come to Guatemala City for the sights, there are some places that are worth visiting while you're here. The Ixchel, Popol Vuh and Archeological **museums** are particularly good, and there are a few impressive buildings in Zona 1 as well as some more outlandish modern structures dotted across the southern half of the city.

If you're interested to see how the rich let their hair down, head for the Zona Viva in Zona 10, while Zona 1 is the place to see the big city streetlife – hawkers, market vendors, evangelical preachers and prostitutes are all here in abundance.

Zonas 1 and 2: the old city

The hub of the old city is **Zona 1**, which is also the busiest and most claustrophobic part of town. This is the run-down **centro histórico**, a squalid world of low-slung, crumbling nineteenth-century town houses and faceless concrete blocks, broken pavements, car parking lots and plenty of noise and dirt. Though the city authorities largely left Zona 1 to rot for decades, tentative signs of regeneration are beginning to emerge, as a committed group of planners and architects attempt to preserve the capital's heritage, and clusters of new bars and cafés are opening in historic buildings. It's a process that will take decades to achieve, as the area remains beset by social problems and plagued by pollution and noise from thundering fume-belching buses, but the streets, thick with street vendors and urban bustle, do harbour a certain brutal fascination and are undeniably the most exciting part of the capital.

The Parque Central and around

Zona 1's northern boundary runs just behind the Palacio Nacional, taking in the **Parque Central**, a square that forms the country's political and religious

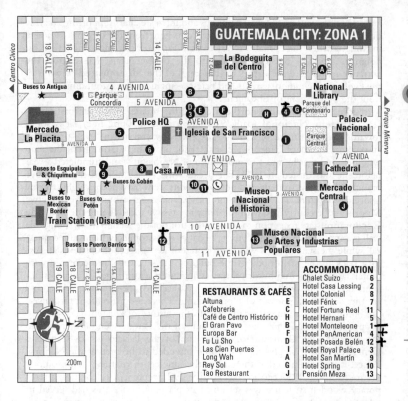

Map: GUATEMALA CITY: ZONA 1

RESTAURANTS & CAFÉS

Altuna	E
Cafebreria	C
Café de Centro Histórico	H
El Gran Pavo	B
Europa Bar	F
Fu Lu Sho	D
Las Cien Puertes	I
Long Wah	A
Rey Sol	G
Tao Restaurant	J

ACCOMMODATION

Chalet Suizo	6
Hotel Casa Lessing	2
Hotel Colonial	8
Hotel Fénix	7
Hotel Fortuna Real	11
Hotel Hernani	5
Hotel Monteleone	1
Hotel PanAmerican	4
Hotel Posada Belén	12
Hotel Royal Palace	3
Hotel San Martín	9
Hotel Spring	10
Pensión Meza	13

centre, as well as being the point from where all distances in Guatemala are measured. This plaza, currently concealing a large underground car park, was originally the scene of a huge central market, which now operates from a covered site behind the cathedral (see below). Nowadays the square is a strangely soulless place, patronized by bored taxi-drivers, *lustradores* (shoeshiners) and pigeons, that only really comes alive on Sundays and public holidays when a tide of Guatemalans descend on the square to stroll, chat and snack or to visit the *huipil* market. Yet there is a new national spirit detectable here now, as soldiers chat with the local Maya, and you may even hear politics being discussed – something almost unthinkable a decade or so ago. Next to the giant Guatemalan flag in the centre of the square is a small box containing an **eternal flame** dedicated to "the anonymous heroes for peace", which has made the parque a place of pilgrimage for many Guatemalans.

Most of the imposing structures that face the parque today were put up after the 1917 earthquake, with the notable exception of the blue-tile-domed **Cathedral** (daily 8am–1pm & 3–7pm; free), which was completed in 1868. For years its grand facade, merging the Baroque and the Neoclassical, dominated the square, dwarfing all other structures. Its solid, squat form was designed to resist the force of earthquakes and, for the most part, it has succeeded. In 1917 the bell towers were brought down and the cupola fell, destroying the altar, but the central structure, though cracked and patched over the years, remains intact. Inside there are three main aisles, all lined with arching pillars, austere colonial paintings and intricate altars supporting an array of saints. Some of this collection was brought here from the original cathedral in Antigua when the capital was moved in 1776. However, the cathedral's most poignant aspect is outside: etched into the twelve pillars that support the entrance railings are the names of thousands of the "**disappeared**" victims of the civil war – children, parents and priests – including an astounding number from the department of El Quiché.

Presiding over the entire northern end of the square, the gargantuan stone-faced **Palacio Nacional** (daily 9am–noon & 2–4.30pm; free) faces south towards the neon maze of Zona 1. The palace was started in 1939 under the auspices of President Ubico – a characteristically grand gesture from the man who believed that he was a reincarnation of Napoleon – and completed a year before he was ousted in 1944. For decades the palace housed the executive branch of the government, and periodically its steps have been fought over by assorted coupsters. The interior of the palace is set around two attractive Moorish-style courtyards, with the most impressive rooms being the **Salas de Recepción** (state reception rooms), at the front of the second floor. Along one wall is a row of flags and the country's coat of arms, topped with a stuffed quetzal, while the stained-glass windows represent key aspects of Guatemalan history. Back in the main body of the building the stairwells are decorated with murals, again depicting historical scenes, mixed in with images of totally unrelated events: one wall shows a group of idealized pre-conquest Maya, and another includes a portrait of Don Quixote. There are plans afoot to convert the building into a museum dedicated to the history of Guatemala.

Opposite the cathedral, the western side of the Parque Central merges into the **Parque del Centenario**, former site of the Palacio de los Capitanes Generales. A long single-storey building intended to be used as the National Palace, it was completed at the end of the nineteenth century, then promptly destroyed in the 1917 earthquake. For the 1921 centenary celebration a temporary wooden structure was set up in its place, but once this had served its purpose it went up in flames. After that it was decided to create a park instead, though today's stone-flagged expanse is unremarkable in the extreme, with an ugly, concrete, shell-shaped bandstand which is occasionally used for live concerts and evangelical get-togethers. Looming over the western side of the Parque del Centenario is the hulking Sixties-style **Biblioteca Nacional** (National Library), housing the archives of Central America.

Around the back of the cathedral is the concrete **Mercado Central** (Mon–Sat 6am–6pm, Sun 9am–noon), with a miserable mini-plaza and car park on its roof. Taking no chances, the architect of this building, which replaced an earlier version destroyed in the 1976 earthquake, apparently modelled the structure on a nuclear bunker, sacrificing any aesthetic concerns to the need for strength. Inside, you'll find textiles, leatherware and jewellery on the top floor; fruit, vegetables, snacks, flowers and plants in the middle; and **handicrafts**, mainly basketry and *típica*, in the basement. Unexpectedly, the market is a pretty good spot to buy traditional weaving, with a comprehensive range of cloth from all over the country on offer. It is only visited by a trickle of tourists so prices are reasonable and the traders very willing to bargain. This was once the city's main food market but these days it's just one of many, and by no means the largest.

Two blocks east of the market and one block south along 9 Avenida, you reach one of the city's less well-known museums, **Museo Nacional de Historia**, 9 C 9–70, Zona 1 (Tues–Sun 9am–4pm; US$1.30), which features a selection of artefacts relating to Guatemalan history, including documents, clothes and paintings. Probably the most interesting displays are the photographs by Eadweard Muybridge, who, in 1875, was one of the first people to undertake a study of the country. Less impressive is the **Museo Nacional de Artes y Industrias Populares**, half a block away at 10 Av 10–72 (Tues–Sun 9am–noon & 2–4pm; US$1.30), with its small, sadly neglected collection of painting, weaving, ceramics, musical instruments and Maya masks.

Along 6 and 7 avenidas

The garish heart of Zona 1 is formed by **6 and 7 avenidas**, running south of the parque central, thick with clothes shops, restaurants, cinemas, neon signs and bus fumes. What you can't buy in the shops is sold on the pavements, while *McDonald's*, *Wimpy* and *Pizza Hut* are all very much part of the scene. It's here that most people head on a Saturday night, when the traffic has to squeeze between hordes of pedestrians. By 11pm or so, though, the streets are largely deserted, left to the cigarette sellers and prostitutes.

Heading down 7 Avenida, the main **post office** (see p.88) at the junction of 12 Calle is a spectacular Moorish-style building with a marvellous arch that spans the road. From here it's short walk to **Casa Mima** at the corner of 14 Calle and 8 Avenida (Mon–Sat 9am–12.30pm & 2–5pm; US$2), an immaculately restored late nineteenth-century town house. Inside there's a terrific collection of original Moderne, Art Deco and French neo-Rococo furnishings, offering a fascinating glimpse of a wealthy middle-class household. There are excellent explanatory leaflets, and usually an English-speaking guide, plus a delightful little café, with good coffee and cookies, on the rear patio.

A block and a half west of here up 14 Calle are the **Police Headquarters**, which occupy an outlandish-looking mock castle complete with imitation medieval battlements. Next door, on 6 Avenida the church of **Iglesia de San Francisco** is famous for its carving of the Sacred Heart, which, like several other of its paintings and statues, was brought here from Antigua. Building began in 1780, but was repeatedly interrupted by seismic activity – it's said that cane syrup, egg whites and cow's milk were mixed with the mortar to enhance its strength. For the most part the church fared well, but in 1917 a tremor brought down one of the arches, revealing that the clergy had used the roof cavity to store banned books.

South along 6 Avenida, things go into a slow but steady decline as the commercial chaos starts to get out of control. A mass of electrical shops line the road and the pavements become increasingly swamped by temporary stalls, many selling clothes. On the left-hand side of 6 Avenida, beneath the trees, **18 Calle** becomes distinctly sleazy, the cheap food stalls and shoeshine boys now mixed in with grimy nightclubs and "streap-tease" joints. By night the streets are patrolled by prostitutes and the local hotels are protected by prison-like grilles. Night or day it's best avoided, but if you really want to delve into the sleaze take nothing of value and a minimum of cash. At the corner of 18 C and 9 Av, the **eastern bus terminal** is the depot for buses to the Mexican border and Petén, while the surrounding streets are home to a number of bus company offices. On the east side of an open square just off 18 Calle lie the derelict remains of the **train station**, from where trains used to leave for Tecún Umán and Puerto Barrios. The station was mysteriously burnt down in 1996, with all its documents and records going up in smoke the night before auditors were due to start investigating the finances of the state railway company. A fifty-year lease has since been awarded to a North American company to revitalize Guatemala's railway system, but currently there are only a few freight trains running, and sporadic tourist day trips (see p.120 under Travel details) which run from a different station. Further east, past the station, lies **Zona 5**, a run-down residential suburb.

Back on 6 Avenida, at the junction of 18 Calle, you'll see the **Tipografía Nacional**, the government's printing press and media centre, a wonderful, crumbling building, where bureaucrats beaver away at their task of disseminating information and propaganda. A little further along 6 Avenida, **La Placita**, the main food market (daily 6am–6pm), is housed in a vast, multicoloured hangar. Traders who can afford it pay for a space inside, while those who can't spread themselves along the surrounding streets, which are littered with rubbish and soggy with rotten fruit. At the end of this extended block the character of the city is radically transformed as the ageing and claustrophobic streets of Zona 1 give way to the broad avenues of Zona 4 and the Centro Cívico.

Into Zona 4: the Centro Cívico

At the southern end of the old city, separating it from the newer parts of town, the **Centro Cívico**, also known as the **Centro Municipal**, marks the boundary between zones 1 and 4. At this point the avenidas from the north merge at a couple of roundabouts, from where they fan out into the more spacious southern city. Bunched around these junctions a collection of multistorey office blocks house the city's main administrative buildings, including the **Banco de Guatemala** on 7 Avenida, bedecked with bold modern murals and stylized glyphs designed by Dagoberto Vásquez – the images recount the history of Guatemala and the conflict between Spanish and Maya. Just to the south you'll find the main office of **Inguat** (see p.19) and opposite is the lofty landmark **Teatro Nacional**, also referred to as the Miguel Ángel Asturias cultural centre, one of the city's most prominent and unusual structures. Completed in 1978, and built on top of the former **San José Fortress**, it's still surrounded by the original battlements. The design is along the lines of a huge ship, painted blue and white, with portholes as windows. Finding an entrance that isn't locked is not always easy, but it's well worth the effort for the superb **views** across the city. The building is also home to the little-visited **Military Museum** (Mon–Fri 8.30am–5pm), a strange homage to the Guatemalan army. Reached through the main theatre gate on 24 Calle, this small collection of weapons and uniforms is really only of interest to would-be *comandantes*.

North to Zona 2 and the Parque Minerva

North of the old city centre is Zona 2, bounded by a deep-cut ravine that prevents the sprawl from spreading any further in this direction. Three blocks north of the Parque Central, 6 Avenida passes a small residential square, the location where **Monsignor Juan José Geradi** (see Contexts, p.467) was bludgeoned to death on April 26 1998, two days after publishing his REMHI report into the civil war atrocities. There's a modest stone and bronze monument to Geradi in the square, and flowers and candles are often laid at the garage door of his former residence where the murder was committed. Next to the house, on the east side of the square, the modern Iglesia de San Sebastián is another place of pilgrimage, and services are held here on the anniversary of his death.

Continuing north along 6 Avenida, it's a further 1.5km to the **Parque Minerva,** also known as the Hipódromo del Norte (daily 9am–5pm; US$2), a park and sports complex on the edge of the city where fairs take place on public holidays and fiestas. Its main point of interest, however, is a newly restored **relief map of the country**, which covers 2500 square metres and has a couple of special viewing towers. The map was finished in 1905 and designed to have running water flowing in the rivers, although the taps are usually shut off.

Its vertical scale is out of proportion to the horizontal, making the mountains look incredibly steep. It does nevertheless give you a good idea of the general layout of the country, from the complexity of the highlands to the sheer enormity of Petén. Unsurprisingly, given the perpetual border squabbles between the two countries, Belize is included as Guatemalan territory. You can get to Parque Minerva on bus #1 or #46 from anywhere along 5 Avenida in Zona 1.

The new city

The southern half of the city is far more spacious, though while you may have more room to breathe, the air is no less noxious. Roughly speaking, the **new city** divides into two, split down the middle by 7 Avenida. The eastern half, centred on Avenida La Reforma, is the smartest part of the city, with banks, hotels, restaurants, boutiques and walled residential compounds – the natural habitat of Guatemala's wealthy elite. The western half of the new town, incorporating the bus terminal, zoo and airport, is less exclusive.

The east: around 7 Avenida and Avenida La Reforma

Heading to the south of the Centro Cívico and into Zona 4 proper, 6 Avenida runs into the modern city, with Ruta 6 branching off to the east, towards Avenida La Reforma, crossing 7 Avenida beside the landmark **Edificio El Triangulo**. From here, 7 Avenida heads south beneath the illuminated **Torre del Reformador**, at the junction of 2 Calle. Guatemala's answer to the Eiffel Tower, this steel structure was built along the lines of the Parisian model, in honour of President Barrios, who transformed the country between 1871 and 1885; a bell in the top of the tower is rung every year on June 30 to commemorate the Liberal victory in the 1871 revolution.

Pushing its way southeast, Ruta 6 passes the **Iglesia Yurrita**, an outlandish building designed in an exotic neo-Gothic style that belongs more to horror movies than to the streets of Guatemala City. It was finally completed in 1944, forty years after it was originally commissioned as a private chapel by a rich philanthropist, Felipe Yurrite Casteñeda. His house, in the same style, stands alongside. The church, also known as **Nuestra Señora de las Angustias**, is usually open to the public (Tues–Sun 7am–noon & 4–6pm), and is well worth a look as the inside – which contains a fabulous carved wooden altar – is just as wild as the exterior.

Ruta 6 meets Avenida La Reforma at a busy roundabout marked by the Cine Reforma, which has been both a cinema and an evangelical church, but is now a theatre and music venue. On the opposite side of Avenida La Reforma are the **Botanical Gardens** (Mon–Fri 8am–3.30pm; US$1.20) of the San Carlos University; the entrance is on 0 Calle. Inside you'll find a beautiful, small garden with a selection of species, all neatly labelled in Spanish and Latin. There's also a small, but not terribly exciting, **Natural History Museum** housing a collection of stuffed birds, including a quetzal and an ostrich, along with geological samples, wood types, live snakes, some horrific pickled rodents and a small library that includes books in English.

Far more interesting, however, are the two privately owned **museums** on the campus of the University Francisco Marroquín reached by following 6 Calle Final off Avenida La Reforma, heading east. **Museo Ixchel** (Mon–Fri 8am–5.50pm, Sat 9am–12.50pm; US$2.50, students US$1) is a striking, purpose-built edifice designed loosely along the lines of a Maya temple. Probably the capital's best museum, the Ixchel is dedicated to Maya culture, with particular emphasis on traditional weaving. It contains a stunning collection of

△ Overview of Agua volcano

hand-woven fabrics, including some very impressive examples of ceremonial costumes, with explanations in English. There's also information about the techniques, dyes, fibres and weaving tools used, and the way in which costumes have changed over the years. Although the collection is by no means comprehensive, and the costumes lose some of their impact and meaning when taken out of the villages where they're made, this is a fascinating exhibition. The building also houses a large library, and permanent exhibitions of paintings by Guatemalan artist Andrés Curruchich, who painted scenes of rural life around San Juan Comalapa (see p.131), and Carmen Peterson, who depicted traditional costumes on canvas. Don't miss the very good miniature *huipil* collection in the basement.

Right next door on the third floor of the *auditorio* building, is the city's other private museum, the excellent **Popol Vuh Archeological Museum** (Mon–Fri 9am–5pm, Sat 9am–1pm; US$2.50, no student discount). Standards here are just as high as at the Ixchel, but this time the subject is archeology, with an outstanding collection of artefacts from sites all over the country. The small museum is divided into Preclassic, Classic, Postclassic and Colonial rooms and all the exhibits are of top quality. The Preclassic room contains some stunning ceramics, stone masks and *hongo zoomorfo* (sculptures shaped like mushroom heads), while highlights of the Classic room include an altar from Naranjo, some lovely incense burners, and a model of Tikal. In the Postclassic room is a replica of the Dresden Codex, one of only three extant pre-conquest Maya books, while the Colonial era is represented by assorted ecclesiastical relics and processional crosses.

Back on Avenida La Reforma heading south, you pass the **Politecnica**, built in the style of a toy fort and still in use by the military. Beyond this is the smart part of town, where you'll find leafy streets filled with boutiques and travel agents, the American embassy (see p.88), banks, office blocks, sleek hotels and the offices of American Express (see p.86). While there's a steady flow of traffic along Avenida La Reforma, the surrounding area has clearly escaped the Third World, with quiet streets and mown lawns. A little to the east, around 10 Calle and 3 Avenida, is the so-called **Zona Viva**, a tight bunch of expensive hotels, restaurants and nightclubs and, at the bottom of La Reforma, the upmarket **Los Próceres** shopping mall. If you've spent some time in the impoverished highland villages, the ostentation on show in this little enclave will come as quite a shock to the system.

Out to the west side of Avenida La Reforma, **Plaza España** sits at the junction of 7 Avenida and 12 Calle. Now marked by a fountain, this crossroads was once the site of a statue of King Carlos III of Spain, torn down when independence was declared. At the four corners of the plaza you can still see some superb, tiled benches dating from colonial times.

To get to Avenida La Reforma from Zona 1, take bus #82 from 10 Avenida, past the Iglesia Yurrita, and all the way along Avenida La Reforma. La Reforma is a two-way street, so you can return along the same route.

Zona 14

Heading further south into Zona 14, the end of Avenida La Reforma is marked by a giant roundabout known as **Parque Independencia**, or **Plaza Obelisco**, at the junction with 20 Calle. Straight ahead, beyond this point the road continues as **Avenida las Américas**, where things become even more exclusive, with many of the large walled compounds belonging to embassies. Heading down Avenida las Américas you'll pass the Instituto Geográfico Militar on the right (see p.68), and two cinema complexes, including one of Guatemala's best movie houses, the Cine Magic Place (see p.85). At the southern end of the avenida, behind a statue of Pope John Paul II, is the **Plaza Berlin**, from where there are stunning views of the Pacaya volcano – it's a popular spot with picnicking families at weekends. Running parallel to Avenida las Américas, 14 Calle – better known as **Avenida Hincapié** – gives access to the **domestic air terminal**, opposite the junction with 18 Calle.

To the east, the main highway to the border with El Salvador runs out through Zonas 10 and 15. As the road leaves the city it climbs a steep hillside and passes through one of the most exclusive and expensive residential districts in the country, where every house has a superb view of the city below, and most are ringed by ferocious fortifications. Out beyond this, at the top of the hill, is Guatemala's main motor-racing track.

West of 6 Avenida

Out to the west of 6 Avenida it's quite another story, and while there are still small enclaves of upmarket housing, and several expensive shopping areas, things are really dominated by transport and commerce. A disused railway track, lined with bedraggled slums, runs out this way, with the airport, the zoo and the infamous Zona 4 bus terminal all rubbing shoulders. Of these, you're most likely to be visiting the **Zona 4 Bus Terminal**, at 1 Calle and 4 Avenida, the country's most impenetrable and intimidating jungle, a brutal swirl of petty thieves, hardware stores, bus fumes and sleeping vagrants.

Around the terminal the largest **market** in the city spreads across several blocks. If you can summon the energy it's a real adventure to wander through this maze of alleys, but don't carry too much money as it's a risky part of town. To get to the bus terminal from Zona 1, take any of the buses marked "terminal" from 4 Avenida or 9 Avenida, all of which pass within a block or two.

Behind the bus terminal, the railway tracks head off towards the coast, and behind these is **Avenida Bolívar**, an important traffic artery that runs out to the **Trébol junction**, where it meets the main highways from the western highlands and the Pacific coast. Up above the bus terminal here, just off Avenida Bolívar, is the **Santuario Expiatorio**, also known as the Iglesia Santa Cecilia de Don Bosco, a superb modern church designed (by a then unqualified Salvadorean architect) in the shape of a fish. It's part of a church-run complex that includes clinics and schools, and is well worth a browse, above all for the fantastic mural running down the side of the interior which depicts the Crucifixion and Resurrection with vivid realism.

Further to the south in **Zona 13**, the **Parque Aurora** houses the city's remodelled **zoo** (Tues–Sun 9am–5pm; US$1.20), where you can see African lions, Bengal tigers, Indian elephants, crocodiles, giraffes, hippos, monkeys and all the Central and South American big cats including some well-fed jaguars. Most of the larger animals seem to have a reasonable amount of space, but many smaller animals do not. To get here, take bus #63.

On the other side of the Parque Aurora, reached along 7 Avenida, is a collection of state-run **museums** (all Tues–Fri 9am–4pm, Sat & Sun 9am–noon & 1.30–4pm). The best of these is the **Museo Nacional de Arqueología y Etnología** (US$5), which has a world-class selection of Maya artefacts, though the design and displays are somewhat antiquated. The collection has sections on prehistoric archeology and ethnology and includes some wonderful stelae and panels from Machaquila and Dos Pilas, spectacular jade masks from Abaj Takalik and a stunning wooden temple-top lintel from Tikal. However, it's the exhibits collected from Piedras Negras, one of the remotest sites in Petén, that are most impressive. Stela 12, dating from 672 AD, brilliantly depicts a cowering captive king begging for mercy, and there's a monumental carved stone throne from the same site, richly engraved with superb glyphs and decorated with a twin-faced head. Right opposite the archeological museum, the city's **Museo Nacional de Arte Moderno** (US$1.70) also suffers from poor presentation and layout but can boast some imaginative geometric paintings by Dagoberto Vásquez, vibrant semi-abstract work by the indigenous artist Rolando Ixquiac Xicará and a collection of startling exhibits by Efraín Recinos including a colossal marimba–tank sculpture. There's also a permanent collection of the bold Cubist art and massive murals of Carlos Mérida, Guatemala's most celebrated artist, which draws strongly on ancient Maya tradition. Finally, the **Museo Nacional de Historia Natural** (US$1.70) is probably the most neglected of the trio of museums, featuring a range of mouldy-looking stuffed animals from Guatemala and elsewhere and a few mineral samples. There's a much-mothballed plan to remodel the whole Parque Aurora area, including massive reforestation, to make the complex more appealing for visitors, though all there is for now is a touristy handicraft market on 11 Avenida. To get here, take bus #63 from 4 Avenida or #83 from 10 Avenida.

The final point of interest in the southern half of the city is the **Ciudad Universitária**, the campus of San Carlos University, in Zona 12. A huge, purpose-built complex, it is heavily decorated with vivid political graffiti. The San Carlos University, originally founded in Antigua by Dominican priests in 1676, is probably the best in Central America; it has an autonomous constitution and is entitled to five percent of the government's annual budget. The university also has a long history of radical dissent and anti-government protest, and hundreds of students here were victims of repression and political killings – many right-wing politicians still regard the campus as a centre of subversion. Buses marked "Universitária" travel along 4 Avenida through Zona 1 to the campus.

Zona 7: the ruins of Kaminaljuyú

Way out on the western edge of the city, beyond the stench of the rubbish dump, is the long thin arm of Zona 7, a well-established but run-down part of town that wraps around the ruins of **Kaminaljuyú** (daily 9am–4pm; US$4). Archeological digs on this side of the city have revealed the astonishing proportions of a Maya city that once housed around fifty thousand people and includes more than three hundred mounds and thirteen ball courts. Unlike the massive temples of the lowlands, these structures were built of adobe, and most of them have been lost to centuries of erosion and a few decades of urban sprawl. Today the archeological site, incorporating only a tiny fraction of the original city, is little more than a series of earth-covered mounds, a favourite spot for football and romance. A couple of sections have been cut into by archeologists, and by peering through the fence you can get some idea of what lies beneath the grassy exterior, but it's virtually impossible to get any impression of Kaminaljuyú's former scale and splendour.

To get to the ruins, take bus #35 from 4 Avenida in Zona 1; alternatively, any bus with a small "Kaminaljuyú" sign in the windscreen passes within a block or two.

A history of Kaminaljuyú

Despite its nondescript appearance, Kaminaljuyú, once the largest Maya city in the Guatemalan highlands, is a particularly important site. Its history falls neatly into two sections: a first phase of indigenous growth, and a later period during which migrants from the north populated the site.

In the Late Preclassic era, 400 BC to 100 AD, the city had already grown to huge proportions, with some two hundred flat-topped **pyramids**, the largest reaching a height of about 18m. Beneath each of these lay entombed a member of the nobility; a few have been unearthed to reveal the wealth and sophistication of the culture. The corpses were wrapped in finery, covered in cinnabar pigment and surrounded by an array of human sacrifices, pottery, jade, masks, stingray spines, obsidian and quartz crystals. A number of carvings have also been found, proving that the elite of Kaminaljuyú were fully literate at a time when other Maya had perhaps no notion of writing. Many of the gods, the ceramic styles and the hieroglyphic forms from these early days at Kaminaljuyú are thought to predate those found at later centres such as Tikal and Copán. But the power of the city, pre-eminent during the Late Preclassic era, faded throughout the second and third centuries, and the site may even have been abandoned.

Kaminaljuyú's renaissance took place shortly after 400 AD, when the Guatemalan highlands suffered a massive influx of migrants from the north and fell under the domination of Teotihuacán in central Mexico. The migrants seized the city of Kaminaljuyú and established it as their regional capital, giving them control of the obsidian mines and access to the coastal trade routes and the lowlands of Petén. With the weighty political and economic backing of Teotihuacán the city once again flourished, as the new rulers constructed their own temples, tombs and ball courts. Numerous artefacts have been found from this period, including some pottery that's thought to have been made in Teotihuacán itself, along with endless imitations of the style. Kaminaljuyú's new-found power also played a crucial role in shaping the lowlands of Petén: it was only with the backing of the great Teotihuacán–Kaminaljuyú alliance that Tikal was able to grow so large and so fast. This role was considered of such importance that some archeologists suggest that Curl Nose, one of the early rulers at Tikal (who ascended to power in 387 AD), may actually have come from Kaminaljuyú. The fortunes of Kaminaljuyú itself, however, were so bound up with those of its northern partner that the fall of Teotihuacán around 600 AD weakened and eventually destroyed the city.

Kaminaljuyú has most recently been reclaimed as an important sacred site by Maya shamen and activists, and you may well stumble across a religious ceremony going on in the grassy plazas. Poignantly, this was also the setting chosen by the indigenous leader Rigoberta Menchú (see p.469) to celebrate her 1992 Nobel Peace Prize, when thousands thronged to the old capital.

Eating, drinking and entertainment

Despite its status as capital and the largest city in Central America, Guatemala City isn't a great place for indulging. Most of the population hurry home after dark and it's only the very rich who eat, drink and dance until the small hours. There are, however, **restaurants** everywhere in the city, invariably reflecting the type of neighbourhood they're in, most concentrating on quantity rather than quality. Movie-watching is hugely popular, with a good selection of cinemas; nightclubs and bars are concentrated in Zona 10.

Restaurants and cafés

When it comes to eating cheaply in Guatemala City, stick to **Zona 1**, where the restaurants tend to reflect the fact that most people have little money to spare. At **lunchtime** you'll find set-price, three-course menus all over the central zone for less than US$2 a head including a *fresco* drink; try the area west of the Parque Central or around the post office, in particular. There's a cluster of **Chinese** restaurants on 6 Calle, between 4 and 3 Avenidas, a patch that ranks as the city's Chinatown, while a few **Italian** restaurants have also sprung up, as have a couple of specifically **vegetarian** places, despite the fact that this is a city obsessed with meat-eating. Cheap and filling food is also sold from stalls around all the bus stations and markets, and on many of the streets in the centre. In the smarter parts of town, particularly **Zonas 9** and **10**, the emphasis is more on upmarket cafés and glitzy dining, and there is more choice here with Mexican, Middle Eastern, Chinese and Japanese options.

Fast food is widely available with plenty of choice, the vast majority being US chains. There's a *McDonald's* at 10 C 5–56, Zona 1, and 7 Av 14–01, Zona 9, and a *Pizza Hut* at 6 Av & 12 C Zona 1 (for delivery ☎230 3394 in Zona 1, ☎ 332 0939 in Zona 9). Home-grown breeds include *Burger Shops*, 6 Av 13–40, Zona 1, and the slightly cheaper *Pollo Campero*, the Guatemalan version of *KFC*, with branches throughout the city.

Zona 1

Altuna 5 Av 12–31. Spanish/Basque food in a wonderfully civilized old colonial mansion. Very strong on fish and seafood, but also pasta and Castilian treats like Manchego cheese and *jamón serrano*. Not cheap, but worth a splurge for the elegant ambience.

Cafebreria 5 Av 13–32. Part bookshop, part internet café, serving coffee, snacks and more substantial dishes on a quiet covered patio. The owner plans to open a budget hotel upstairs.

Café de Centro Histórico 6 Av 9–50. Stylish café on the upper floor of a beautifully restored 1930s building replete with original tiles, wood panelling and evocative monochrome photographs. Simple menu of inexpensive Guatemalan dishes, pies and salads, plus great coffee.

Europa Bar 11 C 5–16. The most popular ex-pat hangout in Zona 1, set inauspiciously beneath a multistorey car park. Primarily a bar, with CNN and sports on screen, but there are also cheapish eats. Owner Judy is a mine of local information. You can trade US dollars here and make local calls. Closed Sun.

Fu Lu Sho 6 Av and 12 C. Popular, inexpensive Chinese restaurant with an Art Deco interior, opening onto the bustle of 6 Avenida.

☛ **El Gran Pavo** 13 C 4–41. Massive portions of genuinely Mexican, moderately priced food. It's riotous on the weekend when mariachi bands prowl the tables. Also at 6 C 3–09, Zona 9; 15 Av 16–72, Zona 10; and 13C and 6 Av, Zona 10.

Long Wah 6 C 3–75, west of the Palacio Nacional. One of the best of the many Chinese restaurants in this neighbourhood, with a good, inexpensive menu.

Rey Sol south side of Parque Centenario. "Aerobic" breakfasts (sic), very good selection of vegetarian dishes and licuados. The shop sells wholemeal bread, granola and veggie snacks.

Tao Restaurant 5 C 9–70. The city's best-value three-course veggie lunch. There's no menu; you just eat the meal of the day at tiny tables around a plant-filled courtyard.

Zona 4

Cafe Restaurant Pereira inside the Gran Centro Comercial mall, 6 Av and 24 C. Just a couple of blocks west of Inguat, this is a very popular comedor with excellent set meals of typical Guatemalan food. Also at Av la Reforma 14–43, Zona 9.

Zonas 9 and 10

Los Alpes 10 C 1–09, Zona 10. A haven of peace, this garden café has superb pastries, pies and crêpes and a relatively inexpensive breakfast menu considering the smart location. Closed Mon.

Los Antojitos Av la Reforma 15–02, Zona 9. Good, moderately priced Central American food – try the *chiles rellenos* or guacamole.

Donde Mikel 13C 5–19, Zona 10. Elegant, expensive Spanish restaurant popular with the nation's elite, with delicious sizzling *camarones* (shrimp) and meats served *a la plancha* (grilled). Closed Sun.

Jake's 17 C 10–40, Zona 10. Lunch and dinner from an international menu, very strong on fish and with terrific sweets. Pleasant, candle-lit atmosphere, excellent service and correspondingly high prices. Closed Sun & Mon.

La Lancha 13 C 7–98, Zona 10. French-owned restaurant, with a superb menu of very reasonably priced traditional Gallic dishes, plus a daily special, and a tremendous wine list, including champagne.

Open for lunch Mon–Fri, dinner Thurs & Fri only.

Luigi's Pizza 4 Av 14–20, Zona 10. Very popular, moderately priced Italian restaurant, serving delicious pizza, pasta and baked potatoes.

Olivadda 12 C 4–51, Zona 10. Very smart restaurant with a stylish interior and a leafy terrace garden, majoring in authentic, moderately priced Mediterranean fare.

Palace 10 C 4–40, Zona 10. Pasta and snacks, cakes and pastries in a cafeteria atmosphere. Inexpensive.

Piccadilly Plaza España, 7 Av 12–00, Zona 9. One of the most popular continental restaurants with tourists and Guatemalans alike. Decent range of pastas and pizzas, served along with huge jugs of beer. Moderate prices. Also in Zona 1 on 6 Av and 11 C.

Puerto Barrios 7 Av 10–65, Zona 9. Excellent, but pricey, seafood restaurant in a slightly comical boat-like building.

Tamarindos 11 C 2–19A, Zona 10. Uber-chic bar-restaurant with modish Italian furniture, sensitive lighting, European chill-out music and a very hip, moneyed clientele. The pan-Asian menu matches the site with delicious, beautifully presented Thai-, Malay- and Chinese-influenced dishes set at far from outrageous prices – expect to pay around US$15 a head.

Vesuvio Pizza 18 C 3–36, Zona 10. Huge pizzas with plenty of mouth-watering toppings, cooked in a traditional, wood-burning oven.

Zona 13

Café de la Libre 7 Av & 13C, Zona 13. Pleasant, if pricey, vegetarian place next to Libreria del Pensativo. Good lunch specials.

Drinking and nightlife

Despite appearances, Guatemala City quietens down very quickly in the evenings, and **nightlife** is not one of its strengths. What little action there is is divided between the edgy appeal of Zona 1 and the glitz of Zona 10 – some of the best are reviewed below.

The best bet for a night out in **Zona 1** is to start somewhere like *Las Cien Puertes* or *El Tiempo* and then head to *Altos del Cairo* close by to see a band, or check out what's on at *La Bodeguita*. Alternatively, if you crave the low life, then stroll on down 18 Calle, to the junction with 9 Avenida, and you're in the heart of the red-light district, where the bars and clubs are truly sleazy.

Zona 10 is where the wealthy go to have fun and it's anything but an egalitarian experience. *Sesto Senso* is a good place to head for, while there's a strip of bars along 1 and 2 avenidas in the Zona Viva, plus plenty of dance clubs. House music is firmly established in Guatemala, though you'll be lucky to get anything other than the commercial "handbag" strain; most DJs spin a mix of pan-Latin sounds and rave hits, with the merengue of the Caribbean often spiced up with raggamuffin vocals; plus there are specialist clubs for salsa fanatics. The city's premier reggae bar is *La Gran Comal* on Via 4 between 6 Avenida and Ruta 6, Zona 4. Radiating rhythm, it's relaxed, but not as worn-out as the clubs of Zona 1. It's a favourite haunt of black Guatemalans from Lívingston and the Caribbean coast, and well worth a visit.

Bars and clubs

Altos del Cairo first floor, 9 C 6–10, Zona 1. Raucous drinking den with simple bench seating, draught beer, and rock, pop and salsa nights.

La Bodeguita del Centro 12 C 3–55, Zona 1 (☎230 2976). Large, leftfield venue with live music, comedy, poetry and all manner of arty events. Free entry in the week, around US$4 at weekends. Definitely worth a visit for the Ché Guevara memorabilia alone.

Las Cien Puertes Pasaje Aycinena, 9 C between 6 and 7 Av, Zone 1. Funky, artistic bar in a beautiful run-down colonial arcade. Good Latin sounds, very moderate prices and some imaginative Guatemalan cooking. Recommended.

El Establo 14 C 5–08, Zona 10. Large, stylish European-owned bar with polished wood interior, good food and a soundtrack of decent jazz and Western music.

Kahlua 15 C and 1 Av, Zona 10. Currently one of the most happening clubs in town with two dance floors and a chill-out room. Attracts a young crowd with a reasonable mix of dance and Latin pop.

Sesto Senso 2 Av 12–81, Zona 10. Hip, lively bar-restaurant with superb menu of global food,

Gay Guatemala City

Guatemala City's small **gay** scene is mostly underground and concentrated around a few (almost entirely male) venues. In *Zona 1*, *El Metropole* at 6 C & 3 Av, *Eclipso* at 12 C & 6 Av, and *Ephebus* at 4 C 5–30, are all small, intimate clubs which play great dance and house music. Over in *Zona 4*, *Pandora's Box*, Via 3 & Ruta 3, is the city's largest gay club, and plays mainstream latin dance and western pop sounds, but nevertheless has a great atmosphere. There are no specifically lesbian clubs or bars in the city.

plus great coffee and snacks, and often some live music, including Garífuna punta, in the evening.
Shakespeare's Pub 13 C 1–51, Zona 10. Small basement bar, with friendly staff, mainly catering to older ex-pat North Americans.
El Tiempo Pasaje Aycinema, 9 C between 6 and 7 Av, Zona 1. Very lively bar in the heart of the historic centre that's a magnet for the city's bohemian youth, hedonists and thinkers, where there are sporadic music jams, protest poetry readings and the like.
Xtreme 3 Av and 13 C, Zona 10. Industrial decor, with a dark interior of steel and aluminium, plus a tooth-loosening sound system make this club one of the coolest places in town. The Latin dance, house and chart pop attracts a rich, young crowd.

Cinemas

Most movies shown in Guatemala City are in English with Spanish subtitles. Often they're the very latest releases from the US, which tend to arrive in Central America before they reach Europe. There are **four cinemas on 6 Avenida** between the main plaza and 8 Calle, and these and a selection of others scattered throughout the city are listed below – the best for sound quality include the Magic Place and the Cine Tikal Futura. For **art house movies**, La Cúpula regularly shows quirky European, Latin American and classic productions; check the *Guatemala Post* for weekly listings. The main cinema programmes are listed in the two national newspapers, *El Gráfico* and *Prensa Libre*.

Cine Las Américas Av las Américas, between 8 & 9 calles, Zona 13.
Cine Bolívar Av Bolívar & 35 C, Zona 8.
Cine Capitol 6 Av & 12 C, Zona 1.
Cine Capri 8 C & 3 Av, Zona 1.
Cine Lido 11 C 7–34, Zona 1.
Cine Lux 11 C & 6 Av, Zona 1.
Cine Magic Place Av las Américas, Zona 13.
Cine Palace opposite the Capitol.
Cine Plaza 7 Av 6–7 C, Zona 9.
Cines Taurus, Leo and Aires 9 C & 4 Av, Zona 1.
Cine Tikal Futura Tikal Futura, Calzada Roosevelt, Zona 11.
Cine Tropical Av Bolívar 31–71, Zona 8.
La Cúpula 7 Av 13–01, Zona 9.

Listings

Airlines Airline offices are scattered throughout the city, with many along Avenida la Reforma. It is fairly straightforward to phone them and there will almost always be someone in the office who speaks English. Aerocaribe, see Mexicana, below; Aerovías, Av Hincapié 18 C, Zona 13 ☎ 332 5686, airport ☎ 332 7470; Air Canada, 12 C 1–25, Zona 10 ☎ 335 3341; American Airlines, *Hotel El Dorado*, Av la Reforma 15–45, Zona 9 ☎ 334 7379; Aviateca, see Taca, below; British Airways, 1 Av 10–81, Zona 10, 6th floor of Edificio Inexa ☎ 332 7402; Continental, 12 C 1–25, Zona 10, Edificio Géminis 10, 12th floor of Torre Norte ☎ 331 3341; Copa, 1 Av 10–1, Zona 10 ☎ 361 1567; Delta, 15 C 3–20, Zona 10, Centro Ejecutivo building ☎ 337 0642; Iberia, Av la Reforma 8–60, Zona 9 ☎ 334 3816, airport ☎ 332 5517; Inter, see Taca below; Lacsa, see Taca below; Jungle Flying, Av Hincapié & 18 C, domestic terminal, Hangar 21, Zona 13 ☎ 360 4917; ✉ jungleflying@guate.net; Mexicana, 13 C 8–44, Zona 10, Edificio Edyma ☎ 333 6048; Nica, see Taca below; Taca Group (Aviateca, Inter, Lacsa, Nica), Av Hincapié 12–22, Zona 13 ☎ 334 7722; Tikal Jets, La Aurora airport, international terminal

☎ 334 5631; United Airlines, Av la Reforma 1–50, Zona 9, Edificio el Reformador ☎ 332 2995. **American Express** Diagonal 6 10–01, Centro Gerencial Las Margaritas, Zona 10 (Mon–Fri 8.30am–5pm; ☎ 339 2877, ⑨ 339 2882).
Baggage There's no central left-luggage facility, so you'll have to entrust any baggage to your hotel.
Banks and exchange At the airport, Banco Del Quetzal (Mon–Fri 6am–8pm, Sat & Sun 6am–6pm) gives a good rate, takes most European currencies, and has a 24-hour Mastercard and Cirrus cashpoint; Visa and Plus cardholders should head for the nearby 24-hour Bancared cashpoint. In Zona 1, Credomatic, on the corner of 5 Av and 11

C, gives Visa and Mastercard cash advances (Mon–Fri 8.30am–7pm, Sat 9am–1pm) and will cash travellers' cheques. In Zona 10, head for the Centro Gerencial Las Margaritas, at Diagonal 6 10–01, where there are numerous banks where you can cash travellers' cheques, three 24-hour cashpoints for Visa and Plus cards and another, inside the Banco de Central América (Mon–Fri 9am–5pm, Sat 9am–1pm), that accepts Mastercard and Cirrus cards.
Books Perhaps the pleasantest bookshop in town is Sopho's, Av la Reforma 13–89, Zona 10, where there's a decent selection of English-language fiction and literature – you can also get good coffee

Moving on from Guatemala City

To get to the **international terminal** of **Aurora airport** from Zona 1, either take bus #83 from 10 Avenida (30min) or take a taxi (around US$10); from Zona 10 a taxi is around US$6. There's a US$30 departure tax on all international flights, payable in either quetzals or dollars. The **domestic terminal** is in the same complex but only reached via Avenida Hincapié; you'll need to take a taxi to reach it. Note that all Taca and Tikal Jets internal flights leave from the international terminal. The domestic departure tax is US$0.80.

If you're leaving by **first-class bus**, departures are from the bus company offices. Most are spread around the streets surrounding the old train station at 18 C and 9 Av in **Zona 1**, where there are first-class departures to Puerto Barrios, Cobán, the Pacific highway, eastern highlands, the Mexican border and Petén. Moving on by **second-class bus**, the main centre is the chaotic **Zona 4 terminal**, where services run to all parts of the country. To get there, take any city bus marked "terminal"; you'll find these heading south along 4 Avenida in Zona 1.

Buses from Guatemala City

The abbreviations we've used for the bus companies are as follows:

KQ	King Quality	**TA**	Transportes Alamo
L	Lituega	**TB**	Ticabus
LA	Líneas Américas	**TD**	Transportes Dulce María
LD	Línea Dorada	**TE**	Transportes Escobar y
LH	Los Halcones		Monja Blanca
MI	Melva Internacional	**TG**	Transportes Galgos
P	Pulmantur	**TM**	Transportes Marquensita
RO	Rutas Orientales	**TR**	Transportes Rebuli
RZ	Rápidos Zacaleu	**TV**	Transportes Velásquez
SJ	San Juanera		*see table below*

To	Company	Bus stop	Frequency	Journey time
Antigua	various (2nd)	18 C & 4 Av, Zona 1	15min	1hr
Belize City	LD	16 C 10–55, Zona 1	Thurs & Sun at 8pm	12hr
Chichicastenango	various (2nd)	Zona 4 terminal	30min	3hr 30min
Chiquimula	RO	19 C & 9 Av, Zona 1	15 daily	3hr 30min
Cobán	TE	8 Av 15–16, Zona 1	14 daily	4hr 30min
Cubulco	TD (2nd)	19 C & 9 Av, Zona 1	10 daily	5hr

here. Over the road in Zona 9 the Librería del Pensativo, 7 Av and 13 C, Edificio La Cúpula, is worth a browse, while in Zona 1 try Arnel, in the basement of the Edificio El Centro on 9 C, corner of 7 Av. Finally Géminis, 3 Av 17–05, Zona 14, is worth a visit if you're in the south of the city.

Car rental Renting a car in Guatemala is quite expensive and you should always keep a sharp eye on the terms: there are usually large penalties if you damage the vehicle. Jeeps can be rented for a little under US$55 a day and cars start from US$35. Adaesa Renta Autos, 4 C A 16–57, Zona 1 ⊤ 220 2180, ⓔ masifre@hotmail.com; Americar, 6 Av 3–95, Zona 10 ⊤ 361 8641, ⓦ www.america.com; Autorrentas (Budget agent), Av Hincapié 11–01, Zona 13 ⊤ 332 2024, ⓔ budget@infovia.com; Avis, 6 Av 11–24, Zona 9 ⊤ 334 1057, ⓔ avis@guate.net; Hertz, 7 Av 14–76, Zona 9 ⊤ 334 2540, ⓔ rentauto@guate .net; Rental, 12 C 2–62, Zona 10 ⊤ 361 0672, ⓕ 334 2739 – the only company to rent motor-bikes; Tabarini, 2 C A 7–30, Zona 10 ⊤ 332 2161, ⓕ 334 1925; Thrifty, Av la Reforma 8–33, Zona 10 ⊤ 332 1220, ⓔ thrifty@guate.net.

Dentist Central Dentist de Especialistas, 20 C 11–17, Zona 10 ⊤ 337 1773 is the best dental clinic in the country, and superb in emergencies. Prices are reasonable.

To	Company	Bus stop	Frequency	Journey time
Escuintla	various (2nd)	Zona 4 terminal	30min	1hr 15min
Esquipulas	RO	19 C & 9 Av, Zona 1	15 daily	4hr
Flores	various (1st/2nd)	17 C & 8 Av, Zona 1	16 daily	9hr
	LD (1st)	16 C 10–55, Zona 1	3 daily	9hr
Huehuetenango	LH (1st)	7 Av 15–27, Zona 1	3 daily	5hr 30min
	TV (1st)	20 C 1–37, Zona 1	9 daily	5hr 30min
	RZ (1st)	9C 11–42, Zona 1	3 daily	5hr 30min
Jalapa	various (2nd)	22 C 1–20, Zona 1	12 daily	2hr 30min
La Mesilla	TV (1st)	20 C 1–37, Zona 1	9 daily	7hr
Monterrico	various (2nd)	Zona 4 terminal	5 daily	4hr
Panajachel	TR (2nd)	21 C 1–54, Zona 1	11 daily	3hr
Puerto Barrios	L (1st)	15 C 10–40, Zona 1	18 daily	5hr 30min
Quetzaltenango	LA (1st)	2 Av 18–74, Zona 1	6 daily	4hr
	TA (1st)	21 C 1–14, Zona 1	5 daily	4hr
	TM (1st)	1 Av 21–31, Zona 1	8 daily	4hr
	TG (1st)	7 Av 19–44, Zona 1	6 daily	4hr
	SJ (2nd)	Zona 4 terminal	10 daily	4hr 30min
Rabinal	TD (2nd)	19 C & 9 Av, Zona 1	10 daily	4hr 30min
Salamá	TD (2nd)	19 C & 9 Av, Zona 1	10 daily	3hr 30min
San Salvador	MI (1st)	3 Av 1–38, Zona 9	11 daily	5hr
	TB (1st)	11 C 2–72, Zona 9	1 daily	5hr
	KQ (1st)	Col. Vista Hermosa II, Zona 15	2 daily	5hr
	P (1st)	Hotel Raddison Suites, 1 Av 12–43, Zona 10	2 daily	5hr
Santa Cruz del Quiché	various (2nd)	Zona 4 terminal		4hr
Tecún Umán	various (1st)	19 Av & 8 C, Zona 1	30min	5hr
Talismán	various (1st)	19 Av & 8 C, Zona 1	30min	5hr 30min
Tapacula	LD (1st)	16 C 10–55, Zona 1	2 daily	7hr
	TG (1st)	7 Av 19–44, Zona 1	2 daily	7hr
Zacapa	RO	19 C & 9 Av, Zona 1	15 daily	3hr

Doctors Your embassy should have a list of bilingual doctors, but for emergency medical assistance, there's the Centro Médico, a private hospital with 24-hour cover, at 6 Av 3–47, Zona 10 ☎332 3555. They can also provide booster vaccinations.

Embassies Most of the embassies are in the southeastern quarter of the city, along Avenida la Reforma and Avenida las Américas, and they tend to open weekday mornings only unless otherwise indicated. Belgium, 15 C A 14–44, Zona 10 (Mon–Fri 8.30am–1pm) ☎368 1150; Belize, Av la Reforma 1–50, 8th Floor, Suite 803, Edificio el Reformador, Zona 9 (Mon–Fri 9am–1pm & 2–5pm) ☎334 5531 or 331 1137; Brazil, 18 C 2–22, Zona 14 ☎337 0949; Canada, 13 C 8–44, 8th floor, Edificio Edyma Plaza, Zona 10 (Mon–Thurs 8am–4.30pm, Fri 8am–1.30pm) ☎333 6102; Chile, 14 C 15–21, Zona 13 ☎332 1149; Colombia, 12 C 1–25, Zona 10 ☎335 3602; Costa Rica, Av la Reforma 8–60, 3rd floor, Torre 1, Edificio Galerías Reforma, Zona 9 ☎ & ☎332 0531; Denmark (consulate) 7 Av 20–36, Zona 1 (Mon–Fri 9am–2pm) ☎238 1091; Ecuador, 4 Av 12–04, Zona 14 ☎337 2902; El Salvador, 4 Av 13–60, Zona 10 ☎366 2240; Germany, 20 C 6–20, Edificio Plaza Marítima, Zona 10 ☎338 0028; Honduras, 12 C 1–25, 12th floor, Edificio Géminis, Zona 10 ☎338 2068; Mexico, 15 C 3–20, Zona 10 (Mon–Fri 9am–1pm & 3–5pm) ☎333 7254 or 333 7255; Netherlands 16 C 0–55, 13th floor, Torre Internacional, Zona 10 ☎367 4761; Nicaragua, 10 Av 14–72, Zona 10 ☎368 0785; Norway, 6 Av 11–77, Zona 10 (Mon–Fri 9am–noon) ☎332 9296; Panamá, 5 Av 15–45, Torre 2, Edificio Centro Empresarial, Zona 10 ☎333 7176; Perú, 2 Av 9–67, Zona 9 ☎331 8558; South Africa, 10 Av 6–20, Zona 10 (Mon–Fri 9am–noon & 2–5pm) ☎334 1531; Sweden, 8 Av 15–07, Zona 10 (8am–1pm & 2–4pm) ☎333 6536; Switzerland, 4 C 7–73, Zona 9 (Mon–Fri 9–11.30am) ☎331 3726; UK, 16 C 0–55, 11th floor, Torre Internacional, Zona 10 (Mon–Fri 9am–noon & 2–4pm) ☎367 5425; US, Av la Reforma, 7–01, Zona 10 (Mon–Fri 8am–5pm) ☎331 1541; Venezuela, 8 C 0–56, Zona 9 ☎331 6505.

Emergencies Police ☎120; Fire ☎123; Red Cross ☎125.

Immigration The main immigration office (*Migración*) is conveniently located on the second floor of the Inguat HQ at 7 Av 1–17, Zona 4 ☎634 8476 (Mon–Fri 9am–3pm). For more details about visa extensions see Basics p.18.

Internet Guatemala City is under-endowed with internet cafés compared with Antigua, and rates are much higher, typically around US$5 an hour. In Zona 1, Cafebreria at 5 Av 13–32 is well set up, while in Zona 10 head for the Próceres shopping mall at 16 C and 2 Av, where you can surf at Café Virtual at ground level or Wizards on the third floor.

Language courses Of the several Spanish schools based in Guatemala City, the best is probably the IGA (the Guatemalan American Institute), on Ruta 1 and Via 4, Zona 4 (☎331 0022, ☎334 4392, no website). Easy, Blvd Los Próceres 9–67, Zona 10 (☎337 3970, ☎365 9150, no website), also gets good reports, though generally speaking, you're better off learning Spanish in Antigua, Quetzaltenango or one of the other centres (see Basics, p.47).

Laundry Lavandería Obelisco, Av la Reforma 16–30, next to the Samaritana supermarket (Mon–Fri 8am–6.45pm, Sat 8am–5.30pm), charges around US$3 for a self-service wash and dry, and there's also a self-service laundry at 4 Av 13–89, Zona 1.

Libraries The best library for English books is in the IGA (Guatemalan American Institute) at Ruta 1 and Via 4, Zona 4. There's also the National Library on the west side of the Parque del Centenario, and specialist collections at the Ixchel and Popol Vuh museums.

Newspapers Guatemalan newspapers are sold everywhere on the streets, but foreign titles are hard to come by. Copies of *Time* and *Newsweek* (and sometimes *The Economist*) are usually on sale on the south side of the main plaza, and the British Embassy often has copies of the *Times*, *Independent* and *Guardian* newspapers. American papers are more readily available: both the *Hotel Panamerican*, 9 C 5–63, Zona 1, and the *Camino Real* on Av la Reforma stock a selection. *Central American Report* is available from 7 Av 2–05, Zona 1.

Pharmacies Farmacia Osco, 16 C and 4 Av, Zona 10.

Photography Colour transparency and colour and monochrome print film is easy to buy, though expensive. There are several camera shops on 6 Avenida in Zona 1. Foto Sittler, 12 C 6–20, Zona 1, and La Perla, 9 C and 6 Av, Zona 1, repair cameras and offer a three-month guarantee on their work.

Police The main police station is in a bizarre castle-like structure on the corner of 6 Av and 14 C, Zona 1. In an emergency dial ☎120.

Post office The main post office is at 7 Av and 12 C (Mon–Fri 8.30am–6.30pm, Sat 8.30am–4.30pm). Note the Lista de Correos system is no longer very reliable in Guatemala.

Telephone You can make long-distance phone calls and send faxes from Telgua, one block east of the post office (daily 7am–midnight).

Tours Excellent walking tours of the historic centre of the city are organized by Antañona, 11 Av 5–59, Zona 1 ℡238 1751, @walkingtour@hotmail.com; tours leave from their offices Mon–Fri at 9.30am and cost US$10 per person. Plenty of agencies offer other guided city tours that usually include the main museums and sites and transport, including Clark Tours – see "Travel agents", below.

Travel agents There are plenty in the centre and along Avenida la Reforma in Zonas 9 and 10; flights to Petén can be booked through all of them. Clark Tours, Diagonal 6 10–01, 7th floor, Torre 2, Las Margaritas, Zona 10 ℡339 2888, ℱ339 2909, ⊛www.clarktours.com, organize trips to many parts of the country; Ecotourism & Adventure Specialists, 4 Av A 7–95, Zona 14 ℡337 0009, ⊛www.ecotourism-adventure.com, offer well coordinated trips to Petén and many remote parts of the country; Maya Expeditions, 15C A. 14–17 Zona 10, ℡ & ℱ363 4965 ⊛www.mayaexpeditions.com, specialize in ecotourism adventure and rafting trips; Viajes Tivoli, 6 Av 8–41, Zona 9 ℡339 2260, @viajes@tivoli.com.gt, or 12 C 4–55, Zona 1 ℡238 4771, is a good all-round agent with competitive rates for international flights.

Work Hard to come by. The best bet is teaching at one of the English schools, most of which are grouped on 10 and 18 calles in Zona 1. Check the classified sections of the *Guatemala Post* and *Revue*.

Around Guatemala City

Leaving the capital in any direction, you'll quickly escape its polluted, hectic atmosphere. In the event you're not dashing off straight away to Antigua, there are a couple of destinations suited to day-trips from the city, while the rest of the surrounding hills are easily explored using other towns as a base.

To the south the main road runs to Escuintla and the Pacific coast, passing through a narrow valley that separates the cones of the Pacaya and Agua volcanoes. Out this way is **Lago de Amatitlán**, a popular weekend resort just half an hour from the capital. A few kilometres to the south of the lake is the village of **San Vicente Pacaya**, from where you can climb Pacaya itself, one of Guatemala's three active cones, currently very lively, spouting smoke, gases, rocks and a plume of lava.

To the northwest of the capital, the villages of **San Juan Sacatepéquez** and **San Pedro Sacatepéquez**, both have impressive markets, while further northwest lie the ruins of **Mixco Viejo**, the ancient capital of the Poqomam Maya.

South of the city

Heading out through the southern suburbs, the **Carretera al Pacífico** runs past the clover-leaf junction at El Trébol and leaves the city through its industrial outskirts. There's a swathe of new housing projects, and elaborate advertising posters on empty lots sing the merits of suburban life. Further south lies the small town of **Villa Nueva**, a place a lot older than its name suggests, beyond which the valley starts to narrow, overshadowed by the volcanic cones of Agua and Pacaya.

Lago de Amatitlán

A few kilometres east of the highway, **Lago de Amatitlán** nestles at the base of the Pacaya volcano, encircled by forested hills. It's a superb setting, but one that's been sadly undermined by the abuses the lake has suffered at the hands of holidaymakers. In the not-too-distant past its delights were enjoyed by a handful of the elite, whose retreats dotted the shoreline, but since then bungalows have proliferated at an astonishing rate, and the waters of the lake are grossly polluted. The wealthy have moved on, seeking their seclusion at Río

Dulce and Lake Atitlán, while here at Amatitlán the weekends bring buses from the capital every ten minutes or so, spewing out families who spend the day eating, drinking, barbecuing, boating and swimming. If you want to enjoy the view and some peace and quiet, then come during the week, but if you prefer to watch Guatemalans at play drop by on a Sunday.

Where the road arrives at the lakeshore, the beach is lined with grimy comedores and tiendas. Taking a **boat trip** across the lake is a popular pastime, as is a dip in the thermal baths which are reputed to cure rheumatism and arthritis. Considerably more healthy than the black waters of the lake, however, are the lakeshore pools, where during daylight hours you can pay a small fee to take a dip in cleaner waters. High above the lake, to the north, is the **Parque de las Naciones Unidas** (the United Nations Park, formerly the Parque El Filón), reached from the lakeside by an Austrian-made bubble-lift that looks strangely out of place so far from the ski slopes. The trip up there, and the park itself, offer incredible views of the lake and the volcanic cones. The lift operates on Saturday and Sunday only.

A kilometre or so from the lake but closer to the highway is the village of **AMATITLÁN**, where you'll find a seventeenth-century church housing El Niño de Atocha, a saintly figure reputed to have miraculous powers, as well as a collection of **hotels** and **restaurants**, including the *Hospedaje Don Leonel*, 8 C 3–25 (❷), and *Hospedaje Kati* (❷), which also serves good, simple food.

Buses run from the capital to Lake Amatitlán every fifteen minutes or so, from 20 Calle and 3 Avenida in Zona 1 and return from the plaza in Amatitlán and the lakeshore. The journey takes around 45 minutes.

The Pacaya volcano

Heading further down the valley towards the Pacific coast, a branch road leaves the main highway to the left (east), heading into the hills to the village of **SAN VICENTE PACAYA**. From here you can climb the **Pacaya volcano**, one of the smallest and most impressive of Guatemala's peaks. At a height of just 2250m, Pacaya is the country's most dramatically active volcano, spitting out clouds of rock and ash in the region's most dramatic sound and light extravaganza. The current period of eruption began in 1965, although colonial records show that it was also active between 1565 and 1775. Today it certainly ranks as the most accessible and exciting volcano in Central America, and a trip to the cone is an unforgettable experience.

The best time to watch the eruptions is **at night**, when the sludge that the volcano spouts can be seen in its full glory as a plume of brilliant orange. Though it is possible to **climb** the cone independently, virtually everyone now chooses to join a group with a guide and an armed guard. Antigua is the best place to organize a trip, which usually costs around US$7 a head.

Four **buses** leave the Zona 4 terminal in Guatemala City for San Vicente, from where it's a further ninety-minute walk to San Francisco, though infrequent buses and pick-ups also travel this route.

The route

Whether you decide to go with a guided tour or not, you'll follow the track from the main highway, winding up through lush coffee plantations and clouds of dust to the village of San Vicente. It's a fairly miserable place, but if you're planning to climb the cone and make it back down the same day, then you may want to find somewhere to stay. There's no hotel in the village and people don't seem particularly friendly, but it's worth asking around for a room anyway – if you don't succeed you can always try one of the villages higher up.

Safety on the Pacaya volcano

Before setting out on the climb to the peak of Pacaya, you should bear in mind that the volcano has been the scene of a number of **attacks**, rapes, murders and robberies. Though incidents have decreased in recent years, tours now come complete with armed guards. While most people climb the volcano without encountering any trouble, it is worth checking the current security situation with your embassy or at the tourist offices in Guatemala City or Antigua and keeping an eye on the Antigua noticeboards, where recent incidents are usually publicized. Virtually all the daily tours (no matter who you book with) are coordinated by Gran Jaguar Tours, 4 C Poniente 30 (℡832 2712, ⓦwww.granjaguar.com) in Antigua; they depart around 1.30pm and return by around 10.30pm.

To climb the volcano you need to rejoin the dirt road (which actually bypasses San Vicente) and then turn left at the fork after 100m or so. You'll come to a second bedraggled village, **Concepción El Cedro**, where you want to keep straight on, walking up the track to the right of the church. This track heads around to the left as it leaves the village, and then climbs in a narrow rocky gully, coming out at the village of **San Francisco**, the last settlement and the highest point accessible to motor vehicles. Here, about an hour from the start, you'll pass the last tienda and your last chance of finding a bed for the night – ask in the tienda and they'll point you towards someone with a room to rent.

From San Francisco the path is a little harder to follow, but it's only another couple of hours to the top. After you pass the tienda the path goes up to the right, beside an evangelical church, above which you need to head diagonally across the open grassland – bearing to the left. From this left-hand corner a clear path heads on towards the cone, through thickish forest and slippery cinder until you reach the top.

Scrambling up through the forest you suddenly emerge on the lip of an exposed ridge from where you can see the cone in all its brutal beauty. In front of you is a massive bowl of cooled lava, its fossilized currents flowing away to the right, and opposite is the cone itself, a jet black triangle that occasionally spouts molten rock and sulphurous fumes. From here you can head on around to the left, across lava fields and between the charred stumps of trees. The path runs around the lip of the bowl to a concrete post, and then up the side of the cone, which is a terrifying but thrilling ascent, eventually bringing you face to face with the eruptions. The ascent certainly shouldn't be attempted when Pacaya is highly active – check with your guide about the state of the eruptions before setting out.

Onwards to the coast: Palín

Continuing towards the coast the main highway passes through **PALÍN**, whose name derives from the word *palinha*, meaning water that holds itself erect, a reference to a nearby waterfall. Home to a tiny pocket of Poqomam-speaking Maya, the town was once famous for its weaving, but these days the only *huipiles* you'll see are the purples of the village of Santa María de Jesús, connected to Palín by a rough back road.

The best time to visit Palín is for its Wednesday morning **market**, which takes place under a magnificent ceiba tree in the plaza. Buses pass through every ten minutes or so, heading between the capital and the coast, so it's worth stopping off even if you just happen to be passing. Guatemala's first **motorway** (US$1 toll per car) starts just outside of town, offering a speedy route between Palín with the southern town of Esquintla, avoiding the slow lorries that clog the old road.

...thwest of the capital lies a hilly area that, despite its proximity, is lit-
... y the influence of the city. Here the hills are still covered by pine
... heading out this way you'll find a couple of interesting villages;
...ere badly scarred by the 1976 earthquake, but today boast markets well
worth visiting. Further afield are the **Mixco Viejo** ruins, impeccably restored
but seldom visited.

San Pedro Sacatepéquez and San Juan Sacatepéquez

Leaving the city to the northwest you travel out through the suburb of Florida.
Once you escape the confines of the city the road starts to climb into the hills,
through an area that's oddly uninhabited. To the south of the city the high
ground has been colonized by the rich, but here there are only one or two
mansions, hidden in the forest.

The first of the two villages you come to is **SAN PEDRO
SACATEPÉQUEZ**, which had to be almost completely rebuilt after the
earthquake. The Friday market here, though not very large, is still worth a
browse. Another 6km takes you over a ridge and into the village of **SAN
JUAN SACATEPÉQUEZ**. As you approach, the road passes a profusion of
makeshift greenhouses where flowers are grown, an industry that has become
the local speciality. The first carnation was brought to Guatemala by Andrés
Stombo some sixty years ago. He employed the three Churup brothers, all from
San Juan, and seeing how easy it was they all set up on their own. Since then
the business has flourished, and there are flowers everywhere in San Juan. By
far the best time to visit is for the Friday market, when the whole place springs
into action and the village is packed. Keep an eye out for the *huipiles* worn in
San Juan, which are unusual and impressive, with bold geometric designs of
yellow, purple and green.

Buses to both villages run every twenty minutes or so from the Zona 4 terminal in Guatemala City.

Mixco Viejo

Beyond San Juan the road divides, one branch heading north to El Chol and
Rabinal (one bus a day takes this route, leaving the Zona 4 terminal in
Guatemala City at 5am), the other branch going northwest towards **Mixco
Viejo** and **Pachalum**. Heading out along this western route the scenery
changes dramatically, leaving behind the pine forests and entering a huge, dry
valley. Small farms are scattered here and there and the *Politecnica*, Guatemala's
military academy, is also out this way. About an hour beyond San Juan, in a massive valley, are the ruins of Mixco Viejo.

The ruins

MIXCO VIEJO was the capital of the Poqomam Maya, one of the main pre-
Conquest tribes. The original Poqomam language has all but died out – it's
now spoken only in a few isolated areas and in the villages of Mixco and
Chinautla – and the bulk of their original territory is swamped by Kaqchikel
speakers. The site itself is thought to date from the thirteenth century, and its
construction, designed to withstand siege, bears all the hallmarks of the troubled times before the arrival of the Spanish. Protected on all sides by deep
ravines, it can be entered only along a single-file causeway. At the time the
Spanish arrived, in 1525, this was one of the largest highland centres, with nine
temples, two ball courts, and a population of around nine thousand.

The Spanish historian Fuentes y Guzmán actually witnessed the conquest of the city, so for once there's a detailed account. At first Alvarado sent only a small force, but when this was unable to make any impact he launched an attack himself, using his Mexican allies, two hundred Tlaxcala warriors. With a characteristic lack of subtlety he opted for a frontal assault, but his armies were attacked from behind by a force of Poqomam fighters who arrived from Chinautla. The battle was fought on an open plain in front of the city, and by sunset the Spanish cavalry had won the day, killing some two hundred Poqomam men, although the city remained impenetrable. According to Fuentes y Guzman the Poqomam survivors then pointed out a secret entrance to the city, allowing the Spanish to enter virtually unopposed and to unleash a massacre of its inhabitants. The survivors were resettled at a site on the edge of the city, in the village of Mixco Viejo, where Poqomam is still spoken.

Today the site has been impressively restored, with its plazas and temples laid out across several flat-topped ridges. Like all the highland sites the structures are fairly low – the largest temple reaches only about 10m in height – and devoid of decoration. It is, however, an interesting site in a spectacular setting, and during the week you'll probably have the ruins to yourself, which gives the place all the more atmosphere. Mixco Viejo is by no means an easy place **to reach**, as there's no public transport at all to anywhere near the ruins. Swiss Travel, in the *Chalet Suizo* in Guatemala City, organize **tours** of the site (see p.69), or try the tour operators on p.89. Alternatively, if you can muster enough people it's worth **renting a car** (see p.87). There are some attractive shelters where you can **camp** overlooking the ruins.

From Guatemala City to Sumpango

Heading out to the west from Guatemala City along the Carretera Interamericana to Chimaltenango, you travel through one of the central highland valleys, where a number of large villages are devoted to market gardening. The villages themselves are particularly scruffy, but their fields are meticulously neat and well taken care of, churning out a wide range of vegetables for both the domestic and export markets.

Leaving Guatemala City, the first place you pass is **MIXCO**, a village now absorbed into the capital's suburban sprawl. Founded in 1525 to house Poqomam refugees from Mixco Viejo, Mixco still has a large Maya population. Next along the way is **SAN LUCAS SACATEPÉQUEZ**, just before the turning for Antigua. The village dates back to before the Conquest but these days bears the scars of the 1976 earthquake and serves the weekend needs of city dwellers, with cheap comedores and family restaurants lining the highway.

Beyond this is **SANTIAGO SACATEPÉQUEZ**, whose centre lies a kilometre or so to the north of the highway. The road to Santiago actually branches off the highway at San Lucas Sacatepéquez – and buses shuttle back and forth along the branch road. (Alternatively, you can walk to Santiago from a point overlooking it on the highway, 2km west of San Lucas.) The best time to visit Santiago is on November 1, for a local fiesta to honour the **Day of the Dead**, when massive paper kites are flown in the cemetery to release the souls of the dead from their agony. The festival is immensely popular, and hundreds of Guatemalans and tourists come every year to watch the spectacle. The kites, made from paper and bamboo, are massive circular structures, measuring up to 6–7m in diameter. Teams of young men struggle to get them aloft while the crowd looks on with bated breath, rushing for cover if a kite comes crashing to the ground.

At other times of the year, there are **markets** in Santiago on Tuesday and Sunday and the town has a small local **museum** (Mon–Fri 9am–4pm, Sat & Sun 9am–noon & 2–4pm), just below the plaza, which is crammed with tiny Maya figurines, clay fragments and pots, all donated by local people from their homes and fields. Also on display is the Guatemalan peso, dating from 1909, a traditional costume from 1901, small paper kites and a stuffed quetzal.

The neighbouring village of **SUMPANGO**, 6km west along the Interamericana, has an identical Day of the Dead tradition – so every few years, when there's not enough wind and the kites at Santiago fail to rise to the occasion, everyone heads there in the hope of better weather.

You'll have no problem reaching either Santiago Sacatepéquez or Sumpango on fiesta day, when travel agencies and language schools send fleets of minibuses up to the villages from Antigua; to get there by public transport take any bus as far as San Lucas Sacatepéquez on the Interamericana and catch a connection there.

Antigua and around

Superbly situated in a sweeping highland valley, suspended between the cones of Agua, Acatenango and Fuego volcanoes, is one of the Americas' most enchanting colonial cities: **ANTIGUA**. In its day this was one of the great cities of the Spanish empire, ranking alongside Lima and Mexico City and serving as the administrative centre for the *Audiencia de Guatemala*, which encompassed all of Central America and Mexican Chiapas.

These days Antigua is a haven of tranquillity. Offering a welcome break from the unrelenting energy of the capital, it has become the country's foremost tourist destination, a favoured hang-out for travellers to recharge. It's almost inevitable that you'll run into someone here that you met in a bar in Mexico City or on a beach in Honduras. Aside from the lively bar scene and a great choice of restaurants, the main attraction is the relaxed ambience and the beauty of Antigua itself. Another factor is the city's **language schools**, some of the best and cheapest in all Latin America, drawing students from around the globe and now a fundamental part of the local economy. The ex-pats, including Europeans, Americans, South Americans and Asians, contribute to the town's cosmopolitan air, mingling with locals selling their wares in the streets and the middle-class Guatemalans who come here at weekends to eat, drink and enjoy themselves. The downside is that while it's a great place to wind down and eat well for a few days if you've been travelling hard, after a while this civilized, isolated world can seem a little too smug and comfortable. After a few days of sipping cappuccinos and munching cake, you could almost forget that you're in Central America at all.

Some history

Antigua was actually the third capital of Guatemala. The Spanish settled first at the site of **Iximché** in July 1524, so that they could keep a close eye on their Cakchiquel allies. In November 1527, when the Kaqchikel rose up in defiance of their new rulers, the capital was moved into the Almolonga valley, to the site of **Ciudad Vieja**, a few kilometres from Antigua. In 1541, however, shortly after the death of Alvarado, this entire town was lost beneath a massive mud slide. Only then did the capital come to rest in Antigua, known in those days as *La Muy Noble y Muy Leal Ciudad de Santiago de los Caballeros de Goathemala.*

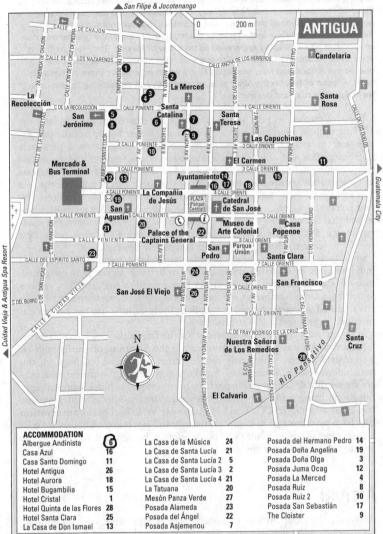

▲ *San Filipe & Jocotenango*

ANTIGUA

▼ *San Juan del Obispo & Santa María de Jesús*

ACCOMMODATION					
Albergue Andinista	6	La Casa de la Música	24	Posada del Hermano Pedro	14
Casa Azul	16	La Casa de Santa Lucía 2	5	Posada Doña Angelina	19
Casa Santo Domingo	11	La Casa de Santa Lucía 3	2	Posada Doña Olga	3
Hotel Antigua	26	La Casa de Santa Lucía 3	21	Posada Juma Ocag	12
Hotel Aurora	18	La Casa de Santa Lucía 4	21	Posada La Merced	4
Hotel Bugambilia	15	La Tatuana	20	Posada Ruiz	8
Hotel Cristal	1	Mesón Panza Verde	27	Posada Ruiz 2	10
Hotel Quinta de las Flores	28	Posada Alameda	23	Posada San Sebastián	17
Hotel Santa Clara	25	Posada del Ángel	22	The Cloister	9
La Casa de Don Ismael	13	Posada Asjemenou	7		

Here, despite the continued threat from the instability of the bedrock – the first earthquake came after just twenty years – the capital settled and began to achieve astounding prosperity.

As the heart of colonial power in Central America, Antigua grew slowly but steadily. One by one the religious orders established themselves, competing in the construction of schools, churches, monasteries and hospitals. Bishops built grand palaces that were soon rivalled by the homes of local merchants and corrupt government officials. When the English friar Thomas Gage visited Antigua in 1627, he was shocked by the wickedness of Spain's empire:

Great plenty and wealth hath made the inhabitants as proud and vicious as are those of Mexico. Here is not only idolatry, but fornication and uncleanliness as public as in any place of the Indies. The mulattoes, Blackamoors, mestizos, Indians, and all common sort of people are much made on by the greater and richer sort, and go as gallantly apparelled as do those of Mexico. They fear neither a volcano or mountain of water on the one side, which they confess hath once poured out a flood and river executing God's wrath against sin there committed, nor a volcano of fire, on the other side, roaring with and threatening to rain upon them Sodom's ruin and destruction.

The city reached its peak in the middle of the eighteenth century, after the 1717 earthquake prompted an unprecedented building boom, and the population rose to around fifty thousand. By this stage Antigua was a genuinely impressive place, with a university, a printing press, a newspaper, and streets that were seething with commercial and political rivalries. But as is so often the case in Guatemala, **earthquakes** brought all of this to an abrupt end. For the best part of a year the city was shaken by tremors, with the final blows delivered by two severe shocks on September 7 and December 13, 1773. The damage was so bad that the decision was made to abandon the city in favour of the modern capital: fortunately, despite endless official decrees, there were many who refused to leave and Antigua was never completely deserted.

Since then the city has been gradually repopulated, particularly in the last hundred years or so. As Guatemala City has become increasingly congested, many of the conservative middle classes have moved to Antigua. They've been joined by a large number of resident and visiting foreigners attracted by the city's relaxed and sophisticated atmosphere, lively cultural life, the benign climate and largely traffic-free streets.

In recent years concern has mounted for the fate of the city's ancient architecture. Antigua was the first planned city in the Americas, originally built on a rigid grid pattern, with neatly cobbled streets and grand buildings. Of this tremendous colonial legacy, some buildings now lie in atmospheric ruin, others are steadily decaying, and many have been restored as hotels or restaurants. Efforts are being made to preserve this unique legacy, especially after Antigua was listed as a UNESCO World Heritage site in 1979. Local **conservation** laws have been brought in to protect the city and extensions to houses are subject to tight planning controls as every effort is being made to preserve the architectural grandeur of the past.

Arrival

Antigua is laid out on the traditional grid system, with avenidas running north–south, and calles east–west. Each street is numbered and has two halves,

Tourist crime in and around Antigua

While there is no need to be paranoid, visitors to the heavily touristed areas around Antigua and Lake Atitlán (covered in Chapter 2, p.154) should be aware that **crime against tourists** – including robbery and rape – does occur infrequently. Pay close attention to security reports from your embassy and follow the usual precautions. In particular, avoid walking alone, especially at night or to isolated spots during the day. If you want to visit viewing spots such as the *cruce* overlooking Antigua, inform the **tourist police** (see below) and they will accompany you or even give you a ride there on one of their motorbikes or trucks. Though there have been very few attacks on people hiking around Lake Atitlán recently, it's still safer to walk in a group. Similarly, don't amble around Panajachel alone late at night. In the more remote highlands, where foreigners are a much rarer sight, attacks are extremely uncommon.

either a north and south (*norte/sur*) or an east and west (*oriente/poniente*), with the plaza, the **Parque Central**, regarded as the centre. Despite this apparent simplicity, poor street lighting, the recent revival of using old street names, and a local law banning overhanging signs – a bid to preserve the colonial character – ensure that most people get lost here at some stage. However, the town is small and if you get confused, remember that the Agua volcano, the one that hangs most immediately over the town, is to the south.

Arriving by bus, whether from Guatemala City or Chimaltenango, you'll end up in the main **bus terminal**, a large open space beside the market, three long blocks to the west of the plaza. The noise, fumes and bustle of this part of town are similar to any other in Guatemala, and you may well be greeted by a hustler or two trying to push a hotel or language school. To get to the centre of town, cross the broad tree-lined street outside the terminal and walk straight up the street opposite (4 Calle Poniente), which leads directly to the plaza.

Information

The **tourist office** (daily 8am–6pm; ℡ & ℻ 832 0763), on the south side of the plaza, dispenses excellent, if occasionally overly cautious, information. Most members of the team speak good English and will provide you with a free map and recommend city walks and itineraries. You'll find the **tourist police** just off the Parque Central on 4 Avenida Norte (℡ 832 7290), who will help you with any difficulties; twice daily, officers escort visitors up to the Cerro de la Cruz, which offers a panoramic view of Antigua and the surrounding volcanoes.

The most comprehensive **guidebooks** devoted to Antigua and the surrounding area are *Antigua For You*, by Barbara Balchin De Koose, which gives detailed information on the town's history and colonial ruins, and *Antigua Guatemala: The City and its Heritage* by Elizabeth Bell. Both are available from bookshops in town (see p.109). Though **guides** of the human variety are often to be found in the plaza, hustling for business, it's better to take a city tour (see p.111).

Noticeboards in various popular tourist venues advertise everything from happy hours to private language tuition, apartments, flights home and shared rides. Probably the most useful are those at *Doña Luisa's* restaurant, 4 C Oriente 12, and the Rainbow Reading Room, 7 Av Sur 8. The US organization,

Amerispan, 6 Av Norte 40 (☎ & ⓕ832 0164; ⓔamerispan@guate.net), also has a decent resource centre with good maps and general information dispensed by a helpful team who know Antigua and the country well, though their trips can be a bit pricey.

Accommodation

There are nearly a hundred hotels in Antigua, and they come in enough permutations to suit every pocket, though be warned that rooms get extremely scarce (and prices increase) around Holy Week (see p.100). Would-be guides often greet arriving bus passengers with offers of a hotel; be aware, though, that they get paid a commission if you take a room, so if you arrive at the hotel with one in tow your bargaining powers have already been affected – only at very busy times is it worth taking one of these guides up. Many of the budget hotels are situated in the streets around the market and bus terminal, and so can be noisy; hotels located in all other parts of the city are much more tranquil.

Budget options

Albergue Andinista 6 Av Norte 34 ☎ & ⓕ832 3343, ⓔdrrios@intelnet.net.gt. Secure rooms and apartments, a little bare but serviceable, grouped around a small garden. The engaging owner also provides luggage storage and advice on volcano climbing. ❸

La Casa de Santa Lucía Alameda Santa Lucía Sur 5 ☎832 6133. Recently refurbished hotel with secure, spacious rooms with dark wood furnishings, all with private hot-water bath, hence it's very popular. You'll have to ring the bell to get in; guests are given a key. ❸

La Casa de Santa Lucía 2 Alameda Santa Lucía Norte 21, **La Casa de Santa Lucía 3**, 6 Av Norte 43 A, and **La Casa de Santa Lucía 4**, Alameda Santa Lucía 5 (no phones). Almost carbon copies of the original, above. Spacious rooms with twin beds and private hot showers, and extremely well priced. Ring the bell for entry. ❷

Hotel Bugambilia 3 C Oriente 19 ☎832 5780, ⓦwww.theantiguajournal.com. Clean, safe place in a quiet location with parking, but rooms are a little plain. The owners are very helpful and hospitable. Snacks available. ❸

Hotel la Casa de Don Ismael 3 C Poniente 6 ☎832 1939. Attractively presented rooms with towels and soap provided, a lovely little garden, free mineral water and free tea or coffee in the morning. Communal bathrooms are brightly painted and kept spotless. Very fair prices. ❷

Hotel Cristal Av del Desengano 25 ☎832 4177. Good-value family-run hotel with pleasant balcony overlooking a flower-filled courtyard. Rooms with or without private bath – hot water and use of kitchen included. The only drawback is its site on the main road out of town – the whole building shakes as buses thunder past, so it's not the place to stay if you're worried about earthquakes. ❷

Hotel Posada Doña Olga Callejón Campo Seco 3A ☎832 0623. Exceptionally good value new guest house, with very clean rooms, all with private bath, and a rooftop sun terrace. ❷

Hotel Santa Clara 2 Av Sur 20 ☎ & ⓕ832 0342. Tranquil location on the east side of town and very spacious, comfortable rooms, most with two double beds and all with private bath, set around a pleasant little courtyard. Parking. ❸

Posada Alameda Alameda Santa Lucía Sur 18 ☎832 7349, ⓔalameda@intelnet.net.gt. Good new hotel close to the bus terminal, with six comfortable rooms, all with cable TV, plus baggage storage and security boxes. ❸

Posada de Doña Angelina 4 C Poniente 33 ☎832 5173. Popular budget choice. Many of the 42 rooms are a bit gloomy, but there's usually space here. Close to the bus terminal, so not the most tranquil place in town. Run by a dynamic señora and there's a secure store room where you can leave your baggage. ❷/❸

Posada Juma Ocag Alameda Santa Lucía Norte 13 ☎832 3109. Superb, very well managed new place. The nine cheery, comfortable rooms represent excellent value: all have wardrobes and private bath, and are draped with local fabrics. Book ahead. ❸

Posada Ruiz Alameda Santa Lucía Norte 17 and **Posada Ruiz 2** 2 C Poniente 25 (no phones). Pretty grim, small rooms with no frills, but rates are extremely cheap and both are a short stumble from the bus terminal. ❶

Mid-range options

La Casa de la Música 7 C Poniente 3 ☏832 0335, ⓦwww.lacasadelamusica.centroamerica .com. Sumptuous guest house with a selection of very attractive bedrooms and characterful suites, all with fireplaces and antique furniture. There's a large garden, with plenty of space for children to play, a guests' lounge with an extensive library and plenty of family games. Very friendly and efficient service, breakfast is included and additional meals are also available. ⑥/⑦

Hotel Aurora 4 C Oriente 16 ☏ & ⓕ832 0217. Antigua's original hotel is set in an attractive, colonial building with rooms grouped around a lovely grassy courtyard and fountain. It's a little old-fashioned, but comfortable enough; breakfast is included. ⑥

Posada Asjemenou 5 Av Norte 31 ☏832 2670, ⓔcangeletti@hotmail.com. Comfortable rooms §with a colonial feel, set around a courtyard with or without private bath. ④/⑤

Posada del Hermano Pedro 3 C Oriente 3 ☏832 2089, ⓕ832 2090. Comfortable hotel in a huge, tastefully converted colonial mansion just behind the main square. The pleasant rooms all have cable TV. ⑥

Posada La Merced 7 Av Norte 43a ☏832 3197, ⓔposadalamerced@hotmail.com. Large refurbished hotel with a good choice of attractive rooms (some set around a pretty garden patio at the rear) that all enjoy spotless private bathrooms and nice decorative touches. The very helpful Kiwi owner is a good source of local information. ④

Posada San Sebastián 3 Av Norte 4 ☏ & ⓕ832 2621. Very quiet, charming establishment. Each room is individually decorated with antiques, there's a gorgeous little bar and the location is very convenient. Excellent value. ⑥

La Tatuana 6 Av Sur 3 ☏832 1223, ⓔlatatuana @micro.com.gt. Small hotel with bright, imaginatively decorated rooms, all with private bath, and comfortable beds. Extremely good value for the price. ④

Luxury accommodation

Antigua Spa Resort San Pedro El Panorama, on road to Cuidad Viejo ☏832 3960, ⓕ832 3968, ⓦwww.antiguaspa.com. Antigua's spa offers a sumptuous environment, volcano views and very attractive rooms with pine furnishings and log fires. There are first-class exercise facilities, a lovely pool, and lots of opportunities for indulgence in the form of herbal wraps, milk almond baths and body massages. ⑨

Casa Azul 4 Av Norte 5 ☏832 0961, ⓕ832 0944, ⓦwww.infoguate.com/casazul. Choice location, just off the plaza, with huge, very stylish rooms in a converted colonial mansion. Facilities include sauna, Jacuzzi and a delightful small rooftop pool. ⑧

The Cloister 5 Av Norte 23 ☏ & ⓕ832 0712, ⓦwww.thecloister.com. Small, elegant hotel, set almost under Antigua's famous arch, with beautifully furnished rooms around a flowering courtyard. There's a real air of tranquillity here, plus a well-stocked private library and reading room. ⑧/⑨

Hotel Antigua 8 C Poniente 1 ☏832 0288, ⓕ 832 0807, ⓦwww.hotelantigua.com.gt. Venerable establishment, popular with Guatemala's elite families, and decorated with tasteful colonial-style furniture. There's a large swimming pool set in expansive gardens, and the pleasant rooms have open fires to ward off the winter chill. US$112 including breakfast. ⑨

Hotel Casa Santo Domingo 3 C Oriente 28 ☏832 0140, ⓕ832 0102, ⓦwww .casasantodomingo.com.gt. Spectacular colonial convent, sympathetically converted into a hotel and restaurant at a cost of several million dollars. Rooms and corridors are bedecked in ecclesiastical art and paraphernalia and there's no lack of luxury. Probably the most atmospheric hotel in Guatemala. High-season rates start at US$132, but there are substantial discounts at quiet times of the year. ⑨

Hotel Quinta de las Flores C del Hermano Pedro 6 ☏832 3721, ⓕ832 3726. A little out of town, but the attractive, tastefully decorated rooms and the spectacular garden, with a swimming pool and many rare plants, shrubs and trees, make it a wonderful place to relax. ⑦

Mesón Panza Verde 5 Av Sur 19 ☏ & ⓕ832 2925, ⓔmpv@infovia.com.gt. Small, immaculately furnished hotel in a colonial-style building that is also home to one of Antigua's premier restaurants. Supremely comfortable suites, some with four-poster beds, plus good-value doubles. Small swimming pool, faultless service and a healthy breakfast included in the price. ⑥/⑧

Posada del Ángel 4 Av Sur ☏832 5303, ⓕ832 0260, ⓦwww.posadadelangel.com. Uniquely homely and luxurious B&B with five stunning suites, all with sumptuous furniture, oriental rugs and textiles, and fireplaces. There's also a small heated lap pool, and a library. Numerous heads of state have stayed here, including President Clinton and ex–President Arzú of Guatemala. US$130–175. ⑨

①

Semana Santa in Antigua

Antigua's **Semana Santa (Holy Week) celebrations** are perhaps the most extravagant and impressive in all Latin America. The celebrations start with a procession on Palm Sunday, representing Christ's entry into Jerusalem, and continue through to the really big processions and pageants on Good Friday. On Thursday night the streets are carpeted with meticulously drawn patterns of coloured sawdust, and on Friday morning a series of processions re-enacts the progress of Christ to the Cross accompanied by melancholic music from local brass bands. Setting out from La Merced, Escuela de Cristo and the village of San Felipe, teams of penitents wearing peaked hoods and accompanied by solemn dirges and clouds of incense carry images of Christ and the Cross on massive platforms. The pageants set off at around 8am, with the penitents dressed in either white or purple. After 3pm, the hour of the Crucifixion, they change into black.

It is a great honour to be involved in the procession, but no easy task as the great cedar block carried from La Merced weighs some 3.5 tonnes, and needs eighty men to lift it. Some of the images displayed date from the seventeenth century and the procession itself is thought to have been introduced by Alvarado in the early years of the Conquest, imported directly from Spain.

Check the exact details of events with the tourist office, who should be able to provide you with a map detailing the routes of the processions. During Holy Week hotels in Antigua are often full, and the entire town is always packed on Good Friday. But even if you have to make the trip from Guatemala City or Lago de Atitlán, it's well worth coming here for the event, especially on the Friday.

The City

In accordance with its position as the seat of colonial authority in Central America, Antigua was once a centre of secular and religious power, trade and, above all wealth. Here the great institutions competed with the government to build the country's most impressive buildings. Churches, monasteries, schools, hospitals and grand family homes were constructed throughout the city, all with tremendously thick walls to resist earthquakes. Today Antigua has an incredible number of ruined and restored **colonial buildings**, and although these constitute only a fraction of the city's original architectural splendour, they do give an idea of its former extravagance. Mentioned below are only some of the remaining examples; armed with a map from the tourist office you could spend days exploring the ruins (most charge a small entrance fee). However, the prospect of visiting the lot can seem overwhelming; if you'd rather just see the gems, make La Merced, Las Capuchinas, the Casa Popenoe and San Francisco your targets.

The Parque Central

As always, the focus of the colonial city was its central plaza, the **Parque Central**. Old prints show it as an open expanse of earth, which in the rainy season turned into a sea of mud. For centuries it served as the hub of the city, bustling with constant activity: a huge market spilled out across it, cleared periodically for bullfights, military parades, floggings and public hangings. The calm of today's shady Parque Central is relatively recent, and the risqué mermaid fountain, originally set to one side so as not to interfere with the action, was moved to the centre in 1936.

The most imposing of the surrounding structures is the **Cathedral of San José**, on the eastern side, its intricate facade evocatively illuminated at night. The first cathedral on this site was begun in 1545, using some of the vast fortune left by Alvarado's death. However, the execution was so poor that the structure was in a constant state of disrepair, and an earthquake in 1583 brought down much of the roof. In 1670 it was decided to start on a new cathedral worthy of the town's role as a capital city. For eleven years the town watched, as conscripted Maya laboured and the most spectacular colonial building in Central America took shape. The scale of the new cathedral was astounding: a vast dome, five naves, eighteen chapels, and a central chamber measuring 90m by 20m. Its altar was inlaid with mother-of-pearl, ivory and silver, and carvings of saints and paintings by the most revered of European and colonial artists covered the walls.

The new cathedral was strong enough to withstand the earthquakes of 1689 and 1717, but its walls were weakened and the 1773 earthquake brought them crashing to the ground. Today, two of the chapels have been restored as the **Church of San José**, which opens off the Parque Central; inside it is a figure of Christ by the colonial sculptor Quirio Cataño, who also carved the famous Black Christ of Esquipulas (see p.287). Behind the church, entered from 5 Calle Oriente, are the remains (entrance fee US$0.40) of the rest of the structure, a mass of fallen masonry, rotting beams, broken arches and hefty pillars, cracked and moss-covered. Buried beneath the floor are some of the great names of the Conquest, including Alvarado, his wife Beatriz de la Cueva, Bishop Marroquín and the historian Bernal Díaz del Castillo. At the very rear of the original nave, steps lead down to a burial vault that's regularly used for Maya religious ceremonies, an example of the coexistence of pagan and Catholic beliefs that's so characteristic of Guatemala.

Along the entire south side of the Parque Central runs the squat two-storey facade of the **Palace of the Captains General**, with a row of 27 arches along each floor. It was originally built in 1558, but as usual this first version was destroyed by earthquakes and in 1761 it was rebuilt, only to be damaged again in 1773, and finally restored along the lines of the present structure. The palace was home to the colonial rulers and also housed the barracks of the dragoons, the stables, the royal mint, law courts, tax offices, great ballrooms, a large bureaucracy, and a lot more besides. Today it contains the local government offices, the headquarters of the Sacatepéquez police department and the tourist office.

Directly opposite, on the north side of the plaza, is the **Ayuntamiento**, the city hall, also known as the *Casa del Cabildo* or town house. Dating from 1740, its metre-thick walls balance the solid style of the Palace of the Captains General. Unlike most others, this building survived earlier rumblings and wasn't damaged until the 1976 earthquake, although it has been repaired since. The city hall was abandoned in 1779 when the capital moved to its modern site, but it later housed the police headquarters; now that they've moved across the plaza the building is again used by the city's administration. If you climb to the upper level of the building there's a wonderful vista of the three volcanoes that ring the city, especially fine at sunset.

The Ayuntamiento also holds a couple of minor museums. The first of these is the **Museo de Santiago** (daily 9am–6pm; US$1.30, Sun free), which houses a collection of colonial artefacts, including bits of pottery, a sword said to have been used by Alvarado, some traditional Maya weapons, portraits of stern-faced colonial figures, and some paintings of warfare between the Spanish and the Maya. At the back of the museum is the old city jail, beside which there used to be a small chapel where condemned prisoners passed their last moments before being hauled off to the gallows in the plaza. Also under the arches of the city hall is the **Museo del Libro Antiguo** (same hours and fees as above), in the rooms that held the first printing press in Central America.

This arrived here in 1660, from Puebla de los Ángeles in Mexico, and churned out the first book three years later. A replica of the press is on display alongside some copies of the works produced on it.

South and east of the plaza

Across the street from the ruined cathedral, in 5 Calle Oriente (Calle de La Universidad), is the old **Seminario Tridentino**, one of the great colonial schools. It was founded at the start of the seventeenth century for some fifteen students, and later expanded to include the Escuela de Guadalupe, a special school for indigenous Maya of high birth, so that local people could share in the joys of theology. The structure is still in almost perfect condition, but it's now divided up into several separate homes, so the elaborate stucco **doorway** – one of the city's finest – is all you'll get to see.

A little further up the same street is the **University of San Carlos Borromeo**, which now houses the **Museo de Arte Colonial** (Tues–Fri 9am–4pm, Sat & Sun 9am–noon & 2–4pm; US$3.20). The founding of a university was first proposed by Bishop Marroquín in 1559, but met with little enthusiasm as the Jesuits, Dominicans and Franciscans couldn't bear the thought of a rival to their own colleges. It wasn't until 1676 that the plan was authorized, using money left by the bishop, and classes began in 1681 with seventy students applying themselves to everything from law to the Kaqchikel language. For a while only pure-blooded Castilians were admitted, but entry requirements were later changed to include a broader spectrum of the population. After the 1751 earthquake the university's original building was beyond repair and the rector of the Seminary donated the house next door to his own. Since then the university has moved to Guatemala City, and in 1832 this building became a grammar school, and then, in 1936, a museum. The Moorish style courtyard, deep-set windows and beautifully ornate cloisters make it one of the finest architectural survivors in Antigua. The museum contains a good collection of dark and brooding religious art, sculpture, furniture, murals depicting life on the colonial campus, and a seventeenth-century map of Antigua by the historian Antonio de Fuentes y Guzmán.

Further up 5 Calle Oriente, between 1 and 2 avenidas, is the house that once belonged to Bernal Díaz del Castillo, one of the soldiers who served under Alvarado in Mexico and Guatemala, and who, in his later years, wrote an account of the Conquest. Just around the corner, on 1 Avenida Sur, is the **Casa Popenoe** (Mon–Sat 2–4pm; US$0.90), a superbly restored colonial mansion, which not only gives a welcome break from church ruins, but also an interesting insight into domestic life in colonial times. The house, set around a well-tended, grassy courtyard, was originally built in 1634 by the Spaniard Don Luis de las Infantes Mendoza, who came to Antigua to serve as the supreme court judge. Needless to say it was badly damaged over the years and eventually abandoned, until 1932, when Doctor Wilson Popenoe, a United Fruit company scientist, began its comprehensive restoration. Dr Popenoe and his wife Dorothy painstakingly sifted through the rubble and, piece by piece, restored the building to its former glory, filling it with an incredible collection of colonial furniture and art. Among the paintings are portraits of Bishop Marroquín and the menacing-looking Alvarado himself. Every last detail has been authentically restored, down to the original leather lampshades painted with religious musical scores and the great wooden beds decorated with a mass of accomplished carving. The kitchen and servants' quarters have also been carefully renovated, and you can see the bread ovens, the herb garden and the pigeon loft, which would have provided the original occupants with their mail service. A narrow staircase leads up from the pigeon loft to the roof, from where there are spectacular views over the city and volcanoes. Dr Popenoe died in 1972, but two of his daughters still live in the house.

A block to the south, on 6 Calle Oriente, two churches face each other at opposite ends of the slim, palm-tree-lined **Parque Unión**, a pretty plaza frequented by típica textile street vendors, washerwomen and fast-food friers. At the western end is the **San Pedro Church** and hospital. Originally built in 1680, and periodically crammed full of earthquake victims, the church was finally evacuated in 1976 when one of the aftershocks threatened to bring down the roof. Reconstruction was completed in 1991 and the facade now has a polished perfection that's strangely incongruous in Antigua. At the other end of the plaza is the convent and church of **Santa Clara**, founded in 1699 by nuns from Puebla in Mexico. In colonial times this became a popular place for well-to-do young ladies to take the veil, as the hardships were none too hard, and the nuns earned a reputation for their cooking, by selling bread to the aristocracy. The huge original convent was totally destroyed in 1717, as was the second in 1773, but the current building was spared in 1976 and its ornate facade (floodlit at night) remains intact. In front of Santa Clara are the huge arches of an open-air *pila*, a washhouse where village women gather to scrub, rinse and gossip.

Walking around the front of the church down 2 Avenida Sur and then left, along 7 Calle Oriente, you arrive at **San Francisco** (daily 8am–6pm), one of the few ruined churches to have come back into service. The latest phase of its reconstruction began in 1960 and is still the subject of much controversy. The nave has been restored in its entirety, but the ornate mouldings and sculpture have been left off, so although you get a rough idea of its former splendour, it would actually have been considerably more decorative. One of the oldest churches in Antigua, the earliest building on this site was begun in 1579 by the Franciscans, the first religious order to arrive in the city. It grew into a vast religious and cultural centre that included a school, a hospital, music rooms, a printing press and a monastery, covering four blocks in all. All of this, though, was lost in the 1773 earthquake. The **ruins** (same hours, US$0.30) of the monastery, which are among the most impressive in Antigua, are surrounded by pleasant grassy verges with good picnicking potential.

Inside the church are buried the remains of **Hermano Pedro de Betancourt** (a Franciscan from the Canary Islands who founded the Hospital of Belén in Antigua), and pilgrims from all over Central America come here to ask for the benefit of his powers of miraculous intervention. Hundreds of little plaques and photographs, as well as a handful of disused crutches, all clustered around the shrine, give thanks for miracles performed. Hermano Pedro's remains have been moved around several times over the years, most recently in October 1990, some 323 years after his death, when he was put into a newly built Chapel of the True Cross, on the north side of the altar. Across the nave, on the south side of the church, there is a **museum** dedicated to Hermano Pedro (daily 8am–noon & 2–4pm; US$1), featuring clothes, sandals and a moneybag that belonged to him.

Heading out of town to the south, in the direction of the Agua volcano, you can follow the **Stations of the Cross**, twelve little chapels (all now in assorted states of disrepair) signifying Christ's route to crucifixion at Calvary. Along the way you pass the cracked remains of **Nuestra Senora de Los Remedios** and at the far end is **El Calvario**, a small functioning church with magnificently thick walls. Outside the church, sunk in the middle of the road and looking oddly out of place, stands a beautifully carved stone fountain.

North of the Parque Central

Setting out northwards from the Parque Central, along 4 Avenida Norte, you'll find the hermitage of **El Carmen**, down to the right past the first block. This was originally one of the city's great churches, first built in 1638 and rebuilt many times since: the top half of the facade finally collapsed in 1976 but the remains hint at its former glory. Back on 4 Avenida and another block to the north lies the church and convent of **Santa Teresa**, originally founded by a Peruvian philanthropist for a group of Carmelite nuns from Lima. These days it serves as the city jail.

A block further to the east, at the junction of 2 Calle Oriente and 2 Avenida Norte, is the site of **Las Capuchinas** (Tues–Sun 9am–5pm; US$1.30), the largest and most impressive of the city's convents, whose ruins are some of the best preserved but least understood in Antigua. The Capuchin nuns, who came from Madrid, were rather late on the scene, founding the fourth convent in the city in 1726. They were only granted permission by the colonial authorities on the condition that the convent would exact no payment from its novices. The Capuchin order was the most rigorous in Antigua. Numbers were restricted to 25, with nuns sleeping on wooden beds with straw pillows. Once they had entered the convent it's thought the women were not allowed any visual contact with the outside world; food was passed to them by means of a turntable and they could only speak to visitors through a grille.

The ruins are the most beautiful in Antigua, with fountains, courtyards and massive earthquake-proof pillars. The tower or "retreat" is the most unusual feature, with eighteen tiny cells set into the walls of its top floor, each having its own independent sewage system. Two of the cells have been returned to their original condition to demonstrate the harshness of the nuns' lives. The lower floor is dominated by a massive pillar that supports the structure above and incorporates seventeen small recesses, some with rings set in the walls. Theories about the purpose of this still abound – as a warehouse, a laundry room, a communal bath or even a torture chamber – though most scholars now agree that it probably functioned as a storage room, and the rings were meat hooks. The exterior of this architectural curiosity is also interesting, ringed with small stone recesses that represent the Stations of the Cross.

A couple of blocks to the west, spanning 5 Avenida Norte, is the **arch of Santa Catalina**, which is all that remains of the original convent founded here in 1609. By 1697 it had reached maximum capacity with 110 nuns and six novices, and the arch was built in order that they could walk between the two halves of the establishment without being exposed to the pollution of the outside world. Somehow it managed to defy the constant onslaught of earthquakes and was restored in the middle of the nineteenth century, and is now a favoured, if clichéd, spot for photographers as the view to the Volcán de Agua is unobstructed from here.

Walking under the arch and to the end of the street, you reach the church of **La Merced**, which boasts one of the most intricate and impressive facades in the entire city. It has been beautifully restored, painted mustard yellow and white, and crammed with plaster moulding of interlaced patterns. Look closely and you'll see the outline of a corn cob, a design not normally seen on Catholic churches and probably added by the original Maya labourers. The church is still in use, but the cloisters and gardens lie ruined, exposed to the sky. In the centre of one of the courtyards is a monumental tiered fountain with four pools that's known as the *Fuente de Pescados*; the pools were used by the Mercedarian brothers for breeding fish. The colonial fountain in front of the church is worth a look for its superbly preserved carved decoration.

Further out to the northeast along 1 Avenida Norte, the badly damaged ruins of the churches of **Santa Rosa**, **Candelaria** and **Nuestra Señora de los Dolores del Cerro** are of interest to ruined church buffs only.

West of the Parque Central

The last of the ruins lie over to the west of the plaza, towards the bus station. At the junction of 4 C Poniente and 6 Avenida Norte stands **La Compañia de Jesús**, an educational establishment and church that was operated by the Jesuits until the King of Spain, feeling threatened by their tremendous and growing power, expelled them from the colonies in 1767. Earlier this century the market moved here from the plaza, and was housed in the cloisters until the 1976 earthquake: nowadays most of the ruins are closed off, though a number of rather touristy artesanía stalls have recently moved back in.

Turning to the right in front of the bus station, walk to the end of the tree-lined Alameda Santa Lucía, and you reach the spectacular remains of **San Jerónimo**, a school built in 1739. Well-kept gardens are woven between the huge blocks of fallen masonry and crumbling walls and the site is regularly used as a spectacular site for classical music concerts. Down behind San Jerónimo a cobbled road leads to the even more chaotic ruin **La Recolección**, where the middle of the church is piled high with the remains of the roof and walls. Recolectos friars first arrived here and asked for permission to build in 1685, but it wasn't until 1701 that they started the church, and a further fourteen years before it was finished. Only months after its completion, the church was brought to the ground by a huge earthquake. This second version was destroyed in 1773 and has been steadily decaying ever since.

On the southern side of the bus station, along Avenida Alameda de Santa Lucía, is an imposing monument to **Rafael Landivar** (1731–93), a Jesuit composer who is generally considered the finest poet of the colonial era. Along with the other members of his order he was banished from the Americas in 1767. Walking back to the plaza along 5 Calle Poniente, you'll pass the **Iglesia de San Agustín**, the remains of a vast convent complex that once occupied about half the block but has stood derelict since the earthquake of 1773, after which the Augustinians followed the government in the exodus to Guatemala City.

Volcano tours from Antigua

A number of outfits in Antigua run guided tours to climb the **Pacaya volcano** near Guatemala City (see warning, p.91). These trips cost US$7–10 per person, and enable you to visit the volcano at night without having to camp out. They all leave Antigua in the early afternoon to climb the volcano, coming back down in the dark and returning to Antigua at around 11pm. Though the spectacle is astounding there has historically always been an element of danger involved and not just from falling rocks and ash – a number of cowboy outfits used to offer trips to Pacaya and set up "robberies" of their own tourists. Things have been much more secure recently with no reported incidents for some time, though you could always check with your embassy (see p.88) before you set off. Virtually all the tours are now organized by Gran Jaguar Tours, 4 C Poniente 30 (℡832 2712, ⊛www.granjaguar.com), no matter who you book with.

For more serious volcano climbing, you should consult Daniel Ramírez Ríos, at *Albergue Andinista*, 6 Av Norte 34 (see p.98), who is the best and most experienced volcano guide in the country. Though he no longer leads trips, he's happy to help out with practical information, and find guides and equipment.

Eating

In Antigua the choice of food is even more cosmopolitan than the population, and you'll be able to munch your way around the world in a number of authentic **restaurants** for a few dollars a time, or dine in real style for around half what it would cost back home. The only thing that seems hard to come by is an authentic Guatemalan comedor, which may be a relief if you've been subsisting on eggs and beans in the mountains. Because Antigua boasts such a wide variety of restaurants to suit every budget we have categorized them according to the price of a full meal with drinks: in places marked inexpensive you'll pay under US$5, moderate is US$5–10, and expensive refers to places charging more than US$10.

If you're after a takeout, the best **deli** is *Deliciosa*, 3 C Poniente 2, where you'll find lots of gourmet treats from all over the world (at a price) and some decent wine. Specializing in Spanish produce, *La Alhambra*, directly behind the Cathedral on 3 Avenida, is another good place, and there's a nice patio where you can eat your *bocadillo*.

Cafés

Bagel Barn 5 C Poniente 2, just off the plaza. A good spot for a coffee and cake pit stop as well as tasty, if pricey, bagels, sandwiches and homemade soup; takeouts also available.

Café Condesa west side of plaza; pass through the Casa del Conde bookshop. Extremely civilized, though pricey, place to enjoy an excellent breakfast, coffee and cake or full lunch. The gurgling fountain and period charm create a nice tone for the long, lazy Sunday brunches favoured by Antiguan society. Alternatively, grab a *latte* from the adjoining take-away window.

Café la Fuente in La Fuente, 4 C Oriente 14. Vegetarian restaurant–café where you can eat stuffed aubergine and falafel or sip good coffee in one of the most attractive restored courtyards in town. On Saturdays village women set up a *huipil* market around the central fountain.

Café Sol 1 C Poniente 9. Simple courtyard café that bakes its own bread. Healthy snacks and tasty sandwiches and cakes. Also has in-house email, fax and phone facilities.

Caffé [sic] Opera 6 Av Norte 17. Expensive café with lavish wall-to-wall operatic paraphernalia, comfortable seating and a tiled floor. Superb, strong coffee, croissants, ice cream and sandwiches are on offer, accompanied by the odd dose of loud opera. Closed Wed.

La Cenicienta 5 Av Norte 7. Bizarre Guatemalan attempt to re-create a Victorian tearoom – fine for quiche, cakes and sweet snacks though the coffee is very weak. No smoking.

Cookies Etc 3 Av Norte & 4 C Oriente. Twenty one varieties of yummy cookies on offer, as well as sandwiches, muffins and free coffee refills. Takeouts available.

Destino 1 Av Sur 8. Diminutive café pit-stop, popular with language students, that's ideal for a caffeine hit or a slab of homemade cake, though the convivial American owner will also rustle up a bacon sandwich for those in need.

Fernando's Kaffee 7 C Poniente 11. Simple outdoor premises but unquestionably the finest coffee in town – ground, roasted and served by a Guatemalan perfectionist – plus delicious homemade pastries and cakes. Fernando's opening hours are a little erratic, though it should be open daily 7am–6pm.

Jugocentre Peroleto Alameda Santa Lucía Norte 36. Excellent budget hole-in-the-wall cabin with cheap, healthy breakfasts, fruit juices and yummy cakes.

Pasteleria Okrassa 6 Av Norte 29. Great for croissants, cinnamon rolls and healthy drinks – try the raspberry juice.

Rainbow Reading Room 7 Av Sur 8. Relaxed bohemian atmosphere in this favourite travellers' hangout. Great vegetarian menu of creative salads and pasta dishes, epic smoothies and decent cappuccinos matched by friendly, prompt service. Also home to one of Antigua's best travel agents, a good secondhand bookshop, and regular musical jams.

Sopho's Café 5 C Poniente 15. Stylish and very tranquil little café, with snacks and very creamy cappuccinos, where you can browse the magazines and books of the adjoining bookshop.

Restaurants

Beijing 6 Av Sur and 5 C Poniente. Antigua's best Chinese and East Asian food, prepared with a few imaginative twists. Good noodle dishes, soups and Vietnamese spring rolls. Moderate.

Café Flor 4 Av Sur 1. Reasonable Thai, Indonesian and Indian style food. Not the most authentic cooking, though the portions are huge, and the atmosphere relaxed and convivial. Closed Sun. Moderate.

Café Panchoy 6 Av Norte 1B. Good-value cooking with a real Guatemalan flavour – top steaks and some traditional favourites like *chiles rellenos* served around an open kitchen. Excellent margari-

tas. Closed Tues. Moderate.

Café-Pizzeria Asjemenou 5 C Poniente 4. A favourite for its legendary breakfasts. Also very strong on pizza and calzone, but the service can be erratic. Daily 9am–10pm. Moderate.

Caffé Mediterraneo 6 C Poniente 6A. Real Italian cooking, with fresh pasta, bruschetta and decent

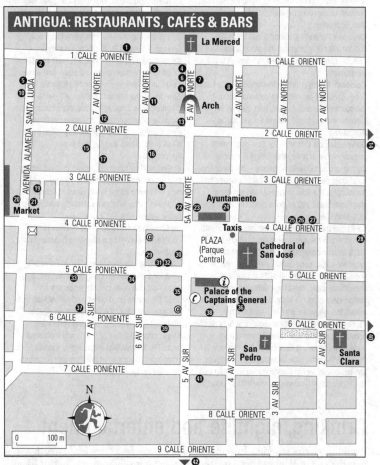

ANTIGUA: RESTAURANTS, CAFÉS & BARS

RESTAURANTS			
Beijing	34	La Casserole	14
Café Flor	36	La Escudilla	24
Caffé Mediterraneo	38	La Fonda de la Calle Real	23
Café Panchoy	29	La Fonda de la Calle Real 2	18
Café Peroleto	10	La Fonda de la Calle Real 3	22
Café-Pizzeria Asjemenou	32	Panza Verde	42
Casa de las Mixtas	19	Quesos y Vinos	6
Comedor Típico Antigüeño	21	San Jerónimo	2
Doña Luisa's	26	Su Chow	4
El Sereno	8	Weiner	20
Frida's	7	Welten	28

BARS & CLUBS	
El Afro	39
Dante's	1
Equinoccio	15
La Canoa	31
La Casbah	9
La Chimanea	12
Macondo's	13
Mono Loco	35
Picasso's	17
Riki's Bar	24

CAFÉS	
Café Opera	16
Condesa	30
Cookies etc	25
Destino	40
Fernando's Kaffee	5
Jugocentro Peroleto	41
La Fuente	27
Pasteleria Okrassa	11
Rainbow Reading Room	37
Sol	3
Sopho's Café	33

107

wine. Very civilized and popular with Antigua's resident foodies. Closed Tues. Moderate.

Casa de las Mixtas 1 Callejón, off 3 C Poniente. A basic comedor, but nicely set up with attractive decor and cooking that's executed with more flair than most. Open early until 7.30pm. Inexpensive.

La Casserole Callejón de la Concepción 7. This elegant French-owned restaurant, set in a pretty patio location, serves the finest Gallic cuisine in Antigua. Leave room for the epic desserts. Closed Mon. Expensive.

Ceviches Peroleto Alameda Santa Lucía 36. Popular with Guatemalans, this place specializes in *ceviche*, plus Peruvian pickled fish and shrimp. Inexpensive.

Comedor Típico Antigüeño Alameda Santa Lucía Sur 5. Excellent canteen-like comedor, opposite the bus terminal and market, with bargain set lunches and meals; all include a soup starter. Inexpensive.

Doña Luisa's 4 C Oriente 12. One of the most popular places in town. The setting is relaxed but the menu could do with a revamp – the basic lineup of chile con carne, baked potatoes, salads and hamburgers is a little uninspired. An adjoining shop sells bread and pastries baked on the premises. Moderate.

La Escudilla 4 Av Norte 4. Tremendous courtyard restaurant, in the same premises as *Riki's Bar*, that's usually extremely busy on account of the excellent-value, good-quality food. The pasta is good, the US$3 all-day, all-night set meal is exceptional value, salads are delicious and vegetarians have plenty of tasty choices. You may have a wait, though, when it's busy. Inexpensive.

La Fonda de la Calle Real upstairs at 5 Av Norte 5, over the road at 5 Av Norte 12 and a third restaurant (the nicest location) at 3 C Poniente 7. Probably the most famous restaurant in Antigua, and patronized by Bill Clinton during his 2000 visit. Try the excellent Guatemalan specialities, including

pepián (spicy meat stew) and *caldo real* (chicken soup) or the sizzling grilled meats. Closed Wed. Moderate to expensive.

Frida's 5 Av Norte 29. Lively atmosphere and the best Mexican food in town – a tasty selection of enchiladas, fajitas etc. Decorated with 1950s Americana. Moderate.

Panza Verde 5 Av Sur 19. One of Antigua's most exclusive restaurants. Exemplary European cuisine, professional service and a nice setting, with well-spaced tables grouped around a courtyard garden. Try the trout or sea bass meunière. Expensive.

Quesos y Vinos 5 Av Norte 32. Very stylish Italian-owned restaurant with a reliable reputation for good homemade pasta and pizza, and wines from Europe and South America. Moderate.

San Jerónimo Alameda Santa Lucía Norte and 1 C Poniente. As it opens at 7am, this pleasant, simple patio-based comedor is a good bet for an early breakfast, though the friendly owners also serve tasty, cheap lunches and snacks. Inexpensive.

El Sereno 4 Av Norte 16. Superb colonial setting with beautiful dining rooms and a lovely roof terrace with some of the finest views in Antigua. Extensive menu with many seasonal specialities plus a decent wine list. Expensive.

Su Chow 5 Av Norte 38. Good Chinese food, cooked and served by a charming Belizean family. Inexpensive.

Weiner Alameda Santa Lucía Sur 8. Especially good for a well-priced, filling breakfast, this bar-restaurant also does lunchtime specials for US$2.50, serves good coffee and herbal teas and has a fair selection of bottled beers. Inexpensive.

Welten 4 C Oriente 21. Exclusive restaurant spread over a number of rooms and a covered patio. The international menu with a marked European influence is let down by an exorbitantly priced wine list. Expensive.

Drinking, nightlife and entertainment

Evening activity is somewhat curtailed in Antigua by a "dry law", which forbids the sale of alcohol after 1am, though there's usually somewhere that flouts this regulation. The places listed below on 5 and 7 Avenidas Norte are particularly popular with the gringo crowd and all open at around 7pm. Antigua's **dance scene** is burgeoning, drawing a big crowd from Guatemala City. The venues tend to be very quiet Monday to Wednesday, busy Thursday and heaving at weekends. For a less raucous atmosphere, try one of the simple bars on Alameda de Santa Lucía, or catch a film at one of the many video cinemas in town.

Bars and clubs

El Afro 6 C Poniente 9. Funky sociable bar, usually crammed at weekends with a salsa-stepping crowd, though space is tight for really serious dancing.

La Canoa 5 C Poniente between 4 and 5 avenidas. A small, unpretentious club where people come to dance to mainly Latin sounds. Merengue is the main ingredient, spiked with a dash of salsa and reggae; they also play a few tracks of Western and Latin pop/rock. Good mix of locals and foreigners and reasonable drink prices, though perennial licensing problems mean it's shut down from time to time. US$2 at weekends, free in the week.

La Casbah 5 Av Norte 30. The most controversial place in town, attracting a well-heeled crowd from Antigua and Guatemala City. The venue, in the ruins of an ancient church, is spectacular and the music can occasionally match the site, with deep bassline-driven dance mixes. Gay night on Thurs. Drinks are expensive. Mon–Wed free, Thurs, Fri & Sat around US$3.50.

La Chimanea 7 Av Norte 7. One of the more popular bars, though the music selection is disturbingly eclectic – expect everything from Rod Stewart to Black Sabbath.

Dante's 7 C Poniente 6B. Arguably the hippest place in town, this large, stylish bar hosts live bands and regular Cuban and house music club nights.

Equinoccio 7 Av Norte and 2 C Poniente. Bar-cum-club that's *the* place to groove to Latin music – predominantly merengue and salsa, but occasionally a little Cuban hip hop – with a dark bar zone and a large dancefloor. Moderate drink prices.

Macondo's 5 Av Norte and 2 C Poniente. Probably the closest thing Antigua has to a pub, though the themed nights (Wed is ladies' night) and constant visual barrage of music videos are not so pub-like.

Mono Loco 2 Av Norte 6B. Popular gringo bar, with full US and some EU sports coverage, though the music selection can be banal.

Picasso's 7 Av Nrte 16. No-nonsense drinking-hole that can get quite lively in high season. Usually closed Sun.

Riki's Bar 4 Av Norte 4. Unquestionably the most happening place in town due to the excellent site inside *La Escudilla* restaurant, the eclectic funk, nu jazz and downbeat music policy and the unrivalled happy hour (7–9pm), which means this place is packed most nights.

Cinemas

There is no movie theatre in Antigua, but a number of small video **cinemas** show a range of Western films daily – *Trainspotting*, *Salvador* and *Buena Vista Social Club* are on almost permanently. Fliers with weekly listings are posted on noticeboards all over town. The main cinemas are: Cinema Bistro, 5 Av Sur 14; Cinemaya, 6 C Poniente 7; and Maya Moon, 6 Av Norte 1A, while the Proyecto Cultural El Sitio, 5 C Poniente 15, also shows a good choice of Latin American and art-house movies.

Listings

Adventure sports Maya Mountain Bike Tours, 3 C Poniente and 7 Av Norte ☎832 3743, ⓦwww.mayanbike.com, has an excellent range of two-wheeler trips, and offers bike rental, plus whitewater rafting; Old Town Outfitters, 6 C Poniente 7 ☎832 4243, ⓦwww.bikeguatemala.com, runs mountain bike excursions and rock-climbing trips for all levels, and offers tent, sleeping bag, pack and bike rental. **Art workshops** Artguat, Callejón López 22 ☎832 6403, ⓕ832 6925, ⓦwww.artguat.org. Well-structured courses in painting, back-strap weaving, natural dye techniques and photography.

Banks and exchange Banco Industrial, 5 Av Sur 4, just south of the plaza (Mon–Fri 8.30am–7pm, Sat 8am–5pm), with a 24-hr ATM for Visa and Plus cardholders; Banco del Agro, north side of the plaza (Mon–Fri 9am–8pm, Sat 9am–6pm); Lloyds, in the northeast corner of the plaza (Mon–Fri 9am–5pm), which changes sterling travellers' cheques. Note that the Banco del Quetzal Mastercard/Cirrus cashpoint on the north side of the plaza routinely accepts cards but fails to dispense money.

Bookstores Casa Andinista, 4 C Oriente 5A ☎832 0161; Casa del Conde ☎832 3322 and Un Poco de Todo are both on the west side of the plaza, and Sopho's inside the El Sitio Cultural Centre 5 C Poniente 15. The Rainbow Reading Room, 7 Av Sur 8, has by far the largest selection of secondhand books.

Car and bike rental Avis, 5 Av Norte 22 ⊤ & ⓕ 832 2692, and Tabarini, 2 C Poniente 19A ⊤ & ⓕ 832 3091, ⓦ www.centroamerica.com/tabarini, both have similar prices with cars from around US$45 a day and jeeps from US$60, including

unlimited mileage and insurance. La Ceiba, 6 C Poniente 15 ⊤ 832 0077, rents out motorbikes from US$25 a day. Aviatur, 5 Av Norte 35 ⊤ & ⓕ 832 2642, and Maya Mountain Bike Tours and Old Town Outfitters (see "Adventure sports", above) rent mountain bikes for around US$8 a day or US$25 weekly.

Cigars and cigarettes There's an incredible selection of cigars, cigarettes and rolling papers on sale at the International Smoke Shop, 4 C Poniente 38B.

Studying Spanish in Antigua

Antigua's **language-school** industry is big business, with a couple of dozen established schools, and many more less reliable set-ups, some operating in the front room of someone's house. Whether you're just stopping for a week or two to learn the basics, or settling in for several months in pursuit of total fluency, there can be no doubt that this is one of the best places in Latin America to learn Spanish: it's a beautiful, relaxed town, lessons are cheap and there are several superb schools.

Choosing a school

Before making any decisions, you could drop into **Amerispan**, 6 Av Norte 40 (⊤ & ⓕ 832 0164, ⓔ amerispan@guate.net; in US ⊤ 1-800/879-6640, ⓕ 215/985-4524, ⓦ www.amerispan.com), which selects schools throughout Latin America to match the needs and requirements of students, and provides advice and support. The website ⓦ www.guatemala365.com is another excellent source of information, with school rankings and lots of independent, practical advice.

The tourist office in Antigua also has a list of "approved schools", most of which are professional and reliable but this is as much a product of bribery and influence as a reflection of professional integrity. Note that the Rigoberta Menchú school has no connection at all with Rigoberta or her foundation. The following schools are well established, recommended and towards the top end of the price scale, charging between US$130 and US$190 per week for four hours daily one-on-one tution and full family-based lodging and meals.

Academia Antigüeña de Español, 1 C Poniente 33 (⊤ 832 2685, ⓦ www.granjaguar .com/antiguena).

APPE, 6 C Poniente 40 (⊤ 832 0720, ⓦ www.guacalling.com/appe).

Centro America Spanish Academy inside La Fuente, 4 C Oriente 14 (⊤ & ⓕ 832 6268, ⓦ www.quik.guate.com/spanishacademy).

Centro Lingüístico de la Fuente, 1 C Poniente 27 (⊤ & ⓕ 832 2711, ⓦ www .delafuenteschool.com).

Centro Lingüístico Maya, 5 C Poniente 20 (⊤ & ⓕ 832 0656, ⓦ www.travellog .com/guatemala/antigua/clmaya/school.html).

Christian Spanish Academy, 6 Av Norte 15 (⊤ 832 3922, ⓕ 832 3760, ⓦ www .learncsa.com).

Probigua, 6 Av Norte 41B (⊤ & ⓕ 832 0860, ⓦ http://probigua.conexion.com).

Projecto Lingüístico Francisco Marroquín, 7 C Poniente 31 (⊤ 832 2886, ⓦ www.plfm-antigua.org).

San José El Viejo, 5 Av Sur 34 (⊤ 832 3028, ⓕ 832 3029, ⓦ www.guate.net/spanish).

Sevilla, 1 Av Sur 8 (⊤ & ⓕ 832 0442, ⓦ www.sevillantigua.com).

Tecún Umán Linguistic School, 6 C Poniente 34 A (⊤ & ⓕ 831 2792, ⓦ www .tecunuman.centramerica.com).

La Unión, 1 Av Sur 21 (⊤ & ⓕ 832 7337, ⓦ www.launion.conexion.com).

City tours Author Elizabeth Bell has an office inside the Casa Santo Domingo (☎832 0140, ex 341 ✉elizbell@guate.net), and leads excellent historical walking tours around the town. Geovany, at Monarcas, 7 Av Norte 15A (☎ & ⓕ832 4779, ⓦwww.angelfire.com/mt/monarcastravel) leads fascinating tours looking at the Maya influence on Antiguan architecture and the flora around the city.

Cultural centre El Sitio, 5 C Poniente 15 (☎832 3037), has an active theatre, art gallery and cinema and regularly hosts exhibitions and concerts – see the *Revue* or *Guatemala Post* for details of current events

Gym La Fábrica, C Del Hermano Pedro 16 (☎832 0486), has excellent facilities, including running machines, weights, and dance, aerobics, step and martial arts classes. Very reasonable daily, weekly, monthly or annual rates (Mon–Sat 6am–10pm).

Horse riding Ravenscroft Stables, 2 Av Sur 3 (☎832 6229) in the village of San Juan del Obispo, on the road up to Santa María de Jesús.

Internet There are over twenty places where you can send and receive email; rates are set at around US$1.50 an hour though there are discounts for heavy users. The best set-up places include La Ventana, 5 Av Sur 24 (daily 8am–9pm), and Enlaces, 6 Av Norte 1 (daily 9am–9.30pm). Conexión, in the La Fuente cultural centre at 4 C Oriente 14 (daily 8am–8pm), is probably the best place to head for real computer queries and techie expertise.

Laundry There are over a dozen in Antigua. Among them, Rainbow Laundry, 6 Av Sur 15 (Mon–Sat 7am–7pm), is friendly and reliable; a large wash typically costs around US$2.50.

Libraries La Biblioteca Internacional de Antigua, on the west side of the plaza, has an extensive collection of English fiction, biography, travel, art, geography and reference books. Temporary/monthly memberships are available. CIRMA (*Centro de Investigaciones Regionales de Mesoamérica*) is a research centre and library with facilities for students of Central America, whose work it also publishes. The library and reading room are to one side of a gorgeously peaceful courtyard at 5 C Oriente 5.

Moving on from Antigua

Because of its small size, and its position off the Interamericana, few **bus routes** originate in Antigua. If you're heading to anywhere in the east of the country, take the first bus to Guatemala City and change there. If you're heading into the western highlands, except Panajachel, it's usually best to catch the first bus to Chimaltenango (see p.130) and get another connection there. The main bus destinations are as follows:

Guatemala City (1hr). A constant flow of buses leaves for the capital (Mon–Sat 4am–7.30pm, Sun 6am–8pm)

Ciudad Vieja (hourly; 20min)

Chimaltenango via Parramos (every 30min; 40min)

Escuintla via El Rodeo (6 daily; 1hr 30min)

Panajachel (1 daily at 7am; 2hr 30min)

San Antonio Aguas Calientes (every 30min; 20min)

Santa María de Jesús (every 30min; 30min)

Yepocapa and **Acatenango** (5 daily; both 40min).

Shuttles

Minibus **shuttle services** run from Antigua to many parts of the country, and can be booked through most travel agents, including Adventure Travel Viareal (see "Listings", p.112). Shuttles are a lot more expensive than public buses but much more comfortable and quicker. There are frequent airport and Guatemala City shuttles for US$7–10 depending on the time of day; Chichicastanango (around US$12) is well served on market days (Thurs & Sun); and there's usually a daily service to Panajachel (around US$12). For Copán in Honduras (around US$30), try Monarcas (see p.112). Shuttles to the Río Dulce (around US$25) and Monterrico (around US$20) run at weekends and when there is enough demand – normally three people is sufficient.

Medical care There's a 24-hour emergency service at the Santa Lucía Hospital, Calzada Santa Lucía Sur 7 (℡ 832 3122). Also, Dr Aceituno, who speaks good English, has his surgery at 2 C Poniente 7 (℡ 832 0512).

Pharmacies Farmacia Santa María, west side of the plaza (daily 8am–10pm).

Police The police HQ is on the south side of the plaza, next to the tourist office (℡ & Ⓕ 832 0572). The tourist police are just off the plaza on 4 Avenida Norte (℡ 832 7290).

Pool hall 3 C Poniente 4–5 A. Very much a male-dominated institution, although tourists of either sex are welcome, providing they can handle the smell.

Post office Alameda de Santa Lucía opposite the bus terminal (Mon–Fri 8am–4.30pm). DHL is at 6 Av Sur 16 (℡ 832 3718, Ⓕ 832 3732, Ⓔ ecastill @gtl-co.gt.dhl.com), and Quick Shipping is at 3 Av Norte 26 (℡ 832 2595).

Shopping If you're interested in seeing *huipiles* from more than one hundred villages, head for Nim Po't, 5 Av Norte 29, which sells some of the finest in the country at reasonable prices. The warehouse-like store is something of a museum of contemporary Maya weaving, with a stunning array of complete costumes, as well as books on Maya culture. La Fuente centre, at 4 C Oriente 14, has a number of upmarket clothing and handicraft stores, while Al Pie del Volcán, on 4 Av Norte 7, also sells quality handicrafts. For the most fun and the lowest prices, check out the open-air market in Parque Unión on 6 C Oriente 2–3 Av Sur, or the stalls at the junction of 4 C Poniente and 6 Av Norte.

Supermarket La Bodegona at 4 C Poniente and Alameda de Santa Lucía.

Swimming pool *Hotel Radisson Antigua*, 9 C south of town on road to Ciudad Vieja, has two pools that non-guests can use for US$5 per day; you also get access to a small gym and sauna. There are also two beautiful but chilly spring-fed pools (daily 7am–4pm; US$1) at El Pilar, on the edge of town on the road to Santa Mariá de Jesús. Past the Stations of the Cross you come to a large

school on the left; follow the track that cuts off to the left just before it.

Taxis On the east side of the plaza close to the cathedral, or call ℡ 832 0479.

Telephones The Telgua office is just south of the plaza on 5 Avenida Sur (daily 7am–10pm), but rates are higher here than anywhere else and you'll have to queue. Several places now offer internet-linked phone facilities, including La Ventana (see "Internet", above) enabling you to call North America for US$0.25 a minute or Europe and the rest of the world for a little more, though lines can be fuzzy. The cheapest conventional phone connections are at Kall Shop, 6 Av Sur 12A (daily 8am–8pm), where you can call North America for US$0.25 a minute, Western Europe for US$0.45, and Australia and New Zealand for US$0.64 a minute.

Travel agents There are dozens of travel agents in Antigua; the following are the most professional and reliable. The Rainbow Travel Center, 7 Av Sur 8 (daily 9am–6pm; ℡ 832 4202, Ⓕ 832 4206, Ⓔ rainbowtravel@gua.gbm.net), is fully computerized and has some of the best deals in town, as well as friendly and efficient staff. Viajes Tivoli, at 4 C Oriente 10, on the west side of the plaza (Mon–Sat 9am–6pm; ℡ 832 4274, Ⓕ 832 5690, Ⓔ antigua@tivoli.com.gt) is another recommended all-rounder. Monarcas, 7 Av Norte 15A (℡ & Ⓕ 832 4779, Ⓦ www.angelfire.com/mt/monarcastravel), is a highly recommended specialist agency with some fascinating Maya culture and ecology tours and daily connections to Copán, Honduras. Adventure Travel Center Viareal, 5 Av Norte 25B (℡ & Ⓕ 832 0162, Ⓔ viareal@guate.net), is particularly good for adventure and sailing trips and shuttle bus services. Perfect for backpackers, Quetzalventures (contact by phone and email only: ℡ 832 4345, Ⓦ www.quetzalventures.com), offers a number of good, inexpensive trips to Petén and the Verapaz highlands; all profits aid Guatemalan street children. Vision Travel, 3 Av Norte 3 (℡ 832 3293, Ⓕ 832 1955, Ⓦ www.guatemalainfo.com), has very high standards of service and is consistently recommended.

Around Antigua: villages and volcanoes

The countryside surrounding Antigua is superbly fertile and breathtakingly beautiful. The valley is dotted with small villages, ranging from the ladino coffee centre of Alotenango to the traditional indigenous village of Santa María de Jesús, while there are two new museums in Jocotenango just north of Antigua. None is more than an hour away and all make interesting day-trips. For the more adventurous, the **volcanic peaks** of Agua, Acatenango and Fuego offer strenuous but superb hiking.

San Antonio Aguas Calientes

To the south of Antigua the Panchoy valley is a broad sweep of farmland, over-shadowed by three volcanic cones and covered with olive-green coffee bushes. A single, poorly maintained road runs out this way, eventually reaching Escuintla and the Pacific coast, and passing a string of villages as it goes.

The first of these, a couple of kilometres from Antigua, is the indigenous village of **SAN ANTONIO AGUAS CALIENTES**, set to one side of a steep-sided bowl beneath the peak of Acatenango. San Antonio is famous for weaving, characterized by its complex floral and geometric patterns, and there's a new indoor textile market next to the plaza where you can find a complete range of the local output. This is also a good place to learn the traditional craft of back-strap weaving; if you're interested, the best way to find out about possible tuition is simply by asking the women in the market.

Adjoining San Antonio is the village of **SANTA CATARINA BARA-HONA** which has a modest ruined colonial church. Out on the edge of the village there's also a small **swimming pool** (Tues–Sun 9am–6pm) – the perfect place for a (chilly) dip. To get to the pool, walk along San Antonio's main street until you come to the plaza in Santa Catarina and continue up the street that goes up to the church, and it's signposted from there, a five minute walk away up a hill to the left. There's a decent **comedor**, the *Restaurante y Cafeteria Gaby*, two blocks east of the plaza. **Buses** from the terminal in Antigua run a regular service to San Antonio and Santa Catarina.

Ciudad Vieja and Alotenango

Three kilometres beyond San Antonio is **CIUDAD VIEJA**, a scruffy and unhurried village with a distinguished past: it was near here that the Spanish established their second capital, Santiago de los Caballeros, in 1527. Today, however, there's no trace of the original city, and all that remains from that time is a solitary tree, in a corner of the plaza, which bears a plaque commemorating the site of the first mass ever held in Guatemala. The plaza also boasts an eighteenth-century colonial church that has recently been restored.

The Spanish settled at first near the Kaqchikel capital of Iximché. Within a year, however, the Kaqchikel had turned against them, and the Spanish decided to base themselves elsewhere, moving their capital to the valley of Almolonga, 35km to the east between the Acatenango and Agua volcanoes. Here, on St Celia's Day 1527, in a landscape considered perfect for pasture and with plentiful supplies of building materials, the first official capital, **Santiago de los Caballeros**, was founded. The new city was built in a mood of tremendous confidence, with building plots distributed according to rank and the suburban sites given over to Alvarado's Mexican allies. Within twenty years things had really started to take shape, with a school, a cathedral, monasteries, and farms stocked with imported cattle. But while the bulk of the Spaniards were still settling in, their leader, the rapacious **Alvarado**, was off in search of action. His lust for wealth and conquest sent him to Peru, Spain and Mexico, and in 1541 he set out for the Spice Islands, travelling via Jalisco, where he met his end, crushed to death beneath a rolling horse. When news of his death reached his wife **Doña Beatriz**, at home in Santiago, she plunged the capital into an extended period of mourning, staining the entire palace with black clay, inside and out. She went on to command the officials to appoint her as her husband's replacement, and on September 9, 1541, became the first woman to govern in the Americas. On the official declaration she signed herself as *La sin ventura*

Doña Beatriz, and then deleted her name to leave only *La sin ventura* (the unlucky one) – a fateful premonition.

Following the announcement of Alvarado's death the city had been swept by storms, and before the night of Beatriz's inauguration was out an earthquake added to the force of the downpour. A tremor shook the surrounding volcanoes and from the crater of the Agua volcano a great wave of mud and water slid down, accelerating as it surged towards the valley floor, sweeping away the capital, and killing Doña Beatriz. Today the exact site of the original city is still the subject of some debate, but the general consensus puts it about 2km to the east of Ciudad Vieja, though it's probable that one of the suburbs would have reached out as far as the modern village.

A further 10km down the valley, the ragged-looking village of **ALOTE-NANGO** is dwarfed by the often steaming, scarred cone of the Fuego volcano, which has been in a state of constant eruption since the arrival of the Spanish. A path leads from the village up the volcano, but it's extremely hard to find and follow, so unless you're with a guide it's a lot easier to climb Acatenango instead, using La Soledad as a starting point (see below).

Beyond Alotenango, a smooth newly paved highway continues down the valley to **Escuintla** (see p.243), passing the village of El Rodeo. Six daily buses connect Antigua and Escuintla (1hr 30min).

To get to Ciudad Vieja or Alotenango, there's a steady stream of **buses** leaving from outside the terminal in Antigua: the last one returns from Alotenango at around 7pm.

Acatenango and Fuego volcanoes

To the south of Antigua, just a short way beyond Ciudad Vieja, a road branches off to **SAN MIGUEL DUEÑAS**, a dried-out, scrappy-looking sort of place where the roads are lined with bamboo fences and surrounded by coffee fincas. There's little to delay you in San Miguel itself, but a kilometre before the village the Valhalla Organic Farm (daily 7am–5pm) is well worth investigating. Owned by an eccentric American, Lorenzo Gottschamer, the farm has five hectares of macadamia nut trees, and welcomes visitors. A short tour will reveal all the secrets of nut harvesting and roasting, and there's a chance to sample delicious madacamia pancakes or buy cosmetics and chocolates. San Miguel Dueñas is also the best starting point for climbing the Acatenango and Fuego volcanoes. **Buses** head out to San Miguel every half-hour or so from the terminal in Antigua, but once you progress beyond the village, traffic becomes scarce. If you're making for the volcanoes then you may have to consider either taking a taxi from Antigua to La Soledad (around US$12) or hitching from San Miguel Dueñas; alternatively, it's a two hour walk.

Climbing Acatenango

The trail for **Acatenango** starts in **LA SOLEDAD**, an impoverished village perched on an exposed ridge high above the valley. Walking up the road from San Miguel Dueñas, you come upon a cluster of bamboo huts, with a soccer field to the right. Here you'll find a small tienda and the last tap – so fill up on water. A short way beyond the tienda a track leads up to the left, heading above the village and towards the wooded lower slopes of Acatenango. It crosses another largish trail and then starts to wind up into the pine trees. Just after you enter the trees you have to turn onto a smaller path that leads away to the right; 100m or so further on, take another small path that climbs to the left. This brings you onto a low ridge, where you meet a thin trail that leads to the left, away up the volcano – this path eventually finds its way to the top, somewhere between six and nine hours away. At times it's a little vague, but most of the way it's fairly easy to follow.

There are two other important spots on the ascent, the **campsites**, which are also the easiest places to lose the trail. The first, a beautiful grassy clearing, is about ninety minutes up – the path cuts straight across, so don't be tempted by the larger track heading off to the right. Another ninety minutes above this is the second campsite, a little patch of level ground in amongst the pine trees. You're now about halfway to the top.

The trail itself is an exhausting climb, a thin line of slippery volcanic ash that rises with unrelenting steepness through thick forest. Only for the last 50m or so does it emerge above the tree line, before reaching the top of the lower cone. Here there's a radio mast and a small yellow hut, put up by the Guatemalan Mountaineering Club, where you can shelter from the freezing nights – though at weekends it may be full. To the south, another hour's gruelling ascent, is the main cone, a great grey bowl that rises to a height of 3975m. From here there's a magnificent view out across the valley below. On the opposite side is the Agua volcano, and to the right the fire-scarred cone of Fuego. Looking west you can see the three cones that surround Lake Atitlán, and beyond that the Santa María volcano, high above Quetzaltenango.

When it comes to getting down again, the direct route towards Alotenango may look invitingly simple but is in fact very hard to follow. It's easiest to go back the same way that you came up.

Climbing Fuego

In the unlikely event that you have any remaining energy you could continue south and climb the neighbouring active cone of **Fuego** (3763m). The volcano is certainly impressive and when the English friar Thomas Gage saw it in 1678, he was inspired to make a comparison with the neighbouring peak of Agua:

This volcano or mountain (whose height is judged full nine miles to the top) is not so pleasing to the sight, but the other which standeth on the other side of the valley opposite unto it is unpleasing and more dreadful to behold. For here are ashes for beauty, stones and flints for fruits and flowers, baldness for greenness, barrenness for fruitfulness. For water whisperings and fountain murmurs, noises of thunder and roaring of consuming metals; for running streams, flashingly of fire; for tall and mighty trees and cedars, castles of smoke rising in height to out-dare the sky and firmament; for sweet and odiferous and fragrant smells, a stink of fire and brimstone, which are still in action striving within the bowels of that ever burning and fiery volcano.

As Gage indicates, Fuego can be very violent, and has erupted recently, so it's essential to check the current safety situation before attempting the climb. Walking down and up the dip between the two peaks takes a good few hours, and you should always be wary of getting too close to Fuego's cone as it oozes overpowering sulphur fumes and occasionally spits out molten rock. Descending from Fuego is fairly problematic, too, as the trail that leads down to Alotenango is hard to find. The bottom of the gully, though it may look tempting, is impassable – the actual trail is on the Fuego side of this dip. The only way to be really sure of a trouble-free descent is to go back over Acatenango and down the way you came up.

Fuego can also be climbed by a direct ascent from the village of Alotenango, but the climb is very hard going and the trail difficult to follow. Hire a guide if you plan to take this route.

San Juan del Obispo, Santa María de Jesús and the Agua volcano

East of Antigua the smooth paved road to Santa María de Jesús runs out along a narrow valley, sharing the shade with acres of coffee bushes. Before it starts to climb, the road passes the village of **SAN JUAN DEL OBISPO**, invisible from the road but marked by what must rank as the country's finest bus shelter, beautifully carved in local stone. The village is unremarkable in itself, although it does offer a good view of the valley below. What makes it worth a visit is the **Palacio de Francisco Marroquín**, who was the first Bishop of Guatemala. The place is currently home to about 25 nuns, and if you knock on the great wooden double doors one of them will come and show you around. Marroquín arrived in Guatemala with Alvarado and is credited with having introduced Christianity to the Maya, as well as reminding the Spaniards about it from time to time. On the death of Alvarado's wife he assumed temporary responsibility for the government, and was instrumental in the construction of Antigua. He died in 1563, having spent his last days in the vast palace that he'd built for himself here in San Juan. The palace, like everything else in the region, has been badly damaged over the years, and serious reconstruction only began in 1962. The interior, arranged around two small courtyards, is spectacularly beautiful and several rooms still contain their original furniture. Attached to the palace is a fantastic church and chapel with ornate wood carvings, plaster mouldings and austere religious paintings. There's also an excellent English-owned **stables** here (see p.111 Antigua "Listings" for more information), a block from the palacio.

There are regular **buses** to San Juan from the market in Antigua (7.30am–6.30pm; 20min) terminating in the churchyard. Alternatively you could catch one heading for Santa María de Jesús and ask the driver to drop you here.

Santa María de Jesús

Up above San Juan the road arrives in **SANTA MARÍA DE JESÚS**, starting point for the ascent of the Agua volcano. Perched high on the shoulder of the volcano, the village is some 500m above Antigua, with magnificent views over the Panchoy valley and east towards the smoking cone of Pacaya. It was founded at the end of the sixteenth century for the Maya transported from Quetzaltenango: they were given the task of providing firewood for Antigua and the village earned the name *Aserradero*, lumber yard. Since then it has developed into a farming community where the women wear beautiful purple *huipiles*, although the men have recently abandoned traditional costume. The village has a certain scruffy charm, with the only place **to stay** being the hospedaje *El Oasis* (T832 0130; ❶), just off the plaza on the road into town; it's a friendly, clean institution that serves meals – beans, eggs and tortillas – as simple as the rooms.

Buses run from Antigua to Santa María every hour or so from 6am to 6.30pm, and the trip takes thirty minutes. Beyond Santa María, the road continues down the east side of the volcano to the village of Palín (see p.91), on the Guatemala City–Escuintla highway. Very few buses cover this route, but you shouldn't have to wait long to hitch a lift on a pick-up or truck.

The Agua volcano

Agua is the easiest and by far the most popular of Guatemala's big cones to climb: on Saturday nights sometimes hundreds of people spend the night at the summit. It's an exciting ascent with a fantastic view to reward you at the top. The trail starts in Santa María de Jesús (see above) – to reach it, head straight across the plaza, between the two ageing pillars, and up the street opposite the church doors. Take a right turn just before the end, and then continue past the cemetery and out of the village. From here on it's a fairly simple climb on a clear path, cutting across the road that goes some of the way up. The climb can take anything from four to six hours, and the peak, at 3766m, is always cold at night: there is shelter (though not always room) in a small chapel at the summit, however, and the views certainly make it worth the struggle.

Antigua to Chimaltenango

As an alternative to the main highway from Guatemala City, a second, smaller road connects Antigua with the Carretera Interamericana, this time intersecting it at **Chimaltenango** (see p.130). The nearest of the villages, **SAN FELIPE DE JESÚS**, is so close that you can walk there: just a kilometre or so north of Antigua following 6 Avenida Norte (or catch one of the minibuses from the bus terminal). San Felipe has a small Gothic-style church housing a famous image of Christ, Jesús Sepultado, said to have miraculous powers. Severely damaged in the 1976 earthquake, the church has been well restored since, and there's a fiesta here on August 30 to celebrate the anniversary of the arrival of the image in 1670. The village's other attraction is a **silver workshop**, where silver mined in the highlands of Alta Verapaz is worked and sold. To find the workshop, follow the sign to the *Platería Típica La Antigüeña*.

Merging into San Felipe to the west, the grimy suburb of **JOCOTENANGO**, "place of bitter fruit", is set around a huge, dusty plaza where there's a magnificent, but crumbling, dusty pink Baroque church. In colonial times Jocotenango was the gateway to Antigua, where official visitors would be met to be escorted into the city. Long notorious for its brothels and gangs, Jocotenango main industries are coffee production and wood carving: there's an excellent selection of bowls and fruits in the family-owned Artesanías Cardenas Barrios workshop on Calle San Felipe, where they have been working at the trade for five generations.

Joco's newest attractions are 500m west of the plaza, down a dirt road. **Casa K'ojom** (ⓦwww.kojom.com; daily 9am–5pm; US$2.50 including tour) is a purpose-built museum dedicated to Maya culture, especially music. The history of indigenous musical traditions is logically presented from its pre-Columbian origins, through sixteenth-century Spanish and African influences – which brought the marimba, bugles and drums – to the present day, with audio-visual documentaries of fiestas and ceremonies. Other rooms are dedicated to the village weavings of the Sacatepéquez department and the cult of Maximón (see box below). Next door, the **Museum of Coffee** (daily 9am–5pm; US$2.50), based in the Finca la Azotea, a 34-hectare plantation dating from 1883, offers a look around a working organic coffee farm. All the technicalities of husking, sieving and roasting are clearly explained and you're served a cup of the aromatic home-grown brew after your tour. **Buses** from the Antigua terminal pass Jocotenango every thirty minutes on their way to Chimaltenango.

Another 4km brings you to **SAN LORENZO EL TEJAR**, which has some superb hot springs. To reach the springs turn right in the village of **San Luis Las Carretas**, and then right again when the road forks: they're at the end of a narrow valley, a couple of kilometres from the main road. If you want to

The wicked saint of San Andrés Itzapa

San Andrés shares with the western highland villages of Zunil (see p.192) and Santiago Atitlán (see p.167) the honour of revering **San Simón** or Maximón, the wicked saint, whose image is housed in a pagan chapel in the village. You'll find it surrounded by drunken men, cigar-smoking women and hundreds of burning candles, each symbolizing a request. Uniquely in Guatemala, this San Simón attracts a largely ladino congregation and is particularly popular with prostitutes. Inside the dimly lit shrine, the walls are adorned with hundreds of plaques from all over Guatemala and Central America, thanking San Simón for his help. For a small fee, you may be offered a *limpia*, or soul cleansing, which involves one of the resident women workers beating you with a bushel of herbs, while you share a bottle of local firewater, *aguardiente*, with San Simón (it dribbles down his front) and the attendant, who will periodically spray you with alcohol from her mouth. If you want to sample the San Simón experience, you have to do so between sunrise and sunset, as he is believed to sleep at other times – indeed above the entrance to his *casa* is a sign saying "San Simón 6am–6pm".

bathe in the sulphurous waters you can either use the cheaper communal pool or for a dollar or so rent one of your own – a little private room with a huge tiled tub set in the floor. The baths are open daily from 6am to 5pm, except Tuesday and Friday afternoons, when they are closed for cleaning; Sundays can get very busy with local families.

From San Luis the main road climbs out of the Panchoy valley through **Parramos**, a dusty, overgrown farming village with a wonderful new rural retreat, *La Posada de mi Abuelo* (Ⓦ www.ecotourism-adventure.com/posadade .htm), offering horse riding and comfortable bungalow accommodation. A couple of kilometres beyond Parramos a side road branches to **SAN ANDRÉS ITZAPA**, one of the many villages badly hit by the 1976 earthquake. Tragically, San Andrés also hit the headlines at the end of 1988, when it was the scene of the largest massacre since the return of civilian rule, when 22 corpses were found in a shallow grave. Today, however, San Andrés' main claim to fame is as home to the cult of San Simón, or Maximón (see box above). To pay San Simón a visit, head for the central plaza from the branch road into the village, turn right when you reach the church, walk two blocks, then up a little hill and you should spot street vendors selling charms, incense and candles. If you get lost, ask for the *Casa de San Simón*. The other point of interest in the village is the particularly intricate weaving of the women's *huipiles*. The patterns are both delicate and bold, similar in many ways to those around Chimaltenango. San Andrés' Tuesday market is also worth a visit.

To get to San Andrés Itzapa, take any **bus** heading to Chimaltenango from the terminal in Antigua (every 20min 5.30am–7pm; 40min). Get the driver to drop you off where the dirt road leaves the highway, from where you can hitch or walk for thirty minutes to the village. Alternatively catch one of the hourly buses to San Andrés Itzapa from the market in Chimaltenango (6am–5pm; 20min).

After the turning for San Andrés, the main road drops through pine trees to the **Laguna de Los Cisnes**, a small boating lake surrounded by cheap comedores and swimming pools, popularly known as *Los Aposeutos*. The lake is very popular with the people of Antigua and Chimaltenango, who flood out here every weekend and public holiday. Above the lake is the local army base, and beyond that the Carretera Interamericana and **Chimaltenango**, 19km and 45 minutes from Antigua.

Fiestas

The region around Guatemala City and Antigua is not prime fiesta territory but a few villages, listed below, have some firmly established traditions and there are some dramatic celebrations. Also listed are some events in the surrounding villages, which aren't necessarily covered in the text but may well be worth visiting if you're in the area around fiesta time.

January

The fiesta year in the region around Guatemala City starts from the 1st to 4th in the village of **Fraijanes**. **Santa María de Jesús**, near Antigua, has an excellent fiesta from the 1st to 5th, with the main action on the first two days. There's also a fiesta in **San Pedro Ayampuc** some time in the month, on a different date each year.

February

Antigua celebrates the first Friday in Lent and there's a huge pilgrimage to the village of San Felipe de Jesús on the same day.

March

Villa Canales has its fiesta from the 6th to 14th, while **San Pedro Pinula** celebrates from the 16th to 20th, with the main day on the 19th. **San José del Golfo** has a fiesta from the 18th to 20th, its main day also being the 19th. **Holy Week**, at Easter, is celebrated throughout the country but with extreme fervour in **Antigua**: here the main processions are marched over carpets of painted sawdust and involve huge numbers of people engulfed in clouds of incense.

April

The only April fiesta is in **Palencia**, from the 26th to 30th.

May

May 1, Labour Day, is marked in the capital by marches and protests, while the fiesta in **Amatitlán** is from the 1st to 7th, with the main day on the 3rd.

June

Comalapa, on the Interamericana, has a fiesta on the 24th. **San Juan Sacatepéquez** has a June fiesta from the 22nd to 27th, with the main day on the 24th. **Yepocapa** parties from the 27th to 30th, with the main day on the 29th.

July

Antigua has a one-day fiesta on the 25th in honour of Santiago. **Palín** has a traditional fiesta from the 24th to 30th, which climaxes on its final day.

August

In **Jocotenango** the fiesta is for a single day on the 15th. **Mixco**, an interesting Poqomam village on the western side of town, has its fiesta on the 4th, while the main **Guatemala City** fiesta, involving all sorts of parades and marches, is on the 15th.

November

The 1st is the scene of intense action in **Sumpango** and **Santiago Sacatepéquez** where they fly massive paper kites in the village cemeteries. **San Catarina Pinula** celebrates from the 20th to 28th, with the main day on the 25th. **San Andrés Itzapa** has a fiesta from November 27 to December 1.

December

The year ends with a fiesta in **Chinautla**, from the 4th to 9th, with the main day on the 6th, and **Villa Nueva**, where they have a fiesta from the 6th to 11th, which climaxes on its final day.

Travel details

Buses

Guatemala City is at the transport heart of the country with even the smallest of villages being connected to the capital. Hence there are literally thousands of buses into and out of the city. Most of these are covered in the "Travel details" of other chapters, but for the main **bus services** from Guatemala City see the "Moving on" box on p.86; for buses from Antigua, see p.111.

Planes

There are frequent **international flights** from Guatemala City's Aurora airport to Mexico, Central America and North America, and at least ten daily flights to Flores in Petén, the only other international airport in the country. Most of these leave in the early morning at around 7am. Tickets for the 50-minute flight can be bought from virtually any travel agent in the capital (see p.89) or Antigua (see p.112) and cost from US$75 return. Tikal Jets (see Guatemala City "Listings" on p.85) operate the only twin jet engined planes; their flights cost around US$100 return.

Trains

There are currently no passenger train services in Guatemala except a tourist day-trip from the capital to the isolated settlement of **Agua Caliente** in the Motagua valley, 25km east from the capital. These trips, which started in 2001, cost a hefty US$45 per person. For more details, contact one of the Guatemala City travel agents on p.89, or Antigua's on p.112.

The western highlands

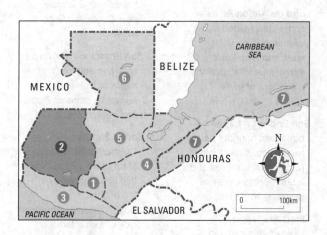

CHAPTER 2 # Highlights

※ **Chichicastenango** – Hunt for textiles and souvenirs at this scenic town's legendary market. p.135

※ **The Ixil triangle** Hike the hillside trails of this remote, intensely traditional indigenous region. p.146

※ **Lago de Atitlán** An awesome steep-sided crater lake, ringed by volcanoes and diminutive indigenous villages, with a plethora of idyllic places to chill. p.154

※ **San Pedro La Laguna** A bohemian hangout *par excellence*, replete with budget guesthouses and a burgeoning travellers' scene. p.169

※ **Quetzaltenango** Guatemala's civilized second city makes an excellent base for studying Spanish, and any number of fascinating day-trips. p.179

※ **Fuentes Georginas** A blissfully relaxing natural spa, with steaming hot pools framed by lush ferns and forest, situated halfway up a volcano near Quetzaltenango. p.192

※ **San Francisco el Alto** Its weekly market is a maelstrom of highland humanity, animals, fruit and vegetables. p.195

※ **Todos Santos Cuchumatán** A sleepy Mam Maya village nestled in a high valley in the mighty Cuchumatanes mountain range, with a famous textile tradition. p.215

2

The western highlands

Guatemala's **western highlands**, stretching from the outskirts of Antigua to the Mexican border, are perhaps the most beautiful and captivating part of the country. The region is defined by two main features: a chain of awesome volcanoes that lines its southern side, and the high mountain ranges that form the northern boundaries. The greatest of these are the **Cuchumatanes**, whose granite peaks rise to some 3837m. Strung between these two natural barriers is a series of spectacular twisting ridges, lakes, gushing streams and deep valleys.

It's an astounding landscape, blessed with tremendous fertility but cursed by instability. Of the thirteen cones that loom over the western highlands, three volcanoes are still active: **Pacaya**, **Fuego** and **Santiaguito**, all oozing plumes of sulphurous smoke and occasionally spewing out showers of molten rock. Two major **fault lines** also cut through the area, making earthquakes a regular occurrence. The most recent major quake occurred around **Chimaltenango** in 1976 – it left 25,000 dead and around a million homeless. But despite its sporadic ferocity the landscape is outstandingly beautiful, with irrigated valleys and terraced hillsides carefully crafted to yield the maximum potential farmland.

The highland landscape is controlled by many factors, all of which affect its appearance. Perhaps the most important is **altitude**. At lower levels the vegetation is almost tropical, supporting dense forests, **coffee**, **cotton**, **bananas** and **cacao**, while higher up the hills are often wrapped in cloud and the ground is sometimes hard with frost. Here trees are stunted by the cold, and **maize** and potatoes are grown alongside herds of grazing sheep and goats. The seasons also play their part. In the rainy season, from May to October, the land is superbly green, with young crops and lush forests of **pine**, **cedar** and **oak**, while during the dry winter months the hillsides gradually turn to a dusty yellow.

Accommodation price codes

All accommodation listed in this guide has been graded according to the following price scales. These refer to the price in US dollars of the cheapest double room in high season. For more details see p.34.

❶ Under US$5	❸ US$15–25	❼ US$60–80
❷ US$5–10	❺ US$25–40	❽ US$80–100
❸ US$10–15	❻ US$40–60	❾ Over US$100

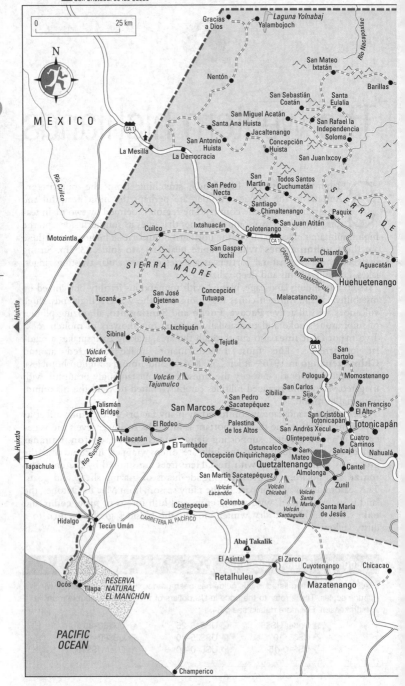

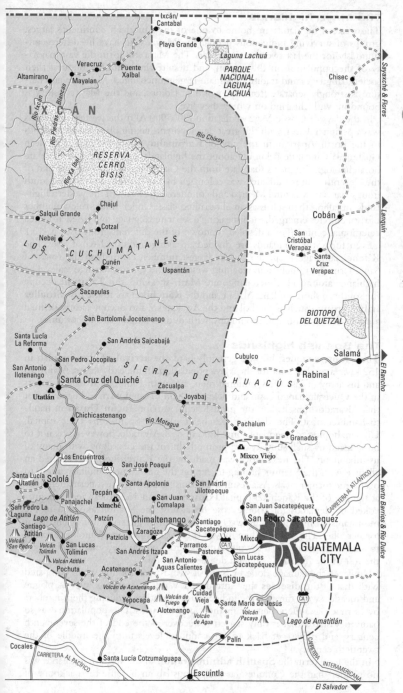

Sayaxché & Flores

Lanquín

El Rancho

Puerto Barrios & Río Dulce

El Salvador ▼

Ixcán/Cantabal

Playa Grande

Laguna Lachuá

PARQUE NACIONAL LAGUNA LACHUÁ

Chisec

Veracruz

Altamirano

Mayalan

Puente Xalbal

Río Ixcán

Río Piedras Blancas

IXCÁN

Río Xal Ibal

Río Chixoy

RESERVA CERRO BISIS

Chajul

Salquil Grande

Cotzal

Nebaj

LOS CUCHUMATANES

Cunén

Uspantán

Cobán

San Cristóbal Verapaz

Santa Cruz Verapaz

Sacapulas

San Bartolomé Jocotenango

BIOTOPO DEL QUETZAL

Santa Lucía La Reforma

San Andrés Sajcabajá

San Pedro Jocopilas

SIERRA DE CHUACÚS

Cubulco

Salamá

San Antonio Ilotenango

Santa Cruz del Quiché

Zacualpa

Joyabaj

Rabinal

Utatlán

Chichicastenango

Río Motagua

Pachalum

Granados

Los Encuentros

CA 1

San José Poaquil

Mixco Viejo

Santa Lucía Utatlán

Sololá

Santa Apolonia

San Martín Jilotepeque

CARRETERA AL ATLÁNTICO

Tecpán

Panajachel

Iximché

San Juan Comalapa

San Juan Sacatepéquez

San Pedro Sacatepéquez

San Pedro La Laguna

Lago de Atitlán

Patzún

Chimaltenango

Santiago Sacatepéquez

Mixco

Santiago Atitlán

Volcán San Pedro

Volcán Tolimán

San Lucas Tolimán

Patzicía

Zaragoza

Parramos

GUATEMALA CITY

Volcán Atitlán

San Andrés Itzapa

Pastores

San Lucas Sacatepéquez

Pochuta

Acatenango

San Antonio Aguas Calientes

Antigua

CA 1

Yepocapa

Volcán de Acatenango

Volcán de Fuego

Cuidad Vieja

Santa María de Jesús

Alotenango

Volcán de Agua

Volcán Pacaya

Lago de Amatitlán

Cocales

CARRETERA AL PACÍFICO

Santa Lucía Cotzumalguapa

Palín

CARRETERA INTERAMERICANA

Escuintla

The Maya highlands

The western highlands are home to one of the American continent's largest groups of surviving indigenous people, the **Maya**, who have lived here continuously for the last two thousand years. The Maya still form the vast majority of the population in this region, and despite the Spanish Conquest their society, languages and traditions remain largely unchanged. Maya life and culture is strongly separate from the world of ladinos, and the Maya's history is bound up with the land on which they live.

In the days of Classic Maya civilization (300–900 AD) the western highlands was a peripheral area, with the great developments taking place in the lowlands to the north. Apart from the city of **Kaminaljuyú**, on the site of modern Guatemala City, little is known about the highlands at this time, and there are no archeological remains that date from the Classic period. Towards the end of the eleventh century the area was colonized by the **Toltec**, who moved south from what is now central Mexico and conquered the Maya of the western highlands, installing themselves as an elite ruling class. Under Toltec rule a number of rival empires emerged, each speaking a separate language and based around a ceremonial centre. (For a detailed rundown of the different groups, see p.413.)

Even today the highlands are divided up along traditional tribal lines. The **K'iche'** language is spoken by the largest number, centred on the town of Santa Cruz del Quiché and reaching west into the Quetzaltenango valley. The highlands around Huehuetenango are **Mam**-speaking, the **Tz'utujil** occupy the southern shores of Lake Atitlán, and the **Kaqchikel** are to the east. **Smaller tribal groups**, such as the Ixil and the Awakateko, also occupy clearly defined areas in the Cuchumatan mountains, with distinct languages and costumes.

The Spanish highlands

Though pre-conquest life was certainly hard, the **arrival of the Spanish** in 1523 was a total disaster for the Maya population. In the early stages, **Alvarado** and his army of just a few hundred men, met with a force of K'iche' warriors in the Quetzaltenango basin and defeated them in open warfare. Legend has it that Alvarado himself slew the great K'iche' warrior **Tecún Umán** in hand-to-hand combat. The defeated K'iche' took the Spanish to their capital, Utatlán, hoping to negotiate some kind of deal. Alvarado, however, was not to be seduced by such subtlety and promptly burnt the city along with many of its inhabitants. The next move was made by the **Kaqchikel**, who formed an alliance with the Spanish, hoping to exploit the newcomers' military might to overcome former rivals. As a result the Spanish made their first permanent base at the site of the Kaqchikel capital **Iximché**. But in 1527 the Kaqchikel, provoked by demands for tribute, rose up against the Spanish and fled to the mountains, from where they waged a campaign of guerrilla war against their former allies. The Spanish then moved their capital into the Almolonga valley, to a site near the modern town of Antigua, from where they gradually brought the rest of the highlands under a degree of control.

However, the damage done by Spanish swords was nothing when compared with that of the **diseases** they introduced. Waves of smallpox, typhus, plague and measles swept through the indigenous population, reducing their numbers by as much as ninety percent in the worst hit areas. The population was so badly devastated that it only started to recover at the end of the seventeenth century, and didn't get back to pre-conquest levels until the middle of the twentieth century.

In the long term the **Spanish administration** of the western highlands was no gentler than the Conquest, as indigenous labour became the backbone of the Spanish empire. Guatemala offered little of the gold and silver that was available in Peru or Mexico, but there was still money to be made from **cacao** and **indigo**. Maya labourers were forced to travel to the Pacific coast to work the plantations, while priests moved them from their scattered homes into new villages and attempted to transform them into devout Catholics. At the heart of all this was the colonial capital of **Antigua**, then known as Santiago de los Caballeros, from where the whole of Central America and Chiapas (now part of Mexico) was administered. In 1773 the city was destroyed by a massive earthquake, and the capital was subsequently moved to its modern site.

Independent highlands

By the time the Spanish left Guatemala, in 1821, three centuries of colonial rule had left a permanent imprint on the western highlands, and the entire social structure had been radically transformed. The Spanish had attempted to remove the power of large regional centres, replacing it with that of the Church, but a lack of clergy, particularly in the seventeenth and eighteenth centuries, had enabled the villages to establish their own authority and allowed traditional religion to continue. As a result of this the Maya population had developed strong village-based allegiances: these, along with the often bizarre hybrid of Catholicism and indigenous beliefs, are still at the heart of highland life.

At the village level, **independence** brought little change. Ladino authority replaced that of the Spanish, but the indigenous people were still required to work the coastal plantations and when labour supplies dropped off they were simply press-ganged (or more subtly lured into debt) and forced to work, often in horrific conditions. It's a state of affairs that has changed little even today, and remains a major burden on the Maya population.

In the last few decades fresh pressures have emerged as the Maya have been caught up in waves of political violence. In the late 1970s **guerrilla movements** began to develop in opposition to military rule, seeking support from the indigenous population and establishing themselves in the western highlands, particularly the departments of El Quiché, Huehuetenango, Sololá and Totonicapán. The Maya became the victims in this process, as they were caught between the guerrillas and the army. A total of 440 villages were destroyed; arond 180,000 died and thousands more fled the country, seeking refuge in Mexico. Indigenous society has also been besieged in recent years by a holy tidal wave of American **evangelical churches** (see p.454), whose influence undermines local hierarchies, dividing communities and threatening Maya culture.

With the signing of the 1996 **peace accords** between the guerrillas and the government, however, political tensions have lifted and there is evidence of a new self-confidence within the highland Maya population. Though most people remain desperately poor, a reawakened sense of pride in Maya identity seems to be coming to the fore, and is particularly evident in the work and writings of Rigoberta Menchú (see p.469) and Gaspar Pedro Gonzáles. With the guerrilla groups now disbanded and the army back in their barracks, the threats, intimidation and deaths that the native population suffered during the war years have largely ceased.

Due to a nationwide lack of confidence in the corrupt and ineffective **legal system**, however, and with the population no longer fearful of repercussions, the rule of law has begun to be threatened. Whole communities have taken justice into their own hands to resolve simmering local disputes, suspected thieves and criminals are reguarly lynched, land-hungry peasants have squatted finca farmland. Angry mobs rioted in August 2001, torching municipal buildings in a protest again tax increases. Travellers in the region are unlikely to be affected by these incidents; indeed, the more remote highland areas are some of the safest parts of the country, as tightly controlled communual life regulates behaviour and outsiders are easily spotted.

Even in a climate of institutionalized racism and bitter poverty **Maya society** remains largely intact, though the allure of "El Norte" (the USA) is increasingly enticing more and more jobless young men away from the highlands.

Market days

Throughout the western highlands **weekly markets** are the main focus of economic and social activity, drawing people from the area around the town or village where they're held. Make an effort to catch as many market days as possible – they're second only to local fiestas in offering a glimpse of a way of life unchanged for centuries.

Monday
Chimaltenango; San Juan Atitán; Santa Bárbara; Zunil.

Tuesday
Chajul; Comalapa; Olintepeque; Patzún; Salcajá; San Andrés Semetabaj; San Antonio Ilotenango; San Lucas Tolimán; San Marcos; San Pedro Jocopilas; Totonicapán; Yepocapa.

Wednesday
Almolonga; Chimaltenango; Colotenango; Cotzal; Huehuetenango; Momostenango; Palestina de Los Altos; Patzicía; Sacapulas; San Sebastián.

Thursday
Aguacatán; Chichicastenango; Chimaltenango; Jacaltenango; La Libertad; Nebaj; Panajachel; Patulul; Patzite; Patzún; Sacapulas; San Juan Atitán; San Luis Jilotepeque; San Mateo Ixtatán; San Miguel Ixtahuacán; San Pedro Necta; San Pedro Pinula; San Rafael La Independencia; Santa Bárbara; Santa Cruz del Quiché; Soloma; Tajumulco; Tecpán; Totonicapán; Uspantán; Zacualpa.

Friday
Chajul; Chimaltenango; San Andrés Itzapa; San Francisco el Alto; San Lucas Tolimán; Santiago Atitlán; Sololá; Tacaná.

Saturday
Almolonga; Colotenango; Cotzal; Ixchiguan; Malacatán; Nentón; Palestina de los Altos; Patzicía; Santa Clara La Laguna; Santa Cruz del Quiché; Todos Santos Cuchumatán; Totonicapán; Yepocapa.

Sunday
Aguacatán; Cantel; Chichicastenango; Chimaltenango; Cuilco; Huehuetenango; Jacaltenango; Joyabaj; La Libertad; Malacatancito; Momostenango; Nahualá; Nebaj; Nentón; Ostuncalco; Panajachel; Patzite; Patzún; Sacapulas; San Bartolo; San Carlos Sija; San Cristóbal Totonicapán; San Juan Comalapa; San Luis Jilotepeque; San Martín Jilotepeque; San Mateo Ixtatán; San Miguel Acatán; San Miguel Ixtahuacán; San Pedro Necta; Santa Bárbara; Santa Cruz del Quiché; Santa Eulalia; Sibilia; Soloma; Tacaná; Tecpán; Tejar; Uspantán; Yepocapa; Zacualpa.

Despite this phenomenon, many traditional structures are still in place, local languages still spoken, native costume still worn, and certain isolated villages still use the 260-day Tzolkin Maya calendar. It is this unique culture, above all else, that is Guatemala's most fascinating feature. Maya society is inward-looking and conservative, operating, in the face of adversity, on its own terms. Rejecting ladino commercialism, the Maya see trade as a social function as much as an economic one, with life centring on the village and its own civil and religious hierarchy, and subsistence farming of maize and beans remaining at the heart of Maya existence.

Visiting Maya **villages** during the week, you may find them almost deserted – their permanent populations are generally small, though they may support five or ten times as many scattered rural homesteads. It's on **market** and **fiesta** days however, when the villages fill to bursting, and you can most clearly sense the values of the Maya world – in the subdued bustle and gossip of the market or the intense joy of celebration.

Where to go

Travelling in the western highlands you're spoilt for choice, with beautiful verdant scenery yielding up atmospheric highland **villages** of adobe houses and whitewashed colonial churches at every turn. In addition to the colourful market towns and spectacular mountainscapes for which the region is famed, there are a few **historical sites**, such as the pre-conquest cities of Iximché, Utatlán and Zaculeu, which, although they don't bear comparison to Tikal and the lowland sites, are nevertheless fascinating in their own way.

Travelling west from Guatemala City, the Carretera Interamericana (Pan-American highway) sweeps through a densely populated region around the scruffy town of Chimaltenango before climbing steadily into the highlands. Just north of the highway in the department **El Quiché** is the renowned market town of **Chichicastenango** and the ruins of **Utatlán**, near the departmental capital of **Santa Cruz del Quiché**. To the south of Quiché, **Lake Atitlán** is the jewel of the western highlands, ringed by volcanoes and some of the country's most traditional villages, and reached via the colourful town of **Sololá**, and **Panajachel**, a booming lakeside resort. To the north are the wildly beautiful peaks of the **Cuchumatanes**, between which nestle the towns of the **Ixil triangle**, remote and intensely traditional communities at the end of a tortuous bus journey. Heading on to the west you pass the strongly traditional town of **Nahualá** and go up over the mountains to Guatemala's second city, **Quetzaltenango** (Xela), an ideal base for visiting local villages or climbing the near-perfect volcanic cone of **Santa María**. Beyond this, the border with Mexico is marked by the departments of **San Marcos** and **Huehuetenango**, both of which offer superb mountain scenery, dotted with isolated villages, the pick of which is the traditional **Todos Santos Cuchumatán**.

There's a constant flow of **buses** along the Carretera Interamericana, some branching off onto minor roads to more remote areas. Travelling on these roads can sometimes be a gruelling experience, particularly in northern Huehuetenango and El Quiché, but the scenery makes it well worth the discomfort. The most practical plan of action is to base yourself in one of the larger places and then make a series of day-trips to markets and fiestas, although even the smallest of villages will usually offer some kind of accommodation.

Into the highlands: the Carretera Interamericana

The serpentine **Carretera Interamericana** forms the main artery of transport in the highlands, and the highway and its junctions will inevitably become very familiar. Often it's easiest to catch the first local bus to the Carretera Interamericana then flag down one of the buses heading along the highway, though there are also some direct bus services, and a few tourist shuttle buses, between the main centres.

There are three major junctions on the highway which you'll soon get to know. The first of these is **Chimaltenango**, an important town and capital of its own department, from where you can also make connections to or from Antigua. Continuing west, **Los Encuentros** is the next main junction, where one road heads off to the north for Chichicastenango and Santa Cruz del Quiché and another branches south to Panajachel and Lake Atitlán. Beyond this the highway climbs high over a mountainous ridge before dropping to **Cuatro Caminos** (p.195), from where side roads lead to Quetzaltenango, Totonicapán and San Francisco el Alto. The Carretera Interamericana continues on to Huehuetenango before it reaches the Mexican border at La Mesilla. Virtually every bus travelling along the highway will stop at all of these junctions and you'll be able to buy fruit, drink and fast food from an army of vendors, some of whom will storm the bus looking for business, others being content to dangle their wares at your window from the street.

Chimaltenango and around

CHIMALTENANGO was founded by Pedro de Portocarrero in 1526, on the site of the Kaqchikel centre of Bokoh, and was later considered as a possible site for the new capital. It has the misfortune, however, of being positioned on a continental divide; it suffered terribly from the earthquake in 1976, which shook and flattened much of the surrounding area. Today's town, its centre just to the north of the main road, is dominated by that fact, and like so much of the region its appearance testifies to rapid and unfinished reconstruction, with dirt streets, breeze block walls and an air of weary desperation. But it remains busy, a regional centre of transport and trade whose prosperity is boosted by the proximity of the capital.

The town's **plaza** is an odd mix of architectural styles, with a police station that looks like a medieval castle, a church that combines the Gothic and the Neoclassical, and a superb colonial fountain positioned exactly on the continental divide – half the water drains to the Caribbean, the other half to the Pacific. "Chimal's" second focal point is the Carretera Interamericana itself, which cuts through the southern side of the town, dominating it with an endless flow of trucks and buses. The town extracts what little business it can from this stream of traffic, and the roadside is crowded with cheap comedores, mechanics' workshops, and sleazy bars that become brothels by night.

The **post office** (Mon–Fri 8am–4.30pm), Banco de Occidente (Mon–Fri 8.30am–7pm, Sat 8.30am–1pm) and Telgua (7am–midnight) are all on the plaza, and if you want **to stay** here the *Hotel La Predilecta*, a block to the south on 9 C (**2**), has pleasant, simple rooms and safe parking. The best place **to eat** is at *La Casa de las Legendas* at Km 56 on the Carretera Interamericana itself, where you can choose from an excellent selection of grilled meats and Guatemalan specialities. Chimal has a suprisingly decent community **website**

(@ www.chimaltenango.com), with plenty of information in Spanish about the central highlands and the town itself.

Buses passing through Chimaltenango run to all points along the Pan-American Highway: for Antigua they leave every twenty minutes between 5.30am and 7pm from the market in town – though you can also wait at the turn-off on the highway. To get here from Guatemala City, take any bus heading to the western highlands from the Zona 4 bus terminal.

San Martín Jilotepeque

To the north of Chimaltenango a rough dirt road runs through 19km of plunging ravines and pine forests to the village of **SAN MARTÍN JILOTE-PEQUE**. San Martín had to be rebuilt following the 1976 disaster, but the sprawling Sunday market is well worth a visit and the weaving here, the women's *huipiles* especially, is some of the finest you'll see – with intricate and ornate patterning, predominantly in reds and purples.

Buses to San Martín leave the market in Chimaltenango hourly from 4am to 4pm for the forty-minute trip and the last one returns at about 4pm, though there's a good clean **hospedaje** (②) just north of the market if you get stuck here. To the north of San Martín the road continues to **Joyabaj** (see p.144). Only three daily buses cover this route from the capital, though it's usually possible to catch a ride in a pick-up at other times.

San Juan Comalapa, Patzicía and Patzún

Heading west from Chimaltenango, a series of turnings lead off the Carretera Interamericana to interesting but seldom-visited villages. The first of these, 16km to the north of the road, on the far side of a deep-cut ravine, is **SAN JUAN COMALAPA**. The village was founded by the Spanish, who brought together the populations of several Kaqchikel centres. A collection of eroded pre-Columbian sculptures is displayed in the plaza, where you'll also find a small monument to Rafael Alvarez Ovalle, a local man who composed the Guatemalan national anthem, below the fine, recently restored Baroque church that dates from colonial times.

In the last few decades the villagers of Comalapa have developed something of a reputation as **folk artists**, and there are several galleries in the streets around the plaza where their work is exhibited and sold. The whole thing started with Andrés Curuchich (1891–1969), who painted simple scenes documenting village life, such as fiestas, funerals and marriages, with a clarity that soon attracted the attention of outsiders. Throughout the 1950s he became increasingly popular, exhibiting in Guatemala City, and later as far afield as Los Angeles and New York, and was awarded Guatemala's highest civilian honour, the Order of the Quetzal. Inspired by his example and the chance of boosting their income, forty to fifty painters are now working here, including two or three women – although success is considerably more difficult for them as painting is generally perceived as a man's task. There is a permanent exhibition devoted to the paintings of Andrés Curuchich at the Museo Ixchel in Guatemala City (see p.77). Comalapan **weaving** is also of the highest standards, using styles and colours characteristic of the Chimaltenango area. Traditionally the weavers work in silk and an untreated natural brown cotton called *cuyuxcate*, although these days they increasingly use ordinary cotton and synthetic fibres.

As ever, the best time to visit is for the **market**, on Sunday, which brings people out in force. **Buses** to Comalapa run hourly from Chimaltenango (1hr) and the service is always better on a market day. There's nowhere to stay in the village and the last bus back leaves at 4pm.

Patzicía and Patzún: a route to the lake

Further to the west another branch road runs down towards Lake Atitlán, connecting the Carretera Interamericana with several small villages. At the junction with the main road is **PATZICÍA**, a ramshackle urban sprawl of breeze blocks and concrete. Despite its bedraggled appearance the village has a history of independent defiance, and in 1944 it was the scene of a Maya uprising that left some three hundred dead. Villagers were led to believe that Maya people throughout Guatemala had risen up against their ladino rulers, and charged through the village killing any they could set hands on. Armed ladinos, arriving from the capital, managed to put down the uprising, killing the majority of the rebels. Ironically enough, over a hundred years earlier, in 1871, the Declaration of Patzicía was signed here, setting out the objectives of the liberal revolution.

PATZÚN, 11km from the main highway heading towards Lake Atitlán, suffered terrible losses in the 1976 earthquake. A monument in the plaza remembers the 172 who died, and a new church stands beside the shell of the old one, somehow making an even more poignant memorial. Traditional costume is still worn here and the colourful Sunday market is well worth a visit. Outside the twin churches the plaza fills with traders, with the majority of the women dressed in the brilliant reds of the local costume.

Beyond Patzún it's possible to continue all the way to the small village of Godínez, high above the northern shore of Lake Atitlán, and from there along the road to Panajachel and San Lucas Tolimán. Four daily buses, plus some tourist shuttles, make this trip, but the road is fairly rough, plunging down the side of a thickly forested ravine. If you're driving you should also bear in mind that it has been the scene of a number of armed robberies and attacks, though incidents have decreased in recent years. **Buses** to Patzún leave the Zona 4 terminal in Guatemala City every hour or so, and you can pick them up in Chimaltenango or at the turning for Patzicía.

Tecpán and Iximché

The small town of **TECPÁN** lies just a few hundred metres south of the Carretera Interamericana, ninety minutes or so from Guatemala City. This may well have been the site chosen by Alvarado as the first Spanish capital, to which the Spanish forces retreated in August 1524, after they'd been driven out of Iximché. Today it's a modest place of little interest, though it has a substantial number of restaurants and guest houses that cater for a mainly Guatemalan clientele; travellers, however, are unlikely to do more than pass through on the way to the ruins. Tecpán again suffered severely in the 1976 earthquake, and in the centre a new church stands alongside the cracked remains of the old one.

The ruins of **Iximché**, the pre-conquest capital of the Kaqchikel, are about 5km south, on a beautiful exposed hillside site, isolated on three sides by plunging ravines and surrounded by pine forests. From the early days of the Conquest the Kaqchikel allied themselves with the conquistadors, so the structures here suffered less than most at the hands of the Spanish. Since then, however, time and weather have taken their toll and the majority of the buildings, originally built of adobe, have disappeared, leaving only a few stone-built pyramids, clearly defined plazas and a couple of ball courts. Nevertheless the site, which housed a population of around ten thousand, is strongly atmospheric, and its grassy plazas are marvellously peaceful, especially during the week, when you may well have the place to yourself.

The Kaqchikel Maya were originally based further west, around the modern town of Chichicastenango, and the Kaqchikel language is still spoken through-out the central highlands and along the eastern side of Lake Atitlán. But when their villages came under the control of the K'iche', the Kaqchikel were the first to break away, moving their capital to Iximché in order to establish their independence. They founded the new city in about 1470 and from that time on were almost continuously at war with other tribes. Despite this, they man-aged to devote a lot of energy to the building and rebuilding of their new cap-ital, and trenches dug into some of the structures have revealed as many as three superimposed layers. War may, in fact, have helped the process, as most of the labour was done by slaves captured in battle. When the Spanish arrived, the Kaqchikel were quick to join forces with Alvarado in order to defeat their old enemies, the K'iche'. Grateful for the assistance, the Spanish established their first headquarters near here on May 7, 1524, – probably where Tecpán stands today. The Kaqchikel referred to Alvarado as *Tonatiuh*, the son of the sun, and as a mark of respect he was given the daughter of a Kaqchikel king as a gift.

On July 25, 1524, the Spanish renamed the new settlement **Villa de Santiago**, declaring it their new capital. But within months the Kaqchikel had risen in rebellion, outraged by Alvarado's demands for tribute. Alvarado retali-ated by burning Iximché, and forcing the Kaqchikel to flee into the mountains from where they waged a guerrilla war against the Spanish until 1530. The Spanish capital was moved from Tecpán to the greater safety of Ciudad Vieja, a short distance from Antigua (see p.113). For 450 years the ruins slumbered peacefully until the predominantly Maya organization the CUC (Peasant Unity Committee) met here in February 1980 and issued the **Declaration of Iximché**. Provoked by the massacre of their leaders during a peaceful occupa-tion of the Spanish embassy in Guatemala City, the declaration identified this atrocity as the latest episode in more than four centuries of state-sponsored genocide against the Maya race. The storming of the embassy led to the out-raged Spanish government breaking off diplomatic relations with Guatemala for five years.

The site

The **ruins of Iximché** (daily 8am–5pm; US$3.40) are made up of four main plazas, a couple of ball courts and several small pyramids. In most cases only the foundations and lower parts of the original structures were built of stone, while the upper walls were of adobe, with thatched roofs supported by wooden beams. You can make out the ground plan of many of the buildings, but it's only the most important all-stone structures that still stand. The most significant buildings were those clustered around courts A and C, which were probably the scene of the most revered rituals. On the sides of **Temple 2** you can make out some badly eroded murals, the style of which is very similar to that used in the codices.

It's thought that the site itself, like most of the highland centres, was a ceremo-nial city used for religious rituals, and, indeed, Maya worship still takes place here down a small trail through the pine trees behind the final plaza. The site was thought to have been inhabited only by the elite, with the rest of the population living in the surrounding hills and coming to Iximché only to attend festivals and to defend the fortified site in times of attack. Archeological digs here have unearthed a number of interesting finds, including the decapitated heads of sac-rifice victims, burial sites, grinding stones, obsidian knives, a flute made from a child's femur, and large numbers of incense burners. There was surprisingly little sculpture, but most of it was similar to that found in the ruins of Zaculeu and Mixco Viejo, both of which were occupied at around the same time.

Getting to Iximché

To get to Iximché, take any bus travelling along the Carretera Interamericana between Chimaltenango and Los Encuentros, and ask to be dropped at Tecpán, from where you can walk to the site. From Guatemala City any of the buses going to Sololá, Quiché, Totonicapán or Xela will do: they leave the Zona 4 terminal about every fifteen minutes, and pass through Chimaltenango. If you're coming from Los Encuentros take any bus heading for Guatemala City.

To get to the ruins simply walk through Tecpán and out the other side of the plaza, passing the Centro de Salud, and follow the road through the fields for about 5km, an hour or so on foot. With any luck you'll be able to hitch some of the way, particularly at weekends when the road can be fairly busy. You can **camp** at the site, but bring your own food, as the small shop sells little apart from drinks – Iximché's shady location is perfect for a picnic or barbeque. If you're not planning to camp, be back on the Carretera Interamericana before 6pm to be sure of a bus onwards.

El Quiché

At the heart of the western highlands, sandwiched between the Verapaces and Huehuetenango, is the department of **El Quiché**. Like its neighbours, El Quiché encompasses the full range of Guatemalan scenery. In the south, only a short distance from Lake Atitlán, is a section of the sweeping central valley, a fertile and heavily populated area that forms the upper reaches of the Motagua valley. To the north the landscape becomes increasingly dramatic, rising first to the **Sierra de Chuacús**, and then to the massive, rain-soaked peaks of the **Cuchumatanes**, beyond which the land drops away into the inaccessible rain-forests of the **Ixcán**.

The department takes its name from the greatest of the pre-conquest tribal groups, the **K'iche'**, for whom it was the hub of an empire. From their capital **Utatlán**, which stood just west of the modern town of Santa Cruz del Quiché, they overran much of the highlands and were able to demand tribute from most of the other tribes. Although by the time the Spanish arrived their empire was in decline, they were still the dominant force in the region and challenged the conquistadors as soon as they entered the highlands, at a site near Quetzaltenango. They were easily defeated though, and the Spanish were able to negotiate alliances with former K'iche' subjects, playing one tribe off against another, and eventually overcoming them all. Today these highlands remain a stronghold of Maya culture and the department of El Quiché, scattered with small villages and mountain towns, is the scene of some superb fiestas and markets.

For the Spanish, however, this remote mountainous terrain, with little to offer in the way of plunder, remained an unimportant backwater: only in later years, when large-scale commercial farming began on the Pacific coast, did it grow in importance as a source of cheap labour. This role has had a profound impact on the area for the last two hundred years and has forced the population to suffer horrific abuses. Perhaps not surprisingly the region became a noted centre of guerrilla activity in the late 1970s, and subsequently the scene of unrivalled repression. The Catholic Church suffered terribly in El Quiché in the late 1970s and early 1980s, when priests, who were often connected with the co-operative movement, were singled out and murdered. The situation was so serious that Bishop Juan Geradi withdrew all his priests from the department in 1981. They have since returned to their posts, but the bishop himself was later assassinated in April 1998.

For the traveller El Quiché has a lot to offer, in both the accessible south and the wilder north. **Chichicastenango**, one of the country's most popular destinations, is the scene of a vast twice-weekly market but remains a pivotal centre of Maya religion. Beyond this, at the heart of the central valley, is the departmental capital of **Santa Cruz del Quiché**, stopping-off point for trips to a string of smaller towns and to the ruins of **Utatlán**. Further to the north the paved road ends and the mountains really begin. Travelling here can be hard work but the extraordinary scale of the scenery makes it all well worthwhile. Isolated villages are set in superb highland scenery, sustaining a wealth of indigenous culture and occupying a misty, mysterious world of their own. Passing over the Sierra de Chuacús, and down to the Río Negro, you reach **Sacapulas** at the base of the **Cuchumatanes**. From here you can travel across the foothills to Cobán in the east or Huehuetenango to the west, or for real adventure up into the mountains to the three towns of the **Ixil triangle** – **Nebaj**, **Chajul** and **Cotzal**.

The road for Chichicastenango and the department of El Quiché leaves the Carretera Interamericana at Km127.3, the **Los Encuentros** junction. From here it descends the southern volcanic ridge and runs into the central valley, a land suspended between the volcanoes and the mountains.

Chichicastenango

Heading north from Los Encuentros, the road drops down through dense, aromatic pine forests, into a deep ravine housing a tributary of the river Motagua. Just beyond the bridge over the river, a sign marks the spot where Jorge Carpio, newspaper owner and cousin of the president, was shot and killed on July 3, 1993. The assassination was seen as a warning to President Ramiro de León Carpio (see p.433) not to challenge the established power structure dominated by the army, landowners and big business. Carpio, a former human rights ombudsman, did little to upset the status quo for the rest of his presidential term.

The road begins a tortuous ascent from the valley floor around endless switchbacks until it reaches **CHICHICASTENANGO**, 17km from the Los Encuentros junction. Known as Guatemala's "Mecca del Turismo", this compact and traditional town of cobbled streets, adobe houses and red-tiled roofs has its day-to-day calm shattered twice a week by the **Sunday** and **Thursday markets** – Sunday is the busiest. As the town is conveniently placed a short hop from the highway, the market attracts a myriad of tourists and commercial traders on day-trips out of Antigua, Panajachel and Guatemala City, as well as Maya weavers from throughout the central highlands. For many years the market and town managed to coexist happily, but recently the invasion of outsiders has begun to dominate and now threatens to undermine Chichicastenago's unique identity – you may find yourself embroiled in one of the country's very few traffic jams outside the capital, as traders, tourists and locals all struggle to reach the town centre.

CHICHICASTENANGO

N

Buses to Santa Cruz
★ Buses to Interamericana
& Guatemala City

Banco
Industrial

Centro
Comercial

El Calvario   Plaza

Museo Rossbach   Santo Tomás
Former Monastery

0   200 m

ACCOMMODATION
Colonial El Centro	7
Hospedaje El Salvador	8
Hospedaje Girón	3
Hotel Chalet House	2
Hotel Chugüilá	4
Hotel Posada Belen	9
Hotel Santo Tomás	5
Maya Inn	6
Posada El Arco	1

RESTAURANTS AND CAFÉS
Buenadventura	C
Casa San Juan	E
Comedor Gumarcaj	B
La Fonda del Tzijolaj	D
La Villa de Los Cofrades	A

Mask
Shop

Pascual Abaj

▼ Los Encuentros & Guatemala City

The market is by no means all that sets Chichicastenango apart, however, and for the local Maya population it's an important centre of culture and religion. Long before the arrival of the Spanish this area was inhabited by the Kaqchikel, whose settlements of Patzak and Chavier were under threat from the all-powerful K'iche'. In a bid to assert their independence, the Kaqchikel abandoned the villages in 1470 and moved south to Iximché (see p.132), from where they mounted repeated campaigns against their former masters. Chichicastenango itself was founded by the Spanish in order to house K'iche' refugees from Utatlán to the north, which they conquered and destroyed in 1524. The town's name is a Nahuatl word meaning "the place of the nettles", accorded it by Alvarado's Mexican allies.

Over the years Maya culture and folk Catholicism have been treated with a rare degree of respect in Chichicastenango, although inevitably this blessing has been mixed with waves of arbitrary persecution and exploitation. Today the town has an incredible collection of Maya artefacts, parallel indigenous and ladino governments, and two churches that make no effort to disguise their acceptance of unconventional pagan worship. Traditional weaving is also adhered to in Chichicastenango and the women wear superb *huipiles*, heavily embroidered with flower motifs. The men's costume of short trousers and jackets of black wool embroidered with silk is highly distinguished, although it's very expensive to make and these days most men opt for western dress. However, for Sundays and fiestas a handful of *cofradres* (elders of the religious hierarchy) still wear the traditional clothing and parade through the streets bearing spectacular silver processional crosses and antique incense burners.

Chichicastenango's appetite for religious fervour is especially evident during the **fiesta** of Santo Tomás, from December 14 to 21. While it's not the most spontaneous of fiestas it's certainly spectacular, with attractions including the *Palo Volador* (in which men dangle by ropes from a twenty-metre pole; see p.144), a live band or two, a massive procession, traditional dances, clouds of incense, gallons of *chicha*, and endless deafening fireworks. On the final day, all babies born in the previous year are brought to the church for christening. Easter, too, is celebrated here with tremendous energy and seriousness.

Arrival and information

There's no bus station in Chichi, as it's known, so the corner of 5 C and 5 Av operates loosely as a terminal. **Buses** heading between Guatemala City and Santa Cruz del Quiché pass through here every twenty minutes or so, stopping for a few minutes to load up passengers. In Guatemala City buses leave from the terminal in Zona 4, from 4am to about 5pm. Coming from Antigua, you can easily connect with these buses in Chimaltenango, while on market days several **shuttle services** run the whole route. From Panajachel you can take any bus up to Los Encuentros and change there, or, on market days there are several direct buses, supplemented by a steady flow of tourist shuttles.

There's a small Inguat **tourist information** office (daily 8am–noon & 2-6pm; ☎756 1015) beside Santo Tomás church on 8 Calle; they usually have a good stock of leaflets about the department. If you're bitten by market fever and need to **change money**, there's no problem in Chichi, even on a Sunday. Try Banco Ejército on 6 Calle (Tues–Sun 9am–5pm) or, for Visa card holders, almost opposite, Banco Industrial (Mon 10am–2pm, Wed–Sun 10am–5pm). *Hotel Santo Tomás* also offers exchange. The **post office** (Mon–Fri 9am–5.30pm) is behind the church on 7 Avenida, and **Telgua** (Mon–Fri 8am–6pm, Sat 9am–1pm) is on 6 Avenida. Try Acses at 6 C 4–52 for **internet** connections, where rates are set at US$4 per hour.

Accommodation

Accommodation can be in short supply on Saturday nights in Chichicastenango, before the Sunday market, but you shouldn't have a problem on other days. Hotel prices can also be inflated on market days, though at other times you can usually negotiate a good deal.

Colonial El Centro 8 C and 6 Av ☎756 1249. Friendly, family-owned guest house, very close to the plaza, with clean inexpensive rooms, some with private bath. ❷

Hospedaje Girón 6 C 4–52 ☎756 1156, ℱ756 1226. Pretty, well-priced pine-trimmed rooms, with or without private bath, plus parking. Good value for single travellers. ❸/❹

Hospedaje El Salvador 5 Av 10–09 ☎756 1329. Decent budget hotel, with a vast warren of bare but cleanish rooms, a bizarre external colour scheme, and cheap prices. Insist that the owners turn on the hot water. ❷

Hotel Chalet House 3C C 7–44 ☎756 1360, ✉multiple@concyt.gob.gt. Excellent new hotel in a quiet street on the north side of town. The ten rooms are all very clean and have nice touches like highland wool blankets and textiles, plus com-

fortable beds and private bathrooms. There's also a tiny dining room where you can get breakfast, and a rooftop terrace. ❹

Hotel Chugüilá 5 Av 5–24 ☎756 1134, ℱ756 1279. Attractive, if rather old-fashioned, rooms, all on different levels and some with fireplaces. Lovely greenery and pot plants everywhere. Secure parking. ❺

Hotel Posada Belen 12 C 5–55 ☎ & ℱ756 1244. Not the most attractive rooms, though half have private bath and many have good views. Cable TV available for a little extra. ❷/❸

Hotel Santo Tomás 7 Av 5–32 ☎756 1061, ℱ756 1306. Very comfortable, well-appointed rooms set around two colonial-style courtyards. Rooms 29–37 are the ones to book if you can – they have great mountain views. Restaurant, swimming pool, sauna and Jacuzzi. ❼

137

Maya Inn 8 C and 3 Av ☎756 1176, ℱ756 1212.
Chichi's oldest tourist hotel offers very comfortable
rooms with old-fashioned period furnishings and
fireplaces. Though its character is undeniable,
prices are a bit steep, and you pity the staff
decked out in mock-traditional dress. ⑧
Posada El Arco 4 C 4–36 ☎756 1255. Superb

new guest house, run by friendly English-speaking
brothers. Seven huge, attractive rooms with good
wooden beds, reading lights and attractive decor,
including local Maya fabrics. Rooms 6 and 7 have
access to a pleasant terrace. Beautiful garden,
with grassy lawn and avocado trees, and stunning
countryside views. ④

The Town

Though most visitors come here to see the market, Chichicastenango also
offers an unusual insight into traditional religious practices in the highlands. At
the main **Santo Tomás Church**, in the southeast corner of the plaza, the local
K'iche' Maya (called *Maxeños*) have been left to adopt their own style of worship, blending pre-Columbian and Catholic rituals. The church was built in
1540 on the site of a Maya altar, and rebuilt in the eighteenth century. It's said
that indigenous locals became interested in worshipping here after Francisco
Ximénez, the priest from 1701 to 1703, started reading their holy book, the
Popul Vuh (see below). Seeing that he held considerable respect for their religion, they moved their altars from the hills and set them up inside the church.
Today, this ancient, unique hybrid of Maya and Catholic worship still takes
place in the church.

Before entering the building it's customary to make offerings in a fire at the
base of the steps or burn incense in perforated cans, a practice that leaves a
cloud of thin, sweet smoke hanging over the steps. Inside is an astonishing
scene of avid worship. A soft hum of constant murmuring fills the air, as the
faithful kneel to place candles on low-level stone platforms for their ancestors
and the saints. For these people the entire building is alive with the souls of the
dead, each located in a specific part of the church. The place of the "first
people", the ancient ancestors, is beneath the altar railing; former officials are

Chichicastenango's market

There's been a **market** at Chichicastenango for hundreds, if not thousands, of years,
and despite the twice-weekly invasions the local people continue to trade their
wares alongside the tourist-geared stalls. On market days Chichicastenango's
streets are lined with stalls and packed with buyers, and the choice is overwhelming, ranging from superb quality Ixil *huipiles* to wooden dance masks, and including
pottery, gourds, machetes, belts and a gaudy selection of recently invented "traditional" fabrics. You can still pick up some authentic and beautiful weaving, but you
need to be prepared to wade through a lot of trash and to haggle hard – easier said
than done, but your chances are better before 10am when the tourist buses arrive
from the capital, or in the late afternoon once things have started to quieten down.
The best of the stuff from the local villages is generally held in the centre of the plaza
and is far more interesting than the bulk of the stalls. Prices are pretty competetive
here, but for a real bargain you need to head further into the highlands, while
Panajachel is a better bet for *típica* clothes.

For a brilliant vantage point for a typical Maya market, however, head for the
indoor balcony on the upper floor of the **Centro Comercial** building on the north side
of the plaza. You'll be able to gawp down on the villagers below as they haggle and
chat over bunches of spring onions and pick out costumes from all over the highlands. At this vegetable market, you'll see *huipiles* from the Atitlán villages of San
Antonio and Santa Catarina Palopó and from even as far away as Chajul; the funky
"space cowboy" shirts and pants are worn by men from the neighbouring Sololá area.

around the middle of the aisle; ordinary folk to the west in the nave; and deceased native priests beside the door. Alongside these, and equally important, are the Catholic saints, who receive the same respect and are continuously appealed to with offerings of candles and alcohol. Last, but by no means least, certain areas within the church, and particular patterns of candles, rose petals and *chicha*, are used to invoke specific types of blessings, such as those for children, travel, marriage, harvest or illness. Don't enter the building by the front door, which is reserved for *cofrades* and senior church officials, but through the **side door**. It's deeply offensive to take **photographs** inside the building – don't even contemplate it.

Beside the church is a former monastery, now used by the parish administration. It was here that the Spanish priest Francisco Ximénez became the first outsider to be shown the **Popol Vuh**, the holy book of the K'iche'. His copy of the manuscript is now housed in the Newberry Library in Chicago: the original was lost some time later in the eighteenth century. The text itself was written in nearby Utatlán shortly after the arrival of the Spanish, and is a brilliant poem of over nine thousand lines that details the cosmology, mythology and traditional history of the K'iche'. Broadly speaking it's split into two parts; the first is an account of the creation of man and the world, culminating in an epic struggle beween the wizard twins Hunahpú and Xbalanqué and the Death Lords of the Maya underworld, with the twins ultimately triumphing and the cycle of creation being born. The second part describes the wanderings of ancestors of the K'iche' as they migrate south and settle in the highlands of Guatemala. The opening lines give an impression of the book's importance, and the extent to which it sets out to preserve a threatened cultural heritage:

This is the beginning of the Ancient World, here in this place called Quiché. Here we shall ascribe, we shall implant the ancient word, the potential and source of everything done in the citadel of Quiché.

And here we shall take up the demonstration, revelation, and account of how things were put in shadow and brought to light...We shall write about this amid the preaching of God, in Christendom now. We shall bring it out because there is no longer a place to see it, a Council book.

Translation by Dennis Tedlock

On the south side of the plaza, on market day often hidden by stalls, the newly renovated **Rossbach Museum** (Tues, Wed, Fri & Sat 8am–noon & 2–4pm, Thurs & Sun 8am–1pm & 2–4pm; US$0.15) houses a broad-ranging collection of pre-Columbian artefacts, mostly small pieces of ceramics (including some demonic-looking incense burners), jade jewellery and stone carvings, some as old as two thousand years. A second room, due to open in 2002, will be dedicated to local artesanías, including weavings, masks and carvings.

Facing Santo Tomás across on the west side of the plaza, the whitewashed **El Calvario** chapel is like a miniature version of Chichi's main church. Inside, the atmosphere is equally reverential as prayers are recited around the smoke-blackened wooden altar, and women offer flowers and stoop to kiss a supine image of Christ, entombed inside a glass cabinet, which is paraded through the street during Holy Week. The steps are also the scene of incense-burning rituals and the chapel is considered good for general confessions and pardons.

The cemetery and the shrine of Pascual Abaj

The town **cemetery**, down the hill behind El Calvario, offers further evidence of the strange mix of religions that characterizes Chichicastenango. The graves are marked by anything from a grand tomb to a small earth mound, and in the centre is a Maya shrine where the usual offerings of incense and alcohol are made. At the back, in a large yellow building, is entombed the body of Father Rossbach.

The churches and cemetery are certainly not the only scenes of Maya religious activity, however, and the hills that surround the town, like so many throughout the country, are topped with shrines. The closest of these, less than a kilometre from the plaza, is known as **Pascual Abaj**. The site is regularly visited by tourists, but it's important to remember that the ceremonies held here are deeply serious and you should still keep your distance and be sensitive about taking any **photographs**. The shrine is laid out in a typical pattern with several small altars facing a stern pre-Columbian sculpture. Offerings are usually overseen by a *brujo*, a type of shaman, and range from flowers to sacrificed chickens, always incorporating plenty of incense, alcohol and incantations. In 1957, during a bout of religious rivalry, the shrine was raided and smashed by reforming Catholics, but the traditionalists gathered the scattered remains and patched them together with cement and a steel-reinforcing rod.

To get to Pascual Abaj, walk down the hill beside the Santo Tomás church, take the first right, 9 Calle, and follow this as it winds its way out of town. You'll soon cross a stream and then a well-signposted route takes you through the courtyard of a workshop making wooden masks. If a ceremony is in progress you may be able to pick out Pascual Abaj by a thin plume of smoke. Continue to follow the path uphill for ten minutes through a dense pine forest to the shrine.

Eating

If you've come from Panajachel or Antigua, the dining scene here may seem rather dull. What is on offer is simple, good-value Guatemalan comedor nosh, which means lots of *pollo frito, carne asada* and *huevos y frijoles*. Even at the smarter restaurants, such as the *Hotel Santo Tomás* or the *Maya Inn*, the food is unlikely to excite real gastronauts. The plaza on **market day** is the place for some authentic highland food – try one of the makeshift comedores, which sell cauldrons of stew, rice and beans.

Buenadventura upper floor, inside the Centro Comercial. Bird's-eye view of the vegetable market; simple, no-nonsense food and the breakfasts are the cheapest in town.

Café-Restaurant La Villa de Los Cofrades 6 C and 5 Av, first floor. Good set meals – soup, a main dish and salad, fries and bread – for under US$4; superb breakfasts and real coffee.

Casa San Juan west side of plaza, beside the El Calvario chapel. Stylish bar-restaurant with a brightly painted interior and plenty of artwork, with good, imaginative Guatemelan cooking, including a US$2.50 set meal. Live music some nights.

Comedor Gumarcaj opposite the *Hotel Santo Tomás*. Simple, scruffy but cheap and friendly comedor that serves up a mean chicken and chips and lush licuados.

La Fonda del Tzijolaj upper floor in the Centro Comercial. Yes, the name's unpronounceable, but the food is probably the best in town and the balcony views of the church of Santo Tomás and the market are excellent. Try the delicious *chiles rellenos*.

Moving on from Chichicastenango

Direct buses head **to Guatemala City** every twenty minutes or so (3hr), the last one leaving at around 6pm, and seven buses daily head westwards to Quetzaltenango between 6am and 3pm (2hr 30min). **For Antigua**, catch a Guatemala City-bound bus and change at Chimaltenango, except on market days when you can get a direct shuttle, if funds permit. If you're **heading north**, it's often quickest to take the first bus to Santa Cruz del Quiché (every 20min; 30min), from where buses go to Nebaj.

Santa Cruz del Quiché and around

The capital of the department, **SANTA CRUZ DEL QUICHÉ**, lies half an hour north of Chichicastenango. A good paved road connects the two towns, running through pine forests and ravines, and past the **Laguna Lemoa**, a lake which, according to local legend, was originally filled with tears wept by the wives of K'iche' kings after their husbands had been slaughtered by the Spanish. Santa Cruz del Quiché itself is a pretty uneventful place where not a lot happens. It is, however, the transport hub for the department and the most direct route to the Ixil Triangle, as well as being the only practical place to base yourself for a visit to the nearby ruins of **Utatlán**.

The Town

Dominating the central **plaza** of Santa Cruz del Quiché is a large colonial church, built by the Dominicans with stone from the ruins of Utatlán. The clock tower beside it is also said to have been built from Utatlán stone, stripped from the temple of Tohil. In the middle of the plaza a defiant statue of the K'iche' hero Tecún Umán stands prepared for battle. His position is undermined somewhat by an ugly urban tangle of hardware stores, *panaderías* and trash that surrounds the plaza, as well as the spectacularly ugly, looming presence of the breeze block, tin-roofed **market** building. The market here takes place on the same days as in Chichicastenango – Thursday and Sunday – and sprawls over most of the area south and east of the plaza, spreading down to the bus station. Palm weaving is a local speciality, and Maya people can often be seen threading a band or two as they walk through town. Many of the palm hats on sale throughout the country were put together here, but if you want to buy you'll have to look hard and long to find one that fits a gringo head.

Practicalities

The **bus terminal**, a large open affair, is about four blocks south and a couple east of the central plaza. Connections are generally excellent from Quiché, with a stream of second-class **buses** to Guatemala City leaving every twenty minutes between 3.30am and 5pm (3hr 30min); all pass through Chichicastenango (30min) and Los Encuentros (1hr). Other points in the highlands are equally well served, with regular services to Nebaj between 8.30am and 4pm (every 1hr 30min; 3hr 30 min), hourly buses to Joyabaj from 6am to 4pm (2hr 30min), four daily buses to Uspantán between 9am and 2pm (5hr), and regular buses to Quetzaltenango leaving between 3am and 1pm (3hr). Two **banks** will change your travellers' cheques: Banco Industrial at the northwest corner of the plaza (Mon–Fri 8.30am–5.30pm, Sat 8.30am–12.30pm), which also advances cash on Visa, and Banco G&T Continental, 6 A 3–00 (Mon–Fri 9am–7pm, Sat 9am–1pm), where Mastercard holders can obtain cash. If you're heading into the Ixil triangle (see p.146), you may want to stock up on **film**: try Kodak or Fuji, both one block northeast of the central church.

Accommodation

There's a limited range of **hotels** in Quiché, none of them luxurious. The cheapest are very grim and right beside the bus terminal; most of the others are between the terminal and the plaza.

Hospedaje Tropical 1 Av and 9 C. Extremely basic place; no hot water but dirt cheap. ❶

Hotel Maya Quiché 3 Av 4–19, Zona 1 ☎755 1464. A friendly place with big clean rooms, some with bathroom. ❷/❸

Hotel Rey K'iche' 8 C 0–39, Zona 5 ☎ 755 0824. Two blocks north, one east from the terminal. Well-run, extremely clean and welcoming place with 26 rooms, most with cable TV and private bath, plus a good comedor. **②** / **③**
Hotel San Pascual 7 C 0–43, Zona 1 ☎ 755 1107. Walk up 1 Avenida, and turn left into 7 Calle.

Large, clean rooms and equally well-kept communal bathrooms. **②** – **③**
Posada Calle Real 2 Av 7–36, two blocks from the terminal. Good-value budget deal: rooms are smallish but clean and the bathrooms (with reliable hot water) are well scrubbed. **②**

Eating and drinking

For **food**, there's not much choice here and very little to get excited about. Most restaurants and cafés are grouped around the plaza, where you'll also find a number of bakeries that sell a pretty uninspiring range of dry pastries and cakes. In the morning, between the church and clock tower, you'll find a señora dispensing freshly squeezed orange juice for a few quetzales a glass. The smartest place in town is *El Torito Steakhouse*, 7 C 1–73, just southwest of the plaza, a real carnivore's delight, specializing in steaks and meat platters, served with soup as a starter. The sausages are very tasty here, the fried chicken's good and the whole place is bedecked in kitsch cowboy decor. On the west side of the plaza, *La Pizza de Ciro* does reasonable pizzas (which taste fine if you've come from remote Nebaj and pretty poor if you've journeyed from cosmopolitan Antigua), and the friendly *Café La Torré* serves good coffee, snacks and delicious quesadillas. Finally, for friendly service, cheap breakfasts and no-nonsense comedor grub, there's *Restaurante Las Rosas*, on 1 Av 1–28.

The ruins of Utatlán (K'umarkaaj)

Early in the fifteenth century, riding on a wave of successful conquest, the K'iche' king Gucumatz (Feathered Serpent) founded a new capital, K'umarkaaj. A hundred years later the Spanish arrived, renamed the city **Utatlán**, and then destroyed it. Today the **ruins** (daily 8am–5pm; US$2) can be visited, about 4km to the west of Santa Cruz del Quiché.

According to the Popol Vuh, Gucumatz was a lord of great genius, assisted by powerful spirits: "The nature of this king was truly marvellous, and all the other lords were filled with terror before him… And this was the beginning of the grandeur of the K'iche', when Gucumatz gave these signs of his power. His sons and his grandsons never forgot him." And there's no doubt that this was once a great city, with several separate citadels spread across neighbouring hilltops. It housed the nine dynasties of the tribal elite, including the four main K'iche' lords, and contained a total of 23 palaces. The splendour of the city embodied the strength of the K'iche' empire, which at its height boasted a population of around a million.

By the time of the Conquest, however, the K'iche' had been severely weakened and their empire fractured. They first made contact with the Spanish on the Pacific coast, suffering a heavy defeat at the hands of Alvarado's forces near Quetzaltenango, with the loss of their hero Tecún Umán. The K'iche' then invited the Spanish to their capital, a move that made Alvarado distinctly suspicious. On seeing the fortified city he feared a trap and captured the K'iche' leaders, Oxib-Queh and Beleheb-Tzy. His next step was characteristically straightforward: "As I knew them to have such a bad disposition to service of his Majesty, and to ensure the good and peace of this land, I burnt them, and sent to burn the town and destroy it."

The site

Utatlán is not as immediately impressive as some of the Petén ruins, but its dramatic situation, surrounded by deep ravines and pine forests, the stunning views across the valley and its fascinating historical significance make up for the lack of huge pyramids and stellae. There has been little restoration since the Spanish destroyed the city, and only a few of the main structures are still recognizable, most buried beneath grassy mounds and shaded by pine trees. The small **museum** has a scale model of what the original city may once have looked like.

The central plaza is almost certainly where Alvarado burned alive the two K'iche' leaders, in the year 1524. Nowadays it's where you'll find the three remaining **temple buildings**, the Great Monuments of Tohil, Auilix and Hacauaitz, which were simple pyramids topped by thatched shelters. In the middle of the plaza there used to be a circular **tower**, the Temple of the Sovereign Plumed Serpent, but these days just its foundations can be made out. The only other feature that is still vaguely recognizable is the **ball court**, which lies beneath grassy banks to the south of the plaza.

Perhaps the most interesting thing about the site today is that *brujos*, Maya shamen, still come here to perform religious rituals, practices that predate the arrival of the Spanish by thousands of years. The entire area is covered in small burnt circles – the ashes of incense – and chickens are regularly sacrificed in and around the plaza.

Beneath the plaza is a long constructed **tunnel** that runs underground for about 100m. Inside are nine shrines, the same number as there are levels of the Maya underworld, Xibalbá. At each shrine devotees pray, but it is the ninth one, housed inside a chamber, that is most actively used for sacrifice, incense and alcohol offerings. Why the tunnel was constructed remains uncertain, but local legends suggest that it was dug by the K'iche' to hide their women and children from the advancing Spanish whom they planned to ambush at Utatlán. Others believe it represents the seven caves of Tula mentioned in the Popul Vuh (see p.139). Whatever the truth, today the tunnel is the focus for Maya rituals and a favourite spot for sacrifice, the floor carpeted with chicken feathers, and candles burning in the alcoves at the end. To get to the tunnel follow the signs to *la cueva* (the cave); the entrance is usually littered with empty incense wrappings and *aguardiente* liquor bottles. Tread carefully inside the tunnel, as some of the side passages end abruptly with precipitous drops. If a ceremony is taking place you'll hear the mumbling of prayers and smell incense smoke as you enter, in which case it's wise not to disturb the proceedings by approaching too closely.

To **get to** Utatlán from Santa Cruz de Quiché you can walk or take a taxi (expect to pay around US$7 for a return trip, with an hour at the ruins). It's a pleasant forty-minute stroll, heading south from the plaza along 2 Avenida, then turning right down 10 Calle, which will take you all the way out to the site. You're welcome to **camp** close to the ruins, but here there are no shower facilities or food available.

A rough road continues west from the ruins to San Antonio Ilotenango and from there to Totonicapán. A fair amount of traffic passes along this back route, which takes in some superb high ground.

East to Joyabaj

A good, smooth paved road runs east from Santa Cruz del Quiché, beneath the impressive peaks of the **Sierra de Chuacús**, through a series of interesting villages set in beautiful rolling farmland. The first of the villages is **CHICHÉ**, a sister village to Chichicastenango, with which it shares costumes and traditions, though the market here is on Wednesday. Next is **CHINIQUE**, followed by the larger village of **ZACUALPA**, which has Thursday and Sunday markets in its beautiful broad plaza. The village's name means "where they make fine walls", and in the hills to the north are the remains of a pre-conquest settlement. There's a pensión down the street beside the church should you want to stay here.

The last place out this way is the small town of **JOYABAJ**, again with a small archeological site to its north. During the colonial period Joyabaj was an important staging post on the royal route to Mexico, but all evidence of its former splendour was lost when the earthquake in 1976 almost totally flattened the town and hundreds of people lost their lives: the crumbling facade of the colonial church that stands in front of the new prefabricated version is one of the few physical remains. In recent years the town has staged a miraculous recovery, however, and it is now once again a prosperous traditional centre: the Sunday **market**, which in fact starts up on Saturday afternoon, is a huge affair well worth visiting, as is the **fiesta** in the second week of August – five days of unrelenting celebration that includes some fantastic traditional dancing and the spectacular *Palo Volador*, in which "flying" men or *ángeles* spin to the ground from a huge wooden pole; a pre-conquest ritual now performed in only two other places in the country. Though the fiesta is in many ways a hybrid of Maya and Christian traditions, the *ángeles* symbolize none other than the wizard twins of the Popul Vuh (see p.139) who descend into the underworld to do battle with the Lords of Death.

While the town may have recovered economically, the remote **Maya villages** beyond are still suffering great hardship through lack of any services – from roads to hospitals. Many inhabitants have survived terrible massacres during the early 1980s and have received little assistance rebuilding their lives. You may, therefore, be interested in supporting the community by enrolling in a language school, the XOY Centre at C de la Hospital (☎763 0407) in Joyabaj, where students can stay with local families and learn Spanish or K'iche' for US$130 per week including full board and accommodation.

It's possible to **walk** from Joyabaj, over the Sierra de Chuacús, to Cubulco in Baja Verapaz. It's a superb but exhausting hike, taking at least a day, though it's perhaps better done in reverse (as described on p.301).

Practicalities

Buses run between Guatemala City and Joyabaj, passing through Santa Cruz del Quiché, about every forty minutes (8am–3.30pm from the capital and 3am–3pm from Joyabaj). There are a few basic **pensiones**, among which the *Hospedaje Mejia* (●), on the plaza in Joyabaj is one of the best, and plenty of scattered **comedores**.

For Panajachel and connections to the Pacific coast, **buses** leave Joyabaj twice daily in the morning, heading for Cocales. It's also possible to get back to the capital along two rough and seldom-travelled routes. The first of these is **via San Martín Jilotepeque** on the daily bus that leaves Joyabaj at 2am; the second option – one daily bus at 2.30pm – takes you **to Pachalum**. In Pachalum, there's the excellent, clean *Hotel Nancy* (●) northwest of the plaza; buses leave for the capital at 2am, passing within an hour's walk of Mixco Viejo – and the driver may let you sleep in the bus while you wait.

To the Cuchumatanes: San Andrés Sajcabaja, Sacapulas and Uspantán

The land to the north of Santa Cruz del Quiché is sparsely inhabited and dauntingly hilly. About 17km northeast of town, only accessed by a rough dirt track, the *Posada San Rafael* (℡755 1834 & 755 1734, ℻755 3121; ❹/❺) is a wonderful new rural hotel, set in the grounds of an old finca in the village of **SAN ANDRÉS SAJCABAJA**, deep in the glorious Quiché hills. The French–Guatemalan owners offer horse riding to the minor Maya ruins of Xepatzac and Agua Colorada, indigenous villages, hot springs and waterfalls and serve up delicious organic food. If you call first, there's a good chance that someone will pick you up from Santa Cruz del Quiché, as very few buses run up this way; alternatively ask around at the bus station to see if there's a pick up leaving for San Andrés. The journey takes an hour.

Heading out of Santa Cruz, the road passes through San Pedro Jocopilas before skirting the western end of the Sierra de Chuacús and eventually dropping to the isolated town of **SACAPULAS**, an hour and a half from Quiché. Set in a spectacular position on the river Negro beneath the dusty foothills of the Cuchumatanes, Sacapulas has a small colonial church, and a good market is held every Thursday and Sunday beneath a huge ceiba tree in the plaza. Some of the women still wear impressive *huipiles* and tie their hair with elaborate pom-poms, similar to those of Aguacatán.

Since long before the arrival of the Spanish, **salt** has been produced here in beds beside the Río Negro, a valuable commodity that earned the town a degree of importance. Legend has it that the people of Sacapulas originally migrated from the far north, fleeing other savage tribes. The town's original name was Tajul, meaning "hot springs", but the Spanish changed it to Sacapulas, "the grassy place", as they valued the straw baskets made locally. Along the river bank, downstream from the bridge, there are several little pools where warm water bubbles to the surface, used by local people for washing. On the opposite bank trucks and buses break for lunch at some ramshackle comedores and fruit stalls.

Getting to Sacapulas is not hard – you can catch any of the **buses** that leave Santa Cruz del Quiché for Uspantán or Nebaj. **Leaving Sacapulas** can be difficult: the four daily buses for Quiché leave between 2am and 6am so you may have to **hitch**. Wait by the bridge as traffic heading for Quiché can turn left or right after crossing the river. There's a daily Transportes Rivas bus to Huehuetenango at 5am (4hr) and four buses to Uspantán (2hr 30min) between 1pm and 5pm, but all services in this remote region are erratic and subject to delays and cancellations. Hitchhike by truck or pick-up whenever possible and expect to pay the same rate as you would on the bus.

At least if you get stuck, there's a reasonable place to **stay**: the *Restaurant Río Negro*, on the south side of the bridge, offers basic but clean rooms (❶). The cook, Manuela, serves good **meals** (menus in English and Spanish) and excellent banana, pineapple and papaya milkshakes. *Panadería Karla*, near the square, does good choco-bananas and the street comodores serve tasty tamales and enchiladas.

East to Uspantán, and on to Cobán

East of Sacapulas a dirt road rises steeply, clinging to the mountainside and quickly leaving the Río Negro far below. As it climbs, the views are superb, with tiny riverside Sacapulas dwarfed by the sheer enormity of the landscape. Eventually the road reaches a high valley and arrives in **USPANTÁN**, a remote staging post on the back road from Huehuetenango and Cobán. Lodged in a chilly gap in the mountains and often soaked in steady drizzle, this scruffy place is the focus for the Uspanteko language, one of Guatemala's more obscure and most threatened Maya dialects that's only now spoken by 3000 people locally. Rigoberta Menchú, the Maya woman who won the 1992 Nobel Peace Prize (see p.469), is from Chimel, a tiny village in this region, but probably the only reason you'll end up here is in order to get somewhere else. With the **bus for Cobán** (5hr) and San Pedro Carchá (5hr 20min) leaving at 3am, the best thing to do is go to bed, or try and hitch a lift. There are three friendly pensiones – all are basic but clean and very cheap – *Casa del Viajero* (❶), just southeast of the plaza, *Galindo* on 5 Calle (❶) and *La Uspanteka* (❶) on 4 Calle. **Buses** for Uspantán, via Sacapulas, leave Quiché at 9am, 11am, noon and 2pm, returning at 11.30pm, 1am, 2am and 3am – a five-hour trip.

The Ixil triangle: Nebaj, Chajul and Cotzal

High up on the spine of the Cuchumatanes, in a landscape of steep hills, bowl-shaped valleys and gushing rivers, is the **Ixil triangle**. Here the three small towns of Nebaj, Chajul and Cotzal, remote and extremely traditional, share a language spoken nowhere else in the country. This triangle of towns forms the hub of the **Ixil-speaking region**, a massive highland area which drops away towards the Mexican border and contains at least 100,000 inhabitants. These lush and rain-drenched hills are hard to reach and notoriously difficult to control, and today's relaxed atmosphere of highland Maya colour and customs conceals a bitter history of protracted conflict. It's an area that embodies some of the very best and worst characteristics of the Guatemalan highlands.

On the positive side are the beauty of the landscape and the strength of indigenous culture, both of which are overwhelming. When Church leaders moved into the area in the 1970s they found very strong communities in which the people were reluctant to accept new authority for fear that it would disrupt traditional structures, and women were included in the process of communal decision-making. Counterbalancing these strengths are the horrors of the human rights abuses that took place here during the civil war, which must rate as some of the worst anywhere in Central America.

Before the **Conquest** the town of Nebaj was a sizeable centre, producing large quantities of jade and possibly allied in some way to Zaculeu (see p.207). The Spanish Conquest was particularly brutal in these parts, however. After several previous setbacks, the Spaniards eventually managed to take Nebaj in 1530, by which time they were so enraged that not only was the town burnt to the ground but the survivors were condemned to slavery as punishment for their resistance. In the years that followed, the land was repeatedly invaded by the Lacandón Maya from the north and swept by devastating epidemics. Things didn't improve with the coming of independence, when the Ixil were regarded as a source of cheap labour and forced to work on the coastal plantations. It is estimated that between 1894 and 1930 six thousand labourers migrated annually to work on the harvest, suffering not only the hardship of the actual work, but also exposure to a number of new diseases. Many never returned, and even today large numbers of local people are forced to migrate in search of work, and conditions on many of the plantations remain appalling (see p.231). In the late 1970s and early 1980s, the area was hit by waves of horrific violence (see p.148) as it became the main theatre of operation for the **EGP**

△ Nebaj man relaxing outside the town church

(the Guerrilla Army of the Poor). Caught up in the conflict, the people have suffered enormous losses, with the majority of the smaller villages destroyed by the army and their inhabitants herded into "protected" settlements. With the peace accords, a degree of normality has returned to the area, and new villages are being rebuilt on the old sites.

Despite this terrible legacy, the fresh green hills are some of the most beautiful in the country and the three towns are friendly and accommodating, with a relaxed and distinctive atmosphere in a misty world of their own.

Nebaj and around

NEBAJ is the centre of Ixil country and by far the largest of the three settlements, a beautiful old town of white adobe walls and cobbled streets. The weaving done here is unusual and intricate, its greatest feature being the women's *huipiles*, which are a mass of complex geometrical designs in superb greens, yellows, reds and oranges, worn with brilliant red *cortes* (skirts). The women also wear superb headcloths decorated with "pom-pom" tassles that they pile up above their heads, though few men still wear traditional dress preferring to buy secondhand North American clothes from the market. The men's ceremonial jackets, which are dusted down for fiestas, are formal-looking

The EGP in the Ixil triangle

Of the entire western highlands the Ixil triangle was one of the areas most devastated by the bitter **civil war** of the late 1970s and early 1980s. During this period the entire area became a desperate battleground and by the time the dust settled virtually all the smaller villages had been destroyed, 15–20,000 people had been killed and tens of thousands more displaced.

The severity of the violence is a measure of the success of the **EGP** (*Ejército Guerrillero de los Pobres* – The Guerrilla Army of the Poor), who fought the army in northern Quiché for more than two decades. The EGP first entered the area in 1972, when a small group of guerrilla fighters (some of whom had been involved in the 1960s guerrilla campaign) crossed the Mexican border to the north and began building links with local people. At the time there was little military presence in the area and they were able to work swiftly, impressing the Ixil Maya with their bold plans for political and social revolution. In 1975 they opened their military campaign by assassinating Luis Arenas, the notorious owner of Finca La Perla, to the north of Chajul, where hundreds of labourers were kept in a system of debt bondage. The EGP shot Arenas in front of hundreds of his employees as he was counting the payroll. According to the EGP, "shouts of joy burst from throats accustomed for centuries only to silence and lament, and with something like an ancestral cry, with one voice they chanted with us our slogan, *"Long live the poor, death to the rich."*

These early actions prompted a huge response from the **armed forces**, who began killing, kidnapping and torturing suspected guerrillas and sympathizers. The organization was already well entrenched, however, and the army's brutality only served to persuade more and more people to seek protection from the guerrillas. By late 1978 the EGP were regularly occupying villages, holding open meetings and tearing down the debtors' jails. In January 1979 they killed another despised local landowner, Enrique Brol, of the Finca San Francisco near Cotzal, and the same day briefly took control of Nebaj itself, summoning the whole of the town's population, including the western travellers staying at *Las Tres Hermanas*, to the central plaza, while they denounced the barbaric inequalities of life in the Ixil.

and ornately decorated, modelled on those worn by Spanish officers – some of the finest red cloth, often used in both the jackets and the women's sashes, originates in Germany and keeps its colour incredibly well. The people of Nebaj are keen to establish a market for their weaving, but most of them can't afford to travel as far as Chichicastenango, and so as soon as you arrive in town you'll probably be hassled by an army of young girls, desperate to sell their clothing. You'll also find an excellent shop, selling goods produced by the Ixil weaving co-op, on the main square.

Nebaj's plaza is the focal point for the community and houses the major shops, municipal buildings, and the police station. There's little to do in the town itself, though the small **market**, a block to the east of the church, is worth investigation. It's fairly quiet most days, but presents the best photographic opportunities in town as Nebajeños go about their daily business. On Thursday and Sunday the numbers swell and traders visit from out of town selling North American secondhand clothing, stereos from Taiwan and Korea and chickens, eggs, fruit and vegetables from the highlands. If you're in town for the second week in August you'll witness the **Nebaj fiesta**, which includes processions, dances, drinking, fireworks and a *marimba*-playing marathon.

Predictably, the army responded with a wave of horrific attacks on the civilian population. Army units swept through the area, committing random atrocities, burning villages and massacring thousands of their inhabitants, including women and children. Nevertheless, the strength of the guerrillas continued to grow and in 1981 they again launched an attack on Nebaj, which was now a garrison town. Shortly afterwards the army chief of staff, Benedicto Lucas García (the president's brother), flew into Nebaj and summoned a meeting of the entire population. In a simple speech he warned them that if they didn't "clean up their act" he'd bring five thousand men "and finish off the entire population".

President Lucas García was overthrown by a military coup in early 1982 and the presidency of **General Ríos Montt** saw a radical change in the army's tactics. Ríos Montt used civilian patrols to ensure the loyalty of the people and placed them in the front line of the conflict. Villagers were given ancient M1 rifles and told to protect their communities from the guerrillas. Meanwhile, the army began aggressive sweeps through the highlands, but instead of burning villages and terrorizing the population they brought people back into Nebaj to be fed and eventually settled in new "model" villages. This new approach revealed that many people of the Ixil were in fact determined to remain neutral and had only taken sides in order to ensure their survival. Relatively quickly, whole communities adapted to the new situation and rejected contact with the guerrillas.

The guerrillas were hit extremely hard and for a brief period responded with desperate acts. On June 6, 1982, guerrillas stopped a bus near Cotzal and executed thirteen civil patrol leaders and their wives; eleven days later a guerrilla column entered the village of Chacalté, where the new civil patrol had been particularly active, and killed a hundred people, wounding another thirty-five.

The army's offer of amnesty, twinned with a continuous crackdown on the guerrillas, soon drew refugees out of the mountains: between 1982 and 1984 some 42,000 people turned themselves in, fleeing a harsh existence under guerrilla protection. By 1985 the guerrillas had been driven back into a handful of mountain strongholds in Xeputul, Sumal and Amachel, all to the north and west of Chajul and Cotzal. Skirmishes continued until the mid-1990s, but since the Peace Accords the conflict has ceased. Ex-guerrillas and former civil patrol members have resettled the old village sites and begun the task of rebuilding communities.

Practicalities

Getting to Nebaj is straightforward with **buses** leaving Santa Cruz del Quiché every ninety minutes between 8.30am and 4pm (4hr), plus a daily service from Huehuetenango (6hr). **Leaving** Nebaj is more problematic, with the schedules being designed to get locals to the early morning market, so buses leave at 11pm, midnight and 1am for Quiché and at 1.45am to Huehuetenango. There should also be a morning bus to Quiché at 7am, but don't count on it and, as usual in these parts, all the timetables are subject to frequent changes, so check at the terminal before you want to leave.

Getting around the Ixil triangle has become much easier in the last few years, with two late morning buses running to Chajul (1hr) and one to Cotzal (50 min) on Thursdays and Sundays. Pick-ups, the odd truck and development agency four-wheel drives also supplement the buses between Nebaj and Chajul and Cotzal. On market days in Chajul (Tues and Fri) and Cotzal (Wed and Sat), there are also early morning buses leaving Nebaj.

There is a **bank**, Bancafé, 2 Av 46, near the market (Mon–Fri 8.30am–4pm, Sat 9am–1pm), which exchanges both cash and travellers' cheques; and next door a new **internet café** with modern terminals, good rates and discounted international call facilities.

Accommodation

You'll find little in the way of luxury in Nebaj, although what there is does have an inimitable charm and prices here are some of the lowest in the country. There are few street signs, so you'll probably have to rely on the gang of children who act as guides – none of the hotels in town is more than a few minutes' walk from the terminal. You should have no problem finding a hotel room in Nebaj, except during the August fiesta, when many families rent out rooms to visitors.

Hospedaje Esperanza northwest of the plaza. Friendly, simple but very basic for the price and you'll have to pay extra for a hot shower. Not the best deal in town but a good place to stay if you're interested in learning to weave – ask the owner's daughter about lessons. ❷

Hospedaje Ilebal Tenam three minutes from the plaza on the road to Chajul/Cotzal. Tremendous hospedaje with two floors of simple but very clean rooms, exhilaratingly hot showers and safe parking. ❶

Hospedaje Las Tres Hermanas a block northwest of the plaza. Despite its damp rooms, ancient mattresses and shabby apperance, this is one of the most famous hotels in Guatemala. During the troubles of the 1970s and 1980s this place put up a virtual who's who of international and Guatemalan journalists including Victor Perera, George Lovell and Ronald Wright (see p.482). It is still run by two of the original three sisters, who must have some stories to tell. ❶

Hotel Ixil on the main road south out of town. The large, bare rooms are a little on the damp side, though the setting is pleasant, around a courtyard in a nice old colonial house, and there's a warmish shower. Better quality rooms, with private bath and hot showers, are available in a nearby house if you ask the friendly staff. ❶–❷

Hotel Posada de Don Pablo one block west of the plaza, opposite *Irene's* comedor. Attractive hotel, with smallish but spotless, pine-trimmed rooms, comfortable beds, private bathrooms and safe parking. ❸

Nuevo Hotel Ixal three blocks south of the plaza. Good, secure little hotel with a charming courtyard. The pleasing rooms have private baths, and those on the upper floor enjoy mountain views. ❷

Posada Maya Ixil four minutes northwest of the plaza, just off the road to Chajul/Cotzal. Excellent new hotel, easily the smartest in town, with real character. Large, comfortable rooms, decorated with vibrant local textiles and rustic furniture and pottery, with private bath. ❸

Eating

As for **eating**, the best comedors in town, serving cheap, tasty Guatemalan food, are *Irene's*, just off the main square, and *Pasabien* by the bus terminal, with several others in the plaza itself. The *Maya-Inca* on 5 Calle is owned by a friendly

Peruvian–Guatemalan couple and serves delicious Peruvian and local dishes, though the portions are small; there are also reasonable pizzas at *Cesar's* on 2 Avenida opposite Bancafé. Alternatively, some village women offer home-cooked Ixil-style meals for tourists for around US$2 per person, or there's always something to eat at the market. For entertainment, most of the raving in town is courtesy of Nebaj's burgeoning neo-Pentecostal church scene, with four-hour services involving much wailing and gnashing of teeth.

Walks around Nebaj

In the hills that surround Nebaj there are several beautiful **walks**, with one of the most interesting taking you to the village of **Acul**, two hours away. Starting from the church in Nebaj, cross the plaza and turn to the left, taking the road that goes downhill between a shop and a comedor. At the bottom of the dip it divides, and here you take the right-hand fork and head out of town along a dirt track.

Just after you pass the last houses you'll see some pre-Columbian burial mounds to your right. These are still used for religious ceremonies, and if you take a close look you'll find burnt patches marking the site of offerings. Since the mounds are usually planted with maize they can be a bit difficult to spot, but once you get up higher above the town they're easier to make out.

Beyond this the track carries on, switchbacking up a steep hillside, and heads over a narrow pass into the next valley, where it drops down into the village. **ACUL** was one of the original so-called "model villages" into which people were herded after their homes had been destroyed by the army, and despite the spectacular setting – and the efforts of the United Nations, amongst others, to improve the standard of living – it's a sad and weary place. If you walk on through the village and out the other side you arrive at the Finca San Antonio, a bizarre Swiss-style chalet set in a neat little meadow. An Italian family have lived here for more than fifty years, making some of the country's best cheese, and visitors are welcome to have a look around – especially if they buy some produce. José Azzari who founded the finca died in 1990, at the ripe old age of 99, though his sons continue to farm here.

A second, shorter walk takes you to a beautiful little **waterfall**, La Cascada de Plata, about an hour from Nebaj, though there's no swimming here. Take the road to Chajul and turn left just before it crosses the bridge, a kilometre or two outside Nebaj. Don't be fooled by the smaller version you'll come to shortly before the main set of falls.

A third half-day circular walk climbs up the steep eastern edge of the natural bowl that surrounds Nebaj to the village of **COCOP** and back to the main Nebaj–Cotzal road. Starting from *Bancafe*, on 2 Avenida, in the centre of town, continue until the end of the road, turn right, and then first left downhill to the bridge. Cross the bridge, and continue walking until you reach the pueblo of Xemamatzé on the edge of Nebaj. This village used to be home to a huge internment camp where Ixil villagers who had surrendered to the army were subject to lengthy "repatriation" treatment before being allowed to return to their native villages. In Xemamatzé take the well-trodden trail uphill just after the *Pepsi tienda* sign, which climbs steadily for about an hour to 2300m. Back across the valley there are spectacular views towards Nebaj. When you eventually come to a maize field, bear left and continue round the mountain. The path grips the side of the slope and twists and turns, then gradually starts to descend as the small village of Cocop comes into view below. The village has recently been rebuilt on old foundations, after it was razed to the ground during the civil war, and 98 villagers were massacred by the army. Today it's a pretty little settlement in a delightful position beside a gurgling river, with a single shop where you can buy a warm fizzy drink. To head back, walk straight ahead from the shop past the Emmanuel church for a lovely hour's stroll along the V-shaped valley through sheep-filled meadows. At the end of the trail is the village of Río Azul on the main Cotzal–Nebaj road from where you can wait for a pick-up, truck or bus, or hike back to Nebaj in an hour an a half.

West to Salquil Grande

Another possible excursion from Nebaj takes you to the village of **SALQUIL GRANDE**, 23km to the west. A road runs out this way, through the village of Tzalbal, and across two huge and breathtaking valleys. New villages, built to replace those burnt to the ground by the army, pepper the hillsides, their tin roofs still clean and almost rust-free. They are inhabited by people who spent the war years either starving in the mountains or shut away in the refugee camps of Nebaj. **Trucks** run out to Salquil Grande from the market in Nebaj at around 6am on most days, and certainly for the Tuesday market. There's nowhere to stay in the village but the trucks usually return a couple of hours later. Continuing west from Salquil Grande, a very rough road runs some 44km to join up with the main Huehuetenango to Barillas road, a spectacular way of reaching the Paquix junction for the turn-off for Todos Santos Cuchumatán.

The landscape around Salquil Grande is supremely beautiful and best enjoyed on foot. A good hike takes you to the little village of **Parramos Grande** in around two hours. Starting from the statue of a soldier on the edge of Salquil Grande, you want to take the path to the right and when this divides take a left through the *milpa*, heading downhill. Along the way you pass a couple of beautiful waterfalls, so if the sun's shining you can always pause for a chilly dip.

San Juan Cotzal and Chajul

To visit the other two towns in the Ixil triangle it's best to coincide your visit with **market** days when there is more traffic on the move (Cotzal's is on Wednesday and Saturday; Chajul's on Tuesday and Friday). On market days, regular morning **buses** leave Nebaj for the two towns from 4am. Buses should return daily to Nebaj from San Juan Cotzal at 6am and 1am, and from Chajul at 11.30am and 12.30pm. Plenty of **pick-ups** supplement these buses; the last usually leaves Chajul at 3.30pm (though you'll have to share the covered trailer with firewood and vegetables) as do aid agency and MINUGUA (United Nations) four-wheel drives. Sunday is also a good day to travel because villagers from the other two Ixil towns visit Nebaj for its weekly market, heading back after 11am.

SAN JUAN COTZAL is the closer town to Nebaj, forty minutes to over an hour away depending on the state of the road. The town is beautifully set in a gentle dip in the valley, sheltered beneath the Cuchumatanes and often wrapped in a damp blanket of mist. In the 1920s and 1930s this was the largest and busiest of the three Ixil towns, as it was from here that the fertile lands to the north were colonized. Once a road reached Nebaj in the 1940s, however, Cotzal was somewhat eclipsed, although there is still a higher concentration of ladinos here. Cotzal attracts very few Western travellers, so you may find many people assume you're an aid worker or attached to a fundamentalist church.

There is little to do in the town itself but there is some great hill walking closeby. If you want to **stay** there is a small, very basic unmarked pensión called *Don Polo* (❷), two blocks from the church, or you may find the farmacia in the corner of the plaza will rent you a room (❶). *La Maguey* **restaurant**, in a front room a block behind the church, serves up reasonable, if bland, food.

Walking from Cotzal to Chajul

Though there is a newish unpaved road beween Cotzal and Chajul it's also possible to hike (approx 2hr 30min) an indirect route through some beautiful Ixil scenery before joining the road for the last two or three kilometres. From Cotzal church take the road downhill that leaves Cotzal for the *Finca San Francisco*, passing a school and a football pitch on your right. Just before the bridge, leave the road and take the path that follows the Río Tichum for about five minutes, until you reach another bridge. Cross the second bridge and take the left-hand path uphill through maize fields; the right-hand path leads to the village of Xepalma. After thirty minutes you'll reach a ridge, marking the border between two municipalities, from where you can see the white bulk of Chajul's church. Continue down a muddy path through woodland and you'll come to a large fenced-off field. Turn to the left and follow the fence until you reach a large path; turn right here and you'll shortly reach the Cotzal–Chajul road. From here, it's about an hour to Chajul: turn right and follow the road down a small valley before climbing very steeply to the village.

Last but by no means least of the Ixil settlements is **CHAJUL**, replete with a good stock of old adobe houses, their wooden beams and red-tiled roofs blackened by the smoke of cooking fires. It is also the most traditional and least bilingual of the Ixil towns. The streets are usually bustling with activity: you'll be met by an army of small children, and the local women gather to wash clothes at the stream that cuts through the middle of the village. Here boys still use blowpipes to hunt small birds, a skill that dates from the earliest of times but is now little used elsewhere. The women of Chajul dress entirely in red, filling the streets with colour, and wear earrings made of old coins strung up on lengths of wool. The traditional red jackets of the men are a rare sight these days. Make sure you visit the shop run by the local weaving co-operative, called *Va'l Vaq Quyol,* between the church and the market, where you will find some of the best quality, handmade textiles in the country at very decent prices.

The colonial church, on the plaza, a huge old structure full of gold leaf and massive wooden beams, is home to the **Christ of Golgotha** and the target of a large pilgrimage on the second Friday of Lent – a particularly good time to be here. The two angels that flank the image were originally dressed as policemen, after a tailor who'd been cured through prayer donated the uniforms so that his benefactor would be well protected. Later they were changed into army uniforms, and recently they've been toned down to look more like boy scouts.

Chajul's plaza was the place where Rigoberta Menchú, in her autobiography (see p.469), describes the public execution of her brother at the hands of the army. According to Menchú, her brother and several other suspected communists and labour organizers were brought before the town's population by the army, all showing signs of hideous torture. She describes the commander delivering an anti-communist lecture then ordering the prisoners to be burnt alive. Although there is no doubt that atrocities took place, painstaking investigation by author David Stoll, and evidence by EGP member Mario Payeras, contradicts Menchú's version of events – eye witnesses testify that the prisoners were machine-gunned, the date of the killings is in dispute, as is the fact that Menchú was there at all. Though the show trial execution was horrific enough under any circumstances, the reliablity of Menchú's account has undoubtedly come into question.

The *Hospedaje Cristina* (❶) initially looks a pretty depressing option if you want somewhere to **stay** for the night, though it has some half-decent rooms on the upper floor. Alternatively, the new *Hospedaje Esperanza* (**❶**), close to the church, is basic but clean, or you could ask at the post office where one of the workers rents out rooms (**❶**). Some other families also rent out beds in their houses to the steady trickle of travellers now coming to Chajul; you won't have to look for them, they will find you. For **eating**, there's an assortment of simple comedores and food stalls scattered around the marketplace.

Beyond the triangle: the Ixcán

To the north of the Ixil triangle is a thinly populated area known as the **Ixcán**, which drops away towards the Mexican border to merge with the Lacandón rainforests. Again this area, formerly an EGP stronghold, was heavily fought over until the mid-1990s, but the Ixcán has long been one of Guatemala's great untamed frontiers. In the 1960s and 1970s land-hungry migrants from Quiché and Huehuetenango began moving into the area to carve out new farms from the forest. After a few years of extreme hardship, and assisted by Maryknoll missionaries, they established thriving communities. The land yielded two crops a year and produced an abundance of fruit, coffee and cardamom. The settlers built health clinics and churches, established a system of radio communication and a transport network and began applying for collective land titles. However, in the early 1970s the EGP moved into the area and the 1980s saw it devastated by bitter fighting, in which virtually every village was burnt to the ground and thousands fled to Mexico.

Now many refugees and ex-guerrillas have returned to the northern Ixcán and there are a number of new villages and resettlement camps. The rough route across the very northern part of Ixcán from Playa Grande to Barillas is covered on pp.212–213, though currently no routes link this road with the Ixil.

Lago de Atitlán

Lake Como, it seems to me, touches the limit of the permissibly picturesque; but Atitlán is Como with the additional embellishments of several immense volcanoes. It is really too much of a good thing. After a few days of this impossible landscape one finds oneself thinking nostalgically of the English Home Counties.

Aldous Huxley, *Beyond the Mexique Bay* (1934)

Whether or not you share Huxley's refined sensibilities, there's no doubt that Lake Atitlán is astonishingly beautiful, and most people find themselves captivated by its scenic excesses. Indeed the effect is so overwhelming that a handful of gringo devotees have been rooted to its shores since the 1960s. The lake, just three hours from Guatemala City and a few kilometres south of the Carretera Interamericana, rates as the country's number one tourist attraction. It's a source of national pride, and some Guatemalans claim that it ranks with the Seven Wonders of the World.

The water itself is an irregular shape, with three main inlets. It measures 18km by 12km at its widest point, and shifts through an astonishing range of blues, steely greys and greens as the sun moves across the sky. Hemmed in on all sides

LAGO DE ATITLÁN

San José Chacayá
Sololá
Santa Lucía Utatlán
Santa Cruz La Laguna
San Jorge La Laguna
San Andrés Semetabaj
Jaibalito
Tzununá
Panajachel
San Marcos La Laguna
Santa Catarina Palopó
San Pablo La Laguna
Santa María Visitacion
Godínez
San Pedro La Laguna
San Antonio Palopó
San Juan La Laguna

Lago de Atitlán

Volcán San Pedro 3020 m

CERRO DE ORO

Agua Escondida

N

Santiago Atitlán
San Lucas Tolimán

Volcán Tolimán 3158 m

0   5km

Volcán Atitlán 3537 m

Pochuta

Patzicía & Patzún

Cocales (25 km) & Carretera al Pacífico ▼

by steep hills and massive volcanoes, it's at least 320m deep and has no visible outlet, draining as it does through an underground passage to the Pacific coast. In the morning the surface of the lake is normally calm and clear, but by early afternoon the *xocomil*, "the wind that carries away sin", blows from the coast, churning the surface and making travel by boat a hair-raising experience. A north wind, say the Maya, indicates that the spirit of the lake is discarding a drowned body, having claimed its soul.

Another astonishing aspect of Atitlán is the strength of Maya culture still evident in its lakeside villages. Despite the holiday homes and the thousands of tourists that venture here each year, many of the villages in the region remain intensely traditional – **San Antonio Palopó**, **Santiago Atitlán** and **Sololá**, in the hills above the lake, are some of the very few places in the entire country where Maya men still wear the native *traje* costume. Around the southwestern shores, from Santiago to San Pedro, the indigenous people are **Tz'utujil** speakers, the remnants of one of the smaller pre-conquest tribes, whose capital was on the slopes of the San Pedro volcano. On the other side of the water, from San Marcos to Cerro de Oro, **Kaqchikel** is spoken, marking the western barrier of this tribe.

There are thirteen villages on the shores of the lake, with many more in the hills behind, ranging from the cosmopolitan resort-style **Panajachel** to tiny, isolated **Tzununá**. The villages are mostly subsistence farming communities, and it's easy to hike and boat around the lake staying in a different one each night. The lakeside area has been heavily populated since the earliest of times, but it's only relatively recently that it has attracted large numbers of tourists. For the moment things are still fairly undisturbed, except in Panajachel, and the beauty remains overwhelming, though some of the new pressures are decidedly threatening. The fishing industry, once thriving on the abundance of small fish and crabs, has been crippled by the introduction of **black bass**, which eat the smaller fish and water birds and are, moreover, much harder to catch. These fish stick to the deeper water and have to be speared by divers – their introduction was intended to create a sport-fishing industry. The increase in population has also had a damaging impact on the shores of the lake, as the desperate need to cultivate more land leads to deforestation and accompanying soil erosion.

In 1955 the Atitlán basin was declared a national park to preserve its wealth of cultural and natural characteristics, but this seems to have had little effect on development. Beginning in the early 1990s the shores suffered through yet another invasion, as the wealthy Guatemala City crowd abandoned the blackened waters of Lake Amatitlán and moved across to Atitlán. Weekend retreats are still springing up around the shores and Saturday afternoons see the waters dotted with speedboats and skiers.

Where to go

You'll probably reach the lake through Panajachel, a small town on the northern shore which is now dominated by tourism. It makes a good base for exploring the surrounding area, either heading across the lake or making day trips to **Chichicastenango**, **Nahualá**, **Sololá** and **Iximché**. Panajachel has an abundance of cheap hotels and restaurants and is well served by buses. To get a sense of a more typical Atitlán village, however, travel by boat to Santiago Atitlán or San Antonió Polopó, while for an established travellers' scene and a surplus of cheap hotels, try **San Pedro**. **Jailbalito**, **Santa Cruz** and **San Marcos** are the places to head for if you're seeking real peace and quiet and some good hikes.

All things Atitlán seem to be covered in the excellent lake **website** Ⓦ www.atitlan.com, including good accommodation options, and plenty of historical and cultural information.

Sololá and around

A couple of kilometres to the west of Los Encuentros, at the El Cuchillo junction, the road for Panajachel branches off the Carretera Interamericana. Dropping towards the lake it arrives first at **SOLOLÁ**, the departmental capital and the gateway to the lake, which is perched on a natural balcony some 600m above the water. Overlooked by the majority of travellers, the town itself isn't much to look at: a wide central plaza with a recently restored clock tower on one side and a modern church on the other. But Sololá is, nonetheless, a fascinating place and the **Friday market** (there's also a smaller one on Tuesdays) is one of Central America's finest, a mesmeric display of colour and commerce. Aldous Huxley described the market here as "a walking museum of fancy dress". From as early as 5am the plaza is packed, drawing traders from all over the highlands, as well as thousands of Sololá Maya, the women covered in striped red cloth and the men in their outlandish "space cowboy" shirts, woollen aprons and wildly embroidered trousers. Weaving is a powerful creative tradition in the lives of Sololá Maya and each generation develops a distinctive style based upon previous designs.

In common with only a few other places in the country, Sololá has parallel indigenous and ladino governments, and is one of Guatemala's largest Maya towns. Tradition dominates daily life here and the town is said to be divided into sections, each administered by a Maya clan, just as it was before the Conquest. Little is known about the details of this system, though, and its secrets are well kept. The town's symbol, still to be seen on the back of the men's jacket, is an abstraction of a bat, referring to the royal house of Xahil, who were the rulers of the Kaqchikel at the time of the Conquest. The pre-Conquest site of **Tecpán–Atitlán**, which was abandoned in 1547 when Sololá was founded by the Spanish, is to the north of town.

Another interesting time to visit Sololá is on Sunday, when the **cofradías**, the elders of the indigenous religious hierarchy, parade through the streets in ceremonial costume to attend the 10am Mass. They're easily recognizable, carrying silver-tipped canes and wearing broad-brimmed hats and particularly elaborate jackets. Inside the church the sexes are segregated, and the women wear shawls to cover their heads.

Sololá practicalities

There are several simple **hotels** in Sololá: the *Hotel Santa Ana*, a block uphill from the plaza at 6 Av 8–35, has plain rooms around a pleasant courtyard (❷); there's the similar *Hotel Paisaje*, also a block above the plaza at 9 C between 6 and 7 avenidas (❷); and the *Hotel La Posada del Viajero*, on the plaza, is again basic but a bit overpriced (❷). The first two have comedores, and there are a few other simple **places to eat** scattered around town, although you can always eat in the market during the day.

There's a **post office** (Mon–Fri 8am–4.30pm) on the plaza and a Banco G&T Continental at 9 C and 5 Av (Mon–Fri 9am–6pm, Sat 9am–12.30pm). For **bus** times refer to the Panajachel schedules, as all buses travelling between Panajachel and Los Encuentros pass through Sololá. There are also minibuses that run regularly between Sololá and Los Encuentros. The last bus to Panajachel passes through Sololá at around 6.30pm.

Nearby villages

Several other villages can be reached from Sololá, most of them within walking distance. About 8km to the east is **Concepción**, an exceptionally quiet farming village with a spectacularly restored colonial church. Restoration work was completed in 1988 and the facade is still a shiny white. The walk out there, along a dirt track skirting the hills above Panajachel, offers superb views across the lake.

Four kilometres to the west of Sololá, along another dirt road and across a deep-cut river valley, **San José Chacayá** has a tiny colonial church with thick crumbling walls but little else. Another 8km further along the track is **Santa Lucía Utatlán**, which can also be reached along a dirt track that branches off the Pan-American Highway. From Santa Lucía the road continues around the lake, set back from the ridge of hills overlooking the water, to Santa María Visitación and **Santa Clara La Laguna**. The latter is connected by a steep trail to San Pablo La Laguna on the lakeshore below: if you're planning to walk to San Pablo via Santa Clara set out early as it's a full day's hike.

On the hillside below Sololá is **San Jorge La Laguna**, a tiny hamlet perched above the lake, whose inhabitants have been chased around the country by natural disasters. The village was founded by refugees from the 1773 earthquake in Antigua and the original lakeside version was swept into the water by a landslide, persuading the people to move up the hill.

Panajachel

Ten kilometres beyond Sololá, separated by a precipitous descent, is **PANAJACHEL**. Over the years what was once a small Maya village has become something of a resort, with a sizeable population of long-term foreign residents, whose numbers are swollen in the winter by an influx of North American seasonal migrants and a flood of tourists. Back in the 1960s and 1970s, Panajachel was the premier Central American hippie hang-out and developed a bad reputation among some sections of Guatemalan society as a haven for drug-taking gringo drop-outs. Today, however, "Pana" is much more integrated into the tourism mainstream and is as popular with Guatemalans (and Mexicans and Salvadoreans) as Westerners. The lotus-eaters and crystal-gazers have not all deserted the town, though – many have simply reinvented themselves as capitalists, owning restaurants and exporting handicrafts. There is much talk about Lake Atitlán being one of the world's few vortex energy fields along with the Egyptian pyramids and Machu Pichu. Though you are unlikely to see fish swimming backwards or buses rolling uphill to Sololá, the lake does have an undeniable draw and attracts a polyglot population of healers, therapists and masseurs to Panajachel. In many ways it's this **gringo** crowd that gives the town its modern character and identity – vortex energy centre or not.

Not so long ago (although it seems an entirely different age) Panajachel was a quiet little village of **Kaqchikel** Maya, whose ancestors were settled here after the Spanish crushed a force of Tz'utujil warriors on the site. In the early days of the Conquest the Franciscans established a church and monastery in the village, using it as the base for their regional conversion campaign. Today the old village has been enveloped by the new building boom, but it still retains a traditional feel, and most of the Maya continue to farm in the river delta behind the town. The Sunday market, bustling with people from all around the lake, remains oblivious to the tourist invasion.

For travellers Panajachel is one of those inevitable destinations, and although no one ever owns up to actually liking it, everyone seems to stay for a while. The old village is still attractive and although most of the new building is fairly nondescript, its lakeside setting is superb. The main **daytime activity** is either shopping – weaving from all over Guatemala is sold with daunting persistence in the streets here, but you'll need to bargain hard as prices can be high – or simply hanging out. There's an amazing selection of places to eat and drink or surf the internet, plus reasonable swimming and sunbathing at the **public beach**, where you can also rent a kayak for a few hours (mornings are usually much calmer) or even scuba-dive with ATI Divers (see "Listings", p.163). The water, however, is much cleaner on the other side of the lake around San Marcos (see p.173) and Santa Cruz (see p.175), so you may want to pay a few

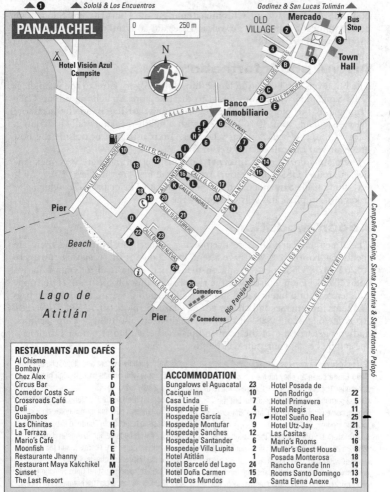

PANAJACHEL

0   250 m

N

OLD VILLAGE

Mercado

★ **Bus Stop**

Town Hall

Å **Hotel Visión Azul Campsite**

Banco Inmobiliario

CALLE REAL

CALLE DE LOS ÁRBOLES

CALLE PRINCIPAL

Alleyway

CALLE EL CHALÍ

CALLE EL CHALÍ

CALLE SANTANDER

CALLE DEL EMBARCADERO

CALLE RANCHO GRANDE

AVENIDA EL FRUTAL

CALLE LONDRES

CALLE 15 DE FEBRERO

CALLE BUENAS NUEVAS

CALLE DEL RÍO

CALLE LOS SALPORES

CALLE DEL CEMENTERIO

Pier

Beach

Lago de Atitlán

CALLE DEL LAGO

Comedores

Río Panajachel

Pier ◆ **Comedores**

▲ *Campaña Camping, Santa Catarina & San Antonio Palopó*

ⓘ

RESTAURANTS AND CAFÉS

Al Chisme	C
Bombay	K
Chez Alex	F
Circus Bar	D
Comedor Costa Sur	A
Crossroads Café	B
Deli	O
Guajimbos	I
Las Chinitas	H
La Terraza	G
Mario's Café	L
Moonfish	E
Restaurante Jhanny	N
Restaurant Maya Kakchikel	M
Sunset	P
The Last Resort	J

ACCOMMODATION

Bungalows el Aguacatal	23	Hotel Posada de	
Cacique Inn	10	Don Rodrigo	22
Casa Linda		Hotel Primavera	5
Hospedaje Eli	4	Hotel Regis	11
Hospedaje García	17	Hotel Sueño Real	25
Hospedaje Montufar	9	Hotel Utz-Jay	21
Hospedaje Sanches	12	Las Casitas	3
Hospedaje Santander	6	Mario's Rooms	16
Hospedaje Villa Lupita	2	Muller's Guest House	8
Hotel Atitlán	1	Posada Monterosa	18
Hotel Barceló del Lago	24	Rancho Grande Inn	14
Hotel Doña Carmen	15	Rooms Santo Domingo	13
Hotel Dos Mundos	20	Santa Elena Anexe	19

dollars to use the swimming pool and private beach at *Vision Azul* (see below), in the bay before Panajachel. You can also drop by Pana's stylish new **Museo Lacustre** (Sun–Fri 8am–7pm, Sat 8am–6pm; US$4.50, students US$2.60), located in the grounds of the *Hotel Posada de Don Rodrigo* (see p.162) on Calle Santander, dedicated to the Panajachel and Atitlán region. There are very well-presented displays, in Spanish and English, outlining the turbulent geological background that led to the creation of the lake, plus an interesting collection of Maya artefacts including Preclassic and Classic-era ceramics and some wonderfully grotesque ceremonial incense burners.

Alternatively, if you're seduced by the bohemiam ambience and easy-going pace of lakeside life, Panajachel now boasts a number of new language schools where you can **study Spanish** (see p.163). Panajachel also makes a comfortable base for exploring the lake and the central highlands. The markets in

Nahualá on Sunday and **Chichicastenango** on Thursday and Sunday are both within an hour or two's travel, and the ruins at **Utatlán** and **Iximché** can also be visited as day-trips.

Arrival and information

The bus drops you beside the Banco Inmobiliario, very close to the main drag, Calle Santander, which runs down to the lakeshore. Straight ahead, up Calle Principal, is the old village. The Inguat **tourist office** is on the lakeshore (Mon–Sat 9am–5pm; ⓣ762 1392), with English-speaking staff, basic hotel information, and boat and bus schedules. **Taxis** usually wait outside the post office, or you can call one on ⓣ762 1571.

There are a dozen or so **internet** cafés in Pana and rates are very inexpensive, at around US$1.40 an hour. Amongst the best are the *Green Earth*, midway along Calle Santander, and *Café Pulcinella* at C Principal 0–72, which also bakes a mean pizza and sells Chianti by the glass.

Accommodation

The streets of Panajachel are overflowing with cheap **hotels**, and there are plenty of "**rooms**". If you have a tent, first choice is the *Campaña* **campsite** (ⓣ762 2479; US$2 per person), on the corner of the road to Santa Catarina and Calle del Cementerio over the river bridge (just off the map). Here happy campers will find kitchen and storage facilities and there are also sleeping bags and tents for rent. Second choice is a nice lakeside plot at the *Hotel Visión Azul* (ⓣ & ⓕ762 1426; US$8 for two), where there are also full hook-up facilities, and you get free use of the pool and private beach. Don't bother camping at the public beach: your stuff will be stolen.

Budget accommodation

Casa Linda down an alley off the top of C Santander. Popular backpackers' retreat where the central garden is undeniably beautiful but the rooms, some with private bath, are a shade pricey for a hospedaje. ❷/❸

Las Casitas C Principal, near the market ⓣ & ⓕ762 1224, ⓔhotelcasitas@yahoo.com. Very clean, friendly and safe, plus free email access for guests. Rooms are tastefully decorated and have good-quality beds and reading lamps; most have private bath. An upstairs dormitory is planned. ❸

Hospedaje Eli Callejón del Pozo, off Calle de los Arboles ⓣ762 0148. Ten clean, cheap rooms overlooking a pretty little garden in a quiet location. ❶

Hospedaje García C el Chali ⓣ762 2187. An abundance of featureless but perfectly reasonable budget rooms. ❷

Hospedaje Montufar down an alley off the top of C Santander ⓣ762 0406. Quiet location and the rooms are cleaned with true evangelical zeal by a very accommodating family. Doubles and triples available. ❷

Hospedaje Sanches C El Chali. Quiet position and the clean rooms are a little larger than most. ❶

Hospedaje Santander C Santander ⓣ762 1304, ⓦwww.atitlan.com/roomssantander.htm. Leafy courtyard, friendly owners and clean, cheap rooms, some with private bath, though hot showers are a little extra. ❶/❷

Hospedaje Villa Lupita Callejón El Tino ⓣ762 1201. Impressive new family-run hotel, on a quiet alley close to the church. Fourteen excellent-value rooms, all with bedside lights, rugs and mirrors, some with private bath. There's a sun terrace and free purified water for guests. ❷/❸

Hotel Doña Carmen just off Calle Rancho Grande ⓣ762 2035, ⓔlosgarcia10@hotmail.com Nicely situated in a quiet corner of town, this pleasant family-run place offers simple, clean budget rooms, some with private bath, set off a huge shady garden. ❷

Hotel Sueño Real C Ramós ⓣ762 0608, ⓕ762 1097. Excellent new hotel, very close to the lakeshore in a quiet location, owned by a friendly, helpful family. The seven attractive, secure rooms – all with private bath – represent superb value for money. ❸

Mario's Rooms C Santander ⓣ762 1313. Good choice of pleasant, very clean rooms, some airy and light with private bath, others more basic. Hot water on request for a few quetzales. ❷/❸

Posada Monterosa C Monterrey ⓣ762 0055. Attractive little hotel, with ten spotless rooms, all with pine furnishings and private bath, and safe car parking. ❸

Rooms Santo Domingo down a path off Calle Monterrey ☎762 0236. One of the cheapest places in town, set well away from the hustle. Very simple wooden rooms all face a charming little garden, and more expensive options upstairs with private bath. ❶ /❸

Santa Elena Anexe C Monterey 3–06 ☎762 1114. Safe, pleasant, ramshackle place with an abundance of children and parrots. Very cheap for single travellers, though hot showers are extra. ❶

Mid-range accommodation

Bungalows el Aguacatal C Buenas Vistas ☎762 1482. These recently refurbished twin-bedroom prefab cabins, which sleep four, are a good option for families or small groups (some have kitchens). They are just off the beach, but it's essential to book ahead at weekends when prices rise too. ❹ /❺

Cacique Inn C del Embarcadero ☎762 1205, ⓕ762 2053. Tranquil position away from the crowds, with a decent-sized swimming pool, and pleasant garden. Large, comfortable rooms with fireplaces. ❻

Hotel Dos Mundos C Santander ☎762 2078, ⓕ762 0127, ⓦwww.atitlan.com/dos_mundos.htm. Italian-owned hotel, just off the main drag, offering comfortable rooms set in a private garden, where there's also a small swimming pool; breakfast is included. The attached *Lanterna* restaurant is recommended for authentic Italian cuisine at moderate prices. ❻

Hotel Primavera C Santander ☎762 2052, ⓕ762 0171, ⓦwww.atitlan.com/primavera.htm The design of this minimalist hotel is almost revolutionary for Guatemala – all blond wood, magnolia walls and a notable absence of típica textiles or rustic clichés. Elegant rooms, a tiny Zen-like garden zone and a classy restaurant, *Chez Alex*, downstairs. Very good value, too. ❺

Hotel Regis C Santander 3–47 ☎762 1149, ⓕ762 1152, ⓦwww.atitlan.com/regis.htm. Age-old colonial-style establishment with pleasant individual bungalows and rooms, all with cable TV, though the real attraction is the wonderful natural hot spring in the grounds. ❻

Hotel Utz-Jay C 15 de Febrero ☎762 0217, ⓕ762 1358, ⓦwww.atitlan.com/utz-jay.htm. Outstanding new hotel set in a large, tranquil garden, with five very stylish adobe-and-stone houses (all sleep up to four and have private bath), decorated with nice homely touches. In-house *tuj* herbal sauna, plus a selection of excellent tours available. Book ahead, though there may be more rooms shortly as the owners are busy constructing accommodation next door. ❹

Muller's Guest House C Rancho Grande ☎762 2442, ⓦwww.atitlan.com/muller.htm. Tasteful Swiss-owned guest house where the rooms, with quality modern European furnishings, are set around a grassy garden. Breakfast is included. ❺ –❻

Rancho Grande Inn C Rancho Grande ☎762 2255, ⓕ762 2247, ⓦwww.atitlan.com/ranchogrande .htm. A long-standing Panajachel institution with very attractive, nicely appointed bungalows, superbly kept gardens and helpful staff. Breakfast included. ❻

Boats

All the lakeside villages are served by small fast boats called **lanchas**, which have largely replaced larger, slower ferry boats. Lanchas do not run to a fixed schedule but depart when the driver has enough passengers to cover his fuel costs, so you may have to wait around a while, sometimes up to an hour at quiet times of the year. There are two **piers** in Panajachel. The pier at the end of Calle Rancho Grande is for Santa Catarina (10min), San Antonio (15min), San Lucas (30min), Santiago Atitlán (40min) and lake tours. The second pier, at the end of Calle del Embarcadero, is for all villages on the northern side of the lake: Santa Cruz (10min), Jaibalito, Tzununá and San Marcos (20min); some services continue on to San Pablo, San Juan and San Pedro (30min). There are also direct lanchas to San Pedro which cut straight across the lake in a white-knuckle twenty-minute ride, leaving from both piers, though most regularly from the second. The last boats on all these routes leave around 6.30pm.

Unfortunately, **rip-offs** are the rule for tourists: you'll be asked for two or three times what locals normally pay, so unless you can convince the boat owners that you're a resident, expect to pay around US$1.30 per trip. Another scam is charging more for the last boat of the day. **Tours of the lake**, visting San Pedro, Santiago Atitlán and San Antonio Palopó, can be booked in virtually any travel agent (see below); all leave around 9am and return by 4pm; they cost US$8–10 per person.

Luxury accommodation

Hotel Atitlán on the lakeside, 1km west of the centre ☎ & ⓕ 762 1441 or 762 1416, ⓦ www .hotelatitlan.com. The swankiest hotel in the Panajachel area with a stunning lakeside location, lovely gardens and a swimming pool. Rooms are very comfortable and tastefully decorated. A double costs US$120. ❾

Hotel Barceló del Lago right on the lakeshore ☎ 762 1555, ⓕ 762 1562, ⓦ www.atitlan.com /barcelo.htm. Opulent, all-inclusive colossus complete with pool, Jacuzzi and gym. Very corporate,

"international" flavour – only the great volcano views remind you you're in Guatemala. Doubles US$110 low season, US$162 high season. ❾

Hotel Posada de Don Rodrigo C Santander, facing the lake ☎ & ⓕ 762 2322 or 762 2329, ⓦ www.centramerica.com/posadadedondodrigo Colonial-style hotel by the lakeside, with a large outdoor pool, sauna and squash court. Most of the accommodation in the main block is on the small side, so try to book a room in the superb new wing (room nos 301–311) – they're supremely spacious and boast bathtubs and stunning volcano views. ❽

Eating, drinking and entertainment

Panajachel has an abundance of **restaurants**, all catering to the cosmopolitan tastes of its floating population. You'll have no trouble finding tasty Chinese, Italian, Mexican and Mediterranean dishes. For really cheap and authentically Guatemalan food there are plenty of comedores on and just off the new beach promenade and close to the market in the old village.

Cafés and restaurants

Bombay halfway down C Santander. Eclectic vegetarian food which, despite the name, has little Indian about it. Indonesian *gado-gado,* epic pitta-bread sandwiches (try the falafel), and organic coffee, plus a US$3 daily set menu.

Chez Alex halfway along C Santander. Unquestionably the flashest place in town, with an over-designed peach interior and gilt plates and cutlery. Heavyweight menu, majoring in European classics – the food's good, though not outstanding. Expensive.

Las Chinitas towards the northern end of Calle Santander. Excellent pan-Asian cuisine in a pretty patio setting. Nonyan (Malay–Chinese) cooking is the main draw, with Thai and Japanese dishes at moderate prices. Closed Mon.

Al Chisme C de los Árboles. A smart, European-style restaurant and bar adorned with black and white photographs of former customers. Delicious food including bagels, sandwiches, crêpes and pasta, but all a little pricey. Closed Wed.

Circus Bar C Los Árboles. Pizza is the speciality here but it also does steaks, salads and pasta and a daily set menu. Nice setting, with gingham tablecloths and walls covered with old prints. Prices are moderate, and there's live music in the evenings.

Comedor Costa Sur near the church in the old town. Clean and attractive comedor, loudly bedecked with Mexican blankets. Great breakfasts, lunchtime dishes and licuados.

Crossroads Café C del Campanario 0–27. Easily the finest coffee in town, selected, blended and roasted by perfectionists. A multitude of combina-

tions and flavourings possible, including lattes and mochas, plus real hot chocolate and fresh pastries. Closed Mon and for siesta 1–2pm.

Deli southern end of C Santander. Excellent range of healthy meals and snacks: salads, sandwiches, pastries, bagels, cakes, wine and tea in a pretty garden setting. Service is friendly, but often lethargic.

Guajimbos midway down C Santander, on the west side. Ideal for a South American-style feast, all the meat – including kebabs, *chorizo* and giant steaks – is barbecued on a giant *parrilla.*

The Last Resort C el Chali. Looks vaguely like an English pub, but does the best American buffet breakfasts in town. Also pasta, steaks and vegetarian dishes, served in huge portions.

Mario's Café halfway down Calle Santander. A limited range of low-cost food: huge salads, delicious yoghurt and pancakes.

Moonfish upper floor, C Principal 0–72. Scruffy-chic bohemian dive popular with travelling scenesters, with a fine line-up of inexpensive tempe, burritos and sandwiches, plus yoghurt licuados. Eclectic sounds – drum 'n' bass, reggae, rock – plus live music some nights.

Restaurante Jhanny halfway down C Rancho Grande. Ignore the fairylights and head inside for a superb Guatemalan-style *menú del día* (US$2.50); tables are nicely arranged around a little garden.

Restaurant Maya Kakchikel C el Chali 2–25. Bright little comedor, great for Guatemalan food, though the owners also serve up excellent filling breakfasts and crêpes.

Sunset lakeside, at the end of C Santander. The expansive lake views are the main draw here, but the mid-priced menu is also pretty good, majoring

in Tex-Mex grub, seafood and sandwiches. There's live music here some nights.
La Terraza northern end of C Santander. One of the finest restaurants on the lake, with a classy European menu plus a few Asian-influenced dishes. Quite formal, and expensive.

Nightlife

Panajachel has a gregarious party spirit at weekends and during the main holiday season, when many young Guatemalans head to the lake to drink and flirt, though things are less lively at other times. Pana's prime bar and dance scene is centred around the southern end of Calle de los Árboles, where there's a cluster of busy places including the long-running *Circus Bar*, *Porque No* and *El Aleph* for **live music**, plus the *Chapiteau* **nightclub**. For a less frenetic environment head for *Moonfish* or *The Last Resort* (see "Cafés and Restaurants", above), or *Ubu's Cosmic Cantina*, on Calle de los Árboles, where there's a big screen for sports fans, movie buffs and news addicts. Finally, there are occasional **poetry** recitals at *Delante's Bookshop* off Calle Buenas Nuevas, video **movies** at Carrot Chic and Turquoise Buffalo on Calle de los Árboles, and a **pool hall** in the old village, near the post office.

Listings

Banks and exchange Banco Inmobiliario, at C Santander and C Principal (Mon–Fri 9am–7pm, Sat 9am–12.30pm), or Banco Industrial, on C Santander, which has a 24-hr ATM for Visa card holders. Try the AT travel agency or *Hotel Regis*, both on C Santander, for Mastercard transactions.

Bicycle rental Moto Servicio Queche, C de los Árboles and C Principal, rents mountain bikes for US$1 an hour, US$5 a day.

Bookstores Delante, down an alley off C Buenas Vistas, has a friendly atmosphere and a very comprehensive selection of secondhand books. The Gallery, on C de los Árboles, stocks a reasonable choice of secondhand titles and a few interesting new books in English; or try *Café Pizzeria Pulcinella* (see "Restaurants" above), where they have a book exchange.

Language schools Escuela Jabel Tinamit, off C Santander (☎762 0238, ⓦhttp://members.nbci .com/learnspanish), and Jardín de América, Calle 14 de Febrero (☎ & ⓕ762 2637, ⓦwww.atitlan .com/jardin.htm), both offer 20 hours of tuition and family board and lodgings for US$140 per week, though you're welcome to stay in a hotel if you prefer. For private lessons, contact Mariluz Mendía (☎762 2458, ⓔMariluz_Mendia@hotmail.com), a qualified Spanish teacher who gives structured lessons for US$4 per hour.

Laundry Lavandería Automatico, C de los Árboles 0–15 (Mon–Sat 7.30am–6pm); US$3.50 for a full load washed, dried and folded.

Medical care Dr Edgar Barreno speaks good English; his surgery is down the first street that branches to the right off C de los Árboles (☎762 1008).

Motorbike rental Moto Servicio Queche, C de los Árboles and C Principal (☎762 2089), rents 185cc bikes for US$6 an hour, US$25 for 24 hours, US$100 for the week.

Pharmacy Farmacia La Unión, C Santander.

Police On the plaza in the old village (☎762 1120).

Post office In the old village, down a side street beside the church (Mon–Fri 8am–4.30pm) or try Get Guated Out, on C de los Árboles (☎762 0595, ⓔgguated@c.net.gt), for bigger shipments.

Shopping Panajachel has dozens of shops and stalls selling a huge range of ethnic trousers, shirts, waistcoats and *huipiles*, on C Santander alone.

Taxis Usually wait outside the post office, or you can call one on ☎762 1571.

Telephone To make a phone call or send a fax, check first with businesses in C Santander for the best rates; many advertise discounted calls. Otherwise, Telgua (daily 7am–midnight) is near the junction of C Santander and C 15 de Febrero.

Travel agents Rainbow Travel, C Principal near the junction with C Santander (☎762 1302), is a good all-rounder, with competitive international flight prices; Sevicios Turisticos Atitlán, C Santander, near C 14 de Febrero (☎762 2075, ⓕ762 2246, ⓦwww.atitlan.com), is another recommended agent.

Water sports Canoes, kayaks and windsurfers can be rented on the main beach. Scuba divers can dive the lake with ATI Divers who are based in Santa Cruz (see p.175) but also have a branch in Pana on C Santander, almost opposite Banco Inmobilario (☎ & ⓕ762 2646, ⓔsantacruz @guate.net); one fun-dive is US$25 while a PADI Open Water course is US$160.

Around Panajachel

About 2km west of Panajachel, the **Reserva Natural Atitlán** (8am–5pm, US$3.20, students US$2) is a privately run forest reserve covering more than a hundred hectares on the steep slopes of the lake. Also known as the Finca San Buenaventura, the reserve's land used to form one of the largest coffee farms in the Atitlán region. There are several walking trails (20–75 minutes) through dense foilage, and viewing platforms from where small mammals like possums and kinkajous are often spotted. Inside the reserve there's a **butterfly park** with 35 species, including golden orange monarchs and blue morphos, plus a breeding laboratory, and there are also orchid gardens and aviaries. To **get to** the reserve head for the *Hotel Atitlán* (see p.162), from where signposted trails lead to the adjacent reserve.

Elsewhere around the lake

The villages that surround the lake are all easily accessible. For an afternoon's outing, head along the shore southeast of Panajachel to **San Antonio** and **Santa Catarina Palopó**. If you want to spend a day or two exploring the area then it's well worth crossing the lake to **Santiago Atitlán**, and going on to **San Pedro la Laguna**. It's perfectly feasible to walk round the whole lake in four to five days; alternatively, you could cut out a section or two by catching a boat between villages. Perhaps the finest **walking** is on the western side, between San Pedro and Santa Cruz (around a six-hour hike). These southern and western shores are by far the most beautiful, and it would be a shame to visit the lake without seeing them.

The eastern shore

There are two roads around the lake's eastern shore from Panajachel: one clings to the shoreline while the other runs parallel up along the ridge of hills towards Godínez. Beside the lake, backed up against the slopes, are a couple of villages, the first of which, **SANTA CATARINA PALOPÓ**, is just 4km from Panajachel. The people of Santa Catarina used to live almost entirely by fishing and trapping crabs, but these days the black bass have put an end to all that and they've turned to farming and migratory work, with many of the women travelling to Panajachel and Antigua to peddle their weaving. The women's *huipiles* here are unusual in that they have dazzling zigzags in vibrant shades of turquoise or purple, though the traditional design was predominantly red with tiny geometric designs of people and animals. The changes are partly due to a North American who visited the village in the 1970s and commissioned a *huipil* to be made in purple, blue and green as opposed to the traditional colours. These new shades became very popular in the village and are now worn almost universally.

Much of the shoreline as you leave Santa Catarina has been bought and developed, and great villas, ringed by impenetrable walls and razor wire, have come to dominate the environment. Here you'll find the landmark *Hotel Villa Santa Catarina* (℡762 1291, ℻762 2013, ⓦwww.villasdeguatemala.com; ❼), which enjoys a prime lakeside plot, with 31 very comfortable **rooms**, two banqueting halls, a pool and restaurant. A kilometre beyond Santa Catarina, high above the lakeshore, the extremely luxurious new *Casa Palopó Hotel* (℡762 2270, ⓦwww.casapalopo.com; doubles US$120, suites US$150; ❾) offers stunning accommodation in a converted villa. Beyond here, the road winds around the shore for another 2km until you reach another upmarket place, the *San Tomas Bella Vista Retreat* (☎762 1566, ⓦwww.santomasatitlanlodge.guate.com; ➐), with fourteen attractive bungalows, all boasting great views, plus a pool and restaurant. Continuing along the lakeside road, just as the steep profile of San Antonio comes into view, the road dips and there is a beautiful secluded little beach almost hidden among the reeds. San Antonio is a further 2km from here.

Two kilometres on from the beach, **SAN ANTONIO PALOPÓ** is a larger and more traditional village, squeezed in beneath a steep hillside. The village is also on the tour group itinerary, which has encouraged some persistent sales techniques on the part of the inhabitants. The hillsides above San Antonio are well irrigated and terraced, reminiscent of rice paddies, and most men wear the village *traje* of red shirts with vertical stripes and short woollen kilts. Women wear almost identical shirts, made of the same fabric with subtle variations to the collar design. The whitewashed central church is worth a look; just to the left of the entrance are two ancient bells, while inside is a model of the birth of Jesus, San Antonio-style, with Joseph wearing the village costume.

One of the best ways to visit the two villages is on foot from above the lake. Catch a bus from Panajachel towards Godínez, and get off at the *mirador* about a kilometre before Godínez. From here you can enjoy some of the best lake views of all, and there are various paths that lead to San Antonio (about a thirty-minute walk) through vegetable terraces of spring onions and tomatoes. Alternatively, you can catch a pick-up from Panajachel, via Santa Catarina to San Antonio; they leave when full (you shouldn't have to wait more than 30 minutes) between 6am and 6pm from Calle Principal. The last pick-up returns to Panajachel from San Antonio at around 5pm.

If you decide **to stay** in San Antonio, there are two options: the fairly upmarket *Hotel Terrazas del Lago* (☎762 1288, ⒻF762 0157; ➒), down by the water, which has comfortable rooms and beautiful views, or the very simple but clean pensión (➊) owned by Juan López Sánchez, near the entrance to the village. Try the comedor below the church for a cheap **meal**.

The higher road – to Godínez and beyond to San Lucas Tolimán

The higher of the two roads heads back into the rich river delta behind Panajachel, before climbing up above the lake to **SAN ANDRÉS SEMETABAJ**, where there's a fantastic ruined colonial church. A path opposite the church's main entrance leads back to Panajachel, winding down through fields and coffee bushes – a nice walk of an hour or so. Beyond San Andrés the road curves around the edge of the ridge, offering an incredible sweeping view of the lake below and the irregular cone of the Tolimán volcano opposite, and arriving eventually in Godínez. A short way before is the *mirador* mentioned above, from where paths leads down to the lakeside village of San Antonio Palopó.

At **GODÍNEZ**, a ramshackle and wind-blown village, the road divides, one way running out to the Carretera Interamericana (through Patzicía and Patzún – though if you're driving, you should bear in mind there have been occasional attacks and robberies on this road), and the other on around the lake to the village of **SAN LUCAS TOLIMÁN** in the southeast corner. Set apart from the other villages in many ways, this is probably the least attractive of the lot. The surrounding land is almost all planted with coffee, which dominates the flavour of the place. The indigenous people take a poor second place to the sizeable ladino population, and the easy-going atmosphere of the lake is tempered by the influence of the Pacific coast. The setting, however, is as spectacular as always. The village is at the back of a small inlet of reed beds, with the Tolimán volcano rising above. Both the Tolimán and Atitlán **volcanoes** can be climbed from here, though taking a guide is recommended as the trails are difficult to find – ask at your hotel or the town hall. The main **market** day here is on Friday, which is certainly the best time to drop by, although unfortunately it clashes with the market in Santiago.

If you need somewhere to **stay**, head for the *Hotel Villa Real Internacional*, on 7 Av 1–84 (⊕722 0102; ❸–❹), with reliable hot showers, safe parking and a restaurant, or the *Hotel Brisas del Lago* (❸), down by the lake, which has similar facilities. By far the most luxurious place in San Lucas is the *Pak'ok Marina and Resort* (⊕206 7561 & 334 6076, ⑤334 6075, ⑩www.virtualguatemala .com/patok; ❼), a spectacular new hotel located in the grounds of an old coffee finca, with lovely gardens, colonial-style rooms and apartments, and a pool. For good, inexpensive food, the best place is the *Café Tolimán* by the lake, or *La Fonda* close to the plaza.

San Lucas is the junction of the coast road and the road to Santiago Atitlán, and **buses** regularly thunder through in both directions. On the whole, they head out towards Cocales and the coast and on to Guatemala City in the early morning, with the last bus at about 3pm, while there are hourly buses to Santiago between 5am and 6pm. There are also five daily buses between here and Panajachel (1hr) running mostly in the morning; the last one leaves at 4pm. Lanchas, which don't run to a fixed schedule, also connect San Lucas with Panajachel (30min; US$2), some calling in at San Antonio and Santa Catarina on the way.

Santiago Atitlán

In the southwest corner of the lake, set to one side of a sheltered horseshoe inlet, **SANTIAGO ATITLÁN** is overshadowed by the cones of the San Pedro, Atitlán and Tolimán volcanoes. It's the largest and most important of the lakeside villages, and also one of the most traditional, being the main centre of the Tz'utujil-speaking Maya. At the time of the Conquest the Tz'utujil had their fortified capital, **Chuitinamit-Atitlán**, on the slopes of San Pedro, while the bulk of the population lived spread out around the site of today's village. Alvarado and his crew, needless to say, destroyed the capital and massacred its inhabitants, assisted this time by a force of Kaqchikel Maya, who arrived at the scene in some three hundred canoes.

Today Santiago is an industrious but relaxed sort of place, in a superb setting, and if you're planning a trip around the lake it's probably best to spend the first night either here or in San Pedro. During the day the town becomes fairly commercial, its **main street**, which runs from the dock to the plaza, lined with weaving shops and art galleries. There's nothing like the Panajachel overkill, but the persistence of underage gangs can still be a bit much, particularly during the Friday morning **market**. By mid-afternoon, once the ferries have left, things revert to normal and the whole village becomes a lot more friendly.

There's little to do in Santiago other than stroll around soaking up the atmosphere, though the old colonial Catholic **church** is well worth a look for its fascinating Maya religious detail. The huge altarpiece, carved when the church was under *cofradía* control, culminates in the shape of a mountain peak and a cross, which symbolizes the Maya world tree. In the middle of the floor is a small hole which villagers believe to be the centre of the world, while dozens of statues of saints (all bedecked in indigenous atire) line the walls. The church

Holy smoke

Easter celebrations are particularly special in Santiago, and as Holy Week draws closer the town comes alive with expectation and excitement. **Maximón** (see p.192 & p.455) maintains an important role in the proceedings. On the Monday of Holy Week his image is taken to the lakeshore where it is washed, on the Tuesday he's dressed, and on the Wednesday the image is housed in a small chapel in the plaza. Here he waits until Good Friday, when the town is the scene of a huge and austere religious procession, the plaza packed out with everyone dressed in their finest traditional costume. Christ's image is paraded solemnly through the streets, arriving at the church around noon, where it's tied to a cross and raised above the altar. At around 3pm it's cut down from the cross and placed in a coffin born by penitents, who emerge from the church for a symbolic confrontation in the plaza between Christ and Maximón, who is carried out of an adjoining chapel by his bearer.

The presence of Maximón, decked out in a felt hat and Western clothes, with a cigar in his mouth, is scorned by reforming Catholics and revered by the traditionalists. The precise **origin** of the saint is unknown, but he's also referred to as San Simón, Judas Iscariot and Pedro de Alvarado, and always seen as an enemy of the church. Some say that he represents a Franciscan friar who chased after young indigenous girls, and that his legs are removed to prevent any further indulgence. "Max" in the Mam dialect means tobacco, and Maximón is always associated with ladino **vices** such as smoking and drinking; more locally he's known as *Rij Laj*, the powerful man with a white beard. Throughout the year he's looked after by a *cofradía*; if you feel like dropping in to pay your respects to him ask for "*La Casa de San Simón*", and someone will show you the way. Take along a packet of cigarettes and a bottle of *Quezalteca* for the ever-thirsty saint and his minders, who will ask you to make a contribution to fiesta funds. For details on visiting San Simón in Zunil and for a warning about the gravity of the process, see p.192.

is also home to a stone memorial commemorating **Father Stanley Rother**, an American priest who served in the parish from 1968 to 1981, and was a committed defender of his parishioners in an era when in his own words, "shaking hands with an Indian has become a political act". Branded a communist by President García, he was assassinated by a paramilitary death squad. His body was returned to his native Oklahoma for burial, but not before, with his family's consent, his heart was removed and buried in the church of Santiago Atitlán. There's an informative article about Santiago's church at Ⓦ www.mesoweb.com.

As is the case in many other parts of the Guatemalan highlands, the Catholic Church in Santiago is locked in bitter rivalry with several evangelical sects, who are building churches here at an astonishing rate. Their latest construction, right beside the lake, is the largest structure in town. Folk Catholicism also plays an important role in the life of Santiago and the town is well known as one of the main places where Maya pay homage to **Maximón**, the drinking and smoking saint (see box above).

The traditional **costume** of Santiago, still worn a fair amount, is both striking and unusual. The men wear long shorts which, like the women's *huipiles*, are white- and purple-striped, intricately embroidered with birds and flowers. Some women also wear a *xk'ap*, a band of red cloth approximately 10m long, wrapped around their heads, which has the honour of being depicted on the 25 centavo coin. Sadly, this headcloth is going out of use and on the whole you'll probably only see it at fiestas and on market days, worn by the older women.

Around Santiago: volcanoes and the nature reserve

The land around Santiago is mostly volcanic, with only the odd patch of fertile soil mixed in with the acidic ash. Farming, fishing and the traditional industry, the manufacture of *cayucos* (canoes), are no longer enough to provide for the population, and a lot of people travel to the coast, or work on the coffee plantations that surround the volcano. The Tolimán and Atitlán **volcanoes** can both be climbed from here (or San Lucas Tomilán), but you'll need up to a couple of days to make it to the top of the latter. It's always best to take a guide to smooth the way as there have been robberies. If you're looking for a guide, ask in the hotel *Chi-Nim-Ya* (see below), or at one of the restaurants.

If you're here for the day then you can walk out of town along the track to San Lucas Tolimán, or rent a **canoe** and paddle out into the lake – just ask around at the dock. To the north of Santiago is a small island which has been designated a **nature reserve**, originally for the protection of the *poc*, or **Atitlán grebe**, a flightless water bird. The *poc* used to thrive in the waters of the lake but two factors have now driven it into extinction: the overcutting of the reeds where it nests and the introduction of the fierce black bass, which ate all the young birds – although the reserve is surrounded by an underwater fence to keep out the marauding fish. Despite the disappearance of the *poc*, the island is still a beautiful place to spend an hour or two and is an interesting destination if you're paddling around in a canoe.

The expulsion of the army from Santiago Atitlán

Santiago Atitlán's recent history, like that of so many Guatemalan villages, is marked by trouble and violence. The village assumed a unique role, however, as the first in the country to successfully **expel the armed forces**. Relations between the army and the village had been strained since a permanent base was established there in the early 1980s, when the ground above the village was used extensively by ORPA guerrillas. The army accused the villagers of supporting the insurgents and attempted to terrorize the population into subservience. Throughout the 1980s villagers were abducted, tortured and murdered – a total of around three hundred were killed over eleven years.

Under civilian rule the guerrilla threat dropped off considerably and the people of Santiago grew increasingly confident and resentful of the unnecessary army presence. Matters finally came to a head on the night of December 1, 1990, when two drunken soldiers shot a villager. The men fled to the army base on the outskirts of the village but were followed by an unarmed crowd that eventually numbered around two thousand. The six hundred soldiers inside the garrison clearly believed they were about to be overwhelmed and opened fire on the crowd, killing thirteen people, including three children, and wounding another twenty. After this incident some twenty thousand villagers signed a petition calling for the expulsion of the army from Santiago and, after intense international pressure, the army finally withdrew, shutting down the base.

Difficulties then arose with the police, when, on December 6, the local civil patrol discovered a group of policemen on a suspicious night-time mission. A mob soon surrounded the police station and the police were similarly forced to leave. New recruits were sent from Guatemala City to replace them, however, but for two weeks the residents refused to sell them any food and it was a month before they agreed to allow them to use the public toilet – for a monthly fee of US$4.

In June 1991, Santiago's example was followed by neighbouring San Lucas Tolimán, where the killing of a community leader by a soldier led to the army's expulsion. Other villages in sensitive areas, including Joyabaj and Chajul, subsequently took steps to shut down army bases. The 1996 Peace Accords went some way to curtailing military interference in civilian affairs, a measure designed to keep the army off the streets.

Santiago Atitlán practicalities

Boats to Santiago leave from the beach in Panajachel at 5.45am, 9.30am, 11.30am and 3pm – the trip takes about an hour – but there are also unscheduled lancha services at other times. The village is also astonishingly well connected by **bus** with almost everywhere except Panajachel (see below); buses depart seven times daily between 2.30am and 3pm from Santiago's central plaza and head via San Lucas Tolimán and Cocales to Guatemala City.

Thanks to the steady flow of tourists, Santiago offers the full range of **accommodation**. A long running backpackers' favourite, the *Hotel Chi-Nim-Ya* (☎721 7131; ❶/❷), on the left as you enter the village from the lake, is a good deal and perennially popular; some rooms have private bath. The good-value *Hotel Tzutuhil*, in the centre of town (☎721 7174; ❷), is a five-storey concrete building with spectacular views from the top floor and a restaurant. For something special, there are a number of good options; all can be reached by water taxi from the dock, or by road. The *Posada de Santiago*, on the lakeshore 1km south of the town (☎ & ☎721 7167, ⓦwww.atitlan.com/posada.htm; ❻), is a luxury, American-owned bed and breakfast, with rooms in stone cabins, each with its own log fire, a few budget rooms and a fine restaurant. A kilometre north of the dock, the *Bird House* (☎716 7440, ⓔthebirdhousetk@hotmail.com; ❸/❹) is another excellent place to stay, with attractive rooms and apartments, nice lakeside gardens, a library and great home-made food. About 500m further north, *Hotel Bambú* (☎416 2122, ⓦwww.virtualguatemala.com/bambu; ❺) has beautiful thatch-roofed stone bungalows and rooms, plus an excellent restaurant with Spanish and Basque specialities. Next door, there's quite a scene developing at *Las Milpas* (☎416 3395, ⓔlas_milpas@hotmail.com; ❸), a great new bohemiam retreat-cum-hotel run by an ex-Grateful Dead roadie, with four comfortable cabañas, camping (US$4 per person), a hot tub and sauna, tasty vegetarian food, plenty of live music and full moon cruises.

There are several **restaurants** at the entrance to the village, just up from the dock, all fairly similar. In the centre of the village you can eat at the *Hotel Tzutuhil* or, if you really want to dine in style, head out to the restaurant in the *Posada de Santiago* or *Hotel Bambú*.

San Pedro La Laguna

Around the other side of the San Pedro volcano is the village of **SAN PEDRO LA LAGUNA**, which has now usurped Panajachel to become the pivotal centre of Guatemala's travelling scene. Generally, this status involves little more than playing host to the few dozen colourful foreigners who have set up home here and providing a plentiful supply of marijuana to keep the young gringo visitors happy. This isn't Goa, but more than anywhere else in Guatemala, it has a distinctive bohemian feel about it. Despite a rather maniacal evangelical presence, things here seem very mellow, though it has not always been so. Crack cocaine arrived here in the early 1990s, and the locals got so fed up with wasted gringos that they wrote to a national newspaper demanding that the freaks leave their village. Today things have settled down again, and the mostly evangelical locals and the travellers seem to rub along reasonably well together.

San Pedro has also started to establish itself as a **language school** centre in recent years, the beautiful location drawing increasing numbers of students, though the quality of tuition is pretty variable at present. Of the four (or more) schools in San Pedro, the best are Casa Rosario, just south of Santiago Atitlán dock (☎767 5795, ⓦwww.worldwide.edu/ci/guatemala/schools/34451.html), and the San Pedro Spanish School, which is located between the piers (℡703 1100, ⊛www.spanish–schools.com)

Again, the setting is spectacular, with the San Pedro volcano rising to the east and a ridge of steep hills running behind the village. To the left of the main beach, as you look towards the lake, a line of huge white boulders juts out into the water – an ideal spot for an afternoon of swimming and sunbathing. Tradition isn't as powerful here and only a few elderly people, mostly men, wear the old costume, although there is a sense of permanence in the narrow cobbled streets and old stone houses. The people of San Pedro have a reputation for driving a hard bargain when trading their coffee and avocados, and have managed to buy up a lot of land from neighbouring San Juan, with whom there's endless rivalry. They're also famed for the *cayucos* (canoes) made from the great cedar trees that grow on the slopes of the San Pedro volcano.

The **San Pedro volcano**, which towers above the village to a height of some 3020m, is largely coated with tropical forest and can be climbed in four to five hours; get an early start in order to see the views at their best and avoid the worst of the heat. The peak itself is also ringed by forest, which blocks the view

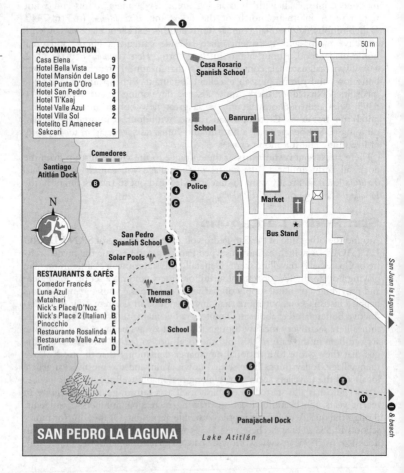

ACCOMMODATION

Casa Elena	9
Hotel Bella Vista	7
Hotel Mansión del Lago	6
Hotel Punta D'Oro	1
Hotel San Pedro	3
Hotel Ti'Kaaj	4
Hotel Valle Azul	8
Hotel Villa Sol	2
Hotelito El Amanecer Sakcari	5

RESTAURANTS & CAFÉS

Comedor Francés	F
Luna Azul	I
Matahari	C
Nick's Place/D'Noz	G
Nick's Place 2 (Italian)	B
Pinocchio	E
Restaurante Rosalinda	A
Restaurante Valle Azul	H
Tintin	D

SAN PEDRO LA LAGUNA   Lake Atitlán

over San Pedro, although an opening on the south side gives excellent views of Santiago. Most of the village **guides** are reliable – including Samuel Cumatz Batzin (☎762 2487), who can often be found at *Casa Elena* (see below) – and it's well worth utilizing their services, as the foliage is dense and the route can be tricky to find. Unfortunately there have been sporadic **attacks** on the volcano; it's best to ask around to assess the current situation before you start climbing. A neighbouring peak to the west of San Pedro, nicknamed "Indian Nose", is another popular excursion, offering stunning vistas of the lake and its three volcanoes – any of the guides will be happy to take you there. Guides charge US$5-8 per person for these hikes; the exact cost depends the numbers involved and your bargaining powers.

If you'd rather do something less exhausting, Excursion Big Foot (☎204 6267), just left of the Panajachel dock, rents out **horses** for US$2.50 an hour, **bicycles** for US$10 a day and **canoes** for US$2 for two hours, or you could just soak yourself at the **thermal baths**. Two sets of pools, adjacent to each other halfway between the two docks, offer a real opportunity to relax – the better of these, Thermal Waters (☎206 9658, ✉thermalwaters@hotmail.com; open late afternoon only; US$2.50 per person) – is run by Antonio, a long-term Canadian resident, who also offers fine organic vegetarian food and camping spots (see below). There's also a **weaving school** where you can create you own *huipil* if you have the patience, though getting together a scarf or cushion cover is quite enough for most.

Arrival and information

There are **two docks** in San Pedro. All boats from Panajachel and villages on the north side of the lake, including Santa Cruz and San Marcos, arrive and depart from the Panajachel dock on the north side of town, while boats from Santiago Atitlán use a separate dock a ten-minute walk away. Three daily **buses** from Guatemala City's Zona 4 terminal run to San Pedro, returning at 3am, 5am and noon; there's also a daily service from Quetzaltenango. There are also regular pick-ups around the lake as far as San Marcos and up to Sololá, but none towards Santiago Atitlán.

Most of the village is centred around the Catholic church in the centre of town, where you'll find the **marketplace** (busiest on Thurs and Sun), **post office** and, a block to the south, Banrural (Mon–Fri 9am–5.30pm, Sat 9am–12.30pm) which will change travellers' cheques. There are very few phone lines in town, and consequently just one place, Solar Pools, between the docks, currently offers international call and **email** facilities – most visitors head into Panajachel where there are much speedier and cheaper connections.

Accommodation

San Pedro has some of the cheapest accommodation in all Latin America, with a number of basic, clean **guest houses** that charge less than US$3 a person per night, plus **camping** at Thermal Waters, halfway between the docks (US$1.30 per person; see above). There's nothing much in the way of luxury, but there are a few new comfortable options. If you plan to stay around for a while then you might want to consider **renting a house**, which works out incredibly cheap; try the noticeboard in *D' Noz* bar above *Nick's Place*. To locate any of the hotels listed below, let one of the local children guide you through the coffee bushes; a tip of a quetzal or two is appropriate.

Casa Elena left after *Nick's Place*. Nine tidy rooms with twin beds, some right on the lakeshore. Owned by a friendly Maya family. ❶

Hotel Bella Vista turn left after *Nick's Place*, by the docks. Pretty decent budget hotel with really cheap rates and clean, bare rooms. The mattresses are foam slabs, though. ❶

Hotelito El Amanecer Sakcari between the docks ☎812 1113. Friendly, family-run place with ten attractive tiled rooms, all with private bath. Most of the rooms have wonderful lake views. ❷

Hotel Mansión del Lago right above the Panajachel dock ☎811 8172. Bulky, somewhat obtrusive new place, with spotless, excellent-value rooms that are unquestionably the smartest in town: all have nice pine beds, private bath and balcony areas with lake outlooks. ❷–❸

Hotel Resort Punta d'Oro 500m north of Santiago Atitlán dock ☎208 1836, ⓦwww.atitlan.com /puntadeoro. Fine lakeside position with grassy grounds that stretch to a little beach. The rooms, all with kitchen facilities, are a little shabby for the price, however. Jacuzzi, small pool and canoe rental. ❺

Hotel San Pedro close to the Santiago Atitlán dock, next door to the *Villa Sol*. Set above the police station, this should be be the safest place in town. Clean rooms, some with private bath. ❷

Hotel Ti'Kaaj near the Santiago Atitlán dock. Very basic rooms, but the lovely shady garden, replete with orange trees and hammocks, certainly helps compensate. ❶

Hotel Valle Azul turn right at the Panajachel dock ☎207 7292. Hulking concrete monster of a hotel, but the views are excellent and the good-value rooms, some with private bath, are reasonable enough. ❶/❷

Hotel Villa Sol beside the Santiago Atitlán dock ☎334 0327, ⓕ360 0994. Plenty of space here, but the 42 clean, perfunctory rooms are set in somewhat souless twin-deck blocks. Bizarrely – despite the location – none enjoy lake views. ❶/❷

Eating and drinking

The steady flow of gringo travellers has given San Pedro's **cafés and restaurants** a decidedly international flavour, and most places are excellent value for money. Vegetarians are well catered for, though there are also a few typical Guatemalan comedores in the centre of the village and by the Santiago Atitlán dock. The San Pedro **drinking** scene is centred around the English-owned *D'Noz* bar, above *Nick's Place*, where you'll find an eclectic musical selection including a good slice of techno and drum 'n' bass, plus free video movies (nightly, at 7pm) and tasty food. Between the docks there are more drinking holes, including the Dutch-run *Tony's Sports Bar* and *Torj's Bar* over the pathway. The guys at *D'Noz* also organize DJ-driven techno and hard house **full moon parties** on the lakeside close to San Pedro most months of the year, though events are sometimes cancelled in the rainy season.

Cafés and restaurants

Café Luna Azul 400m west of the Panajachel dock. Wonderful lakeside location, with a good dock for swimming and sunning, plus great breakfasts, lunches and treats – try the chocolate fudge cake. Open daily 9am–4pm.

Comedor Francés between the docks. Reasonably priced Gallic fare – coq-au-vin at less than US$2 and yummy crêpes.

Matahari turn right from the Santiago Atitlán dock. The best comedor in San Pedro, with tasty line-up of Guatemalan dishes and amazingly good fries.

Nick's Place by the Panajachel dock. Great-value grub (chicken and chips at US$2) and a lakefront location make this the most popular place in town. There's another branch serving Italian food beside the Santiago dock.

Pinocchio between the two docks. Consistently good Italian, where you can feast on bruschetta and pasta in a pretty garden setting.

Restaurante Rosalinda a short walk uphill from the Santiago Atitlán dock. Excellent comedor – fresh lake fish, grilled meats and a warm welcome.

Restaurante Ti'Kaaj opposite the eponymous hotel. Stunning views of the lake and volcanoes from the upper floor and a lovely garden out front, too. Famous for its burgers, though it also does great breakfasts and pasta.

Restaurante Valle Azul overlooking the lake. Popular for daytime chilling and tasty snacks and drinks.

Tintin between the docks. Pleasant patio setting and a delicious menu of pitta bread sandwiches, Thai and Indonesian dishes.

The northern shore

The **northern side** of the lake harbours a string of isolated villages, including some of the most traditional settlements of the Central Highlands. From San Pedro, a rough road runs as far as Tzununá and from there a spectacular path continues all the way to Sololá. Non-direct lanchas to Panajachel will call in at any village en route, but the best way to see this string of isolated settlements is **on foot**: it makes a fantastic day's walk. A narrow strip of level land is wedged between the water and the steep hills most of the way, but where this disappears the path is cut into the slope providing dizzying views of the lake below. To walk from San Pedro to Santa Cruz takes between five and six hours and if you want some really rewarding hiking, this is the section of the lake to head for. At several of the villages along the way tiendas sell Coke and biscuits, so there's no need to carry gallons of water. There's a good choice of accommodation along the way, in San Marcos, Jaibalito and Santa Cruz.

From San Pedro you follow a dirt road to **SAN JUAN LA LAGUNA**, just 2km or so away at the back of a sweeping bay surrounded by shallow beaches. The village specializes in the weaving of *petates*, mats made from lake reeds, and there's a large weaving co-op, Las Artesanías de San Juan, where they welcome visitors and have plenty of goods for sale – if you walk from the dock it's signposted on the left. On the other side of the street is the simple *Hospedaje Estrella del Lago* (**❶**) with eleven secure rooms, none with private bath, while uphill, in the centre of the village, you'll find a quiet comedor, *Restaurant Chi'nimaya*, and a very under-used branch of *Nick's Place*, a quiet sibling restaurant to that in San Pedro, serving North American-style sandwiches and meals. Behind the church and basketball court, there's a shrine to **Maximón** (see p.167), the San Juan branch of the evil saint's property portfolio. Dressed in local garb, he attracts fewer visitors here than elsewhere, so you may want to bring him some liquor or a cigar. Leaving San Juan, you'll pass below the Tz'utujil settlement of **SAN PABLO LA LAGUNA**, perched high above the lake a fifteen-minute walk away, and connected to the Carretera Interamericana by a tortuous road. The village's traditional speciality is the manufacture of rope from the fibres of the maguey plant; you can sometimes see great lengths being stretched and twisted in the streets. Continuing along the lakeside road, however, the route cuts through extensive coffee plantations and past terraced fields planted with spring onions.

San Marcos La Laguna

Guatemala's premier New Age centre, the tiny village of **SAN MARCOS LA LAGUNA**, is about a two-hour walk from San Pedro, or a twenty-minute ride in one of the regular pick-ups that bump along the road between the villages. The land close to the lakeshore, densely wooded with banana, mango, jocote and avocado trees, is where San Marcos' bohemian hotels and guest houses have been sensitively established, while the Maya village is centred on higher ground away from the shore. Apart from a huge new stone church, built to replace a colonial original destroyed in the 1976 earthquake, there are no sights in the Maya village. Though distinctly polarized, relationships between the two communities remain reasonably good.

San Marcos has a decidedly tranquil appeal – there's little in the way of partying and no bar scene at all. The main draw is the *Las Pirámides* yoga and meditation retreat (see "Accommodation", below), with a surplus of auxiliary practitioners and masseurs, plus the requisite organic bakery and healing centre. It may also be possible to study Spanish here in the near future as the San Pedro-based Casa Rosario school (see p.169) is planning to open a branch locally. There's excellent swimming from a number of wooden jetties by the lakeshore, and a mesmerizing view of Atitlán's three volcanoes, including a perspective of the double-coned summit of Tolimán, plus a glimpse of the grey 3975-metre peak of Acatenango, over 50km to the east.

Accommodation

To **get to** any of the places listed below, disembark at the westernmost of San Marcos' two docks, where *Posada Schumann* and *Las Pirámides* have jetties (look out for the mini-pyramid), and all accommodation is signposted from there.

Hotel Quetzal ☎306 5039. Good-value private rooms and a small dormitory in a sturdy-looking two-storey house. Children welcome. ❷

Hotel San Marcos. Six cheap and perfunctory but clean rooms in a concrete block, none with private bath. ❷

El Paco Real ☎801 2297. Attractive French-owned place, with pleasant, well-constructed stone bungalows, some sleeping up to four, set in a garden dotted with chairs. No private bathrooms, but the communal facilities are kept spotless. Terrific in-house restaurant. ❸

Las Pirámides ☎205 7151, ⓦwww.laspiramides .com.gt. Meditation retreat set in leafy grounds, where monthly courses beginning the day after full moon (though you can also enrol on a daily or weekly basis) include hatha yoga, healing and meditation techniques, plus days of fasting and silence and plenty of esoteric pursuits. All accommodation is in comfortable pyramid cabañas, and there's delicious vegetarian food. US$10–12 per person per day including all courses but not food.

Posada Schumann cell phone ☎202 2216. Stylish, solar-powered hotel with a wonderful lakeside plot and accommodation in rooms or stone bungalows (sleeping between two and six); numbers 8 and 10 have stupendous volcano views. Very friendly management, decent restaurant, private wooden jetty for sunbathing and swimming, plus a Maya sauna. ❹/❺

Unicornio Quirky English–Guatemalan-owned set-up with small A-frame huts in a nice garden, with a kitchen and a sauna. Massages available. ❷

Eating

There's a limited choice of places to eat in San Marcos, with inexpensive Guatemalan food available at the *Comedor Marquensita* and *Sonoma* close to the church, and pretty decent pizza and pasta at *Rudy's Place* at the back of the village, though it's best to order in advance and come back later. Otherwise, any of the hotels closer to the lakeshore have restaurants attached, with superb but pricey French food at *El Paco Real*. There's also excellent healthy eating (including delicious sandwiches and salads) at *Las Pirámides*, while *Posada Schumann* also has a good menu.

Tzununá to Paxanax

Beyond San Marcos, the villages en route have a greater feeling of isolation, and you'll find the people surprised to see you and often eager for a glimpse of passing gringos. Nowhere is this more true than in **TZUNUNÁ**, the next place along the way, where the women run from oncoming strangers, sheltering behind the nearest tree in giggling groups. They wear beautiful red *huipiles* striped with blue and yellow on the back. The village originally sat at the lakeside, but after it was badly damaged by a flood in 1950 the people rebuilt their homes on the higher ground. Here the road indisputably ends, giving way to a narrow path cut out of the steep hillside, which can be a little hard to follow as it descends to cross small streams and then climbs again around the rocky outcrops.

The next, slightly ragged-looking place is **JAIBALITO**, an isolated lakeside settlement nestled between soaring *milpa*-clad slopes. Though the village remains resolutely Kaqchikel – very little Spanish is spoken and few women have ever journeyed beyond Lago de Atitlán – the opening of two new **hotels** means that outside influence is growing. Almost lost amongst the coffee bushes, 70m north of the main pathway, the Norwegian-owned *Vulcano Lodge* (☎410 2237, ⓦwww.atitlan.com/vulcano.htm; ❹/❺) is tranquil and beautifully maintained, its well-tended garden bursting with bougainvillea and flowering scrubs and scattered with sun loungers and hammocks. There's a bright little restaurant decorated with antique *huipiles*, and a choice of spotless, comfortable double rooms and very stylish two-bedroomed suites with balconies, ideal for families. Heading west, it's a steep five-minute walk up along the cliff path to the spectacularly sited *La Casa del Mundo* (T204 5558, F762 2333, Wwww .atitlan.com/casamundo.htm; rooms ❹/❺, suite ❾). It's a simply magnificent place, the culmination of twelve years' work by the warm North American host family, with a range of atmospheric accommodation including a budget room, doubles (rooms 1 and 3 have the best views), detached stone cabins, and a glorious suite with private Jacuzzi, kitchen and balcony. Guests can rent kayaks – the hotel boasts its own dock – and use the lakeside hot tub. **Lanchas** between Panajachel and San Pedro stop at the village pier about every half-hour.

From Jaibalito it's around an hour to Santa Cruz along a stunning, easy-to-follow path gripping the steep hillside. Set well back from the lake on a shelf 100m or so above the water, **SANTA CRUZ LA LAGUNA** is the largest in this line of villages with a population of around 4000. If you arrive here by boat it may appear to be just a collection of **hotels**, as the village is higher up above the lake. There isn't much to see in Santa Cruz, apart from a fine sixteenth-century church, and most people spend their time here walking, swimming or just chilling out with a book.

On the shore, opposite a line of wooden jetties, you'll find the *Iguana Perdida* (Wwww.atitlan.com/iguana.htm; ❷–❸), owned by English–American couple Dave and Deedle, with undoubtedly the most convivial atmosphere in Lago de Atitlán. The rooms are fairly basic, ranging from dorms (US$2.75) to twin-bedded doubles, but it's the gorgeous, peaceful site overlooking the lake and volcanoes that really makes this place. Dinner is a wholesome three-course communal affair (US$4.50) and the *Iguana* is also home to Lago de Atitlán's only **dive school**, ATI Divers (in Panajachel T762 2646, Wwww.atitlan.com), a professional PADI outfit that can train all levels up to assistant instructor. Next door is another good place, the slightly more expensive and comfortable *Hotel Arca de Noé* (cell phone T306 4352, Wwww.atitlan.com/arcadenoe.htm; ❸–❺), with a selection of attractive rooms, most with private bath, and uninterrupted views of the lake from the spacious terraced gardens. There's good home cooking here as well, with large breakfasts for US$4 and dinner for US$7. On the other side of the main dock, the *Posada Abaj* (Wwww .atitlan.com/abaj; ❹) offers beautiful, peaceful gardens, decent, though unexceptional, rooms and a restaurant. However, service standards are not always the highest, and perhaps consequently the hotel is less popular than the others and much more subdued.

There's some spectacular hiking in the hills behind Santa Cruz, including a forty-minute hike to a lovely **waterfall**, reached by following a trail that cuts inland from the village football pitch, which is located ten minutes' west of the lakeside hotels on the path towards Jaibalito. Alternatively, you could walk up through the village **to Sololá**, along a spectacular and easy-to-follow path that takes around three hours, and from there catch a bus back to Panajachel. If you want to do this walk in the other direction – **from Sololá to Santa Cruz** – you should head west out of Sololá along the dirt road towards San José Chacayá and, as you come up out of the river valley, about 1km out of Sololá, follow the track branching off to the left. The track can be very hard to find as there are many leaving Sololá in this direction, so ask around before committing yourself to any particular direction, but once you've found the right trail, it's a straightforward (though slippery in the rainy season) descent to Santa Cruz.

Following the lakeshore beyond Santa Cruz, a path wriggles along the waterfront past luxury villas for a kilometre to the small bay of **PAXANAX**, ringed by about twenty holiday homes, where a magnificent and superb-value luxury guest house, *Villa Sumaya* (⊤762 0488; ⓦwww.villasumaya.com; ❺/❻) enjoys a prime site with stupendous lake views. All the seven rooms, and one suite, have stylish decor and balconies with hammocks, and there's a fine Mediterranean restaurant, a hot tub and sauna. Expect a warm welcome from Armand and Wendy Boissey, the young French–American couple who own this gorgeous retreat, where guests can also hire kayaks and windsurfers.

Beyond Paxanax the path that runs directly to Panajachel is very hard to follow, and distraught walkers have been known to spend as long as seven hours scrambling through the undergrowth. **Lanchas** will call in at Paxanax if they see you waving from the pier beside *Villa Sumaya*, but as there's very little traffic from here it's often best to retreat back to Santa Cruz to move on.

Along the Carretera Interamericana: Los Encuentros to Cuatro Caminos

Heading west from the Los Encuentros junction to Cuatro Caminos and the Quetzaltenango valley, the Carretera Interamericana runs through some fantastic high mountain scenery. The views alone are superb, and if you have a Sunday morning to spare then it's well worth dropping into Nahualá for the market. **LOS ENCUENTROS** itself is an all-important staging point on the Carretera Interamericana and typical of the junctions along the way, with wooden comedores, an army base, and a team of enthusiastic sales people who besiege waiting buses. Here a branch road heads north to Chichicastenango, while the main highway continues west towards Quetzaltenango, Huehuetenango and the Mexican border. Only a kilometre or so beyond this turning, at the **EL CUCHILLO** junction, a second road runs south to Sololá, Panajachel and the shores of Lake Atitlán.

These junctions are likely to feature heavily in your travels as it's here that you transfer from one bus to another on routes between Panajachel, Chichicastenango and the rest of the country. There are direct buses to and from all of these places, but if their schedule doesn't coincide with yours then it's easier to take any bus to the junction and intercept one going your way – all buses stop here and their destinations are yelled by the driver's assistant, touting for business. The last buses to Chichicastenango, Panajachel and Guatemala City pass through Los Encuentros at around 6pm; if you miss those you'll have to negotiate with a taxi.

Nahualá

West of Los Encuentros and El Cuchillo the Carretera Interamericana runs through some spectacular and sparsely inhabited countryside. The only place of any size before Cuatro Caminos is **NAHUALÁ**, "place of sorcerers", a small and intensely traditional town a kilometre or so to the north of the highway, at the base of a huge, steep-sided and intensely farmed bowl. The unique atmosphere of isolation from and indifference to the outside world makes Nahualá one of the most impressive and unusual K'iche' towns.

The town itself is not much to look at, a sprawl of old cobbled streets and adobe houses mixed with newer concrete structures, but the inhabitants of Nahualá have a reputation for fiercely preserving their independence and have held out against ladino incursions with exceptional tenacity. At the end of the nineteenth century the government confiscated much of their land, as they did throughout the country, and sold it to coffee planters. In protest, the entire male population of Nahualá walked the 150km to Guatemala City and demanded to see President Barrios in person, refusing his offers to admit a spokesman and insisting that they all stood as one. Eventually they were allowed into the huge reception room where they knelt with their foreheads pressed to the floor, refusing to leave until they were either given assurances of their land rights or allowed to buy the land back, which they had done twice before. The action managed to save their land that time, but since then much of it has gradually been consumed by coffee bushes all the same.

On another occasion, this time during the 1930s under President Ubico, ladinos were sent to the town as nurses, telegraph operators and soldiers. Once again the Nahualáns appealed directly to the president, insisting that their own people should be trained to do these jobs, and once again their request was granted. Ubico also wanted to set up a government-run drink store, but the villagers chose instead to ban alcohol, and Nahualeños who got drunk elsewhere were expected to confess their guilt and face twenty lashes in the town's plaza.

These days the ban's been lifted, and if you're here for the fiesta on November 25 you'll see that the people are keen to make up for all those dry years. However, only a handful of ladinos live in the town, and the indigenous Maya still have a reputation for hostility, with rumours circulating about the black deeds done by the local shaman. You don't have much to worry about if you drop in for the **Sunday market**, though, as this is one time that the town is full to bursting and the people seem genuinely pleased to welcome visitors. There is also a smaller market on Thursdays.

The town is also a major centre of artisan craft. The **weaving** is outstanding: the *huipiles*, designed in intricate geometrical patterns of orange on white, particularly impressed the Spanish because they featured a double-headed eagle, the emblem of the Habsburgs who ruled Spain at the time of the Conquest. The men wear bright yellow and pink shirts with beautifully embroidered collars, short woollen "skirts" called *rodilleras*, which are worn with white trousers underneath, also huge hats and leather sandals very similar to those of the ancient Maya. Woollen garments including *capixay* cloaks and jackets are also woven locally. The town is also famous for its woodwork, and Nahualá carpenters churn out a good proportion of the country's hand-carved pine and cedar wood bedsteads and wardrobes.

To **get to Nahualá** take any bus along the Carretera Interamericana between Los Encuentros and Cuatro Caminos, and get off at the *Puente Nahualá*, from where it's a kilometre or so up the path behind the old bus shelter. There are a few very basic pensiones (all ❶) in the centre of town, but it's easier to visit on a day-trip from Chichicastenango, Panajachel or Quetzaltenango.

Santa Catarina and the Alaskan heights

Beyond Nahualá the road continues west, climbing a mountainous ridge and passing the entrance road to **SANTA CATARINA IXTAHUACÁN**, a sister and bitter rival of Nahualá, just north of the highway. Santa Catarina used to be located on notoriously unstable land on the south side of the Carretera Interamericana, only moving to its present position in December 2000 after huge sink holes swallowed up and destroyed several houses. The costumes and traditions of Santa Catarina and Nahualá, which are together known as the **Pueblos Chancatales**, are fairly similar, and they're both famous as producers of *metates*, the stones used for grinding corn. These days much corn-grinding is done by machine and they've turned to making smaller toy versions and rustic wooden furniture – both of which you'll see peddled by the roadside.

Just west of Santa Catarina, the road bottoms out on a flat plateau high up in the hills – one of the most impressive sections of the Carretera Interamericana. Known as **Alaska**, this exposed tract of land, where the men of both Nahualá and Santa Catarina farm wheat and graze sheep, shines white with frost in the early mornings. At more than 3000m, almost on a level with the great cones, the view is of course fantastic – this is one of the highest points anywhere on the highway (second only to the Cerro de la Muerte in Costa Rica, which reaches 3300m). Away to the east a string of volcanoes runs into the distance, and to the west the Totonicapán valley stretches out below you.

Further on, as the road drops over the other side of the ridge, the Quetzaltenango valley opens out to the left, a broad plain reaching across to the foot of the Santa María volcano. At the base of the ridge the highway arrives at the Cuatro Caminos crossroads, the crucial junction of the extreme western highlands. Turning right here leads to Totonicapán, left to Quetzaltenango, and straight on for Huehuetenango and the Mexican border.

Quetzaltenango and around

To the west of Lake Atitlán the highlands rise to form a steep-sided ridge topped by a string of forested peaks. On the far side of this is the **Quetzaltenango basin**, a sweeping expanse of level ground that forms the natural hub of the western highlands. The Quetzaltenango basin is perhaps the most hospitable area in the region, encompassing a huge area of fertile farmland that has been densely populated since the earliest of times. Originally it was part of the Mam kingdom, administered from their capital **Zaculeu** (at a site adjacent to the modern city of Huehuetenango), but sometime between 1400 and 1475 the area was overrun by the K'iche', and was still under their control when the Spanish arrived. Today the western side of the valley is Mam-speaking and the east K'iche'. It was here that the conquistador Pedro de Alvarado first struggled up into the highlands, having already confronted one K'iche' army on the coast and another in the pass at the entrance to the valley. Alvarado and his troops came upon the abandoned city of Xelajú (near Quetzaltenango) and were able to enter it without encountering any resistance. Six days later they fought the K'iche' in a decisive battle on the nearby plain, massacring the Maya warriors – legend has it that Alvarado himself killed the king Tecún Umán in hand-to-hand combat. The old city was then abandoned and the new town of Quetzaltenango established in its place. The name means "the place of the quetzals" in Nahuatl, the language spoken by Alvarado's Mexican allies. Quetzals may well have existed here then, but the name is more likely to have been chosen because of the brilliant green quetzal feathers worn by the K'iche' nobles and warriors, including, no doubt, Tecún Umán himself.

It's easy to spend a week or two exploring this part of the country; making day-trips to the markets and fiestas, basking in hot springs, or hiking in the mountains. Nowadays the valley is heavily populated, with three major towns: the departmental capital of **Quetzaltenango** (Xela) – the obvious place to base yourself, with bus connections to all parts of the western highlands – and the textile centres of **Salcajá** and **San Cristóbal Totonicapán**. In the surrounding hills are numerous smaller towns and villages, mostly indigenous agricultural communities and weaving centres. To the south, straddling the coast road, are **Almolonga**, **Zunil** and **Cantel**, all overshadowed by volcanic peaks, where you'll find superb natural hot springs, including **Fuentes Georginas**, a wonderful natural spa. To the north are **Totonicapán**, capital of the department of the same name, and **San Francisco el Alto**, a small market town perched on an outcrop overlooking the valley. Beyond that, in the midst of a pine forest, lies **Momostenango**, the country's principal wool-producing centre. Throughout this network of towns and villages Maya culture remains strong, based on a simple rural economy that operates in a series of weekly markets, bringing each town to life for one day a week. Leaving Quetzaltenango you can head west to the rather neglected, little-visited department of **San Marcos** – a potential **route to Mexico** by the coastal crossing, and the home of the country's highest volcano, Tajumulco. You could also follow the Carretera Interamericana to **Huehuetenango**, and cross into Mexico from there.

Set in some of the finest highland scenery, the area offers excellent **hiking**. The most obvious climb is the **Santa María volcano**, towering above Quetzaltenango itself. It's just possible to make this climb as a day-trip, but to really enjoy it, and increase your chances of a good view from the top, you should plan to take two days, camping on the way. If you haven't the time, energy or equipment for this then try instead the hike to **Laguna Chicabal**, a small lake set in the cone of an extinct volcano. The lake is spectacularly beautiful, and can easily be reached as a day-trip from Quetzaltenango, setting out from the village of **San Martín Sacatepéquez**.

Quetzaltenango (Xela)

Totally unlike the capital, and only a fraction of its size, Guatemala's second city, **QUETZALTENANGO (XELA)**, has the subdued provincial atmosphere that you might expect in the capital of the highlands, its edges gently giving way to corn and maize fields. Bizarre though it may seem, Quetzaltenango's character and appearance is vaguely reminiscent of a Northern English industrial town – grey, cool, slightly dour and culturally conservative. Ringed by high mountains, and bitterly cold in the early mornings, the city wakes slowly, only getting going once the warmth of the sun has made its mark. The main plaza, heavily indebted to Neoclassicism, is a monument to stability, with great slabs of grey stone that look reassuringly permanent, defying a history of turbulence and struggle. The heart of town has the calm order of a regional administrative centre, while its outskirts are ruffled by the bustle of a Maya market and bus terminal. Locally, the city is usually referred to as Xela (pronounced "shey-la"), a shortening of the K'iche' name of a nearby pre-conquest city, Xelajú. Meaning "under the ten", the name is probably a reference to the surrounding peaks.

A brief history

Under colonial rule Quetzaltenango flourished as a commercial centre, benefiting from the fertility of the surrounding farmland and good connections to

San Pedro & San Marcos

Cuatro Caminos & Guatemala City

▼ Almolonga

the port at Champerico. When the prospect of independence eventually arose, the city was set on deciding its own destiny. After the Central American Federation broke with Mexico in 1820, Quetzaltenango declared itself the capital of the independent state of **Los Altos**, which incorporated the modern departments of Huehuetenango, Sololá, San Marcos and Totonicapán. But the separatist movement was soon brought to heel by President Carrera in 1840, and a later attempt at secession, in 1848, was put down by force. Despite having to accept provincial status, the town remained an important centre of commerce and culture, consistently rivalling Guatemala City. The coffee boom at the end of the last century was particularly significant, as Quetzaltenango controlled some of the richest coffee land in the country. Its wealth and population grew rapidly, incorporating a large influx of German immigrants, and by the end of the nineteenth century Quetzaltenango was firmly established as an equal to Guatemala City.

All this, however, came to an abrupt end when the city was almost totally destroyed by the massive **1902 earthquake**. Rebuilding took place in a mood of high hopes; all the grand Neoclassical architecture dates from this period. A new rail line was built to connect the city with the coast, but after this was washed out in 1932–33 the town never regained its former glory, gradually falling further and further behind the capital.

Today, nevertheless, Quetzaltenango has all the trappings of wealth and self-importance: the grand imperial architecture, the great banks, and a list of famous sons. But it is completely devoid of the rampant energy that binds Guatemala City to the all-American twenty-first century. Instead the city finds itself suspended in the late nineteenth century, with a calm, dignified air that borders on the haughty. Quetzaltecos have a reputation for formality and politeness, and pride themselves on the restrained sophistication of their cultured semi-provincial existence.

The city arguably now eclipses the capital as **educational centre**, with eight universities and more than a hundred private colleges that attract high-school students from all over the country, and from as far away as El Salvador. Since the early 1990s, the city has also established itself as one of Latin America's principal **language school** hubs, and can now boast around seventy Spanish schools (see p.185). This growing influx of international students and travellers had brought a cosmopolitan influence to the city's bars, restaurants and cultural life, and many visitors find themselves seduced by the relatively easy-going character of the place, making firm local friendships, and end up staying a lot longer than planned.

Arrival and information

Unhelpfully for the traveller, virtually all buses arrive in and depart from nowhere near the centre of Quetzaltenango. If you arrive by **second class bus** you will almost certainly end up in the chaotic **Minerva bus terminal** on the western side of the city, on the northern side of the Parque Minerva, just off 6 Calle. It's quite a way from the centre – about 15min or so depending on traffic – so you'll need to catch a local bus to and from the plaza. Local buses heading into town stop on the other side of the road, on 4 Calle. Separating the two is a large covered market: walk down the passage that runs through the middle of this, and on the south side cross a large patch of open ground to reach the road. Any of the small buses going to the left will take you to the plaza – look out for a "parque" sign on the front of the bus. Local buses run Mon–Sat 6am–9pm, Sun 8am–9pm, and charge 75 centavos – you need to have some change to hand.

First-class or pullman buses come and go from the office of the particular company. Líneas Américas is on 7 Av 3–33, in Zona 2, just off Calzada Independencia, on the eastern side of town (☎761 2063 or 761 4587); Alamo is at 14 Av 14–04, Zona 3 (☎761 7117); while the Galgos terminal is at C Rodolfo Robles 17–43, Zona 1 (☎761 2248). An extremely useful transport hub is a roundabout called the **rotunda** at the far end of Calzada Independencia, where virtually all long-distance buses stop on their way to and from the city.

The official **tourist office** (Mon–Fri 8am–1pm & 2–5pm, Sat 8am–noon; ☎761 4931) is on the main plaza. Here you can pick up a map of the town and get information on trips to the surrounding villages. In addition, the owners of Casa Iximulew travel agency, 15 Av 5 C, Zona 1 (☎763 5270 or 765 1308), are always keen to point tourists in the right direction and know the area very well; they have a full bus timetable and also run tours to the villages and volcanos around Xela. There's an excellent **website** (ⓦ www.xelapages.com) devoted to the city and region, with comprehensive hotel and accommodation listings, lots of good cultural information and a useful chat room-cum-noticeboard.

Orientation and city transport

Quetzaltenango is laid out on a standard grid pattern, somewhat complicated by a number of steep hills. Basically, **avenidas** run north–south, and **calles** east–west. The oldest part of the city, focused around the plaza, is made up of tightly grouped narrow streets while in the newer part, reaching out towards the Minerva terminal and sports stadium, the blocks are larger. The city is also

Quetzaltenango transport connections

As the focus of the western highlands, Quetzaltenango is served by literally hundreds of buses. **Getting to Quetzaltenango** is fairly straightforward: there are direct pullmans from Guatemala City, and at any point along the Carretera Interamericana you can flag down a bus to take you to Cuatro Caminos, from where buses leave for Quetzaltenango every twenty minutes (the last at around 7pm). Coming from the coast you can catch a bus from the El Zarco junction, Mazatenango or Retalhuleu. **Leaving the city**, there are plenty of direct buses, or you can head for the Cuatro Caminos junction and go on from there.

Pullman buses

Líneas Américas has daily buses to Guatemala City at 5.15am, 9.30am, 11am, 1.10pm, 2.15pm, 3.30pm & 8pm from their terminal at 7 Av 3–33, Zona 2 (☎761 2063) in Quetzaltenango. Buses from Guatemala City to Quetzaltenango run at 8am, 10.30am, 12.30pm, 3pm, 5.30pm and 7.30pm. The Guatemala City office is at 29 Av 18–47, Zona 1 (☎232 1432).

Alamo has buses to Guatemala City from Monday to Saturday at 4.30am, 6.30am, 8am, 10.15am and 2.30pm from 4 C 14–04, Zona 3 in Quetzaltenango (☎767 7117). On Sundays, buses leave at 8am, 2pm, 2.30pm and 3pm. From Guatemala City, buses leave daily from their terminal at 21 C 0–14, Zona 1 (☎251 4838) at 8am, 10.30am 12.30pm, 3pm and 5.30pm with an extra service at 7.30pm from Mondays to Saturdays.

Galgos has services at 3am (Monday only) and daily at 4.15am (and 5am Tues–Sat), 8.30am, 10am, 12.30pm, 3pm and 4.15pm from their offices at C Rodolfo Robles 17–43, Zona 1, in Quetzaltenango (☎761 2248). From Guatemala City buses leave at 5.30am, 8.30am, 11am, 12.30pm, 2.30pm, 5pm and 7pm from 7 Av 19–44, Zona 1 (☎253 4868). On Sundays, it's essential to book ahead for services to Guatemala City. See p.181 for details of bus terminals in Quetzaltenango.

divided up into **zones**, although for the most part you'll only be interested in 1 and 3, which contain the plaza and the bus terminal respectively.

When it comes to **getting around** the city, most places are within easy walking distance (except the bus terminal). To get to the Minerva terminal you can take any bus that runs along 13 Avenida between 8 Calle and 4 Calle in Zona 1. To head for the eastern half of town, along 7 Avenida, catch one of the buses that stops in front of the Casa de la Cultura, at the bottom end of the plaza. You pay the driver; have some small change handy.

Accommodation

Once you've made it to the plaza you can set about looking for somewhere to stay. Most of the **hotels** in town are a little gloomy, even at the top end of the market, and not especially good value for money. However, all but one of the places listed below are within ten minutes' walk of the centre.

Casa Argentina 12 Diagonal 8–37, ☎761 2470, ⓔ casaargentina@trafficman.com. The most popular budget place in town with 25 comfortable single rooms, two dorms (US$3 per bed), a kitchen and very friendly owners who are an excellent source of information. Home of Quetzaltrekkers (see p.188) and assorted resident gringos. ❷

Casa Kaehler 13 Av 3–33, ☎761 2091. Attractive place with spotless rooms set around a patio,

some with private bath. Decent value, secure and very central, but be sure to book ahead as it's always popular. ❷

Casa Mañen 9 Av 4–11 ☎765 0786, ⓕ765 0678, ⓦ www.comeseeit.com. Very stylish, luxury boutique hotel, with helpful owners, that's also exceptional value for money. Beautifully presented rooms, some with fireplaces, all with *ikat* fabrics and rugs and cable TV, plus two huge split-level

Second-class buses

Buses for **Zunil** (25min) leave every thirty minutes between 8am and 6pm from the corner of 10 C and 9 Av, Zona 1. For **San Francisco el Alto** (45min), **Totonicapán** (50min), **Huehuetenango** (2hr 30min) and **Guatemala City** (4hr) there are buses every thirty minutes from the Minerva terminal – all pass via the rotunda, where you should be able to get on though you're unlikely to get a seat as they're usually full by this stage. Also from Minerva, there are daily buses about every thirty minutes to **Mazatenango** (2hr), **Retalhuleu** (1hr 20min) and **Coatepeque** (1hr 45min), and hourly services to **San Marcos** (2hr).

There are also buses from the Minerva terminal to **Panajachel** at 6.15am, 8am, 10am, 11am, noon, 1pm, 2.15pm and 3.15pm (2hr 30min), and one to **San Pedro la Laguna** at noon (2hr 30min). Services to **Momostenango** leave hourly (1hr 15min). For all but the Pacific destinations and San Marcos, you can also catch these buses at the rotunda. **⑤**

Heading for **Santa Cruz del Quiché** and **Chichicastenango**, you can catch any bus going to Guatemala City and change at the Los Encuentros junction, though fairly regular buses leave from the terminal between 6.30am and 4pm.

For **Antigua**, catch any Guatemala City-bound bus and change at Chimaltenango.

To get to **the Mexican border at Talismán** (3hr 30min), it's possible to travel via San Marcos to the border in a day, but the quickest route is to take a bus heading for the coast or Coatepeque, and intercept a pullman on the Carretera Pacífico.

To **the Mexican border at La Mesilla** there are hourly buses until 4pm (4hr).

Flights

Taca flies daily from Quetzaltenango **to Guatemala City** at 9am and 3pm. **From Guatemala City** flights leave at 8.15am and 2.15am. The flight takes 40 minutes and costs US$48. Cancellations are quite common and if you are making an international connection it's highly preferable to travel a day before your departure.

---

suites with sofas and fridges. Wonderful rooftop terrace with Jacuzzi. Breakfast is included in the price. **⑥/⑦**

Hotel del Campo Carretera al Pacífico Km 224, Zona 5, 4km from the town centre ☎761 1663, ℱ761 0074. Huge, modern, three-star hotel with a swimming pool and a decent restaurant. Though it's good value, it's only really an option if you have your own transport. **⑤**

Hotel Casa Florencia 12 Av 3–61 ☎761 2811, ⓦwww.xelapages.com/florencia/index.htm. The lobby isn't going to win any design awards, but the nine large rooms with wood-panelled walls and fitted carpets are comfortable enough, and all come with private bath. **④**

Hotel Modelo 14 Av A 2–31 ☎761 2529, ℱ763 1376 ⓦwww.xelapages.com/modelo/index.htm. Civilized and quiet, but a bit gloomy for the price and decidedly old-fashioned. The nicest rooms face a small garden courtyard, or try the separate annexe which is better value. **④/⑤**

Hotel Occidental 7 C 12–23 ☎765 4069. In a good location just off the plaza, large plain rooms with good beds, some with private bath. **②/③**

Hotel Río Azul 2 C 12–15 ☎ & ℱ763 0654, ℮rioazul@c.net.gt. Very reminiscent of an English boarding house, but spotless and welcoming. All rooms have private bath. **③**

Hotel Villa Real Plaza 4 C 12–22 ☎761 4045, ℱ761 6780. Comfortable modern hotel across the plaza from the *Bonifaz*, to which it is a modern(ish) rival, but the decor and ambience are a little soulless. **⑥**

Pensión Altense 9 C 8–48 ☎761 2811. Just above the budget range, this place has plenty of clean, spacious rooms, all with private bath. Safe parking. **③**

Pensión Andina 8 Av 6–07 ☎761 4012. Very cheap and centrally located, the rooms are pretty plain but fairly clean – some have private bath. Hot water 6–9am only. **①/②**

Pensión Bonifaz northeast corner of the plaza ☎761 2182, ℱ761 2850. The hotel, founded in 1935, has character and comfort, a reasonable (though overpriced) restaurant and a quirky bar. Very much the backbone of Quetzaltenango society, with an air of faded upper-class pomposity, but still one of the best places in town. **⑥**

▲ *Minerva Bus Terminal*   ▲ *Mercado La Democracia*

CENTRAL QUETZALTENANGO

N

Teatro Roma
Teatro Municipal
Cine Paraíso
Casa Verde

19 AVENIDA
15 AVENIDA
14 AVENIDA
14 AVENIDA

2 CALLE
2 CALLE

CALZADA SINFOROSO AGUILAR

3 CALLE
3 CALLE
2 CALLE

4 CALLE

5 CALLE

DIAGONAL 12

6 CALLE

DIAGONAL 11

7 CALLE

Mercado Las Flores

PLAZA

Municipalidad

13 AVENIDA
12 AVENIDA
1 AVENIDA
10 AVENIDA
6 AVENIDA

Cathedral

DIAGONAL 13

Casa de la Cultura

8 CALLE

9 CALLE

Rotunda

RESTAURANTS & CAFÉS

Artura's Restaurant	A
Blue Angel Video Café	L
Café Baviera	G
Café Colonial	M
Café El Mana	H
Café La Luna	K
Cardinali's	D
Deli Crêpe	C
El Rincón de los Antojitos	E
La Polonesa	F
La Salida	O
La Taquería	J
Royal Paris	B
Sagrado Corazón	N
Salón Tecún	I

ACCOMMODATION

Casa Argentina	9
Casa Kaehler	3
Casa Mañen	7
Hotel Casa Florencia	4
Hotel Modelo	1
Hotel Occidental	8
Hotel Río Azul	2
Hotel Villa Real Plaza	5
Pensión Altense	11
Pensión Andina	10
Pensión Bonifaz	6

10 CALLE
11 CALLE

★ **Buses to Zunil**   ★ **Buses to Rotunda**

0   100 m

Staying with a Maya family

Quetzaltenango is the base for **Fundación Kanil**, 6 C 18, Zona 1 (☎ & ℱ 761 3269). This non-profit organization is run in association with Maya community leaders in remote areas of the departments of Quiché, Huehuetenango and Quetzaltenango, and provides an excellent opportunity to spend time with an indigenous family, either as a language student in Joyabaj (see p.144), or simply as a **guest** of a particular village. Expect to pay approximately US$80–100 per person per week, less if there are several of you. The money is paid direct to the *alcalde* (mayor) of the community, who distributes it between your host family, the community, aid projects and Fundación Kanil.

The City

There aren't many things to do or see in Quetzaltenango, but if you have an hour or two to spare then it's well worth wandering through the streets, soaking up the atmosphere and taking in the museums. The hub of the place is, obviously enough, the **central plaza**, officially known as the **Parque Centro América**. A mass of false Greek columns, imposing banks and shoeshine boys, with an atmosphere of wonderfully dignified calm, the plaza is the best place to appreciate the sense of self-importance that accompanied the city's rebuilding after the 1902 earthquake. The buildings have a look of defiant authority, although there's none of the buzz of business that you'd expect – except on the first Sunday of the month when it plays host to a good artesanías market, with blankets, basketry and piles of *típica* weavings for sale.

Studying Spanish in Quetzaltenango

Quetzaltenango is now one of the most popular places in the world to **study Spanish**, having literally dozens of language schools, many of a very high standard. Though the days are long gone when schools could boast about the absence of foreigners in the town, Quetzaltenango is still less visited than Antigua and its relatively large population (130,000) means that you shouldn't have to share a family home with other gringos if you don't want to.

Many Quetzaltenango schools claim to fund community and enviromental projects, like supporting village libraries and clean water programmes. However, whilst most genuinely do assist development work, there are cowboys whose financial aid never gets through to the people they claim to support. Always ask to see evidence of the projects they profess to be involved with before you enrol. Virtually all schools have a **student liaison officer** who speaks English to act as a go-between for students and teachers.

All the schools below offer intensive Spanish classes and the chance to live with a local family (usually with full board). In addition, they often run trips to places of interest around Quetzaltenango and hold lectures on local political and social issues. For four or five hours' individual tuition from Monday to Friday and seven nights' full-board accomodation in a family, you can expect to pay from US$120 to US$140 a week, often a little more in July and August. The following schools are all well established and employ professional teachers. The tourist office also has a list of officially recognized language schools.

For background information about studying Spanish in Guatemala see Basics, p.47.

ALM 15 Av 6-75, Zona 1 ☎761 2877, ℻763 2176, ⒲http://travel.to/alm. Also has branches in Antigua and Monterrico.

Casa de Español Xelajú, Callejón 15, Diagonal 13–02, Zona 1 ☎761 5954, ℻761 5953, ⒲www.casaxelaju.com

Centro Bilingüe Amerindía (CBA) 7 Av 9–05, Zona 1 ☎761 1613, ⒲www.xelapages .com/cba

Centro Maya de Idiomas 21 Av 5–69 Zona 3 ☎767 0352, ⒲www.centromaya.org. Also offers classes in six Maya languages and helps operate a school in Todos Santos.

Educación para Todos 12 Av 1–78, Zona 3 ☎ & ℻765 0715, ⒲www.xelapages .com/paratodos

English Club International Language School Diagonal 4 9–71, Zona 9 ☎763 2198. Also classes in K'iche' and Mam.

Escuela Juan Sisay 15 Av 8–38, Zona 1 ☎ & ℻763 1318, ⒲www.juansisay.com

Guatemalensis 19 Av 2–14, Zona 1 ☎ & ℻765 1384, ⒲www.infovia.com.gt/gssxela

Kie–Balam Diagonal 12 4–46 ☎761 1636, ℻761 0391, ⒲www.super-highway.net /users/moebius

La Paz 2 C 19–30, Zona 1 ☎761 4243, ⒲www.xelapages.com/lapaz

Pop Wuj 1 C 17–72, Zona 1 ☎761 8286, ⒲www.popwuj.org

Proyecto Lingüístico Quetzalteco de Español 5 C 2–40, Zona 1 ☎761 2620, ⒲www.inforserve.net/hermandad/montana.html. Also has sister schools on the Pacific coast and in Todos Santos Cuchumatán.

Sakribal 10 C 7–17, Zona 1 ☎ & ℻761 5211, ⒲http://kcyb.com/sakribal

The Greek columns were probably intended to symbolize the city's cultural importance and its role at the heart of the liberal revolution, but today many of them do nothing more than support street lights. The northern end of the plaza is dominated by the grand Banco de Occidente, complete with sculptured flaming torches. On the west side is Bancafé, and the impressive but crumbling **Pasaje Enriquez**, which was planned as a sparkling arcade of upmarket shops, spent many years derelict, but has now been partially renovated. Inside you'll find Xela's most hip spot, the *Salón Tecún Bar*, a friendly place for meeting other travellers, plus a frenetically busy cybercafé and a travel agency.

At the bottom end of the plaza, next to the tourist office, is the **Casa de la Cultura** (Mon–Fri 8am–noon & 2–6pm, Sat 9am–1pm; US$1), the city's most blatant impersonation of a Greek temple, with a bold grey frontage. The main part of the building is given over to an odd mixture of local exhibits. On the ground floor, to the left-hand side, you'll find a display of assorted documents, photographs and pistols from the liberal revolution and the State of Los Altos (see p.420), sports trophies and a room dedicated to the marimba. Upstairs there are some modest Maya artefacts, historic photographs and a bizarre natural history room, where amongst the dusty displays of stuffed bats and pickled snakes you can see the macabre remains of assorted freaks of nature, including a four-horned goat.

Along the eastern side of the plaza is the **Cathedral**, with a new cement version set behind the spectacular crumbling front of the original. There's another unashamed piece of Greek grandeur, the **Municipalidad** or town hall, a little further up. Take a look inside at the courtyard, which has a neat little garden set out around a single palm tree. Back in the centre of the plaza are rows and circles of redundant columns, a few flowerbeds, and a monument to President Barrios, who ruled Guatemala from 1873 to 1885.

In the bottom corner of the plaza, between the cathedral and the Casa de la Cultura, the old **Mercadito** still functions, although nowadays it's eclipsed by the larger market near the bus terminal in Zona 3. Beside it, there's a grim three-storey shopping centre, the **Centro Comercial Municipal**.

Beyond the plaza

Away from the plaza the city spreads out, a mixture of the old and new. The commercial heart is 14 Avenida, complete with pizza restaurants and neon signs. At the top of 14 Avenida, at its junction with 1 Calle, stands the newly restored **Teatro Municipal**, another spectacular Neoclassical edifice. The plaza in front of the theatre is dotted with busts of local artists, including Osmundo Arriola (1886–1958), Guatemala's first poet laureate, and Jesús Castillo, "the re-creator of Maya music" – another bid to assert Quetzaltenango's cultural superiority. On clear days, there's a spectacular perspective of the Volcán Santa Maria from the steps of plaza.

Further afield, the city's role as a regional centre of trade is more in evidence. Out in Zona 3 is the **La Democracia Market**, a vast covered complex with stalls spilling out onto the streets. A couple of blocks north of the market stands the modern **Iglesia de San Nicolás**, at 4 C and 15 Av, a bizarre and ill-proportioned neo-Gothic building, sprouting sharp arches.

Another Greek-style structure stands right out on the edge of town, also in Zona 3: the **Minerva Temple** makes no pretence at serving any practical purpose, but was built to honour President Barrios's enthusiasm for education. Beside the temple is the little **zoo** (Tues–Sun 9am–5pm; free), doubling as a childrens' playground. Crammed into the tiny cages are a collection of foxes, sheep, birds, monkeys, wild boar and big cats, including a pair of miserable-looking lions, who have miraculously managed to raise a family. Below the temple are the sprawling **market** and **bus terminal**, and it's here that you can really sense the city's role as the centre of the western highlands, with indigenous traders from all over the area doing business, and buses heading to or from every imaginable village and town. To get to this side of the city, take any of the local buses that run along 13 Avenida between 8 Calle and 4 Calle in Zona 1.

Eating, drinking and entertainment

There are more than enough **restaurants** to choose from in Quetzaltenango, with four reasonable pizza places on 14 Avenida alone. Note that very few places open before 8am in the morning, so forget early breakfasts. After dark, things are generally quiet in the week, but there are a number of lively **bars** that fill up at the weekend, plus a small club scene, with a couple of venues in the centre of town and other alternatives in the suburbs.

Restaurants and cafés

Artura's Restaurant 14 Av 3–09, Zona 1. Dark, cosy atmosphere, with traditional, moderately priced food and a separate, fairly civilized bar for drinking.

Blue Angel Video Café 7 C 15–22, Zona 1. Popular gringo hangout with a daily video programme. An intimate, friendly place where you can eat great vegetarian food. Daily 2.15pm–11pm.

Café Baviera 5 C 12–50, Zona 1, a block from the plaza. Spacious, pine-panelled coffee house, dripping with photographic nostalgia. Quality cakes and decent coffee, though the set breakfasts are a little pricey. Open daily 8am–8pm.

Café Colonial 13 Av and 7 C, Zona 1. Large café-cum-restaurant serving tasty barbecued meats, decent sandwiches and rich licuados.

Café El Mana 13 Av and 5 C, Zona 1. Tiny, very friendly, family-run café with an excellent selection of inexpensive breakfasts (including *mosh* porridge, pancakes and granola), lunches and real coffee. Closed Sun.

Cardinali's 14 Av 3–41, Zona 1. Without doubt the best Italian food outside the capital, at reasonable prices. Make sure you are starving when you eat here because the portions are huge. For a delivery dial ☎761 0924.

Deli Crêpe 14 Av and 3 C, Zona 1. Looks a bit gloomy from the outside, but wait till you try the licuados, pancakes and delicious sandwiches.

La Luna 8 Av 4–11, Zona 1. Stylish new place, ideal for a relaxing cup of coffee and a yummy cake. They also do very fine chocolates.

Pan y Pasteles 18 Av and 1 C, Zona 1. The best bakery in town, run by Mennonites whose fresh pastries and breads are used by all the finest restaurants. Tues & Fri only, 9am–6pm.

Pensión Bonifaz corner of the plaza, Zona 1. Always a sedate and civilized spot for a cup of tea, a cake and rubbing shoulders with the town's elite, though the restaurant is overrated and best avoided. Expensive.

La Polonesa 14 Av 4–55, Zona 1. Great little place with an unbeatable selection of set lunches (with daily specials) all at under US$2, served on nice, solid wooden tables.

El Rincón de los Antojitos 15 Av and 5 C, Zona 1. Run by a French–Guatemalan couple, this friendly little restaurant nevertheless sticks to an almost purely Guatemalan menu, with specialities such as *pepián* (spicy chicken stew) and *hilachas* (beef in tomato sauce).

Royal Paris 14 Av A 3–06, Zona 1. Superb, moderately priced French-owned restaurant with a winsome menu of really flavoursome dishes including cassoulet and onion soup, plus snacks like croque monsieur. Special weekday lunches are a steal at US$2.

Sagrado Corazón 9 C 9–00, Zona 1. Excellent little comedor, with great-value breakfasts, filling meals and very friendly service.

La Salida 9 Av and 10 Av Zona 1. Diminutive vegetarian café, with delicious food including tempe and tofu, Oriental treats like *pad thai*, wholesome soups, and lassis. No alcohol. Closed Wed.

La Taquería 8 Av 5 C, Zona 1. Best Mexican food in town, served in a pleasant courtyard patio setting. Try the enchiladas or the *caldo Tlalpeño* soup. Moderate prices and cheap litres of beer.

Drinking and nightlife

Considering the size of Quetzaltenango, there's not that much going on in the evenings and the streets are generally quiet by about 9pm. There are a few **bars** worth visiting, however. At the popular *Salón Tecún*, on the west side of the plaza, you can down *cuba libres*, enjoy draught beer and great bar food, and listen to the latest sounds imported by the gringo bar staff. At the more sedate but classy *Don Rodrigo*, 1 C and 14 Av, you'll find leather-topped bar stools, more draught beer and good, but pricey sandwiches. The *Casa Verde* (also known as the *Green House*), at 12 Av 1–40 (☎763 0271), has a lively cultural programme including theatre, dance and poetry readings plus salsa nights at weekends. Close to the Teatro Municipal, there are a cluster of new hip places including the bar *El Zaguan*, at 14 Av A and 1 C, Zona 1, and the **club** *Bukana's*, almost next door, for salsa and merengue. Of the clubs on the outskirts of town, the *Music Center* attracts a loyal young local clientele, while *Loro's* appeals to an older crowd.

Quetzaltenango is a also good place to catch movies, with a number of **cinemas**, though you shouldn't have to stray further than the excellent Cine Paraíso on 14 Avenida A, near the Teatro Municipal, which shows a very varied selection of independent movies from all over the world, plus the odd quality Hollywood production. For **theatre** head for the refurbished Teatro Roma, also on 14 Avenida A, which often stages interesting productions. To find out **what's on** in Xela, pick up a copy of the free listings magazine *Fin de Semana*, available in many bars and cafés.

Listings

Banks and exchange Banco Inmobiliario, Banco de Occidente and Bancafé (with the longest opening hours: Mon–Fri 8.30am–8pm, Sat 10am–1.30pm) are all in the vicinity of the plaza and will change travellers' cheques. Banco Industrial, also in the plaza, has an ATM that takes Visa.

Bike and car rental Guatemala Unlimited, 12 Av and 1 C, Zona 1 (℡761 6043), has mountain bikes for around US$6 a day; or try the Vrisa bookstore (see below).

Books Vrisa, 15 Av 3–64, opposite Telgua and the post office, has over 4000 used titles, plus a newsroom with *Newsweek* and *The Economist*, a message board, espresso coffee and bike rental.

Internet There are at least a dozen places in Xela where you can surf the net (all open roughly 9am–9.30pm), including Maya Communications, above *Salón Tecún* in the Plaza Central; Casa Verde, 12 Av 1–40, Zona 1; and Alternativas at 16 Av 3–35, Zona 3. Prices hover around US$1.40 an hour.

Laundry MiniMax, 4 Av and 1 C, Zona 1 (Mon–Sat 7am–7pm); US$2 for a full-load wash and dry.

Medical care Doctor de León at the San Rafael Hospital, 9 C 10–41, Zona 1 (℡761 4414), speaks English. For emergencies, the Hospital Privado is at C Rodolfo Robles 23–51, Zona 1 (℡761 4381).

Mexican consulate Mexican Consulate, 9 Av 6–19, Zona 1 (Mon–Fri 8–11am & 2.30–3.30pm). A Mexican tourist card costs US$1. Hand in your paperwork in the morning and collect in the afternoon.

Photography For camera repairs try Fotocolor, 15 Av 3–25, or one of the several shops on 14 Avenida.

Post office At the junction of 15 Av and 4 C (Mon–Sat 8am–4.30pm).

Taxis Rulitaxsa ℡761 5001 or 761 1925, available 24hr.

Telephone office The best rates in town are at Kall Shop, 8 Av 4–24 Zona 1, where calls to the USA and Canada are US$0.25 and to Europe US$0.45 per minute. Maya Communications (see "Internet", above) is also competitive. You'll pay much more at the main Telgua office, 15 Av and 4 C (daily 7am–10pm).

Tours and travel agencies Adrenalina Tours, inside Pasaje Enríquez, Plaza Central (℡761 0924, ⓦhttp://adrenalinatours.xelaenlinca.com), offers city tours, daily transport to Fuentes Georginas and volcano climbing. Casa Iximulew, 15 Av and 5 C, Zona 1 (℡765 1308, ⓔiximulew@trafficman.com), runs organized trips to most of the volcanoes and sights around Xela. The Guatemalan Birding Resource Center, 7 Av 19–18, Zona 1 (℡767 7339), offers excellent guided tours to the surrounding countryside. Guatemala Unlimited, 12 Av and C 35, Zona 1 (℡ & ℡761 6043, ⓦwww .guatemalaunlimited.centroamerica.com), has tours all over the country. Quetzaltrekkers, inside *Casa Argentina* (see "Accommodation", p.182), offers hiking trips to volcanoes and to Lago de Atitlán, with all profits going to a street children charity.

Weaving classes For textile weaving classes contact the Ixchel school at 8 Av 4–24, Zona 1 (℡765 3790).

Olintepeque and the old road towards Huehuetenango

To the north of Quetzaltenango, perched on the edge of the flat plain, is the small textile-weaving town of **OLINTEPEQUE**. According to some accounts this was the site of the huge and decisive battle between the Spanish and K'iche' warriors, and legend has it that the Río Xequijel, the "river of blood", ran red during the massacre of the K'iche'. These days, however, it's better known as a peaceful little village with a small colonial church and a market on Tuesdays. **Buses** for Olintepeque (20min) leave from the Minerva terminal in Quetzaltenango every thirty minutes.

Olintepeque was a staging post on the old road to Huehuetenango, and although only local traffic heads this way nowadays you can still follow the route. Leaving Olintepeque the road climbs the steep hillside onto a plateau, arriving at the village of **SAN CARLOS SIJA**, 22km from Quetzaltenango and the hub of a fertile yet isolated area. There's nowhere to stay in San Carlos, but seven buses a day connect it with Quetzaltenango – leaving from the Minerva terminal – the last returning at about 4pm. The only real reason to come out here is for the wonderful views, or to visit the small Sunday market. Heading on from San Carlos, you can hitch a ride to the Carretera Interamericana, just 10km away, where there's plenty of traffic to Quetzaltenango via Cuatro Caminos or on to Huehuetenango. The old road itself continues more or less due north, rejoining the Carretera Interamericana about 40km before Huehuetenango – though there's very little traffic on this route.

Volcán Santa María

Due south of Quetzaltenango, the perfect cone of the **Volcán Santa María** rises to a height of 3772m. From the town only the peak is visible, but seen from the rest of the valley the entire cone seems to tower over everything around. The view from the top is, as you might expect, spectacular, and if you're prepared to sweat out the climb you certainly won't regret it. It's possible to climb the volcano as a day-trip, but to really see it at its best you need to be on top at dawn, either sleeping on the freezing peak, or camping at the site below and climbing the final section in the dark by torchlight. Either way you need to bring enough food, water and stamina for the entire trip, and you should be acclimatized to the altitude before attempting it. For more **information on climbing** Santa María, or any of the volcanoes in the region, contact Casa Iximulew (see opposite) or Adrenalina Tours. Sadly, you should also check the current security situation with either of these tour operators, as there have been robberies reported.

Climbing the cone

To get to the start of the climb you need to take a local bus to **Llanos del Pinal**, a twenty-minute ride: buses leave every hour or so between 7am and 5.30pm from the Minerva terminal in Quetzaltenango. The village is set on a high plateau beneath the cone, and the bus driver will drop you at a crossroads from where you head straight down the road towards the right-hand side of the volcano's base. After passing a small plaque dedicated to the Guatemalan

Mountaineering Club, the track bears up to the left, quickly becoming a rocky trail. At the end of a confined rocky stretch, a few hundred metres in length, the path crosses a more open grassy area and then curves further around to the left. All the way along this first section painted arrows mark the way – those signs painted with a fierce "NO" mean exactly what they say and you should backtrack until you find an alternative.

As you push on, the path continues to climb around to the left, up a rocky slope and under some trees, arriving at a flat and enclosed grassy area about the size of small football pitch. There's a grass bank to the right, a wooded area to the left, and a big boulder at the other end. This point is about ninety minutes to two hours from the start, and is an ideal place to **camp** if you want to make the final ascent in the hours before dawn. The path cuts off to the right from here, leaving from the start of this level patch of grass. (Another path heads across the grass, but this isn't the one for you.) From here on, the route is a little harder to follow, but it heads more or less straight up the side of the cone, a muddy and backbreaking climb of two or three hours: avoid the tempting alternative that skirts round to the right.

At the top of the cone is a mixture of grass and volcanic cinder, usually frozen solid in the early morning. The highest point is marked by an altar where the Maya burn copal and sacrifice animals, and on a clear day the **view** will take your breath away – as will the cold if you get here in time to watch the sun rise. In the early mornings the Quetzaltenango valley is blanketed in a layer of cloud, and while it's still dark the lights of the city create a patch of orange glow; as the sun rises, its first rays eat into the cloud, revealing the land beneath. To the west, across a chaos of twisting hills, are the cones of Tajumulco and Tacaná, marking the Mexican border. But most impressive is the view to the east. Wrapped in the early morning haze are four more volcanic cones, two above Lake Atitlán and two more above Antigua. The right-hand cone in this second pair is Fuego, which sometimes emits a stream of smoke, rolling down the side of the cone in the early morning. If you look south, you can gaze down over the smaller cone of **Santiaguito**, which has been in constant eruption since 1902. Every now and then it spouts a great grey cloud of rock and dust hundreds of metres into the air.

South towards the coast: Almolonga to Zunil

The most direct route from Quetzaltenango to the coast takes you through a narrow gash in the mountains to the village of **ALMOLONGA**, sprawled around the sides of a steep-sided, flat-bottomed valley just 5km from Quetzaltenango. Almolonga is K'iche' for "the place where water springs", and streams gush from the hillside, channelled to the waiting crops. This is the market garden of the western highlands, where the flat land is far too valuable to live on and is parcelled up instead into neat, irrigated sections.

In **markets** throughout the western highlands the women of Almolonga corner the vegetable trade; it's easy to recognize them, dressed in their bold, orange zigzag *huipiles* and wearing beautifully woven headbands. The village itself has markets on Wednesday and Saturday mornings – the latter being the larger one – when the elongated plaza is ringed by trucks and crammed with people, while piles of scrubbed radishes and gleaming carrots are swiftly traded between the two. The Almolonga market may not be Guatemala's largest, but it has to be one of the most frenetic, and is well worth a visit. While you're here, it's also worth dropping into the village **church**, an arresting banana yellow-and-white affair that backs onto the plaza. Inside, beneath the cupola, there's a wonderfully gaudy gilded altar complete with a silver statue of a crusading San Pedro, complete with bible, set behind protective bars. Pay the caretaker a quetzal and the whole altar lights up in a riot of technicolour fluorescent tubes, including a halo for the saint.

A couple of kilometres beyond the village lie **Los Baños**, where about ten different operations offer a soak in waters heated naturally by the volcano; two good ones are *Fuentes Saludable* and *El Recreo* (daily 5am–10pm). For a dollar you get a private room, a sunken concrete tub, and enough hot water to drown an elephant. In a country of lukewarm showers it's paradise, and the baths echo to the sound of indigenous families who queue barefoot for the pleasure of a good scrub. Below the baths is a communal pool, usually packed with local men, and a *pila* where the women wash their clothes in warm water. Below the road between the baths and the village there's a warm swimming pool known as *Los Chorros* – follow the sign to *Agua Tibia* – which you can use for a small fee.

If on the other hand you'd prefer to immerse yourself in steam, then this too emerges naturally from the hillside. To get to the **vapores**, as they're known, get off the bus halfway between Quetzaltenango and Almolonga at the sign for *Los Vahos*, and head off up the track. Take the right turn after about a kilometre, follow this track for another twenty minutes, and you'll come to the steam baths. Here you can sweat it out for a while in one of the cubicles and then step out into the cool mountain air, or have a bracing shower to get the full sauna effect.

Buses run to Almolonga from Quetzaltenango every twenty minutes, leaving from the Minerva terminal in Zona 3 and stopping to pick up passengers at the junction of 9 Av and 10 C in Zona 1. They pause in Almolonga itself before going on to the baths, and, although the baths stay open until 10pm, the last bus back is at around 7.30pm. Beyond *Los Baños* the road heads through another narrow gully to join the main coast road in Zunil. If you're bound for Zunil, plenty of buses pass this way.

Cantel, Zunil and the Fuentes Georginas

Most buses to the coast avoid Almolonga, leaving Quetzaltenango via the **Las Rosas** junction and passing through **CANTEL FÁBRICA**, an industrial village built up around an enormous textile factory. The factory's looms produce a range of cloths, using indigenous labourers, German dyes, English machinery and a mixture of American and Guatemalan cotton. The village was originally known as Chuijullub, a K'iche' word meaning "on the hill", and this original settlement (now called Cantel – Cantel Fábrica simply means "Cantel Factory") can still be seen on a height overlooking the works.

A kilometre beyond Cantel on the road to Zunil is the **Copavic glass factory**, one of Guatemala's most successful co-operatives. Copavic uses one hundred percent recycled glass and exports the finished product all over the world. Visitors are welcome to see the glass-blowers in action (Mon–Fri 8am–1pm), or visit the factory shop (Mon–Fri 8am–5pm & Sat 8am–noon), which sells a fine selection of glasses, vases, jugs and other assorted goods.

Further down the valley is **ZUNIL**, another centre for vegetable growing. As at Almolonga, the village is split in two by the need to preserve the best land.

Visiting San Simón in Zunil

Zunil's reputation for the worship of **San Simón** is well founded, and as in Santiago Atitlán (see p.167) with a minimum of effort you can pay a visit to the man himself. Every year on November 1, at the end of the annual fiesta, San Simón is moved to a new house; discreet enquiries will locate his current home. Here his effigy sits in a darkened room, dressed in Western clothes, and guarded by several attendants, including one whose job it is to remove the ash from his lighted cigarettes – this is later sold off and used to cure insomnia, while the butts are thought to provide protection from thieves. San Simón is visited by a steady stream of villagers, who come to ask his assistance, using candles to indicate their requests: white for the health of a child, yellow for a good harvest, red for love and black to wish ill on an enemy. The petitioners touch and embrace the saint, and just to make sure that he has heard their pleas they also offer cigarettes, money and rum. The latter is administered with the help of one of the attendants, who tips back San Simón's head and pours the liquid down his throat, presumably saving a little for himself. Meanwhile, outside the house a small fire burns continuously and more offerings are given over to the flames, including whole eggs – if they crack it signifies that San Simón will grant a wish.

If you **visit San Simón** you will be expected to contribute to his upkeep (US$0.50 or so). While the entire process may seem chaotic and entertaining, it is in fact deeply serious and outsiders have been beaten up for making fun of San Simón – so proceed with caution.

David Dickinson

The plaza is dominated by a beautiful white colonial church with twin belfries and a magnificent Baroque facade – complete with a Buddha-like figure, a quetzal and vines – inside which is an intricate silver altar protected behind bars. The women of Zunil wear vivid purple *huipiles* and carry incredibly bright shawls, and for the Monday market the plaza is awash with colour. Just below the plaza is a **textile co-operative** (Mon–Sat 8.30am–5pm, Sun 2–5pm), where hundreds of women market their beautiful weavings; lessons are also offered here. Zunil is also one of the few remaining places where **Maximón** (or San Simón), the evil saint, is avidly worshipped. In the face of disapproval from the Catholic Church, the Maya are reluctant to display their Judas, who also goes by the name Alvarado, but his image is usually paraded through the streets during Holy Week, dressed in Western clothes and smoking a cigar. At other times of year you can meet the man himself (see above box).

In the hills above Zunil are the **Fuentes Georginas**, a spectacular set of luxuriant hot springs, owned by the Xela department, and named after the dictator Jorge Ubico (1931–44). A turning to the left off the main road, just beyond the entrance to the village, leads up into the hills to the baths, 8km away. You can walk it in a couple of hours, or rent a truck from the plaza in Zunil – prices are fixed at US$5 for the trip, no matter how many passengers hitch a ride. It's an exhilarating journey to the natural spa, up a smooth paved road which switchbacks through magnificent volcanic scenery. If you're not staying the night you'll have to arrange the return trip (another US$5) a few hours later with the driver. The baths (US$1.30) are surrounded by fresh green ferns, thick moss and lush forest, and to top it all there's a restaurant with a well-stocked bar (with decent wine) beside the main pool. It's easy to spend an afternoon or more here soaking up the scene, though you can also rent one of the very pleasant rustic stone **bungalows** for the night (no phone; ❸), complete with bathtub, two double beds, fireplace and barbecue.

Buses to Cantel and Zunil run from Quetzaltenango's Minerva bus terminal every thirty minutes or so, though you can also catch a bus from the centre of town beside the Shell gas station at 10 C and 9 Av in Zona 1. The last bus back from Zunil leaves at around 6.30pm. All buses to the coastal town of Retalhuleu also pass through this way.

West to Ostuncalco, and towards the coast via San Martín Sacatepéquez

Heading west from Quetzaltenango, a good paved road runs 15km along the valley floor, through **San Mateo**, to the prosperous village of **SAN JUAN OSTUNCALCO**, the commercial centre for this end of the valley. The large Sunday market draws people from all the surrounding villages; here you can see the furniture made locally from wood and rope, painted in garish primary colours. The village's other famous feature is the *Virgen de Rosario*, in the church and reputed to have miraculous powers. Barely 2km away, on the far side of the coast road, is the quiet, traditional village of **CONCEPCIÓN CHIQUIRICHAPA**, which hosts a very local market on Thursday, attended by only a few outsiders and conducted in hushed tones.

Buses and minibuses run every thirty minutes between Quetzaltenango and Ostuncalco. If you find yourself enchanted by the place, there's a very relaxed **guest house** at the entrance to the village: *Ciprés Inn*, 6 Av 1–29 (☎761 6174; ❸), a beautiful wooden house that looks as if it ought to be in New England, and which boasts huge double beds, a restaurant and a garden. Beyond the village the road splits, one branch running to Coatepeque on the coast, and the other over a high pass north to San Marcos and San Pedro Sacatepéquez. The road to the coast climbs into the hills and through a gusty pass before winding down to **SAN MARTÍN SACATEPÉQUEZ**, also known as San Martín Chile Verde, an isolated Mam-speaking village set in the base of a natural bowl and hemmed in by steep, wooded hills. The village was abandoned in 1902 when the eruption of the Santa María volcano buried the land beneath a metre-thick layer of pumice stone, killing thousands. These days both the people and fertility have returned to the land, and the village is once again devoted to farming. The men of San Martín wear a particularly unusual costume, a long white tunic with thin red stripes, ornately embroidered around the cuffs and tied around the middle with a red sash; the women wear beautiful red *huipiles* and blue *cortes*.

A three-hour hike from San Martín brings you to **Laguna Chicabal**, a spectacular lake set in the cone of the Chicabal volcano which is the site of Maya religious rituals. To get there, head down the side of the purple-and-blue church and turn right onto the signposted track at the end, which takes you out of the village. Once the track has crossed a small bridge take the path that branches off to the right, and follow this as it goes up and over a range of hills, then drops down and bears around to the left – several kilometres from the village. Beyond the lip the path carries on past the park offices (entrance US$1.40) and then through a forest, curving around to the right before finally cutting up to the left and crossing over into the cone itself. All of a sudden you come into a different world, eerily still, disturbed only by the soft buzz of a hummingbird's wings or the screech of parakeets. From the rim the path drops precipitously, through thick, moist forest, to the water's edge, where charred crosses and bunches of fresh-cut flowers mark the site of ritual sacrifice. On May 3 every year *brujos* from several different tribes gather here for ceremonies to mark the fiesta of the Holy Cross; at any time, but on this date especially, you should take care not to disturb any ceremonies that might be taking place – the site is considered holy by the local Maya. Note also that fog can be a problem in February, making it easy to get lost.

San Martín can be visited either as a day-trip from Quetzaltenango or on the way to the coast – if you want to **stay**, the woman who runs the *Centro de Salud* has a room that she rents out (❶). **Buses** run along the road between Coatepeque (for the coast) and Quetzaltenango every 45 minutes or so, with the last passing San Martín in both directions at about 5pm; pick-ups are also pretty frequent. From Quetzaltenango buses for Coatepeque leave from the Minerva terminal in Zona 3.

Quetzaltenango to Cuatro Caminos

Between the Cuatro Caminos junction and Quetzaltenango, lined along the road, is the small ladino town of **SALCAJÁ**, one of Guatemala's main commercial weaving centres, producing much of the cloth used in the dresses worn by Maya women. The lengths of fabric are often stretched out by the roadside, either to be prepared for dyeing or laid out to dry, and on market day they're an exceptionally popular commodity.

Salcajá's other claim to fame is that (according to some historians at least) it was the site of the first Spanish settlement in the country, and its church is therefore regarded as the first Catholic foundation in Guatemala. If you're staying in Quetzaltenango and travelling out to the surrounding villages then the sight of Salcajá will become familiar as you pass through heading to and from Cuatro Caminos. But the ideal time to stop off is for the market on Tuesday.

A few kilometres beyond Salcajá the main road turns sharply to the right, beside a filling station. At this point a road branches off to the left, running to the edge of the valley and the village of **SAN ANDRÉS XECUL**. Bypassed by almost everything, and enclosed on three sides by steep dry hills, it is to all appearances an unremarkable farming village – but two features set it apart. The first is little more than rumour and hearsay, set in motion by the artist Carmen Petterson when she was painting here in the 1970s. She claimed to have discovered that a "university" for *brujos* was operating in the village, attracting young students of shamanism from K'iche' villages throughout the country. There's little sign of this in the village itself, though, except perhaps for an atmosphere that's even more hushed and secretive than usual. The second feature is the **village church**, a beautiful old building with incredibly thick walls. Its facade is painted an outrageous mustard yellow, with vines dripping plump, purple fruit, and podgy little angels scrambling across the surface – you can see some of the detail on the rear cover of this guide. Less orthodox religious ceremonies are conducted at hundreds of small altars in the slopes around San Andrés, one of which is up a hill just above the village's smaller yellow church.

A few daily **buses** leave the Minerva terminal in Quetzaltenango for San Andrés; it's easier, though, to take any bus as far as the filling station beyond Salcajá and hitch a ride from there.

Cuatro Caminos and San Cristobal Totonicapán

At **CUATRO CAMINOS** the Carretera Interamericana is met by the main roads from Quetzaltenango and Totonicapán. This is the most important junction in the western highlands and you'll find all the usual characteristics of Guatemalan road junctions, including the cheap motels, the hustlers, the outrageously priced fruit and the shanty-like comedores. More importantly, up until about 7pm there's a stream of **buses** heading for Quetzaltenango, Huehuetenango, Guatemala City and smaller villages along the way. Wherever you are, this is the place to make for in search of a connection.

One kilometre to the west, the ladino town of **SAN CRISTÓBAL TOTONICAPÁN** is built at the junction of the Sija and Salamá rivers. Similar in many ways to Salcajá, San Cristóbal is a quiet place that holds a position of importance in the world of Maya tradition as a source of fiesta costumes, which can be rented from various outfitters. If you'd like to see one of these you can drop in at 5 C 3–20, where they rent costumes for around US$50 a fortnight, depending on age and quality. The colonial church, on the other side of the river, has been restored by the local wheat-growers' association and contains some fantastic ancient altars, including ornate silverwork and images of the saints. Look out especially for the silver figure of St Michael. The market here is on Sunday. **Buses** going to San Francisco el Alto pass by the village – they leave from the Minerva terminal and pass the rotunda in Quetzaltenango.

San Francisco el Alto and Momostenango

From a magnificent hillside setting, the small market town of **SAN FRANCISCO EL ALTO** overlooks the Quetzaltenango valley. It's worth a visit for the view alone, with the great plateau stretching out below and the cone of the Santa María volcano marking the opposite side of the valley. At times a layer of early morning cloud fills the valley, and the volcanic cone, rising out of it, is the only visible feature.

An equally good reason for visiting the village is the **Friday market**, the largest weekly market in the country. Traders from every corner of Guatemala make the trip, many arriving the night before, and some starting to sell as early as 4am by candlelight. Throughout the morning a steady stream of buses and trucks fills the town to bursting; by noon the market is at its height, buzzing with activity.

The town is set into the hillside, with steep cobbled streets connecting the different levels. Two areas in particular are monopolized by specific trades. At the very top is an open field used as an animal market, where everything from pigs to parrots changes hands. The teeth and tongues of animals are inspected by the buyers, and at times the scene degenerates into a chaotic wrestling match, with pigs and men rolling in the dirt. Below this is the town's plaza, dominated by textiles. These days most of the stalls deal in imported denim, but under the arches and in the covered area opposite the church you'll find a superb selection of traditional cloth. (For a really good view of the market and the surrounding countryside, pay the church caretaker a quetzal and climb up to the church roof.) Below, the streets are filled with vegetables, fruit, pottery, furniture, cheap comedores and plenty more. By early afternoon the numbers start to thin out, and by sunset it's all over – until the following Friday.

San Francisco practicalities

There are plenty of **buses** from Quetzaltenango to San Francisco, leaving every twenty minutes or so from the rotunda; the first is at 6am, with the last bus back leaving at about 5pm. If you'd rather stay in town, the cheapest **accommodation** is at the *Hospedaje Central* (**①**), on the main street, a roughish sort of place that fills with market traders. The *Hotel Vista Hermosa*, 3 Av 2–22, a block or so below the plaza (**☎**738 4030; **②**), looks smartish from the outside but is run-down, though, as its name suggests, some of the front rooms have magnificent views. Finally, the newest hotel in town is the *Hotel Galaxia* (**②**), which is very neat, clean and hospitable, some of the rooms having private bathrooms and views to rival the *Vista Hermosa*. San Francisco goes to bed at around 7.30pm, so if you're stuck here for an evening you might want to see what's showing at the Cine García. Nearby, there's a Banco G&T Continental, which may be persuaded to change travellers' cheques.

Momostenango

Above San Francisco a smooth paved road continues over the ridge, dropping down on the other side through lush pine forests. The road is deeply rutted, and the journey painfully slow, but within an hour you arrive in **MOMOS-TENANGO**. This small, isolated town is the centre of wool production in the highlands, and *Momostecos* travel throughout the country peddling their blankets, scarves and rugs. Years of experience have made them experts in the hard sell and given them a sharp eye for tourists. The wool is also used in a range of traditional costumes, including the short skirts worn by the men of Nahualá, and San Antonio Palopó, and the jackets of Sololá. The ideal place to buy Momostenango blankets is in the **Sunday market**, which fills the town's two plazas.

A visit at this time will also give you a glimpse of Momostenango's other feature: its rigid adherence to tradition. Opposite the entrance to the church, people make offerings of incense and alcohol on a small fire, muttering their appeals to the gods. The town is famous for this unconventional folk-Catholicism, and it has been claimed that there are as many as three hundred Maya **shamans** working here. Momostenango's religious **calendar**, like that of only one or two other villages, is still based on the 260-day *Tzolkin* year – made up of thirteen twenty-day months – that has been in use since ancient times. The most celebrated ceremony is *Guaxaquib Batz*, "Eight Monkey", which marks the beginning of a new year. Originally this was a purely pagan ceremony, starting at dawn on the first day of the year, but the Church has muscled in on the action and it now begins with a Catholic service the night before. The next morning the people make for Chuitmesabal (Little Broom), a small hill about 2km to the west of the town. Here offerings of broken pottery are made before age-old altars (Momostenango means "the place of the altars"). The entire process is overseen by *brujos*, shamans responsible for communicating with the gods. At dusk the ceremony moves to Nim Mesabal (Big Broom), another hilltop, where the *brujos* pray and burn incense throughout the night.

As a visitor, however, even if you could plan to be in town at the right time, you'd be unlikely to see any of this, and it's best to visit Momostenango for the market, or for the fiesta on August 1. If you decide to stay for a day or two then

△ Santo Tomás church, Chichicastenango

you can take a walk to the *riscos*, a set of bizarre sandstone pillars, or beyond to the **hot springs** of Pala Chiquito. The springs are about 3km away to the north, and throughout the day weavers work there washing and shrinking their blankets – it's always best to go early, before most people arrive and the water is discoloured by soap.

Practicalities

The best **place to stay** in Momostenango is the *Hotel Estiver*, 1C 4–15, Zona 1 (☎736 5036; ❷), with clean rooms, some with private bath, great views from the roof and safe parking. For **eating**, there are plenty of small comedores on the main plaza or try the one inside the *Hospedaje Paglóm* (which also has very basic rooms; ❶) for a good feed. There's a Bancafé **bank** at 1C and 1 Av (Mon–Fri 9am–4pm), which accepts Visa, cash and travellers' cheques.

Buses run here from Quetzaltenango, passing through Cuatro Caminos and San Francisco el Alto on the way. They leave the Minerva terminal in Quetzaltenango hourly from 7am to 5pm (1hr 15min) and from Momostenango between 6am and 3pm. On Sunday, special early-morning buses leave Quetzaltenango every thirty minutes from 6am: you can also catch them at the rotunda.

Totonicapán

TOTONICAPÁN, capital of one of the smaller departments, is reached down a direct road leading east from Cuatro Caminos. Entering the village you pass one of the country's finest *pilas* (communal washing places), ringed with Gothic columns. Surrounded by rolling hills and pine forests, the town stands at the heart of a heavily populated and intensely farmed region. There is only one point of access and the valley has always held out against outside influence, shut off in a world of its own. In 1820 it became the scene of one of the most famous **Maya rebellions**. The early part of the nineteenth century had been marked by a series of revolts throughout the area, particularly in Momostenango and Totonicapán; the largest of these erupted in 1820, sparked by demands for tax. The indigenous people expelled all of the town's ladinos, crowning their leader Atanasio Tzul the "king and fiscal king", and making his assistant, Lucas Aquilar, president. His reign lasted only 29 days before it was violently suppressed – a stone memorial commemorates the event in the town's southern plaza.

Tensions in the town boiled over again in August 2001, after the Portillo government announced a two percent increase in VAT, as angry demonstrations ignited into widespread **rioting** during which FRG (Portillo's party) offices, a bank, the local tax office, the mayor's house and a radio station were burnt down. The riots were only quelled when a state of emergency was declared and army tanks were sent in to Totonicapán to restore order – the most serious incidents in a wave of national protests.

Rebellions aside, Totonicapán is normally a quiet place whose faded glory is ruffled only by the Tuesday and Saturday markets, which fill the two plazas to bursting. Until fairly recently a highly ornate traditional costume was worn here. The women's *huipiles* were some of the most elaborate and colourful in the country, and the men wore trousers embroidered with flowers, edged in lace, and decorated with silver buttons. Today, however, all this has disappeared and the town has instead become one of the chief centres of commercial weaving. Along with Salcajá it produces much of the *jasped* cloth worn as skirts by the majority of indigenous women: the machine-made *huipiles* of modern Totonicapán are used throughout the highlands as part of the universal costume. To take a closer look at the work of local artisans, head for the town's **visitor centre**, the Casa de la Cultura, on 8 Av 2–17 (Mon–Sat 9.30am–5pm; Ⓦhttp://larutamayaonline.com/aventura.html). It organizes pricey tours of the town (US$6–14) and classes in weaving and wood carving (US$21–49 per person, depending on class size); the funds raised help benefit the community. The only other sight here is located just north of the two plazas: a grand, though somewhat faded municipal **theatre** – a Neoclassical structure echoing the one in Quetzaltenango and currently undergoing restoration.

There are good connections between Totonicapán and Quetzaltenango, with buses shuttling back and forth every half-hour or so. Totonicapán is very quiet after dark, but if you want to stay, the best **hotel** is the *Hospedaje San Miguel*, a block from the plaza at 8 Av and 3 C (☎766 1452; ❷/❸). It is pretty comfortable and some rooms have bathrooms and TV, but beware price rises before market days. The *Pensión Blanquita* (❶) is a friendly and basic alternative opposite the gas station at 13 Av and 4 C. For somewhere **to eat**, there are plenty of comedores scattered around both plazas, or try *La Hacienda Steakhouse* at 8 Av and 4 C, where they also offer good *pinchos* (kebabs) and tacos. **Buses** for Totonicapán leave Quetzaltenango between 6am and 5pm, passing the rotunda and Cuatros Caminos, or else take any bus to Cuatros Caminos and change there.

The Department of San Marcos

Leaving Quetzaltenango to the west, the main road heads out of the valley through San Mateo and Ostuncalco and climbs a massive range of hills, dropping down on the other side to the village of Palestina de Los Altos. Beyond this it weaves through a U-shaped valley to the twin towns of **San Marcos** and **San Pedro Sacatepéquez**. These towns form the core of the country's westernmost department, a neglected area that once served as a major trade route and includes Guatemala's highest volcano and a substantial stretch of the border with Mexico. There's little to detain you in either place, but they make useful bases for a trip into the mountainous countryside to the north.

San Pedro Sacatepéquez and San Marcos

SAN PEDRO SACATEPÉQUEZ is the larger and busier of the two towns, a bustling and unattractive commercial centre with a huge plaza that's the scene of a market on Thursday and Sunday. In days gone by this was a Maya settlement, famed for its brilliant yellow weaving, in which silk was used. Over the years the town has been singled out for some highly questionable praise: in 1543 the King of Spain, Carlos V, granted the headmen special privileges as thanks for their assistance during the Conquest, and in 1876 the town was honoured by President Rufino Barrios, who with a stroke of his pen raised the status of the people from Indians to ladinos.

A dual carriageway road connects San Pedro with its sister town of San Marcos, 2km west. Along the way, a long-running dispute about the precise boundary between the two towns has been solved by the construction of the departmental headquarters at **La Unión**, halfway between the two. The building, known as the **Maya Palace**, is an outlandish and bizarre piece of architecture that goes some way to compensate for the otherwise unrelenting blandness of the two towns. The structure itself is relatively sober, but its facade is covered in imitation Maya carvings. Elaborate decorative friezes run around the sides, two great roaring jaguars guard the entrance, and above the main doors is a fantastic clock with Maya numerals and snake hands. The **buses** that run a continuous shuttle service between the two towns can drop you at the Maya Palace. A few kilometres away there's a spring-fed **swimming pool**, where you can while away an hour or two: to get there walk from the plaza in San Pedro down 5 Calle in the direction of San Marcos, and turn left in front of the Templo de Candelero along 2 Avenida. Follow this road through one valley and down into a second, where you take the left turn to the bottom. The pool – marked simply *Agua Tibia* – is open from 6am to 6pm, and there's a small entrance fee.

SAN MARCOS, officially the capital of the department, once stood proud and important on the main route to Mexico, but these days articulated lorries roar along the coastal highway and the focus of trade has shifted to San Pedro, leaving San Marcos to sink into provincial stagnation.

Practicalities

Most of the activity and almost all the transport are based in **San Pedro**. The cheapest **place to stay** is the *Pensión Mendez*, a very basic place at 4 C and 6 Av (❶). The *Hotel Samaritano*, 6 Av 6–44 (❷), is a clean but characterless modern building, though definitely better than the *Hotel Bagod*, on 5 C and 4 Av (❶). Finally, the newish *Hotel Tacaná*, 3 C 3–22 (❷), is good value, and some of its rooms have private showers. In **San Marcos** the *Hotel Palacio*, on 7 Av, opposite the police station (❶), is an amazing old place, its rooms decaying and very musty with peeling wallpaper. There's also a relatively luxurious hotel, the *Pérez*, at 9 C 2–25 (☎760 1007; ❸), a very dignified and longstanding establishment that's excellent value and has its own restaurant.

There are plenty of cheap **comedores** in San Pedro, fewer in San Marcos. For real Italian food in San Pedro, head for *La Cueva de los Faraones*, at 5 C 1–11, or in San Marcos, try *Mah Kik* behind the Chevron station, an elegant, subdued and fairly expensive place. Both towns have **cinemas**: the Cine T'manek on the plaza in San Pedro, and the Cine Carua, beside the *Hotel Pérez* in San Marcos. There are **banks** on both plazas.

Second-class **buses** run hourly from San Pedro to Malacatán, Quetzaltenango (both 1hr 30min) and Guatemala City, between 5am and 5pm, from a small chaotic terminal one block behind the church. *Marquensita* pullmans go direct from San Marcos to Guatemala City, passing through the plaza in San Pedro eight times daily from 2.30am until 4pm.

To Tacaná and the high country

To the northwest of San Pedro is some magnificent high country, strung up between the Tajumulco and Tacaná volcanoes and forming an extension of the Mexican Sierra Madre. A rough dirt road runs through these mountains, connecting a series of isolated villages that lie exposed in the frosty heights.

Leaving San Pedro the road climbs steeply, winding up through thick pine forests and emerging onto a high grassy plateau. Here it crosses a great boggy expanse to skirt around the edge of the Tajumulco **volcano**, whose 4220-metre peak is the highest in Guatemala. It's best climbed from the roadside hamlet of Tuchan, from where it's about four hours to the summit – not a particularly hard climb as long as you're acclimatized to the altitude.

Quetzaltrekkers, in Quetzaltenango (☎761 2470; see p.188 for full details), conducts tours up Tajumulco.

Up here the land is sparsely inhabited, dotted with adobe houses and flocks of sheep and goats. The rocky ridges are barren and the trees twisted by the cold. At this altitude the air is thin and what little breath you have left is regularly taken away by the astonishing views which – except when consumed in the frequent mist and cloud – open up at every turn. The village of **IXCHIGUÁN**, on an exposed hillside at 3050m, is the first place of any size, surrounded by bleak rounded hills and in the shadow of the two towering volcanic cones. Buses generally stop here for lunch, giving you a chance to stretch your legs and thaw out with a steaming bowl of *caldo*.

Moving on, the road climbs to the **CUMBRE DE COTZIL**, a spectacular pass which reaches some 3400m and marks the highest point on any road in Central America. From here on it's downhill all the way to the scruffy village of **TACANÁ**, a flourishing trading centre that signals the end of the road – 73km from San Marcos and less than 10km from the Mexican border. Cross-border ties are strong and at the end of 1988 the inhabitants threatened to incorporate themselves into Mexico if the road to San Pedro wasn't paved, claiming that this had been promised to them by the Christian Democrats in the run-up to the 1985 election. Up above the village, spanning the border, is the **Tacaná volcano** (4064m), which can be climbed from the village of Sibinal. It last erupted in 1855, so it should be safe enough. Unless you're setting out to climb one of the volcanoes there's not much to do out this way, but the bus ride alone, bruising though it is, offers some great scenery. Three **buses** a day leave the terminal in San Pedro for Tacaná, at 9am, 11am and noon, returning at 3am, 5am and 11am. The trip takes about five hours, and there is also a bus service to Sibinal and Concepción Tutuapa – at similar times. In Tacaná, the *Hotel El Trébol* (❶), on the entrance road, is a basic place **to stay** where they also do good food. Right in the village, you'll also find the *Hospedaje Los Ángeles* (❶) and the *Pensión Celajes Tacanecos* (❶).

Heading on from Tacaná, pick-ups provide links with Cuilco (from where there are regular buses to Huehuetenango) and to a remote crossing point on the Mexican border called Niquimiul.

Towards the Mexican border

The main road through San Pedro continues west, through San Marcos and out of the valley. Here it starts the descent towards the Pacific plain, dropping steeply around endless hairpin bends and past acre after acre of coffee bushes. Along the way the views towards the ocean are superb. Eventually you reach the sweltering lowlands, passing through San Rafael and El Rodeo with their squalid shacks for plantation workers. About an hour and a half out of San Pedro you arrive in **MALACATÁN**, a relatively sedate place by coastal standards. If you get stuck here on your way to or from the border, try the *Pensión Lucía* (☎776 9415; ❷) or the *Hotel América* (❶), both on the plaza, or *Hotel Don Arturo*, 5 C & 7 Av (☎776 9169; ❹), for somewhere more comfortable. Contrary to popular belief, there is no Mexican consul in Malacatán, but if you need to change money, you can do so at a branch of the Bancafé (Mon–Fri 8.30am–5.30pm, Sat 8.30–1pm).

Buses between Malacatán and San Marcos run every hour from 5am to 5pm. There are trucks and minibuses every half-hour from Malacatán to the border at Talisman, and plenty of pullmans pass through on their way between the border and the capital.

Huehuetenango and the Cuchumatanes

The **department of Huehuetenango**, slotted into the northwest corner of the highlands, is a wildly beautiful part of the country that's bypassed by the majority of visitors. The area is dominated by the mountains of the **Cuchumatanes** but, also includes a limestone plateau in the west and a strip of dense jungle to the north. The vast majority of this is inaccessible to all but the most dedicated of hikers but, with adequate time and a sense of adventure, this can be one of the most rewarding and spectacular parts of the country.

The **Carretera Interamericana**, cutting through from Cuatro Caminos to the Mexican border, is virtually the only paved road in the department, and if you're heading through this way you'll get a glimpse of the mountains, and perhaps a vague sense of the isolating influence of this massive landscape. With more time and energy to spare, a trip into the mountains to **Todos Santos Cuchumatán**, or even all the way out to **San Mateo Ixtatán**, reveals an exceptional wealth of Maya culture. It's a world of jagged peaks and deep-cut valleys, where Spanish is definitely the second language and traditional costume is still rigidly adhered to. Heavily populated before the Conquest, the area has pre-Columbian ruins scattered throughout the hills, with the largest at **Zaculeu**, immediately outside **Huehuetenango**, a surprisingly lively town with good budget hotels and some decent restaurants and cafés.

Despite the initial devastation, the arrival of the Spanish had surprisingly little impact in these highlands, with some of the communities remaining amongst the most traditional in Guatemala. A visit to these mountain villages, either for a market or fiesta (and there are plenty of both), offers one of the best opportunities to see Maya life at close quarters.

Heading on from Huehuetenango you can be at the **Mexican border** in a couple of hours, reach Guatemala City in five or six, or use the back roads to travel across the highlands through **Aguacatán** towards Santa Cruz del Quiché, Nebaj or Cobán.

From Cuatro Caminos to Huehuetenango

Heading northwest from Cuatro Caminos, the Carretera Interamericana climbs steadily, passing the entrance to San Francisco el Alto and stepping up out of the Xela valley onto a broad plateau thick with fields of wheat and dotted with houses. The only village along the way is **POLOGUÁ**, where they have a small weekly market, a pensión – the *Pologuita* (❶) – and a fiesta from August 21 to 27.

About a kilometre before the village, a dirt track leads north to **SAN BARTOLO**, a small agricultural centre down amongst the pine trees, some 12km from the road. The place is virtually deserted during the week, but on Sundays the farmers who live scattered in the surrounding forest gather in the village for the market. There is a small unmarked pensión and some thermal springs a couple of kilometres away. Another track, branching from the first a couple of kilometres before San Bartolo, connects the village with Momostenango, which is about two hours' walk. From Quetzaltenango to San Bartolo there are five daily buses, plus services which continue on to Momostenango on market days.

Beyond Pologuá the road turns towards the north and leaves the corn-covered plateau, crossing the crest of the hills and skirting around the rim of a huge sweeping valley. To the east a superb view opens out across a sea of pine forests, the last stretch of levellish land before the mountains to the north. Way out there in the middle is Santa Cruz del Quiché and closer to hand, buried in the trees, lies Momostenango. Once over the ridge the road winds its way down towards Huehuetenango. The first place inside the department is the ladino village of **Malacatancito**, where Mam warriors first challenged the advancing Spanish army in 1525.

Huehuetenango

In the corner of a small agricultural plain, 5km from the main road at the foot of the mighty Cuchumatanes, **HUEHUETENANGO**, capital of the department of the same name, is the focus of trade and transport for a vast area. Nonetheless, its atmosphere is provincial and relaxed. The name is a Nahuatl word meaning "the place of the old people", and before the arrival of the Spanish it was the site of one of the residential suburbs that surrounded the Mam capital of Zaculeu (see p.207). Under colonial rule it was a small regional centre with little to offer other than a steady trickle of silver and a stretch or two of grazing land. The supply of silver dried up long ago, but other minerals are still mined, and coffee and sugar have been added to the area's produce.

Arrival and information

Like all Guatemalan towns, Huehuetenango, known simply as Huehue, is laid out on a grid pattern, with avenidas running one way and calles the other. It's

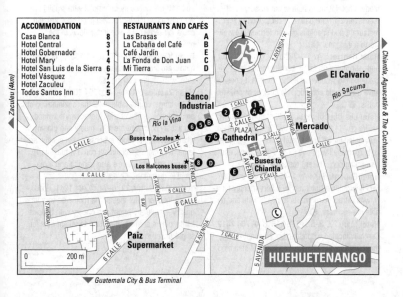

fairly small so you shouldn't have any real problems finding your way around, particularly once you've located the plaza.

Most buses arrive at the **bus terminal**, halfway between the Carretera Interamericana and town. Minibuses make constant trips between the town centre and the bus terminal, or you can take the larger bus, heading for **Chiantla**, just beyond Huehue, via the town centre.

You'll probably be coming **to Huehuetenango** from elsewhere in the highlands, in which case you might be able to pick up a direct bus somewhere along the Carretera Interamericana – or you can catch any bus to Cuatro Caminos, where you'll be able to get one to Huehuetenango. There's also a regular service, with hourly departures, from the terminal in Quetzaltenango.

Coming direct **from Guatemala City** the best way to travel is by pullman. Los Halcones runs buses at 7am, 2pm and 5pm from its offices at 7 Av 15–27, Zona 1, Guatemala City. Also highly recommended is Transportes Velásquez, 20 C 1–37, Zona 1 (☏473 6005) in Guatemala City, who runs pullmans to Huehuetenango eleven times a day from 5.20am until 5.30pm, with an extra service on Fridays at 6.30pm. Five of the morning departures continue on to the Mexican border at La Mesilla. There are also second-class departures every hour from the main bus terminal in Zona 4. There's also one daily Taca **flight** from Guatemala City to Huehue, via Santa Cruz del Quiché (US$55; one hour).

Coming **from the Mexican border** at La Mesilla, there's a bus every hour from 4am to 4pm.

Accommodation

Huehuetenango has a good range of **hotels**, most of which are good value and attractive, though there are no luxury options. Most of the real cheapies are scruffy, chaotic places clustered around 1 Avenida, and geared mainly towards market traders.

Casa Blanca 7 Av 3–41 ☏ & ☏769 0777. Modern hotel, though built in colonial style; all rooms have private bath and cable TV. The fine restaurant and spacious garden terrace are well worth a visit, too. ❺

Hotel Central 5 Av 1–33 ☏764 1202. Classic budget hotel, with large, scruffy rooms in a creaking old wooden building, though it does have a fantastic comedor. No singles or private baths. ❶

Hotel Los Chuchumatanes 3km north of town centre ☏764 9356, ☏764 2815. Huehuetenango's finest hotel boasts 55 bungalow-style rooms, all with two large double beds, and a swimming pool. Decent restaurant, too. ❻

Hotel Gobernador 4 Av 1–45 ☏ & ☏764 1197. Excellent budget hotel run by a very friendly family, with attractive rooms, some with bath, and reliable hot showers. ❷

Hotel Mary 2 C 3–52 ☏764 1618, ☏764 7412. Centrally located with small but pleasant rooms, most with private shower, and loads of steaming hot water. ❷/❸

Hotel San Luis de la Sierra 2 C 7–00 ☏ & ☏ 764 1103. Spotless modern hotel with small but very attractive rooms, all with good showers and cable TV; some have wonderful views of the mountains. ❹

Hotel Vásquez 2 C 6–67 ☏764 1338. Cell-sized rooms around a bare courtyard, but clean and safe, with secure parking. ❷

Hotel Zaculeu 5 Av 1–14 ☏764 1086, ☏764 1575. Large, comfortable hotel that's something of an institution. Some of the older rooms surrounding a leafy courtyard are a bit musty and gloomy, while those in the more expensive new section are larger and more spacious. All come with cable TV and private bath. There's also parking and a reasonable restaurant. ❹/❺

Todos Santos Inn 2 C 6–74 ☏764 1241. Good, secure budget hotel though the rooms do vary in quality – some are bright and cheery with bedside lights, others are less attractive. Excellent deal for single travellers. ❷

The Town

Today's Huehuetenango has two quite distinct functions – and two contrasting halves – each serving a separate section of the population. The large majority of the people are ladinos, and for them Huehuetenango is an unimportant regional centre far from the hub of things, a mood summed up in the unhurried atmosphere of the attractive **plaza** at the heart of the ladino half of town, where shaded walkways are surrounded by administrative offices. Overlooking it, perched above the pavements, are a shell-shaped bandstand, a clock tower and a grandiose Neoclassical church, a solid whitewashed structure with a facade that's crammed with Doric pillars and Grecian urns. In the middle of the plaza there's a **relief map** of the department with flags marking the villages. The details are vague and the scale a bit warped, but it gives you an idea of the mass of rock that dominates the region, and the deep river valleys that slice into it.

A few blocks to the east, the town's atmosphere could hardly be more different. Here the neat little rows of arches are replaced by the pale green walls of the **market**, hub of the Maya part of town, where the streets are crowded with traders, drunks and travellers from Mexico and all over Central America. This part of Huehuetenango, centred on 1 Avenida, is always alive with activity, its streets packed with people from every corner of the department and littered with rotten vegetables.

Eating and drinking

Most of the better **restaurants** are, like the accommodation, in the central area, around the plaza. For a **drink** head to *Mi Tierra*, which is a sociable place for a beer, or try *"Café-Bar"* next door.

Las Brasas 4 Av 1–55. Reasonably good Chinese food and steaks, but a bit overpriced.

La Cabaña del Café 2 C, opposite *Hotel Vásquez*. Logwood café with an excellent range of coffees (including cappuccino), great cakes and a few snacks.

Café Jardín 4 C and 6 Av. Friendly place serving inexpensive but excellent breakfasts, milkshakes, pancakes and the usual chicken and beef dishes. Open daily 6am–11pm.

La Fonda de Don Juan 2 C 5–35. Attractive place with gingham tablecloths, serving good, if slightly pricey, pizza and pasta, and a reasonable range of beers.

Hotel Central 5 Av 1–33. Very tasty, inexpensive set meals. Particularly good, filling and inexpensive breakfast.

Mi Tierra 4 C 6–46. Attractive little restaurant set in a covered patio with nice decor and a good atmosphere. The flavoursome menu is more imaginative than most – great for house salads, *churrascos* (barbecued meat) and cheesecake – plus very cheap healthy breakfasts. Also has internet facilities and a good noticeboard.

Listings

Banks Banco G&T Continental is on the plaza (Mon–Fri 9am–8pm, Sat 10am–1pm), Bancafé is a block to the south (Mon–Fri 8.30am–8pm, Sat 9am–3pm), and there's a Banco Industrial on 6 Av 1–42 (Mon–Fri 9am–7pm, Sat 9am–1pm) with a Visa and Plus network ATM.

Immigration Inside the Farmacia el Cid at 4 C on the southern side of the plaza (daily 8am–12.30pm & 2–7.30pm; ☎764 1353 & 764 1366).

Internet Génesis at 2 C 6–37 and Mi Tierra at 4 C 6–46 both charge around US$3.80 an hour.

Language schools Huehuetenango is a good place to learn Spanish as you don't rub shoulders with many other gringos. Almost everywhere offers a package of tuition and accommodation with a family for around US$125 a week. One of the best schools is Insituto El Portal, 1 C 1–64, Zona 3 (☎ & ℱ764 1987, ⊛www.guatemala365.com/english /schools/schu003.htm), while Casa Xelajú, is another good option – contact their Quetzaltenango school (see p.185) for more information. Two other schools, Fundación XXIII, at 6 Av 6–126, Zona 1

(☎764 1478 ⓦ www.worldwide.edu/ci/guatemala /schools/10024.html) and Xinabajul, 6 Av 0–69 (☎ & ⓕ764 1518; www.spanish-schools.com/huehue /inf/infoe.htm), have moderate reputations. Abesaida Guevara de López gives good private lessons: call ☎764 2917.

Laundry The best is in the Turismundo Commercial Centre at 3 Av 0–15 (Mon–Sat 9.30am–6.30pm).

Mexican consulate In the Farmacia El Cid, on the plaza at 5 Av and 4 C (daily 8am–12.30pm & 2–7.30pm). They'll charge you US$1.30 for a tourist card that's usually free at the border, though few nationalities now need one at all.

Post office 2 C 3–54 (Mon–Fri 8am–4.30pm).

Shopping Superb weaving is produced throughout the department and can be bought in the market here or at Artesanías Ixquil, on 5 Av 1–56, opposite the *Hotel Central*, where both the prices and quality are high. If you have time, though, you'd be better advised to travel to the villages and buy direct from the producers.

Supermarket There's a large branch of Paiz on the southwestern outskirt of town at 6 C and 10 Av.

Telephone Telgua is at 4 Av 6–54 (daily 7am–10pm), though it may move back to its former location next to the post office.

Moving on from Huehuetenango

All transport, except to the village of San Juan Atitán and the Zaculeu ruins, leaves from the **main bus terminal** on the edge of town. To get there from the town centre, take either a minibus or the Chiantla bus from the *parada servicio urbano* just past the *Café Jardín*, or on 6 Av, between 2 and 3 C. The outdoor terminal is dusty and scruffy, but well laid out, each bus company with its own office, so you can easily get the latest timetable information; don't believe all the times painted on the walls, though. Note also that it is standard practice to buy your ticket from the office, before boarding the bus, even for second-class buses. Generally, there are more buses in the mornings to all destinations.

Buses to the **Mexican border** (2hr) leave every half-hour from 5.30am onwards, with the last one departing at 7pm. For Coatepeque and the Mexican border at Tecún Umán, 15 buses leave daily between 3am and 5pm. For anywhere along the **Pacific Highway**, eleven Velásquez buses leave between 2am and 3pm along this alternative route to Guatemala City. There are buses every half-hour to **Quetzaltenango** (2hr), with the first one leaving at 4.30am, and the last at 6pm. To **Guatemala City** (6hr), there are hourly second-class departures from 2.15am to 4pm plus the luxury Los Halcones buses that leave from their own terminal on 7 Av 3–62 (☎764 2251) at 4.30am, 7am and 2pm. If you want to go to **Antigua**, take a capital-bound bus and change at Chimaltenango; for **Lake Atitlán** or **Chichicastenango** change at Los Encuentros.

More remote destinations are also served. Heading north, into the **Cuchumatanes mountains**, there are several companies offering buses for **Barillas** (7hr) at 7am, 8am, 9am, 11.30am, noon and 10pm, as well as regular departures to San Miguel Acatán, Soloma and San Mateo Ixtatán (see p.213 for details). The **Todos Santos** (2hr 45 min) buses leave at 5.45am, 11.30am, 12.30pm, 2pm and 4pm with afternoon buses often continuing on to San Martín and Jacaltenango. La Paisanita buses for **Nentón** (4hr) leave at 5.30am, 9.30am and 1.30pm, the last departure continuing on to **Gracias a Dios** (7hr 30min), in the isolated northwest. (It's currently not wise to enter Mexico at the remote Gracias a Dios border post because of political tension in the area.) You should always check these schedules, however, prior to your planned day of departure.

To the west, buses head for isolated **Cuilco** (3–4hr) at 5am and 2pm. Heading east and northeast, there are hourly buses for **Aguacatán** (1hr 15min) and one daily to **Sacapulas** (4hr) at 12.45pm, where you can make a connection for the Ixil towns or Uspantán. A daily direct bus to **Nebaj** (6hr), departs at 11.30am, also going via Aguacatán and Sacapulas.

Zaculeu

A few kilometres to the west of Huehuetenango are the ruins of **ZACULEU**, capital of the **Mam**, who were one of the principal pre-conquest highland tribes. The site (daily 8am–6pm; US$3.20) includes several large temples, plazas and a ball court, but unfortunately it has been restored with an astounding lack of subtlety (or accuracy). Its appearance – more like an ageing film set than an ancient ruin – is owed to a latter-day colonial power, the **United Fruit Company**, under whose auspices the ruins were reconstructed in 1946 and 1947; the company is, of course, notorious for its heavy-handed practices throughout Central America, and the Zaculeu reconstruction is no exception. The walls and surfaces have been levelled off with a layer of thick white plaster, leaving them stark and undecorated. There are no roof-combs, carvings or stucco mouldings, and only in a few places does the original stonework show through. Even so, the site does have a peculiar atmosphere of its own and is worth a look; surrounded by trees and neatly mown grass, with fantastic views of the mountains, it's an excellent spot for a picnic.

Not all that much is known about the early history of Zaculeu as no Mam records survived the Conquest, but the site is thought to have been a religious and administrative centre housing the elite, while the bulk of the population lived in small surrounding settlements or scattered in the hills. Zaculeu was the hub of a large area of Mam-speakers, its boundaries reaching into the mountains as far as Todos Santos and along the Selegua and Cuilco valleys, an area throughout which Mam remains the dominant language.

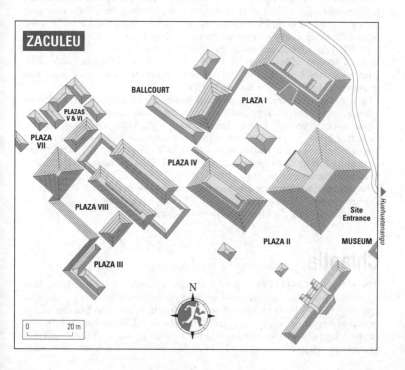

To put together a history of the site means relying on the records of the K'iche', a more powerful neighbouring tribe. According to their mythology, the K'iche' conquered most of the other highland tribes, including the Mam, some time between 1400 and 1475: the Popol Vuh tells that "our grandfathers and fathers cast them out when they inserted themselves among the Mam of Zakiulew". The K'iche' maintained their authority under the rule of the leader Quicab, but following his death in 1475 the subjugated tribes began to break away from the fold. As a part of this trend the Mam managed to reassert their independence, but no sooner had they escaped the clutches of one expansionist empire than the **Spanish** arrived with a yet more brutal alternative.

For the first few months the Spaniards devoted themselves to conquering the K'iche', still the dominant force in the highlands. But once they'd achieved this they turned their attention to the Mam, especially after being told by Sequechul, leader of the K'iche', that a plan to burn the Spanish army in Utatlán had been suggested to his father by **Caibal Balam**, king of the Mam. In answer to this, Pedro de Alvarado despatched an army under the command of his brother Gonzalo to mete out punishment. It was met by about five thousand Mam warriors near the village of Malacatancito, and promptly set about a massacre. Seeing that his troops were no match for the Spanish, Caibal Balam withdrew them to the safety of Zaculeu, where they were protected on three sides by deep ravines and on the other by a series of walls and ditches. The Spanish army settled outside the city, preparing themselves for a lengthy siege, while Gonzalo offered the Maya a simple choice – they either became Christians "peacefully" or faced "death and destruction".

Attracted by neither option they struggled to hold out against the invading force. At one stage a relief army of eight thousand arrived from the mountains, but again they were unable to ruffle Gonzalo's well-disciplined ranks. Finally, in mid-October, after about six weeks under siege, his army starving to death, Caibal Balam surrendered to the Spanish. With the bitterest of ironies a bastardized version of his name has been adopted by one of Guatemala's crack army regiments – the "Kaibils", who have been held responsible for numerous massacres during the 1970s and early 1980s.

Excavations at the site have unearthed hundreds of burials carried out in an unusual variety of ways; bodies were crammed into great urns, interred in vaults and even cremated. These burials, along with artefacts found at the site, including pyrite plaques and carved jade, have suggested links with the site at Nebaj. There's a small **museum** on site (daily 8am–noon & 1–6pm) with examples of some of the burial techniques used and some interesting ceramics found during excavation.

To get to Zaculeu from Huehuetenango, take one of the pick-ups or buses that leave from 7 Avenida between 2 and 3 calles – make sure it's a Ruta 3 bus heading for Ruinas Zaculeu (not Zaculeu central).

Chiantla

The village of **CHIANTLA** is backed right up against the mountains, 5km to the north of Huehuetenango. The main point of interest here is the colonial church, built by Dominican friars, which is now the object of one of the country's largest pilgrimages, annually on February 2, in honour of its image of the **Virgen del Rosario**. Legend has it that the image of the Virgin was given to the church by a Spaniard named Almengor, who owned a silver mine in the hills. Not only did the mine proceed to yield a fortune, but on his last visit to it, just after Almengor had surfaced, the entire thing caved in – thus proving the power of the Virgin. She is also thought to be capable of healing the sick, and at any time of the year you'll see people who've travelled from all over Guatemala asking for her assistance. A mural inside the church depicts a rather ill-proportioned Spaniard watching over the Maya toiling in his mines, while on the wall opposite the Maya are shown discovering God. The precise connection between the two is left somewhat vague, but presumably the gap is bridged by the Virgin. This is also the town where Rigoberta Menchú (see p.469) attended convent school, according to her biographer David Stoll, though the Nobel Laureate has always denied receiving a formal education.

Buses from Huehuetenango to Chiantla travel between the main bus terminal and Chiantla every fifteen minutes between 6am and 6.30pm. You can catch one as it passes through the town centre, or wait at the Calvario (by the junction of 1 Av and 1 C), instead of heading out to the terminal.

The Cuchumatanes

The **Cuchumatanes**, rising to a frosty 3837m just to the north of Huehuetenango, are the largest non-volcanic peaks in Central America. The mountain chain rises from a limestone plateau close to the Mexican border, reaches its full height above Huehuetenango, and falls away gradually to the east, continuing through northern Quiché to form part of the highlands of Alta Verapaz. Appropriately enough the name translates as "that which was brought together by great force", from the Mam words *cucuj*, to unite, and *matan*, superior force.

The mountain scenery is magnificent, ranging from wild, exposed craggy outcrops to lush, tranquil river valleys. The upper parts of the slopes are barren, scattered with boulders and shrivelled cypress trees, while the lower levels, by contrast, are richly fertile, cultivated with corn, coffee and sugar. Between the peaks, in the deep-cut valleys, are hundreds of tiny villages, isolated by the enormity of the landscape. This area had little to entice the Spanish, and even at the best of times they only managed to exercise vague control, occasionally disrupting things with bouts of religious persecution or disease, but rarely maintaining a sustained presence. Following the initial impact of the Conquest, the people were, for the most part, left to revert to their old ways, and their traditions are still very powerful today, showing through in the fiestas, costumes and folk-Catholicism.

More recently the mountains were the scene of bitter fighting between the army and the guerrillas. In the late 1970s and early 1980s the area was struck by a wave of violence and terror that sent thousands fleeing across the border to Mexico. These days things have calmed down, and most families have returned from exile and begun rebuilding their communities.

The region offers a good chunk of Guatemala's most spectacular scenery and fascinating villages. A single rough road runs through the range, climbing the steep south face, crossing the exposed central plateau and dropping into the isolated valleys to the north. Travel here is not easy – distances are large, hotels and restaurants basic at best, buses are packed and frequent cloudbursts often make the roads impassable – but if you can summon the energy it's an immensely rewarding area, offering a rare glimpse of Maya life and some of the country's finest fiestas and markets. The mountains are also ideal for hiking, particularly if you've had enough of struggling up volcanoes.

The most accessible of the villages in the vicinity, and the only one yet to receive a steady trickle of tourists, is **Todos Santos Cuchumatán**, which is also one of the most interesting. At any time of year the Saturday market here is well worth visiting, and the horse race fiesta on November 1 has to be one of the most outrageous in Guatemala. From here, you can walk over the hills to **San Juan Atitán** and **Santiago Chimaltenango**, or head on down the valley to **San Martín** and **Jacaltenango**. Further into the mountains are the villages of **Soloma** and **San Mateo Ixtatán**, both of which have markets on Thursday and Sunday. Another good hike takes you from **San Miguel Acatán** along the edge of the hills to Jacaltenango. Beyond San Mateo Ixtatán the road comes to an end a few kilometres past **Barillas**, a ladino town from where the jungle lowlands beyond are being colonized.

Huehuetenango to Barillas

Heading north out of Huehuetenango, the road for the mountains passes through Chiantla before starting to climb the arid hillside, and as the bus sways around the switchbacks, the view across the valley is superb. In the distance you can sometimes make out the perfect cone of the Santa María volcano, towering above Quetzaltenango some 60km to the south.

At the top of the slope the road slips through a pass into the *región andina*, a desolate grassy plateau suspended between the peaks, strewn with boulders and segregated with neat earth walls. At this height the air is cool, thin and fresh, the ground often hard with frost and occasionally dusted with snow. In the middle of the plain is the *Comedor de los Cuchumatanes*, where buses stop for a chilly lunch before pressing on through Paquix, junction for the road to Todos Santos. Shortly before the road reaches the comedor a rough track branches off to the east, climbing through the mountains for 44km to Salquil Grande – the road is often impassable, but if you're in search of an unpredictable adventure it makes a spectacular trip.

Beyond Paquix the road runs through a couple of magical valleys, where great grey boulders lie scattered among ancient-looking oak and cypress trees, their trunks gnarled by the bitter winds. A few families manage to survive the rigours of the altitude, collecting firewood and tending flocks of sheep. Sheep have been grazed here since they were introduced by the Spanish, who prized this wilderness as the best pasture in Central America, though you are unlikely to find lamb on a menu up here or anywhere in Guatemala.

Continuing north the road gradually winds down off the plateau, emerging on the other side at the top of an incredibly steep valley. Here the track clings to the hillside, cut out of the sheer rock face that drops hundreds of metres to the valley floor. This northern side of the Cuchumatanes contains some of the most dramatic scenery in the entire country, and the road is certainly the most spine-chilling. A little further down, as if to confirm your worst fears, the rusting wreck of a bus lies a hundred metres or so beneath the road.

The first village reached by the road is **SAN JUAN IXCOY**, an apple-growing centre drawn out along the valley floor. There's no particular reason for breaking the journey here, but there is a small pensión (❶), where you can get a bed and a meal. In season, around the end of August, passing buses are besieged by an army of fruit sellers. This innocent-looking village has a past marked by violence. On the night of July 17, 1898, following a dispute about pay, the Maya of San Juan murdered the local labour contractor, and in a desperate bid to keep the crime secret they slaughtered all but one of the village's

The Maya priests of the Cuchumatanes

The high peaks and rugged terrain of the Cuchumatanes guard one of the country's most traditional Maya cultures. Ethnographer Krystyna Deuss has been studying Maya rituals in these remote communities for more than ten years, focusing her attention on the prayer-makers, who occupy a position parallel to that of local priests. Here she explains their role and some of the key rituals surrounding their office.

Some of the purest **Maya rituals** today can be found among the Q'anjob'al of the northwestern Cuchumatanes. The office of *alcalde resador* (chief prayer-maker) still exists here and the 365-day *Haab* calendar is used in conjunction with the 260-day *Tzolkin*. The former ends with the five days of *Oyeb ku*, when adult souls leave the body; the return of the souls on the fifth day brings in the new year. As this always falls on a day of *Watan*, *Lambat*, *Ben* or *Chinax*, these four day lords are referred to as the "Year Bearers" or "Chiefs". Depending on the community, the *Haab* year begins either at the end of February or the beginning of March, coinciding with the corn planting season.

The duty of the **alcalde resador** is to protect his village from evil and ensure a good harvest by praying for rain at planting time and for protection against wind, pest and disease while the corn is maturing. His year of office – during which he and his wife must remain celibate – begins on January 1, the day all the voluntary municipal officials change, and in the towns of Santa Eulalia, Soloma and San Miguel Acatán where traditions are particularly strong, he lives in a house which has been especially built for him. Traditionalists regularly visit to ask for prayers and to leave gifts of corn, beans, candles and money. On the altar of the house stands the **ordenanza**, a chest that not only contains religious icons but also ancient village documents, a throwback to the time when religious and civil authorities worked as one. The chest now serves both as a symbol of authority and as a sacred object, and can only be opened by the *alcalde resador*, in private, once a year. The *resador*'s whole day is spent in prayer: at his home altar before the *ordenanza*, in church and at sacred village sites marked by crosses. Prayers for rain are often accompanied by the ritual sacrifice of turkeys whose blood is poured over the candles and incense destined to be burned at the sacred places the following day. These ceremonies are not open to the general public.

Festivals more in the public domain happen on January 1 when the incumbent *resador* hands over to his successor. In **Soloma** after an all-night vigil the *ordenanza* is carried in procession to the middle of the market square and put on a makeshift altar under a pine arch. When the incoming group arrives there are prayers and ritual drinking and they receive their wooden staffs of office, after which the outgoing *resador* (usually a man in his sixties or seventies) is free to leave for his own home. The new *resador*'s group stays in the marketplace praying, collecting alms and drinking until 3pm, when they carry the *ordenanza* back to the official residence in a somewhat erratic procession. Notwithstanding a further night of vigil and ceremonial drinking, at 7am the following morning, the *resador* sets out on his first prayer-round to the sacred mountains overlooking the town.

In **San Juan Ixcoy** the year-end ceremonies differ in that the new *resador* is not appointed in advance. Here the outgoing group carries the *ordenanza* to a small chapel outside the church on the night of the 31st and leaves it in the care of a committee of traditionals. The usual all-night vigil with prayers, ritual drinking and collecting alms continues throughout the following day while everyone waits anxiously for a candidate to turn up. As the office of *resador* is not only arduous, and with dwindling support from the community, also expensive, the post is not always filled on January 1. The *ordenanza* sometimes stays locked in the chapel for several days before a volunteer (usually an ex-prayer maker) takes on the office again rather than let the *ordenanza* and the tradition be abandoned.

Krystyna Deuss – Maya: the Guatemalan Indian Centre, London

ladino population. The authorities responded mercilessly, killing about ten Maya for the life of every ladino. In local mythology the revolt is known as *la degollación*, the beheading.

Over another range of hills and down in the next valley is **SOLOMA**, largest, busiest and richest of the villages in the northern Cuchumatanes, with a population of around three thousand. Its flat valley floor was once the bed of a lake, and the steep hillsides still come sliding down at every earthquake or cloudburst. Soloma translates (from Q'anjob'al, the dominant language on this side of the mountains) as "without security", and its history is blackened by disaster; it was destroyed by earthquakes in 1773 and 1902, half burnt down in 1884, and decimated by smallpox in 1885. The long white *huipiles* worn by the women of Soloma are similar to those of San Mateo Ixtatán and the Lacandones, and are probably as close as any in the country to the style worn before the Conquest. These days they are on the whole donned only for the **market** on Thursday and Sunday, which again is by far the best time to visit.

About four hours from Huehuetenango, Soloma makes a good place to break the trip. The *Hotel Caucaso* is first choice here – an excellent, moderately priced **hotel** (❷/❸), where some rooms have private bath and cable TV – though there are other options including the *Hotel San Antonio* (☎780 6191; ❷) at the edge of town, or as a last resort, the scruffy *Hospedaje San Juan* (❶). Hourly **buses** leave the terminal in Huehuetenango for Soloma, or you can catch any bus bound for either San Rafael La Independencia, San Sebastian Coatan and Barillas.

Leaving Soloma the road climbs again, on a steadily deteriorating surface, over another range of hills, to the hillside village of Santa Eulalia. Beyond, past the junction to San Rafael La Independencia, it heads through another misty, rock-strewn forest and emerges on the other side at **SAN MATEO IXTATÁN**, the most traditional, and quite possibly the most interesting, of this string of villages. Little more than a thin sprawl of wooden-tiled houses on an exposed hillside, it's strung out beneath a belt of ancient forest and craggy mountains. The people here speak **Chuj** and form part of a Maya tribe who occupy the extreme northwest corner of the highlands and some of the jungle beyond; their territory borders that of the Lacandon, a jungle tribe never subjugated by the Spanish, who constantly harassed these villages in colonial times. The only industry is the manufacture of salt from some communally owned springs in the hills, and life at these heights is hard at the best of times. The only time to visit, other than for the fiesta on September 21, is on a market day, Thursday or Sunday. For the rest of the week the village is virtually deserted. The women here wear unusual and striking *huipiles*, long white gowns embroidered in brilliant reds, yellows and blues, radiating out from a star-like centre. The men wear short woollen tunics called *capixay*, often embroidered with flowers around the collar and quetzals on the back. Below the village is the beautiful Maya ruin of **Xolcol**, the unrestored remains of a small pyramid and ball court, shaded by a couple of cypress trees. If you decide to **stay**, there are several extremely basic *pensiones* – the best of which is *El Águila* (❶), run by the very friendly family who also operate the *Comedor Ixateco*. To the northwest of San Mateo a road cuts high across the mountain and is the start of a beautiful hike to Yalambojoch (see below).

Beyond San Mateo the road drops steadily east to **BARILLAS**, a ladino frontier town in the relative warmth of the lowlands. Further on still, the land slopes into the Usumacinta basin through thick, uninhabited jungle. Rough tracks penetrate a short distance into this wilderness (and a local bus runs out as far as San Ramón), opening it up for farming, and eventually a road will run east across the **Ixcán** (the wilderness area that stretches between here and the jungles of Petén) to Playa Grande (see p.316). The cheapest place **to stay** in Barillas is the *Tienda las Tres Rosas* (❶) while the *Hotel Monte Cristo* (❶) costs not much more.

Buses to Barillas, passing through all the villages en route, are operated by a number of companies including Autobuses del Norte, Rutas Barillenses and Transjosue and leave at 7am, 8am, 9am, 11.30am, noon, 10pm and 11.30pm from Huehuetenango, taking around eight hours to reach Barillas. All buses leave from Huehue's main bus terminal, and it's well worth buying your ticket in advance as they operate a vague system of seat allocation. It's a rough and tortuous trip, the buses usually filled to bursting and despite recent road improvements it's a long, slow bumpy ride once you're past the Paquix junction. Buses leave Barillas for Huehuetenango at 11pm, 11.30pm, 12.30am, 1.30am, 5am, 8am and 10am.

Hiking from San Mateo to Yalambojoch

The great forested peaks looming to the west of San Mateo Ixtatán are in fact a narrow spur of the Cuchumatanes and can easily be crossed in a day. In a matter of hours you're up on top of the ridge, in a misty world of forest and high pasture, while over on the other side you soon drop onto a low-lying limestone plateau from where you can catch a bus back to Huehuetenango.

The main road from San Mateo to Barillas heads on around the side of the mountain, dipping into a narrow gulley. At the bottom of this dip – less than a kilometre east of the centre of San Mateo – another road branches off to the left, climbing into the hills. Following this you pass right over the spine of the Cuchumatanes, through high alpine pastures and beautiful pine and white oak forests, the older trees draped in mosses, ferns and bromeliads. Sadly, the trees are being cut down at a phenomenal rate to provide firewood for the nearby villages, although this does mean you may be able to catch a ride on one of the lumber lorries.

After a couple of hours' walk you emerge from the forest at the top of a huge, steep-sided valley, beside the tiny settlement of **Chizbazalum**. Sticking with the road, you want to cross the top of the valley, which drops away beneath you. Individual houses, maize fields and herds of sheep are scattered across this enormous landscape and many of the young shepherds are armed with blowpipes, a tradition probably inherited from the lowland Maya to the north. (The only other area that hunters use blowpipes is in Chajul in the Ixil triangle, where they were heavily influenced by Lacandón Indians.) The focus of this dispersed community is the village of **Patalcal**, where the road divides – you want to bear right and head up and onto the next shoulder. The road pushes out along this high ridge, but again it splits and you need to branch right. Here too the high ground is forested, but the trail soon starts to drop again, zigzagging down towards the village of Bulej – five or six hours' walk from San Mateo. If it's a clear day the views are superb, with the Mexican plateau mapped out below and the Lagunas de Montebello catching the light.

BULEJ itself is a remote settlement that acts as a centre for the surrounding farming communities of scattered wooden buildings and fruit trees. If you happen to be here in June then the entire place will be in bloom, while in August it is awash with pears and apricots. You shouldn't have any trouble finding a place to stay here and there is a shop on the main square selling soft drinks and biscuits. If you decide to press on, then it's another couple of hours of steep descent to the village of **YALAMBOJOCH**, which is right down on the plateau and the point you finally meet up with the road from Huehuetenango.

The recent history of Yalambojoch is bound up with that of Finca San Francisco, a smaller village along the road some 3km to the east. In 1982 the army massacred around three hundred people in San Francisco (see Contexts, p.464) and the entire population of the surrounding area fled for their lives, crossing the border into Mexico. After more than a decade people started to return, and life in Yalambojoch is beginning to return to normal. Despite all this horror you'll find the people warm and welcoming, and although they are very poor you shouldn't have any trouble finding somewhere to stay – offer to pay about US$2 per person. The village of **FINCA SAN FRANCISCO** is itself also well worth a look – just follow the road to the east. Along the way you can stop off for a chilly dip in a beautiful crystal-clear stream, and in the village itself there is a small Maya temple, which is also the site of a plaque commemorating those who died in the massacre.

Transportes Chiantlequita **buses** connect Yalambojoch and Huehuetenango. They leave the bus terminal in Huehuetenango at 5am, 12.30pm and 1.20pm, passing through Yalambojoch after about seven hours, before spending the night at Finca Gracias a Dios, metres from the Mexican border. The next morning two buses leave Gracias a Dios at 3am and one at 7am for the journey back to Huehuetenango, and pass through Yalambojoch.

San Rafael La Independencia, San Miguel Acatán and on foot to Jacaltenango

Between Santa Eulalia and San Mateo Ixtatán a branch road cuts off to the left, heading over the spine of the Cuchumatanes and curving around the other side to **SAN RAFAEL LA INDEPENDENCIA**, a small village perched on a cold outcrop. In San Rafael you'll find a couple of comedores and a Thursday market but probably nowhere to stay: however, if you ask in the office of the bus company they'll usually be able to find you a concrete floor on which you can spend the night. There are **buses** to San Rafael from Huehue at 2.30am, 11.15am and 4.30pm, which return at 3am and 9am and 11.30pm. From San Rafael you can walk on down the valley, following the road or taking the path towards the larger village of **SAN MIGUEL ACATÁN**. Here there are a couple of comedores, a Sunday market and a small pensión in the house behind the Municipalidad. **Buses** leave Huehuetenango for San Miguel at 1pm and 3.30pm, returning at midnight and 2am. Confirm all schedules in Huehuetenango before you travel, as the poor roads in this region affect services and punctuality.

From San Miguel Acatán, a spectacular walk takes you along the edge of the mountains to Jacaltenango (see p.218). Setting out from San Miguel, cross the river and follow the trail that bears to the right as it climbs the hill opposite. At the fork, halfway up, take the higher path that crosses the ridge beside a small shelter. On the other side it drops down into the head of the next valley. Here you want to follow the path down the valley on the near side of the river, and through the narrow gorge to an ancient wooden bridge. Cross the river and climb up the other side of the valley, heading down towards the end of it as you go. The path that heads straight out of the valley runs to Nentón, and the other path, up and over the ridge to the left, heads towards **Jacaltenango**. Along the way there are stunning views of the rugged peaks of the southern Cuchumatanes and the great flat expanse that stretches into Mexico – on a clear day you can see the Lagunas de Montebello, a good 50km away, over the border. On the far side of the ridge the path eventually drops down to Jacaltenango through the neighbouring village of San Marcos Huista: some eight or nine tough but worthwhile hours in all from San Miguel.

Todos Santos Cuchumatán

If you turn off at the **Paquix** junction, about 20km from Huehuetenango, you can follow a road heading west to **TODOS SANTOS CUCHUMATÁN**. This western road slopes down through **La Ventosa**, a narrow gulley lined with pine and cedar trees, where almost immediately you'll begin to see the traditional red costume of Todos Santos: the men in their red-and-white striped trousers, black woollen breeches and brilliantly embroidered shirt collars; the women in dark blue *cortes* and superbly intricate purple *huipiles*. Further down, at the bottom of the steep-sided, deep-cut river valley, is the village itself – a single main street with a few tiendas, a scruffy plaza, a church, some language schools and a loose collection of houses and corn fields. Above the village flocks of sheep are grazed and below it the crops are farmed. Todos Santos was originally put on the map by the writer Maud Oakes (whose *The Two Crosses of Todos Santos* was published in 1951) and photographer Hans Namuth, who has been recording the faces of the villagers for more than forty years.

It's the endurance of tradition and the isolation that have made the village so attractive to visitors, and photographers in particular, though such attention has not always been welcome. In April 2000, an angry mob attacked and killed a Japanese tourist and his Guatemalan guide here, believing that the former, who was taking pictures of local children, was a Satanist baby stealer. Though the perpetrators have been jailed, and the community as a whole was stunned and deeply remorseful, the depth of misunderstanding serves to highlight the cultural chasm between this remote, highly superstitious mountain community and the developed world. There have been no incidents since, but obviously it's important to respect local sensitivities and be very judicious about taking photographs, particularly of children.

As usual, most of the people the village serves don't actually live here. The immediate population is probably around twelve hundred, but there are perhaps ten times that many in the surrounding hills who are dependent on Todos Santos for trade, supplies and social life. This population is more than the land can support, and many travel to the coast in search of work. All over the country you'll see them, always dressed in *traje* – traditional costume. However, there's one event that brings them all home, the famous November 1 **fiesta**

Learning Spanish or Mam in Todos Santos

Todos Santos is now home to three **language schools** where you can learn Spanish or Mam. Despite the fact that Spanish is the second language here, and students get a limited chance to practise it with their Mam-speaking host families, if you're looking for **cultural exchange** you'll find the courses highly rewarding – especially if you don't mind pretty basic living conditions. Some students can be placed with ladino, Spanish-speaking families, though these houses are in short supply. Courses at all the schools consist of four to five hours' tuition a day and accommodation and meals with a local family, all for between US$100 and US$120 a week. A percentage of the profits from all the schools goes to local development projects.

The original school, set up in the early 1990s, is the Proyecto Lingüístico de Español/Mam Todos Santos, a branch of the excellent Quetzaltenango-based language centre (to contact them see p.185); it's located a block east of the parque. A block west of the parque, Nuevo Amanacer is another good school, which aids women's projects and also offers weaving classes; contact the Centro Maya de Idiomas in Quetzaltenango for more information (see p.185). Finally, Hispano Maya (🌐www.personal.umich.edu/~kakenned) is the newest school in town, though there are no reports from ex-students about the quality of tuition available yet.

for All Saints (*todos santos*). For three days the village is taken over by unrestrained drinking, dance and marimba music. The event opens with an all-day **horse race**, which starts out as a massive stampede. The riders tear up the course, thrashing their horses with live chickens, pink capes flowing out behind them. At either end of the run they take a drink before burning back again. As the day wears on some riders retire, collapse, or tie themselves on, leaving only the toughest to ride it out. On the second day, "The Day of the Dead", the action moves to the cemetery, with marimba bands and drink stalls setting up amongst the graves for a day of intense ritual that combines grief and celebration. On the final day of the fiesta the streets are littered with bodies and the jail packed with brawlers. You can see some of the community's historic costumes, tools, and traditional idols, if the local **museum**, just off the main square (US$1 donation), has reopened. There's also an excellent community **website** – ⓦwww .stetson.edu/~rsitler/TodosSantos – dedicated to the Todos Santos region.

If you can't make it for the fiesta then the Saturday **market**, although nothing like as riotous, also fills the village, and the night before you might catch some marimba. During the week the village is fairly quiet, although it's a pleasant and peaceful place to spend some time and the surrounding scenery is unbelievably beautiful. Moreover, since the **language schools** opened in Todos Santos (see box on p.215), a small but lively "gringo-scene" has developed, revolving around *Comedor Katy* and the schools' evening events. This is either a bonus or spoils the whole place – depending on your point of view.

Todos Santos is one of the few places where people are still said to use the 260-day *Tzolkin* calendar, which dates back to Maya times. Above the village – follow the track that goes up behind the *Comedor Katy* – is the small Maya site of **Tojcunanchén**, where you'll find a couple of grass-covered mounds sprouting pine trees. The site is occasionally used by *brujos* for the burning of incense and the ritual sacrifice of animals.

Practicalities

Buses leave Huehuetenango for Todos Santos from the main bus terminal five times a day at at 5.45am, 11.30am, 12.30pm, 2pm and 4pm – get there early to mark your seat and buy a ticket. Some carry on through the village, heading further down the valley to Jacaltenango and pass through Todos Santos on the way back to Huehuetenango; ask around for the latest schedule.

The best places **to stay** are *Hospedaje Casa Familiar* (❷), 30m above the main road past *Comedor Katy*, where views from the terrace café are breathtaking, and *Hospedaje Las Ruinas* (❶), further up the track on the right, which has four large rooms in a large twin-storey concrete structure. Turning left just before you reach the *Casa Familiar* brings you to the orange *Hotel Mam*, another good option with hot showers (❶), while the new *Hotelito Todos Santos* (❷), just east of the plaza, is a fairly decent choice with cleanish rooms. There are two other very cheap "hotels" in Todos Santos, *Hospedaje La Paz* and *Las Olguitas* (both ❶), but both are also extremely rough.

Comedor Katy does tasty, cheap **meals**, though you can also find good food at the *Casa Familiar* or try the gringo-geared restaurant-cafés *Cuchumatán* or *Tzolkin* nearby. There's a **post office** and a Banrural **bank** (Mon–Fri 8.30am–5pm & Sat 9am–1pm) in the plaza that will change travellers' cheques.

Though most of the fun of Todos Santos is in simply hanging out, it would be a shame not to indulge in a traditional **smoke sauna** (*chuc*) while you're here. Most of the guest houses will prepare one for you. If you want to take a shirt, pair of trousers or *huipil* home with you, you'll find an excellent co-op selling quality **weavings** next to the *Casa Familiar*.

Hikes from Todos Santos

The scenery around Todos Santos is some of the most spectacular in all Guatemala and there's no better place to leave the roads and set off on foot. In a day you can walk across to **San Juan Atitán**, and from there continue to the Carretera Interamericana or head on to **Santiago Chimaltenango**. From the highway you'll be able to catch a bus back to Huehuetenango for the night, and if you make it to Santiago you shouldn't have any problem finding somewhere to stay. This is the more interesting walk, particularly if you set out early on a Thursday morning and arrive in San Juan before the market there has finished.

Alternatively, you can walk down the valley from Todos Santos to **San Martín** and on to **Jacaltenango**, a route which offers superb views. There's a hotel in Jacaltenango, so you can stay the night and then catch a bus back to Huehuetenango in the morning.

Walking to San Juan Atitán

The village of **SAN JUAN ATITÁN** is around five hours from Todos Santos, across a beautiful isolated valley. The walk follows the path that bears up behind the *Comedor Katy*, passes the ruins and climbs steeply above the village through endless muddy switchbacks, bearing gradually across to the right. You reach the top of the ridge after about an hour and if the skies are clear you'll be rewarded by an awesome view of the Tajumulco and Tacaná volcanoes. Here the path divides: to the right are the scattered remains of an ancient cloud forest and a lovely grassy valley, while straight ahead is the path to San Juan, dropping down past some huts, through beautiful forest. The route takes you up and down endless exhausting ridges, through lush forests, and over a total of five gushing streams, only the first and third of which are bridged.

Beside the first stream is an idyllic spot where a family have set up home – they may allow you to **camp** here especially if you share your rations. Between the fourth and fifth streams, about three hours' from Todos Santos, you'll find an ideal place for a **picnic** overlooking the valley. Having crossed the thinly inhabited valley the path swings up to the left and on to the top of another pass, about three and a half hours from Todos Santos. From here you can see the village of San Juan, strung out along the steep hillside in a long thin line, though it is still more than an hour's walk away. To head down into the village follow one of the left-hand trails that goes out along the hillside and then drops down amongst the houses. There are several paths to choose from – all cross a series of deep ravines before emerging onto the main track that runs through the village.

Built on treacherously unstable land, San Juan is regularly hit by landslides that sweep whole houses into the valley below. The government has proposed that the entire village be moved, but the people have so far resisted this idea. It's an intensely traditional place: all the men wear long woollen coats (similar in style to the habits worn by Spanish friars), red shirts and plain white trousers. The high-backed sandals worn by both the men and the women, and also by a lot of people in Todos Santos, are a style depicted in ancient Maya carving – they are also worn in some of the villages around San Cristóbal de las Casas in Chiapas, Mexico.

Like most of these mountain villages, San Juan is a pretty quiet place, active only on market days, Monday and Thursday. The central square has a giant palm tree and a pretty garden, and from the marketplace, below the health centre, there are spectacular views across the valley.

If you want to **stay**, the *Hospedaje San Diego*, on the hill above the plaza (❶), makes a very basic but friendly place to rest, and the family may cook you supper on request. Alternatively, there's the *Hospedaje Jímenez*, beside the church (❶). For **food**, the small comedor beneath the *San Diego* serves up reasonable meals, but watch out for the fearsome *picante* sauce. Next morning you can catch a pick-up to Huehuetenango – they leave every couple of hours or so from 6am (1hr) – or walk back. From Huehuetenango, the pick-ups for San Juan leave from outside the *Cafetería Tucaná*, 2 C 2–15, around noon. Get there early for a space. In this direction the journey takes around and hour and a half.

On to Santiago Chimaltenango

SANTIAGO CHIMALTENANGO, which everyone in the region simply calls "Chimbal", makes a good alternative destination. If you want to go straight here from Todos Santos, turn right when you reach the top of the pass overlooking San Juan, head along the side of the hill and over another pass into a huge bowl-like valley. The village lies on the far side. If you're coming from San Juan, follow the track straight through the village and you'll come to the same pass in just over an hour. From the top of the pass, follow the main track down into the valley as it bears around to the right, towards the village – about one and a half hours from the top. Although not as traditional as the other villages of the region, Chimbal does retain some character, with narrow cobbled streets and adobe houses juxtaposed with modern concrete structures.

Ask at the main terminal in Huehuetenango for information on buses to and from Santiago Chimaltenango, otherwise you will have to walk on down the valley through coffee plantations to the village of San Pedro Necta, and beyond to the Carretera Interamericana, which should take two or three hours. *Mini Tienda La Benedición* below the market is a friendly **place to stay** (❶).

From Todos Santos to San Martín and Jacaltenango

Heading down the valley from Todos Santos the road arrives at the one-street village of **SAN MARTÍN**, a three-hour walk away. It is inhabited entirely by ladinos, but has a Friday market that attracts indigenous people from the land all around, including many from Todos Santos. A little beyond the village the road down the valley divides, with a right fork that leads 11km around the steep western edge of the Cuchumatanes. On a clear day there are spectacular views, reaching well into Mexico. At the end of the old road, on a rocky outcrop, is the poor and ragged village of **Concepción Huista** from where a road plunges to Jacaltenango, the final destination of one of the Todos Santos buses, which returns from there to Huehuetenango at about 3am.

Perched on a plateau overlooking the limestone plain that stretches out across the Mexican border, **JACALTENANGO** is the heart of an area that was once very traditional, inhabited by a small tribe of Akateko speakers. Several notable books about Maya customs were researched here in the early twentieth century, including the classic *The Year Bearer's People* by Douglas Byers (for more on the Maya year bearers, see the box on p.211). More recently, the village's most famous son, Víctor Montejo, documented his highly emotive experiences during the dark days of the civil war, when he worked here as a teacher, in his book *Testimony: Death of a Guatemalan Village* (see "Books" in Contexts, p.483).

Things have calmed down considerably since then, however, and in recent years the surrounding land has been planted with coffee, and waves of ladinos have swelled the population of the town. Today the place has a calm and fairly prosperous feel to it. There are two pensiones – one in the large tienda on the corner of the plaza and the other up the hill opposite it – and plenty of cheap comedores along the side of the market, which is at its busiest on Sunday.

The town can also be reached by a branch route that leaves the Carretera Interamericana close to the Mexican border. A **bus** usually leaves Huehuetenango for Jacaltenango at 12.30pm, but you should always check the timetable at the terminal.

East to Aguacatán

To the east of Huehuetenango, a dirt road turns off at Chiantla to weave along the base of the Cuchumatanes, through dusty foothills, to **AGUACATÁN**. This small agricultural town is strung out along two main streets, shaped entirely by the dip in which it's built. The village was created by Dominican friars, who in the early years of the Conquest merged several smaller settlements inhabited by two distinct peoples. The remains of one of the pre-conquest settlements can still be seen a couple of kilometres to the north, and minute differences of dress and dialect linger – indeed the village remains loosely divided along pre-Columbian lines, with the Chalchitek to the east of the market and the Awakatek to the west. The language of Awakateko (used by both) is spoken only in this village and its immediate surrounds, by a population of around 15,000. During the colonial period gold and silver were mined in the nearby hills, and the Maya are said to have made bricks of solid gold for the king of Spain, to persuade him to let them keep their lands. Today the town is steeped in tradition and the people survive by growing vegetables, including huge quantities of garlic, much of it for export.

Aguacatán's vast Sunday **market** gets under way on Saturday afternoon, when traders arrive early to claim the best sites. On Sunday morning a steady stream of people pours down the main street, cramming into the market and plaza, and soon spilling out into the surrounding area. Around noon the tide turns as the crowds start to drift back to their villages, with donkeys leading their drunken drivers. Despite the scale of the market its atmosphere is subdued and the pace unhurried: for many it's as much a social event as a commercial one.

The traditional costume worn by the women of Aguacatán is unusually simple: their skirts are made of dark blue cotton and the *huipiles*, which hang loose, are decorated with bands of coloured ribbon on a plain white background. This plainness, though, is set off by the local speciality – the *cinta*, or headdress, an intricately embroidered piece of cloth combining blues, reds, yellows and greens, in which the women wrap their hair.

Aguacatán's other attraction is the source of the **Río San Juan**, which emerges from beneath a nearby hill, fresh and cool. The source itself, bubbling up beneath a small bush and then channelled by concrete walls, looks a bit disappointing to the uninitiated (though as far as cavers and geologists are concerned, it's a big one), but if you have an hour or two to kill it's a good place for a chilly swim – for which you have to pay a small fee. To get there walk east along the main street out of the village for about a kilometre, until you see a sign directing you down a track to the left. Follow this round a sharp bend to the left and then take the right turn, towards the base of the hills. From the village it takes about twenty minutes.

Hourly **buses** run from Huehuetenango to Aguacatán passing by the Calvario in Huehuetenango, at the junction of 1 Av and 1 C; the first bus leaves at 6am and the last at about 4pm. The 25-kilometre journey takes around an hour. In Aguacatán the best places **to stay** are the *Nuevo Amanecer* (**2**) or the

Hospedaje Aguateco (**❶**), both of which are small and very simple; if they're full try the *Hospedaje La Paz* (**❶**). **Beyond Aguacatán** the road runs out along a ridge, with fantastic views stretching out below. Eventually it drops down into the Chixoy valley, to the riverside town of **Sacapulas** (p.145).

West to the Mexican border

From Huehuetenango the Carretera Interamericana runs for 79km through the narrow Selegua valley to the Mexican border at **La Mesilla**. Travelling direct this takes about two hours on one of the buses that thunder out of Huehuetenango every hour or so between 5am and 6pm. Along the way, just off the main road, are some interesting traditional villages, largely oblivious to the international highway that carves through their land. Most are best reached as day-trips out of Huehuetenango.

The first of these, 20km from Huehuetenango, is **San Sebastián Huehuetenango**, a quiet little place barely 200m north of the highway. The village was the site of a pre-conquest centre, and of a settlement known as Toj'jol, which was swept away by the Río Selegua in 1891. Further on the road runs through a particularly narrow part of the valley known as **El Tapón**, the cork, and past a turning for San Juan Atitán (12km) and another for San Rafael Petzal, 2km from the main road. Beyond this it passes roads that lead to Colotenango, Nentón and Jacaltenango.

You pass one last roadside village, La Democracia, before reaching the border at **LA MESILLA**. If you get stuck here, there's **accommodation** at the newish *Hotel Maricruz* (**❷**), which is clean, with private bathrooms and a restaurant, or at the slightly cheaper *Hospedaje Marisol* (**❷**). The two sets of customs and immigration are 3km apart; taxis run between the immigration points, and on the Mexican side you can pick up buses via the border settlement of **Ciudad Cuauhtemoc** to **Comitán**, or even direct to **San Cristóbal de las Casas**. Heading into Guatemala, the last bus leaves La Mesilla for Huehuetenango at around 5pm, and wherever you're aiming for in Guatemala, it's best to take the first bus to Huehue and change there.

Colotenango, San Ildefonso Ixtahuacán and Cuilco

The most important of the villages reached from the highway is **COLOTE-NANGO**, perched on a hillside 1km or so south from the main road. The municipality of Colotenango used to include San Rafael and San Ildefonso, until 1890 when they became villages in their own right. Ties are still strong, however, and the red *cortes* worn by the women of all three villages are almost identical. Colotenango remains the focal point for the smaller settlements, and its Saturday market is the largest in the Selegua valley. From early Saturday morning the plaza is packed, and the paths that lead into the village are filled with a steady stream of traders, indigenous families, cattle, chickens, reluctant pigs and the inevitable drunks. Here you'll see people from all of the surrounding villages, most of them wearing traditional costume. The village is also worth visiting during Holy Week, when elaborate and violent re-enactments of Christ's Passion take place (the bravest of villagers takes the role of Judas, and is shown no mercy by the rest), and for its fiesta from August 12 to 15.

To get to Colotenango from Huehuetenango take any **bus** heading towards the Mexican border, and ask the driver to drop you at the village. They'll usually leave you on the main road just below, from where you have to cross the bridge and walk up the hill. The journey from Huehuetenango takes around 45 minutes.

On to San Ildefonso and Cuilco

Behind Colotenango a dirt road goes up over the hills and through a pass into the valley of the Río Cuilco. Here it runs high above the river along the top of a ridge, with beautiful views up the valley: below you can make out the tiny village of San Gaspar Ixchil, which consists of little more than a church and a graveyard.

Another few kilometres brings you to the larger village and mining centre of **SAN ILDEFONSO IXTAHUACÁN**. Similar in many ways to Colotenango, it has a large and traditional Maya population. In 1977 the place achieved a certain notoriety after its miners were locked out of the mine because they'd tried to form a union. In response to this they decided to walk the 260km to Guatemala City in order to put their case to the authorities. At the time this was a bold gesture of defiance and it captured the imagination of the entire nation. When they eventually arrived in the capital 100,000 people turned out to welcome them.

Beyond San Ildefonso the road slopes down towards the bottom of the valley and crosses the river before arriving at **CUILCO**, a sizeable ladino town 36km from the Carretera Interamericana that marks the end of the road. The Mexican border is just 15km away, and the town maintains cross-border trade links both inside and outside the law. Beyond today's village are the ruins of an earlier settlement known as **Cuilco Viejo**. Cuilco has also earned itself something of a reputation, although this time it's for producing heroin. As a result of the successful anti-drug campaigns in Mexico, many poppy growers have moved across the border, and the area produces a substantial amount of opium.

Buses run between Huehuetenango and Cuilco at 5am and 2pm, returning at 7am and 8.30am, so if you come out this way you'll probably end up having to **stay**: the *Hospedaje Osorio* (❶) is on the main street. If the roads are in reasonable condition, trucks and pick-ups run south from Cuilco to the mountain village of Tacaná, from where there is a regular bus service to San Pedro.

North to Nentón and Jacaltenango

A short distance before the border, from the roadside village of **Camoja Grande**, a dirt road leads off to the north, running parallel to the border. It heads across a dusty white limestone plateau to the village of **Nentón**, and right up into the extreme northwest corner of the country, to **Gracias a Dios** and Yalambojoch. Although there are **buses** (two a day to Jacaltenango, three to Gracias a Dios), the only reason to venture out this way would be to walk back into the Cuchumatanes. It's also may be possible to use a remote unofficial **border crossing** into Mexico at Gracias a Dios, though as a result of high levels of tension in the area because of the Zapatista rebellion, it's currently best to use the regular border point at La Mesilla. If you do make it over the border here, it's a ten-minute walk from Gracias a Dios to Carmixan in Mexico and bus services do connect.

Halfway between the Carretera Interamericana and Nentón, at the junction of Cuatro Caminos, a branch road heads east towards the mountains, through lush foothills, passing the entrance to **Santa Ana Huista**. It then continues through rich coffee country to **San Antonio Huista** – with the *Pensión Victoria* (❶) should you want to stay – and ends up in Jacaltenango, from where you can walk to Todos Santos (see p.215).

Fiestas

The **western highlands** are the home of the traditional Guatemalan fiesta. Every village and town, however small, has its own saint's day, around which a fiesta is based that can last anything from a day to two weeks. All of these involve traditional dances that mix pre-Columbian moves with more modern Spanish styles, and each fiesta has its own speciality, whether it's a horse race or a firework spectacular.

January

January is a particularly active month, kicking off in **El Tumbador**, in the department of San Marcos, where there's a fiesta from the 3rd to 8th, and in **San Gaspar Ixchil**, a tiny village on the road to Cuilco in the department of Huehuetenango, where they have their fiesta from the 3rd to 6th. In **Sibilia**, in the department of Quetzaltenango, there's a fiesta from the 9th to 15th, with the main day on the 13th, and **Santa María Chiquimula**, near Totonicapán, has its fiesta from the 10th to 16th, in honour of the Black Christ of Esquipulas. **Nentón**, to the northwest of Huehuetenango, has a fiesta from the 13th to 16th, and **La Libertad**, to the west of Huehuetenango, from the 12th to 16th. In the central highlands **Chinique**, east of Santa Cruz del Quiché, has a very traditional fiesta from the 12th to 15th, with the final day as the main day. **Colomba**, in the department of Quetzaltenango, has one from the 12th to 16th. The village of **San Antonio Ilotenango**, west of Santa Cruz del Quiché, has its fiesta from the 15th to 17th (the main day). **San Sebastián Coatan**, in the department of Huehuetenango, has a fiesta from the 18th to 20th. **Santa Lucía La Reforma**, in the department of Totonicapán, has its fiesta from the 19th to 21st. The village of **Ixtahuacán**, on the road to Cuilco in the department of Huehuetenango, has a traditional fiesta from the 19th to 24th. **San Pablo La Laguna**, on the shores of Lake Atitlán, has a fiesta from the 22nd to 26th, with the main day on the 25th. **San Pablo**, in the department of San Marcos, has its fiesta from the 23rd to 27th. The village of **Chiantla**, just north of Huehuetenango, celebrates from January 28 to February 2, with the final day as the main day, and finally **Jacaltenango**, to the west of Huehuetenango, also has a fiesta that starts on the 28th and goes on until February 2.

February

The celebratory season in February starts in **Cunén**, in the department of Quiché, with a fiesta from the 1st to 4th, with the main day on the 2nd. **Ostuncalco**, in the department of Quetzaltenango, has a fiesta on the 8th. **Santa Eulalia** in Huehuetenango has its fiesta from the 8th to 13th, with the main day on the 8th, and **Patzité**, in Quiché, has a fiesta from the 6th to 10th, in which the main action is also on the 8th. **Palestina de Los Altos**, in the department of San Marcos, has a fiesta celebrating the first Friday in Lent.

March

In March things start off in **San Jose El Rodeo**, in the department of San Marcos, where they have a fiesta from the 14th to 20th, with the main day on the 19th. **San José Poaquil**, near Chimaltenango, has a fiesta on the 19th. The second Friday in Lent is marked by huge pilgrimages to **Chajul** and **La Democracia**. Holy Week is celebrated throughout the country but **Santiago Atitlán** is well worth visiting at this time to see Maximón paraded through the streets, usually on the Wednesday.

April

San Marcos has its fiesta from the 22nd to 28th, with the main day on the 25th, **San Jorge La Laguna** celebrates on the 24th, and **San Marcos La Laguna** on the 25th. **Barillas,** far to the north of Huehuetenango, has a fiesta from April 29 to May 4, and both **Zacualpa** and **Aguacatán** have moveable fiestas to mark forty days from Holy Week. **Zacualpa** also has a moveable fiesta at some stage during the month. Finally,

La Esperanza, in the department of Quetzaltenango, has its fiesta from April 30 to May 4.

May
Cajola, a small village in the department of Quetzaltenango, has its fiesta from the 1st to 3rd, with the final day as the main day. **Uspantán** has a busy and traditional fiesta from the 6th to 10th, with the main day on the 8th. **Santa Cruz La Laguna**, on the shores of Lake Atitlán, has its fiesta from the 8th to 10th, with the main day on the last day, as does **Santa Cruz Balanya**, in the department of Chimaltenango. **Patzún** has a fiesta on the 20th.

June
Things start to hot up again in June, starting in **San Antonio Palopó**, to the east of Panajachel, which has a fiesta from the 12th to 14th, with the main day on the 13th. The same days are celebrated in **San Antonio Huista**, while **San Juan Ixcoy**, in the department of Huehuetenango, has its fiesta from the 21st to 25th, with the main day on the 24th. **Olintepeque**, a few kilometres from Quetzaltenango, has its fiesta from the 21st to 25th. Towards the end of the month there are two very interesting fiestas high up the mountains: the first, at **San Juan Cotzal**, a very traditional village to the north of Nebaj, lasts from the 22nd to 25th, with the main day on the 24th; the second, in remote **San Juan Atitán** near Huehuetenango, runs from the 22nd to 26th, with the main day on the 24th. **Comalapa**, near Chimaltenango, has a fiesta on the 24th; **San Juan la Laguna**, on the shores of Lake Atitlán, from the 23rd to 26th, with the main day on the 24th; **San Pedro Sacatepéquez** from the 24th to 30th; and the isolated village of **Soloma**, to the north of Huehuetenango, from the 26th to 30th, with the main day on the 29th. At the end of the month two villages share the same dates: **San Pedro Jocopilas** to the north of Santa Cruz del Quiché, and **San Pedro La Laguna** on Lake Atitlán have fiestas from the 27th to 30th, with the main day on the 29th. Finally in **Almolonga**, near Quetzaltenango, there's a fiesta from the 28th to 30th, with the main day on the 29th. Corpus Christi celebrations, held throughout Guatemala in June, are particularly spectacular in **Patzún**.

July
In July things start off in **Santa María Visitación**, near Sololá, where they have a fiesta from the 1st to 4th, with the main day on the 2nd. In **Huehuetenango** there's a fiesta from the 12th to 17th, and in **Momostenango** from July 21 to August 4 – a traditional celebration that is worth going out of your way for, especially on the 25th. The village of **Tejutla**, high above San Marcos, has a fiesta from the 22nd to 27th, with the main day on the 25th, as does **San Cristóbal Totonicapán**, in the department of Totonicapán. **Chimaltenango** has a fiesta from the 22nd to 27th, with the main day on the 26th; **Malacatancito**, a small ladino town on the border of the department of Huehuetenango, celebrates from the 23rd to 26th, with the last day as the main day. **Santiago Atitlán's** fiesta, from the 23rd to 27th, is most enjoyable on the 25th. **Patzicía** has a fiesta from the 22nd to 27th, with the main day on the 27th, and **Santa Ana Huista**, in the department of Huehuetenango, has its fiesta from the 25th to 27th, with the main day on the 26th. Finally **Ixchiguan**, in the department of San Marcos, has a fiesta from the 29th to 31st, with the final day the main day.

August
August is a particularly good month for fiestas and if you're in the central area you can visit three or four of the very best. The action starts in **Sacapulas**, which has a fiesta from the 1st to 4th, with the last day as the main day. **Santa Clara La Laguna** has its fiesta from the 10th to 13th, with the main day on the 12th. **Joyabaj** has its

continues overleaf

fiesta from the 9th to 15th, with the last day as the main day. This is the first of August's really special fiestas and sees Joyabaj filled with Indians from throughout the valley: traditional dances here include the *Palo Volador*, in which men swing from a huge pole. The second major fiesta is in **Sololá**, from the 11th to 17th, with the main day on the 15th. The next is in **Nebaj**, where the fiesta is from the 12th to 15th, with the main day on the last day. In **Colotenango**, near Huehuetenango, they have a fiesta from the 12th to 15th, with the final day as the main day. **Cantel**, near Quetzaltenango, has a fiesta from the 12th to 18th, the main day on the 15th, and **Tacaná** has a fiesta from the 12th to 15th, the main day on the 15th. In **Santa Cruz del Quiché** there's a fiesta from the 14th to 19th, with the main day on the 18th. **San Bartolo** has its fiesta from the 18th to 25th, climaxing on the 24th, while **Salcajá** has a fiesta from the 22nd to 28th, with the principal day the 25th. **Sipacapa**, in the department of San Marcos, has its fiesta from the 22nd to 25th, and **Sibinal**, in the same department, has its fiesta from the 27th to 30th, with the main day on the 29th.

September

The fiesta in **Quetzaltenango** lasts from the 12th to 18th, with the main day on the 15th. **San Mateo**, to the west of Quetzaltenango, has a fiesta on the 21st, **San Mateo Ixtatán**, to the north of Huehuetenango, from the 17th to 21st, with the last day the main day, and the departmental capital of **Totonicapán** from the 24th to 30th, with the main day on the 29th. **San Miguel Acatán**, in the department of Huehuetenango, has a fiesta from the 25th to 30th, with the main day also on the 29th. Finally **Tecpán** has its fiesta from September 26 to October 5.

October

The action in October starts up in **San Francisco el Alto**, which has its fiesta from the 1st to 6th, with its main day on the 4th. **Panajachel** has a fiesta from the 2nd to 6th, which also has its main day on the 4th. **San Lucas Tolimán**, on the shores of Lake Atitlán, has its fiesta from the 15th to 20th, with the main day on the 18th.

Travel details

Buses

Travel in the western highlands is fairly straightforward. Along the **Carretera Interamericana** there's an almost constant stream of buses heading in both directions: certainly between about 8am and 6pm you should never have to wait more than twenty minutes. The major towns are generally just off the highway, and it's the main connections to these that are covered below: other more local schedules have been given in the text. The best way to explore the western highlands is to base yourself in one of these main towns and make a series of day-trips into the surrounding area.

Chimaltenango

From **Chimaltenango** (the junction for Antigua) there are buses in both directions along Carretera Interamericana every twenty minutes, and local buses to Antigua (40min) every twenty minutes

between 5.30am and 6.30pm.

Buses to **Chimaltenango** (40min) leave Antigua every 20min (5am–7pm), from where you can get regular connections to Chichicastenango and Quiché, Panajachel, Quetzaltenango and Huehuetenango. Buses to Patzicía and Patzún pass through Chimaltenango every hour or so.

Santa Cruz del Quiché and Chichicastenango

To **Santa Cruz del Quiché** via Chichicastenango. Buses leave from Guatemala City every 30min (4am–4pm; 3hr) from the terminal in Zona 4. Along the way they can be picked up in Chimaltenango or at **Los Encuentros**, the junction for this part of the country. There are also hourly buses from Quetzaltenango, and five daily buses from Panajachel to Santa Cruz del Quiché.

Finally the fiesta in **Todos Santos Cuchumatán**, one of the best in the country, starts on October 21 and continues into the first few days of November.

November

The 1st is the scene of intense action in **Todos Santos Cuchumatán** featuring a wild and alcoholic horse race, the climax of celebrations that began in October and continue until November 2nd. **San Martín Jilotepeque** has its fiesta from the 7th to 12th, with the main day on the 11th. **Malacatancito**, in the department of Huehuetenango, has a fiesta from the 14th to 18th, with the last day as the main day. **Nahualá** has a very good fiesta from the 23rd to 26th, with the main day on the 25th. **Santa Catarina Ixtahuacán**, in the department of Sololá, has its fiesta from the 24th to 26th, with the principal day on the 25th. **Zunil** has a fiesta from the 22nd to 26th, again with the chief action on the 25th, and **Santa Catarina Palopó** has a fiesta on that day. Finally **Cuilco**, **San Andrés Semetabaj** and **San Andrés Xecul** all have their fiestas from November 27 to December 1. The main day in Cuilco is on the 28th, and in the San Andreses on the 30th.

December

Santa Bárbara, in the department of Huehuetenango, has its fiesta from the 1st to 4th. **Huehuetenango** has a fiesta from the 5th to 8th, again with the last day as the main one, as does **Concepción Huista**, in the department of Huehuetenango. **Concepción**, in the department of Sololá, has its fiesta from the 7th to 9th, and **Malacatán**, in the department of San Marcos, has a fiesta from the 9th to 14th. **Santa Lucía Utatlán**, in Sololá, has its fiesta from the 11th to 15th, with the main day on the 13th. **Chichicastenango** has its fiesta from the 13th to 21st, with the last day as the main day. This is another very large and impressive fiesta, with an elaborate procession and a mass of fireworks. Chichicastenango's sister village, **Chiché**, has its fiesta from the 25th to 28th, with the last day as the main day. From the 7th December men dressed as devils chase around highland towns, particularly in those around Quetzaltenango, and the night of the 7th is celebrated with bonfires throughout the country – The Burning of the Devil.

From Santa Cruz del Quiché buses leave the main bus terminal for **Nebaj** (4hr) at 8.30am, 10am, 11.30am, 1pm, 2.30pm and 4pm. Buses to **Uspantán** (5hr), which all pass through **Sacapulas** (2hr), leave Quiché at 11am, 1pm, 2pm and 4pm returning at 1am, 3am and 9am. **From Uspantán** there are buses for **San Pedro Carchá**, a few kilometres from Cobán (5hr), at 3am and 3.30am, returning at 10am and noon. Direct buses from Santa Cruz to **Quetzaltenango** (3hr) leave hourly between 3am and 2pm; at other times go to Los Encuentros and change there. Buses to **Joyabaj** (2hr) pass through Santa Cruz (hourly; 9am–5pm). The last bus back from Joyabaj leaves at 4pm.

Lake Atitlán

Buses **to Panajachel** (3hr 30min) via **Sololá** are run by the Rebuli company, whose offices in Guatemala City are at 21 C 3–24, Zona 1. There are direct buses between Guatemala City and Panajachel (hourly; 6am–4pm); at other times you can travel via Los Encuentros. There is one daily bus at 7am from Antigua to Panajachel (3hr), which returns at 10.45am. **From Panajachel** there are daily departures to **Quetzaltenango** (2hr 30min) at 5am, 6am, 7am, 8am, 9am and 10am plus an extra service at 3pm on Sundays, and five buses a day to **Cocales** (2hr 30min) between 10.30am and 4.15pm, all via **San Lucas Tolimán**. Buses to **Chichicastenango** leave Panajachel hourly from 6.45am; with extra services on market days.

There are also direct buses six times daily (from 2.30am and 2pm) between Guatemala City and **Santiago Atitlán** along the coastal highway, but this is a very slow route.

To get to **Nahualá** from Lake Atitlán, take any bus heading along the Carretera Interamericana to the west of Los Encuentros.

Quetzaltenango

Pullman buses **to Quetzaltenango** (4hr) via Chimaltenango, Los Encuentros and Cuatro

Caminos from Guatemala City are run by a number of companies: see box on p.87 for full details. There are also second-class buses to Quetzaltenango every half-hour from the Zona 4 terminal in Guatemala City until 4pm.

From Quetzaltenango second-class buses leave hourly from the Minerva terminal in Zona 3, for San Pedro, San Marcos, Retalhuleu and Mazatenango; and every thirty minutes for Huehuetenango and Guatemala City. Details of buses to the smaller towns are given in the relevant chapters. From Quetzaltenango to the Mexican border (2hr), it's quickest to take a bus to Mazatenango or Coatepeque, and then catch another from there.

San Marcos

Transportes Marquensita runs pullman buses to San Marcos from 21 C 12–41, Zona 1, Guatemala City (5hr 30min) at 6am, 6.30am, 8.40am, 11am, noon, 3.30pm, 4pm and 5pm, as well as additional second-class services throughout the day. Eight pullmans plus extra second-class buses make the return journey to Guatemala City between 2.30am and 4pm.

From San Marcos there are hourly buses to Quetzaltenango (1hr 30min), and Malacatán (1hr 30min), from where regular buses leave for the Mexican border at Talisman bridge.

Huehuetenango

Los Halcones pullman buses to Huehuetenango leave daily at 7am, 2pm and 5pm, from 7 Av 15–27, Zona 1, Guatemala City (5hr 30min), returning from Huehue at 4.30am, 7am and 2pm. Transportes Velásquez runs 8 buses daily from 20 C 1–37, Zona 1, Guatemala City to Huehuetenango at 5.20am, 7.30am, 8.30am, 9.30am, 10.30am, 11.30am, 12.15pm, 2.30pm, 3.30pm, 4.30pm and 5.30pm (plus a 6.30pm departure on Fridays) returning from Huehue at 2am, 3am, 8.30am, 10.30am, 12.15pm, 2.30pm, 3.30pm and 4.30pm.

Second-class buses to Huehuetenango run from Zona 4 terminal in Guatemala City every hour and the Minerva terminal in Quetzaltenango every half-hour or so.

From Huehuetenango, there are buses to the border at La Mesilla every 30min or so until 7pm.

The Pacific coast

MEXICO

BELIZE

CARIBBEAN
SEA

6

2

5

7

1

4

HONDURAS

3

N

PACIFIC OCEAN

EL SALVADOR

0   100km

CHAPTER 3 # Highlights

3

The Pacific coast

A chain of volcanoes divides the cool air of the mountains from a sweltering strip of low-lying, tropical, ladino land, some 300km long and 50km wide. Known simply as **La Costa Sur** this featureless yet supremely fertile coastal plain – once a wilderness of swamp, forest and savannah – is today a land of vast fincas, uninteresting commercial towns and small seaside resorts scattered along an unrelentingly straight, black sand shoreline.

Prior to the arrival of the Spanish, the Pacific coast was similar in many ways to the jungles of Petén, and certainly as rich in wildlife and archeological sites. However, while the jungles of Petén have lain undisturbed, the Pacific coast has been ravaged by development. Today its large-scale agriculture – including sugar cane, palm oil, cotton and rubber plantations – accounts for a substantial proportion of the country's exports. Only in some isolated sections, where mangrove swamps have been spared the plough, can you still get a sense of the maze of tropical vegetation which once covered it. Little, if any, of the original dry tropical forest remains, although in several areas, including the **Monterrico Reserve**, the unique swampy coastal environment is protected, offering a refuge to sea turtles, iguanas, crocodiles and an abundance of bird life.

As for the archeological sites, they too have largely disappeared, though you can glimpse the extraordinary art of the **Pipil** (see p.231) around the town of Santa Lucía Cotzumalguapa. Totally unlike the sites in the highlands and Petén – and nowhere near as spectacular – these ceremonial centres are almost lost in fields of sugar cane, though some are still regularly used for religious rituals and reveal a hotchpotch of carvings. The one site in the area that ranks with those elsewhere in the country is **Abaj Takalik**, outside Retalhuleu. For a fascinating insight into the Preclassic era of the Pacific littoral, the ruins are well worth a detour on your way to or from Mexico, or as a day-trip from Xela or Retalhuleu. The site is only in the early stages of excavation, but already its significance has been clearly established. In addition, recent discoveries at **La Nueva**, near the border with El Salvador, prove that the area is hiding a lot

Accommdation price codes

All accommodation listed in this guide has been graded according to the following price scales. These refer to the price in US dollars of the cheapest double room in high season. For more details see p.34.

❶ Under US$5	❹ US$15–25	❼ US$60–80
❷ US$5–10	❺ US$25–40	❽ US$80–100
❸ US$10–15	❻ US$40–60	❾ Over US$100

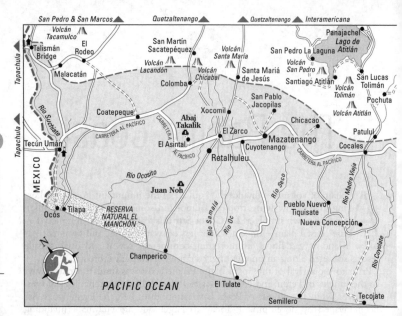

more archeological secrets, and that the Maya world extended further than was once thought.

The main attraction of the region should be the **coastline**, though sadly much of it is mosquito-ridden and dotted with filthy palm huts, pig-pens and garbage, with dangerous currents and poor surfing conditions. The hotels are some of the country's worst, so if you're desperate for a quick dip and a fresh shrimp feast, you're far better off taking a day-trip from the capital or from Quetzaltenango. The one glorious exception is the nature reserve of **Monterrico**, which harbours an attractive village and maybe the country's finest beach, with a superb stretch of clear, clean sand.

The main transport link in this region is the coastal highway, the **Carretera al Pacífico** (CA-2), the country's fastest and busiest road. This is the usual route for pullman buses speeding between Guatemala City and the Mexican border, so travel is normally swift and comfortable.

Some history

The earliest history of the Pacific coast remains something of a mystery, with the only hints being offered by the remnants of two distinct languages: **Zoquean**, still spoken by a tiny population on the Mexico–Guatemala border, and **Xincan**, which is thought to have been spoken throughout the eastern area of Guatemala but can now only be heard in an isolated part of the Zacapa department. However, the extent to which these languages are evidence of independent tribes, and how these tribes might have lived, remains mere speculation. It's generally held that the sophisticated Olmec culture – in what is now Mexico – spread along the Pacific coast, giving birth to the **Ocós** and **Iztapa** cultures, which thrived here some time around 1500 BC. These were small, village-based societies that developed considerable skills in the working

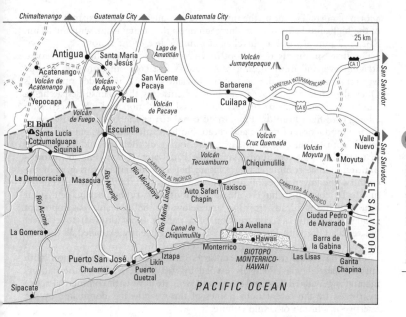

of stone and pottery. It's also generally believed that the great cultural developments of the Maya, including writing and the Maya calendar, reached the southern area of the Maya region via the Pacific coast.

What is certain is that some time between 400 and 900 AD the entire coastal plain was overrun by the **Pipil**, who migrated south from the Central Highlands and Veracruz area of Mexico, possibly driven out by the chaos that followed the fall of Teotihuacán. (The Pipil language is actually an antiquated form of Nahuatl, the official language of the Aztec empire.) These migrants brought with them their architectural styles and artistic skills, and the remains of their civilization show that they used a foreign calendar and worshipped the gods familiar in Mexico. The Pipil built half a dozen sites, all compact ceremonial centres with rubble-filled pyramids. Their main produce was cacao, from which they extracted the beans to make a chocolate drink and to use as

Migrant workers on the Pacific coast

Though the towns of the Pacific coast are quintessentially ladino in temperament and climate, it's the Maya from the highlands who form the backbone of the region's agricultural workforce. Families and whole communities fled the repression and bullets of the civil war to live along the coast in semi-permanent exile, while thousands more arrive each year to provide essential seasonal labour. In the past the Maya were forcibly recruited, but today the shortage of land in the mountains drives them to migrate "voluntarily" for several months a year in search of employment. In addition to working in burning conditions for a pittance, many economic migrants face ritual exploitation from the finca henchmen, who routinely underpay and overcharge workers for food and drink, pharmacy bills and tool hire. Malaria and pesticide poisoning are also rife.

a form of currency. But by the time of the Conquest the ever-expanding tribes of the highlands had started to encroach upon the coastal plain, with the Mam, K'iche', Tz'utujil and Kaqchikel all claiming a slice of the action.

The first **Spaniards** to set foot in Guatemala did so on the Pacific coast, arriving overland from the north. Alvarado's first confrontation with K'iche' warriors came here in the heat of the lowlands, before he headed up towards Quetzaltenango. Once they'd established themselves, the Spanish despatched a handful of Franciscans to convert the coastal population, and were faced with a long, hard fight from the Pipil. In **colonial times** the land was mostly used for the production of indigo and cacao, and for cattle ranching, but the inhospitable climate and accompanying disease soon took their toll, and for much of that era the coast remained a miserable backwater. It was only after **independence** that commercial agriculture began to dominate this part of the country. The lower slopes of the mountains, known as the *Boca Costa*, were the first to be covered in huge coffee plantations; later, rubber, banana and sugar cane plantations spread across the land below. By 1880 the area was important enough to justify the construction of a railway (now disused) to connect Guatemala City with Puerto San José, and subsequently extended all the way to the Mexican border.

Today the coastal strip is the country's most intensely farmed region, with entire villages being effectively owned by vast fincas. Much of the nation's income is generated here and the main towns are alive with commercial activity, ringed by the ostentatious homes of the wealthy and dominated by the assertive machismo of ladino culture.

Crossing the border

Approaching the coast from the Mexican border you face some of the very worst that the region has to offer. Breathless and ugly **Coatepeque** is typical of the towns you'll find, though **Retalhuleu** is somewhat more attractive and sedate. If you plan to spend any time on the coast, aim for the area south of Escuintla, but if you just want to head for the beach then **El Tulate** and **Champerico** are both within easy reach of Quetzaltenango and the border.

The Talismán Bridge and Tecún Umán

The coastal border with Mexico is the busiest of Guatemala's frontiers, with two crossing points, Talismán and Tecún Umán, both open 24 hours. Tourist cards for either country can be obtained at the immigration posts, but if you require a visa you'll need to get hold of one beforehand – there's a Guatemalan consulate in Tapachula on the Mexican side, and Mexican consulates in Retalhuleu, Quetzaltenango, Huehuetenango and Guatemala City.

The northernmost of the two crossings is the **Talismán Bridge**, also referred to as El Carmen, where the customs and immigration posts face each other from opposite banks of the Río Suchiate. This tends to be the more relaxed of the two as there's nothing here but a few huts and a couple of basic pensiones, and it's also marginally better for first-class buses to Guatemala City. There's little difference on the Mexican side, as both crossings are thirty minutes from Tapachula, and well connected to it by a stream of minibuses. On the Guatemalan side, a regular flow of trucks, minibuses and buses leaves for **Malacatán**, where you'll find hotels and buses for San Marcos and the western highlands. If you're heading for Guatemala City there's usually a bus waiting at the border – if not, go to Malacatán and catch one from there.

The **Tecún Umán** crossing, on the edge of the dusty and bustling border town of Ciudad Tecún Umán, is favoured by most Guatemalans and all commercial traffic. The town has an authentic frontier flavour with all-night bars, lost souls, contraband and moneychangers, and its streets are almost permanently choked by a chaos of articulated lorries and buses, with cycle rickshaws snaking through the traffic. Everything and everyone is on the move, mostly trying to get out as soon as possible. If you do get stuck, there are plenty of cheap **hotels** and restaurants – the *Hotel Vanessa 2* has reasonable, cheap rooms with fans (❷), or you could try the *Hospedaje Marcel 2* (❷) or the *Hotel Don José*, 2 C 3–42 (☎776 8164; ❷). Again, there's a steady stream of buses connecting the border with Guatemala City, Coatepeque and Retalhuleu.

South to Ocós and Tilapa

South of Tecún Umán a rough dirt road, running parallel to the border, bounces through clouds of thick white dust and past endless palm-oil plantations to **OCÓS** on the beach. The village is one of the most forlorn and miserable in the country, with sand streets that run past rows of squalid palm huts. Before the Conquest this was the site of a Mam settlement called Ucez, and prior to that it was part of the so-called Ocós culture, a network of small fishing and farming villages which was one of the earliest civilizations on the Pacific coast, existing here from 1250 to 1150 BC. There is no evidence of this nowadays, however, and if you do end up in Ocós you'll probably want to leave immediately, as the only accommodation in town is horrific.

The quickest way out is to take the boat across the Río Naranjo to the simple resort town of **TILAPA**, a much better bet for spending an hour or two by the sea. It has a decent beach, largely devoid of rubbish, as well as a row of comedores dispensing good, fresh prawns and fish, and Gallo beer. The coastline here forms part of the **Reserva Natural El Manchón**, which covers some 30km of prime turtle-nesting beach and extends around 10km inland to embrace a belt of swamp and mangrove, which is home to crocodiles, iguanas, kingfishers, storks, white herons, egrets and an abundance of fish. If you're interested in exploring you shouldn't have any trouble finding a boatman willing to take you on a tour of the canals and lagoons. There's a lonely Peace Corps worker stationed here to look after the reserve who's sure to appreciate some company and bound to be a good source of local information (just ask for the "gringo").

Although the only pensión is very basic, with reed mats to sleep on, a new eco-hotel is being constructed, with twelve comfortable rooms, by local landowner Guillermo Aguirre – it should be open in late 2001. You may choose **to stay** in Tilapa rather than risk getting stranded on a back road in the dark wating for a bus back to Quetzaltenango. **Buses** run between Tilapa and Coatepeque every hour or so from 5am to 6pm, and several times a day between Coatepeque and Ocós.

The coastal highway: Coatepeque and Retalhuleu

East from the Mexican border, **COATEPEQUE** is the first place of any importance on the main road, a furiously busy, purely commercial town where most of the locally produced coffee is processed. The action is centred on the

bus terminal, an intimidating maelstrom of sweat, mud and energetic chaos: buses run every thirty minutes from here to the two border crossings, hourly between 4am and 5pm to Quetzaltenango (via Santa María and Zunil), and hourly from 2.30am to 6pm to Guatemala City. Local buses also run regularly to **Colomba**, in the coffee-producing foothills of the highlands, with some continuing on to Quetzaltenanago via San Martín Sacatepéquez (approximately hourly).

Coatepeque practicalities

One of the best places to **stay** in Coatepeque is the *Hotel Villa Real*, 6 C 6–57 (T775 1308, F775 1939; ❹), a modern hotel with clean rooms and secure parking. A bit cheaper is the family-run *Hotel Baechli*, 6 C 5–35 (T775 1483; ❹), which has plain rooms with fans and TV, plus secure parking, while the *Hotel Lee*, on 4 Avenida (❸) just below the plaza, is basic, but also offers secure parking. At the budget end of the market there's the *Europa* (❷), at 6 C and 4 Av, just off the plaza, and the *Pensión La Batalla* (❶), just below the bus terminal on 2 Calle.

For **changing money**, there's a branch of the Banco del Occidente (Mon–Fri 9am–7pm, Sat 9am–1pm) on the central plaza, with several more banks nearby. The **Telgua** office (daily 7am–10pm) is on 5 Avenida at the corner of 7 C, and there's a **cinema** a short distance from the plaza, down the hill on 4 Av.

Retalhuleu and around

Beyond Coatepeque lies the most densely populated section of the Pacific coast, centred on **RETALHULEU**, the region's largest town. The town is usually referred to as **Reu** (pronounced "Ray-oo"), which is what you should look for on the front of buses. Set a few kilometres south of the Carretera al Pacífico and surrounded by the walled homes of the wealthy, Retalhuleu has managed to avoid the worst excesses of the coast, protected to some extent by a combination of wealth and tradition. The town was founded by the Spanish in the early years of the Conquest, when they merged the villages of Santa Catarina Sacatepéquez and San Antonio. Maya women from these two villages maintained, until recently, the tradition of wearing no blouse – though they were banned from appearing topless in public. This traditionalism marks a real division in the town between a ladino population said to be proud of a lineage untainted by indigenous blood, and the Maya who have repeatedly risen up against their control.

Today, however, things seem astonishingly peaceful, and Retalhuleu is something of an oasis of civilization in the chaos of life on the coast. Its plaza epitomizes all this, with towering Greek columns on a shiny white *municipalidad*, a covered bandstand and an attractive colonial church. The mood is relaxed and easy-going and in the warmth of the evening young couples nestle in the bushes, birds squawk in the trees and BMWs glide through the streets. If you have time to kill, pop into the local **Museo de Arqueología y Etnología** in the *municipalidad* (Tues–Sun 8am–1pm & 2–5pm; US$0.20). Rooms are divided into Preclassic, Classic and Postclassic Maya periods and display an amazing collection of anthropomorphic figurines, mostly heads. Many show a strong Mexican influence in their design, with large earplugs a common feature. Upstairs, a fascinating collection of ancient photographs, dating back to the 1880s, provides an excellent historic record of the town's changing streetscapes and industries, demonstrating the extent to which its leading citizens tried to create a bourgeois haven among the festering plantations.

Retalhuleu practicalities

Budget **accommodation** is in short supply in Retalhuleu. The best hospedaje is *Hotel Hillman* at 7 Av 7–99 (❷), where most rooms have a private bath. Elsewhere, rates go up steeply: the *Hotel Modelo*, 5 C 4–53 (☎771 0256; ❸), has decent basic but clean rooms with private bath, while over the road the good-value *Hotel Astor*, 5 C 4–60 (☎771 0475, ✉hotelastor@infovia.com.gt; ❹), has rooms with fan, TV and bath, set around a pleasant courtyard. If you want a bit more luxury, try the modern *Hotel Posada de Don José*, 5 C 3–67 (☎771 0180, ⓦwww.don-jose.com; ❹), which has good a/c rooms, a reasonable restaurant and a pool.

The **plaza** is the hub of the town's activity. Here you'll find three **banks**, including the Banco del Agro and, close by, the Banco Industrial, with a 24-hour Visa ATM, along with the **post office** (Mon–Fri 8am–4.30pm); the **Telgua** office (daily 7am–10pm) is just around the corner. The best **restaurants** are also on the plaza: try the *Cafetería la Luna* for inexpensive Guatemalan favourites, or, for cakes and pastries, *El Volován*.

Buses running along the coastal highway almost always pull in at the Retalhuleu terminal on 7 Av and 10 C, a ten-minute walk from the plaza. There's a half-hourly service to and from Guatemala City, the Mexican border and Quetzaltenango, and there are also regular buses to Champerico and El Tulate. Retalhuleu has the only **Mexican consulate** on the Pacific coast, at 5 C and 3 Av (Mon–Fri 4–6pm).

Abaj Takalik

The area around Retalhuleu was heavily populated before the arrival of the Spanish and has been the scene of a number of recent archeological digs which have cast fresh light on the development of early Maya civilization, showing in particular the way it was influenced by other cultures from the north. The site of **Abaj Takalik** (daily 9am–4pm; US$3.20), 15km west of Retalhuleu, is a case in point, having already provided firm evidence of **Olmec** influence, which reached the area in the first century AD. The large site is still currently being excavated, with four main groups of ruins and around seventy mounds in the main part of the site; archeologists have unearthed enormous stelae, several of them very well preserved, dating the earliest monuments to around 126 AD. The remains of two large **temple platforms** have also been cleared, and what makes a visit to this obscure site really worthwhile are the carved sculptures, stelae and altars found around their base, particularly the rare and unusual representations of frogs and toads (monument 68), and even an alligator (monument 66). Amongst the finest carving is stela 5, which features two standing figures separated by a hieroglyphic panel, dated to 126 AD. Look out for a giant Olmec head, too, showing a man of obvious wealth with great hamster cheeks. A kilometre away, close to a river bank, are two more stelae, both still regularly used for pagan religious worship. There is a small building which acts as the site **musuem**, containing a model of Abaj Takalik along with assorted carvings and ceramics. You should be able to get a warm fizzy *agua* near the entrance, but there's no food available.

To **get to Abaj Takalik**, take a local bus from Reu to **El Asintal**, a small village 15km to the west, from where it's a four-kilometre walk to the site through coffee and cacao plantations. If you're driving, take the highway towards Mexico from Reu and turn right at the sign to the site.

The Parque Acuático Xocomil

North of Retalhuleu on the Carretera al Pacífico, the **El Zarco** junction is the start of one of the country's most scenic roads, which heads up into the highlands towards Quetzaltenango. Some 12km north of the junction is the gargantuan new water park, **Parque Acuático Xocomil** (daily 8am–6pm, US$10), which has been landscaped into the foothills of the highlands. The vast complex contains an abundance of water slides, wave pools and "lazy rivers" (artificial rivers) amidst grounds replete with fake Maya temples and copious greenery, and is very popular with Guatemalan families. **Buses** between Retalhuleu and Quetzaltenango pass the water park every thirty minutes in daylight hours.

Beyond the water park it's a stunning, hour-long ride up **to Quetzaltenango**, climbing more than 1500m up into the highlands, past dense forests, skirting the Santa María volcano and the village of Zunil. Heading **east** along the Carretera al Pacífico from the El Zarco junction there's a constant stream of buses bound for Guatemala City or El Salvador via Mazatenango and Escuintla.

Champerico

South from Retalhuleu a paved road heads to the beach at **CHAMPERICO**, which, though it certainly doesn't feel like it, is the country's third port. Founded in 1872, it was originally connected to Quetzaltenango by rail and enjoyed a brief period of prosperity based on the export of coffee. In 1934 Aldous Huxley passed through, but was distinctly unimpressed: "Then suddenly, vast and blank, under a glaring white sky, the Pacific. One after another, with a succession of dreary bumps, the rollers broke on a flat beach." Huxley was fortunate enough to board a steamer and escape what he called "the unspeakable boredom of life at Champerico". If anything, things have got worse, as barely any trade passes through the port these days, and the rusting pier, the only feature to disturb the coastline, will doubtless soon sink beneath the waves. Champerico still supports a handful of fishermen, but spends most of its time waiting for the weekend, when hordes of weary city dwellers descend on the coast. The **beach** is much the same as anywhere else, and although its sheer scale is impressive and there are lifeguards, it's essential to watch out for the dangerous undertow. On a more positive note, delicious **meals** are widely available: try the *Restaurant Monte Limar* or the *Alcatraz* for fried shrimp and fish, or, for a treat, feast on paella at the *Hotel Miramar* at 2 C and Av Coatepeque (☎773 7231; ❷), which also has a fantastic wooden bar – the best place is town to tackle your thirst – and dark, windowless **rooms**. Alternative places to stay include the *Martita*, just over the street (❷), though it's nothing special, or the *Hospedaje Buenos Aires* (❶), a very seedy little boarding house.

Buses run between Champerico and Quetzaltenango every hour or so from 7am to noon, passing through Retalhuleu. The last bus for Retalhuleu leaves Champerico at 6.30pm. Coming the other way, there are direct buses from 7am onwards. If you're heading anywhere else, catch a bus from Champerico to Retalhuleu and then another along the coastal highway.

Cuyotenango to Cocales

Beyond Retalhuleu the highway runs east to **CUYOTENANGO**, one of the older settlements along the road, having started life as a pre-conquest Kaqchikel village before becoming an important colonial town. The narrow streets and some of the older buildings bear witness to this distinguished past, but the thunder of the highway, which cuts right through the town, overwhelms all else, and its larger neighbours, Mazatenango and Retalhuleu, have long since consumed any importance that Cuyotenango once held.

Another branch road turns off for the beach here, heading 45km south to **EL TULATE**, where the village and the ocean are separated from the mainland by a narrow expanse of mangrove swamp. The beach itself, lined with palm trees, is another featureless strip of black sand, though the waves are a little less brutal here than at other beaches along this stretch of coast. The village's isolation is a definite bonus, though the only places **to stay** are on the reed mattresses in the shacks adjoining the open-air fried fish 'n' shrimp restaurants. **Buses** struggle down to El Tulate every hour or so from Mazatenango and Retalhuleu, with the last bus back to Mazatenango at 5pm and the last to Retalhuleu at 6pm: small boats meet the buses to ferry passengers from the end of the road to the village.

Back on the highway, the next stop is **MAZATENANGO**, another seething commercial town. There are two sides to "Mazate", as it's generally known. The main street, which runs down the side of the market, past the filling stations and bus terminal, is characteristic of life along the coastal highway, redolent of diesel fumes and cheap commercialization. The other half of town, centred on the plaza, is quieter, calmer and more sophisticated, with long shaded streets. There's no particular reason to linger in Mazatenango, but if you do find yourself here for the night, budget **accommodation** options include the *Hotel Sarah*, beside the old train station, which offers good-value simple rooms with private bath (❷). If you want somewhere more comfortable, head for the *Hotel Alba*, on the main highway heading for Mexico (☎872 0264; ❹), which also has secure parking. For **food**, try *Maxim's*, 6 Av 9–23, which specializes in barbecued meat and Chinese dishes, or *Croissants Pastelería* on the plaza, for coffee and cakes. There are a couple of cinemas in Mazatenango and plenty of **banks**.

Buses can be caught at the small terminal above the market on the main street, or outside the filling stations on the highway, which is where most of the pullmans stop. Services run regularly in both directions along the coastal highway – and also to Quetzaltenango, El Tulate, Chicacao and Pueblo Nuevo Tiquisate – every hour or so from 8am to 4pm.

East to Cocales

Continuing east from Mazatenango the main road passes the turn-off for Chicacao, a coffee centre with close links to Santiago Atitlán (see p.166), and **PUEBLO NUEVO TIQUISATE**, once the local headquarters of the all-powerful United Fruit Company, whose banana plantations stretched almost as far as its political influence. The company, now owned by Del Monte, planted huge numbers of bananas in this area after its plantations on the Caribbean coast were hit by disease, although modern techniques have enabled many to be switched back to their original locations. The branch road heading this way offers an interesting glimpse of sugar cane plantations and the very different houses of the workers (dormitories) and managers (great wooden houses on stilts, painted a neat New England-style green and white). If you want to **stay** overnight before heading south to the coast, your best bet is the *Hotel El Viajero* (☎884 7189; ❸), which has simple but decent rooms with fan and TV, plus secure parking. From here you can either drive, hitch or take a local bus to El Semillero or El Tecojate. The better beach is at **El Semillero**, where there's a sweeping expanse of dark sand that's the location for full-moon parties organized by the Rainbow Gathering tribe, a big hippie party collective. You'll need to bring along all supplies, water and blankets – check in the *Moonfish* café in Panajachel (see p.162) for details of the latest events.

About 30km beyond Mazatenango is **COCALES**, a crossroads town from where a road and **buses** runs north to Santiago Atitlán, Panajachel and San Lucas Tolimán. If you're heading this way you can wait for a connection at the junction, but don't expect to make it all the way to Panajachel unless you get here by 1pm. The best option is take the first pick-up or bus to Santiago Atitlán and catch a boat from there to other points around the lake. The last bus to Santiago leaves Cocales at around 4pm, but plenty of pick-ups also run this route.

From Cocales, a road also heads south to the agricultural centre of **NUEVA CONCEPCIÓN**, an inconspicuous little place that catapulted into the headlines in the 1980s as the home parish of Guatemala's most radical and controversial priest, **Padre Andrés Girón**, who founded the country's first significant land reform movement since the Arbenz government of 1949–54. During the civil war, Girón spoke out eloquently on behalf of campesinos and led fifteen thousand peasants in a four-day march to Guatemala City. He received numerous death threats for his troubles but, undeterred, has since entered politics.

Santa Lucía Cotzumalguapa and around

Another 23km along the Carretera al Pacífico brings you to **SANTA LUCÍA COTZUMALGUAPA**, a pretty uninspiring Pacific town a short distance north of the highway. The main reason to visit is to explore the **archeological sites** that are scattered in the surrounding cane fields, though you should bear in mind that getting to them is not easy unless you rent a taxi.

Santa Lucía Cotzumalguapa

Pullman **buses** passing along the highway will drop you at the entrance road to town, ten minutes' walk from the centre, while second-class "direct" buses from the capital go straight into the terminal, a few blocks from the plaza. Buses to Guatemala City leave the terminal hourly from 3am to 4pm, or you can catch a pullman from the highway.

As usual, the **plaza** is the main point of interest. Santa Lucía's shady square is disgraced by one of the ugliest buildings in the country (in a very competitive league), a memorably horrific green and white concrete municipal structure. Just off the plaza, you'll find several cheap and scruffy **hotels**: the *Pensión Reforma*, 4 Av 4–71 (❶), true to its name, is owned by some friendly but fearsome Catholics – the light switches are outside the rooms and if there's any suggestion of immoral activities they'll switch your light on; even the bathrooms are separate sex. Around the corner at 5 C 4–35 the *Hospedaje El Carmen* (❶) is another budget option, with thirteen tiny but clean rooms. The nearest upmarket place is the *Caminotel Santiaguito* (☎882 5435, ℻882 2285; ❺), a slick motel at km 90.5 on the main highway, with a swimming pool (non-guests can swim here for US$2.80) and a restaurant. Alternatively, the *El Camino*, across the road from here (☎882 5316; ❸–❹), is a little expensive for what you get, though some rooms have a/c.

For **food**, the *Comedor Lau* on 3 Avenida serves reasonable Chinese meals, or there's a huge *Pollo Campero* on the north side of the plaza. *Sarita* on 3 Avenida does great ice creams, while *Cevichería La Española*, on 4 Avenida a block south of the plaza, is the best bet for a drink and fresh seafood. The only other non-sleazy night-time entertainment is watching a **film** at the *Cine Victoria* on 3 Avenida. The *Kodak Club,* also on 3 Avenida, stocks slide film, and at least three **banks** will change your travellers' cheques – Banco Corporativo, on the plaza, accepts most varieties.

Sites around Santa Lucía Cotzumalguapa

A tour of the **sites** around Santa Lucía Cotzumalguapa can be an exhausting and frustrating process, taking you through a sweltering maze of cane fields. Doing the whole thing on foot is certainly the cheapest way, but also by far the hardest. Note that wandering about the cane fields alone is never a good idea, though if you are determined to, do so in the mornings when, as locals would say, "the thieves are still sleeping". You're far better off taking a round trip by taxi instead – you'll find plenty in the plaza in varying degrees of decrepitude – and if you bargain well it need not be prohibitively expensive (reckon on around US$10 all in). Make sure the trip includes all the sites and fix a firm price beforehand. If you only want to see one of the sites, **Bilbao** is just a kilometre or so from the centre of town and features some of the best carving. The sites are covered below, with directions, in the best order for visiting them on foot, but it's still fairly easy to get lost. If you do, just ask for *las piedras*, as they tend to be known locally.

Bilbao

Bilbao lies just north of Santa Lucía Cotzumalguapa. In 1880, more than thirty Late Classic stone monuments were removed from this site, and nine of them, probably the very finest of the Pacific coast stelae, deemed far too good to waste on Guatemala, were shipped to Germany. One was lost at sea and the others are currently on display in the Dahlem Museum in Berlin. Four sets of stones are still visible in situ, however, and two of them, both beautifully preserved slabs of black volcanic rock, perfectly illustrate the magnificent precision of the carving.

To get to the site, walk uphill from the plaza along 4 Avenida and bear right at the end, where a dirt track takes you past a small red-brick house and along the side of a cane field. About 200m further on is a fairly wide path leading left into the cane for about 20m. This brings you to two large stones carved in bird-like patterns, with strange circular glyphs arranged in groups of three: the majority of the glyphs are recognizable as the names for days once used by the people of southern Mexico. Numbers are expressed only by dots and circles, without the bar that was used by the Maya to represent five. This is further evidence that the Pipil, who carved these stones some time between 400 and 900 AD, had more in common with the tribes of the far north than with those of the Guatemalan highlands or Petén.

The same cane field contains two other sets of stones, reached along similar paths further up this side of the field. The first of them is badly eroded, so that it's only possible to make out the raised border and little or nothing of the actual carving. But the second is the best of the lot, a superbly preserved set of figures and interwoven motifs. The Mexican migrants who were responsible for all this shared with the Maya a fascination for the ball game, and on this stone a player is depicted, reaching up to decidedly Mexican divinities – a fairly clear indication that the game was regarded as a form of worship. The player is wearing a heavy protective belt, which would have been made from wood and leather, and you can clearly make out several birds and animals, as well as pods of cacao beans – which were used as currency.

△ Fishing near Livingston

There's one final stone hidden in the cane, which can be reached by heading back down the side of the field and turning right at the bottom, along the other side. Here you'll come across yet another entrance, opposite Casa no. 13, which brings you to the last carving, featuring another well-defined set of figures. The face of this stone has been cut into, presumably in an attempt to remove it.

Finca El Baúl

The second site is also out on the northern side of town, though somewhat further afield in the grounds of the **Finca El Baúl**. The finca is about 5km from Santa Lucía Cotzumalguapa and has its own collection of artefacts, as well as a small but fascinating site out in the cane fields. To get there from the last of the Bilbao stones, walk on beyond Casa no. 13 and onto the tarmacked road (if you're coming out of town this is a continuation of 4 Av). At the T-junction straight ahead of you turn to the right and follow the road for some 3km until it comes to a bridge. Cross this and take the right-hand fork for another kilometre or so, passing all the houses. Once out here a dirt track crosses the road: turn right along this to the base of a small hill. The site is on top of this hill, but you need to walk round to the other side to find the path up.

Once there you'll see two **stones** dating from the Classic period. The first is propped against a tree, carved in low relief, and depicts a standing figure wearing a skirt and a spectacular headdress, possibly that of Huhuetéotl, the fire god of the Mexicans, who supported the sun. Surrounding the figure are a number of carved circles, one seemingly bearing the date "8 deer". The second stone is a massive half-buried head, in superb condition, with a wrinkled brow, huge cheesy grin and patterned headdress, which again probably represents Huehuetéotl. The site has a powerful, mysterious atmosphere and is still used for religious ceremonies and by women seeking children and safe birth. In front of the stones is a set of small altars on which local people make animal sacrifices, burn incense and leave offerings of flowers. Recent excavations here have revealed a network of buried causeways – one stretches to the north to a site called **Gloria**, where some giant carved stones have been unearthed – you can view these in the Popul Vuh museum in Guatemala City (see p.79). El Baúl also makes an ideal shaded spot for a **picnic** lunch, with fine vistas towards the twin peaks of volcanos Agua and Fuego to the north.

The next place of interest is the **finca** itself, a further 3km away. This can be reached by continuing down the dirt track that exits the site, crossing a tarmacked road and walking through the sugar cane for about ten minutes until you emerge onto another road; here you should turn right for the finca's main building. At the gate, explain to the guards that you're here to see *el museo*, then walk beyond the rows of shanty-like huts to the huge furnace, behind which the main administration building is protected by further armed guards. Ask in here to see the collection, which is housed in a special compound under lock and key: despite the fierce-looking security measures the staff are always willing to oblige. The carvings include some superb heads, a stone skull, a massive jaguar and an extremely well-preserved stela of a ball-court player (monument 27) dating from the Late Classic period. Alongside all this antiquity is the finca's old steam engine, a miniature machine that used to haul the cane along a system of private tracks. A visit is also interesting for the rare glimpse it offers of a working finca, where about nine hundred people are employed. They even have their own **bus** service from town, which you may be able to hitch a ride on – buses leave from the Tienda El Baúl, a few blocks uphill from the plaza in Santa Lucía Cotzumalguapa, four or five times a day, the first at around 7am and the last either way at about 6pm.

Finca Las Ilusiones

The remaining site is on the other side of town, at the **Finca Las Ilusiones**, home to another private collection of artefacts and some stone carvings. To get there walk east along the highway for about a kilometre, out beyond the two Esso stations and past a small football field to the north of the road. After this a track leads off to the left (north) to the finca itself. Outside the buildings you'll see some copied carvings and several originals, including some fantastic stelae. The building to the left houses a small museum – ask around for the man who looks after the key. Inside is a tiny room crammed with literally thousands of small stone carvings and pottery fragments, including a striking statue of a pot-bellied figure (monument 58), probably from the middle Preclassic era. There are more carvings leaning against the walls of a private courtyard, reached by crossing the bridge and turning to the left. If you manage to get a peep you'll see many figures with the flattened foreheads that are so common in Maya art, along with others that look like nothing you'd expect to find in the Maya heartland. If you want to learn more about the latest archeological investigations around Santa Lucía Cotzumalguapa, consult the **website** Ⓦ www.famsi.org.

La Democracia and the coast at Sipacate

Heading east from Santa Lucía Cotzumalguapa the coastal highway arrives next at **Siquinalá**, a run-down sort from where another branch road heads to the coast. Along the way, 9km to the south, **LA DEMOCRACIA** is of particular interest as the home of another collection of archeological relics. To the east of town lies the archeological site of **Monte Alto**, and many of the best pieces which have been found there are now spread around the town plaza under a vast ceiba tree. These so-called "fat boys" are massive stone heads with simple, almost childlike faces, grinning with bizarre, Buddha-like contentment. Some are attached to smaller rounded bodies and rolled over on their backs, clutching their swollen stomachs like stricken Teletubbies. The figures resemble nothing else in the Maya world, but are strikingly similar to the far more ancient Olmec sculptures found near Villahermosa in the Gulf of Mexico. Debate continues to rage in academic circles about the precise origins of these traits, but for the moment even less is known about these relics than about the sites around Santa Lucía Cotzumalguapa, though it now seems likely that they date from the mid-Preclassic period, possibly from as far back as 500 BC. Also on the plaza, the town **museum** (Tues–Sun 8am–noon & 2–5pm; US$0.60) houses carvings, ceremonial yokes worn by ball-game players, pottery, grinding stones, a wonderful jade mask and a few more carved heads.

The road continues 21km further south to **La Gomera**, a mid-sized agricultural centre where buses usually wait for a while, and beyond to the coast at **SIPACATE**. The beach here is separated from the village by the black waters of the Canal de Chiquimulilla, across which boats ferry a steady stream of passengers. Sipacate is a pretty scruffy place **to stay**, but if you're determined to visit, *La Costa* (❷), in the village, has reasonable rooms set around a grassy lawn, while the beachside *Rancho Carillo* (❹) is more comfortable, with cabañas and a decent restaurant – they also run fishing trips.

Buses to Sipacate and La Democracia from both Guatemala City and Santa Lucía Cotzumalguapa pass through Siquinalá. However, the direct buses from Guatemala City are very slow, so if you want to head down this way the best thing to do is catch a bus to Siquinalá and wait outside the market there for one heading to La Democracia and Sipacate. Note that the trip from the main highway to Sipacate can take as long as two hours, with the last bus back to the highway leaving at 5pm.

East from Escuintla towards El Salvador

The eastern section of the Pacific coast is dominated by **Escuintla**, the region's largest town, and **Puerto San José**, formerly its most important port. If you're heading for the coast from Guatemala City this is probably the route you'll take, and it's a fairly easy day-trip. Neither town is particularly attractive, however, and you're unlikely to stay more than a single night, if that. Further to the east is **Monterrico**, an impressive beach where you'll find the coast's most important wildlife reserve, a protected area of mangrove swamps that's home to some superb birdlife. Beyond that the coastal highway runs to the border with El Salvador, with branch roads heading off to a couple of small seashore villages.

Escuintla

At the junction of the two principal coastal roads, **ESCUINTLA** is the largest and most important of the Pacific towns. There's nothing to do here but you do get a good sense of what life on the coast is all about, dominated as it is by a heady cocktail of pace, energy, squalour, dirt and commerce. Escuintla lies at the heart of the country's most productive region, both industrially and agriculturally, and the department's resources include cattle, sugar, cotton, light industry and even a small Texaco oil refinery. The town is also one of the oldest on the Pacific coast, built on the site of a pre-conquest Pipil settlement. Its modern name is a contraction of the Pipil word *Isquitepeque*, meaning "the hill of the dogs", a name given to the village because of the dog-like animals the Pipil kept for meat. These days there's no lack of commercial bustle in Escuintla's streets, though it seems as though the inhabitants, swept up in all the hubbub, have completely forgotten about the town itself, leaving it to crumble around them and fall into its current state of advanced decay.

Below the plaza, a huge, chaotic daily **market** sprawls across several blocks, spilling out into 4 Avenida, the main commercial thoroughfare, which is also notable for a lurid blue mock-castle that functions as the town's police station.

Practicalities

Buses to Escuintla leave the Trébol junction in Guatemala City every thirty minutes or so from 4am to 7pm. In Escuintla, they leave at the same times from 8 C and 2 Av. Services to other destinations depart from one of two other terminals: for places **en route to the Mexican border**, buses run through the north of town and stop by the Esso station opposite the Banco Uno (take a local bus up 3 Av); buses for the **coast road and inland route to El Salvador** are best caught at the main terminal on the south side of town, at the bottom of 4 Avenida (take a local bus down 4 Av). From the latter, buses leave every twenty minutes for Puerto San José and Iztapa, hourly for the eastern border, and six times daily for Antigua, via El Rodeo.

Banks are plentiful in Escuintla, and include Banco Industrial, at 4 Av and 6 C, Lloyds, at 7 C 3–07, and Banco del Occidente and Banco Immobiliario, both on 4 Avenida. Escuintla also has a couple of **consulates** – El Salvador is on 16 C 3–20, and Honduras is on 6 Av 8–24.

There are plenty of cheap **hotels** near 4 Avenida, most of them sharing the general air of dilapidation. The *Hospedaje El Centro* (**①**), on 3 Avenida a block behind the market, is one of the better really cheap places, while the *Hospedaje Oriente*, 4 Av 11–30 (**①**), is slightly more upmarket. For more luxury, the *Hotel Izcuintla*, 4 Av 6–30 (**③**), offers overhead fans and private baths, while *Hotel*

Costa Sur, 4 Av and 12 C (☎888 1819; ❸), is recommended, not least for its air-conditioning and secure parking. For real peace and quiet, head for the *Hotel La Villa* (☎888 0395, ℉888 1523; ❹–❺), a very dignified hotel boasting a gorgeous, dark wooden bar-restaurant and a small pool, plus some rooms with a/c – it's a few blocks from the bustle of the town centre at 3 Av 3–21. Finally, if money is no object you could try the rather overpriced *Sarita* motel on Avenida Centroamérica, at the junction of the coastal highway and the Guatemala City road (☎888 0482 or 888 1959; ❻), which has a nice pool.

Again, 4 Avenida is the place to head if you're looking for something **to eat**, being lined with restaurants offering anything from Guatemalan seafood feasts to the inevitable *ch'ao mein* and burgers, with the best deal being the US$2 lunch specials at *Pizzería al Macarone,* 4 Av 6–103. There are two **cinemas** in town – the Rialto at 5 C and 3 Av, and the Lux on 7 C, opposite the bank.

To the coast: Puerto San José

South from Escuintla the coast road heads through acres of cattle pasture to **PUERTO SAN JOSÉ**, which opened as a port in 1853 and was once Guatemala's main shipping terminal, funnelling goods to and from the capital. Now, however, it has been made virtually redundant by the container port of Puerto Quetzal, a few kilometres to the east, and both town and port are somewhat run down and sleazy. The main business is local tourism: what used to be rough sailors' bars now pander to the needs of the rowdy day-trippers from the capital who fill the beaches at weekends.

The shoreline is separated from the mainland by the **Canal de Chiquimulilla**, which starts near Sipacate, west of San José, and runs as far as the border with El Salvador, cutting off all the beaches in between. For the most part the canal is nothing more than a narrow strip of water, but in some places it fans out into a maze of mangrove swamps, providing a home for a wide array of wildlife.

In San José the main resort area is on the other side of the canal, directly behind the beach. This is where you'll find all the **bars** and **restaurants**, most of them crowded at weekends with big ladino groups feasting on seafood and playing the jukebox until the small hours. The **hotels**, most of them in the same area, are not so enjoyable, catering as they do to a largely drunken clientele. Prices are usually high and standards low – in the cheapest digs you'll be lucky if you get a sheet, and will have to make do with a bare reed mat. You're really better off sampling the delights of San José as a day-trip from the capital, but if you do need to stay, one of the better deals is at the *Casa San José Hotel,* on Avenida del Comercio (☎776 5587; ❹), where you'll find a pool and restaurant; for something cheaper, there's the basic *Viñas del Mar,* right on the beach (❸). If you want to spend a few days on the coast then head along to Iztapa or Monterrico.

Buses between the plaza in San José and the Zona 4 bus terminal in Guatemala City run every hour or so all day, with most services continuing on to Iztapa. Uniquely in Guatemala, Puerto San José has adopted Thai **tuk tuks** (motorized three-wheeler auto-rickshaws) as taxis – you can buzz about the place Bangkok-style for a few quetzales a trip.

Chulamar and Likín

Leaving San José and following the coast in either direction brings you to the beach resorts of Guatemala's wealthy elite, who abandoned Puerto San José to the day-trippers long ago and established themselves instead in their own enclaves, with holiday homes built in a pale imitation of California. The first of these enclaves is **CHULAMAR**, about 5km west of Puerto San José, which can be reached only by private car or taxi. Here you'll find another strip of sand separated from the land by the muddy waters of the canal. There are two **hotels** on the beach: the extremely swanky new *Radisson Villas del Pacífico* (☎881 1028; ❾), with three pools, manicured grounds and luxurious rooms – a room plus all meals and drinks costs US$160 per day during the week, US$200 at weekends – or the very faded holiday camp-style *Hotel Santa María del Mar* (☎225 2002; ❺), which has a pool, though the concrete family rooms are nothing special.

East of San José, past the container terminal at **Puerto Quetzal**, is the second of the area's upmarket resorts, **BALNEARIO LIKÍN**. Here a complete residential complex has been established, based around a neat grid of canals and streets. The ranks of second homes have speedboats and swimming pools, and the entire compound comes complete with an armed guard. There are no buses to Likín itself, but any of those going from San José to Iztapa will drop you at the entrance. Like all these places it's deserted during the week, when there are no boats to shuttle you to the beach, but at weekends you can drop by to watch the rich at play.

Iztapa and along the coast to Monterrico

Further east the road comes to an end at **IZTAPA**, another venerable port that now serves the domestic tourist industry. Of all the country's redundant ports Iztapa is the oldest, as it was here that the Spanish chose to harbour their fleets. In the early days Alvarado used the port to build the boats that took him first to Peru and then on the trip to the Spice Islands from which he never returned. In 1839 the English explorer and diplomat John Lloyd Stephens passed through on his way to Nicaragua and found the inhabitants far from happy: "The captain of the port as he brushed them away (the swarming moschetoes), complained of the desolation and dreariness of the place, its isolation and separation from the world, its unhealthiness, and the misery of a man doomed to live there."

While for some this might serve as a fitting summary of the entire Pacific coast, these days there are certainly places that it describes better than Iztapa. If not exactly beautiful, the village is at least one of the nicer Pacific beach resorts, smaller and quieter than San José but with none of the elitism of Likín or Chulamar. The beach itself, a bank of black sand, is on the other side of the Canal de Chiquimulilla. A handful of boatmen provide a regular shuttle service across the canal for a quetzal per passenger or US$2 per vehicle to the settlement of **Pueblo Viejo**. Just above the dock in Pueblo Viejo there's a small reptile breeding centre, where slumberous-looking iguanas and caimen are fattened up in concrete tanks before being released into the wild; visitors are free to take a look around.

There are also several reasonable **hotels** in Iztapa and Puerto Viejo, another rarity in this part of the country. In Iztapa, the welcoming, family-run *Sol y Playa Tropical* (☎881 4346; ❹) is a good deal, with rooms (all with private bath) set around a small pool. The cheapest deal is at the *Hotel María del Mar* (☎881 4055; ❶–❷), opposite the post office, which has clean rooms with fans – some also have private baths. The *Hotel Brasilia*, 1 C 4–27 (❷), over in Puerto Viejo, has even fewer pretensions, with basic, fanless second-floor rooms looking down over a huge bar and dance floor. Yelix, the owner of the Bike Center, a repair shop down the road from the *Hotel María del Mar* in Iztapa, rents out **bikes** for US$5 per day. **Buses** run from the Zona 4 bus terminal in Guatemala City to Iztapa every hour or so (5am–5pm).

Beyond Iztapa a smooth, newly paved road traces the 25km coastline from Pueblo Viejo to Monterrico, through a littoral landscape punctuated with loofa farms. Thanks to the improved road, large swathes of this unspoilt coastline are now being snapped up by property developers from the capital, so you may pass a hotel or two by the time you read this. From Pueblo Viejo, four **buses** a day should go to **Monterrico** – usually at 9am, 11am, 1.30pm and 4pm, although the buses are old and the schedule uncertain at the best of times. Buses leave Monterrico for Pueblo Viejo at 2.30am, 6am, noon and 3pm.

Monterrico: the beach and nature reserve

The setting of **MONTERRICO** is one of the finest on the Pacific coast, with the scenery reduced to its basic elements: a strip of dead straight sand, a line of powerful surf, a huge empty ocean and an enormous curving horizon. The village is scruffy, but friendly and relaxed, and is separated from the mainland by the waters of the Canal de Chiquimulilla, which weaves through a fantastic network of mangrove **swamps**. Mosquitoes can be a problem during the wet season.

Beach apart, Monterrico's chief attraction is the nature reserve, the **Biotopo Monterrico-Hawaii**, which embraces the village, Baule beach – an important turtle nesting ground – and a large slice of the swampland behind, covering a total area of some 2800 hectares. Sadly, however, the reserve's officially protected status does not prevent mounds of domestic rubbish being dumped in it, nor the widespread theft of turtle eggs. That said, it's well worth making your way to Monterrico, if only for the fantastically beautiful ocean view, though if you intend to swim it's worth remembering that there's a vicious **undertow** along the entire southern coast of Guatemala. Lifeguards are posted here at weekends, but swimmers regularly get into trouble and drownings are not uncommon.

It's also possible to **study Spanish** in Monterrico at the ALM language school – for more details contact their offices in Quetzaltenango (see p.185).

Getting to Monterrico

There are two ways to **get to Monterrico**: either the slower route by ferry and bus from Iztapa (see above) or from Taxisco (see p.251) on the coastal highway. From Taxisco, trucks and buses run the 17km south to La Avellana, from where boats shuttle passengers (US$0.40) and cars (US$12) back and forth to Monterrico on the opposite side of the mangrove swamp. There's a steady flow of traffic between Taxisco and La Avellana, with the last bus leaving Taxisco at 6pm and La Avellana at 5pm – though if you don't want to wait for a bus it's usually easy enough to hitch a ride with a truck or a car. There are also four **direct buses** between La Avellana and the Zona 4 bus terminal in Guatemala City (around 3hr 30min), leaving La Avellana between 4am and 9am and Guatemala City between 9am and 2pm – you can check the schedule in the *Hotel Baule Beach*. An altogether easier, though pricey, option if you're staying in Antigua is to use one of the **shuttle bus** services (see p.211) which leave every Friday afternoon and return on Sundays around 3pm.

On **arriving** at the dock in Monterrico, follow the meandering dirt track through some coconut palms towards the slumbering, tropical village centre. You'll pass a series of tiendas, a farmacia, a football pitch and plenty of pigs, chickens and dogs. Continue past a group of open-air restaurants and you'll soon hear the pounding of the Pacific and see what all the fuss is about: **Baule beach**.

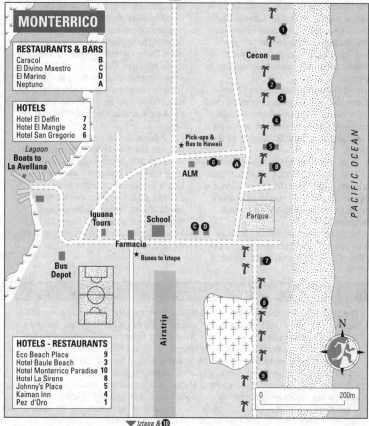

▲ Hawaii

MONTERRICO

RESTAURANTS & BARS
Caracol	B
El Divino Maestro	C
El Marino	D
Neptuno	A

HOTELS
Hotel El Delfin	7
Hotel El Mangle	2
Hotel San Gregorio	6

Lagoon
Boats to La Avellana

Pick-ups & Bus to Hawaii

ALM

Iguana Tours

School

Farmacia

Buses to Iztapa

Parque

PACIFIC OCEAN

Bus Depot

Airstrip

HOTELS - RESTAURANTS
Eco Beach Place	9
Hotel Baule Beach	3
Hotel Monterrico Paradise	10
Hotel La Sirena	8
Johnny's Place	5
Kaiman Inn	4
Pez d'Oro	1

N

0   200m

▼ Iztapa & ⑩

Accommodation

There's a pretty good range of **accomodation** in Monterrico, with almost everything concentrated right on the beach. As there are **no phones** in Monterrico it isn't easy to book in advance; you'll do best if you try accommodation that has email addresses or reservation numbers in Guatemala City. As with most places on the coast, prices can increase by around fifty per cent at **weekends**, and finding a bed may involve trudging through the sand from place to place.

Eco Beach Place turn right at the beach and walk for 250m (cell phone ☎ 309 2505, in Guatemala City ☎ 369 1116 or 365 7217). Very attractive new guest house, run by a friendly Italian–Guatemalan guy, set away from the others, with large comfortable doubles – all but one have private bath. There's good grub, a nice lounge and bar area, and stunning Pacific vistas from the verandah. ④

Hotel Baule Beach next door to the *Kaiman* (in Guatemala City ☎ 478 3088, ⓔ baulebeach @hotmail.com). For many years this was a very

popular place, but a recent change in management has seen service levels plummet and a general air of decay set in. All rooms have private bath and mosquito net, and there's also a tiny pool. Avoid the food. ③

Hotel El Mangle beside the *Hotel Baule Beach* (in Guatemala City ☎ 369 8958 or 514 6517, ⓕ 369 7631). Friendly place with thirteen very pleasant but small budget rooms – all have private shower, fan, nice wooden furniture and a little terrace with hammocks – and there's a small pool. ④

Hotel Monterrico Paradise 2km outside the village, on the road to Iztapa (in Guatemala City ☎478 4202, ☎478 4595). Spacious bungalows with two double beds and private bath, plus a pool. The restaurant, though decent, charges silly prices. It's most easily reached with your own transport. **❼**

Hotel San Gregario behind *Johnny's Place* (in Guatemala City ☎238 4690). Large modern block with a swimming pool and recently renovated motel-style rooms – they're a little souless but comfortable enough, and all come with a/c and bath. **❺**

Hotel La Sirena turn right at the beach and walk for 100m (no phone). Huge, unattractive concrete hotel which nonetheless offers a decent choice of digs, from tiny twin-bed rooms to larger apartments. There's also a pool and a reasonable restaurant. **❷**–**❹**

Johnny's Place turn left when you reach the ocean and it's the first place you'll come to (cell phone ☎206 4702, ⓦwww.backpackamericas .com/johnnys.htm). Selection of reasonable, though not wildly attractive, self-catering bungalows sleeping between two and four, each with little bathing pools, plus four gloomy, though cheap rooms. The new management team promises substantial renovation. **❸**/**❺**

Kaiman Inn turn left at beach and walk for 200m. The large rooms have mosquito nets and fans but are a little run-down and can also be noisy. There's a pool and a variable, overpriced Italian restaurant. **❹**

Pez d' Oro the last place as you head east down the beach (cell phone ☎204 5249, in Guatemala City ☎368 3684, ⓔlaelegancia@guate.net). The nicest cabañas in Monterrico – well-spaced, comfortable and tastefully decorated. Most are detached and all have ceiling fans and balconies with hammocks. The pretty swimming pool is shaded by coconut palms and there's also a good Italian restaurant with excellent pasta and wine by the glass. **❺**

The turtles of Monterrico

The huge, sparsely populated expanses of beach around Monterrico are prime nesting sites for three types of **sea turtle**, including the largest of them all, the giant leatherback. The reserve was originally established to protect the turtles from the soup pot and to curb the collection of the eggs, which are considered an aphrodisiac. Further dangers include the turtles include being hunted for their shells, drowned inside fishing nets and poisoned by pollution, especially plastic bags that resemble jellyfish, a favourite food. Turtles almost always nest in the dark, and on a moonless night in egg-laying season you have a good chance of seeing one in Monterrico.

Leatherback (*Dermochelys coriace*). The gargantuan leatherback is by far the largest of the world's turtles, growing to more than 2m in length and weighing up to 900 kilos. Named baule in Spanish, the leatherback gives the beach at Monterrico its name. It feeds almost exclusively on jellyfish, diving as deep as a kilometre beneath the sea in search of its prey. As its name suggests, it's the only turtle not to have a hard exterior shell; instead it has a layer of black, soft, rubbery skin. The leatherback frequents tropical and Arctic waters from Malaysia to Scotland and makes one of the longest migrations of any creature on earth. The species, which has been around for 200 million years, is in severe danger of extinction. It nests at Monterrico between mid-October and late December.

Olive Ridley (*Lepidochelys olivacea*). Spread throughout the tropical waters of the Pacific, Atlantic and Indian oceans, the Olive Ridley is the most numerous of the world's eight species of marine turtle and also one of the smallest, typically around 80cm long and weighing around 35kg. Olive Ridleys gather in huge numbers off favoured beaches to mate, after which the females return en masse to nest. They are common visitors at Monterrico (where they are known as *parlamas*) during their nesting season beween July and December.

East Pacific Black Turtle (*Chelonia agassizi*). The East Pacific black turtle nests only on the Pacific coast between California and Ecuador, and is not found anywhere else in the world. It reaches more than a metre in length and has a characteristic dark heart-shaped shell. Some scientists believe it to be a subspecies of the more common green turtle, which shares a similar shell outline and can be found

Eating and drinking

When it comes to **eating** in Monterrico, most of the hotels on the beach serve food, though prices are expensive at around US$5-8 a main course. Of these, the restaurant at the *Pez d'Oro* is one of the best, with delicious Italian food, or try the restaurant at the *Hotel La Sirena* for a cheaper meal. Inland from here, the *Neptuno* boasts a wonderful setting, but the food is only moderate. For inexpensive eating, the **comedores** in the village are a good bet – the best being the *Divino Maestro*, where they do a superb shark steak with rosemary, with *El Marino* next door a good second choice. For a relaxing **drink**, head for the *Caracol* bar on the beach, which boasts a lethal cocktail list and good tunes; it's run by a friendly Norwegian and Swiss team who can recommend local guides for the Biotopo Monterrico-Hawaii – they also serve up excellent, creatively prepared food including curries and vegetarian dishes.

The Biotopo Monterrico-Hawaii

Monterrico's **mangrove swamp** is a bizarre and rich environment, formed as rivers draining from the highlands find their path blocked by the black sands of the beach and spill out into this enormous watery expanse before finally finding their way to the sea through two estuaries, 30km to the east and west of the village. These dark, nutrient-rich waters are superbly fertile, and four distinct types of mangrove form a dense mat of branches, interspersed with

throughout the tropics. Its nesting season at Monterrico is the same as that of the Olive Ridleys, from July to December.

All the species of turtle use similar **nesting** techniques, hauling themselves up the beach, laboriously digging a hole about 50cm deep with their flippers, and then with great effort depositing a clutch of a hundred or so soft, ping-pong-ball-sized eggs, which they then bury, before racing back into the ocean. The eggs of the two smaller turtles take around fifty days to hatch, those of the leatherback, 72. When their time comes, the tiny turtles, no larger than the palm of your hand, use their flippers to dig their way out and make a mad dash for the water, desperately trying to avoid the waiting seabirds. Even once they are in the water, their existence is still very hazardous for the first few years of their lives, with only one in a hundred making it to maturity.

Watching a turtle lay her eggs at Monterrico should be a memorable experience, but the presence of the local *hueveros* (egg collectors) will probably ensure that it's not. In season, Baule beach is lined with sentries on the lookout for turtles, scanning the waves with torches every minute or so for signs of the marine visitors. When a turtle comes ashore these human vultures leave the creature undisturbed until all its eggs have been laid, then a *huevero* will pick the exhausted beast up (unless it's a leatherback) and dump it elsewhere before delving straight into the nest. Most foreign witnesses are content to take a photo and touch the bewildered creature before it claws its way back to the ocean, though you shouldn't use flash photography as it can upset and disorientate the sensitive turtles. Other braver souls who have challenged the *hueveros* have been threatened with machetes.

Officially the taking of eggs is outlawed, but informally a deal has been done so that out of every clutch of eggs collected, a dozen are donated to the turtle hatchery at the reserve headquarters, from where five thousand baby turtles are released each year. It's hoped that this deal will ease relations between the local community, who sell the eggs for US$2 a dozen, and the conservation aims of the reserve. During nesting season, visitors can also contribute to the scheme by backing a turtle hatchling in the Saturday "turtle race" on the beach. The sponsor of the winning baby turtle gets a dinner for two in one of the shoreside restaurants.

narrow canals, open lagoons, bullrushes and water lilies. The tangle of roots acts as a kind of marine nursery, offering small fish protection from their natural predators, while above the surface the dense vegetation and ready food supply provide an ideal home for hundreds of species of bird and a handful of mammals, including racoons, iguanas, alligators and opossums.

A trip into the swamp is an adventure, taking you through a complex network of channels and beneath a dense canopy of vegetation. The best way to explore the area is with one of the knowledgeable guides from **Iguana Tours** (in Guatemala City ☎238 4690); they have an office opposite the football field in Monterrico. Alternatively, rent a small *cayuco* (US$1.25 per hour) – there are always plenty of children hanging around the dock in Monterrico who'll be willing to paddle you on a trip into the wilds, or you can rent a larger boat with an engine – but you won't see as much because the noise of the engine will frighten off the wildlife. You shouldn't expect to encounter the anteaters and racoons which hang around the swamp whichever way you travel, but you probably will see a good range of bird life, including kingfishers, white herons and several species of duck, with the Palmilla lagoon being a particularly good spot. Failing all else the trip is well worth it just to watch the local fishermen casting their nets.

The **headquarters** of the Monterrico reserve (daily 8am–noon & 2–5pm), beside the *Hotel Baule Beach*, has some baby turtles in tanks and a dusty collection of jars filled with pickled fish and crustaceans. Next to the headquarters there's a shaded section of sand where the **turtle eggs** are reburied. Once the turtles hatch they are released from buckets directly into the ocean, so that they can avoid the attentions of sea birds. The reserve and research project, run by the government body CECON and the University of San Carlos, is urgently in need of funding, Spanish-speaking volunteers, and contacts with overseas universities. If you're interested in helping out, write to CECON USAC, Reserva Natural Monterrico, 06024 Taxisco, Santa Rosa.

A short **trail** runs from the headquarters along the edge of the reserve, past enclosures of alligators and green iguanas which are also bred for release into the wild. If you turn to the right down the dirt road at the end of the trail you'll pass a shrimp farm on the right before the track eventually meets the beach. It's a good stroll for bird-watching, particularly in the early morning and evening.

East to Hawaii

Further along the beach, about 7km east of Monterrico, is isolated **HAWAII**, another relaxed fishing village which has attracted a handful of regular visitors, notably wealthy Argentinians from Guatemala City who have built second homes on the beach. Locals live by fishing and farming and there's a large **turtle project**, run by ARCAS (Association to Rescue and Conserve Wildlife), which releases ten thousand turtles each year into the wild. Volunteers are always needed (at any time of year, though June to November is the main nesting season), and though they prefer you to get in touch first, you can always just show up. The work is primarily nocturnal, with volunteers walking the beach collecting sea turtle eggs and assisting in the management of the hatcheries. You can also assist in environmental education, mangrove reforestation and caiman and iguana captive-breeding. Accommodation costs US$50 a week (meals not included). Contact ARCAS at 21 Calle 9–44A, Zona 11, Mariscal, Guatemala City (☎ & ⓕ 476 6001, ⓦ www.rds.org.gt/arcas). You can visit Hawaii on a day-trip from Monterrico, by catching a pick-up, the occasional public bus, or by renting a boat from the dock (about US$30 round trip).

From Escuintla to El Salvador

Heading east from Escuintla the coastal highway brings you to **TAXISCO**, a quiet farming centre set to the north of the main road. From here a branch road runs to **La Avellana**, from where you can catch a boat to Monterrico (see p.246). **Buses** to Taxisco leave from the Zona 4 terminal in Guatemala City, calling at Escuintla and usually going on to the El Salvador border. If you get stuck in Taxisco, make for the comfortable *Hotel Jereson* (❸), on the main street.

Shortly before it reaches Taxisco the highway passes one of Guatemala's most unusual tourist sights, the **Club Auto Safari Chapín** (Tues–Sun 9.30am–5pm; US$4.20), Central America's only safari park. The park lies about a kilometre south of the highway (at km 87.5) on land owned by one of the great *fincero* families, whose older generation were enthusiastic big-game hunters, covering the walls of the main hacienda with the heads and skins of animals from every corner of the globe. Their children, however, developed a strong resistance to these exploits and insisted on bringing their animals home alive. The end result is a safari park that includes giraffes, hippos, a pair of black rhinos, African lions, pumas, deer, tapir, antelope, coyotes and a superbly comprehensive collection of Central American animals, snakes and birds. Sadly, their elephant died after he was fed a piece of plastic, but aside from this mishap the animals are active and well cared for and every species, except for the black rhino, has been successfully bred here in captivity.

The park is set up and managed in a very Guatemalan style, catering almost exclusively to domestic tourists, who like to make a day of it, picnicking, feasting in the restaurant and swimming in the pools. The entrance fee entitles you to a swim and a trip through the park in a minibus, although you can drive yourself if you have a car. There is also a small walk-through zoo, laid out around a lake, which is largely devoted to Central American wildlife.

Chiquimulilla and Las Lisas

Beyond Taxisco is **CHIQUIMULILLA**, from where another branch road heads up into the eastern highlands, through acres of lush coffee plantations, to the town of Cuilapa. Chiquimulilla is another fairly nondescript town that serves as a market centre for the surrounding area, but you might easily come here to change buses. If you get stuck, try the *Hotel San Carlos*, Barrio Santiago (✆885 0187; ❷), or the excellent-value *Turicentro Baru* (✆885 0374; ❸), on the main highway at km114.5, which has motel-style rooms, most with a/c and TV, and a pool.

The town is in the heart of ladino cowboy country and superb **leather goods**, including machete cases and saddles, are handcrafted in the market, so you may want to do a little shopping. From the small bus terminal, a block or so from the plaza, there's a steady flow of traffic to both the border and Guatemala City, with departures every hour or so. There are also hourly buses to Cuilapa, departing from the other side of the market.

Heading on towards the border, the highway is raised slightly above the rest of the coastal plain, giving great views to the sea. A few kilometres south of the road, archeological digs in at a long-forgotten Maya site called **La Nueva** have recently yielded some fascinating stellae and evidence that more than five thousand people lived here between the years 250 and 900 AD.

A short distance before the border a side road runs off to the seashore village of **LAS LISAS**, another good spot for spending time by the sea. Like all of these villages, Las Lisas is separated from the mainland by the murky waters of the Canal de Chiquimulilla, again bridged by a shuttle service of small boats.

Fiestas

Ladino culture dominates on the Pacific coast – despite the presence of a massive migrant labour force – so fiestas here tend to be more along the lines of fairs, with parades, fireworks, sporting events and heavy drinking. You'll see very little in the way of traditional costume or pre-Columbian dances, although marimba bands are popular even here and many of the fiestas are still based on local saints' days. Nevertheless, there's no doubt that the people of the coast like to have a good time and know how to enjoy themselves. Allegiances tend to be less local than those of the Maya population and national holidays are celebrated as much as local ones.

January
The year kicks off in **Taxisco** from the 12th to 15th, with a fiesta in honour of the Black Christ of Esquipulas; events include bullfighting and plenty of macho bravado. In **Colomba** (a few kilometres from Coatepeque) a fiesta takes place from the 12th to 16th which honours the same Black Christ and also involves bullfighting. In **Cuyotenango** there's a fiesta from the 11th to 18th, with the main day on the 15th – unlike most coastal fiestas this one includes some traditional dancing.

February
A fiesta takes place in **Tecún Umán** some time during the month.

March
Holy Week is celebrated everywhere in a combination of religious ritual and secular partying, while in **Coatepeque** there's a local fiesta from the 11th to 19th, with the main day on the 15th. In **Puerto San José** there's a fiesta from the 16th to 22nd, with the principal day on the 19th, while **Ocós** has a fiesta some time during the month on a variable date.

April
Chiquimulilla has a fiesta from April 30 to May 4.

July
Coatepeque has a one-day fiesta on the 25th, in honour of Santiago Apostol.

August
The port of **Champerico** holds a fiesta in honour of El Salvador del Mundo, from the 4th to 8th, with the main day on the 6th.

October
Iztapa's fiesta takes place from the 20th to 26th. The 24th is the main day.

November
All Saints' Day, 1 November, is celebrated throughout the country, and people gather in cemeteries to eat and drink and to honour the dead. In **Siquinalá** they have a local fiesta from the 23rd to 26th.

December
Retalhuleu has a fiesta from the 6th to 12th; the main day is the 8th. **Chicacao**'s fiesta, from the 18th to 21st, includes traditional dancing, as the town has close links with Santiago Atitlán. **Escuintla** has a fiesta from the 6th to 15th, with the main day on the 8th, and in **Santa Lucía Cotzumalguapa** the main fiesta is held on the 25th. Finally it's the turn of **La Democracia** on the 31st.

On the sandbank itself the village follows a standard pattern, with a collection of scruffy huts and palm trees behind a beautiful black-sand beach. It's a great place to relax for an afternoon, but accommodation is high in price and very low in quality. **Buses** run between Las Lisas and Chiquimulilla hourly from 9am to 4pm (1hr 30min).

The border with El Salvador
The coastal highway finally reaches the border with El Salvador at **CIUDAD PEDRO DE ALVARADO**. Most of the commercial traffic and all the pull-man buses use the highland route to El Salvador, and consequently things are fairly quiet and easy-going here. Should you get stuck for the night, try the *Hospedaje Yesina* (**❶**), right opposite the immigration post, and there's a selection of basic hotels and comedores on the El Salvador side of the border. There are second-class buses to and from the Zona 4 terminal in Guatemala City every hour or so between 1am and 4pm, all of them going via Escuintla. There's also another branch road from here to the coast, ending up at a couple of small seaside villages, Garita Chapina and Barra de la Gabina.

Travel details

Buses

Buses are the best way to get around on the Pacific coast, and the main highway, from Guatemala City to the Mexican border, is served by a constant flow of pullmans. Heading in the other direction, to the border with El Salvador, there are fewer pullmans, though there is a regular stream of second-class buses. On either of these main routes you can hop between buses and expect one to come along every thirty minutes or so, but if you plan to leave the highways then it's best to travel to the nearest large town and find a local bus from there. If you're heading up into the highlands take any bus to the relevant junction and wait for a connection there – El Zarco for buses to Quetzaltenango and Cocales for Lake Atitlán – but set out early.

The coastal highway
Guatemala City to the Mexican border (5hr). There are buses every thirty minutes or so calling at all the main towns along the coastal highway, including Escuintla, Santa Lucía Cotzumalguapa, Cocales, Mazatenango, Retalhuleu and Coatepeque. The bulk of these leave from the terminal at 19 C and 9 Av, in Zona 1 (watch your bags carefully if you are waiting around here). The main companies to the borders at Talismán and Tecún Umán are Fortaleza del Sur (hourly, 4am–7pm; ☎ 230 3390) and Chinita (11 daily, 8am–6.30pm; ☎ 251 9144), both with offices on 19 Calle between 8 and 9 avenidas, Zona 1, Guatemala City. In addition, Galgos, 7 Av 19–44, Zona 1 (☎ 253 4868) and Línea Dorada, 16 C 10–55, Zona 1 (☎ 232 9658), both run two luxury buses to Tapachula in Mexico, via Talismán. To Taxisco (3hr) and Chiquimulilla (3hr 30min), there are buses every hour or so from the Zona 4 terminal in Guatemala City, many of which go on to the border with El Salvador at Cuidad Pedro de Alvarado (1hr from Chiquimulilla).
Coatepeque to: Retalhuleu (50min); Tecún Umán (40min).
Cocales to: Escuintla (30min).
Escuintla to: Antigua (1hr 30min); Guatemala City (1hr).
Retalhuleu to: Cocales (50min); Mazatenango (30min).

Branching off the coastal highway
To Champerico. From Retalhuleu (every 30min; 1hr 20min); from Quetzaltenango (hourly; 2hr 45min).

To Ocós and Tilapa. From Coatepeque to Tilapa (hourly; 2hr), and to Ocós (4 or 5 daily; 2hr); boats connect the two.

To Puerto San José. Buses leave from the Zona 4 terminal in Guatemala City (every 30 min; 2hr); hourly buses continue on to Iztapa (30min from San José).

To Monterrico. Four daily buses leave Pueblo Viejo (1hr) and three return from Monterrico. Monterrico is better reached from Taxisco, by taking a bus or truck to La Avellana and a boat from there. Buses from Taxisco run hourly (6am–6pm).

To **Las Lisas** (1hr). There are buses from Chiquimulilla (hourly 9am–4pm), most of which start from the Zona 4 terminal in Guatemala City.

To **Ciudad Pedro de Alvarado** (4hr 30min). There are buses every hour or so from the Zona 4 terminal in Guatemala City, which travel via Escuintla and Taxisco. Buses from the border to Guatemala City leave hourly from 6am to 4pm.

East to the Caribbean

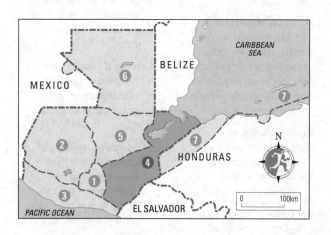

CHAPTER 4

Highlights

✳ **Quiriguá's carvings**
Gawk at the monumental
stelae stones, the largest
in the Maya world, and
the bizarre altars in the
great plaza of this fascinating site. **p.259**

✳ **Hotel del Norte** Enjoy the
faded Caribbean class of
Puerto Barrios' oldest
hotel. **p.266**

✳ **Punta de Manabique** A
Caribbean coast nature
reserve, rich in wildlife
including howler and spi-
der monkeys, and boast-
ing some of Guatemala's
best beaches. **p.267**

✳ **Punta-dancing in
Livingston** Shake your
booty to the Garífuna
beat in this funky
Caribbean town. **p.268**

✳ **Río Dulce** – The boat journey through this soaring,
jungle-clad gorge is an
exhilarating trip. **p.271**

✳ **Hot spring waterfall**
Soak away an afternoon
or two at this exquisite
hot spring-fed waterfall,
on the north bank of
Lago de Izabal. **p.277**

✳ **Eastern highlands** An
evocative landscape of
ancient, eroded volca-
noes, and parched,
cacti-studded hills interspersed with hard-drink-
ing cowboy towns.
p.280

✳ **Volcán de Ipala** Swim in
the azure waters of a
stunning crater lake,
located atop an extinct
volcano. **p.283**

✳ **Esquipulas** A vast basilica that's home to an
ancient carving of a
black Christ – the focus
for the largest pilgrimage
in Central America.
p.287

East to the Caribbean

Connecting Guatemala City with the Caribbean is the **Motagua valley**, a broad corridor of low-lying land that separates the Sierra del Espíritu Santo, marking the border with Honduras, from the Sierra de Las Minas. In fact the valley starts in the central highlands, around Santa Cruz del Quiché, cutting east through a particularly arid section of the mountains and meeting the Carretera al Atlántico (Caribbean Highway) at the El Rancho junction, where the Río Motagua is surrounded by desert. From here on, the valley starts to take its true form, opening out into a massive flood plain with the parallel ridges rising on either side. The land here is fantastically fertile and lush with vegetation at all times of the year, and the air is thick with humidity.

This final section, dampened by tropical heat and repeated cloudbursts, was densely populated in Maya times, when it formed the southern limit of their civilization. The valley served as an important trade route connecting the highlands with the Caribbean coast just as it does today, and it was also one of the main sources of jade. Following the decline of the Maya civilization, however, the area lay disease-infested and virtually abandoned until the end of the nineteenth century. Its revival was part of the masterplan of the **United Fruit Company**, who cleared and colonized the land, planting thousands of acres with bananas and reaping massive profits. At the height of its fortune the company was powerful enough to bring down the government and effectively monopolized the country's trade and transport. Today bananas are still the main crop, though cattle are becoming increasingly important, and the Carretera al Atlántico thundering through the valley is also vital to the region's prosperity, carrying the bulk of foreign trade from both Guatemala and El Salvador.

For the traveller the Motagua valley is the main route to and from Petén, and most people get no more than a fleeting glimpse of it through a bus window. But two of the greatest Maya sites are in this area: **Quiriguá**, just 4km from the main road, and **Copán**, across the border in Honduras (a side trip of a day or two) and covered in depth in Chapter Seven (see p.383).

Accommdation price codes

All accommodation listed in this guide has been graded according to the following price scales. These refer to the price in US dollars of the cheapest double room in high season. For more details see p.34.

❶ Under US$5　　❹ US$15–25　　❼ US$60–80
❷ US$5–10　　　❺ US$25–40　　❽ US$80–100
❸ US$10–15　　　❻ US$40–60　　❾ Over US$100

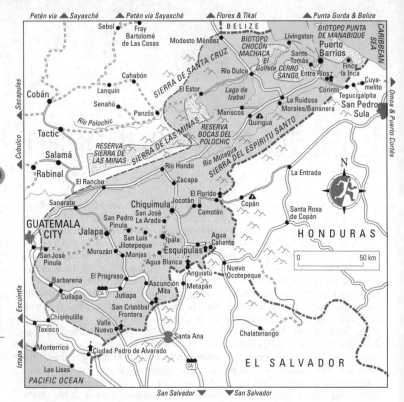

The region to the north of the Motagua valley is dominated by the sub-tropical **Río Dulce** and **Lago de Izabal**, a vast expanse of freshwater ringed by isolated villages, swamps, hot springs and caves. The protected **Reserva Bocas del Polochic**, occupying the western fringes of the lake, harbours a tremendous variety of the region's wildlife (including alligators, iguanas and turtles, as well as large numbers of migratory birds and resident parrots and toucans) and is best reached from the sleepy town of **El Estor**. From Lake Izabal, you can sail to the Caribbean through **El Golfete**, another large freshwater expanse where there's a manatee nature reserve. Beyond here, the Río Dulce runs through spectacular gorges, with jungle towering overhead, to the coast at **Lívingston**, a laid-back seaside town, and home to one of Guatemala's few communities of black Garífuna people. Also on the Caribbean coast, and connected to Livingston by ferry, is the faded, slightly seedy port of **Puerto Barrios**, jumping-off point for the coastal route into Honduras or boats to Belize.

Also covered in this chapter is the **eastern highlands**, a seldom-visited part of the country that spreads to the south and east of the capital and shares little with the highlands of the west. Its dry ladino lands are dominated by ancient, eroded volcanoes and hot, dusty towns. Though the scenery is superb, there is little for the traveller here, save the beautiful isolation of the **Ipala volcano** with its stunning crater lake, and the curious holy town of **Esquipulas**, home of the famous Black Christ, the scene of Central America's largest annual pilgrimage.

The Motagua valley

Leaving Guatemala City, the Carretera al Atlántico also forms the main route to Cobán, until the road divides at the **El Rancho junction** beneath the parched hills of the upper Motagua. Here a branch road climbs into the rain-soaked highlands of the Verapaces while the main highway continues to the Caribbean coast. Heading on down the Motagua valley for another 20km or so the land is bleak, dry and distinctly inhospitable, with the road keeping well to the left of the river and bypassing the villages that line the railway. The first place of any note is the **Río Hondo junction**, a smaller version of El Rancho, where the road divides, with one arm heading south to Esquipulas and the three-way **border** with Honduras and El Salvador, and the main branch continuing on to the coast. Here you'll find an army of food sellers swarming around every bus that stops and a line of comedores, as well as a number of motels scattered around. Río Hondo is home to the large Valle Dorada water park (daily 8am–6pm; US$6 per day), which makes it a popular weekend retreat for Guatemalans: if you stay at the *Valle Dorada* motel, at km 149 (☎941 2542, ℰ941 2543; ❺), you get free use of the slides and pools. For a cheaper bed, try *Hotel Nuevo Pasabien* (☎934 7201, ℰ934 8788, ℰpasabien@infovia.com.gt; ❺), with nice bungalows and a pool, or the simpler *Hotel Santa Cruz* (☎ & ℰ934 7112; ❹), both at km 126.

On down the valley the landscape starts to undergo a radical transformation; the flood plain opens out and the cacti are gradually overwhelmed by a profusion of tropical growth. It is this supremely rich flood plain that was chosen by both the Maya and the United Fruit Company, to the great benefit of both. Here the broad expanse of the valley is overshadowed by two parallel mountain ranges; to the northwest the **Sierra de las Minas**, and over on the other side, marking out the Honduran border, the **Sierra del Espíritu Santo**.

The ruins of Quiriguá

Of one thing there is no doubt; a large city once stood there; its name is lost, its history unknown; and no account of its existence has ever before been published. For centuries it has lain as completely buried as if covered with the lava of Vesuvius. Every traveller from Yzabal to Guatimala [sic] has passed within three hours of it; we ourselves had done the same; and yet there it lay, like the rock-built city of Edom, unvisited, unsought, and utterly unknown.

John Lloyd Stephens (1841)

In 1841 John Stephens was so impressed with the ruins at **Quiriguá** that he planned to take them home, using the Río Motagua to float the stones to the Caribbean so that "the city might be transported bodily and set up in New York". Fortunately, the asking price was beyond his means and the ruins remained buried in the rain forest until 1909, when the land was bought by the United Fruit Company.

Quiriguá emblem glyph

Today things are somewhat different: the ruins themselves are partially restored and reconstructed, and banana plantations stretch to the horizon in all directions. Few travellers visit Quiriguá, which is a shame because whilst it can't compete with the enormity of Tikal, it does have some of the finest of all Maya carving. Only nearby Copán comes close to matching the magnificent stelae, altars and zoomorphs that are covered in well-preserved and superbly intricate glyphs and portraits.

The site is surrounded by a dense patch of lush rainforest, and weather conditions are decidedly **tropical**; cloudbursts are the rule and the buzz of mosquitoes is almost uninterrupted – take repellent.

QUIRIGUÁ

Carretera al Atlántico (3 km) & Quiriguá village

Ticket Office

Café & Museum

P

•A •C •D
•B

•E •F
•G

Jungle

H•

CENTRAL PLAZA

•I
J• •K

Ball Court
M•
•N
P• •O

Grupo Este East Group

Jungle

Acropolis

Banana Plantations

N

Grupo Sur South Group

0   100 m

A brief history of Quiriguá

Quiriguá's history starts a short distance from the existing site, near the hospital in the village, where two stelae and a temple have been unearthed, marking the site of an earlier ceremonial centre. From there it moved to a second location nearby, where another stela has been found, before finally settling at the main site you see today.

The **early history** of Quiriguá is still fairly vague, and all that is certain is that at some time during the Late Preclassic period (250 BC–300 AD) migrants from the north, possibly Putun Maya from the Yucatán peninsula, established themselves as the rulers here. Thereafter, in the Early Classic period (250–600 AD), the centre was dominated by Copán and doubtless valued for its position on the banks of the Río Motagua, an important trade route, and as a source of jade, which is found throughout the valley. At this stage the rulers themselves may well have come from Copán, just 50km away, and there certainly seem to have been close ties between the two sites: the architecture, and in particular the carving that adorns it, makes this very clear.

In the Late Classic period (600–900 AD) Quiriguá really started to come into its own. The site's own name glyph is first used in 731, just six years after its greatest leader, **Cauac Sky**, ascended to the throne. As a member of the long-standing Sky dynasty, Cauac Sky took control of a city that had already embarked upon a campaign of aggressive expansion, and was in the process of asserting its independence from Copán. In 737 matters came to a head when he captured Eighteen Rabbit, Copán's ruler, thus making the final break (see p.385). For the rest of his sixty-year reign the city experienced an unprecedented building boom: the bulk of the great stelae date from this period and are decorated with Cauac Sky's portrait. For a century Quiriguá dominated the lower Motagua valley and its highly prized resources. Cauac Sky died in 771 and was succeeded 78 days later by his son, Sky Xul, who ruled for nineteen years until being usurped by Jade Sky, who took the throne in 790. Under Jade Sky Quiriguá reached its peak, with fifty years of extensive building work, including a radical reconstruction of the acropolis. But from the end of Jade Sky's rule, in the middle of the ninth century, the historical record fades out, as does the period of prosperity and power.

The ruins

Entering the site beneath the ever-dripping trees you emerge at the northern end of the **Great Plaza**. To the left-hand side of the path from the ticket office and new museum is a badly ruined pyramid and directly in front of this are the **stelae** for which Quiriguá is justly famous. The nine stelae in the plaza are the tallest in the Maya world and their carving is arguably the best. The style, similar in many ways to that of Copán, always follows a basic pattern, with portraits on the main faces and glyphs covering the sides. As for the figures, they represent the city's rulers, with Cauac Sky depicted on no fewer than seven (A, C, D, E, F, H and J). Two unusual features are particularly clear: the vast headdresses, which dwarf the faces, and the beards, a fashion that caught on in Quiriguá thirty years after it became popular in Copán. Many of the figures are shown clutching a ceremonial bar, the symbol of office, which has at one end a long-nosed god – possibly Chaac, the rain god – and at the other the head of a snake. The glyphs, crammed into the remaining space, record dates and events during the reign of the relevant ruler.

Largest of the stelae is E, which rises to a height of 8m and weighs 65 tonnes – it was originally sunk about 3m into the ground and set in a foundation of rough stones and red clay, but was reset in 1934 using concrete. The stelae are carved out of an ideal fine-grained sandstone, from a quarry about 5km from the site. The stones were probably rolled to the site on skids, set up, and then worked by sculptors standing on scaffolding. Fortunately for them the stone was soft once it had been cut, and fortunately for us it hardened with age.

Another feature that has earned Quiriguá its fame are the bizarre **zoomorphs**, six blocks of stone carved with interlacing animal and human figures. Some, like the turtle, frog and jaguar, can be recognized with relative ease, while others are either too faded or too elaborate to be accurately made out. The best of the lot is P, which shows a figure seated in Buddha-like pose, interwoven with a maze of others. The zoomorphs are usually referred to as altars and thought to be connected with the stela altar complexes at Tikal, but their size and shape make this seem unlikely.

Around the plaza are several other interesting features. Along the eastern side are some unrestored structures that may have been something to do with Quiriguá's role as a river **port** – since the city's heyday the river has moved at least 1km from its original course. At the southern end of the plaza, near the main zoomorphs, you can just make out the shape of a **ball court** hemmed in on three sides by viewing stands, although the actual playing area is still buried beneath tons of accumulated soil. The **Acropolis** itself, the only structure of any real size that still stands, is bare of decoration. Trenches dug beneath it have shown that it was built on top of several previous versions, the earliest ones constructed out of rough river stones. Apart from these central structures there are a few smaller unrestored complexes scattered in the surrounding forest, but nothing of particular interest.

Quiriguá practicalities

The **ruins** (daily 7.30am–5pm; US$4) are situated some 70km beyond the junction at Río Hondo, and 4km from the main road, reached down a side road that serves the banana industry. All **buses** running between Puerto Barrios and Guatemala City pass by – just ask the driver to drop you at the ruins and you'll end up at the entrance road, about four hours from Guatemala City, from where there's a fairly regular bus service to the site itself, as well as a number of motorbikes and pick-ups that shuttle passengers back and forth. The entrance to the ruins is marked by a ticket office, a couple of cheap food shacks, a coconut vendor or two and a car park. A new site **museum** should also open here some time in 2002.

To get back to the highway, wait until a bus or motorbike turns up. Buses, often packed with plantation workers, are the most likely to stop at the barrier – some go only as far as the road, others all the way to Morales and Bananera.

There's nowhere to stay at the ruins themselves, but there are two **hotels** in the **village** – also known as Quiriguá – about halfway between the site and the main road. To get there ask to be dropped off at the rail line (which crosses the dirt track about 1km from the main road) and walk south along the tracks for a further kilometre; by car the village is reached by a separate entrance road off the main road. Nowadays it's a ramshackle and run-down sort of place, strung out along the railway track, but in the past it was famous for its hospital of tropical diseases, run by the United Fruit Company. This imposing building still stands on the hill above the track, now a state-run workers' hospital. Up beside the hospital is the plaza, where you'll find the surprisingly good *Hotel y Restaurante Royal* (☎947 3639; ❷/❸), with large old rooms downstairs and modern rooms on the upper floor, while the *Hotel el Eden* (☎947 3281; ❷), next to the old station, just off the tracks, is another reasonable budget option, and also serves **meals**.

On to the coast: Puerto Barrios

Heading on towards the Caribbean, another 15km brings you to **La Trinchera**, junction for the branch road to Mariscos (see p.279) on the shores of Lake Izabal. Further down the Motagua valley the road pushes on through a blooming landscape of cattle ranches and fruit trees, splitting again at the junction for the twin towns of **MORALES** and **BANANERA**, a ramshackle collection of wooden huts and railway tracks. These squalid towns are of no interest except as the transport hub of the lower Motagua, served by all the second-class buses for Petén and a regular shuttle of minibuses to and from Río Dulce. There's also, of course, a steady flow of buses for Puerto Barrios and Guatemala City. Note that most fast Litegua buses (see "Puerto Barrios: travel connections", p.267) don't pass through Morales or Bananera. If, for whatever reason, you need **to stay** in Morales, the small *Hotel del Centro* (☎ & ⓕ947 8054; ❹) on Avenida Bandegua is the most comfortable option, and all rooms come with private bathrooms, while the *Pensión Montavlo*, next to the station (❶), is very basic but reasonably clean.

A short distance beyond the turning for Morales/Bananera you pass the **Ruidosa junction**, from where the highway to Petén heads northwest,

Bananera and bananas

The unprepossessing town of Bananera has a special place in the history of Guatemala. It was here that the **United Fruit Company** made its headquarters and masterminded the growth of its massive empire. The company's land is now owned by Bandegua (a subsidiary of Del Monte) who maintain a local headquarters in a neatly landscaped and well-sealed compound and continue to dominate the area. The town is still surrounded by a sea of banana plantations, with crop-dusting planes wafting overhead, a company store that supplies the faithful and a one-hole golf course (at the bottom of the airfield), testifying to the presence of foreign executives.

The United Fruit Company muscled in on the Motagua valley in the early part of this century, developing huge tracts of unused land, waging war on endemic diseases and making millions of dollars in the process. The company's fingers were in so many pies that it became known as "el pulpo", the octopus, and its political lobby was so powerful that it secured exemption from almost all taxes, controlling not only the banana industry but also the country's railways and the crucial port at Puerto Barrios. So profitable was the company that its assets multiplied fourteen times between 1900 and 1930. Its tentacles held Central America so firmly that when the socialist government of Arbenz proposed confiscating the company's unused lands in 1954, the United Fruit Company engineered a coup and replaced the government.

Bandegua, as inheritors of the empire, have largely avoided political controversy until very recently, limiting themselves to exporting around two billion bananas a year. In September 1999, trouble again re-ignited when Bandegua sacked 900 employees in the area, citing a worldwide slump in banana prices, and declining Guatemalan productivity, following the devastation caused by Hurricane Mitch. The sackings prompted unions to call for a mass strike and a roadblock of the Carretera al Atlántico, proposals which in turn sparked violence by gangs of vigilantes, allegations of massive corruption and the ultimate resignation of the union leaders who had called for the strike. Though Bandegua denied any involvement, the suspicion was very clear that the powerful banana lobby was again flexing its muscles and there was an international outcry. The ensuing row drew in President Arzú, the American ambassador and MINUGUA (the UN mission to Guatemala) until the dispute was eventually settled in April 2000 and all the workers were reinstated.

out over the Río Dulce. Another 50km to the northeast and you reach the Caribbean, with the road dividing for the last time, right to the old port of Puerto Barrios and left to Puerto Santo Tomás de Castillo, the modern town and dock.

Puerto Barrios and around

At the final junction on the highway, unless you happen to be driving a banana truck, the turning for **PUERTO BARRIOS** is the one to take. Founded in the 1880s by President Rufino Barrios, the port soon fell into the hands of the United Fruit Company, who used their control of the railways to ensure that the bulk of trade passed this way. Puerto Barrios was Guatemala's main port for most of the twentieth century, and while the Fruit Company was exempt from almost all tax, the users of its port were obliged to pay heavy duties. In the 1930s it cost as much to ship coffee to New Orleans from Guatemala as it did from Brazil. These days the boom is over and the town distinctly forlorn, although you'll still find all the services associated with ports, including a cluster of strip clubs, all-night bars and a brothel or two. The streets are wide, but they're poorly lit and badly potholed, and the handful of fine old Caribbean buildings are now outnumbered by grimy concrete hotels and hard-drinking bars.

Arrival and information

There is no purpose-built bus station in Puerto Barrios. Litegua **buses**, which serve all destinations along the Carretera al Atlántico, have their own terminal in the centre of town on 6 Avenida, between 9 and 10 calles. All second-class buses to Chiquimula and Esquipulas arrive and depart close by from several bays grouped around the central market opposite. Daily Taca **flights** from Guatemala City land at the airstrip 3km northeast from the centre of town. **Taxis** seem to be everywhere in Barrios – drivers toot for custom as they ply the streets.

The **Telgua** office is at the junction of 8 Av and 10 C (daily 7am–midnight) though you'll find the best international rates at Comunitel at 7 C and 5 Av (daily 8am–10pm); the best **internet** café in town is *Cafenet* at 13 C and 6 Av (daily 9am–9pm). There are a number of **banks** to choose from: you'll find Lloyds Bank on the corner of 7 Av and 15 C (Mon–Fri 9am–4pm, Sat 9am–1pm), Banco G&T Continental (for Mastercard) at 7 C and 6 Av (Mon–Fri 9am–7pm, Sat 9am–1pm), and Banco Industrial (with a 24hr Visa-friendly ATM) at 7 Av and 7 C. The **post office** is at 6 C and 6 Av (Mon–Fri 8am–4.30pm).

The Town and around

The main **market**, sprawling around disused railway lines at the corner of 9 Calle and 6 Avenida, is the town's main focus and the best place to start to get a grip of Barrios' modern identity. Here lines of ladino vendors furiously whisk up lush fruit licuado drinks from a battery of blenders, while Garífuna women swat flies from piles of *pan de coco*. A block north of the market at the junction of 7 Calle and 7 Avenida, the tottering remains of the once near-monumental wooden landmark, the **Palacio del Cine y Lavandería** ("Cinema and Laundry Palace"), confirms the port's Caribbean heritage. Heading west along 7 Calle from here, it's about 800m to another magnificent wooden relic, the elegant *Hotel del Norte* (see below), its timber corridors warped by a century of storms and salty air – be sure to take a look inside at the colonial-style bar and dining room. Next to the hotel, there are a tiny park and pier, where you gaze out over the glistening waters of the Bahía de Amatique.

Across the bay from here, 7km west of Puerto Barrios, is **Santo Tomás de Castillo**, the newest port facility in the country. To look at the concrete plaza, the planned housing and the fenced-off docks, you'd never guess that the place had a moment's history, but oddly enough it's been around for a while. It was originally founded by the Spanish in 1604, who inhabited it with some Black Caribs, the survivors of an expedition against pirates on Roatán Island. The pirates in turn sacked Santo Tomás, but it was revived in 1843, when a Belgian colony was established here. Today it's connected by a regular shuttle of local buses to Puerto Barrios, though other than the docks themselves there's nothing much to see.

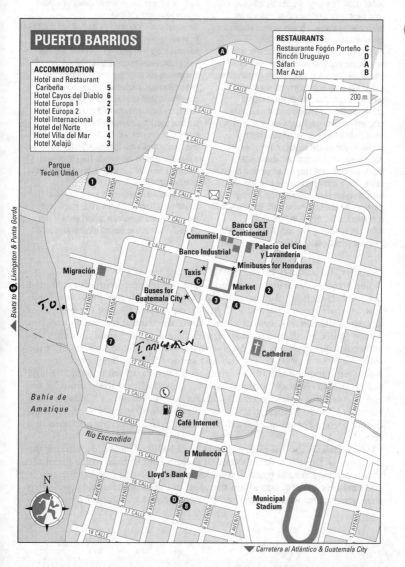

PUERTO BARRIOS

ACCOMMODATION

Hotel and Restaurant Caribeña	5
Hotel Cayos del Diablo	6
Hotel Europa 1	2
Hotel Europa 2	7
Hotel Internacional	8
Hotel del Norte	1
Hotel Villa del Mar	4
Hotel Xelajú	3

RESTAURANTS

Restaurante Fogón Porteño	C
Rincón Uruguayo	D
Safari	A
Mar Azul	B

0   200 m

Parque Tecún Umán

Banco G&T Continental

Comunitel

Banco Industrial

Palacio del Cine y Lavandería

Migración

Taxis

Minibuses for Honduras

Buses for Guatemala City

Market

Cathedral

Bahía de Amatique

Café Internet

Río Escondido

El Muñecón

Lloyd's Bank

Municipal Stadium

N

Carretera al Atlántico & Guatemala City

Boats to 6, Livingston & Punta Gorda

Accommodation

There are few good budget hotels in Puerto Barrios, but in amongst the squalor, there's the odd slice of Caribbean charm. This is a very hot and sticky town so you'll definitely need a fan or a/c in your room.

Amatique Bay Resort and Marina 2km north-east of town centre ☎948 7967, ℻948 7964. New, luxury hotel, set in grassy grounds right on the seafront. Amenities include a fine restaurant, pool and scuba-diving school. ❻

Hotel Caribeña 4 Av between 10 and 11 calles ☎948 0384. This large, friendly place has very good value rooms, with doubles, triples and quadruples available. A quality seafood restaurant, too, which also does cheap breakfasts. ❷

Hotel Cayos del Diablo across the bay, reached by a regular free boat service from the jetty; in Guatemala City ☎333 4633. Lovely Best Western-owned hideaway hotel, discreetly set above a secluded beach. Beautiful thatched cabaña accommodation, swimming pool, a good restaurant, tennis courts and kayaks available for rent. The definitive luxury option on this stretch of coastline, with special packages available. ❻

Hotel Europa 2 3 Av and 12 C ☎948 1292. Ideally placed for the ferry to Lívingston, this is a clean, safe, friendly place where all rooms have fan and private shower. Good prices for single travellers. An almost identical twin, *Hotel Europa 1*, is at 8 Av and 8 C ☎948 0127. Both ❸

Hotel Internacional 7 Av and 16 C ☎948 0367. Very well-priced motel-style set-up, with a small, heat-busting swimming pool. Rooms all have private shower and TV, and come with a choice of either a/c or fan. ❸/❹

Hotel Lee 5 Av & 10 C ☎948 0685. Reasonable choice where the accommodation is spread over several floors, and located just around the corner from the Litegua bus terminal. Some rooms have private bath and TV. ❷/❸

Hotel del Norte 7 C and 1 Av ☎ & ℻948 0087. An absolute gem of a hotel – a magnificent colonial time-warp built entirely from wood. The clap-board rooms aren't especially comfortable or even that private, but there is a nice swimming pool, and the location, overlooking the Caribbean, is magnificent. Best of all is the incredibly classy, mahogany-panelled restaurant and bar – though the food doesn't quite match the decor. ❸–❺

Hotel Villa del Mar 9 C & 7 Av ☎948 1011. Safe and friendly family-run hospedaje positioned above a cafetería close to the market. The fifteen small rooms are bare but serviceable, but only one has a private bath. ❷

Hotel Xelajú 9 C, between 6 and 7 avenidas ☎948 0482. Though it looks a little rough from the outside, this reasonable budget place is safe, has clean rooms, and doesn't allow visiting señoritas. ❷/❸

Eating, drinking and nightlife

When it comes to **eating**, there is an abundance of cheap **comedores** around the market, such as *Cafesama* and *El Punto*, although the *Restaurant Fogón Porteño*, close by on 6 Av and 9 C, has a nicer setting. One of the best places in town is the *Rincón Uruguayo* (closed Mon), where meat is cooked on a giant *parrilla* (grill), South American style, and there are also vegetarian dishes like barbecued spring onions and *papas asados*. It's a ten-minute walk south of the centre at 7 Av and 16 C. For fish and seafood there's plenty of choice: try *Safari*, ten minutes north of the centre on 5 Avenida, which is good, if a little pricey, and serves huge portions; *Mar Azul*, also right on the seafront, at the end of 6 Calle, which is a little cheaper; or *Restaurant La Caribeña*, 4 Av between 10 and 11 calles, which does a superb *caldo de mariscos* (seafood soup). Finally, there is the unique period charm of the *Hotel del Norte* restaurant (see above).

Puerto Barrios also has plenty of **bars**, pool halls and nightclubs, offering the full range of late-night sleaze. None of these is hard to find, with a lot of the action centring around 6 and 7 avenidas and 6 and 7 calles. Merengue, reggae and punta rock are the sounds on the street in Puerto Barrios, and you'll catch a fair selection at weekends in the *Bric a Brac Disco* on 7 C and 7 Av.

There are daily **flights** connecting Puerto Barrios with Guatemala City (1hr; US$54); call Taca (☎334 7722) for more details.

Moving on from Puerto Barrios, there is no Inguat tourist office in town, so you should check at the Litegua terminal for bus schedules. Litegua **pullmans**, some of the country's finest, ply the Carretera al Atlántico to Guatemala City eighteen times daily from 1am to 4pm (5hr). From the capital, buses leave hourly from 6am to 5pm from beside the old train station at 9 Av and 18 C, Zona 1. Tickets for pullmans can be bought in advance, although on the whole it's not necessary. **Second class buses** go from Puerto Barrios to Chiquimula every hour or so from 4am to 4pm: if there's no direct connection take a Guatemala City bus as far as the Río Hondo junction and get a connection there for Copán, Honduras and El Salvador.

From the Muelle Municipal at the end of 12 Calle, a public **ferry** leaves Puerto Barrios for **Lívingston** daily at 10am and 5pm (US$1.40; 90min), returning at 5am and 2pm. Departure times are subject to changes, however, so check them at the dock on arrival if you can. The ferry service is supplemented by a fleet of fast, small **lanchas** which leave when full (generally every 30 minutes or so; US$3; 30min). For Punta Gorda in **Belize**, two boats leave daily at 10am and 2pm (US$11; 1hr 30min) – again, check departure times at the dock beforehand. You have to clear **immigration** before you can buy a ticket, and it's a good idea to do so the day before you ✗ leave. The immigration office is at the end of 9 Calle, two blocks north of the dock (7am–noon & 2–5pm; ☎948 0802); the ticket office is next to the dock. *—bollocks*

4

EAST TO THE CARIBBEAN | On to the coast: Puerto Barrios

Overland to Honduras

Getting to Honduras from Puerto Barrios is now straightforward, and the previous struggle (the "jungle route") through the swamps of the Caribbean coast is no longer necessary. Minibuses depart from the marketplace in Puerto Barrios every half-hour or so between 6.30am and 4.30pm, and head, via the small town of Entre Ríos, to the new Arizona bridge over the Río Motagua (1hr) via a Guatemalan **immigration** point – you may get asked for an unofficial US$1 "exit tax". You then have to catch a pick-up to the border at Corinto inside Honduras a further 8km away, where there's Honduran immigration and plenty of money changers offering fairly reasonable rates. Buses depart from Corinto to Puerto Cortés (3hr 30min) every hour and a half via the pretty village of Omoa. If you set out early from Puerto Barrios, you'll get to San Pedro Sula (see p.390) the same day, and it's certainly possible to make an afternoon flight out to one of the Bay Islands. San Pedro Sula is extremely well connected with Puerto Cortés by Citul buses (every 30min, 5am–7.30pm; 1hr 15min); the Citul terminal is located just across the plaza from immigration. Note that there are plans to construct a joint Guatemalan–Honduran border post close to the Río Motagua in 2002 or 2003, and together with ongoing road improvements inside Honduras, the crossing between the countries should soon be speeded up.

Punta de Manabique

North of Puerto Barrios, the hooked peninsula that juts into the Bahía de Amatique, the **Punta de Manabique**, contains virtually all Guatemala's finest Caribbean beaches and offers superb ecotourism opportunities. Most of the area, covering 66,900 hectares and encompassing the entire coastline around to the border with Honduras, has been designated a nature reserve – managed by the conservation group **Fundary** (see below). It's one of the richest wetland

habitats in Central America and the swamps, mangroves and patches of flooded rainforest are home to caimen, iguana, spider and howler monkeys, peccary
plus a few manatee, some jaguar, tapir and bountiful birdlife. The reserve also
includes over 60,000 hectares of adjacent coastal water and the only coral reef
outcrops in Guatemalan waters.

Around 1,000 people, mainly immigrants from Western Guatemala, eke out
a living in Manabique, surviving by subsistence fishing (mainly for sardines,
which are then salted) and hunting (particularly iguana) and cultivating small
rice paddies. Their livelihood is increasingly under threat from cattle ranchers
who are starting to encroach into the drier lands in the south of the reserve.
Most locals are very poor, and Fundary have been busy establishing basic
health care measures, setting up schools and providing teachers, and raising
environmental awareness. Part of this initiative has been to try and develop
limited **ecotourism** in the area, by establishing a hotel lodge, *El Saraguate* (no
phone, reservations through Fundary, US$8 per bed) which offers basic, clean
dormitory-style accommodation, and a restaurant which serves simple but
excellent meals, including lobster, grilled fish and chicken dishes. From the
lodge there are jungle paths and coastal walks along stunning palm-fringed
white-sand beaches with excellent swimming. Boat trips can also be arranged
along the **Canal Inglés** ("English Channel") – named after British loggers
who dug a ten kilometre trench between Laguna Santa Isabel and the Río
Piteros – which offers superb bird-watching. Local guides can be hired at the
hotel. It's also possible to **camp** (US$3 per person) at the reserve's scientific
research station, which is a kilometre east of the Punta de Manabique in Cabo
Tres Puntos.

To **get to** Manabique, you have two choices. From Puerto Barrios, you first
need to get in touch with Fundary, located on 17 Calle between 5 and 6
avenidas in the town (☎948 0435, ☎ & ℱ948 0944, ℮manabique@intelnet
.net.gt) or at Diagonal 6 17–19 Zona 10, Guatemala City (☎333 4957,
ⓦwww.guate.net/fundarymanabique). They can arrange boats (around US$70
return for up to eight people), the main cost involved in getting to the reserve,
as there are no roads to Manabique. All boats leave from the pier in Puerto
Barrios. Another alternative is to travel to Manabique on a day-trip (around
US$25 per person) from Lívingston, though a minimum of six people is usu-
ally necessary. Tours can be arranged by several travel agents including Exotic
Travel (see opposite) based in the *Bahía Azul* restaurant.

Lívingston and the Río Dulce

North of Puerto Barrios the **Bahía de Amatique** is ringed with a bank of
lush green hills, rising straight out of the Caribbean and coated in tropical rainforest. Halfway between Puerto Barrios and the border with Belize, at the
mouth of the Río Dulce, is **LÍVINGSTON**. Reached only by boat,
Lívingston not only enjoys a superb setting but is also the only **Garífuna** town
in Guatemala, a strange hybrid of Guatemalan and Caribbean culture in which
marimba mixes with Marley. While certainly affected by modernization, this is

also the centre for a number of small and traditional villages strung out along the coast, and it has a powerful atmosphere of its own.

Arrival and information

The only way you can get to Lívingston is **by boat**, either from Puerto Barrios, the Río Dulce, Belize or, occasionally, from Omoa in Honduras. Wherever you come from, you'll arrive at the main dock on the south side of town, where a dreadlocked hotel hustler may greet you – most are not that pushy.

Lívingston is a small place with only a handful of streets, and you can see most of what there is to see in an hour or so. Straight ahead up the hill is the main drag with most of the restaurants, bars and shops, and the **immigration office** (daily 7am–9pm), where you can get an exit stamp if you're heading for Belize or an entrance stamp if you've just arrived, is on the left 300m up the hill. Exotic Travel (℡947 0049, ℮kjchew@hotmail.com), in the same building as the *Bahía Azul* restaurant, and Happy Fish (℡902 7143) just down the road,

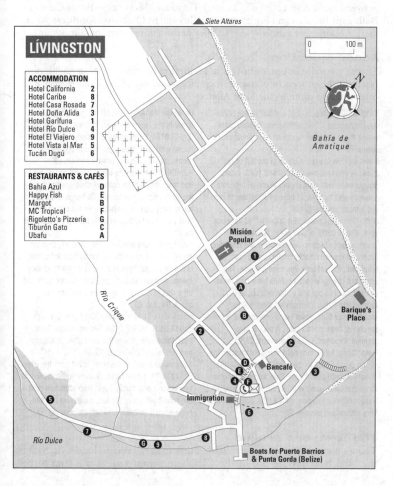

▲ Siete Altares

LÍVINGSTON

0   100 m

ACCOMMODATION
Hotel California	2
Hotel Caribe	8
Hotel Casa Rosada	7
Hotel Doña Alida	3
Hotel Garífuna	1
Hotel Río Dulce	4
Hotel El Viajero	9
Hotel Vista al Mar	5
Tucán Dugú	6

RESTAURANTS & CAFÉS
Bahía Azul	D
Happy Fish	E
Margot	B
MC Tropical	F
Rigoletto's Pizzería	G
Tiburón Gato	C
Ubafu	A

Bahía de Amatique

Río Crique

Misión Popular

Barique's Place

Bancafé

Río Dulce

Immigration

Boats for Puerto Barrios & Punta Gorda (Belize)

are the best **travel agents** in town. The helpful owners of both agencies will arrange a variety of **trips** around the area: up the Río Dulce (US$9); along the coast to the lovely white-sand beach of Playa Blanca (US$10); to the Sapodilla Cayes off Belize (see p.276) for **snorkelling** (US$30); and to the Reserva de Punta Manabique for its beaches and game **fishing** (US$14). All these trips only depart if there are sufficient people; sign up early and be prepared to wait a day or two.

For **changing money**, try the Banco de Comercio, down the road to the left as you walk up the hill from the docks; Bancafé on the main drag; or the Almacen Koo Wong in the centre of town on Sundays. **Telgua** is on the right, up the main street from the docks (daily 7am–midnight), and the **post office** is next door. There are several **internet** facilities in Lívingston try @ or Happy Fish on the main drag, or Explorer Travel which is just west of the dock – rates hover around US$6 an hour.

Scheduled **boats** leave for Puerto Barrios daily at 5am and 2pm (1hr 30min), supplemented by **speedboats**, which leave when full – roughly half-hourly between 6.30am and 5.30pm (25 min). There are also boats to Punta Gorda in **Belize** on Tuesdays and Fridays at 8am (1hr) and to Omoa in **Honduras** when there are sufficient numbers (US$35 per person, min 6 persons; 2hr 30min).

Accommodation

There's a good selection of **hotels** in Lívingston considering its size, with new places in the process of going up, including one next to the *Casa Rosada*, and others on the route to the Siete Altares.

Hotel California turn right just before the *Bahía Azul* restaurant. Clean, vivid green-painted hotel where the reasonable rooms all have private bathrooms. ❷

Hotel Caribe along the shore to the left of the dock, as you face the town ☎ 948 1073. Basic, budget hotel with bare rooms, some with private showers and fans. Avoid downstairs where things get a touch smelly. ❶/❷

Hotel Casa Rosada about 300m left of the dock ☎ & ℻ 947 0303, ℻ 947 0304, ⊛ www .hotelcasarosada.com. Very relaxing and charming American-owned establishment, with a harbourfront plot and lush, spacious grounds. The small but cheery wooden cabins have nice hand-painted touches but are a little overpriced (and lack private bath); alternatively there are very smart duplex bungalows being constructed, all of which will have private bath. A pool is also planned. Excellent vegetarian meals. ❹/❺

Hotel Doña Alida turn right immediately after the *Tucán Dugú*, 250m to the north ☎ & ℻ 947 0027, ℰ hotelalida@hotmail.com. Selection of spacious modern rooms, some with excellent sea views, in a quiet cliffside location, with a little beach below. Very welcoming owners. ❹

Hotel Garífuna turn left off the main street towards the *Ubafu* bar, then first right ☎ 948 1091, ℻ 948 0184. Squeaky-clean, locally owned guest house with good-value, secure and spotless rooms, all with fan and private shower. ❷

Hotel Río Dulce at the top of the hill as you walk into town. Impressive colonial-style wooden building with a newish extension. Go for an upstairs room if you can as the balconies are one of the best places in Lívingston for watching the world go by. ❷

Hotel El Viajero turn left after the dock, past the *Hotel Caribe*. A good choice for backpackers, this is a safe budget hotel with clean if slightly shabby rooms, all with fan and some with private bath, set off a thin strip of garden. There's a shoreside snack bar, too. ❷

Hotel Vista al Mar about 350m left of the dock ☎ 947 0131, ℻ 947 0134. Secure, simple wooden huts, three with private bath, set close to the sea and run by amiable locals. ❷/❸

Tucán Dugú first on the right, uphill from the jetty ☎ 947 0072, ℻ 947 0614, ⊛ www.hoteltucan.com. Lívingston's only luxury hotel, with attractive modern rooms set above the bay, a pleasant bar and restaurant, swimming pool and gardens. ❼/❽

The Town and around

There's not much to do in town itself, other than relaxing in local style. Sadly, the local **beaches** are not of the Caribbean dream variety, and tend to be

strewn with seaweed, but there are plenty of pleasant places to take a swim –
try below the *Hotel Doña Alida* (see above). Everywhere you'll find that the
sand slopes into the sea very gradually. It's best to explore the more isolated
beaches away from town in a group, however, as **attacks** on tourists have been
occasionally reported.

The most popular side trip is to the **Siete Altares**, an imposing series of
waterfalls – much more impressive in the rainy season – 5km northwest of
town. Though incidents have diminished in recent years as police patrols have
increased, you should still not take anything of value; the safest option is to hire
a local guide or visit as part of a **tour** (see below). To **get there** continue down
the street past the *Ubafu* bar and turn right by the *African Place* hotel to the
beach, then follow the sand away from town to the west. After a couple of kilometres, wade across a small river and, just before the beach eventually peters
out, take a path to the left. Follow this inland and you'll soon reach the first of
the falls; to reach the others, scramble up, and follow the water. All of the falls
are idyllic places to swim, but the highest one is the best of all.

Eating and drinking

There are plenty of places to **eat** in Lívingston, two of the best for local food
being *Tiburón Gato* and *Margot's* (where Mama Helén serves up a mean *tapado*).
For a memorable **vegetarian** meal, check out the *Casa Rosada* (see above),
though it's not priced for budget travellers. The *Bahía Azul*, on the main street,
is probably the most popular place in town, with very tasty snacks, decent coffee an excellent terrace for watching Lívingston streetlife – this place also has
a useful noticeboard and a good travel agency. Down in the south side of town,
Rigoletto's Pizzería is pretty authentic and recommended; they also serve vegetarian and Asian dishes. Of the **fried fish** comedores and cookshacks on the
main street, try *Comedor Coni* or the *Lívingston*. For a good **fruit juice**, or a
tropical breakfast, try the *MC Tropical*, opposite the *Río Dulce* hotel.

For evening **entertainment** there are lots of groovy bars, of which *Ubafu* is
usually the most lively, with live drumming and music most night of the week.
There are video movies at the *Black Sheep* next to the *Bahía Azul*, and at
Barique's Place, a dance hall on the beach, you'll hear the deep bass rhythms of
Jamaican reggae and pure Garífuna punta rock.

The Río Dulce

In a few moments we entered the Río Dulce. On each side, rising perpendicularly
from three to four hundred feet, was a wall of living green. Trees grew from the
water's edge, with dense unbroken foliage, to the top; not a spot of barrenness
was to be seen; and on both sides, from the tops of the highest trees, long tendrils
descended to the water, as if to drink and carry life to the trunks that bore them. It
was, as its name imports, a Río Dulce, a fairy scene of Titan land, combining
exquisite beauty with colossal grandeur. As we advanced the passage turned, and
in a few minutes we lost sight of the sea, and were enclosed on all sides by a forest wall; but the river, although showing us no passage, still invited us onward.

John Lloyd Stephens (1841)

Another very good reason for coming to Lívingston is to travel up the **Río
Dulce**, a truly spectacular trip that takes you into the hills behind the town
and eventually brings you to the main road about 30km upriver. The scenery
is the main attraction, but along the way there are several places where you can

stop off for a while. If you really want to do it thoroughly, searching out the river's wildlife or exploring the inlets, then you'll certainly need to rent a boat – you can find them fairly easily in both Lívingston and the town of Río Dulce (see p.276), but make sure that you fix the price (around US$9 per person) and schedule first, so that the boatmen don't try to hurry you.

From Lívingston the river heads into a daunting gorge, between sheer rock faces 100m or so in height. Clinging to the sides is a wall of tropical vegetation and cascading vines, and here and there you might see some white herons or flocks of squawking parakeets. A few kilometres into the gorge there's a spot, known to most boatmen, where warm sulphurous waters emerge from the base of the cliff – a great place for a swim. Afterwards, a friendly spot to stop for fried fish or a snack is the *Restaurante El Viajero*, about level with the mouth of

Garífuna history and culture

The Garífuna trace their history back to the island of **St Vincent**, one of the Windward Islands in the eastern Caribbean. At the time of Columbus' landing in the Americas the islands of the Lesser Antilles had recently been settled by people from the South American mainland, who had subdued the previous inhabitants, the Arawaks. These new people called themselves *Kalipuna*, or *Kwaib*, from which the names *Garífuna,* meaning cassava-eating people, and *Carib* probably derived; St Vincent was then known as Yurimein. The natives the Europeans encountered were descendants of Carib men and Arawak women. A few thousand descendants of the original Caribs still live in Dominica and St Vincent.

In the early seventeenth century Britain, France and the Netherlands vied for control of the islands, fighting each other and the Caribs. The admixture of African blood came in 1635 when two Spanish ships, carrying slaves from Nigeria to their colonies in America, were wrecked off St Vincent and the survivors took refuge on the island. At first there was conflict between the Caribs and the Africans, but the Caribs had been weakened by wars and disease and eventually the predominant race was Black, with some Carib blood, becoming known by the English as the **Black Caribs** – in their language they were *Garinagu*, or *Garífuna*. For most of the seventeenth and eighteenth centuries St Vincent was nominally under British control but in practice it belonged to the Garífuna, and in 1660 with the Treaty of Basse Terre the islands of Dominica and St Vincent were granted "perpetual possession" to the Caribs.

A century later, however, Britain attempted to gain full control of St Vincent, but was driven off by the Caribs, with French assistance. Another attempt twenty years later was more successful, and in 1783 the British imposed a treaty on the Garífuna, allowing them over half of the island. The treaty was never accepted, however, and the Garífuna continued to defy British rule, resulting in frequent battles in which the French consistently lent the Garífuna support. The last serious attempt by the Garífuna to establish their independence took place in 1795, when both sides suffered horrendous casualties. The Garífuna lost their leader, Chief Joseph Chatoyer, and on June 10, 1796, after a year of bitter fighting, the French and Garífuna surrendered to the British.

The colonial authorities could not allow a free Black society to survive amongst slave-owning European settlers, so it was decided to deport the Garífuna population. They were hunted down, their homes (and in the process some of their culture) destroyed, and hundreds died of starvation and disease. The survivors, 4300 Black Caribs and 100 Yellow Caribs, as they were designated by the British, were transported to the nearby island of Balliceaux; within six months over half of them had died, many of yellow fever. In March 1797, the remaining survivors were loaded aboard ships and sent to **Roatán**, one of the Bay Islands, off the coast of Honduras (see p.398). One of the ships was captured by the Spanish and taken to Trujillo, on the mainland, while barely 2000 Garífuna lived to make the landing on Roatán, where the British abandoned them.

the Río Tatín and with great views across the waters. Some boatmen will venture up the Río Tatín, a delightful river tributary, if you ask them, where there's a good new guest house, the *Finca Tatín* (☎902 0831, ⓦwww.geocities.com /fincatatin/index.htm; ➋), set in dense shoreside jungle. Run by hospitable Italians, the four wooden huts are very basic, but the remote, peaceful location is the real draw, and there are kayaks for hire, walking trails to explore, excellent healthy food, and **Spanish classes** available.

Almost opposite is the **Ak'Tenamit Health Centre** (ⓦwww.aktenamit .org), which caters to the needs of around fifty newly established Q'eqchi' Maya villages, whose inhabitants have been driven off the land elsewhere. Until the American Guatemala Tomorrow Fund came to work here, the people had neither schools, medical care, nor much else. Now there is a 24-hour clinic, a

Perhaps in response to pleas for help from the Garífuna, who continued to die on Roatán, the Spanish Commandante of Trujillo arrived and took possession of the island, shipping survivors to Trujillo where they were in demand as labourers. The Spanish had never made a success of agriculture here and the arrival of the Garífuna, who were proficient at growing crops, benefited the colony considerably. The boys were conscripted and the Garífuna men gained a reputation as soldiers and mercenaries. Soon they began to move to other areas along the coast, and in 1802, 150 of them were brought as wood-cutting labourers to southern Belize, from where they moved along the Caribbean coast in to Guatemala.

By the start of the twentieth century, the Garífuna were well established in the Lívingston area, with the women employed in bagging and stacking *cohune* nuts and the men working as fishermen. As in the previous century, the Garífuna continued to travel widely in search of work, and in World War II Garífuna men supplied crews for both British and US merchant ships. Since the 1970s, many have left Central America for the US, and there's now a 50,000-strong population in New York, plus much smaller Garífuna communities in New Orleans, Los Angeles, and even in London. Today most Garífuna live in villages along the Caribbean coast of Honduras (where they number over 100,000) with smaller populations in Belize (around 16,000) and Nicaragua.

Most Garífuna speak Spanish (and some English) plus the unique Garífuna **language** that blends Arawak, French, Yuroba, Banti, and Swahili words. Though virtually all worship at either Catholic or evangelical churches, their Afro-Carib **dugu** (religion) – centred on ancestor worship and comparable in some respects to Haitian voodoo – continues to be actively practised. Dugu is immersed in ritual, and death is seen as the freeing of a spirit, a celebration which involves dancing, drinking and music. Garífuna music, or **punta**, is furiously rhythmic, characterized by mesmeric drum patterns and ritual chanting, and it's very easy to hear its West African origins.

For many Guatemalans, the Garífuna remain something of a national curiosity, a mysterious and somewhat mistrusted phenomenon. They are not only subjected to the same discrimination that plague the Maya population, but also viewed with a strange awe that gives rise to a range of fanciful myths. Uninformed commentators have argued that their society is matriarchal, polygamous, and directed by a secret royal family. Accusations of voodoo and cannibalism are commonplace too, while it's claimed that the women speak a language incomprehensible to the men, passing it on only to their daughters. The prejudices, and the isolated nature of the community – numbering only around 6,000 in Guatemala – mean many young Garífuna are much more drawn to African American (hip hop) and also Jamaican (rastafari) influence rather than Latin culture.

For more on the Garífuna, see the September 2001 feature in the *National Geographic* magazine.

primary school for several hundred children, a new secondary college as well as a self-help programme to train adults in "income generating" crafts. Ecotourism initiatives are also planned. Volunteer doctors, nurses and dentists who can commit themselves for at least one month are very welcome and visitors are invited to take a look around. For more information, see p.49 in "Basics".

After another four kilometres the gorge opens out into a small lake, **El Golfete**, on whose northern shore is the **Biotopo de Chocón Machacas** (daily 7am–4pm; US$5), a government-sponsored nature reserve designed to protect the habitat of the manatee or sea cow, a threatened species that's seen around here from time to time. The manatee is a massive seal-shaped mammal that lives in both sea- and freshwater and, according to some, gave rise to the myth of the mermaid. Female manatees breastfeed their young clutching them in their flippers, but are not as dainty as traditional mermaids, weighing up to a ton. They are exceptionally timid too, so you're unlikely to see one.

The reserve also protects the forest that still covers much of the lake's shore, and there are some specially cut trails where you might catch sight of a bird or two, or if you've plenty of time and patience a tapir or jaguar – if not, you may well encounter a tame monkey kept by one of the reserve workers. The jetty where the boats dock is great to swim from. Visitors are welcome to **camp**, but you'll need to bring your own food and some form of water purification. Alternatively, if you have river transport, you could eat your meals at the *Los Palafitos Restaurant*, just outside the reserve. In a peaceful spot, this comedor does great fish and shrimp meals and sells beers at reasonable prices.

At the western end of the Golfete is another **charity operation**, this one an orphanage for children from the capital, who are often referred here by the judicial system. *Casa Guatemala* is run entirely on donations and with the help of volunteers, who do anything from teach, nurse or instruct in carpentry, sewing or typing. There are up to 150 children of all ages here at any one time and volunteers with the right background, who can stay at least one month (preferably three), are always desperately needed. The work is stressful (starting at 5am daily) and conditions are pretty basic, but for those who can take it, it's time well spent. For contact information see p.49 in "Basics".

Lago de Izabal and around

Heading on upstream, across the Golfete, the river closes in again and passes the marina and bridge at the squalid settlement of **RÍO DULCE TOWN** (sometimes also known as Fronteras), on the northern side of the river. The waterfront away from Río Dulce Town, however, is a favourite playground for wealthy Guatemalans, with boats and hotels that would put parts of California to shame; the shores of **Lago de Izabal** beyond hide increasing numbers of elite properties behind high walls and dense foliage. Here also the road for Petén crosses the river and the boat trip from Lívingston comes to an end.

The very beautiful area along the lush banks of the Río Dulce and Lago de Izabal is fast becoming a tourist destination in its own right, with plenty to keep you occupied for at least a week and a genuinely relaxed atmosphere. A new road around the northern shore of the lake has opened up an interesting route up to the Verapaces (see p.313), passing the idyllic **hot spring waterfall** close to the *Finca El Paraíso* and the towering **Boquerón canyon**. On the western side of the lake, the small town of **El Estor** is an excellent alternative base to explore these sights and the biodiverse wetlands of the **Reserva Bocas**

LAGO DE IZABAL & RÍO DULCE AREA

0   10 km

N

Puerto Cortés
Omoa
Cuyamel
Tegucigalpita
CARIBBEAN SEA
Corinto
SIERRA DEL MERENDÓN
HONDURAS
Finca La Inca
Entre Rios
BIOTOPO PUNTA DE MANABIQUE
Canal Inglés
Laguna Santa Isabel
Puerto Barrios
Santo Tomás
Punta Manabique
Belize (Punta Gorda)
Livingston
Siete Altares
Cayos del Diablo
Cerro San Gil 1267m
CERRO SAN GIL
MONTAÑAS DEL MICO
CARRETERA AL ATLÁNTICO
Morales/Bananera
Río Dulce
BIOTOPO CHOCÓN MACHACAS
El Golfete
Río Chocón Machacas
Cuatro Cayos
Río Dulce
Castillo San Felipe
San Felipe
La Ruidosa Junction
Río Motagua
Poptún & Tikal
Río Sarstún
BELIZE
Modesto Méndez
SIERRA DE SANTA CRUZ
Finca El Paraíso
Denny's Beach
Mariscos
Lago de Izabal
Quiriguá
Quiriguá
Los Amates
Guatemala City
Panzós, Tactic & Cobán
Sebol
El Estor
Boquerón Canyon
RESERVA BOCAS DEL POLOCHIC
Río Polochic
Río Zarquito
RESERVA SIERRA DE LAS MINAS

del Polochic. The new road has now isolated the former ferry hub of **Mariscos**, and neighbouring **Denny's Beach**, on the southern shores of the lake, though you'll have no trouble finding a boatman to take you to either place from Río Dulce. Before you arrange anything, however, ask around about going rates and make sure you fix a price before you set out. The restaurants *Río Bravo* and *Bruno's* or the *Hacienda Tijax* hotel are all good places for gleaning **information**. There's also a useful **website** covering the Río Dulce region, Ⓦ www.mayaparadise.com, with good links and listings.

Practicalities in and around Río Dulce Town

The town of Río Dulce is little more than a truck stop, where traffic for Petén pauses before the long stretch to Flores. Río Dulce is actually the new name given to a couple of older settlements, Fronteras to the north and El Relleno to the south, which have been connected by a monstrous concrete road bridge, obliterating almost any sense of tranquillity in this formerly beautiful area. The road is lined with cheap comedores and stores and you can pick up **buses** here in either direction.

A good **place to stay** for those on a tight budget is *Hotel Backpackers* (Ⓣ 208 1779, Ⓕ 331 9408, Ⓔ casaguatemala@guate.net; ❶–❸), a newish set-up underneath the bridge, on the south side, with dorm beds, private doubles and hammock space. The hotel is owned by the nearby Casa Guatemala children's home, and many of the young staff are former residents. It's a good place to pick up information, and there's a noticeboard detailing yacht crewing opportunities and sailing courses; they also rent canoes. *Hotel Río Dulce*, on the north side of the bridge (Ⓣ 930 3179; ❸), is a comfortable place with spotless double rooms with fans and showers. Very close by, under the bridge, *Bruno's* (Ⓣ 930 5174, Ⓔ rio@guate.net; ❹–❻) offers either modern, comfortable, overpriced rooms with terraces, or less attractive, but cheaper, accommodation; there are also a swimming pool and a bar-restaurant. *Hacienda Tijax*, two minutes by water taxi from the bus stop on the north side of the bridge (Ⓣ 902 0858, Ⓦ www.tijax.com; camping US$2 per person, rooms ❸, cabins ❹, bungalows ❻), is a working teak and rubber farm with a pleasant lakeside plot and tasty, slightly pricey food, as well as hiking trails and horse riding.

As for **restaurants**, *Río Bravo*, on the north side of the bridge, is the best place to meet other travellers (and yachties), eat pizza or pasta and drink the night away – you can also make radio contact with most places around the river and lake from here. *Bruno's* serves up international food and offers the chance to catch up with the latest news and North American sports events – it's very popular with the sailing fraternity; they have **internet** facilities here, too. For cheap grub, there's a strip of pretty undistinguished comedores on the main road close to the bus stop. There are three **banks** in Río Dulce that will change travellers' cheques.

Río Dulce is also the base for **sailing trips**, and most guest houses in town can arrange a tour around the lake with a local boatman. Mornings are the best time for trips, before strong winds whip up dangerous waves later in the day. For the more ambitious, wonderful seven-day adventures on *That*, a nineteen-metre (62ft) trimaran are operated by ATI Divers (Ⓣ & Ⓕ 762 2646, Ⓔ atidivers@yahoo.com) of Santa Cruz, Lago de Atitlán (see p.175); trips leave three times a month, passing through the Río Dulce gorge to the Belize cayes and cost US$390 for snorkellers and US$490 for divers, including all equipment rental, tanks and meals. Alternatively, you can also explore Lago de Izabal's beautiful waterways on four-day sailing excursions (around US$155 per person) aboard John Clarke's 46-foot catamaran. Trips leave every Friday around noon from *Bruno's* bar (see opposite); for more details, contact his Antigua office at 1 Av Sur 11B (☎ & ℱ832 3352, ⓦwww.tikaltravel.com/sailing.htm).

Moving on from Río Dulce, there are buses every half-hour or so to Guatemala City, and to Flores via Poptún until around 6pm. If you're heading towards Puerto Barrios, take the first bus or minibus to La Ruidosa junction (every 30min) and pick up a connection there. Heading to El Estor, there are hourly buses around the lakeshore (1hr 30min) between 6am and 4pm; they all pass the hot springs and Boquerón canyon en route, and some continue on up the Polochic valley towards Cobán and the Verapaces. If you're heading for Lívingston via the Río Dulce gorge, the lancha **boat** captains will quickly find you; services do not run to a fixed schedule but there are several daily (US$10), mostly in the afternoon. Finally, there are **flights** connecting Río Dulce with Guatemala City on Fridays, Saturdays and Sundays. Telephone Taca (☎334 7722) for details, but be warned that cancellations are frequent.

Castillo de San Felipe

Structurally damaged by a large earthquake in July 1997, the **Castillo de San Felipe**, 1km upstream from the bridge, was still closed to visitors at the time of writing, but should reopen in the next few years. Looking like a miniature medieval castle and marking the entrance to Lago de Izabal, the *castillo* is a tribute to the audacity of British pirates, who used to sail up the Río Dulce to raid supplies and harass mule trains. The Spanish were so infuriated by this that they built the fortress to seal off the entrance to the lake, and a chain was strung across the river. If it's open you'll find a maze of tiny rooms and staircases within, plus plenty of canons and panoramic views of the lake.

A kilometre from the castle, close to the waterside village of **SAN FELIPE**, is the *Rancho Escondido* (☎ & ℱ369 2681; ❷–❸), a friendly American–Guatemalan guest house and backpackers' retreat, with hammock space and a restaurant. Even nicer, though a little overpriced, is the nearby *Hotel Vinas del Lago* (☎902 7505, ℱ476 3042; ❼), which offers great views across the lake from its several terraces and also has its own private beach. Both places will come and pick you up if you call or radio from the *Río Bravo* or *Bruno's*.

The hot spring waterfall and Boqueron canyon

Beyond the *castillo*, the broad sweep of Lago de Izabal opens before you, with great views of the fertile highlands beyond the distant shores. Some 25km from Río Dulce, the **hot spring waterfall** (daily 8am–6pm; US$0.65), 300m north of the road, is one of Guatemala's most remarkable natural phenomena. Bathtub-temperature spring water cascades into pools cooled by a separate chilly flow of fresh river water, creating a sublime steamy spa-like environment where it's easy to soak and bathe away an afternoon. Above the waterfall is a series of caves whose interiors are crowded with extraordinary shapes and colours – made even more memorable by the fact that you have to swim by torchlight to see them (bring your own flashlight). Two kilometres south of the waterfall, the *Finca el Paraíso* **hotel** (☎949 7122; ❺/❻) sits on the waterfront, with two rows of large, comfortable, but rarely occupied cabañas and a reasonably good, if pricey, restaurant. The hotel enjoys a delightfully peaceful location and there's good swimming from the black-sand beach. Buses and pick-ups between Río Dulce and El Estor pass the hot springs and hotel hourly in both directions.

Continuing west along the lakeshore it's a further 7km to the **Boquerón canyon**, completely hidden yet just 500m from the road. Near-vertical cliffs soar to over 250m above the Río Sauce which flows through the bottom of the startling jungle-clad gorge, the river bed plotted with colossal boulders. To see Boquerón, you'll have to employ Hugo, a campesino–cum–boatman who lives at the base of the canyon, at the end of a signposted track from the main road, who will paddle you upstream in his logwood canoe for a small fee. The return trip takes around thirty minutes, though it's possible to continue exploring Boquerón – which extends for a further 5km – on foot if you have sturdy footwear and enjoy a scramble.

El Estor

Heading west beyond Boquerón, it's just 6km to the sleepy lakeside town of **EL ESTOR**, allegedly named by English pirates who came up the Río Dulce to buy supplies at "The Store". It's an easy-going, friendly place which was briefly energized in the mid-1960s, prompted by a chance discovery of high-grade nickel deposits, by the International Nickel Company of Canada, which then built and developed the mine and processing plant. After thirteen years of study and delay the plant opened in 1977, functioned for a couple of years at reduced capacity, and was then shut down as a result of technical problems and the plummeting price of nickel. Today the great, ghost-like structure stands deserted just west of the town, surrounded by the prefabricated huts that would have housed its workforce. El Estor itself settled back into provincial stupor after the mine closed down, but is now undergoing a minor revival, at the centre of a regional development boom. Fresh farmlands are being opened up all the time, and the new road to Río Dulce town is bringing in a steady trickle of travellers.

Apart from the pool in the plaza, which harbours fish, turtles and alligators, there's not a lot to see in El Estor itself. However, the town does have a friendly, relaxed atmosphere, particularly in the warmth of the evening when the streets are full of activity, and you could easily spend a few days exploring the surrounding area – including the hot spring waterfall, the Boquerón canyon and Bocas del Polochic – much of which remains undisturbed. For now, however, El Estor remains off the main tourist trail, though there's much local expectation that the town can begin to capitalize on the vast ecotourism potential of the region.

The best contacts for **tours** of the area are Hugo at *Hugo's Restaurant*, or Oscar Paz, who runs the *Hotel Vista del Lago* and is an enthusiastic promoter of the area, who will arrange a boat and guide to explore any of the surrounding countryside, go fishing in the lake or visit the hot springs at *Finca Paraíso*. There are **bikes** to rent at 6 Av 4–26.

Accommodation

Considering the size of the place, there's an excellent choice of quality budget and mid-range **hotels**, much of it excellent value. There's nothing at the top end of the scale.

Hospedaje Santa Clara 5 Av 2–11 ℡948 7244. Owned by the same family as the *Hotel Central*. Very economical place with a warren of basic, clean rooms, some with private bath. ❶ /❷

Hotel Central 5 Av & 2 C, ℡949 7244. Just north of the plaza, this is an excellent deal, with pleasant, spotless modern rooms, each with private bath and fan. An upstairs terrace overlooks the square. ❷

Hotel Ecológico Cabañas del Lago on the lakeshore, 1km west of the centre ℡ & ℻949 7245. In a prime, tranquil lakeside plot, with a private little black-sand beach, these bungalows are very comfortable, spacious and attractive. Hugo, the owner, will take you there if you drop in at his restaurant in the plaza. ❹

Hotel Villela 6 Av 2–06 (no phone). A block from the lakeshore, this is a decent budget deal, with rooms, some with private shower, surrounding a pretty garden. ❷

Hotel Vista del Lago by the lakeside, 2 blocks south of the plaza ℡949 7205. The most atmospheric hotel in town, a beautiful colonial-style wooden building by the dock, claimed by the owners to be the original store that gave the town its name. It offers clean rooms with private bath, the second-floor ones boasting superb views of the lake. The irrepressible owner, Oscar Paz, runs tours of the lake and region. ❸

Posada de Don Juan On the east side of the plaza (no phone). Large rooms, some with new beds and fans, set around a grassy courtyard, with well-maintained bathrooms. ❷

Eating and entertainment

For good, inexpensive snacks and breakfasts try the friendly, clean *Cafetería Santa Clave*, three blocks west of the plaza at 3 C 7–75, or *Hugo's Restaurant*, on the main plaza, for more substantial steaks and burgers. At the lakeside *Restaurant Chaabil* you'll pay extra for the location and they don't serve alcohol, but the fish is good. There's a great **pool hall** just south of the plaza at 2 C and 5 Av where you can play for less than a dollar an hour. Its enthusiastic DJ-minded owner lets rip a frighteningly eclectic mix of rock, pop and dance from colossal speakers most nights. Some 300m east of the *Hotel Vista del Lago*, the Cine Video Allan shows Hollywood **movies** at weekends.

Reserva Bocas del Polochic

Encompassing a substantial slice of lowland jungle on the west side of the lake, the **Bocas del Polochic** nature reserve is one of the richest wetland habitats in Guatemala. The green maze of swamp, marsh and forest harbours at least 224 different species of birds, including golden-fronted woodpeckers, Aztec parakeets and keel-billed toucans. It's also rich in mammals, including howler monkeys, which you're virtually guaranteed to see (and hear), plus rarely encountered manatees and tapirs. There's good accommodation next to the tiny Q'eqchi' village of **SELEMPÍM** in the heart of the reserve – the large mosquito-screened wooden house with bunk beds (US$12 per person per day including three substantial meals) provides villagers with employment. Locals also lead guided walks up into the foothills of the Sierra de Las Minas and conduct kayak tours of the river delta. The drawback is that visitors wanting to get to the reserve have to pay for the fuel costs of the lancha boat – there's no road system. This can amount to US$35 for a day-trip, or as much as US$80 (return) to get to Selempím, though costs are reduced considerably if you can get a group together. To **get to** the reserve contact Defensores de la Naturaleza at 5 Av and 2 C, El Estor (☎949 7237, ✉rbocas@defensores.org.gt), which organize excellent tours into the heart of the refuge and manage the accommodation at Selempím. To visit the zone nearest to El Estor, contact Hugo or Oscar in El Estor (see above), both of whom run good excursions.

Mariscos and Denny's Beach

MARISCOS, the main town on the south side of Lago de Izabal, now sees very few visitors since the road was completed around the northern shore of the lake. In its day, however, it was an important stopping-off point, where travellers heading for the capital would disembark and continue overland. Nowadays there's no longer a ferry service to El Estor, though the odd lancha boat (1hr; US$3.50) does cover the route when enough passengers can be amassed. It's pretty much a one-street town, with cheap, scruffy hotels, a police station, a pharmacy, and a well-stocked supermarket at the pier. One direct bus a day runs from Guatemala City to Mariscos, departing at 2pm from outside the train station at 18 C and 9 Av, returning at 6am. At other times take any bus along the Carretera al Atlántico, ask to be dropped at La Trinchera, and a pick-up will take you from there to Mariscos. If you have **to stay** in Mariscos, the best place is *Hotel Karinlinda* (❷), where some rooms have private bathrooms, or the more basic but still pretty clean *Hospedaje Los Almendras* (❶).

If you're craving a good swim, you can't do better than head for **Denny's Beach**, a ten-minute boat ride from the pier at Mariscos. It's an ideal place to get away from it all with nice cabañas above the sandy beach (no phone; VHF 63; ❸); you can also camp or sling a hammock (both US$2 per person). The open-air bar and restaurant are a little pricey, so bring as many provisions as you can with you. If you call or radio Dennis Gulck, the owner, someone will come and get you from Mariscos, or you could barter with a boatman in Río Dulce.

The eastern highlands

The eastern end of the highlands, connecting Guatemala City with El Salvador, ranks as the least-visited part of the entire country. In this stronghold of right-wing politics the population is almost entirely Latinized, speaking Spanish and wearing Western clothes, although many are by blood pure Maya. Only in a couple of isolated areas do the people still speak Poqomam, the region's indigenous language, which is closely related to Q'eqchi', the language spoken around Cobán. The ladinos of the east have a reputation for behaving like cowboys, and violent demonstrations of macho pride are common.

The landscape lacks the immediate appeal of the western highlands. Not only are its peaks lower, but its features are generally less clearly defined. The volcanoes, unlike the neatly symmetrical cones of the west, are badly eroded, merging with the lower-lying hills. But the lower altitude does have a positive side: the hills are that much more fertile, and the broad valleys are lush with vegetation, similar in many ways to the highlands of El Salvador.

On the whole you're unlikely to head in this direction unless you're on your way to the border with El Salvador, in which case your best bet is to travel directly to **San Salvador** by pullman. It's a route that takes you through the southern side of the eastern highlands, and several companies can get you from one capital to the other in little over five hours. If, however, you decide to explore this part of the country, the best route takes you right through the central area, from **Jutiapa** to **Jalapa**, and then east to **Esquipulas**; near here, you'll find the spectacular volcanic crater lake of **Ipala** which can be climbed in just two hours. The roads are poor in this region but the scenery along the way is superb, taking you across vast valleys and over great ranges of hills.

Alternatively, you can head into the northern side of the eastern highlands, along a good road that branches off the Carretera al Atlántico and connects the towns of **Zacapa**, **Chiquimula** and Esquipulas. From here you can either head on into El Salvador, or make a short trip to the ruins of Copán in Honduras, the very best of the southern Maya sites. The landscape out this way is very different, with dry hills and dusty fields, but once again the population is very urban and Latinized.

From Guatemala City to El Salvador

Although there are several possible routes between the capital and the El Salvadorean border, it's the highland route, passing through Cuilapa, that draws the most traffic. This is not only the fastest connection between the two countries but also offers the most spectacular scenery, weaving through a series of lush valleys. The highway leaves Guatemala City through the southern suburbs of Zona 10, and climbs steeply out of the city, passing the hillside villas of the wealthy. It then reaches a high plateau from where you get a good view of the eastern side of the Pacaya volcano, its cone spraying out rocks and smoke. There are few towns out this way: the only place before **CUILAPA**, some 70km from the capital, is the small roadside settlement of Barberena. Cuilapa's claim to fame is that it is supposedly the very "centre of the Americas" – this doesn't, however, make it an especially interesting place to stop. There are a couple of hotels if you get stuck, including the very pleasant *Turicentro Los Esclavos* (℡ 886 5139, ℗ 886 5158; ❸) on the highway, 4km beyond Cuilapa, where there's a small pool, and good café-restaurant and spotless rooms with TV and fridge. Right next to the hotel is a sixteenth-century stone bridge, one of the oldest in Central America, though it's now dwarfed by an adjacent modern steel replacement. South of Cuilapa, a branch road heads through stunning scenery, between the peaks of Volcán Tecuamburro and Volcán Cruz Quemada to the town of **Chiquimulilla** (buses every hour or so; see p.251).

Eleven kilometres beyond Cuilapa the highway splits at the **El Molino junction**. The southern fork, highway CA8, is the most direct route to the border, heading straight for the crossing at **VALLE NUEVO**, less than 50km away. This road is straight, fast and scenic, but the border crossing is little more than a customs post and there's nowhere to stay when you get there or on the way.

The northern fork, CA-1, is the continuation of the **Carretera Interamericana** (Panamerican Highway). This road is much slower, as it passes through most of the main towns and is served only by second-class buses, but it's also considerably more interesting. If you're heading directly for El Salvador, the southern branch is the one to stick with, and if you wait at the junction a pullman for San Salvador will turn up sooner or later.

The Carretera Interamericana: Jutiapa

Heading west from El Molino, the Carretera Interamericana turns towards the mountains, running through an isolated valley of sugar cane, then climbing onto a high plateau. Here the landscape is more characteristic of the eastern highlands, with its open valleys and low ridges overshadowed by huge eroded volcanoes.

Bypassing the small town of Quesada, the road arrives at **JUTIAPA**. The centre of trade and transport for the entire eastern region, this is a busy and not particularly attractive place, with a steady stream of buses to and from the border and the capital, and to all other parts of the east, from Jalapa to Esquipulas. If you need **to stay**, there are plenty of places to choose from including the clean *Posada de Peregrino* at C 15 de Septiembre 0–30 (℡ 855 1770, ❸), and if you need to **change money** there is a branch of the Banco del Ejército on 5 Calle.

Hourly **buses** pass through Jutiapa heading for the border and for Guatemala City, pulling in at the bus terminal right in the middle of town. Jutiapa is also the starting point for a trip across the eastern highlands to Chiquimula or Esquipulas. The quickest route takes you directly to Esquipulas, through Ipala, and buses from Jutiapa head this way. But if you'd rather take your time and see the best of this part of the country then take a bus to Jalapa, spend the night there, and then press on to Chiquimula.

Asunción Mita and the border at San Cristóbal

Heading on from Jutiapa towards the border with El Salvador the Panamerican Highway runs through El Progreso, where the roads to Jalapa and to Ipala (for the direct route to Chiquimula or Esquipulas) branch off to the north. Beyond here the road drops into yet another vast open valley, and arrives at the small town of **ASUNCIÓN MITA**, 45 minutes from Jutiapa and thirty minutes from the border. Despite its jaded appearance, Asunción has a considerable past: founded, according to Maya records, in 1449, and captured by the Spanish in 1550, it was an important staging post on the royal route to Panamá in colonial times. Nowadays, its only real significance is as the last town before the border; if you arrive in the evening it's easiest to stay the night and cross into El Salvador the next day.

Archeology enthusiasts might want to visit the **ruins** about 4km to the east of Asunción Mita along the main road – opposite the INDECA building. There's not much to see, but if you rummage around in the fields you should be able to find a series of small mounds, which according to legend were built as a monument to Quetzalcoatl by an old man and a young girl who rose out of a lake.

A stream of buses and minibuses connect Asunción Mita with the **border**, 21km south. The actual crossing point is marked by the small town of **SAN CRISTÓBAL**, where you'll find a couple of basic pensiones (❶–❷) and an Inguat desk. The last **bus** for Guatemala City leaves the border at around 5pm, and the last minibus for Asunción Mita leaves at around 6pm.

Jalapa to Ipala

Any trip through the eastern highlands should include the road **between Ipala and Jalapa**, which takes you through some truly breathtaking scenery. This is not actually on the way to anywhere, and it's a fairly long and exhausting trip, but if you've had enough of the tourist overkill of the western highlands and don't mind a bumpy ride, then it makes a refreshing change.

From Jutiapa direct buses run to Jalapa, passing over the shoulder of the Volcán Tahual and through a huge bowl-shaped valley, thick with fields of sugar cane, tobacco and maize. The main towns along the way are **Monjas** and **Morazán**, two busy agricultural centres. **JALAPA** itself is a prosperous but isolated town, resting on a high plateau in the heart of the eastern highlands and surrounded by low peaks and cattle pasture. Set away from all the major roads, its busy bus terminal links all the area's smaller towns and villages. Chances are that you'll arrive here fairly late and have **to stay** the night; not a bad prospect as the *Hotel Casa del Viajero*, at 1 Av 0–70 (☎922 4086; ❷/❸), is a great place: charming, friendly and relaxed, with a good restaurant and rooms with or without bath and TV. If it's full, try *Hotel Méndez*, at 1 C A 1–27 (☎922 4835; ❷), overlooking the bus terminal. The town also has several **banks**, including the Banco Reformador at 1 C 0–98 (Mon–Fri 8.30am-7pm, Sat 8.30–3pm) and the G&T Continental at 1 Av 1–66 (Mon–Fri 9am–7pm, Sat 9am–1pm). The best place to eat in town is the *Restaurante Casa Real* on 1 Calle where they serve huge salads, soups and grilled meats; or try *Antojitos Acuarios* opposite for a cheaper feed.

A paved road runs from Jalapa to **Sanarate**, on the Carretera al Atlántico – much the fastest route back to the capital. Alternatively, there's a very rough road to Guatemala City via Mataquesquintla and San José Pinula – only recommended to the hardy and patient as it takes a full day.

Buses run hourly from Jalapa to Guatemala City from 3am until 4pm via Jutiapa, and until 5pm via Sanarate. Coming from Guatemala City, buses to Jalapa via Sanarate leave from 22 C 1–20, Zona 1, between 4am and 6pm, a journey of just over three hours. Buses leave Jalapa for Chiquimula (6hr) via Ipala every ninety minutes from 5am to 2.30pm.

San Luis Jilotepéque and Ipala

Heading on from Jalapa towards Chiquimula and Esquipulas the road climbs into the hills for the most beautiful section of the entire trip, leading up onto a high ridge with superb views, and then dropping down to the isolated villages of San Pedro Pinula and **SAN LUiS JILOTEPÉQUE**, two outposts of Maya culture. The plaza of San Luís is particularly impressive, with two massive ceiba trees, a colonial church, and a couple of replica stelae from Copán – and on Sundays it's the scene of a vast Maya market. There are three fairly basic pensiones.

Fourteen kilometres beyond San Luís, this back road joins the main road from Jutiapa at **IPALA**. This is an important crossroads, from where buses run to Jutiapa to the south, Jalapa in the west, Chiquimula to the north and Esquipulas in the east. The village itself is a pretty forlorn place with a few shops and a couple of **hotels**, the best of which is the basic *Hotel Ipala Real* (☎923 7107; ❷), where the rooms have cable TV and (very) en-suite showers and toilets. Alternatively, try the basic, pretty dirty-but-cheap *Hospedaje Ipaleco* (❶).

Ipala is built on an open plain at the base of the **Ipala volcano** (1650m), which looks more like a rounded hill. The cone, inactive for hundreds of years, is now filled by a beautiful little **crater lake** ringed by dense tropical forest, and is similar in many ways to the cone of Chicabal near Quezaltenango. The lake is said to contain a unique species of the mojarra fish, which apparently has six prominent spines on its back. It's beautifully peaceful up here and the shores of the lake, which you can walk around in a couple of hours, make a wonderful place to **camp**, though you'll have to bring all your own supplies.

You can climb the volcano from Ipala, via the Finca El Paxte, a distance of around 10km, but the easiest ascent (2hr) is from the south, setting out from close to the village of **Agua Blanca**, a moustache-and-cowboy-hat kind of place. If you're in your own transport, head for the tiny settlement of Sauce, at km 26.5 on the Ipala to Agua Blanca road, park by the small tienda and follow the dirt track up to the summit. By public transport, take a bus from the Zona 4 bus terminal in Guatemala City to Agua Blanca: buses leave at 5am, 7am and noon, returning at 3am, 6am and noon.

The north: Zacapa, Chiquimula and Esquipulas

What is true of the entire eastern highlands is particularly true of the string of towns that runs along the northern side of the mountains. Here eastern machismo is at its most potent and hardly anyone lives outside the towns. The vast majority of the population are ladinos, and furiously proud of it, with a reputation for quick tempers, warm hearts and violent responses. The trio of **Zacapa**, **Chiquimula** and **Esquipulas** are the most accessible towns in the eastern highlands, with a good road and fast bus service from the capital. They also offer access to two particularly interesting sites: the Maya ruins at **Copán** (see p.383) over the border in Honduras, and the shrine of the **Black Christ** in Esquipulas.

The direct road branches off the Carretera al Atlántico at the Río Hondo junction, running through dry, dusty hills to Zacapa, and on through Chiquimula and Esquipulas to the three-way border with Honduras and El Salvador. Before Zacapa the road passes the small, remote town of **ESTANZUELA**, which, oddly enough, has its own museum of paleontology, **El Museo de Paleontología Bryan Patterson** (daily 8am–5pm; free), dedicated to an American scientist who worked in the area for many years. The exhibits, which include the fossil of a blue whale, manatee bones, a giant armadillo shell, and the entire skeleton of a mastodon said to be some fifty thousand years old, are equally unexpected. There are also some more recent pieces such as a small Maya tomb, transported here from a site 66km away, and in the basement some copies of Copán stelae and one or two originals. The museum has a certain amateur charm and is well worth a look if you have half an hour to spare. To get here take any bus between El Rancho and Zacapa – including all the buses heading between Guatemala City and Esquipulas – ask the driver to drop you at the village, and simply walk straight through it for ten minutes, along the main street.

Zacapa

Just 13km from the Río Hondo junction, **ZACAPA** is reached from the main road by twin bridges across the Río Grande. In the dry months this is one of the hottest towns in the country, with maximum temperatures of 35–40°C. Its atmosphere is dominated by two things: ladino culture and the surrounding desert, which is irrigated to produce tobacco. The town is also famous for its rum – Ron Centenario Zacapa, the finest in Central America – and quesadilla cheesecake. There's not much to do in Zacapa, although it's pleasant enough, with a large, busy market, and some hot springs a few kilometres to the south. The town itself stretches out between the old train station and the plaza, a relaxed, tree-lined spot, that boasts some of the finest public toilets in Guatemala. The plaza is also where you'll find the Banco G&T Continental (Mon–Fri 9am–7pm, Sat 9am–1pm), which will cash travellers' cheques, and the **post office** (Mon–Fri 8am–4.30pm); the **Telgua** office is nearby on 5 Calle (daily 7am–midnight). There are two **hotels** of note: the good value, eccentric Chinese-run *Hotel Wong*, 6 C 12–53 (**②**), where the rooms come with or without private bathrooms, and the vast, chintzy *Hotel Miramundo*, 17 Av 5–41, Zona 3 (**T**941 2674, **F**941 0157; **④**), whose rooms have air-conditioning and TV. Zacapa has something approaching an epidemic of Chinese **restaurants**, most of which offer only fair food at inflated prices (around US$5 a meal): the *Po Wing*, on the plaza, is a reasonable option and has an ice-cream parlour attached.

The **bus** terminal in Zacapa is a kilometre or so from the centre; take a local bus if you don't want to walk. From the terminal, buses leave hourly for Guatemala City, Chiquimula and Esquipulas. There are also minibuses that run between the junction at El Rancho and all of the towns out this way: in Zacapa pick them up on 13 Av between 6 and 7 calles, near the *Hotel Wong*; they don't run to any timetable but departures are regular. Coming from Guatemala City there are plenty of buses to Zacapa from the Zona 1 terminal at 19 C and 9 Av.

△ Río Dulce

The hot springs of Santa Marta

The one good reason for stopping off in Zacapa is to take a trip to the **Aguas Thermales Santa Marta**, four or five kilometres south of town. There are no buses out this way so you'll either have to walk (you might be able to hitch some of the way) or go by taxi (around US$3 one way). To get to the hot springs on foot, walk up the street to the right of the church in Zacapa's plaza, past the Banco G&T Continental. After four blocks you come to a small park where you want to take the first left, then the next right and then another left. This brings you onto a track that heads out of town across a small river – stick with this track as it continues through the fields and after about 3km it will start to drop into another small valley. Just as it does so take the left-hand fork, at the end of which you'll find the baths – if you get lost, just ask for *los baños*.

The bathing rooms are set off a small courtyard built in a vaguely colonial style. Inside each room there's a huge tiled tub, filled with naturally heated water and a couple of beds. The tubs cost US$5 to hire, for as many people as you want to fit in, and the very friendly owner Rolando also sells beers, soft drinks and snacks. It's a superbly relaxing experience, sending you to the brink of sleep – if not beyond.

Chiquimula

From Zacapa the main road continues towards the border, heading up over a low pass and into a great open valley. Set to one side of this is the town of **CHIQUIMULA**, an ugly, bustling ladino stronghold. This is the largest of the three northern towns and its huge plaza, shaded by ceiba trees, is permanently congested by the coming and going of assorted traffic. There's little to see here other than a massive ruined colonial **church**, the Iglesia Vieja, on the eastern side of town. Damaged in the 1765 earthquake and left behind as the town has shifted over the years, it retains an impressive Baroque facade.

As Chiquimula is the starting point for routes to Copán in Honduras and back through Ipala to Jalapa, you might well end up **staying**. If so, *Pensión Hernández* at 3 C 7–41 (T & F 942 0708, hotelh@guate.net; ❷/❸) is the first place to try, with plenty of very clean, simple rooms, all with fan and some with TV and private shower. It has safe parking, a small pool and the owner speaks good English. A little further down the road, at 3 C 8–30, *Hotel Central* (T 942 6352; ❸) has five pleasant rooms all with private bath and cable TV, while *Pensión España*, at 3 C 7–81 (❶), is very cheap and basic. A couple of blocks south from here, *Hotel Posada Don Adán* at 8 Av 4–30 (T 942 0549; ❸) is comfortable, if old-fashioned; most of its eighteen large rooms have a/c and cable TV and there's parking here, too.

When it comes to **eating**, there are plenty of good, inexpensive comedores in and around the **market**, which is centred on 3 C and 8 Av, as well as *Magic Burger* and *Cafe Paíz*, both on 3 Calle, for predictable fast food and good fruit juices. For something a little more ambitious, try *Bella Roma*, 7 Av 5–31, which specializes in pizza and pasta. *Las Vegas*, on 7 Avenida off the plaza, with fairly high prices and garish decor, is where the town's upwardly mobile gather – you can forget the cocktails here, but the food's reasonable. Otherwise the only evening entertainment in Chiquimula is at the Cine Liv on the plaza.

For **changing money** there's a branch of the Banco G&T Continental at 7 Av 4–75 (Mon–Fri 9am–7pm, Sat 10am–2pm) and a Bancafé on the north side of the plaza (Mon–Fri 9am–7pm, Sat 9.30am–1.30pm) with an ATM that accepts Visa cards. You can also cash dollars safely at Azujey, the largest of the sombrero shops in the daily market, which is always worth a browse in its own right for its kitsch selection of cowboy gear and leatherware. There's an **internet** café, *Email Center,* at 6 Av 4–51 (daily 9am–9pm), and Telgua is on the corner of the plaza (daily 7am–midnight). The **bus terminal** is at 1A C, between 10 and 11 avenidas, midway between the plaza and the highway; buses to Guatemala City (3hr 30min) and Esquipulas (1hr) leave every half-hour, and hourly to Puerto Barrios (1hr) until 3pm. There are also hourly buses to Jalapa (3hr), via Ipala, from 5am to 6pm, and to the border at El Florido (1hr 30min), for Copán in Honduras until 4.30pm.

Esquipulas

We returned to breakfast, and afterwards set out to visit the only object of interest, the great church of the pilgrimage, the Holy Place of Central America. Every year, on the fifteenth of January, pilgrims visit it, even from Peru and Mexico; the latter being a journey not exceeded in hardship by the pilgrimage to Mecca. As in the east, "it is not forbidden to trade during the pilgrimage", and when there are no wars to make the roads unsafe eighty thousand people have assembled among the mountains to barter and pay homage to "our Lord of Esquipulas".

John Lloyd Stephens (1841)

The final town on this eastern highway is **ESQUIPULAS**, which, now as in Stephens' day, has a single point of interest; it is almost certainly the most important Catholic shrine in Central America. Arriving from Chiquimula the bus winds through the hills, beneath craggy outcrops and forested peaks, emerging suddenly at the lip of a huge bowl-shaped valley centring on a great open plateau. On one side of this, just below the road, is Esquipulas itself. The place is entirely dominated by the four perfectly white domes of the church, brilliantly floodlit at night: beneath these the rest of the town is a messy sprawl

The Esquipulas pilgrimage

The history of the **Esquipulas pilgrimage** probably dates back to before the Conquest, when the valley was controlled by Chief Esquipulas. Even then it was the site of an important religious shrine, perhaps connected with the nearby Maya site of Copán. When the Spanish arrived the chief was keen to avoid the normal bloodshed and chose to surrender without a fight; the grateful Spaniards named the city they founded at the site in his honour. The famed colonial sculptor Quirio Cataño was commissioned to carve an image of Christ for the church constructed in the middle of the new town, and in order to make it more likely to appeal to the local people he chose to carve it from balsam, a dark wood. Another version has it that Cataño was hired by the Maya after one of their number had seen a vision of a dark Christ on this spot. In any event the image was installed in the church in 1595 and soon accredited with miraculous powers. But things really took off in 1737 when the bishop of Guatemala, Pardo de Figueroa, was cured of a chronic ailment on a trip to Esquipulas. The bishop ordered the construction of a new church, which was completed in 1758, and had his body buried beneath the altar.

While all this might seem fairly straightforward, it doesn't explain why this figure has become the most revered in a country full of miracle-working saints. One possible explanation is that it offers the Maya, who until recently dominated the pilgrimage, a chance to combine pre-Columbian and Catholic worship. It's known that the Maya pantheon included several Black deities such as Ek Ahau, the black lord, who was served by seven retainers, and Ek'Chuach, the tall black one, who protected travellers. When Aldous Huxley visited the shrine in 1934 his thoughts were along these lines: "So what draws the worshippers is probably less the saintliness of the historic Jesus than the magical sootiness of his image... numinosity is in inverse ratio to luminosity."

of cheap hotels, souvenir stalls and overpriced restaurants. The pilgrimage, which continues all year, has generated numerous sidelines, creating a booming resort where people from all over Central America come to worship, eat, drink and relax, in a bizarre combination of holy devotion and indulgence.

The principal day of **pilgrimage**, when the religious significance of the shrine is at its most potent, is January 15. Even the smallest villages will save enough money to send a representative or two on this occasion, their send-off and return invariably marked by religious services. These plus the thousands who can afford to come in their own right ensure that the numbers attending are still as high as in Stephens' day, filling the town to bursting and beyond. Buses chartered from all over Guatemala choke the streets, while the most devoted pilgrims arrive on foot (some dropping to their knees for the last few kilometres). There's a smaller pilgrimage annually on March 9, and faithful crowds visit year-round. The town has also played an important role in modern-day politics: it was here that the first **peace accord** initiatives to end the civil wars in El Salvador, Nicaragua and Guatemala were signed in 1987.

Inside the **church** today there's a constant scurry of hushed devotion amid clouds of smoke and incense. In the nave pilgrims approach the image on their knees, while others light candles, mouth supplications or simply stand in silent crowds. The image itself is most closely approached by a separate, side entrance

Fiestas

January
El Progreso (near Jutiapa) kicks off the fiesta year in the eastern highlands. The action lasts from the 12th to 15th; the final day is the most important. **Cabañas** (near Zacapa) has a fiesta from the 19th to 21st, in honour of San Sebastián; the 19th is the main day. **Ipala**'s fiesta, which includes some traditional dances and bullfighting, is from the 20th to 26th: the 23rd is the main day. There's also the great pilgrimage to **Esquipulas** on the 15th.

February
San Pedro Pinula, one of the most traditional places in the east, has a fiesta from the 1st to 4th, in which the final day is the main one. **Monjas** has a fiesta from the 5th to 10th, with the 7th as the main day. **Río Hondo** (on the main road near Zacapa) has its fiesta from the 24th to 28th; the 26th is the principal day. Both **Pasaco** (in the department of Jutiapa) and **Huite** (near Zacapa) have moveable fiestas around carnival time.

March
Jeréz (in the department of Jutiapa) has a fiesta in honour of San Nicolas Tolentino from the 3rd to 5th, with the last day as the main one. There's a smaller day of pilgrimage to the Black Christ of Esquipulas on the 9th. **Moyuta** (near Jutiapa) and **Olapa** (near Chiquimula) both have fiestas from the 12th to 15th. **Morales**, a town with little to celebrate but its lust for life, has a fiesta from the 15th to 21st, with the main day on the 19th. **Jocotán** (halfway between Chiquimula and El Florido) has a moveable fiesta in March.

April
April is a quiet month in the east but **La Unión** (near Zacapa) has a fiesta from the 22nd to 25th.

where you can join the queue to shuffle past beneath it and pause briefly in front before being shoved on by the crowds behind. Back outside you'll find yourself among swarms of souvenir and relic hawkers, and pilgrims who, duty done, are ready to head off to eat and drink away the rest of their stay. Many pilgrims also visit a set of nearby **caves**, Las Cuevas de las Minas (US$0.40), a ten-minute walk south of the basilica, said to have miraculous powers; and there are some **hot baths** – ideal for ritual ablution.

Practicalities

When it comes to staying in Esquipulas, you'll find yourself amongst hundreds of visitors whatever the time of year. **Hotels** probably outnumber private homes and there are new ones springing up all the time. Bargains, however, are in short supply, and the bulk of the budget places are grubby and bare, with tiny monk-like cells – not designed in a spirit of religiosity, but simply to up the number of guests. **Prices** are rarely in writing and are always negotiable, depending on the flow of pilgrims. Avoid **Saturdays** when prices double.

Many of the least expensive places are clustered opposite the church on the other side of the main road, 11 C. The family-run *Hotel Villa Edelmira* (❷/❸), and *La Favorita*, on 10 C and 2 Av (❷), are two of the best simple budget hotels. For a touch more luxury, head for the *Hotel Los Ángeles*, on 2 Avenida, the street

May
Jalapa has its fiesta from the 2nd to 5th, with the 3rd the main day. **Gualán** (which is near Zacapa) has a fiesta from the 5th to 9th.

June
The only June fiesta out this way is in **Usumatlán**, from the 23rd to 26th.

July
Puerto Barrios has its fiesta from the 16th to 22nd, with the main day on the 19th: this has something of a reputation for its (enjoyably) wild celebrations. **Jocotán** (near Chiquimula) has its fiesta from the 22nd to 26th. **Esquipulas** has a fiesta in honour of Santiago Apostol from the 23rd to 27th.

August
Chiquimula has its fiesta from the 11th to 18th, with the main day on the 15th: sure to be a good one, this also includes bullfighting. Over on the other side of the highlands, **Asunción Mita** has a fiesta from the 12th to 15th. **San Luís Jilotepéque** has its one-day fiesta on the 25th.

September
Sansare (between Jalapa and Sanarate) has its fiesta from the 22nd to 25th, with the 24th as the main day.

November
Sanarate celebrates from the 7th to 14th and **Jutiapa** from the 10th to 16th, with the middle day as the main day. **Quesada** (near Jutiapa) has a fiesta from the 26th to 30th.

December
Zacapa has its fiesta from the 4th to 9th, with the main day on the 8th, and **San Luís Jilotepéque** from the 13th to 16th. **Cuilapa** goes wild from the 22nd to 27th, and **Lívingston** has a Caribbean carnival from the 24th to 31st; it is one of the best places in the country to spend Christmas.

just west of church (☎943 1254; ❸), where some rooms have private bath-rooms, or the *Hotel Esquipulao*, next door (❹), a cheaper annexe to the *Hotel Payaquí* (☎943 2025, ⓕ943 1371;❺), where there's a pool and all rooms come with a TV and fan.

There are also dozens of **restaurants** and **bars** to choose from. Breakfast is a bargain in Esquipulas, and you shouldn't have to pay more than US$1.50 for a good feed. There's a decent range of lunch specials later on, though dinner here can be expensive. The *Hacienda Steak House*, a block from the plaza at 2 Av and 10 C, is one of the smartest places in town, while many of the cheaper places are on 11 Calle and the surrounding streets – try the *Taquería Andale* at 2 Av and 10 C for cheap tasty tacos. Among the **banks** in town, Banco Industrial has a branch with a 24-hour ATM at 9 C and 3 Av, and there's also a Banco G&T Continental (Mon–Fri 9am–7pm, Sat 10am–2pm) almost opposite.

Rutas Orientales runs a superb hourly **bus** service between Guatemala City and Esquipulas; its office is on the main street at 11 C and 1 Av. There are also buses across the highlands to Ipala and regular minibuses to the borders with **El Salvador** (every 30min, 6am–4pm; 1hr) and **Honduras** at Aguacaliente (every 30min, 6am–5.30pm; 30min). If you want to get to the ruins of Copán, you'll need to catch a bus to Chiquimula and change there for the El Florido border post (see p.379).

On to the borders: El Salvador and Honduras

The **Honduran** border crossing at **Agua Caliente**, open 24 hours, is just 10km from Esquipulas, and served by a regular shuttle of minibuses and taxis from the main street, that will shuttle you back and forth for a dollar a time (20 min). The **El Florido** crossing, which is more convenient if you're head-ing for the ruins of Copán, is reached by bus from Chiquimula (see p.287). There's a **Honduran consulate** (Mon–Fri 8am–1pm & 3–6pm) in the *Hotel Payaquí*, beside the church, though most nationalities do not need a visa.

The border with **El Salvador** is about 24km from Esquipulas, down a branch road that splits from the main road just before you arrive at the town. Minibuses and buses serve this border too, running every half-hour (45 min), but there's no Salvadorean consulate in Esquipulas.

Travel details

Buses

Bus is the best way to get around the eastern highlands. For the northeastern area simply take a bus to either Puerto Barrios or Esquipulas, as these pass through all the main towns in between. To travel into the central highlands you usually need to catch a bus heading for Jutiapa, and change buses there.

The Motagua valley and Lake Izabal/Río Dulce area

Buses for Puerto Barrios leave Guatemala City hourly from the terminal at 9 Av and 18 C in Zona 1. The very best of these, luxury pullmans, are run by Litegua (5.30am–5pm; US$5.20), whose office is at 15 C 10–40. From Puerto Barrios, Litegua runs 18 buses daily (including nine *especiales*) to Guatemala City (1am–4pm) from its office on 6 Avenida, between 9 & 10 calles. The trip takes about 5hr and tickets can be bought in advance. All buses run past the entrance road for Quiriguá (about 3hr 30min from Guatemala City), and virtu-ally everywhere else along the way except Morales and Bananera: for these you can change at the Ruidosa junction where the road to Petén turns off.

From Puerto Barrios there are also buses to Morales and Bananera every hour or so; to Esquipulas during the morning; to Mariscos at

3pm daily; and to Entre Ríos for Corinto and the Honduras border every 20 minutes (1hr).
From Morales and Bananera there are regular buses and minibuses to Río Dulce, where you can pick up buses to Petén.

To Mariscos there's a direct bus from 18 C and 9 Av in Guatemala City at 6am, and one from Puerto Barrios at 3pm – there are also pick-ups to Mariscos from the La Trinchera junction on the main Caribbean Highway.

The eastern highlands

To Esquipulas half-hourly pullman buses, run by Rutas Orientales, leave from 19 C and 9 Av, Zona 1, in Guatemala City (4am–6pm; 4hr). Buses from Esquipulas to Guatemala City (every 30 min, 2am–6pm) pass by Zacapa and Chiquimula. If you're coming from Puerto Barrios or Petén and want to head out this way, you can pick up one of these at the Río Hondo junction on the Caribbean highway.

From Esquipulas there is also a regular flow of minibuses and buses to the borders with El Salvador (1hr) and Honduras (30min). There are also buses to Jutiapa and Jalapa.

From Chiquimula there are regular daily buses between 6am and 4.30pm to the El Florido border crossing (1hr 30min), from where trucks and buses run to Copán in Honduras. There's also a regular service to Ipala (1hr) and on to Jalapa (4hr) between 5am and 6pm.

To Jutiapa buses leave every hour or so from the Zona 4 bus terminal in Guatemala City between 6am and 4pm; most of them go on to Asunción Mita and San Cristóbal Frontera – the border with El Salvador. The last bus from the border to Guatemala City is at around 4pm. All buses between Guatemala City and Jutiapa pass through Cuilapa, from where there are hourly buses to Chiquimulilla.

From Jutiapa there are buses to all parts of the eastern highlands, including Esquipulas, Ipala and Jalapa.

To San Salvador several companies run a direct service from Guatemala City via the Valle Nuevo border crossing (hourly; 8hr). Companies serving this route include hourly buses run by Melva Internacional, 3 Av 1–38, Zona 9, Guatemala City (just south of the Zona 4 bus terminal) and Tica Bus from 11 C 2–38, Zona 9, Guatemala City.

Boats

From Puerto Barrios to Lívingston there's a daily ferry service at 10am and 5pm (1hr 30min; US$1.40), returning at 5am and 2pm. In addition, a steady shuttle of speedboats operates between Puerto Barrios and Lívingston, leaving when they are full ($2.75).

From Puerto Barrios to Puna Gorda in Belize boats leave daily at 10am and 2pm (1hr 30min; US$11).
From Lívingston up the Río Dulce there are daily sightseeing boats (around 3hr; US$9).
From Lívingston to Omoa in Honduras you can charter a boat from the Bahía Azul restaurant (minimum of 6 people; 2hr 30min; US$36).

Planes

Puerto Barrios to Guatemala City (daily; 1hr).

Río Dulce town to Guatemala City (Fri, Sat and Sun; 1hr 30min).

Cobán and the Verapaces

CHAPTER 5

Highlights

✳ **Fiestas** The towns of Baja Verapaz are famous for their festivals, enlivened by some unique traditional dances, like the Rabinal Achi and Palo Volador. **p.299–300**

✳ **Quetzal** Catch a glimpse of Guatemala's emblematic national bird in the dense cloudforests of the Verapaces. **p.302 and p.310**

✳ **Cobán** Slurp some of the world's finest coffee in the compact, agreeable capital of Alta Verapaz. **p.305**

✳ **Semuc Champey** Cool off in the turquoise pools at this idyllic riverside hideaway. **p.312**

✳ **Rio Cahabón** Go white-water rafting along the Cahabón river, through some of the most breathtaking terrain in Guatemala. **p.313**

✳ **Candelaria caves** An extraordinary limestone cave system, extending for over 18km underground, with some immense chambers to explore. **p.316**

✳ **Laguna Lachuá** An exceptionally beautiful jungle-rimmed crater lake set in a remote area close to the Mexican border. **p.316**

5

Cobán and the Verapaces

While essentially a continuation of Guatemala's western highlands, the mountains of Alta (Upper) and Baja (Lower) Verapaz have always been set apart in a number of ways: certainly, the flat-bottomed Salamá valley and the mist-soaked hills around Cobán are physically unlike any of the country's other mountainous areas. **Baja Verapaz**, the more southerly of these two departments, is sparsely populated, a mixture of deep river valleys, dry hills and lush tropical forest, dotted with tiny hamlets. Just two roads cross the department; one connects the fiesta towns of **Salamá**, **Rabinal** and **Cubulco**, while the other runs from the Eastern Highway up to Cobán. **Alta Verapaz**, the wettest and greenest of Guatemala's highlands, occupies the higher land to the north. Local people say it rains for thirteen months a year here, alternating between straightforward downpour and the drizzle of the *chipi-chipi*, a misty rain that hangs interminably on the hills, although the mountains are now being deforested at such a rate that weather patterns may soon be disrupted. For the moment, however, the area's alpine terrain remains almost permanently moist, coated in resplendent vegetation and vivid with greenery. The capital of Alta Verapaz is **Cobán**, from where roads head north into Petén, west to El Quiché, and east to Lake Izabal.

The **history** of the Verapaces is also quite distinct. Long before the Conquest local Achi Maya had earned themselves a unique reputation as the most bloodthirsty of all the tribes, said to sacrifice every prisoner that they took. Their greatest enemies were the K'iche', with whom they were at war for a century. So ferocious were the Achi that not even the Spanish could contain them by force. Alvarado's army was unable to make any headway against them, and

eventually he gave up trying to control the area, naming it *tierra de guerra*, the "land of war".

The church, however, couldn't allow so many heathen souls to go to waste, and under the leadership of **Fray Bartolomé de Las Casas**, the so-called apostle of the Maya, they made a deal with the conquistadors. If Alvarado would agree to keep all armed men out of the area for five years, the priests would bring it under control. In 1537 Las Casas himself, accompanied by three other Dominican friars, set out into the highlands. Here they befriended the Achi chiefs, and learning the local dialects they translated devotional hymns and taught them to the bemused *indígenas*. By 1538 they had made considerable progress, converting large numbers of Maya and persuading them to move from their scattered hillside homes to the new Spanish-style villages. At the end of the five years the famous and invincible Achi were transformed into Spanish subjects, and the king of Spain renamed the province *Verapaz*, "True Peace".

Since the colonial era the Verapaces have remained isolated and in many ways independent: all their trade bypassed the capital by taking a direct route to the Caribbean, along the Río Polochic and out through Lake Izabal. The area really started to develop with the **coffee boom** at the turn of the century, when German immigrants flooded into the country to buy and run fincas, particularly in Alta Verapaz. By 1914 about half of all Guatemalan coffee was grown on German-owned lands and Germany bought half of the exported produce.

Around Cobán the new immigrants intermarried with local families and established an island of European sophistication. A railway was built along the Polochic valley and Alta Verapaz became almost totally independent. This situation was brought to an end by World War II, when the Americans insisted that Guatemala do something about the enemy presence, and the government was forced to expel the landowners, many of whom were unashamed in their support for Hitler.

Although the Verapaces are now well connected to the capital and their economy integrated with the rest of the country, the area is still dependent on the production of coffee, and Cobán is still dominated by the huge coffee fincas and the wealthy families who own them. Here and there, too, hints of the Germanic influence survive. Taken as a whole, however, the Verapaces remain very much indigenous country: Baja Verapaz retains a small Achi Maya outpost around Rabinal, and in Alta Verapaz the Maya population, largely **Poqomchi'** and **Q'eqchi'** speakers, the two languages of the Poqomam group, is predominant. The production of coffee, and more recently **cardamom** for the Middle Eastern market, has cut deep into their land and their way of life, the fincas driving many people off prime territory to marginal plots. Traditional costume is worn less here than in the western highlands, and in its place many of the *indígenas* have adopted a more universal Q'eqchi' costume, using the loose-hanging white *huipil* and locally made *cortes*.

The northern, flat section of Alta Verapaz includes a slice of Petén rainforest, and in recent years Q'eqchi' Maya have fanned out into this empty expanse, reaching the Río Salinas in the west, heading up into the Petén and making their way across the border into Belize. Here they carve out sections of the forest and attempt to farm, a process that threatens the future of the forest and offers little long-term security for the migrants.

Where to go

Few tourists make it out this way, possibly because the Maya tradition and costumes are not so evident as in the western highlands, but if you've time and energy to spare then you'll find these highlands astonishingly beautiful, with their unique limestone structure, moist, misty atmosphere and boundless fertility. The hub of the area is **Cobán**, an attractive mountain town with good accommodation, coffee houses and restaurants; it's a little subdued once the rain sets in, but is still the place from which to explore and the starting point for several adventurous trips. In August Cobán hosts the **National Folklore Festival**; in Baja Verapaz, the towns of **Salamá**, **Rabinal** and **Cubulco** are also renowned for their fiestas, while **San Jerónimo** has some interesting historic sights. From Cubulco you can continue on foot, over the Sierra de Chuacús, to Joyabaj, a spectacular and exhausting hike.

In isolated patches of **cloudforest** in northern Baja Verapaz you can occasionally see the **quetzal**, Guatemala's national bird and one of Central America's rarest. The **quetzal sanctuary**, just off the Cobán highway, is an accessible and popular place to search, though you may have more luck inside the larger adjacent **Reserva Sierra de las Minas**. Heading out to the east of Cobán there are the exquisite natural bathing pools of **Semuc Champey**, surrounded by lush tropical forest and fed by the azure waters of the **Río Cahabón**, which boasts spectacular white-water rafting possibilities. Cobán is also the starting point for three seldom-travelled back routes: east down the Río Polochic to **Lake Izabal**; north through Pajal and Raxrujá towards **Petén**; and west to **Uspantán** for Santa Cruz del Quiché and Nebaj (or all the way across to Huehuetenango).

Baja Verapaz

A strange but dramatic mix of dry hills and verdant, fertile valleys, Baja Verapaz is crossed by a skeletal road network. The historic towns of **San Jerónimo**, **Salamá**, **Rabinal** and **Cubulco** are all regularly served by buses, and have interesting markets as well as being famed for their fiestas, where you'll see some unique traditional dances. The other big attractions are the **quetzal sanctuary**, on the western side of the Cobán highway, and the forested mountains, waterfalls and wildlife inside the **Reserva Sierra de las Minas** just to the east.

The main approach to both departments is from the Carretera al Atlántico, where the road to the Verapaz highlands branches off at the **El Rancho** junction. Lined with scrub bush and cacti, the road climbs steadily upwards, the dusty browns and dry yellows of the Motagua valley soon giving way to an explosion of green as dense pine forests and alpine meadows grip the mountains. The views from up here are superb, though the mountains can often be shrouded in a blanket of cloud. Some 48km beyond the junction is **La Cumbre de Santa Elena**, where the road for the main towns of Baja Verapaz turns off to the west, immediately starting to drop towards the floor of the Salamá valley. Surrounded by steep, parched hillsides, with a level flood plain at its base, the valley appears entirely cut off from the outside world.

San Jerónimo

At the valley's eastern end lies the large village of **SAN JERÓNIMO**, 4km from La Cumbre junction, which is bypassed by the road for Salamá. In the early days of the Conquest Dominican priests built a church and convent here and planted vineyards, eventually producing a wine lauded as the finest in Central America. In 1845, after the religious orders were abolished, an Englishman replaced the vines with sugar cane and began brewing an *aguardiente* that became equally famous. These days the area still produces cane, and a fair amount of alcohol, although the English connection is long gone.

Thanks to some active promotion by the municipal tourism authority, and a trio of sights, tranquil San Jerónimo is beginning to attract the odd curious visitor. Presiding over the central plaza, the village's seventeenth-century Baroque **church** contains a monumental gilded altar, brought here from France, which was crafted from sheets of eighteen-carat gold. Just down the hill behind the church are the remains of the convent complex, the Hacienda de San Jerónimo, and its sugar mill which has been converted into the **Museo Regional del Trapiche** (Mon–Sat 9am–1pm & 2–5pm; US$1.30). Entrance includes a guided tour (Spanish only) of the old mill premises and an explanation of the refining process. Also of interest is the colonial **aqueduct**, built in

1679, that once supplied the mill's water wheels, with many of its 124 original stone arches still standing; it's on the southeast outskirts of the village, a few minutes' walk from the plaza – just ask the way to the *acueducto antiguo*.

For something **to eat**, *Churrasquitos La Tablita*, three blocks east of the plaza, does delicious barbecued meat, while you can sample the local coffee at *Cafetería del Quiosco* on the south side of the plaza. Regular **minibuses** connect Salamá and San Jerónimo between 6.30am and 7pm.

Salamá

At the western end of the valley is **SALAMÁ**, capital of the department of Baja Verapaz. The town has a relaxed and prosperous air, and like many of the places out this way its population is largely ladino. There's not much to do outside **fiesta time** (Sept 17–21), other than browse in the Sunday market, though a couple of things are worth looking out for. On the edge of town lies a crumbling colonial bridge, now used only by pedestrians, and the old church is also interesting, with huge altars, darkened by age, running down either side. If you decide **to stay**, the pick of the hotels is the modern *Hotel Real Legendario* at 8 Av 3–57 (☎940 0187; ❸), with very clean rooms, all with private bath, good beds and cable TV and a little café, or you could try the *Hotel Tezulutlán* just south of the plaza (☎940 1643; ❸) as a reasonable alternative, though the rooms, set round a courtyard, are less attractive. *Pensión Juárez* (☎940 0055; ❷), a good budget hotel at the end of 5 Calle, past the police station, is cheaper. For **eating**, try one of the places around the plaza: *El Ganadero* is the best restaurant and *Deli-Donus* and *Café Central* both score for coffee and snacks. There's also a Bancafé (Mon–Fri 9am–5pm, Sat 9am–1pm) opposite the church that will cash dollars and travellers' cheques.

To really explore the region you may want to consider getting in touch with Eco-Verapaz, 8 Av 3–20, Zona 2 (☎ & 🖷940 0294 or ☎940 0459), who run excellent hiking, mountain biking, caving, horse riding and cultural trips throughout the department. Prices are around US$40 a day for most activities. Transportes Dulce María **buses** from Guatemala City run hourly to Salamá (3hr 30min) between 3am and 5pm, from 11 Av and 17 C in Zona 1; most continue on to Rabinal (4hr 30min) and Cubulco (5hr 15min). They return from Salamá between 3.30am and 4pm; there's also a steady shuttle of minibuses to and from La Cumbre for connections with pullman buses running between Cobán and Guatemala City.

Rabinal

To the west of Salamá the road climbs out of the valley over a low pass and through a gap in the hills, to **San Miguel Chicaj**, a large traditional village clustered around a colonial church. Beyond here the road climbs again, this time to a greater height, reaching a pass with magnificent views across the surrounding mountain ranges, which step away into El Quiché.

An hour or so from Salamá you arrive in **RABINAL**, another isolated farming town that's also dominated by a large colonial church. Here the proportion of indigenous inhabitants is considerably higher, making both the Sunday market and the fiesta well worth a visit. Founded in 1537 by Bartolomé de Las Casas himself, Rabinal was the first of the settlements in his peaceful conquest of the Achi nation: about 3km northwest, a thirty-minute hike away, are the ruins of one of their fortified cities, known locally as Cerro Cayup. Nowadays the place is best known for its oranges, claimed to be the finest in the country – and they certainly taste like it.

Sights are slim in Rabinal itself, but beside the church the town's small **museum** (Mon–Fri 9am–4pm; free) is worth a visit, with exhibits on traditional medicinal practices, local arts and crafts and the impact of the civil war in the region – there were four massacres in 1982 alone in the Río Negro region north of the town. Rabinal's **fiesta**, running from January 19 to 24, is renowned for its dances, many of them pre-colonial in origin. The most famous of these, an extended dance drama known as the "Rabinal Achi" re-enacts a battle between the Achi and the K'iche' tribes and is unique to the town, performed annually on January 23. Others include the *patzca*, a ceremony to call for good harvests, using masks that portray a swelling below the jaw, and wooden sticks engraved with serpents, birds and human heads. If you can't make it for the fiesta, the Sunday **market** is a good second-best; look out for some high-quality local artesanías, including carvings made from the *árbol del morro* (calabash tree) and traditional pottery.

Of the several fairly basic **hotels** in Rabinal, the best is the *Posada San Pablo* at 3 Av 1–50 (❶ /❷), a decent budget hotel with immaculate rooms, some with private bath. If it's full, try the *Hospedaje Caballeros*, 1 C 4–02 (❶), or for somewhere really comfortable see if the new three-storey *Gran Hotel Rabinal Achi*, also on 1 Calle, due to open in late 2001, is operational yet; if it is, you'll find comfortable rooms, a pool and a café. For an inexpensive **meal** try *Cafetería Mishell del Rosario* on 1 Calle behind the church. The Banrural at 1 C and 3 Av (Mon–Fri 8.30am–5pm, Sat 9am–1pm) will only cash dollars.

Cubulco

Leaving Rabinal the road heads on to the west, climbing yet another high ridge with fantastic views to the left, into the uninhabited mountain ranges. To the north, in one of the deep river valleys, lies the **Chixoy** hydroelectric plant (see p.304) where over three-quarters of Guatemala's electricity is generated.

Another hour of rough road brings you down into the next valley and to **CUBULCO**, an isolated, ladino town, surrounded on all sides by steep, forested mountains. Like Salamá and Rabinal, Cubulco is best visited for its fiesta, this being one of the few places where you can still see the **Palo Volador**, a pre-conquest ritual in which men throw themselves from a thirty-metre pole with a rope tied around their legs, spinning down towards the ground as the rope unravels, and hopefully landing on their feet. It's as dangerous as it looks, particularly when you bear in mind that most of the dancers are blind drunk; every few years an inebriated dancer falls from the top of the pole to his death. The fiesta still goes on, though, as riotous as ever, with the main action taking place on July 23. The best place to stay is the *Hospedaje Pías* (❶) next to the large farmacia in the centre of town, where some rooms have private bath. Avoid the smelly *Posada Morales* (❶). There are several good **comedores** in the market, but the best place to eat is *La Fonda del Viajero* which serves up big portions of Guatemalan food at reasonable prices.

On from Cubulco: the back routes

If you'd rather not leave the valley the same way that you arrived, there are two other options. One bus a day leaves Cubulco at around 9am, heads back to Rabinal and then, instead of going to La Cumbre and the main road, turns to the south, crossing the spine of the Sierra de Chuacús and dropping directly down towards Guatemala City. The trip takes you over rough roads for around eight hours, through El Chol, Granados and San Juan Sacatepéquez, but the mountain views and the sense of leaving the beaten track help to make the journey more appealing.

Hiking from Cubulco to Joyabaj

If you'd rather leave the roads altogether, an even less travelled route takes you out of the valley on foot, also over the Sierra de Chuacús, to Joyabaj in the department of El Quiché. The hike takes between eight and ten hours, but if you have a tent it's probably best to break the trip halfway at the village of **TRES CRUCES** (if you don't have one, you'll probably be able to find a floor to sleep on). The views, as you tramp over a huge ridge and through a mixture of pine forest and farmland, are spectacular.

The hills around Cubulco are covered in a complex network of paths so it's worth getting someone to point you in the right direction, and asking plenty of people along the way – for the first half of the walk it's better to ask for Tres Cruces rather than Joyabaj. Broadly speaking the path bears up to the right as it climbs the hillside to the south of Cubulco, crossing the mountain range after about three hours. On the other side is an open, bowl-shaped valley, where to reach Tres Cruces you walk along the top of the ridge that marks the right-hand side of the valley – heading south from the pass. Don't drop down into the valley until you reach Tres Cruces. The village itself is the smallest of rural hamlets, perched high on the spine of the ridge, and far from the reach of the nearest road. On Thursday mornings the tiny plaza is crammed with traders who assemble for the market, but otherwise there's nothing save a couple of simple tiendas. Beyond Tres Cruces you drop down into the valley that cuts in to the right (west) of the ridge, and then follow the dirt road out of the valley, onto the larger Joyabaj to Pachalum road – turn right for Joyabaj (p.144).

Towards Alta Verapaz: Reserva Sierra de las Minas and Biotopo del Quetzal

Heading for Cobán, and deeper into the highlands, the main road sweeps straight past the turning for Salamá and on around endless tight curves below forested hillsides. The steep slopes on the eastern side of the road form the foothills of the **Reserva Sierra de las Minas**, a mighty dividing mountain range that soars to over 3000m along a slender stretch of land between the Motagua and Polochic valleys. The peaks are often called the "dark mountains" because of the dense blanket of mist that hangs over the hills. Forming one of Guatemala's largest expanse of **cloudforest**, the almost unpopulated region harbours abundant wildlife including howler monkeys, white-tailed deer, coyotes and birds including the emerald toucan, hummingbirds and fairly plentiful numbers of quetzals (see box on p.303).

The reserve is currently well off the tourist trail and is not easy to **get to** independently. The most practical option is to arrange a trip with Defensores de la Naturaleza (see p.478) who manage the area. To get there under your own steam, you first need to get to the village of **San Rafael Chilascó**, which is 12km east of the Cobán highway, via the turn-off at km 145. Monja Blanca buses between Guatemala City and Cobán pass by the turn-off every half-hour between 4am and 6pm, but you may have to wait a while at the junction for a pick-up to the village. Once in San Rafael, contact the village ecotourism committee, who work in conjunction with the Defensores de la Naturaleza, and can organize accommodation (❶) and meals with local families, and guides. You'll need good-quality waterproofs and hiking boots. Trails lead to two spectacular **waterfalls**, El Saltó de Chilascó, which plunges 200m in two drops close to the entrance of the reserve and the Laguneta falls which drop an astounding 350m. There are many rare orchids and a liquidambar forest to admire along the way.

Back on the highway north to Cobán, just before the village of Purulhá at km 161, the **Biotopo del Quetzal** (daily 7am–4pm; US$3.85), is a much easier place to visit, though Guatemala's national bird is actually most common in the forests south of San Pedro Carchá (see p.309). The 1153-hectare nature reserve is designed to protect the habitat of the endangered quetzal and covers a steep area of dense cloudforest, through which the Río Colorado cascades towards the valley floor, forming waterfalls and natural swimming pools. It is also known as the **Mario Dary Reserve**, in honour of one of the founders of Guatemala's environmental movement. A lecturer from San Carlos University, Mario Dary pioneered the establishment of nature reserves in Guatemala and spent years campaigning for a cloud forest sanctuary to protect the quetzal, causing great problems for the powerful timber companies in the process. He was murdered in 1988; an ecological foundation, Fundary, has been set up in his name to manage protected areas, including Punta de Manabique (see p.478).

Visiting the sanctuary

Two paths through the undergrowth from the road complete a circuit that takes you up into the woods above the reserve headquarters (where maps are available for US$0.60). Although there are reasonable numbers of quetzals hidden in the forest, they're extremely elusive. The **best time of year to visit** is just before and just after the nesting season (between March and June), and the best time of day is **sunrise**. In general the birds tend to spend the nights up in the high forest and float across the road as dawn breaks, to spend the days in the forest below, and they can be easily identified by their strange jerky, undulating flight. A good place to look out for them is at one of their favoured feeding trees, the broad-leaved *aguacatillo* which produces a small avocado-like fruit. Whether or not you see a quetzal, the forest itself, usually damp with the *chipi-chipi*, a perpetual mist, is well worth a visit: a profusion of lichens, ferns, mosses, bromeliads and orchids, spread out beneath a towering canopy of cypress, oak, walnut and pepper trees. **Buses** from Cobán and Guatemala City pass the entrance every half-hour, but make sure they know you want to be dropped at the *biotopo* as it's easy to miss – the entrance is at km 161 on the Cobán highway.

There are several places to stay, eat and drink within a few kilometres of the quetzal sanctuary, though **camping** is no longer permitted at the *biotopo* itself. Coming from Guatemala City, the first place you reach is the *Hotel Posada Montaña del Quetzal* at km 156.5 (☎331 0929, ⊛www.medianet.com.gt /quetzal; ❺/❻), which offers very attractive stone and timber bungalows with fireplaces and pleasant rooms with warm private showers and great forest views – there's a restaurant, bar and swimming pool here. Less than a kilometre past the entrance to the reserve (at km 161.5) is the rustic *Hospedaje Ranchito del Quetzal* (☎953 9235; ❷/❸), with clean, basic accommodation with or without private bath, and a simple comedor with a menu usually limited to eggs and beans. Compensating for the no-frills facilities are the quetzals often seen in the patch of forest around the hotel, though staff sometimes insist on charging an entrance fee even if you just want to come in and look around. Alternatively, heading on towards Alta Verapaz, there's a wonderful solitary Swiss-style chalet with full cooking facilities at the *Country Delight Inn* (☎308 7767; sleeps four; US$45 per night) at km 166.5, plus a lovely meadow set aside

The resplendent quetzal

The **quetzal**, Guatemala's national symbol (after which the country's currency is named) has a distinguished past but an uncertain future. The bird's feathers have been sacred from the earliest of times, and in the strange cult of Quetzalcoatl, whose influence spread throughout Mesoamerica, it was incorporated into the plumed serpent, a supremely powerful deity. To the Maya the quetzal was so sacred that killing one was a capital offence, and the bird is also thought to have been the *nahual*, or spiritual protector, of the Maya chiefs. When Tecún Umán faced Alvarado in hand-to-hand combat, his headdress sprouted the long green feathers of the quetzal; when the conquistadors founded a city adjacent to the battleground they named it **Quetzaltenango**, the place of the quetzals.

In modern Guatemala the quetzal's image saturates the country, appearing in every imaginable context. Citizens honoured by the president are awarded the Order of the Quetzal, and the bird is also considered a symbol of freedom, since caged quetzals die from the rigours of confinement. Despite all this, the sweeping tide of deforestation threatens the very existence of the bird, and the sanctuary is about the only concrete step that has been taken to save it.

The more resplendent of the birds, and the source of the famed feathers, is the male. Their heads are crowned with a plume of brilliant green, the chest and lower belly is a rich crimson, and trailing behind are the unmistakeable oversized, golden-green tail feathers, though these are only really evident in the mating season. The females, on the other hand, are an unremarkable brownish colour. The birds nest in holes drilled into dead trees, laying one or two eggs at the start of the rainy season, usually in April or May.

for camping (US$1.30 per person) and, despite the fact that only cold showers are available, it's an idyllic, if isolated, place to spend the night. The little café-restaurant here is one of the best on the highway, with an atypical menu that includes homemade bread and soups, plus wonderfully flavoursome locally reared ham. The owners are also planning to rent out mountain bikes in the future.

Alta Verapaz

Beyond the quetzal sanctuary the main road crosses into the department of Alta Verapaz, and another 13km takes you beyond the forests and into a luxuriant alpine valley of cattle pastures hemmed in by steep, perpetually green hillsides.

The first place of any size is **TACTIC**, a small mainly Poqomchi'-speaking town adjacent to the main road, which most buses bypass. Tactic has earned its share of fame as the site of the **pozo vivo**, the living well. A sign points the way to this decidedly odd attraction, opposite the northern entrance road. The well itself is all but dried up for most of the year, but if you visit in the rainy season you may see the odd swirl in the mud. Legend has it that the water only comes to life when approached, because it harbours the restless soul of a dead Maya beauty who fell in love with a Spanish soldier. After the soldier had died fighting to protect her from the less than honourable attentions of his companions, she chose to be stoned to death rather than marry another.

The colonial **church** in the centre of town, boasting a elaborate facade decorated with mermaids and jaguars, is worth a look, as is the Chi-ixim chapel, high above the town. If you fancy a cool swim, head for the *Balneario Cham-che*, a crystal-clear spring-fed **pool**, on the other side of the main road, opposite the centre of town. The simple *Pensión Central* (❶), on the main street north of the plaza, is a reasonable budget bet, or for a little more comfort try *Hotel Villa Linda* close by (☎953 9216; ❸), where the rooms have private baths. Better still, head for the rustic *Chi'ixim Eco Hotel* at km 182.5 on the highway (☎ & ℱ953 9198; ❹), where all the eight comfortable bungalows have fireplaces and there's a spotless little dining room. For tasty ranch-style **food**, *Café La Granja*, a little further north at km 187, has tempting Guatemalan favourites plus sandwiches and salads, in a great log cabin-style setting.

Further towards Cobán, the turning for Uspantán peels off to the left at the featureless town of **SANTA CRUZ VERAPAZ**. Right by the junction at km 196.5 the huge *Park Hotel* (☎ & ℱ950 4539 or ☎951 3388, ✉parkhotel @intel.net.gt; ❹/❺) is a comfortable place to stay, with large, good-value doubles and suites, many overlooking a fairly miserable mini **zoo** (no charge) with cramped cages of squirrels, pizote, owls and even some spider monkeys. It's very popular with Guatemalan families at weekends. Close by at km 198.5, the *Ecocentro Holanda* (☎952 1269, ℱ952 1771, ✉holanda@intelnet.net.gt; ❹) has pleasant cabañas, a campsite (US$6 per tent) and a children's paddling pool.

Some 10km west of the junction, along the road to Uspantán, **SAN CRISTÓBAL VERAPAZ** is an attractive town surrounded by fields of sugar cane and coffee. It's set on the banks of **Lago de Cristóbal**, a favourite spot for swimming and fishing, although a shoe factory close to the shore has now badly polluted the water. Legend has it that the lake was formed in 1590 as a result of a dispute between a priest and local Maya over the celebration of pagan rites. According to one version the earth split and swallowed the *indígenas*, sealing their graves with the water, while another has it that the priest fled, hurling maledictions so heavy that they created a depression which then filled with water. The Poqomchi'-speaking Maya of San Cristóbal are among the last vestiges of one of the smallest and oldest highland tribes, and you can find out more about their culture at an interesting new **museum**, located just off plaza at C del Calvario 5–03. The Museo Katinamit (Mon–Sat 9am–1pm & 2.30–6pm, Sun 9am–noon; US$0.75) hosts exhibits on the maguey plant, the most important fibre of the region, woven into bags, hammocks and rope, Verapaz flora and fauna and music, and has an exhibition room with handicrafts for sale. The museum building also acts as a base for CECEP (Centro Comunitario Educativo Poqomchi'; ☎950 4030, ✉cecep@intco.com.gt) which organizes **ethno-tourism** trips (US$9 for a half-day tour) of indigenous villages and sights around San Cristóbal, and provides computer classes for locals.

The town knows how to throw a good **fiesta**, held annually on December 8, and is an excellent, almost tourist-free place to head for **Semana Santa**, when a kilometre-long coloured sawdust carpet is created between the main church in the plaza and the Calvario chapel to the west. Try to avoid staying here if you can, as the only **hotel**, the *Pensión San Cristóbal* on 0 Avenida, just up from the plaza, is very grim. Banco Industrial, almost next door at 0 and 1 calles (Mon–Fri 10am–5pm, Sat 10am–2pm), will give advances on Visa credit cards and cashes US dollars.

South of San Cristóbal is the billion-dollar disaster known as the **Chixoy dam** and hydroelectric plant, financed with money borrowed from the World Bank. Though the dam provides Guatemala with a large proportion of its electricity needs, the price of the project has been high. Unchecked deforestation in the area has increased sediment in the river thus reducing the efficiency of the power plant, and the cost of constructing the dam accounts for a sizeable chunk of all Guatemala's considerable foreign debt payments. West from San

Cristóbal the rough road continues to **Uspantán** (in the western highlands) from where buses run to Santa Cruz del Quiché, via Sacapulas, for connections to Nebaj and Huehuetenango. To head out this way you can either hitch a ride in a pick-up pretty easily from San Cristóbal, or catch one of the buses that leave San Pedro Carchá at 10am and noon, passing just above the terminal in Cobán ten minutes later, and reaching San Cristóbal after about another half hour.

Cobán

The heart of these rain-soaked hills and the capital of the department is **COBÁN**, where the paved highway comes to an end. If you're heading up this way, stay in town for a night or two and sample some of the finest coffee in the world in one of Cobán's many genteel cafés. Cobán is not a large place; its suburbs fuse gently with outlying meadows and pine forests, giving the town the air of an overgrown mountain village. When the rain sets in, it has something of a subdued atmosphere and in the evenings the air is usually damp and cool. That said, the sun does put in an appearance most days, and the town makes a useful base to recharge, eat well, sleep well and for all kinds of **ecotourism** possibilities in the spectacular mountains and rivers nearby.

Arrival and information

Transportes Escobar y Monja Blanca, one of Guatemala's best **bus** services, operates half-hourly departures between Guatemala City and Cobán, a journey of four to five hours; its office is at 2 C 3–77, Zona 4 (℡952 1536 or 952 1498). Buses to **local destinations** such as Senahú, El Estor, Lanquín and Cahabón leave from the terminal and streets around the market down the hill behind the town hall. There are also a few long-distance departures to and from San Pedro Carchá (see p.309), a few kilometres away.

It's also possible to **fly** between Guatemala City and Cobán: Inter Airlines, operated by Taca, has daily flights (30min) to and from the capital from the small airstrip a few kilometres southeast of the centre of town. There are also occasional charter flights to the remote departmental airstrips of Playa Grande (Ixcán), Chisec and Fray Bartolomé de Las Casas.

Inexcusably, Inguat currently chooses not to grace Cobán with a tourist office, but luckily a couple of hotels – namely *Hostal d'Acuña*, with helpful staff, a good folder of maps and bus times, and a useful noticeboard, and *Hostal Doña Victoria* (see below for details of both) – more than fill the **information** gap. Another source is the Access office, in the same complex as *Café Tirol*, where both the owners are bilingual and there are plenty of terminals where you can surf the **internet** and check your email. For expert guidance and advice about getting to really remote areas of the Verapaces, contact Proyecto Eco-Quetzal (see "Listings", p.309).

Like many other Guatemalan towns, Cobán is divided into a number of **zonas**, with the northeast corner of the plaza at 1 C and 1 Av as the dividing point. Zona 1 is to the northwest, Zona 2 to the southwest, Zona 3 to the southeast and Zona 4 to the northeast.

Accommodation

Unless you're here for one of the August fiestas you'll probably only pause for a day or two before heading off into the hills, out to the villages, or on to some other part of the country. There are, however, plenty of **hotels** in town, and there's **camping** (US$2.50 per person) at the Parque las Victorias on the

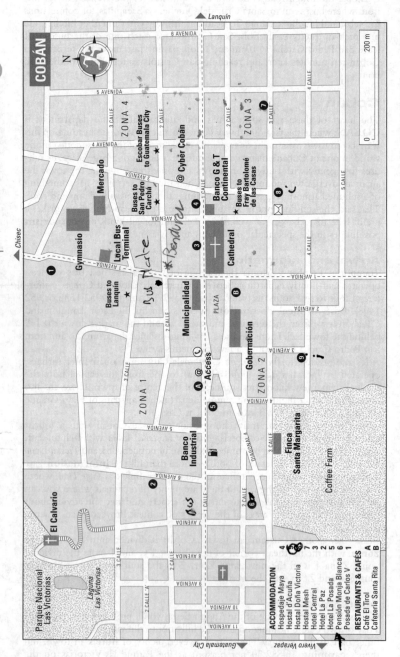

COBÁN

▲ Lanquín

▲ Chisec

N

200 m

0

Parque Nacional
Las Victorias

Laguna
Las Victorias

El Calvario

Gymnasio

Mercado

Local Bus
Terminal

Buses to
Lanquín

Municipalidad

Buses to San Pedro Carchá

Escobar Buses
to Guatemala City

@ Cyber Cobán

Banco G & T
Continental

Buses to
Fray Bartolomé
de las Casas

Cathedral

PLAZA

Gobernación

Banco
Industrial

Finca
Santa Margarita

Coffee Farm

Access

ZONA 1

ZONA 2

ZONA 3

ZONA 4

6 AVENIDA

5 AVENIDA

4 AVENIDA

3 AVENIDA

3 AVENIDA

1 AVENIDA

2 AVENIDA

3 AVENIDA

4 AVENIDA

5 AVENIDA

6 AVENIDA

7 AVENIDA

8 AVENIDA

9 AVENIDA

10 AVENIDA

11 AVENIDA

4 CALLE

3 CALLE

2 CALLE

1 CALLE

5 CALLE

4 CALLE

3 CALLE

2 CALLE

1 CALLE

2 CALLE

3 CALLE

DIAGONAL 4

2 CALLE "A"

3 CALLE

▼ Guatemala City
▼ Vivero Verapaz

ACCOMMODATION	
Hospedaje Maya	4
Hostal d'Acuña	3
Hostal Doña Victoria	7
Hostal Mesh	3
Hotel Central	2
Hotel La Paz	5
Hotel La Posada	6
Pensión Monja Blanca	1
Posada de Carlos V	

RESTAURANTS & CAFÉS	
Café El Tirol	A
Cafetería Santa Rita	B

northwest side of town, which lacks showers, though there are toilets and running water.

Hospedaje Maya 1 C 2–33, Zona 4, opposite the Cine Norte ☎ 952 2380. Large, basic hotel used by local travellers and traders. Bargain rates, warm showers and friendly staff but smelly toilets. ➊

Hostal d'Acuña 4 C 3–17, Zona 2 ☎951 0482, ⓕ952 1547, ⓔuisa@amigo.net.gt. Undoubtedly the most popular budget choice, offering spotless rooms with comfortable bunks. Dorms (US$5.50 per bed) are in the garden of a colonial house and guests can enjoy excellent home cooking on the verandah. They also arrange shuttles and tours. Highly recommended. ➋

Hostal Doña Victoria 3 C 2–38, Zona 3 ☎951 4213, ⓕ952 2213, ⓔaventour@intelnet.com.gt. Beautiful refurbished colonial house dripping with antiques and oozing character. Commodious bedrooms are individually furnished and all come with private bath; the streetside rooms are rather noisy, though. Good café-bar and restaurant. It's also the base of Aventuras Turísticas. The owners also have a second premises at 1 Av 5–34, Zona 1 which is equally as comfortable though the location is not as good. ➎

Hostal Mesh 3 C 4–27, Zona 3 ☎ & ⓕ952 1605, ⓔhostalmesh@hotmail.com. Small hostel with two clean dormitories, with bunk beds (US$4.50) and safety boxes. Breakfast is included, there's a café-bar at the rear and the owners also organize tours of the region. ➋

Hotel Central 1 C 1–79, Zona 4 ☎ & ⓕ952 1442. Germanic decor and friendly staff. The rooms, set around a nice little garden, are a bit gloomy for the price – though they do have reliable hot water and private bath. ➌

Hotel la Paz 6 Av 2–19, Zona 1 ☎952 1358. Safe, pleasant budget hotel run by a very vigilant *señora*. Some rooms have private bath. ➋

Hotel la Posada 1 C 4–12, Zona 2, at the west end of the plaza ☎ & ⓕ952 1495, ⓕ951 0646, ⓔlaposada@c.net.gt. Probably the city's finest hotel, in an elegant colonial building, with a beautiful, antique-furnished interior. The rooms, many with wooden Moorish-style screens and some with four-poster beds, are set around two leafy courtyards and offer all the usual luxuries, though traffic noise can be a problem. Excellent restaurant and café. ➏

Pensión Monja Blanca 2 C 6–30, Zona 2 ☎951 1900 or 952 0531, ⓕ951 1899, ⓦwww.sitio.de /hotelmonjablanca. A wonderfully old-fashioned atmosphere and a variety of rooms, all very quiet and set around two stunning courtyard gardens. The older ones are a little run-down but the others have been nicely refurbished and come with private bath. Don't miss the almost Victorian-style tearoom. ➋/➌

Posada de Carlos V 1 Av 3–44, Zona 1 ☎952 3502, ⓕ951 3501. Mountain chalet-style hotel close to the market, with pine-trimmed rooms and modern amenities including cable TV. Comfortable if not memorable. Check out the lobby photographs of old Cobán. ➍

The Town

Cobán's imperial heyday, when it stood at the centre of its own isolated world, is long gone, and its glory faded. The **plaza**, however, remains an impressive triangle, from which the town drops away on all sides. It's dominated by the **cathedral**, which is worth peering into to see the remains of a massive ancient cracked church bell. A block behind, the **market** bustles with trade during the day and is surrounded by food stalls at night. Hints of the days of German control can also be found here in the architecture, which incorporates the occasional suggestion of Bavarian grandeur.

Life in Cobán revolves around **coffee**: the sedate restaurants, tearooms, trendy nightclubs and overflowing supermarket are a tribute to the town's affluent elite, while the crowds that sleep in the market and plaza, assembling in the bus terminal to search for work, are migrant labourers heading for the plantations. Since the highway linked Cobán with the capital, the *finqueros*, wealthy owners of the coffee plantations, have mostly moved to Guatemala City, but a small residue still base themselves in Cobán. For a closer look at Cobán's principal crop, take the guided tour offered by the **Finca Santa Margarita**, a coffee plantation just south of the centre of town at 3 C 4–12, Zona 2 (Mon–Fri 8am–12.30pm & 1.30–5pm, Sat 8am–noon; US$2). The interesting tour (an English-speaking guide is available) covers the history of the finca, founded by the Dieseldorff family in 1888, examines all the stages of cultivation and production, and includes a walk through the grounds. You also get a chance to sample the crop and, of course, purchase some beans.

One of Cobán's most attractive sights is the church of **El Calvario**, a short stroll from the town centre. Head west out of town on 1 Avenida and turn right up 7 Avenida until you reach a steep cobbled path. You'll pass a number of tiny **Maya shrines** on the way up – crosses blackened by candle smoke and decorated with scattered offerings. There's a commanding view over the town from the whitewashed church, which has a distinctly pagan identity, including both Christian and Maya crosses; inside the church hundreds of corn cobs (sacred in indigenous religion) hang from the roof.

Another place worth visiting lies just outside town: the **Vivero Verapaz** (Mon–Sat 9am–noon & 2–5pm, Sun 9am–noon; US$0.75), a former coffee finca now dedicated to the growing of orchids, which flourish in these sodden mountains. The export of the blooms is illegal in Guatemala but the farm produces some seven hundred indigenous varieties, as well as a handful of hybrids which they've put together themselves, all of which are sold within Guatemala. The plants are nurtured in a wonderfully shaded environment, and a farm worker will show you around and point out the most spectacular buds, which are at their best between November and January. The farm is on the old road to Guatemala City, which you reach by leaving the plaza on Diagonal 4. At the bottom of the hill turn left, go across the bridge and follow the road for 3km. A taxi here from the plaza will cost around US$3.

Eating and drinking

When it comes to **eating** in Cobán you have a choice between fancy European-style restaurants and cafés and very basic, inexpensive comedores. For really cheap food, your best bet, as always, is the **market**, but remember that it's closed by dusk, after which street stalls set up in the plaza selling barbecued meat and warm tortillas.

Bistro Acuña 4 C 3–17, Zona 2. The most relaxed place to eat in town – stunning period setting, uplifting classical music, attentive service and a good place to meet other travellers. A full-scale blowout will cost around US$8 a head but there are many cheaper options, including great cannelloni. Leave room to sample something from the cake cabinet.

Café and Restaurant la Posada inside *Hotel la Posada*, 1 C 4–12, Zona 2, at the west end of the plaza. The smartest restaurant in town with traditional Guatemalan specialities as well as international cuisine. The café on the verandah outside serves superb breakfasts, bagels and muffins.

Café Tirol 1 Calle, on the north side of the plaza. Relatively upmarket by Guatemalan standards, though cheaper than the *Posada*. Serves 52 different types of coffee, pretty good breakfasts, hot chocolate, pancakes and sandwiches. Service can be distracted. Open Tues–Sun 7am–8.30pm.

Cafetería Santa Rita 2 Calle, on the plaza, close to the cathedral. Good comedor with friendly service and decent nosh. Very Guatemalan, in the unlikely event you're sick of all those European-style cafés.

Kam Mun 1 C and 9 Av, Zona 2. Excellent, hyper-hygienic Chinese restaurant, with a good line-up of economical Oriental choices. Open daily noon–9.30pm.

Nightlife and entertainment

Generally speaking Cobán is a pretty quiet place, particularly in the evenings. In addition to the usual cantinas, however, there are some half-decent **bars**: *Tofuba*, at 2 C and 6 Av, is one of the trendiest places with a cosmopolitian atmosphere, modern Latin sounds and good snacks, while *Tacobán*, 1 Av and 4 C, can get lively at weekends with a sociable crowd and house music. The best **club** in town is *Keops*, 5 Av and 3 C, where the merengue and Latin dance draw a funky bunch of groovers. There are two **cinemas**, the CineTuria in the plaza, and the Cine Norte, on 1 Calle.

Listings

Banks and exchange Banco Industrial at 1 C and 2 Av (Mon–Fri 8.30am–7pm, Sat 8.30am–5.30pm) with Visa facilities, or Banco G&T Continental, 1 C and 2 Av (Mon–Fri 9am–7pm, Sat 9am–1pm) for Mastercard.

Car rental Tabarini, 7 Av 2–27, Zona 2 (☎952 1504, ℱ951 3282), and Geo Rentals, a local company, in the same building as *Café Tirol* and Access (☎952 1650).

Email and Internet Cobán is well wired with email facilities. Access, in the same building as the *Café Tirol*, is very central, but for the best rates and speeds head to Cybercoban at 3 Av 1–11, Zone 4.

Laundry La Providence, at the west end of the plaza on Diagonal 4 (Mon–Sat 8am–noon & 2–5pm).

Post office 2 C and 2 Av (Mon–Fri 8am–4.30pm).

Spanish schools If you enjoy Cobán's slightly subdued atmosphere you could spend some time studying Spanish here. Schools include the Active Spanish School, 3 C 6–12 Zona 1 (☎ & ℱ952 1432, ⓦwww.spanish-schools.com/coban/city /ce.htm), and the Instituto Cobán Internacional (INCO Int), 6 Av 5–39, Zona 3 (☎ & ℱ951 2459, ⓦwww.worldwide.edu/ci/guatemala/schools/15017 .html); while Muq'b'ilbe, 6 Av 5–39, Zona 3 (☎951 2459, ⓦwww.guatemala365.com/english /schools/schu005.htm) also offers Q'eqchi' language study. All the schools offers free excursions, with rates starting at US$120 a week for 20 hours' tuition and full board.

Telephones Telgua has its main office in the plaza (daily 7am–midnight).

Tours Proyecto Eco-Quetzal, at 2 C 14–36, Zona 1 (☎ & ℱ952–1047, ℮bidaspeq@guate.net), is a highly recommended adventure and cultural tourism specialist, enabling visitors to really get off the beaten track and visit some beautiful, remote areas of the Verapaces. Trips, all using local guides, include a three-day hike into the Chicacnab cloudforest (see p.310) where quetzals are abundant, and five-day excursions to Laguna Lachuá and the Ixcán. Costs are set at around US$15 per person per day, and it's also possible to opt for a teacher-guide so you can learn Spanish on the trip for US$28 per day. Tours to Semuc Champey, Lanquín, the Rey Marco caves and other destinations in the Verapaces are regularly offered by *Hostal d'Acuña* and Aventuras Turísticas inside the *Hostal Doña Victoria*.

San Pedro Carchá and around

A few kilometres away, **SAN PEDRO CARCHÁ** is a smaller version of Cobán, with silver rather than coffee money firing the economy, and a greater percentage of Maya people. These days the two towns are merging into a single urban sprawl, and many of the buses that go on towards Petén, or even over to Uspantán, leave from Carchá. Some of the Escobar buses from Guatemala City continue to Carchá; others stop at Cobán, in which case you can catch one of the regular shuttle buses between the two. These leave from the terminal in Cobán and from the plaza in Carchá.

In San Pedro Carchá itself the **regional museum** (Mon–Fri 9am–noon & 2–5pm; small fee) in a street beside the church, is worth a visit. It houses a collection of Maya artefacts, dolls dressed in local costumes, and a mouldy collection of stuffed birds and animals, including the inevitable moulting quetzal. Another excursion takes you a couple of kilometres from the centre of town to the **Balneario Las Islas**, a stretch of cool water that's popular for swimming and **camping**, though there are no formal facilities. To get here walk along the main street beside the church and take the third turning on the right. Follow this street for about a kilometre, then take the right-hand fork at the end.

If you want **to stay** in Carchá, try the *Pensión Central*, just off the plaza, or the *Hotel La Reforma*, 4 C 8–45 (both ❷). For **changing money**, there's a branch of the *Banco del Ejército* on the plaza (Mon–Fri 9am–5.30pm, Sat 10am–2pm). **Moving on**, buses to local destinations such as Senahú, El Estor, Lanquín and Cahabón leave from the plaza. Two buses a day (at 10am and noon) leave from beside the *bomberos* for **Uspantán** (pausing just above the terminal in Cobán), where you can get connections to Sacapulas, Nebaj and Quiché. They return from Uspantán at 3am and 3.30am.

Sierra de Caquipec

Southwest of San Pedro Carchá, the dense cloudforests of the **Sierra de Caquipec** probably contain the greatest concentration of **quetzals** (see box on p.303) in Central America. German biologists have established that there are around 26 quetzals per square kilometre (1000 in total) in this thinly populated region, which stretches south towards Tucurú (see p.314), part of which has been declared a habitat sanctuary for Guatemala's national bird. It's now possible to visit the Caquipec mountains as part of an excellent low impact **ecotourism** initiative run by Proyecto Eco-Quetzal (see p.309), staying in the Q'eqchi' Maya village of **Chicacnab**, from where local guides take you into the oak and pine forests where quetzals are abundant. The trips cost US$41 per person for a three-day excursion, which includes (very basic) accommodation, meals and a guide but not public transport from San Pedro Carchá. It's a steep and often very slippy three-hour climb from the village to the forest for quetzal-spotting – you'll need stout walking boots and waterproofs. The guides can also lead you to caves, a lagoon and a viewpoint from where the three towns of Cobán, Carchá and Chamelco can be seen, if the hills aren't wrapped in cloud that is.

San Juan Chamelco

A few kilometres southeast of Cobán, easily reached by regular local buses from the terminal, **SAN JUAN CHAMELCO** is the most important Q'eqchi' settlement in the area. Most of your fellow bus passengers are likely to be women dressed in traditional costume, wearing beautiful cascades of old coins for earrings, and speaking Q'eqchi' rather than Spanish. Chamelco's focal point is a large colonial church, whose facade is rather unexpectedly decorated with twin Maya versions of the Habsburg double eagle – undoubtedly a result of the historic German presence in the region. Inside, you will find the usual hushed devotional tones and flickering candles around the altars. The most significant treasure, the church bell, is hidden in the belfry; it was a gift to the Indian leader Juan Matalbatz from no less than the Holy Roman Emperor Charles V.

The large market around the church sells anything from local farm produce to blue jeans, but very little in the way of crafts, and the best time to visit the village is for its annual **fiesta**, on June 16. A special feature of the festival is the procession, during which participants dress up in a variety of outfits from preconquest Maya costumes to representations of local wildlife, in celebration of the local Q'eqchi' culture and environment.

Not far from Chamelco is a great **place to stay**, *Don Jerónimo's* (☎308 2255, ⓦ www.dearbrutus.com/donjeronimo; ❹ for full board), a vegetarian guesthouse-cum-retreat in sublime countryside, run by a friendly American who has been living off the land for a good twenty years. It's a pleasant five-kilometre walk from Chamelco down a signposted road 150m west of the plaza; alternatively you can catch a pick-up from 0 C and 0 Av heading for the village of Chamil. Just 500m from *Don Jerónimo's* are the **Grutas de Rey Marcos** (daily 9am–5pm; US$3 including guide service, hard hat and boot rental), a series of **caves** discovered in May 1998. The cave system is over a kilometre long, though the tour only takes you a little way into the complex – you have to wade across an underground river at one stage to see some of the best stalactites and stalagmites, including one that's a dead ringer for the leaning tower of Pisa.

△ Old and new water jugs sold at market

East to Lanquín, Semuc Champey and beyond

Northeast of Cobán and San Pedro Carchá a rough, badly maintained road heads off into the hills, connecting a string of coffee fincas. For the first few kilometres the hills are closed in around the road, but as it drops down into the richer land to the north the valleys open out. Their precipitous sides are patched with cornfields and the level central land is saved for the all-important coffee bushes. As the bus lurches along, clinging to the sides of the ridges, there are fantastic views of the valleys below.

The road divides at the **Pajal** junction (43km and up to three hours by bus from Cobán), where one branch turns north to Sebol and Fray Bartolomé de Las Casas and the other cuts down deep into the valley to **LANQUÍN** (another 12km and 45min). This sleepy, modest Q'eqchi' village, where little Spanish is spoken, shelters beneath towering green hills, whose lower slopes are planted with coffee and cardamom bushes. Of the several **pensiones** here, the good, cheap hospedaje-cum-store-cum-comedor, *Divina Providencia* (❶), is the best, offering good grub, steaming hot showers and the only cold beers in town. The clapboard-built rooms are comfortable enough, though you'll probably get to know all about your neighbours' nocturnal pursuits. More luxurious is the *Hotel El Recreo* (☎952 2160, ℻952 2333; ❹), on the entrance road, with a choice of rooms in wooden huts, a restaurant and a pool. There is electricity only between 6pm and 9pm, though, and prices rise at weekends. Perhaps the best place to stay, however, is a ten-minute walk from the village, along the road to Cahabón. *El Retiro* (✉elretirolodge@hotmail.com; ❷) is a wonderful English/Q'eqchi'-owned lodge by the Lanquín river, with camping, palm leaf-thatched cabañas with mosquito screens and hammock space. There's a camp fire and music most nights, and the owners run tours to sights in the region and plan to offer rafting excursions.

The Lanquín caves

Just a couple of kilometres from the village, the **Lanquín caves** are a maze of dripping, bat-infested chambers, stretching for at least 3km underground (daily 8am–noon & 1.30–5pm; US$1.30). To find them, simply walk along the road heading back to Cobán and turn right along a signposted dirt road which turns off towards the river, five minutes after you pass the *Recreo* hotel. A walkway, complete with ladders and chains, has been cut through the first few hundred metres and electric lights have been installed, which makes access substantially easier, though it remains dauntingly slippery. It's also well worth dropping by at dusk, when thousands of bats emerge from the mouth of the cave and flutter off into the night. A small car park near the entrance to the caves has a covered shelter where you're welcome to **camp** or sling your hammock.

Semuc Champey

The other attraction around Lanquín, the extraordinary pools of **Semuc Champey** (US$2.50, parking US$0.75) are harder to reach than the caves, but a great deal more spectacular. **Getting there** can be problematic. If you're very lucky and there are enough tourists in town, you can catch a pick-up at about 8am, returning around noon. Otherwise you can book a tour from Cobán (around US$30 per person) or take the *Hostal d'Acuña* shuttle bus (Wed & Sat, when sufficient demand). Alternatively, Rigoberto Fernández offers a round-trip pick-up service (US$10), which gives you two hours at the pools; you can find him in the unnamed, vivid-green shop beneath the central park.

The hardest option is to walk. It takes around three hours from Lanquín, and can be extremely tough going if the sun is out – take plenty of water. To get there, set out from the village along the gravel road that heads to the south, away from the river. Beyond the houses, this starts to climb back and forth, out of the valley and down into another, then wanders through thick tropical vegetation where bananas, coffee and cardamom plants grow beside scruffy thatched huts. Just as you start to lose hope, the river appears below the road, which heads upstream for a kilometre or so before crossing a suspension bridge. Once you're over the bridge, follow the track uphill for a little way, then bear right and you'll soon come to a car park where you may be asked to buy an entrance ticket. Finally, follow the muddy track that brings you, at long last, to the pools.

This staircase of turquoise waters suspended on a natural limestone bridge has a series of idyllic pools in which you can swim – watch out for the odd sharp edge. The bulk of the **Río Cahabón** runs underground beneath this natural bridge but, if you walk a few hundred metres upstream via a slippery obstacle course of rocks and roots, you can see the aquatic frenzy, where the river plunges into a cavern, cutting under the pools to emerge downstream. If you have a tent or a hammock it makes sense to **stay** the night – there's a thatched shelter, and the altitude is sufficiently low to keep the air warm in the evenings. Be warned, though, it is not safe to leave your belongings unattended.

Beyond Lanquín

Beyond Lanquín the road continues to **CAHABÓN** – which has two basic pensiones, the best being *Hospedaje Carolina* (❶) – another 24km to the east, and from there a very rough road heads south towards Panzós (see p.315), cutting high over the mountains through superb scenery. The municipality here has appointed a tourism officer who can help out with local excursions – drop into the *Ajuntamiento* or call ☎685 0512 and ask for Javier. Two daily **buses** leave at 4am and 12.30pm for the three-hour trip to El Estor (see p.278), while pick-ups ply the route more frequently. Buses to Cahabón, passing through Lanquín, leave Cobán five times daily (6am, 12.30pm, 1pm, 2pm & 3pm; 4hr; returning at 2am, 3am, 4am, noon & 3pm). On Sundays there may only be three buses, the last being the 3pm service to Cobán, which is always packed. Another extremely rough trail connects Cahabón with Senahú (see p.314), which is sometimes negotiable in a four-wheel drive; check with the tourist officer (see above) about current conditions.

Heading north, buses pass Pajal for **Fray Bartolomé de Las Casas** (from where you can head northeast to Poptún) and **Raxrujá** (see p.315) twice each morning (around 6.30am & 8.30am).

Down the Polochic valley to Panzós

If you're planning to head out towards the Caribbean from Cobán, or simply interested in taking a short trip along backroads, then the **Polochic valley** is an ideal place to spend the day being bounced around inside a bus. Travelling the length of the valley you witness an immense transformation as you drop down through the coffee-coated mountains and emerge into lush, tropical lowlands. To reach the head of the valley you have to travel south from Cobán along the main road to Guatemala City; shortly after Tactic at the San Julián junction, you leave the luxury of tarmac and head off into the valley. The scenery is pure Alta Verapaz: V-shaped valleys where coffee commands the best land and fields of maize cling to the upper slopes wherever they can. The villages are untidy-looking places where the Q'eqchi' and Poqomchi' Maya are largely *ladinized* and seldom wear the brilliant red *huipiles* that used to be traditional here.

The first village at the upper end of the valley is **Tamahú**, 15km below which the village of **Tucurú** marks the point where the valley starts to open out and the river loses its frantic energy. High above Tucurú, in the Caquipec mountains to the north, is a large protected area of pristine cloudforest which contains one of the highest concentrations of **quetzals** anywhere in the world, not to mention an array of other birds and beasts, including some very vocal howler monkeys. The reserve is extremely difficult to reach and you really need a four-wheel drive to get you up there – contact Proyecto Eco-Quetzal in Cobán (see p.309) who run excellent tours into these mountains and can arrange accommodation with local families in the region.

Beyond Tucurú the road plunges abruptly, with cattle pastures starting to take the place of the coffee bushes, and both the villages and the people have a more tropical look about them. After 28km you reach **LA TINTA**, a scruffy town with an excellent, very clean new hospedaje, *Hotel Los Ángeles* (❶/❷) right on the highway, where some rooms have private bath. Continuing east, it's just 13km to **TELEMÁN**, the largest of the squalid trading centres in this lower section of the valley; here, the agreeable family-run *Hotel de los Ralda* on the highway (❣875 0074; ❷/❸) offers rooms with hot water and fans, while the *Ampakito Comedor* serves the town's best food.

A side trip to Senahú

From Telemán a sideroad branches off to the north and climbs high into the lush hills, past row upon row of neatly ranked coffee bushes. As it winds upwards a superb view opens out across the level valley floor below, exposing the river's swirling meanders and a series of oxbows and cut-offs.

Set back behind the first ridge of hills, the small coffee centre of **SENAHÚ** sits in a steep-sided bowl high above the Polochic valley. The village itself is a fairly unremarkable farming settlement, but briefly hit the front pages in March 2001 when a 1000-strong mob attacked and brutally murdered a judge who had freed two rape suspects. The army only restored peace after the suspects had been killed and a three-day blockade had isolated the town from the rest of the country.

Today, things seem to have settled down and Senahú is well worth a visit, not least as an ideal starting point for a wander in the Alta Verapaz hills, with superb hikes to the nearby **Cuevas de Seamay**, used by Maya shamen for ceremonies, and to Semuc Champey and Lanquín (see above). Of several simple pensiones, the best are the simple *Edilson* (❶) and, on the central plaza, the pleasant, twelve-room *Hotel El Recreo Senahú* (❣952 2160; ❸), where guides can be arranged. Several **buses** (plus some minibuses) connect Senahú and Cobán daily, leaving the terminal in Cobán at 6am, 10am, noon and 2pm; the first bus returns from Senahú at 11.30pm. Alternatively, you could easily hitch a ride on a pick-up or truck from Telemán.

Two kilometres to the east of Senahú a gravel road, occasionally served by buses, runs to the *Finca El Volcán*, beyond which you can continue towards Semuc Champey (see above), passing the *Finca Arenal* en route. The walk takes two to three days, and with the uncertainty of local weather conditions you can expect to be regularly soaked, but the dauntingly hilly countryside and the superb fertility of the vegetation make it all worthwhile. The best way to find the route is to hire a guide in Senahú, though you do pass several substantial fincas where you can ask for directions. Another hike takes you to Cahabón through some equally stunning lush mountain terrain – ask at the *Edilson* or the *Hotel El Recreo Senahú* for directions. Sometimes you can make this trip in a four-wheel drive.

Panzós

Heading on down the Polochic valley you reach **PANZÓS**, the largest of the valley villages. Its name means "place of the green waters", a reference to the swamps that surround the river, infested with alligators and bird life. It was here in Panzós that the old Verapaz railway from the Caribbean coast ended, and goods were transferred to boats for the journey across Lago de Izabal. In 1978, Panzós made international headlines when a group of campesinos attending a meeting to settle land disputes were gunned down by the army and local police, in one of the earliest and most brutal massacres of General Lucas García's regime. The day before the atrocity, bulldozers had prepared mass graves at two sites outside the town before the demonstrators even arrived. About a hundred men, women and children were killed, and the event is generally regarded as a landmark in the history of political violence in Guatemala, after which the situation deteriorated rapidly. García's interest in the dispute, however, may have been more personal than political, as he owned 78,000 acres of land in the area around Panzós.

North towards Petén

In the far northern section of the Alta Verapaz, the lush hills drop away steeply onto the limestone plain that marks the frontier with the department of Petén. The road network here is rough and ready, to say the least, and each year roads return to jungle while others are cut and repaired. Understandably, then, many maps of the area are riddled with errors. At present, two roads head north: the first from Cobán via **Chisec**, the second from San Pedro Carchá, via Pajal. From the **Pajal** junction it's a slow, very beautiful journey through typical alpine scenery, a verdant landscape of impossibly green mountains, tiny adobe-built hamlets, pasture and pine forests. After three hours or so of twists and turns you'll reach **Sebol**, a beautiful spot on the Río Pasión where waterfalls cascade into the river and a road heads off for **FRAY BARTOLOMÉ DE LAS CASAS**, 5km to the east. This featureless town has been left off many maps, though it boasts several **hospedajes** – the best are the clean *Hotel Diamelas* (❷) and the basic *Pensión Ralíos* (❶) – and a couple of banks. Buses leave Las Casas for Cobán (7hr) four times daily and also head northeast to Poptún (see p.329) daily at 3am (5hr 30min); buses to Las Casas from Cobán are also four-daily. There are also regular flights from the airstrip to Cobán (US$16); check in the *municipalidad* for details of the next departures. Back on the main road, the next stop is the small settlement of **Raxrujá**, where the buses from Cobán terminate, with only pick-ups and trucks continuing north to **Cruce del Pato** and then on, either up to Sayaxché and Petén or west into the Ixcán.

Raxrujá and the Candelaria caves

RAXRUJÁ (spelt locally Raxruhá), 26km southeast of Cruce del Pato, is the best place to get a pick-up, truck or, if you're very lucky, a bus north to Sayaxché and Flores or west to Playa Grande and the Ixcán. Little more than a few streets and an army base straggling round the bridge over the Río Escondido, a tributary of the Pasión, it has the only **accommodation** for miles around, so you may end up staying here; *Hotel Raxruhá* (❶), next to the

Texaco garage, is the best on offer. There are plenty of quite reasonable places to **eat** in town, including the *Comedor Vidalia*, and a Banrural (Mon–Fri 8am–5pm, Sat 9am–1pm) next to *Hotel Raxruhá* which will cash dollars and travellers' cheques. Buses leave for Cobán at 4am and 1pm; buses from Cobán leave at 6am and 8am. Heading north, there are occasional buses but expect to have to travel by pick-up or minibus.

The limestone mountains to the west of Raxrujá are full of caves, including the spectacular **Candelaria** complex 10km out of town, off the road to Chisec. This series of caverns, stretching for around 18km and including some truly monumental chambers – "Tzul Tacca" is over 200m long – is located on private property a short walk from the road, and is guarded by Daniel Dreux, who has set up the **Complejo Cultural de Candelaria** conservation area. Entrance to the complex, including a two-hour tour and a guide to the first cave system, costs US$4 per person, while a two-day tour by lancha costs US$35 per person. Alternatively contact one of the Cobán travel agents (see p.309) or the official agents, PTP, 15 C 3–20, Zona 10 in Guatemala City (℡363 4404, ⓦwww.ptpmayas.com), to organize a trip. The wonderful **accommodation** in the complex (US$50 a day per person including two meals) is often block-booked by French tour groups but you can **camp** close to the entrance at the *Rancho Ríos Escondidos*.

The area beyond Raxrujá, where the rolling foothills of the highlands give way to the flat expanse of southern Petén, is known as the **Northern Transversal Strip** and is the source of much contentious political debate in Guatemala. In the 1970s it was earmarked for development as a possible solution to the need for new farmland and pressures for agrarian reform, but widespread corruption ensured that huge parcels of land, complete with their valuable mineral resources, were dispersed no further than the generals: the land was dubbed "Generals' Strip". Since then oil reserves have been developed around Playa Grande, in the west of the area and the region saw heavy fighting between the army and guerrillas in the late 1980s.

Playa Grande (Cantabál, Ixcán)

Continuing west from Raxrujá, trucks regularly make the 90km journey over rough roads to **Playa Grande** (up to 6hr), a bridging point over the Río Negro. There's nothing here but the bridge, a huge army base and a couple of comedores, but it's a loading point for grain travelling downriver, so you might get a boat.

The town formerly known as **PLAYA GRANDE** (also referred to as **CANTABÁL** or **IXCÁN**), 7km west of the river crossing, is an authentic frontier settlement with cheap hotels, rough bars and brothels, plus a smattering of development agencies. It's also the administrative and transport centre of the region. If you need to **stay**, the best options are the basic but clean *Hospedaje Torre Visión* (➊) or *Pensión Reyna* (➊), which has at least some semblance of a courtyard.

The prime point of interest in this area is the **Parque Nacional Laguna Lachuá**, a stunning little crater lake 8km to the east of Playa Grande. Any truck driver will drop you off at the entrance, which is signposted right by the road – it's a four-kilometre walk from here to the shore. One of the least visited national parks in Central America, this is a beautiful, tranquil spot, the clear, almost circular lake completely surrounded by dense tropical forest (though see below). The lake smells slightly sulphurous, but the water is good for swimming, with curious horseshoe-shaped limestone formations by the edge that make perfect individual bathing pools. You'll see otters and an abundance of

The Xamán massacre

Since 1992, communities of refugees, mainly highland Maya, have been settling in pockets of land in the "frontier" country of northern Alta Verapaz. On the whole, the *repatriados*, some of whom have been in exile in Mexico for decades, have reintegrated peacefully, with one notable exception. In 1994 a group of 206 Mam-, Ixil-, Q'ekchi'-, Q'anjob'al- and K'cihe'-speaking Maya families established a settlement in **Xamán**, near Chisec, as part of a government-sponsored programme. A year later, soldiers entered the community and opened fire indiscriminately, killing eleven and wounding thirty others. Both Amnesty International and MINUGUA (the UN Guatemalan peace mission) immediately held soldiers from Military Barracks Zona 21 responsible. Though the Minister of Defence resigned and the Commander of Military Zona 21 was dismissed days after the killing, it took five years to bring the suspects to trial, illustrating the formidable barriers to justice involving the prosecution of military personnel. The commanding officer and 24 soldiers were eventually found guilty of manslaughter and "complicity to manslaughter" in 1999. Though this was a landmark judgement, the first time that members of the military had ever been successfully prosecuted, the sentences were derisory: between four and five years, commutable by each soldier paying five quetzales (approximately US$0.65) for each day of the sentence – a total of US$975–1218 per soldier.

bird life, but watch out for mosquitoes. There's a large thatched *rancho* by the shore, ideal for camping or slinging a hammock (available for rent). Though fireplaces and wood are provided, you'll need to bring food and drinking water. Canoes are also available for rent.

Despite the Laguna Lachuá being officially protected as national park, thirty percent of the reserve's mahogany trees were illegally cleared by 150 highly organized **loggers** – who were accompanied by armed guards for protection – in February 1999. Park officials who attempted to stop the plunder were forced to suspend patrols after the intruders threatened to lynch them. Though arrests were made, mobs connected with the timber companies quickly freed the loggers from Playa Grande police station where they were being held. They then kidnapped an official of the Nature Conservation Union, holding him until authorities agreed to release a jailed timber merchant. Similar incidents have occurred throughout northern Guatemala, where loggers enjoy virtual impunity from arrest, environmentalists live in fear of their lives, and a nature reserve often amounts to little more than lines on a map.

You can get to Playa Grande **from Cobán** on one of the endless streams of trucks setting out from the corner of the bus terminal – a journey of at least eight hours. Heading south **from Sayaxché** you need to catch a bus or pick-up to Playitas via Cruce del Pato and take another pick-up or truck from there. There are also regular flights from the airstrip in Cobán.

Into the Ixcán

The Río Negro marks the boundary between the departments of Alta Verapaz and Quiché; the land to the west is known as the **Ixcán**. This huge swampy forest, some of which was settled in the 1960s and 1970s by peasants migrating from the highlands, became a bloody battleground in the 1980s. In the last few years, the Ixcán has become a focal **repatriado** settlement as refugees who fled to Mexico in the 1980s are resettled in a string of "temporary" camps west of the river. Travelling further west, across the Ixcán and into northern Huehuetenango, though no longer hazardous, is still fairly ardous, taking two days to get from Playa Grande to Barillas (see p.212). **Veracruz**, 20km (1hr

30min) from Playa Grande, is the first place of note, a *repatriado* settlement at the crossroads beyond the Río Xalbal. Some buses continue to Mayalan, 12km away, across the presently unbridged Río Piedras Blancas. Here the road ends and you'll have to walk the next 15km to **Altamirano** on the far bank of the Río Ixcán – if you're in good shape it'll take about four or five hours. The path is easy to follow, and passes several tiny villages. At the last village, **Rancho Palmeras**, ask for directions to the crossing point on the Ixcán, where boys

Fiestas

The Verapaces are famous for their fiestas, and in Baja Verapaz especially you'll see an unusual range of traditional dances. In addition, Cobán hosts the **National Fiesta of Folklore**, at the start of August, which is attended by indigenous groups from throughout the country.

January
Rabinal's fiesta, famed for its traditional dances, runs from the 19th to 25th, with the most important events taking place on the 23rd (the Rabinal Achi dance) and the 24th. **Tamahú** has a fiesta from the 22nd to 25th, with the 25th being the main day.

May
Santa Cruz Verapaz has a fiesta from the 1st to 4th, including the dances of *Los Chuntos*, *Vendos* and *Mamah-Num*. **Tucurú** celebrates from the 4th to 9th, with the main day on the 8th.

June
Senahú has its fiesta from the 9th to 13th, with the main day on the 13th. In **Purulhá** the action is from the 10th to 13th, which is the principal day. **San Juan Chamelco** has a fiesta from the 21st to 24th, in honour of San Juan Bautista. In **San Pedro Carchá** the fiesta is from the 24th to 29th, with the main day on the 29th: here you may witness the dances of *Moros y Cristianos* and *Los Diablos*. **Chisec** has a fiesta from the 25th to 30th; the main day is the 29th.

July
Cubulco has a very large fiesta from the 20th to 25th, in honour of Santiago Apostol. Dances include the *Palo Volador*, *Toritos*, *Los 5 Toros* and *El Chico Mudo*, among others. **San Cristóbal Verapaz** has a fiesta from the 21st to 26th, also in honour of Santiago.

August
The fiesta in **Cobán** lasts from July 31 to August 6, and is immediately followed by the **National Fiesta of Folklore**. **Tactic** has a fiesta from the 11th to 16th, with the main day on the 15th. In **Lanquín** the fiesta runs from the 22nd to 28th, with the last day as the main day. In **Chajal** the fiesta takes place from the 23rd to 28th, and in **Panzós** it lasts from the 23rd to 30th.

September
Cahabón has a fiesta from the 4th to 8th, with the main day on the 6th. **Salamá** has its fiesta from the 17th to 21st, with the principal day on the 17th. In **San Miguel Chicaj** the fiesta runs from the 25th to 29th, and in **San Jerónimo** it lasts from the 27th right through until October 10th.

December
Santa Cruz El Chol has a fiesta from the 6th to 8th, with the main day on the 8th.

will pole you across the flowing river. Once across, Altamirano is still a few kilometres away up the hill. From here a regular flow of trucks make the thirty-kilometre journey to Barillas, taking at least four hours over some of the worst roads in the country. It's a spectacular journey, though, especially as you watch the growing bulk of the Cuchumatanes rising ever higher on the horizon. You can also get trucks over the border into **Mexico**, taking you to Chajul on the Río Lacantún in Chiapas, but you need a Guatemalan exit stamp first, probably best obtained in Cobán or Flores.

Travel details

Buses

Baja Verapaz

Transportes Dulce María, 11 Av and 17 C, Zona 1, Guatemala City (☎ 253 4618), runs hourly buses from Guatemala City to Salamá (3hr 30min), half of which continue on to Rabinal (4hr 30min) and Cubulco (5hr 30min).

A daily bus from Guatemala City to Cubulco via El Chol leaves the Zona 4 terminal at 10am and from Cubulco on the return journey at 11pm (about 9hr).

Heading for Baja Verapaz from Cobán or from Guatemala City you can also take any bus between the two (see below) and get off at La Cumbre (de Santa Elena) from where minibuses run to Salamá.

Alta Verapaz

Cobán to Guatemala City (4–5hr). First-class pullman services (half-hourly 2am–5pm) calling at all points in between including Biotopo del Quetzal and Tactic, are run by the efficient Transportes Escobar y Monja Blanca, at 8 Av 15–16, Zona 1, Guatemala City (☎ 251 1878), and at 2 C 3–77, Zona 4, Cobán (☎ 952 1536 or 951 3571). Return journeys from Guatemala City to Cobán also leave half-hourly between the same times.

Cobán to Cahabón (4hr). Five buses leave daily at 6am, 11am, 12.30pm, 2pm and 3pm, passing through Lanquín (3hr). The return buses leave Cahabon for San Pedro Carchá and Cobán at 2am, 3am, noon and 2pm, reaching Lanquín an hour later.

Cobán to Fray Bartolomé de Las Casas (7hr). Daily buses leave at 5.30am, 6.30am and 10am with an occasional extra service at midday. The first return bus leaves Las Casas for Cobán at midnight.

Cobán to Panzós (around 8hr). Buses leave daily from the terminal in Cobán at 5.30am, 7am, 8am, 9am, 11am, noon and 1pm. For the return journey, seven buses leave Panzós daily between 2.30am and 4.30pm.

Cobán to Raxrujá (9hr). Two departures daily at 6am and 8am to Raxrujá, from where there are pick-ups to Sayaxché. If you miss the morning Raxrujá buses, take a bus to Las Casas, get off at Sebol and get a pick-up from there.

Cobán to San Cristóbal Verapaz (45min) every thirty minutes from the Cobán terminal.

Cobán to Senahú (around 7hr). Four departures daily at 6am, 10am, noon and 2pm. From Senahú to Cobán the first bus leaves at 11.30pm.

San Pedro Carchá to Uspantán (5hr). Two daily at 10am and noon. From Uspantán there's a connecting bus to Santa Cruz del Quiché, which passes through Sacapulas, for connections to Nebaj (see p.148). Buses for San Pedro Carchá and Cobán leave Uspantán at 3am and 3.30am.

Pick-ups

Cobán to Chisec (3hr 30min) and Playa Grande (8hr); both leave when full from the market.

Domestic flights

Cobán to Guatemala City (1 daily; 30min); Fray Bartolomé de Las Casas and Playa Grande (irregular flights to both).

Petén

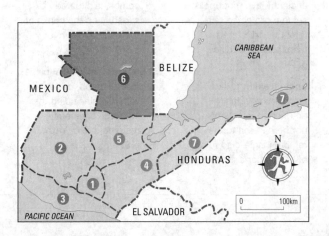

CHAPTER 6 # Highlights

Petén

The vast northern department of **Petén** occupies about a third of Guatemala but contains less than three percent of its population. This huge expanse of swamps, dry savannahs and tropical rainforest forms part of an untamed wilderness that stretches into the Lacandón forest of southern Mexico and across the Maya Mountains to Belize. Totally unlike any other part of the country, much of it is virtually untouched, with ancient ceiba and mahogany trees that tower 50m above the forest floor. Undisturbed for so long, the area is also extraordinarily rich in **wildlife**. Some 285 species of bird have been sighted at Tikal alone, including a wide range of hummingbirds, toucans, blue and white herons, hawks, buzzards, wild turkeys and the motmot (a bird of paradise). Many of these can be seen quite easily in the early morning and evening, when their cries fill the air. Beneath the forest canopy lurk many other species that are harder to locate. Among the mammals are the lumbering tapir, ocelots, deer, coatis, jaguars, monkeys, plus crocodiles and thousands of species of plants, snakes, insects and butterflies.

Recently, however, this position of privileged isolation has been threatened by moves to colonize the country's final frontier. Waves of **settlers**, lured by offers of free land, have cleared enormous tracts of jungle, while oil exploration and commercial logging have brought with them mountains of money and machinery, cutting new roads deep into the forest. The population of Petén, in 1950 just 15,000, is today estimated at over 400,000, a number which puts enormous pressure on the remaining forest. Various attempts have been made to halt the tide of destruction and in 1990 the government declared that forty percent of Petén would be protected as the **Reserva Biósfera Maya** (Maya Biosphere Reserve), although little is done to enforce this. Today, though there are numerous Petén-based environmental groups committed to preserving the remaining forests, activists are subject to routine threats and protective laws are widely ignored.

Accommodation price codes

All accommodation listed in this guide has been graded according to the following price scales. These refer to the price in US dollars of the cheapest double room in high season. For more details see p.34.

❶ Under US$5	❹ US$15–25	❼ US$60–80
❷ US$5–10	❺ US$25–40	❽ US$80–100
❸ US$10–15	❻ US$40–60	❾ Over US$100

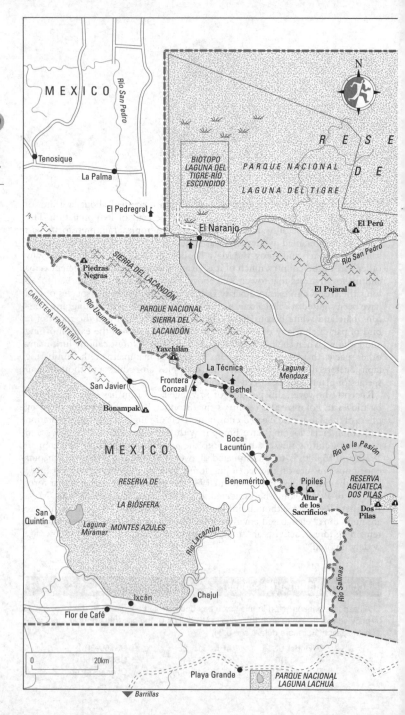

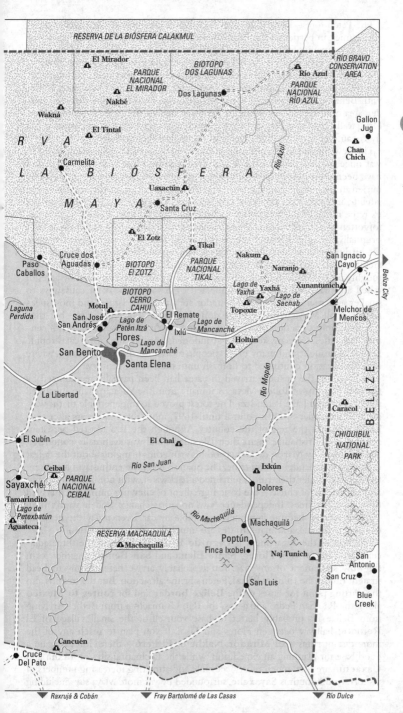

RESERVA DE LA BIÓSFERA CALAKMUL

El Mirador

PARQUE NACIONAL EL MIRADOR

BIOTOPO DOS LAGUNAS

Río Azul

RÍO BRAVO CONSERVATION AREA

Nakbé

Dos Lagunas

PARQUE NACIONAL RÍO AZUL

Wakná

Gallon Jug

El Tintal

Chan Chich

R V A

Carmelita

L A   B I Ó S F E R A

Uaxactún

M A Y A

Santa Cruz

El Zotz

Tikal

Nakum

San Ignacio (Cayo)

Paso Caballos

Cruce dos Aguadas

BIOTOPO EL ZOTZ

PARQUE NACIONAL TIKAL

Naranjo

Belize City

BIOTOPO CERRO CAHUÍ

Lago de Yaxhá

Yaxhá

Xunantunich

Lago de Sacnab

Laguna Perdida

Motul

San José

El Remate

Topoxte

Melchor de Mencos

San Andrés

Lago de Petén Itzá

Ixlú

Lago de Mancanché

Flores

San Benito

Lago de Mancanché

Holtún

Santa Elena

Río Mopán

B E L I Z E

La Libertad

El Subín

El Chal

Caracol

CHIQUIBUL NATIONAL PARK

Ixkún

Ceibal

PARQUE NACIONAL CEIBAL

Río San Juan

Dolores

Sayaxché

Tamarindito

Lago de Petexbatún

Aguateca

Río Machaquilá

Machaquilá

RESERVA MACHAQUILÁ

Machaquilá

Poptún

Finca Ixobel

Naj Tunich

San Antonio

San Cruz

San Luis

Blue Creek

Cancuén

Cruce Del Pato

▼ Raxrujá & Cobán   ▼ Fray Bartolomé de Las Casas   ▼ Río Dulce

The Petén forests historically provided shelter for some of Guatemala's guerrilla armies, in particular the FAR (Rebel Armed Forces) during the civil war. This led to many of the settlers being driven across the border into Mexico and becoming refugees, while the oil industry, too, had to withdraw from some of the worst-hit areas. Today most of the refugees have returned, though there are still small pockets of tension in the region. Many disputes are over land rights, with Belizean troops evicting Guatemalan campesinos from the disputed border area and mass occupations of privately owned fincas by peasant groups. Drug traffickers have also moved into Petén to set up marijuana plantations and fly cocaine in from South America to the region's remote airstrips.

The new interest in the region is in fact something of a reawakening, as Petén was once the heartland of the **Maya civilization**. More than 200 Maya sites have been reported in the region, although many of them remain completely buried in the jungle, and some are known only to locals. In the last few years, satellite imagery has uncovered the remains of a large city, El Pajaral, in the extreme north of the area, while archeological expeditions to two other near-forgotten sites, Cancuén and Wakná, have revealed them to be much larger than originally thought. It's now accepted that the forests of northern Petén were the birthplace of Maya culture, a culture which went on reach the height of its architectural, scientific and artistic achievement during the Classic period, roughly 300–900 AD. Great cities rose out of the forest, surrounded by acres of raised and irrigated fields and connected by a vast network of causeways to smaller settlements. Tikal and El Mirador are among the largest and most spectacular of all **Maya ruins** – Tikal alone has some 3000 buildings – but they represent only a fraction of what was once here. At the close of the tenth century the cities were mysteriously abandoned, possibly due to a catastrophic period of drought, and many of the people moved north to the Yucatán, where Maya civilization continued to flourish until the twelfth century.

By the time the Spanish arrived the area had been partially recolonized by the Itza, a group of Toltec–Maya (originally from the Yucatán) who inhabited the land around Lake Petén Itzá. The forest proved so impenetrable that it wasn't brought under Spanish control until 1697, more than 150 years after they had conquered the rest of the country. Although the Itza resisted persistent attempts to Christianize them, their lakeside capital was eventually conquered and destroyed by Martín de Ursúa and his army, thus bringing about the defeat of the last independent Maya tribe. The Spanish had little enthusiasm for Petén, though, and under their rule it remained a backwater, with nothing to offer but a steady trickle of chicle – the basic ingredient of chewing gum, which is bled from sapodilla trees. Independence saw no great change, and it wasn't until 1970 that Petén became genuinely accessible by car. Even today the network of roads is skeletal, and many routes are impassable in the wet season.

The hub of the department is **Lago de Petén Itzá**, where the three adjacent lakeside towns of **Flores**, **Santa Elena** and **San Benito** together form the only settlement of any size. You'll probably arrive here, if only to head straight out to the ruins of **Tikal**, Petén's prime attraction. But the town is also the starting point for buses to the **Belize border** and for **routes to Mexico** along the Río San Pedro and across the Río Usumacinta from Bethel. Arriving from Belize it's probably better to base yourself at the small village of **El Remate**, halfway between Flores and Tikal. If you plan to reach any of the more distant ruins – **El Mirador**, **Nakbé** or **El Perú** – then Flores is again a good base for planning an expedition, while the fascinating sites of **Yaxhá** and **Uaxactún** are now much more accessible and attracting increasing numbers of visitors. To the south is **Sayaxché**, surrounded by yet more Maya sites including

The idea behind biosphere reserves, conceived in 1974 by UNESCO, is an ambitious attempt to combine the protection of natural areas and the conservation of their genetic diversity with scientific research and sustainable development. The **Reserva Biósfera Maya** (the Maya Biosphere Reserve) created in 1990, covers 16,000 square kilometres of northern Petén: in theory it is the largest tropical forest reserve in Central America.

On the premise that conservation and development can be compatible, land use in the reserve has three designations: **core areas** include the national parks, major archeological sites and the *biotopos*, areas of scientific investigation. The primary role of core areas is to preserve biodiversity; human settlements are prohibited though tourism is permitted. Surrounding the core areas are **multiple-use areas** where inhabitants, aided and encouraged by the government and NGOs, are able to engage in sustainable use of the forest resources and small-scale agriculture. The **buffer zone**, a fifteen-kilometre wide belt along the southern edge of the reserve, is intended to prevent further human intrusion while containing many existing villages.

Fine in theory, particularly when you consider that much of the northern reserve skirts the Reserva Biósfera Calakmul in Mexico and that protected land in Belize forms much of the reserve's eastern boundary. In practice, however, the destruction of Petén's **rainforest** proceeds virtually unchecked. Less than fifty percent of the original cover remains and illicit logging, often conducted from Mexico with the complicity of Guatemalan officials, is reducing it further. Although the soil is thin, poor migrant families from Guatemala's agriculturally impoverished southeastern departments arrive daily to carve out *milpas* – slash-and-burn holdings – in the sparsely settled buffer and multiple-use zones. Oil extraction takes place in core areas in the northwest and new roads are being built. Some areas of the reserve are being allocated for *repatriado* – returning refugee – settlement, causing acrimony between those government departments whose task is to assist the refugees and those whose job it is to protect the reserve.

Although alarming and very real, the threats to the integrity of the reserve are being tackled by a number of government agencies and NGOs, both Guatemalan and international. Foreign funding, from aid programmes and conservation organizations, provides much of the finance for protection, and people living in remote villages realize that their future depends on sustainable use of forest resources. Tourism is an accepted part of the plan and, though most visitors see little outside Tikal and Flores, a trip to the more remote *biotopos* and national parks is possible as guides and the basic infrastructure become more organized.

Ceibal, which boasts some of the best-preserved carvings in Petén, and also the ruined cities of the **Lago de Petexbatún** region. From Sayaxché you can set off down the Río Pasión to **Mexico** and the ruins of **Yaxchilán**, or take an alternative route back to Guatemala City – via Cobán in Alta Verapaz.

Getting to Petén

Most visitors arrive in Petén by bus or plane directly **from Guatemala City**: by air it's a short fifty-minute hop; by bus it can take anywhere between eight and ten hours, despite the recent upgrading of the road between Río Dulce and Flores.

A number of domestic airlines **fly** the route daily and tickets can be bought from virtually any travel agent in the country; prices range between US$70 and US$120 depending on the airline. Some of the planes really are tiny; the largest twin jet-engined craft are operated by Tikal Jets. It's important to assertain which terminal your flight departs from: Taca and Tikal Jets' flights leave from the **international side** while all other airlines depart from their offices inside the airport perimeter (entrance on Avenida Hincapie). Most flights leave between 6am and 7.30am in the morning, enabling day-tripping visitors to spend several hours at Tikal, returning between 3.30pm and 5pm (though there are departures at other times of day). Flights are heavily in demand in the peak tourist season, and overbooking is common at all times of year.

Buses to Flores from Guatemala City are run by six companies, all operating from a pretty sleazy part of Zona 1 between 16 and 17 calles and 8 and 10 avenidas. Between them they operate around thirty buses a day, all of which pass the Río Dulce bridge (for **Lívingston**) after about five hours and Poptún after about six and a half hours. The best buses are the luxurious a/c pullmans run by Línea Dorada which leave daily from 16 C 10–55, Zona 1 (☏ 926 0528, ⓦ www.lineadorada.com) at 9am, 8pm and 9pm; you pay either US$16 for an "economic" bus (which is still very comfortable) or a hefty US$28 for the very flash "luxury" service with meals and movies. (These Línea Dorada buses connect with luxury Mundo Maya services for onward travel to Belize and Chetumal in Mexico.) If you want a reasonably comfortable ride, try Fuente del Norte (☏ 251 3817) or Máxima (☏ 232 4684), both of which run decent buses, from the corner of 9 Av and 17 C for US$13 one-way. Fares are about forty percent cheaper on their standard *corriente* services, but the journey can take ten hours.

Coming **from the highlands**, you can get to Petén along the backroads from Cobán in Alta Verapaz, a long, exhausting and adventurous route covered in more detail on p.315. You can also enter **from Belize** through the border at Melchor de Mencos or **from Mexico** – the most widely used route is now via Frontera Corozal to Bethel, but there are other river routes from Palenque (see p.366) and Tenosique (see p.369) in Mexico.

Guatemala City to Flores

If you don't want to do the 554-kilometre trip from the capital to Flores in one go, it's easy enough to do it in stages. Heading along the Carretera al Atlántico, the first place of interest are the ruins of **Quiriguá** (see p.259) at km 204 on the highway, which are famed for their colossal stelae. Shortly afterwards, the road to Petén turns north at the **Ruidosa junction**, soon crossing the **Río Dulce** at the stopping-off place for the boat to Lívingston. From here it continues through Modesto Méndez and on through San Luis through a degraded landscape of small *milpa* farms and cattle ranches that were untouched jungle a decade or two ago. **Poptún**, 107km short of Flores, is the first place inside Petén that's worth a look: a dusty frontier settlement that's the unlikely embodiment of rustic bliss and organic food, thanks to the proximity of the *Finca Ixobel* (see below).

Finca Ixobel

Some 4km south of Poptún, surrounded by aromatic pine forests in the cool foothills of the Maya Mountains, the *Finca Ixobel* (☏ & ⓕ 927 7363, ⓦ www .fincaixobel.conexion.com) is a working farm that provides **accommodation** to passing tourists. The farm was originally run by Americans Mike and Carole DeVine, but on June 8, 1990, Mike was murdered by the army. This prompted the American government to suspend military aid to Guatemala and, after a drawn-out investigation which cast little light on their motives, five soldiers were convicted of the murder in September 1992. Others involved have managed to evade capture and their commanding officer, Captain Hugo Contreras, escaped from jail shortly after his arrest. Carole fought the case for years and remains at the finca.

Finca Ixobel is a supremely beautiful and relaxing place, where you can swim in the pond, walk in the forest, dodge the resident "attack" macaws and stuff yourself stupid with healthy home-grown food. There are **hikes** into the jungle, horse-riding trips, rafting, 4WD jungle jaunts, and short excursions to nearby caves. Accommodation is in attractive bungalows with private bath (❹), regular rooms (❷/❸), or dorms (US$3.50 per bed), and there's also camping and hammock space (US$3) plus tree houses (❷). You run up a tab for accommodation, food and drink, paying when you leave – which can be a rude awakening. Many travellers are quickly seduced by the tranquil nature of the finca and end up staying much longer than planned, some working as cooks or helpers in exchange for board and lodging. To get to the finca, ask the bus driver to drop you at the gate (marked by a large sign), from where it's a fifteen-minute walk through the pine trees; after dark, it's safest to head for the *Fonda Ixobel 2* restaurant (see below) in Poptún and they'll call a taxi (US$1.50) to drop you off.

Poptún and around

The scruffy town of **POPTÚN** makes a useful stop off on the way to Flores, with a Telgua office, banks, several pensiones. One of the best is the friendly *Hotel Posada de los Castellanos*, in the centre of town (☎927 7222, ℉927 7365; ❷), where all rooms have hot water and a bathroom; the owners run trips to destinations around central Petén including the Reserva Machaquilá and the caves at Naj Tunich. Alternatively, the new *El Tapir Backpackers* at 3 C 4–74 (☎927 7327; ❷) is a good choice, run by Héctor and Carmelina Gómez. They run **tours** from here to the *Finca el Tapir*, a remote 1,200 hectare forest reserve rich with wildlife which they also own. Four-day hikes (US$60) and five-day horseback excursions (US$70) to the forest are offered, plus day-trips by jeep to jungle and caves (US$20 per person) closer to town. The best **food** in Poptún is at the *Fonda Ixobel 2*, which serves good bread and cakes, or try the *Comedor los Claveles* for tasty Guatemalan grub.

The limestone hills surrounding Poptún are riddled with **caves** and coated in lush tropical forest. One of the largest caves contains an underground river and waterfall that you can swim through (if you don't mind leaping into a chilly pool in total darkness); walking trips to this cave system are organized by *Finca Ixobel* (see above). The most impressive, however, is the remote **Naj Tunich** "Stone House", 23km down a rough track from Poptún, close to the Belizean border. At the time of writing the cave system, which is over 1.2km long, was open (daily 8am–5pm; US$2), though it has been periodically closed to all visitors because of the threat from looters. The walls of the cave are decorated with extensive hieroglyphic texts (400 glyphs in total) and **Maya murals**, which, in addition to depictions of religious ceremonies and ball games, include several graphic and well-preserved drawings of erotic scenes, a feature found nowhere else in Maya art. Caves were sacred to the ancient Maya, who believed them to be entrances to Xibalbá, the dreaded underworld, and Naj Tunich was considered one of the most sacred sites of the central Maya region. Many of the glyphic inscriptions were painted by royal scribes from distant cities, including Calakmul in today's Mexico, and the cave was something of a place of pilgrimage for kings eager to secure a favourable passage to the afterlife. Today, trips to Naj Tunich are run by the *Hotel Ecológico*

Villa de los Castellanos (see below) who will have the latest information and can organize a 4WD excursion. If you can't make it to the caves, there's an excellent feature on Naj Tunich in the April 1981 edition of the *National Geographic*.

Six kilometres north of Poptún, just past the village of **Machaquilá**, is the very basic *Cocay Camping* (☎927 7024, ⓦwww.cocay-guesthouse.de; ❶), set in peaceful isolation in thick forest on the banks of the river. It's run by Christina and Paco, former employees at the *Finca Ixobel*, who offer simple stick-and-thatch hut dorms (US$3.40), camping (US$2.80) and vegetarian and European food. Get off the bus at the south side of the river bridge and follow the signs west for ten minutes. Over the bridge to the right, attractively set amongst dense jungle foliage, are the comfortable cabañas of the *Villa de los Castellanos* (☎927 7541, ☎927 7307, www.ecovilla.com; ❺, but ask about special backpacker rates), offering a friendly, comfortable base for adventurous visitors to explore the forests, rivers and caves of central Petén. It's run by the Castellanos family, who've been in Petén since 1720, and Don Placido, the owner, is an excellent source of information – botanical, historical and logistical. He knows Naj Tunich well and organizes trips there, if it's open. The family also organize other tours, including an amazing five-day horseback trip through an area seldom visited by outsiders, across the Reserva Machaquilá, camping at San Miguel caverns and the ruins of Machaquilá, before descending the Río Pasión to Ceibal (see p.359).

Dolores and El Chal

Most of the non-luxury buses to Flores call in at the village of **Dolores**, set back from the road about 20km north of Poptún. Founded in 1708 as an outpost for missionaries working out of Cobán, these days it's a growing town and the area around has been settled by returning refugees and migrants from the eastern highlands. An hour's walk to the north are the unrestored Maya ruins of **Ixkún** (8am–5pm; US$1.80), a mid-sized site made up of eight plazas. Fifteen kilometres north of Dolores a road branches northeast at the village of Sabaneta, making a short cut to the **Belize border**. Some buses from Guatemala to Melchor use this route, though it's liable to flooding and often in bad condition.

A further 30km brings you to the ruins of **El Chal** (daily 8am–5pm; no charge), signed on the west side of the village of the same name, and less than 500m from the road. Call in at the small hut by the entrance to the ruins for a free tour with the guard. The ruins include several plazas and a ball court, and the palace complex, built on a ridge, gives a view of the surrounding countryside. Although some bush has been cleared, the buildings are largely unrestored – the most remarkable features are a couple of stelae and nearby altars with clearly visible glyphs and carved features. If you need **to stay**, there are a couple of basic hotels in the village, the *Medina* and the *Bienestar* (both ❶).

Flores

Although it's the capital of Petén, **FLORES** is an easy-going, sedate place with an old-fashioned atmosphere, quite unlike most towns in the region where commerce and bustle dominate. A cluster of cobbled streets and ageing houses built around a twin-domed church, it sits beautifully on a small island in Lago de Petén Itzá, connected to the mainland by a short (man-made) causeway.

The modern emphasis lies across the water in the twin towns of **SANTA ELENA** and **SAN BENITO**, both of which are ugly, chaotic and sprawling places, dusty in the dry season and mud-bound during the rains. Santa Elena, opposite Flores at the other end of the causeway, is strung out between the airport and the market, and takes in several hotels and banks, the offices of the bus companies and a well-established residential area. San Benito, further west, is at the forefront of the new frontier, complete with rough bars, villains, prostitutes, sleazy hotels and mud-lined streets. The three once distinct towns are now often lumped together under the single name of Flores.

The **lake** is a natural choice for settlement, and its shores were heavily populated in Maya times. The city of **Tayasal**, capital of the Itza, lay on the island that was to become modern Flores. Cortés passed through here in 1525, on his way south to Honduras, and left behind a sick horse which he promised to send for. In 1618 two Franciscan friars arrived to find the people worshipping a large white idol in the shape of a horse called "Tzimin Chac", the thunder horse. Unable to persuade the Maya to renounce their religion they smashed the idol and left the city. Subsequent visitors were less well received; in 1622 a military expedition of twenty men was invited into the city by Canek, chief of the Itza, where they were set upon and sacrificed to the idols. The town was eventually destroyed by Martín de Ursúa and an army of 235 in 1697. The following year the island was fortified in order to be used as an outpost of the Spanish Empire on the Camino Real (Royal Road) to Campeche. For the entire colonial period (and indeed up to the 1960s) Flores languished in virtual isolation, having more contact with neighbouring Belize than the capital.

Today, despite the steady flow of tourists passing through for Tikal, the town retains a genteel air, with residents greeting one another courteously as they meet in the streets. Though it has little to detain you in itself – a leisurely thirty-minute stroll around the cobbled streets and alleyways is enough to become entirely familiar with the place – Flores does offer delightful surroundings and an excellent selection of hotels, restaurants, cybercafés and tour operators.

Arrival

Arriving by bus from Guatemala City you'll be dropped on or near Calle Principal in Santa Elena, just a few blocks from the causeway to Flores, though Línea Dorada buses will continue on to Flores. Coming from the Belize border on Pinita you'll probably be dropped at the *Hotel San Juan*, two blocks south of the causeway in Santa Elena. The **airport** is 3km east of the causeway, a US$2 taxi-ride from town. **Local buses**, known here as *urbanos,* cover the route for Q0.75, but this entails a time-consuming change halfway to get on another bus across the causeway if you're heading to Flores. (Getting **back** to the airport, local buses leave from the Flores end of the causeway about every ten minutes or so.)

Information

The knowledgeable staff at the **Inguat** desk in the arrivals hall at the airport (daily 7am–noon & 3-6pm; ☎926 0533), can give you reasonable maps and good information in English. There's another Inguat office on the central plaza in Flores (Mon–Fri 8am–4.30pm; ☎926 0669), whose staff are helpful but will probably direct you across the plaza to **CINCAP** (Centro de Información sobre la Naturaleza, Cultura y Artesanías de Petén) in the **Castillo de Arismendi** across the plaza (Mon–Fri 9am–1pm & 2–6pm; ☎926 0718), to examine their more detailed maps, books and leaflets about northern Petén. Here at the Castillo, you can see exhibits on historical and contemporary Petén and buy medicinal herbs, collected as part of the effort to promote forest sustainability. This is also the production office of *Destination Petén*, a useful free monthly listings and **information magazine**, available at most hotels and travel agencies.

If you're planning to go on a trip to remote parts of the Reserva Biósfera Maya, the tour agencies listed below (see "Listings", p.336) are usually the best source of logistical information. You should also check with **ProPetén** on Calle Central (Mon–Fri 8am–5pm; ☎926 1370, ℉926 0495, ℮propeten @guate.net) for current information on route conditions, accommodation and

FLORES

0 ────── 200m

Lake Petén Itzá

CALLE FRATERNIDAD
AV. LA LIBERTAD
CALLE LA UNIÓN
Cincap ⓘ
Theatre
Banrural
CENTRAL
AVENIDA FLORES
Catholic Church
Gobernación Departmental
PASAJE...
CALLEJÓN EL RENCHINO
AV. REFORMA
AV. BARRIOS
CALLE EL ROSARIO
CALLE 15 DE SEPTIEMBRE
ⓘ Inguat
ProPetén
Isla Santa Barbara
CALLEJÓN PEDRITO
CALLE 30 DE JUNIO
CALLE CENTRAL
@ Flores Net
EL CRUCERO
CALLE CENTRO AMÉRICA
AVENIDA SANTA ANA
Martsam Travel
Tikal Net
Lanchas to San Benito, San Andrés & San José
Linea Dorada Bus Office
Restaurant Chaltunhá
★ Local Bus to Airport/ Santa Elena/ San Benito
Source: ProPetén

ACCOMMODATION
Casazul   1
Hospedaje Doña Goya   4
Hotel Butterfly Planet   8
Hotel La Casona de la Isla   7
Hotel La Jungla   12
Hotel la Mesa de Los Mayas   9
Hotel Mirador del Lago   6
Hotel Petén   8
Hotel Sabana   2
Hotel La Santana   11
La Casa del Lacandón   3
Posada Tayazal   5

RESTAURANTS & CAFÉS
Crocodile Club   E
El Tucán   G
La Canoa   F
La Luna   A
Las Puertas   C
Maya Princess Café Bar   B
Pizzeria Picasso   D

▼ Causeway to Santa Elena (750 metres approx.)

SANTA ELENA

0 ────── 400m

1 CALLE
1 CALLE A
2 CALLE
SANTA ELENA
3 CALLE
5 AVENIDA
3 CALLE
AVENIDA
Avinsa Travel
SAN BENITO
CALLE PRINCIPAL
Buses to Guatemala City & Poptún
Banco Industrial (ATM)
Hotel Diplomatico Bus Station
@ Tikal Net
4 CALLE (CALLE PRINCIPAL)
4 CALLE A
Market
Buses to Belize
5 CALLE

ACCOMMODATION
Hotel Alonzo   5
Hotel Casa Elena   3
Hotel Jade   1
Hotel Sac-Nicte   2
Hotel Villa Maya   6
Jaguar Inn   4

RESTAURANTS
Mijaro   B
Petenchel   A

▶ Airport, Tikal, Belize & 6

332

guides. They also do **organized trips**, including the "Scarlet Macaw Trail" ("La Ruta Guacamaya"; see p.370), a five-day expedition by truck, horse and boat along rivers and through primary forest, taking in the remote ruins of El Perú and the largest concentration of scarlet macaws in northern Central America.

Accommodation

Accommodation in Flores and Santa Elena has undergone a boom in recent years and the sheer number of new **hotels** keeps prices very competitive. There are several good budget places in Flores itself, making it unnecessary to stay in noisier and dirtier Santa Elena unless your budget is extremely tight. Avoid being press-ganged into staying at the noisy *Hotel San Juan* by their pushy staff – there are a lot of better deals around.

Flores

La Casa del Lacandón on the lakeshore, Calle Fraternidad ☎926 3592. Good new hotel with a selection of accommodation, all with private bath. The downstairs rooms are clean and offer reasonable value, but the upstairs rooms (especially 101 and 105 with stunning lake views) are larger and more attractive. ❸

Casazul close to the northern tip of the island ☎926 1138. Stylishly converted, colonial-style mansion with light, tastefully decorated rooms, all with two double beds, wooden furniture, fridges and a/c. ❻

Hospedaje Doña Goya at the north end of the island ☎926 3538. Excellent family-run budget guest house. Clean, light rooms with fans, some with private bath; the ones at the front have balconies. Also offers a book exchange, a rooftop terrace with hammocks, and trips to nearby caves. Good rates for single travellers. ❷

Hotel Butterfly Planet near the Línea Dorada office ☎926 0357, ✉martsam@guate.net. Clean, inexpensive rooms with shared cold-water bath. Run by Benedicto Grijalva of Martsam Travel, so very good for information and tours. ❷

Hotel la Casona de la Isla Calle 30 de Junio ☎ & ℻926 0593, ⓦwww.corpetur.com. The one with the arresting citrus and powder-blue paint job. Attractive, modern rooms with private bath and a/c, swimming pool and spectacular sunset views from the terrace bar–restaurant. ❺

Hotel la Jungla in the southwest corner of the island ☎926 0634. The best value in this price range, with gleaming tiled floors and private baths with hot water. Also has rooftop views over the town and lake and a good restaurant. ❸

Hotel La Mesa de Los Maya ☎ & ℻926 1240. The hotel is a newish addition to the restaurant, which is a longstanding Flores institution. It's a pleasant place with reasonable prices, though the rooms are a little dark and old-fashioned. ❹

Hotel Mirador del Lago Calle 15 de Septiembre

☎926 3276. Easily the best just-above-budget hotel in Flores, with well-furnished rooms with two beds, private bath and fan. Friendly owner Mimi Salguero (who speaks a little English) keeps the lobby fridge stocked with beer and soft drinks, and has tables on a lakeshore terrace at which to enjoy them. Great sunset views from the roof. ❸

Hotel Petén ☎926 0593, ☎ & ℻926 0692. Friendly, small, modern hotel, with a terrace overlooking the lake. It's run by the ever-helpful Pedro Castellanos, and though the rooms are a shade overpriced and won't win any design awards, they all come with hot water, fans, private bath and lake views. ❺

Hotel Sabana at the northern tip of the island ☎ & ℻926 1248, ⓦwww.sabanahotel.com. Large modern place with a small pool and nice lake views, especially from the restaurant. All 28 rooms have a/c and cable TV and represent good value. ❺

Hotel Santana in the southwest corner of Flores ☎926 0492, ℻926 0662. Recently modernized three-storey building with a small pool and patio overlooking the lake. Very comfortable, spotless rooms with fan and private bath; first-floor rooms have private lakeside terraces and a/c. ❻

Hotel Santa Rita opposite the *Hotel Santana*, close to the southwest corner of Flores ☎926 0710. Decent family-run budget choice, with good-value singles and doubles, though try to book ahead as it's often full. ❷

Posada Tayazal Calle la Unión near the Doña Goya ☎ & ℻926 0568. Well-run budget hotel with decent basic rooms, some with private bath. Shared bathrooms have hot water. Roof terrace, information service and tours to Tikal. ❷

Santa Elena and around

Hotel Alonzo 6 Av 4–99 ☎926 0105. Reasonable budget rooms, some with balconies and a few with private hot- or cold-water bath (the shared bathroom is pretty grubby). There's also a restaurant and a public telephone. ❷/❸

Hotel Casa Elena a block north of the causeway ☎926 2238 & ⓕ926 0097. New executive-style hotel, hardly the most aesthetically pleasing in town, but the rooms are all comfortable with good beds and cable TV. There are also a restaurant, a pool and a rooftop terrace. ❺

Hotel Jade 6 Av. Venerable backpackers' stronghold. Shambolic but the cheapest place in town. ❶

Hotel Sac-Nicté 1 C 4–45 ☎ & ⓕ926 0092. Clean rooms with fans and private shower; those on the second floor have views of the lake. The flexible owners will serve breakfast before the 4am trip to Tikal. ❷

Hotel Villa Maya 10km east of Santa Elena at Lago de Petenchel ☎ & ⓕ926 0086, ⊛www

.villasdeguatemala.com. Sublimely tranquil setting overlooking the Petenchel lagoon, with forty attractive, spacious rooms, a restaurant and a swimming pool. There are hiking trails nearby and guests can hire kayaks, mountain bikes or horses to explore the area. The hotel group also operates the less well-situated *Hotel Villa Maya Internacional* in Santa Elena itself (same contact details). Both ❽

Jaguar Inn Calzada Rodríguez Macal 8–79 ☎ & ⓕ926 0002, ⓔsolis@quetzal.net. Comfortable singles and doubles all with private baths and TV, plus a choice of a/c or fan, but situated a little out of town near the airport. Restaurant, safe parking, and credit cards are accepted. ❹

Eating, drinking and entertainment

Flores unquestionably offers the most cosmopolitan dining in Petén, and there are a number of good **restaurants**, many with delightful lakeside views, though prices are a little higher than elsewhere in Guatemala. Santa Elena has a very limited selection of comedores, so even if you're staying here you may want to cross the causeway for a little more atmosphere. Be warned: many restaurants here serve **wild game**, often listed on menus as *comida silvestre*, and virtually all this has been taken illegally from reserves – avoid in particular ordering items such as *tepescuintle* (paca, a large relation of the guinea-pig), *venado* (deer), or *coche de monte* (peccary, or wild pig).

If you want to experience the dubious thrills of a Petén dancehall, check out *Discoteca Raíces* in Santa Elena for merengue and salsa and western pop and rock. For a quieter place to **drink**, head for the *Maya Princess* or *Las Puertas*.

Flores

La Canoa Calle Centro América. Popular, good-value place, serving pasta, great soups, and some vegetarian and Guatemalan food, as well as excellent breakfasts.

Crocodile Club Calle Centro América, near Martsam Travel and under the same ownership. Bar–restaurant with really good, filling meals (some vegetarian) and bar snacks in a friendly atmosphere. Music, movies, book exchange and information, plus a daily "happy hour" 6.30–8.30pm.

La Luna, at the far end of Calle 30 de Junio. The best restaurant in town, though not that expensive, set in a wonderfully atmospheric old wooden building. Meat, fish and pasta, plus home-made soup and a few vegetarian dishes. It doesn't serve wild game. Also great for an espresso.

Maya Princess Café Bar Avenida la Reforma. An interesting, creatively assembled international menu – teriyaki chicken, salad with basil leaves – and a sociable vibe make this a deservedly popular place. Movies shown at 4pm and 9pm daily, moderate prices.

Pizzeria Picasso across the street from the *Tucán* and run by the same family. Great pizza

served under cooling breezes from the ceiling fans, and they will deliver, call ☎926 0637.

Las Puertas signposted on Calle Santa Ana. Paint-splattered walls and live music as well as very good pasta and healthy breakfasts. Worth it for the atmosphere.

El Tucán a few metres east of the causeway, on the waterfront but reached from Calle Centro America. Good fish, enormous chef's salads, great Mexican food and the best waterside terrace in Flores, but prices are higher than they used to be and there's wild game on the menu.

Santa Elena

Mijaro two locations: one on the road from the causeway, the other round the corner on Calle Principal. The best Guatemalan restaurants in Santa Elena, with good food at local prices and a daily special. You can usually leave luggage here while you look for a room.

Restaurant Petenchel 2 Calle, beyond *Hotel San Juan*, past the park. Simple, good food: the nicest place to eat around the main street. They'll also look after your luggage here if you need to check transport connections or look for a room.

Listings

Banks and currency exchange There's currently only one bank in Flores, Banrural, Avendia Flores (Mon–Fri 8.30am–4pm), where you can cash travellers' cheques. Santa Elena, meanwhile, has a glut of banks along 4 Calle including Banco Industrial (Mon–Fri 8.30am–6pm & Sat 9am–5pm), which has a 24-hour ATM for Visa cards, and Banco G&T Continental (Mon–Sat 8.30am–8pm) for Mastercard transactions. You can also change dollars and cash travellers' cheques at one of the recommended travel agents, below.

Car and bike rental Several firms, including Budget, Hertz and Koka, operate from the airport. All offer cars, minibuses and jeeps, with prices from around US$65 a day for a jeep. Bikes can be rented from Martsam Travel of the *Hotel Butterfly Planet* in Flores, for US$1.25 per hour.

Doctor Centro Medico Maya, 4 Avenida near 3 Calle in Santa Elena, down the street by the *Hotel Diplomatico* (☎926 0180), is helpful and professional, though no English is spoken.

Language schools San Andrés and San José, two very attractive villages on the north shore of the lake, both have good Spanish schools and, since

Moving on from Flores

All the Guatemala City **bus companies** have offices on Calle Principal in Santa Elena, and there are about thirty departures daily to the capital. Línea Dorada have an additional office in Flores on the south side of the island. Heading for **Guatemala City**, most of the more comfortable buses leave in the evening, with Fuente del Norte (☎926 0517) having a good number of departures (8hr 30min; US$13). Línea Dorada (☎926 0070) operates the very best, and most pricey, luxury services (all have a/c and reclining seats, and some include meals and movies) and they leave daily at 10am, 8pm and 10pm (8hr; US$16–28 depending on the bus). For travel **around Péten**, Rosita, Pinita, and Del Rosío have basic buses, which are always crowded. The latter two frequently hike their rates for tourists; you can check ticket prices and departure times in *Destination Petén* or pick up the list of regulated fares at Inguat or CINCAP. It's best to get on Pinita buses in the market, as they are often full by the time they pass the San Juan hotel.

Travelling on **to Belize**, Pinita and Rosita buses leave from the marketplace in Santa Elena eight times daily for Melchor de Menchos (2hr 30min). Most are crowded "chicken buses" though there are also some (fairly beat-up) Pullman services. Pinita buses leave at 5am, 8am and 11am while Rosita buses depart at 5.30am, 7am, 9.30am, 11am, 2pm, 3pm and 6pm. Mundo Maya (☎926 0528) operates an a/c express service leaving daily at 5am, for Belize City (5hr; US$20) and continues to the **Mexican border** at Chetumal (another 4hr; US$35) for connections north to Cancún. San Juan Travel operates a similar service.

For **Naranjo** (and **boats** to La Palma, Mexico), Pinita buses leave at 5am, 7am, 8am, 9am, 11am, 1pm and 2pm, and Del Rosío services at 4.30am, 8.30am, 11.30, 1pm and 1.30pm (5hr). Along with the regular stream of minibuses to **Tikal** run by almost every hotel in Flores and Santa Elena (1hr 15min; US$3.50), there's a daily service run by Pinita leaving at 1pm (2hr) and continuing on to Uaxactún. Pinita also runs buses to **Bethel**, on the Río Usumacinta at 5am, 8am and 1pm (4hr), **San Andrés** at 7am, 8am, noon and 1pm (1hr) and **Sayaxché** (2hr) at 5am, 6am, 8am, 10am, 1pm and 4pm; Del Rosío buses also leave for Sayaxché at 5am and noon. If you're heading for **Cobán**, there are currently no buses via Raxrujá (though Del Rosío are planning to resume a service) so you'll have to head for Cruce del Pato (4hr 30min) on Del Rosio's 5am or 10am buses for Playitas via Sayaxché, and hitch south from Cruce del Pato on a series of pick-ups.

Tickets for **flights** to Guatemala City can be bought at the airport, or from any of the travel agents in Santa Elena and Flores. There are also flights **to Puerto Barrios** (Taca, 1 daily; 45min), **Cancún** (Taca 1, daily; Aerocaribe, 2 daily; 1hr 20min), **Palenque** (Aerocaribe, 3 weekly on Mon Wed and Fri; 50min) and **Belize City** (Tropic Air, 2 daily; Rasca, 1 daily; Maya Island Air, 1 daily; Island Air, 1 daily; 35 min). For details on getting to **Mexico** along the Río San Pedro, see p.369.

few of the villagers speak English, are excellent places to learn and practise the language. Official rates (around US$180 a week for lessons, food and lodging) are more expensive than schools in Antigua or Xela, in highland Guatemala, however. The Eco Escuela in San Andrés (☎ 928 8106, ⓦ www.conservation.org/ecoescuela/about.htm) is larger and has been established longer than the Escuela Bio-Itzá in San José (☎ 928 8142, ⓦ www .conservation.org/ecoescuela/bioitza.htm), but the instruction in the latter is just as good and San José is arguably the prettier village. Lanchas for the villages leave regularly from Flores, and there are buses from Santa Elena.

Laundry Lavandería Amelia, behind CINCAP in Flores; Lavandería Emanuel on 6 Avenida in Santa Elena.

Post office Two doors away from the Inguat office in Flores; on Calle Principal, Banco Continental, in Santa Elena (Mon–Fri 8am–4.30pm).

Telephones and email Telgua is in Santa Elena on 5 Calle, but you're better off using Tikal Net, at 4 C and 6 Av, for all phone, fax and internet facilities; they also have another branch in Flores at Calle Centro América (daily 8.30–10.30pm).

Travel agents and tour operators Every hotel in Flores – and a good many in Santa Elena – seems to be offering tours, but most can simply sell you minibus trips to Tikal or bus and plane tickets. The best travel agent in Flores is Martsam Travel (☎ & ⓕ 926 3225, ⓔ martsam@guate.net), at the western end of Calle Centro América; the owners speak

English, run a daily trip to Yaxhá (p.371) and know neighbouring Belize well. Avinsa (☎ 929 0808, ⓦ www.tikaltravel.com), a few blocks east along Calle Principal in Santa Elena, arranges first-class tours throughout Guatemala and the entire Maya region, and is the only agent able to issue international airline tickets beyond Mexico or Belize; staff speak English and German. Evolution Adventures (☎ 926 0633, ⓔ evolution@internetdetelgua.com .gt), off Calle Centro América, opposite Tikal Net, offers overnight backpacking trips to the more remote ruins of the Reserva Biósfera Maya (such as El Perú, Río Azul and El Mirador and the Petexbatún area), formerly very difficult to reach on your own; it's owned by a Canadian, David Jackaman. Eco Maya, at Calle 30 de Junio in Flores (☎ 926 1363 ⓦ www.ecomaya.com), is also recommended for trips to remote ruins including El Zotz and El Mirador and the Scarlet Macaw Trail. The *Hotel San Juan* travel agency in Santa Elena is not recommended.

Voluntary work ARCAS (Asociación de Rescate y Conservación de Vida Silvestre), the Wildlife Conservation and Rescue Association, located next to the Petencito zoo (☎ 926 2022, ⓔ arcaspeten @intelnet.net.gt), runs a rescue service for animals including spider monkeys, scarlet macaws, iguanas, racoons, margays, parrots and the occasional jaguar taken illegally as pets from the forests. They always need volunteers and the work can be very rewarding, but you'll need to sign up for at least a week (US$80 per person, includes board and lodging).

Around Flores

For most people Flores is no more than an overnight stop, but if you have a few hours to spare, the lake and surrounding hills offer a few interesting diversions. The most obvious excursion is a **trip on the lake**. Boatmen can take you on a circuit that includes a *mirador* and small ruin on the peninsula opposite, and the **Petencito zoo** (daily 8am–5pm) with its small collection of sluggish local wildlife, pausing for a swim along the way. (Note, though, that the concrete waterslide by the zoo can be dangerous and has caused at least one death.) The fee for the trip is negotiable but aim to agree a price of around US$12 an hour, which works out pretty cheap if you can get a group of four or five people together. You'll find the boatmen behind the *Hotel Santana*, in the southwestern corner of Flores, and at the start of the causeway in Santa Elena. If you'd rather paddle around under your own steam you can rent a canoe for around US$2 an hour from below *Hotel La Casona de la Isla*.

Of the numerous **caves** in the hills behind Santa Elena, the most accessible is **Ak'tun Kan** (daily 8am–5pm; US$1) – simply follow the Flores causeway through Santa Elena, turn left when it forks in front of a small hill, and then take the first right. Otherwise known as *La Cueva de la Serpiente*, the cave is the legendary home of a huge snake. The guard may explain some of the bizarre

names given to the various shapes inside, some of which resemble animals and even a marimba.

San Andrés and San José

Though accessible by bus and boat, the traditional villages of **San Andrés** and **San José**, across the lake from Flores, have until recently received few visitors. The pace of life even slower here than in Flores, and the people are courteous and friendly. The streets, sloping steeply up from the shore, are lined with one-storey buildings, some of *palmetto* sticks and thatch, some coated with plaster, and others hewn in brightly painted concrete. Pigs and chickens wander freely.

In the past the mainstay of the economy was the arduous and poorly paid collection of **chicle**, the sap of the sapodilla tree, for use in the manufacture of chewing gum. This involves setting up camps in the forest, and working for months at a time in the rainy season when the sap is flowing. Today, natural chicle has largely been superseded by artificial substitutes, but there is still a demand for the original product, especially in Japan. Other forest products are also collected, including *xate* (pronounced "shatey"), palm leaves used in floral arrangements and exported to North America and Europe, and *pimienta de jamaica*, or allspice. Harvesters (*pimenteros*) use spurs to climb the trees and collect the spice, then dry it over a fire. Since the creation of the Reserva Biósfera Maya (see p.327), however, efforts have been made to provide villagers with alternative sources of income.

Getting to the villages is best achieved by using the lanchas (US$0.50 to San Andrés, 40 min; US$0.75 to San José, 50min) that leave when full from the beach next to the *Hotel Santana* in Flores and from **San Benito**, a suburb of Santa Elena. A chartered *expreso* from Flores or San Benito will cost around US$9. Regular morning **buses** leave for San Andrés from the market in Santa Elena; if they don't continue to San José, it's an easy two-kilometre walk downhill. Lanchas and buses return throughout the day at regular intervals until 5pm.

San Andrés

Most outsiders in **SAN ANDRÉS** are students at the **language school**, the first to be set up in Petén, the Eco-Escuela. Since nobody in the village speaks English a course here is an excellent opportunity to immerse yourself in

Spanish, without the distractions of Antigua, though it may be daunting for absolute beginners. For more information see Flores "Listings" above, p.335.

There are currently no hospedajes in the village, but 3km to the west is the attractive *Hotel Nitún* (℡201 0759, ℻926 0807, ⓦwww.nitun.com; ❻ including transport from Flores), with full-board **accommodation** in very attractive thatched stone cabañas, with hardwood floors and private bathrooms, and a restaurant serving superb food. The hotel is run by Lorena Castillo and Bernie Mittelstaedt, a friendly, knowledgeable couple (both speak perfect English), who also operate Monkey Eco Tours and can organize well-equipped expeditions to remote archeological sites throughout northern Petén. There are several simple **comedores** in San José, including the *Angelita*, at the top of the hill next to the road junction.

San José and around

Just 2km east along the shore from San Andrés, above a lovely bay, **SAN JOSÉ** is even more relaxed than its neighbour. The village is undergoing something of a cultural revival: Itza, the pre-conquest Maya tongue is being taught in the school, and you'll see signs in that language dotted all around. Part of this iniative has been the establishment of the **Asociación Bio-Itza**, a community partnership which has established an excellent new Spanish school (see Flores "Listings" above, p.336), the Bio-Itza, just above the main dock and parque. Here students get twenty hours' one-on-one tuition and family board for US$185 a week, plus the chance to help out with the association's other projects. These include a **women's co-operative** with fifty members, who run a botanical garden where visitors can learn about the use of traditional medicinal plants and their relation to the lunar cycle; it's located a kilometre inland from the centre in a district known as Nuevo San José. The other main project is the management of a 36-hectare **forest reserve**, north of the village, which abuts the Biotopo El Zotz, in the buffer zone of the Reserva Maya Biósfera. The area is rich in wildlife and contains a thatched visitor shelter and some unexcavated minor Maya ruins.

San José's sacred skulls

San José is famous for its two **fiestas**. The first, to mark the patron saint's day, is held between March 10 and 19 and includes parades and fireworks plus an unusual, comical-looking costumed dance during which a girl (*la chatona*) and a horse skip through the village streets. The second fiesta is distinctly more pagan, with a unique mass, celebrated in the church on All Saints' Day (or Halloween) and a festival which continues on into November 1 – The Day of the Dead. For the evening service, one of three venerated human **skulls** (thought to be early founders of the village, though some claim they were Spanish missionaries) is removed from its glass case inside the church and positioned on the altar for the ceremony. Afterwards, the skull is carried through the village by black-clad skullbearers, accompanied by children dressed in traditional Itza *traje* and hundreds of devotees, many carrying candles and lanterns. The procession weaves through the streets, stopping at around thirty homes where prayers are said, chants made and the families ask for blessings. A corn-based drink called *ixpasá* is consumed and special fiesta food eaten in each home, part of a ceremony which can take over a day to complete. The exact origin of the event is unclear, but it clearly incorporates a degree of ancestor reverence (or even worship). After all the houses have been visited, the skull is returned to its case in the church, where it remains, and can be seen with the other two skulls, for the rest of the year.

Some 4km northwest of San José, down a signed track, are the recently restored ruins of the Classic period settlement of **Motul** (free). The site, which was historically allied to Tikal, is fairly spread out and little visited (though there should be a caretaker about), with four plazas. In Plaza B a large stela in front of a looted temple depicts dancing Maya lords. Plaza C is the biggest, with several mounds and court-

Motul de San José emblem glyph

yards, while Plaza D has the tallest pyramid. It's a tranquil spot, ideal for bird-watching, and probably best visited by bicycle from either of the villages. If you'd rather just chill out for a while by the lake, there are secluded spots east of the village, including a rocky beach with good swimming.

If you continue west from San José along the dirt road on the northern side of the lake, you pass the isolated villages of San Román and Jobompiché before eventually reaching El Remate (see below) some 30km away. Pick-ups (but currently no buses) serve this route, though it makes a great and not too demanding excursion by bike – best hired in Flores (see p.335).

El Remate and around

On the eastern shore of Lago de Petén Itzá, 30km from Santa Elena on the road to Tikal, **EL REMATE** offers a pleasant alternative to staying in Flores. Just 2km north of the Ixlú junction on the road to Belize and Melchor, it's a quiet, friendly village, growing in popularity as a convenient base for visiting Tikal, and with several worthwhile places to visit nearby, such as the ruins of **Ixlú** and the **Biotopo Cerro Cahuí**.

Getting to El Remate is easy: every minibus to Tikal passes through the village, while local buses from the market in Santa Elena run to Jobompiché, a village on the lake near the Biotopo Cerro Cahuí (see below), and to Socotzal on the way to Tikal (every 2hr, 8am–5pm). Coming from the Belize border, get off Ixlú – from here you can walk or hitch the 2km to El Remate. Heading to Flores, local buses pass through El Remate at 5.30am, 7.30am and 8am, and a swarm of minibuses from Tikal ply the route from midday onwards.

Accommodation and eating

El Remate is a deservedly popular base between Flores and Tikal, with an excellent range of **accommodation**. Most of the places to stay listed below have a distinctive charm and they're fairly well spaced, with no sense of over-crowding. There are a few simple comedores offering inexpensive Guatemalan **food**, and most of the hotels also provide meals. Places are listed in the order you approach them from the Ixlú junction.

Camping Sal Itzá 100m down a signed track opposite the lakeshore right at the beginning of the village. Simple stick-and-thatch cabins and camping on a steep hillside with lake views. Run by a very friendly family, headed by Juan and Rita, who'll cook tasty local food on request. ❷
El Mirador del Duende high above the lake, reached by a stairway cut into the cliff ©miraduende @hotmail.com. An incredible collection of globular whitewashed stucco cabañas decorated with Maya glyphs, plus space for hammocks and tents. There's a wonderful "chillout" terrace overlooking the lake and a restaurant serving cheap vegetarian food. ❷
La Mansión del Pajaro Serpiente just below *El*

Mirador del Duende ⓣ & ⓕ 926 4446, ©nature @ietravel.com. The most comfortable accommo-dation on the road to Tikal. Stone-built and thatched two-storey cabañas in a tropical garden and smaller rooms, all with superb lake views. Annoyingly, the owners fluctuate their prices according to demand, so bargain at quiet times of the year. Good food and a small swimming pool. ❹–❻
Hotel Ixchel just off the Tikal road close to the junction. Simple but fairly comfortable wood cab-ins, run by a very friendly local family. ❷
Casa de Bruno's Place just past the *Ixchel*, at the junction. Four basic, functional rooms with shared bath, behind the village store. ❷

La Casa de Don David 300m beyond *La Mansión*, right on the junction ☏ 306 2190, ⓦ www.lacasadedondavid.com. Comfortable, spacious and secure wooden bungalows and rooms with private hot-water bath, set in grassy grounds just back from the lakeshore. Owners David and Rosita Kuhn offer great hospitality and home cooking. David is a mine of information about Petén, and can change money, arrange trips, and sell bus tickets for Belize and Guatemala City; the staff know the times of local buses. There are usually a couple of bikes for guests to borrow. ❹

Casa Mobego 500m down the road to Cerro Cahuí on the right. Good budget deal right by the lake. Simple, well-constructed stick-and-thatch cabañas, plus camping, canoe rental, a good, inexpensive restaurant and swimming. ❷

Casa de Doña Tonita 800m down the road to Cerro Cahuí on the right. Four basic clapboard rooms, built high above the lake, with great views.

The owner also runs a pleasant thatched-roofed restaurant next door with vegetarian food and snacks. ❷

El Gringo Perdido on the north shore, 3km from *Don David's* ☏ & ⓕ 334 2305, ⓔ ecoadventure @mail2.guate.net. Long-established place in a supremely tranquil setting offering rooms with bath, and a mosquito-netted bunk, as well as good-value basic cabañas and camping (US$3 per person). The restaurant is less impressive. Guided canoe tours available. ❸–❺

Hotel Camino Real Tikal beyond Cerro Cahuí, 5km from the Tikal highway (in Guatemala City ☏ 926 0207, ⓔ caminor@infovia.com.gt). Luxury option in extensive lakeside grounds with excellent views over the water and a private beach. Rooms are a bit unimaginative and corporate, but there are attendant luxury trappings like electric buggies and a souvenir shop. Free use of kayaks and a guided tour of the Biotopo Cerro Cahuí. US$132 for a double. ❼

Ixlú and the Biotopo Cerro Cahuí

Two kilometres south of El Remate, at the Belize and Melchor road junction, formerly known simply as El Cruce, is the tiny village of **Ixlú**, where you'll find a thatched information hut with toilets. Inside, a large map of the area shows the little restored **ruins of Ixlú**, 200m down a signed track from the road, on the shore of **Lago de Salpetén**. The *Zac Petén* restaurant, on the Melchor side of the junction, is the best place to eat; they'll also let you store your bags. A very basic **campsite** has been built on the lakeshore where you can rent canoes.

On the north shore of the lake, 2km west of the centre of El Remate, the **Biotopo Cerro Cahuí** (daily 7am–5pm; US$3.50) is a 650-hectare wildlife conservation area comprising lakeshore, ponds and some of the best examples of undisturbed tropical forest in Petén. The smallest and most accessible of Petén's *biotopos*, it contains a rich diversity of plants and animals, and is especially recommended for bird-watchers. There are hiking trails, a couple of small ruins and two thatched *miradores* on the hill above the lake; pick up maps and information at the gate where you sign in. Unfortunately there were **attacks** on tourists inside the *biotopo* in late 2000 and early 2001, and though arrests have been made, it's wise to enquire about the current security situation before setting out – check with Inguat in Flores (see p.331) or in the *Casa de Don David*.

Tikal

Towering above the rain forest, **Tikal** is possibly the most magnificent of all Maya sites. The ruins, 68km from Flores down a smooth paved road, are dominated by five enormous temples: steep-sided limestone pyramids that rise to more than 60m above the forest floor. Around them are literally thousands of other structures, many semi-strangled by giant roots and still hidden beneath mounds of earth.

The site itself is surrounded by the **Parque Nacional Tikal**, a protected area of some 370 square kilometres, and is on the edge of the even larger Reserva Biósfera Maya. The trees around the ruins are home to hundreds of species including howler and spider monkeys, toucans and parakeets. The sheer scale of the place is overwhelming, and its atmosphere spellbinding. Whether you can spare as little as an hour or as long as a week, it's always worth the trip.

Getting there

The best way to reach the ruins is in one of the **tourist minibuses** – known as colectivos – that meet flights from the capital and are operated by just about every hotel in Flores and Santa Elena. In addition, a **local bus**, run by Pinita, leaves Santa Elena market at 1pm, passes El Remate about 45 minutes later and arrives at Tikal about 2.30pm; it then continues to Uaxactún (see p.352) a further hour away; it returns from Uaxactún at 6am. There are also fleets of tourist minibus departures at 4am from hotels in Flores and Santa Elena – useful if you want to see the ruins at dawn but would rather not stay at the site. It's usually billed as the "**sunrise at Tikal**" trip, though the appearance of the sun is generally delayed by mist rising from the humid forest and many find the experience slightly disappointing.

If you're travelling **from Belize**, there is usually no need to go all the way to Flores: instead change buses at **Ixlú**, the three-way junction at the eastern end of Lake Petén Itzá (see opposite). The local bus from Santa Elena to Tikal and Uaxactún arrives at about 2pm, and there are plenty of passing minibuses all day long. There have been **robberies** along the road between Tikal and the Belizean border at Melchor in the past, though very few incidents recently. The robbers have been determined, but not violent, and tended to target the tourist minibuses while leaving the local "chicken buses" alone; your risk overall of encountering them is very slim.

Site practicalities

Plane and local bus schedules are designed to make it easy to visit the ruins as a day-trip from Flores or Guatemala City, but if you can spare the time it's well worth staying overnight. Partly because you'll need the extra time to do justice to the ruins themselves, but more importantly to spend dawn and dusk at the site, when the forest canopy bursts into a frenzy of sound and activity. The air fills with the screech of toucans and the roar of howler monkeys, while flocks of parakeets wheel around the temples, and bats launch themselves into the night. With a bit of luck you might even see a grey fox sneak across one of the plazas.

Entrance to the national park costs US$6.40 a day (payable every day you stay at the site; if you arrive after 3pm you'll be given a ticket that's also valid for the next day but you'll only pay the one-day fee). The ruins are **open** daily from 6am to 6pm; extensions to 8pm can be obtained from the *inspectoría* (7am–noon & 2–5pm), a small white hut to the left of the entrance to the ruins.

There are also a **post office**, shops and **visitor centre**, behind the central plaza, where you'll find an overpriced café–restaurant and souvenir stalls. There are **toilets** in the visitors' centre and near Temple IV (bring your own toilet paper).

Three **books** of note are usually available at the visitor centre: William Coe's *Tikal: A Handbook to the Ancient Maya Ruins* is the best guide to the site, while *The Birds of Tikal*, although by no means comprehensive, is useful for identifying some of the hundreds of species you might come across as you wander round. Look out too for *The Lords of Tikal* by Peter D. Harrison, a very comprehensive and readable account of the city's turbulent history. The **website** www.tikalpark.com has lots of useful information about the site and the reserve.

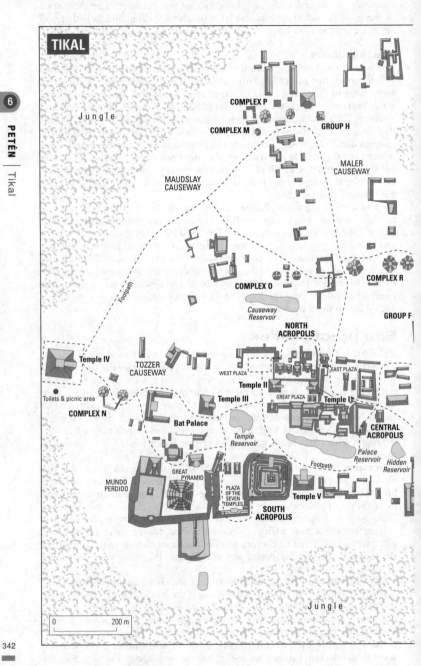

TIKAL

Jungle

COMPLEX P

COMPLEX M

GROUP H

MAUDSLAY
CAUSEWAY

MALER
CAUSEWAY

COMPLEX O

COMPLEX R

*Causeway
Reservoir*

NORTH
ACROPOLIS

GROUP F

Temple IV

TOZZER
CAUSEWAY

WEST PLAZA

EAST PLAZA

Footpath

Toilets & picnic area

Temple II

GREAT PLAZA

Temple I

COMPLEX N

Temple III

Bat Palace

*Temple
Reservoir*

CENTRAL
ACROPOLIS

*Palace
Reservoir*

*Hidden
Reservoir*

Footpath

MUNDO
PERDIDO

GREAT
PYRAMID

PLAZA
OF THE
SEVEN
TEMPLES

Temple V

SOUTH
ACROPOLIS

Jungle

0   200 m

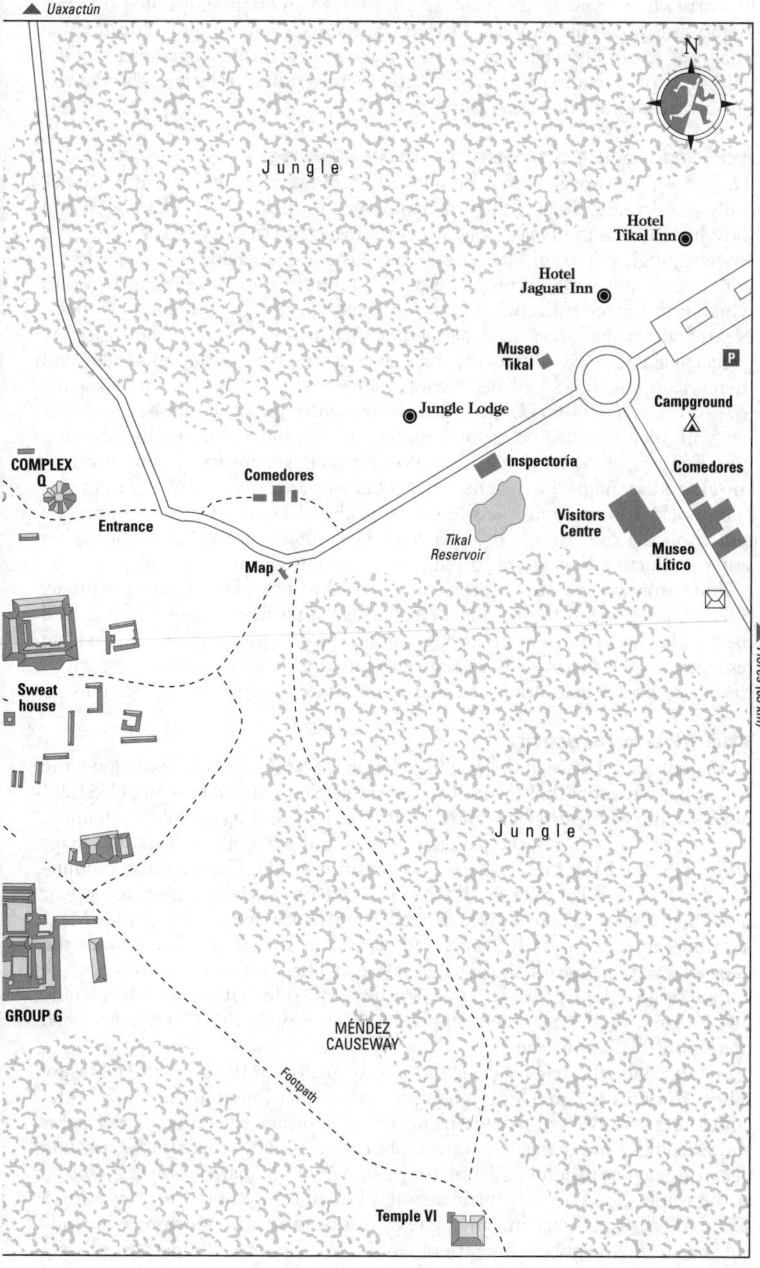

N

Jungle

Hotel
Tikal Inn

Hotel
Jaguar Inn

Museo
Tikal

Jungle Lodge

Campground

COMPLEX
Q

Comedores

Inspectoría

Comedores

Entrance

Visitors
Centre

Tikal
Reservoir

Map

Museo
Lítico

Sweat
house

Flores (63 km)

Jungle

GROUP G

MÉNDEZ
CAUSEWAY

Footpath

Temple VI

A **licensed guide** to show you the site (US$40 for a 4hr tour) is an extremely worthwhile investment if you can afford it. Many, including Eulogio López García and José Luis Morales Monzón, speak excellent English, and they all know the site really well. Obviously, if you can get a group together it doesn't work out to be that expensive. You'll find them waiting for business by the visitor centre and the *inspectoría* gate.

Accommodation, eating and drinking

There are three **hotels** at the ruins, all of them fairly expensive and not especially good value, though they offer discounts out of season. The largest and most luxurious is the *Jungle Lodge* (in Guatemala City ☎476 8775, ⓕ476 0294, ⓦwww.junglelodge.com; ❹/❺), which offers good bungalow accommodation with two double beds but no a/c, and some pretty comfortable "budget" rooms which lack private baths but are often booked up, plus a restaurant and a pool. Next door is the overpriced *Jaguar Inn* (☎926 0002, ⓕ926 2413, ⓦwww.jaguartikal.com; ❺), where the nine bungalows have little verandahs, and there's camping (US$3.20 per person) but no pool. Close by, the *Tikal Inn* (☎926 0065, ⓕ594 6944, ⓔtikalinn@internetdetelgua.com.gt; ❺) is a better bet, with nice thatched bungalows, pleasant rooms and a glorious, heat-busting swimming pool. Alternatively, for US$4.80 you can **camp** or sling a **hammock** under one of the thatched shelters in a cleared space used as a campsite. Hammocks and mosquito nets (essential in the wet season) can sometimes be rented on the spot, or ask at *Jaguar Inn*. The campsite has a shower block, but water is sporadic. It is illegal to camp or sleep out within the ruins.

Three simple **comedores** at the entrance to the site, and a couple more inside, offer a limited menu of traditional Guatemalan specialities – eggs, beans, grilled meat and chicken. For a more extensive and expensive menu, there's an adequate restaurant in the *Jaguar Inn*. It's essential to buy some water before setting out to the ruins, though cold drinks are sold at a number of spots within the ruins.

The site museums

At the entrance, between the *Jungle Lodge* and *Jaguar Inn* hotels (see below), the one-room **Museo Tikal** (Mon–Fri 9am–5pm, Sat & Sun 9am–4pm; US$1.30) houses some of the artefacts found in the ruins, including jewellery, ceramics, obsidian eccentric flints, the jade jewellery found in tumba 116 and the magnificent **Stela 31**, which was inaugurated in 445 AD. This limestone monument shows the Tikal ruler Siyah Chan K'awil ("Stormy Sky") bearing a jaguar head belt and a jade necklace, flanked by two warriors, bearing non-Maya Teotihuacan-style spear throwers and darts and shields decorated with the "goggle-eyed" image of the rain god Tlaloc. The stela was cut to mark the completion of the first *katun* under Stormy Sky's rule, but the lengthy glyphic inscriptions on the rear confirm clear alliance with the Central Mexican metropolis of Teotihuacán.

The museum also has a spectacular reconstruction of the great ruler **Hasaw Chan K'awil's tomb**. This is one of the richest ever found in the Maya world, containing 180 worked jade items in the form of bracelets, anklets, necklaces and earplugs, and delicately incised bones, including the famous carving depicting deities paddling a canoe to the underworld. A larger bone also found at the tomb shows a poignant image of a bound captive, no doubt awaiting a sacrificial death. The accompanying text explains that this unfortunate individual is from the neighbouring city of Calakmul – the other "superpower" state to the north – a city that Hasaw Chan K'awil defeated in a seminal victory in 695 AD, reversing more than a century of subjugation.

The **Museo Lítico** (same hours as Museo Tikal; free), inside the visitor centre, holds nineteen more stelae, though they are presently very poorly labelled and there is no supplementary information in English.

The rise and fall of Tikal

The following account is a summary of the very latest findings based on the interpretations of inscriptions from Tikal itself and texts gathered from numerous other sites throughout the Petén, Mexico and Belize. According to this latest evidence, the first occupants of Tikal arrived around 900 BC, probably attracted by its position raised above surrounding seasonal swamps and by the availability

Tikal emblem glyph

of flint for making tools and weapons. For the next four hundred years, though the village grew and prospered slowly, there's nothing to suggest that it was anything more than a tiny settlement of thatched huts. By 500 BC, however, the first steps of a modest astronomical stone temple had been constructed (which were later used as foundations for the great pyramid in the Mundo Perdido), though burials at this time were still relatively simple and ceramics found had been crudely executed. Tikal remained a minor settlement during the latter years of the Middle Preclassic (800–350BC), while 50km to the north, towering temples were being built at **Nakbé** (see p.357), the first city to emerge from the Petén forest.

It's in the Late Preclassic era, after 250 BC, that the first significant ceremonial structures began to be constructed. The Mundo Perdido structure was enlarged to form a pyramid, and small temples were built in the **North Acropolis**, though the absence of royal burials and the relatively modest size of these buildings mean that Tikal was a peripheral settlement at this stage. Dominating the entire northern region of Petén, the formidable city–state of **El Mirador** (see p.356) was the first Maya "superpower", though its Preclassic hegemony was later to be challenged by a distant, and even more powerful player – **Teotihuacán** in Central Mexico.

By the time of Christ, the **Great Plaza** had begun to take shape and Tikal was already established as an important site with a large permanent population. For the next two centuries, art and architecture became increasingly ornate and sophisticated as the great pyramid was enlarged to over 30m in height, its sides adorned by huge stucco masks. The styles that were to dominate throughout the Classic period were perfected in these early years, and by 200 AD all the major architectural traits had evolved. It's during this period that **Yax Ehb' Xok** ("First Step Shark") established the first ruling dynasty of the city, somewhere between 100 and 200 AD. Though there were earlier kings, the royal lineage established by Yax Ehb' Xok was recognized by all 33 (known) subsequent kings of Tikal, until the record fades in 869 AD.

The closing years of the Late Preclassic era (350–300 AD) were marked by the eruption of the Ilopango volcano in El Salvador, which smothered a huge area of the highlands, including much of Guatemala and Honduras, in a thick layer of volcanic ash. Trade routes were disrupted and alliance patterns altered. The ensuing years saw the decline and abandonment of El Mirador, creating a power vacuum and opening the way for the expansion of several smaller sites. To the south of El Mirador, Tikal and Uaxactún emerged as substantial centres of trade, science and religion. Less than a day's walk apart and growing rapidly, the cities engaged in heated competition.

Matters finally came to a head on January 31, 378 AD, when, during the last year of the reign of Chak Tok Ich'aak's ("Jaguar Paw I"), Tikal's warriors overran Uaxactún. The secret of Tikal's success appears to have been its alliance with Teotihuacán, and the introduction of new warfare technology from Central Mexico. Inscriptions attest that it was the arrival of a somewhat mysterious warrior, **Siyak K'ak'** ("Fire-Born"), "from the west" that helped seal the victory. This general is thought to have been dispatched by the Teotihuacán king, "Spearthrower Owl", armed with the latest technology: an *atlatl* (a wooden sling capable of firing arrows). Recent revaluation of texts suggests that it's probable that the warrior Siyak K'ak' ordered the execution of the old ruler Jaguar Paw I. It's clear that this was nothing less than a Mexican-directed takeover, for the next king installed at Tikal, Yax Nuun Ayin I ("First Crocodile" but also known as "Curl Nose"), was the son of Spearthrower Owl. First Crocodile married into the Tikal dynasty, and started a new royal lineage.

The victory over Uaxactún enabled Tikal to dominate the central Petén for much of the next five hundred years. During this time it became one of the most elaborate and magnificent of all Maya city states, monopolizing the crucial lowland trade routes, its influence reaching as far as Copán in Honduras and Yaxchilán on the Usumacinta. The elite immediately launched an extensive rebuilding programme, including a radical remodelling of the North Acropolis and the renovation of most of the city's finest temples. It's clear that Tikal's alliance with Teotihuacán remained an important part of its continuing power: stelae and paintings from the period show that subsequent Tikal rulers adopted Central Mexican styles of clothing and pottery and warfare.

Yet as Tikal was expanding and growing in size during the fifth century, a formidable rival Maya "superpower" – **Calakmul** "the Kingdom of the Snake" – was emerging in the jungles to the north. Through an aggressive series of regional alliances, Calakmul steadily encircled Tikal with enemy cities, filling the power vacuum in the Maya heartland that had developed as the influence of Tikal's overstretched backer, Teotihuacán, faded. By the Early Classic period, Calakmul had built up a power bloc of vassal states, many previously under the auspices of Tikal, including Naranjo and El Perú (see p.370) and was courting a potentially devastating alliance with **Caracol**, a powerful emerging city to the southeast, in modern Belize.

In an apparent attempt to subdue a potential rival, Wak Chan K'awil, **Double Bird**, the ruler of Tikal, launched an attack (known as an "axe war") on Caracol and its ambitious leader, Yahaw Te, **Lord Water**, in 556 AD. Despite capturing and sacrificing a noble from Caracol, Double Bird's strategy was only temporarily successful. In 562 AD Lord Water (with substantial backing from Calakmul) hit back in a devastating "star war", which crushed Tikal and almost certainly sacrificed Double Bird. The victors stamped their authority over the humiliated nobles of Tikal, smashing stelae, desecrating tombs and destroying written records, ushering in a 130-year "hiatus" during which no inscribed monuments were erected. Yet though Tikal was severely humbled, the city was never completely broken.

Towards the end of the seventh century, however, Calakmul's stranglehold had begun to weaken and Tikal gradually started to recover its lost power under the formidable leadership of Hasaw Chan K'awil, **Heavenly Standard Bearer** (682–723 AD). During his reign the main ceremonial areas, the East Plaza and the North Acropolis, were completely remodelled, reclaimed from the desecration suffered at the hands of Calakmul and Caracol. By 695 AD, Tikal was powerful enough to launch an attack against Calakmul, capturing and executing its king, Yich'aak K'ak' or **Fiery Claw** or **Jaguar Paw**, and severely weakening the alliance against Tikal. The following year, Hasaw Chan

K'awil repeated his astonishing coup by capturing **Split Earth**, the new king of Calakmul, and Tikal regained its position as the dominant city in the Maya world.

Hasaw Chan K'awil's leadership gave birth to a revitalized and powerful ruling dynasty: in the hundred years following his death Tikal's five main temples were built, and his son, Yik'in Chan K'awil or **Divine Sunset Lord** (who ascended the throne in 734 AD), had his father's body entombed in the magnificent **Temple I**. He also constructed Temple VI, remodelled the Central Acropolis and principal city causeways and defeated El Perú and Naranjo in 743 AD and 744 AD, breaking the ring of hostile cities that encircled Tikal. Around this time, at the height of the Classic period, Tikal's population had grown to somewhere over 100,000 (some Mayanists argue for double the figure) spread across a central area covering around thirty square kilometres. Its authority also extended to include a series of vassal states, among them Naranjo, El Perú, Uaxactún and many more minor settlements – a domain of around 500,000 subjects. During this time we know the city was called **Mutul** – "knot of hair" – the name taken from Tikal's emblem glyph, which depicts the rear view of a head, with what appears to be a knotted headband around it.

But within a few years, by the beginning of the ninth century, there were severe signs of crisis across the entire Maya region – perhaps sparked by a catastrophic drought or environmental disaster. Population levels at Tikal plummeted, as people fled the area, and Tikal's last recorded monument is inscribed on Stela 24, completed in 869 AD. What brought about Tikal's final **downfall** remains a mystery, but what is certain is that around 900 AD almost the entire lowland Maya civilization collapsed and that Tikal was effectively abandoned by the end of the tenth century. Afterwards, the site was used from time to time by other groups, who worshipped here and repositioned many of the stelae, but it was never occupied again.

Rediscovery

After its mysterious decline little is known of Tikal until 1695 when Father Avendaño, lost in the maze of swamps, stumbled upon a "variety of old buildings". The colonial powers were distinctly unimpressed by Petén and for the next 150 years the ruins were left to the jungle. In 1848 they were rediscovered by a government expedition led by Modesto Méndez. Later in the nineteenth century a Swiss scientist visited the site and removed the beautifully carved wooden lintels from the tops of Temples I and IV – they are currently in a museum in Basel – and in 1881 the English archeologist Maudslay took the first photographs of the ruins, showing the main temples cloaked in tropical vegetation.

Until 1951 the site could only be reached – with considerable difficulty – on horseback, and although there was a steady trickle of visitors the ruins remained mostly uncleared. Then the Guatemalan army built an airstrip, paving the way for an invasion of archeologists and tourists. The gargantuan project to excavate and restore the site started in 1956, and involved teams from the University of Pennsylvania in the USA and Guatemala's Institute of Anthropology. Most of the major work was completed by 1984, but thousands of minor buildings remain buried by roots, shoots and rubble. There's little doubt that an incredible amount is waiting to be found – as recently as 1996 a workman unearthed a stela (Stela 40, dating from 468 AD) while mowing the grass on the Great Plaza. A ten-year project to restore Temple 5 (at 58m the third highest structure at Tikal) is currently being coordinated with help from the Spanish government, and should be completed by 2007.

The ruins

The sheer scale of the ruins at Tikal can at first seem daunting. The **central area**, with its five main temples, forms by far the most impressive section; if you start to explore beyond this you can ramble seemingly forever in the maze of smaller, **unrestored structures** and complexes. Compared with the scale and magnificence of the main area, they're not that impressive, but armed with a good **map** (the best is in Coe's guide to the ruins, available in the visitor centre), it can be exciting to search for some of the rarely visited outlying sections. Don't even think about exploring the more distant structures without a map; every year at least one tourist gets lost in the jungle.

From the entrance to the Great Plaza

Walking into the ruins the first structures that you come to are the prosaically named **Complex Q** and **Complex R**, two of the seven sets of twin pyramids. Commissioned by Yax Ain II, also known as **Chitam**, one of Tikal's last known rulers, they were built to mark the passing of a *katun* (twenty 360-day years). Twinned pyramids are an architectural feature found only in the Tikal region, with several at the city itself, and a few others found at sites nearby (including Nakúm, Yaxhá and Ixlú). At Complex Q (inaugurated in 771 AD), the first you come to, only one of the pyramids has been restored, with the stelae and altars re-erected in front of it. The stelae at the base of the pyramid are blank, as a result of erosion, but there's a copy of a superbly carved example, **Stela 22** (the original of which can be seen in the Museo Lítico inside the visitor's centre). The carvings on Stela 22 record the ascension to the throne of Chitam II, portrayed in full regalia, complete with an enormous sweeping headdress and the staff of authority.

Following the path as it bears around to the left after the twin temples of **Complex R** (built in 790 AD) you approach the back of Temple I through the **East Plaza**. On the left side, behind a small ball court, is a broad platform supporting a series of small buildings known as the **marketplace**, and in the southeast corner of the plaza stands an imposing temple, beneath which were found the remains of several severed heads, the victims of human sacrifice. Behind the marketplace is the **Sweat House**, which may have been a kind of sauna similar to those used by highland Maya today. Priests and rulers would haven taken a sweat bath in order to cleanse themselves before conducting religious rituals.

From here a few short steps bring you to the **Great Plaza**, the heart of the ancient city. Surrounded by four massive structures, this was the focus of ceremonial and religious activity at Tikal for around a thousand years, and was still in use long after the rest of the city had been abandoned. The earliest part is the North Acropolis; the two great temple–pyramids (which disrupted the city's original north–south axis) weren't built until the eighth century. The plaza covers an area of one and a half acres, and beneath today's grass lie four layers of paving, the oldest of which dates from about 150 BC and the most recent from 700 AD. Temple II can be climbed and is well worth it for the views from the top. At present the steeper stairway on Temple I is roped off, though it may be reopened in the future.

Temple I, towering 44m above the plaza, is the hallmark of Tikal – it's also known as the Jaguar Temple because of the jaguar carved in its door lintel, though this is now in a museum in Basel. The temple was built as a burial monument to contain the magnificent **tomb of Hasaw Chan K'awil**, one of Tikal's greatest rulers, who ascended the throne in 682 AD (see p.346) and defeated the archenemy state of Calakmul. It was constructed shortly after his death in 721 AD, under the direction his son and successor Yik'in Chan K'awil, though it's now thought likely that Hasaw Chan K'awil planned his tomb and burial temple himself. Within the tomb at the temple's core, his remains were found facing north, surrounded by an assortment of jade, pearls, seashells and stingray spines, which were a traditional symbol of human sacrifice. There were also some magnificent bone ornaments, perhaps spoils of victory over Calakmul, depicting a journey to the underworld made in a canoe rowed by mythical animal figures. A reconstruction of the tomb (Tumba 116) is on show in the Museo Tikal.

Architecturally, Temple I was radically different from anything else that had been yet constructed in the Maya region – an unequivocal statement of confidence no doubt designed to reassert Tikal's position as a dominant power. Comprising a series of nine ascending platforms, the style emphasises the vertical dimensions of the temple and draws the eye to the roof comb. To create this soaring effect, hundreds of tons of flint and rubble were poured on top of the completed tomb and the temple was built around this, with a staircase of thick plastered blocks running up the front. The staircase was a skeleton structure, over which the final surface would have been constructed. The whole thing is topped by a three-room building and a hollow roof comb that was originally painted in cream, red and possibly green. On the front of the comb it's just possible to make out a seated figure and a stylized serpent.

Standing opposite, like a squatter version of Temple I, is **Temple II**, also known as the Temple of the Masks for the two grotesque masks, now heavily eroded, that flank the central stairway. The temples were arranged to form a twin pyramid alignment, and their construction marked a seminal change to the ceremonial core of the city. Not only were these new temples the largest structures in the city, but they purposely deflected attention away from the adjacent North Acropolis, rising above the temples where Tikal's elite had been buried for over eight hundred years. It's not exactly certain when Temple II was completed, though it dates from the beginning of the eighth century, and almost certainly predates Temple I by a few years. As yet no tomb has been found beneath this temple, but it's thought to have been built to honour Hasaw Chan K'awil's wife, Lady Twelve Macaw. The structure now stands 38m high, although with its roof comb intact it would have equalled Temple I. It's an easy climb up the staircase to the top, from where the echo is fantastically clear and crisp; and the view, almost level with the forest canopy, is incredible, with the great plaza spread out below.

The **North Acropolis**, which fills the whole north side of the plaza, is one of the most complex structures in the entire Maya world. In traditional Maya style it was built and rebuilt on top of itself, and beneath the twelve temples that can be seen today are the remains of about a hundred other structures. As early as 100 BC the Maya had constructed elaborate platforms supporting temples and tombs here; in about 250 AD the entire thing was torn down and rebuilt as a platform and four vaulted temples, each of which was rebuilt twice during Early Classic times. Archeologists have removed some of the surface to reveal these earlier structures, including two four-metre-high Preclassic **masks**. One facing the plaza, protected by a thatched roof, is clearly visible; the other can be reached by following the dark passageway to the side – you'll need a torch. In 1959 a trench was dug deep beneath the platform of the North Acropolis, unearthing a bizarre burial chamber in which the body of a ruler lay surrounded by nine retainers killed for the occasion, along with turtles, a crocodile and a mass of pottery.

In front of the North Acropolis are two lines of **stelae** with circular altars at their bases, all of which were originally painted a brilliant red. These were once thought to show images of the gods, but it's now known that the carvings are of members of Tikal's ruling elite. These rulers were certainly obsessive in their recording of the city's dynastic sequence, linking it with great historical moments and reaching as far back into the past as possible. Many of the stelae bear the marks of ritual defacement, perpetrated by Caracol and Calakmul during Tikal's hiatus, acts carried out by conquerors as rites of humiliation. Several of the stelae now in the main plaza were set up in their current positions long after the decline of the city by people who still worshipped here.

The Central Acropolis and Temple V

On the other side of the plaza is the **Central Acropolis**, a maze of tiny interconnecting rooms and stairways built around six smallish courtyards. The buildings here are usually referred to as palaces rather than temples, although their precise use remains a mystery. Possibilities include law courts, temporary retreats, administrative centres and homes for Tikal's elite. What we do know is that they were constantly altered and adapted, with rooms, walls and doorways added and repositioned regularly. The large two-storey building in Court 2 is known as **Maler's Palace**, named after the archeologist Teobert Maler who made it his home during expeditions in 1895 and 1904.

Behind the acropolis is the palace reservoir, one of at least twelve clay-lined pools that were fed by a series of channels with rainwater from all over the city. Further behind the Central Acropolis is the soaring outline of **Temple V** (58m) with a imposing central staircase that rises to a single tiny rooftop room. This was the second last of the great temples to be constructed at Tikal, and though it's now thought to date from Yax Ain II's rule (768–794 AD), astonishingly little is known about it – it's not yet clear to whom it was dedicated. More details will undoubtedly emerge, as the temple is currently the subject of a huge restoration project, partly financed by Spain, and due to be completed by 2007. When the work is finished, the view from the top will be superb, with a great profile of Temple 1 and a side view of the central plaza.

From the West Plaza to Temple IV

Behind Temple II is the **West Plaza**, dominated by a large Late Classic palace on the north side, and scattered with various altars and stelae, which, like those in the Great Plaza, owe their present position to Postclassic people, who rearranged many of the smaller monuments. From here the **Tozzer Causeway** – one of the raised routes that connected the main parts of the city – leads west to the unrestored **Temple III** (60m), covered in jungle vegetation. A fragment of Stela 24, found at the base of the temple, dates it at June 24, 810 AD, which marked the end of a *katun*. It was customary to construct twin temples to mark this auspicious event, but by this time it's clear that the Classic Maya were in severe difficulties across the region and just raising the manpower necessary to build Temple III would have been quite an achievement. Around the back of the temple is a huge palace complex, of which only the **Bat Palace** has been restored. Further down the causeway, on the left-hand side, is **Complex N**, another set of Late Classic twin pyramids. In the northern enclosure of the complex, the superbly carved **Stela 16** shows a flamboyantly dressed Hasaw Chan K'awil, who was buried beneath Temple I, depicted with a huge plumed headdress. **Altar 5** at its base bears a sculpted scene of Hasaw presiding over a sacrificial skull and bones with a lord from Maasal, formerly a vassal state of Calakmul, a clear indicator that Tikal had successfully expanded into the orbit of its bitter rival by 711 AD when the altar was completed. The accompanying text mentions the death of Hasaw's wife, Lady Twelve Macaw. Both Altar 5 and Stela 16 are aligned with Temples I and II, the monuments dedicated to Hasaw and his wife in the great plaza.

At the end of the Tozzer Causeway is **Temple IV**, the tallest of all the Tikal structures at a massive 64.6m (212ft). Built in 741 AD by Yik'in Chan K'awil (Hasaw's son), it is thought by many archeologists to be his burial monument, though no tomb has yet been found here. It's most famous for the stunning carved **wooden lintels**, embellished with images of the victorious king and a riot of glyphs, that were built into the top of the temple. Nowadays you'll have to travel to Switzerland to see them – though you can see an excellent replica of Lintel 3 in Guatemala City's archeological museum.

Twin ladders, one for the ascent, the other for the descent, attached to the sides of the temple delineate the route up, past the tangle of roots and trees that grip the sides of the unrestored temple. Slow and exhausting as the climb is, the finest views of the whole site await. All around you the forest canopy stretches out to the horizon, over the ruins of Naranjo towards the Maya mountains of Belize, interrupted only by the great roof combs of the other temples. Given the vistas, it's not surprising that the sunrise tribe gather here in great numbers, and though the humidity and mist usually shroud the visuals somewhat, the dawn jungle chorus rarely fails to disappoint.

From Temple IV the **Maudslay Causeway** leads to **Group H**, which includes two more twin-pyramid structures, and from here the **Maler Causeway** takes you back down to the East Plaza, past yet another set.

The Mundo Perdido, the Plaza of the Seven Temples and the Temple of the Inscriptions

The other main buildings in the centre of Tikal are to the south of the Central Acropolis. Here, reached by a trail from Temple III, you'll find the **Plaza of the Seven Temples**, which forms part of a complex dating back to before Christ. There's an unusual triple ball court on the north side of the plaza, and to the east is the unexcavated South Acropolis. To the west of here is the **Mundo Perdido**, or Lost World, another magical and very distinct section of the site with its own atmosphere and architecture. Little is known about the ruins in this part of the site, but archeologists hope that further research will help to explain the early history of Tikal. The main feature is the **Great Pyramid**, a 32-metre-high structure whose surface hides four earlier versions, the first an astronomical temple from 500 BC. The top of the pyramid offers awesome views towards Temple IV and the Great Plaza and makes an excellent base to watch the visual dramatics at sunrise or sunset.

Finally there's **Temple VI**, also known as Temple of the Inscriptions, reached along the Méndez Causeway from the East Plaza behind Temple I. The temple (only discovered in 1957) is about 1km from the plaza and is another of Yik'in Chan K'awil's constructions, completed in 766 AD. It's a medium-sized temple, famous for its twelve-metre roof comb, on the back of which is a huge hieroglyphic text, only just visible these days. The texts chart the history of the city from a founding date in 1139 BC (which is over two hundred years before the first archeological evidence of settlement) though this date was almost certainly guesswork by the Classic Maya. Temple VI is another candidate as the burial place of Yik'in Chan K'awil, Tikal's most prodigious monument builder, along with Temple IV.

Outside the main area are countless smaller **unrestored structures**. Compared with the scale and magnificence of what you've seen already they're not that impressive, but armed with a good map (the best is in Coe's guide to the ruins), it can be exciting to explore some of the rarely visited outlying sections. Tikal is certain to exhaust you before you exhaust it.

Uaxactún and around

Twenty kilometres north of Tikal, strung out by the side of an airstrip, are the village and ruins of **UAXACTÚN**. With a couple of places to stay, several comedores and a daily bus to Santa Elena, the village is an ideal jumping-off point for the remote northern ruins of **El Zotz** and **Río Azul**. Substantially smaller than Tikal, the site (known as Sia'an K'aan in Maya times) rose to prominence in the Late Preclassic era,

Uaxactún emblem glyph

and grew to become a major player in the Early Classic era. It's known that both Uaxactún and Tikal were overshadowed by the presence of the El Mirador to the north until the first century AD, but once the influence of the Maya world's first superpower started to decline, rivalry between Tikal and Uaxactún took off as both cities began to expand, embarking on grand building programmes. The two finally clashed on January 16, 378 AD, when Tikal's warriors conquered Uaxactún. It's very likely that the key to this victory was the introduction of new warfare technology from Mexico – spearthrowing slings – by the Teotihuacán warrior Siyak K'ak who had just overturned the ruling Tikal dynasty. Tikal's victory at Uaxactún, within days of the arrival of the Mexicans, was to prove a seminal event, announcing the new leader's aggressive intent to the rest of the Petén cities and condemning Uaxactún to six hundred years of subordinate status. Quite simply, Uaxactún never recovered.

The overall impact of the Uaxactún **ruins** (daily 8am–5pm; US$1.80) may be a little disappointing after the grandeur of Tikal, but you'll probably have the site to yourself, giving you the chance to soak up the atmosphere, and there are several large structures to explore. Village children will offer to guide you around; their charm is irresistible – as are the dolls made from corn husks decorated with beads and dried flowers you'll be implored to buy – though their archeological knowledge is limited. A quetzal or two tip is fine.

The most interesting buildings are in **Group E**, east of the airstrip, where three low reconstructed temples – Temples E-1, E-II and E-III – built side by side, are arranged to function as an observatory. Viewed from the top of a fourth temple, the sun rises behind the north temple (E-I) on the longest day of the year and behind the southern one (E-III) on the shortest day. It's an architectural pattern that was first discovered here but has since been found at a number of other sites. This point of observation is above the famous **E-VII sub**, a buried Preclassic temple that was once thought to date back to 2000 BC, though a much later date is now accepted. The pyramid has simple staircases on all sides, the steps flanked by pairs of elaborate **stucco masks** of jaguar and serpent heads. It's clear that this was a sacred monument, a platform for bloodletting and sacrifice, for the jaguar signifies the Jaguar God of the underworld, one of the most powerful deities; the serpent is the fabled "vision serpent".

Over on the other side of the airstrip is **Group A**, a series of larger temples and residential compounds, some of them reconstructed, spread out across the high ground. In amongst the structures are some impressive stelae, each sheltered by a small thatched roof.

Practicalities

A **bus** from Flores passes through Tikal en route for Uaxactún at around 3pm; alternatively, you could take one of the **tours** run by a number of companies based in Flores. **Staying** overnight you have two options: the very basic *EcoCampamento* (☎926 0077 in Flores; rooms ❷) has tents and hammocks (US$3 per person), protected by mosquito nets, under a thatched shelter; the welcoming *Campamento Ecológico El Chiclero* (☎926 1033, ℉926 1095 in Flores; ❷–❸) offers clean rooms with shared bath, or you can camp or sling up a hammock for US$2.50 a head. There's a spacious, screened restaurant and owner Neria Herrera can organize 4WD trips to Río Azul and other sites buried deep in the jungle. Doña Neria is also in charge of the **Museo Juan Antonio Valdes**, in the *El Chiclero* grounds (free at the moment, though a small fee is planned). Guarded only by chicken wire and a padlock, there's an astonishing collection of intact vases, plates and other ceramics crammed onto the wooden shelves. Many of the vessels are decorated with glyphs and animal figures, and some have a hole drilled in the centre to ceremonially "kill" the power they contain. Other items include a beautiful necklace and flint axe heads, polished to a glass-like gleam.

Uaxactún's **guide association** will also arrange **camping trips** to any of the remote northern sites, into the jungle or east to Nakúm and Yaxhá. Equipment is carried on horseback and the price (US$30 per person per day for a group of three or more) includes a guide, horses, camping gear and food. Check at CINCAP or ProPétén in Flores for advice and help with putting together excursions, or contact Evolution Adventures (see p.336).

El Zotz and Río Azul

Away to the north of Tikal, lost in a sea of jungle, are several other substantial **ruins** – unrestored and for the most part uncleared, but with their own unique atmosphere. The bulk of the temples lies beneath mounds of earth, their sides coated in vegetation, and only the tallest roof combs are still visible. A dirt road heads north to Río Azul (a controversial plan is being considered to make this a highway into Mexico) and a track heads west to El Zotz. For the moment these sites remain well beyond the reach of the average visitor – perfect if you're in search of an adventure and want to see a virtually untouched Maya site.

El Zotz

Thirty kilometres west of Uaxactún, along a rough jeep track, sometimes passable in the dry season (by 4WD), is **El Zotz**, a large Maya site set in its own *biotopo* adjoining the Tikal national park. To **get there** you can rent vehicles in Uaxactún, or rent a pack horse, guide, food and camping equipment from Uaxactún's guide association (see above). After about four hours – almost halfway – you come to **Santa Cruz**, where settlers including Pablo Pérez make a living from selling honey and crocodile skins. He'll direct you to the *aguada* for water (you'll need a filter) and will let you camp if you decide to split the journey. At the site itself you'll be welcomed by the guards who look after the *biotopo* headquarters. You can camp here and, with permission, use the kitchen and drinking water. Remember to bring some food to share with the guides.

Totally unrestored, El Zotz has been systematically looted, although there are guards on duty all year now and there's also a CECON biological station close to the ruins. The three main temples are smothered in soil and vegetation, but using the workers' scaffold you can climb to the top of the tallest structure, the **devil's pyramid**, which is spectacular in itself. The roof combs of the Tikal temples, 23km west of here, can be glimpsed on clear days. Zotz means "bat" in Maya and each evening at dusk you'll see tens, perhaps hundreds of thousands of **bats** of several species emerge from a cave near the campsite. It's especially impressive in the moonlight, the beating wings sounding like a river flowing over rapids – one of the most remarkable natural sights in Petén. Keep an eye out too for bat falcons, swooping with talons outstretched in search of their prey.

Walking on, it takes about four and a half hours to get to **Cruce Dos Aguadas**, a crossroads village populated by Q'eqchi' Maya on the bus route from Santa Elena to Carmelita. There are a couple of basic tiendas and comedores here, the best of which is the *Comedor Patojas* where they'll let you sling a hammock or camp. Northwards it's 41km to Carmelita (see p.358) for El Mirador and about the same distance west to Pasos Caballos for El Perú (see p.370; not possible in the rainy season). It's actually a little quicker to get to El Zotz independently if you do this trip in reverse, by getting a bus or pick-up from San Andrés (see p.337) to Cruce Dos Aguadas and walking or hitching from there. Some *xatero* trucks go right past the site and the guards usually know when one will pass by for the return journey. While this route is shorter, entailing less walking, there's also less forest cover than on the route from Uaxactún, and less chance of seeing wildlife.

Río Azul

The remote site of **Río Azul**, almost on the tripartite border where Guatemala, Belize and Mexico meet, was only rediscovered in 1962. The city and its suburbs are thought to have had a population of at least five thousand, scattered over 750 acres. Although totally unrestored, the core of the site resembles Tikal in many ways, though it is smaller. The tallest temple (A-III) stands some 47m above the forest floor, poking

Río Azul emblem glyph

its head out above the treetops and giving magnificent views across the jungle.

Investigations suggest that the site dates back to the Middle Preclassic period, though the population soared in the Early Classic era between 410 AD and 530 AD. This period of rapid expansion coincides with the emergence of the new Teotihuacán–Tikal alliance, and it's clear that the city became a crucial trading centre between the Caribbean coast (where cacao, the Maya currency, was abundant), Tikal and routes to Central Mexico. Río Azul became a strategic outpost of the expanding Tikal empire, defining its northernmost boundaries, and an important defensive ally against the threatening presence of Calakmul, the other regional superpower, 60km to the northwest. It's likely that Tikal's ruler Stormy Sky installed one of his sons here as king. But by the sixth century Río Azul's position on the fringes of Tikal's domain had become alarmingly precarious, and Calakmul's Tuun K'ab' Hix ("Stone Hand Jaguar") overran the city in 530 AD. After this defeat Río Azul was forcibly allied to Calakmul and there followed a long hiatus when no monuments were constructed. Mirroring Tikal's fortunes, the city again saw a surge in population in Late Classic times, as Tikal reclaimed its former sphere of influence. It was again sacked in 830, this time by marauding Puuc Maya from the Yucatán and ended the Classic period as it had began – a much squabbled over outpost city.

Several incredible **tombs** have been unearthed here, lined with white plaster and painted with vivid red glyphs. Tomb 1 is thought to have contained the remains of Stormy Sky's son, while nearby Tombs 19 and 23 contained bodies of warriors dressed in clothing typical of the ancient city of Teotihuacán in central Mexico, further supporting the theory that Tikal derived much of its power from an alliance with this mighty city. Many of these finds, including a richly decorated jar with a curved handle which turns to open the vessel, are displayed in the archeology museum in Guatemala City (see p.80).

Extensive **looting** occurred after the site's discovery, however, robbing even greater burial treasures – a gang of up to eighty men plundering the tombs once the archeological teams had retreated to Flores in the rainy season. During the late 1960s and early 1970s, when the looting business reached its height, Río Azul supplied the international market with unique treasures, including some incredible green jade masks and pendants. The gangs stripped the tombs bare, hacking away many of their elaborately decorated walls and removing some of the finest murals in the Maya world. Despite its chamber being looted in 1981, Tomb 1's walls escaped the worst of the damage and remain mercifully intact. Working with simple tools, several of the robbers are thought to have died when tombs caved in on them, and in due course the bodies, buried alongside their Maya ancestors, will probably be unearthed by archeologists. More recently, several new tombs have been discovered, probably those of noblemen rather than royalty, though, and their murals don't compare with those that have been removed.

Today there are two resident guards, who'll accompany you throughout your visit. The tallest temples are now becoming unsafe to climb, so always heed the advice of the guards. For more information on the site see the recent book *Río Azul: An Ancient Maya City*, by Richard Adams (University of Oklahoma).

Getting there

The **road** that connects Tikal and Uaxactún continues for another 95km north to Río Azul. This route is only passable in the dry season, and can be covered by 4WDs in as little as five hours, depending on the conditions. **Walking** or on **horseback** it's four days each way – three at a push. Trips can be arranged through *El Chiclero* in Uaxactún or through ProPetén and CINCAP or a number of agents in Flores.

Just beyond the halfway point you come to the **Biotopo Dos Lagunas**, an excellent point to take a break. There's a *campamento* for the guards on the shore of one of the lagunas and they'll be happy to let you cook a meal here, or even stay the night – there are basic shelters and showers but you'll need a mosquito net. As always, bring some gifts of food or coffee for the guards – and the crocodiles in the lake will lunge at pieces of bread.

Once you arrive at Río Azul you'll be welcome to stay at the guard's **camp** at **Río Ixcán**, on the far side of the river; in the dry season a truck can drive through the river, otherwise you cross in an old dugout canoe. The ruins themselves are six kilometres from the campsite, along a wide, motorable road shaded by the forest, so take all the food and water you'll need for several hours at the site.

For much of the year the river is reduced to a series of pools, and the road continues another 12km to **Tres Banderas**, where the borders of Guatemala, Mexico and Belize meet. Eventually, it may be possible to get your exit stamp in Uaxactún and continue to Mexico using this route. It's not currently possible to exit Guatemala this way however, and many environmental groups oppose the upgrading of the road, fearing it will bring an invasion of land-hungry settlers who will clear the forest.

El Mirador and around

Still engulfed by the most extensive forests in the Maya region, tight against the Mexican border in the extreme north of the country, are the remains of the first great cities of the Maya. The importance of this remote region is only just beginning to be understood, and it's only very recently that archeologists have begun extensive excavations here, but exciting discoveries have already led to a major rethink about the origins of Maya civilization. The main focus of investigation has been the giant site of **El Mirador**, the first Maya "superpower" famous for its colossal triadic temple complexes. Neighbouring **Nakbé,** the first city to emerge in the Middle Preclassic around 800 BC, and **Wakná** (which was only discovered in 1998) also now have teams of archeologists and workers anxiously trying to piece together the formative history of the Maya.

The conditions are very difficult – marshy mosquito-plagued terrain which becomes so saturated that excavations can only be attempted for five months of the year. However, undoubtedly the greatest challenge facing the archeologists and Guatemalan authorities is to save the ruins from the constant threat from well-organized gangs of **tomb looters** and timber merchants eager to plunder the forest hardwoods. Because of this insecurity, environmentalists and Mayanists are lobbying hard to get the core region declared a **Mirador Basin National Park**. The Univeristy of California has had to recruit 27 armed guards to patrol El Mirador alone; otherwise, according to Richard Hanson, who is leading the excavations here, "we'd lose the whole city".

The sites are all very difficult to **get to** and require a minimum of a five-day hike through dense jungle with pack horses and supplies. Trips can be organized through several tour operators in Flores (see p.336), Guatemala City (see p.89) and also from the village of Carmelita (see below).

El Mirador

El Mirador is perhaps the most exotic and mysterious of all Petén's Maya sites. Encircled by the Petén and Campeche jungles, this massive city matches Tikal's scale, and may even surpass it, although little is known about its history. Rediscovered in 1926, it dates from a period much earlier than Tikal, and came to dominate the Maya region. Occupying a commanding position above the rainforest, at an altitude of 250m, the city was built on Middle Preclassic foundations, and could well have been originally settled by migrants from Nakbé (see below). The city flourished between 200 BC and 150 AD, when it was unquestionably the largest city in Central America, being home to tens of thousands of Maya. Though substantial archeological investigations have only just really begun, it's already clear that the site represents the peak of Preclassic Maya culture, which was far more sophisticated than was once believed.

The core of the site covers some sixteen square kilometres, stretching between two massive pyramids that face each other across the forest on an east–west axis. The site's western side is marked by the massive **Tigre Complex**, made up of a huge single pyramid flanked by two smaller structures, a triadic design that's characteristic of El Mirador's architecture. The base of this complex measures 125m by 135m alone (enough to cover around three football fields), while the height of the 2000-year-old main pyramid touches 70m, making it the tallest structure anywhere in the Maya world. Giant stucco **jaguar masks** have been uncovered on lower flanking temples of the main pyramid, their teeth and claws painted red. In front of the Tigre Complex is El Mirador's sacred hub: a long narrow plaza, the **Central Acropolis**, and a row of smaller buildings. Burial chambers unearthed in this central section had been painted with ferric oxide to prevent corrosion and contained the bodies of priests and noblemen, surrounded by the obsidian lancets and stingray spines used to pierce the penis, ears and tongue in ritual bloodletting ceremonies (see "Contexts", p.450). The spilling of blood was seen by the Maya as a method of summoning and sustaining the gods, and was clearly common at all the great ceremonial centres.

To the south of the Tigre Complex is the **Monos Complex**, another triadic structure and plaza, named after the local howler monkeys that roar long into the night and after heavy rainfall. To the north, the **León Pyramid** and the **Casabel Complex** mark the boundary of the site. Heading away to the east, on the other side of the main plaza and the Central Acropolis, the Puleston Causeway runs some 800m to the smaller East Group, the largest of which (about 2km from the Tigre Complex) is the **Danta Complex**. Another triadic structure, it rises in three stages to a height just below that of the Tigre pyramid, but gives even better views since it was built on higher land. It too has imposing masks built into the side of its temples, including some striking jaguar and vulture heads.

The area **around El Mirador** is riddled with smaller Maya sites, and as you look out across the forest from the top of either of the main temples you can see others rising above the horizon on all sides – including the largest (as opposed to the tallest) Maya pyramid of all: Structure 2 at Calakmul in Mexico. Raised **causeways**, ancient trading routes called *sakbé*, connect many of these smaller sites to El Mirador and some are currently being investigated by visiting archeologists.

Nakbé, El Tintal and Wakná

About 10km to the southeast of El Mirador down one of the *sakbé*, **Nakbé** was the first substantial city to emerge in the Maya region (though it's quite possible that earlier sites have yet to be discovered). There's now definitive evidence that people had settled here to farm by 1000 BC, possibly a few centuries earlier, and that the settlement grew to become a city of many thousands by 400 BC. These dates have necessitated a complete revision of the once-accepted timescale of origin of the Maya civilization in the lowlands, and it's hoped that ongoing research here will reveal much more about the earliest development of Maya calendrics, religion and writing.

Today the site, which has only been partially cleared, is virtually unvisited by anyone except archeologists, *xateros* (palm leaf gatherers) and *chicleros* (rubber tappers). Initial excavation work by Richard Hansen and his UCLA team has revealed that the city had a ceremonial core of **temples**, separated into two groups via a kilometre-long limestone causeway – much like El Mirador. At the eastern end, the temples rise from a platform to peak at 35m, while the western temple reaches 45m (around the same height as Temple I at Tikal, though it was constructed more than 1200 years previously, around 500 BC). The archeologists have also found evidence of skilful stucco work – a huge **mask** (measuring 5m by 8m) was found on the side of one of the temples, though it has since been covered in earth for protection. There are probably hundreds of outlying structures, including residential complexes grouped around plazas, though very limited excavation has yet been undertaken and doubtless many more exciting discoveries will follow.

El Tintal, another Preclassic site, 21km to the southwest of El Mirador, was also connected by a causeway to its giant neighbour, and the ruins, though severely looted, make an ideal campsite on the route to Mirador basin. The unrestored temples here are from a slightly later era, but also arranged in a triadic formation with a central staircase flanked by elaborate stucco masks – some of the earliest examples of Maya sculptural art. Climb to the top of the largest pyramid and there are spectacular views, including El Mirador in the distance.

The other great site in the Mirador basin – **Wakná** or "house of six" – was only discovered in 1998, detected by satellite imagery after careful analysis of aerial photographs detected temple-like mounds in the jungle. It was still up to a ground crew to verify that these anomalies were indeed a Maya ruin, however. Dr Hansen, accompanied by *chicleros*, lead a team to the region and confirmed that the mounds were indeed the remains of a city, later established to be Preclassic in origin. Unfortunately they weren't the first people to discover the site – a trench cut into one of the temples confirmed that looters had been already been active, and had raided a tomb.

Getting to the Mirador basin

Getting to El Mirador area is a substantial undertaking, involving a rough sixty-kilometre bus or pick-up journey from Santa Elena to **Carmelita**, a *chicle-* and *xate*-gathering centre, followed by two days of hard jungle hiking – you'll need a horse to carry your food and equipment. There's basic but clean **accommodation** at the *Campamento Nakbé* (❷), 1.5km before the village, where the large thatched shelters have mosquito nets and hammocks, or, if you have your own tent, you can **camp** (US$2 per person). For a good feed, visit the *Comedor Pepe Toño* in the centre of the village, run by Brenda Zapata, who is a mine of information about the area and can introduce you to the local guides.

The journey – impossibly muddy in the rainy season – is best attempted from mid-January to August; February to April is the driest period. It offers an exceptional chance to see virtually untouched forest, and perhaps some of the creatures that inhabit it. If you want to **organize a trip in advance**, Maya Expeditions (see Guatemala City "Listings", p.89) run excellent trips to all the sites (including Wakná) in the region; all are lead by a prominent archeologist, often Richard Hanson. Far Horizons (see "Basics", p.12) and many of the Flores-based tour operators (including ProPetén and EcoMaya, see p.336) can get you to El Mirador and El Tintal (see above) with five-day **tours** costing around US$200 for two people, including guide, packhorse and digs in Carmelita; add US$50 per person if you want to include Nakbé. It's also possible to travel to the Mirador area **independently**, arranging a guide in Carmelita (about US$30 a day) who will then organize packhorse, food, water and camping gear for you – ask for Luis Morales, president of the Tourist Committee, or speak to Brenda Zapata (see above). The more people you can persuade to join the trip, the cheaper it becomes.

However you decide to plan you trip, the first night after leaving Carmelita is spent – in a simple thatched shelter if you've no tent – by an *aguada* (a waterhole of dubious quality) near the ruins of **El Tintal** (see above), a large site which you'll be able to explore on the way back. Another day's walking brings you to the guards' huts at **El Mirador**, where you are welcome to stay, using their hearth to cook on. You should bring along food or drink for the guards, who spend forty days at a time in the forest, subsisting on beans and tortillas. If you plan to continue on to **Nakbé**, you'll need to budget for another two days' worth of supplies. The only other serious hazards are the *garraptas* (ticks), for which you'll need a pair of tweezers and a trusty companion. Whether you take a tour or go independently, you're advised to examine the information and maps at ProPetén and CINCAP first.

Sayaxché and around

Southwest of Flores, on a lazy bend in the Río Pasión, is **SAYAXCHÉ**, an easy-going settlement that's an ideal base for exploring the forest and its huge collection of archeological remains. A frontier town at the junction of road and river, Sayaxché is an important point of storage for grain and cattle and the source of supplies for a vast surrounding area which is being steadily cleared and colonized. The complex network of rivers and swamps that cuts through the forests here has been an important trade route since Maya times, and there are several interesting ruins in the area. Upstream is **Ceibal**, a small but beautiful site in a wonderful jungle setting, while to the south is **Lago de Petexbatún**, a stunning lakeside setting for the small Maya sites of **Aguateca** and Punta de Chimino, and the trailhead for the substantial ruins of **Dos Pilas** and Tamarindito. A visit to this region offers great opportunities to explore the Petén forest and watch the wildlife, including howler and spider monkeys, crocodiles, iguanas and toucans.

Sayaxché practicalities

Getting to Sayaxché from Flores is very straightforward, with several Pinita **buses** (5.30am, 8am, 10am, 1pm & 4pm; 2hr) and two Del Rosío services (5am and 10am) plying the fairly smooth 62-kilometre dirt road. At other times hitching a ride in a **pick-up** is not too difficult, or there are a number of travel agencies offering tours (around US$30 for a day-trip to Ceibal, US$60 per person for Ceibal and Aguateca, including a night at Lago de Petexbatún) from Flores. A ferry takes you over the Río Pasión, directly opposite Sayaxché.

Hotels in Sayaxché are on the basic side. The *Guayacán* (☎926 6111; ❸), right beside the river, is the first you come to, with plain functional rooms, some with private bath, and lovely sunset views from the terrace. For a cheaper room, head right from the dock to the friendly *Hotel Posada Segura* (❷) which has decent, clean rooms, some with private bath; alternatively, head left down the street above the *Guayacan* to the basic but cheap *Hospedaje Mayapan* (❶), where you may be able to rent a **bike** for visiting Ceibal. There are plenty of reasonable places to **eat** in the central area, the best being *Restaurant Yaxkín* (closes 8pm), where the portions are huge, and *El Botanero* set in a attractive thatched house, where they also have full bar. There is also decent food at *Guayacan* and at *La Montaña*, 100m south on the same street, a restaurant owned by the knowledgeable and helpful Julián Mariona, who can arrange **trips** to the nearby ruins and fishing expeditions (both around US$45 a day). Plenty of **boatmen** are eager to take you up- or downriver, though they tend to see all tourists as walking cash-dispensers and quote very high rates. Try Pedro Méndez Requena of Viajes Don Pedro (☎ & ⓕ928 6109), who offers **tours** of the area from his office on the riverfront. You can change travellers' cheques at Banora, a block up from the *Guayacan*.

The ruins of Ceibal (Seibal)

The most accessible and impressive of the sites near Sayaxché is **Ceibal** (sometimes spelt "Seibal") which you can reach by land or river. By boat it's easy enough to make it there and back in an afternoon. Not much commercial river traffic heads upstream, however, so you'll probably have to **rent a boat** – ask around at the waterfront and be prepared to haggle: boats take up to six people and generally charge around US$40–50 for the round trip including two hours at the ruins. The hour-long

Ceibal emblem glyph

boat journey is followed by a short walk through towering rainforest. **By road** Ceibal is just 17km from Sayaxché. Any transport heading south out of town towards Cruce del Pato passes the entrance road to the site, from where it's an eight-kilometre walk through the jungle to the ruins. About halfway along the road, you'll pass a sign denoting the start of the protected area of the Ceibal cultural monument, though this status hasn't prevented some *campesinos* clearing a chunk of forest. Visiting Ceibal should be a day-trip, but if you're unlucky you may end up stranded at the entrance road waiting for a truck back. If you haven't hired a boat and decide to try and return by river, be prepared to wait a long time for a ride. If you have a tent or hammock (with mosquito net), you might as well stay – bring food to share with the guards and you'll always be welcome.

Surrounded by forest and shaded by huge ceiba trees, **the ruins** of Ceibal are partially cleared and restored, and beautifully landscaped into a mixture of open plazas and untamed jungle. Although it can't match the enormity of Tikal, and many of the largest temples lie buried under mounds, Ceibal does have some outstanding carving, superbly preserved due to the use of hard stone. The two main plazas are dotted with lovely **stelae**, centred on two low platforms. Fragments of stucco found on these platforms suggest that they were originally decorated with ornate friezes and painted in brilliant shades of red, blue, green, pink, black and beige. During the Classic period Ceibal was a relatively minor site, but it grew rapidly between 830 and 910 AD, possibly after falling under the control of Putun colonists from what is now Mexico. In this period it grew to become the largest southern lowland site, with an estimated population of around 10,000. Outside influence is clearly visible in the carving here: speech scrolls, straight noses, waist-length hair and serpent motifs are all decidedly non-Maya. The architecture also differs from other Classic Maya sites, including the round platforms that are usually associated with the Quetzalcoatl cult. The five fine stelae set around the radial A-3 temple in the plaza were all commissioned in 849 AD to commemorate the Maya year 10.1.0.0.0. Just east of the plaza, the crudely carved but unusual monkey-faced Stela 2 is particularly striking, beyond which, straight ahead down the path, lies Stela 14, another impressive sculpture. If you turn right here and walk for ten minutes, you'll reach the only other restored site, a massive circular stone **observation** platform, used for astronomy and superbly set in a clearing in the forest.

Lago de Petexbatún

A similar distance to the south of Sayaxché is **Lago de Petexbatún**, a spectacular expanse of water ringed by dense forest and containing plentiful supplies of snook, bass, alligator and freshwater turtle. The shores of the lake abound with wildlife and Maya remains and though the ruins themselves are small and unrestored, they do make interesting goals as part of a trip into the forest. Their sheer number suggests that the lake was an important trading centre for the Maya.

If you can get together a group of three or four it's well worth arranging a boat and guide to take you on a **two- or three-day trip** around the lake. The simplest way to do this is to ask Julián at *La Montaña* in Sayaxché or the folks at the *Chiminos Island Lodge* (see below). There are plenty of options – touring the lake on foot, by boat or on horseback, wandering in the jungle, fishing or bathing in the natural warm springs on the lakeshore – but whichever you opt for you'll need a guide. It's cheapest to **stay** at the sites themselves, camping or

△ Details of house facade, Flores

sleeping in a hammock, although if you do feel the need for a little luxury there are **hotels** around the lake. Owned by Julián, the *Posada El Caribe*, on the river before it enters the lake (☎928 6114, ☏928 6168; full board ❼) offers clean, screened cabins, reasonable food and boat trips to Aguateca; negotiate rates in advance. On the west side of the lake, the spectacularly located *Chiminos Island Lodge* (☎335 3506, ☏335 2647, ☯www.chiminosisland.com; US$75 per person, including all meals) has a Maya ruin (see below) virtually on the premises and comfortable wood and thatch cabañas. Owner Mynor Pinto arranges superb guided trips to the many remote sites in the Petexbatún area.

Aguateca and Punta de Chiminos

Aguateca (daily 8am–5pm; US$3.20, includes entrance to all the Petexbatún sites), a minor site perched on a high outcrop at the southern tip of the lake, was only rediscovered in 1957. The settlement remains completely unrestored, although in recent years it has been the subject of intense archeological investigation. Throughout the Late Classic period Aguateca was closely aligned with (or controlled by) nearby Dos Pilas, the dominant city in the southern Petén, reaching its peak in the eighth century, when the latter was developing an aggressive policy of expansion. Indeed, Aguateca may have been a twin capital of an ambitious Petexbatún state. Military successes, including a conclusive victory over Ceibal in 735 AD, were celebrated at both sites with remarkably similar stelae – Aguateca's Stela 3 showing the Dos Pilas ruler Master Sun Jaguar in full battle regalia, including a Teotihuacán-style face mask. After 761 AD, however, Dos Pilas began to lose control of its empire and the members of the elite moved their headquarters to Aguateca, attracted by its strong defensive position. Despite the construction of 5km of walls around the citadel and its agricultural land, their enemies soon caught up with them, and sometime after 790 AD Aguateca itself was overrun.

Surrounded by dense tropical forest and with superb views of the lake, Aguateca has a magical atmosphere. You can clearly make out the temples and plazas, dotted with well-preserved stelae. The carving is superbly executed, the images including rulers, captives, hummingbirds, pineapples and pelicans. If you ask the two guards who live here, they'll give you an enthusiastic and well-informed tour, explaining the meaning of the various images and showing you the stelae shattered by looters who hoped to sell the fragments. Aguateca is also the site of the only known **bridge** in the Maya world, which crosses a narrow gash in the hillside, but it's not that impressive in itself.

The guards always welcome company and if you want to **stay** they'll find some space for you to sling a hammock or pitch a tent, but you'll need to bring a mosquito net and food. To reach the site from Sayaxché by boat takes a couple of hours, but as the boatmen usually charge around US$120 for the round trip you'll either need a large group or deep pockets. Aguateca is also accessible by truck in the dry season (see p.359).

A couple of kilometres to the north, jutting out from the west shore of the lake, is a club-shaped peninsula known as **Punta de Chiminos**. This site was the final refuge of the last of the Petexbatún Maya in the Late Classic era, as the region descended into warfare and chaos at the beginning of the ninth century. Here they constructed some formidable defences across the narrow stem of the peninsula including three rock-hewn trenches, and nine metre ramparts which created man-made citadel. The point is now the spectacular location for the lovely *Chiminos Island Lodge* (see above).

Dos Pilas and around

Some 12km west of the northern tip of Lago de Petexbatún, still buried in the jungle, is another virtually unreconstructed site – **Dos Pilas** – which has one of the most fascinating and best documented histories of any Maya city. Only established around 640 AD, the founders were a renegade group from Tikal, who fled the great city during its dark ages, the 130-year hiatus that followed its defeat by Calakmul. The leader of this breakaway tribe, a lord called B'alaj Chan K'awil ("Lightening Sky") was clearly a brazen individual. Even though he claimed membership of the Tikal royal line, he swore a treacherous allegiance with Calakmul in 648 AD, in an attempt to launch a rival dynasty at Tikal. Dos Pilas clashed with Tikal several times in the years afterwards, as Tikal sought to humble the upstart Dos Pilas ruler. Though B'alaj Chan K'awil ultimately failed in his bid to claim the Tikal lineage, he did repel Tikal in 679 AD, a victory which he celebrated by commissioning several new stelae and launching a substantial reconstruction of the plaza.

Dos Pilas emblem glyph

Dos Pilas continued to throw its weight around for another century, provoking a series of battles with neighbouring cities, defeating Ceibal in 735 AD, and capturing lords from Yaxchilán and Motul. Monuments including three hieroglyphic stairways were built, though by the latter half of the eighth century the region was becoming so unstable (probably due to attacks by Putun Maya from Mexico) that the rulers fled Dos Pilas in 761 AD. Squatting farmers continued to occupy the site for a few more years, tearing down the temple structures to build elaborate defensive walls in a vain attempt to keep out the invaders, but by the early ninth century Dos Pilas was abandoned completely. If you want to find out more about the history of Dos Pilas, there's a masterful account about the city's place in Classic Maya politics in Simon Martin and Nikolai Grube's *Chronicle of the Maya Kings and Queens* (Thames and Hudson; see "Books", p.487).

Sadly, today the remains of the city are less than spectacular, as many temples were partly dismantled during the chaos of the late eighth century. Nevertheless there's some superb carving to admire, including several wonderful stelae and four **hieroglyphic stairways**, now protected by thatched shelters grouped around the grassy plaza. On the south side of the plaza are the ruins of a palace, while on the east side a rich tomb was discovered under Temple L-51, probably belonging to the ruler Itzamnaaj K'awiil. Encircling the remains of this ceremonial core, it's still possible to make out the remains of the fortifications, a double defensive wall and stockade that the final occupiers erected.

Getting to Dos Pilas is by no means straightforward, or cheap. It's best to try and organize transport in Sayaxché or Flores (see p.330), where several tour operators offer trips to the Ceibal and the Petexbatún region. Either way you'll have to travel from Sayaxché, and then via a 45-minute speedboat trip to the *Posada El Caribe* (see above) followed by a further 12km on foot to the ruins. The hike takes you past the small site of **Arroyo de Piedra**, where you'll find a plaza and two fairly well-preserved stelae, and the ruins of **Tamarindito** where another hieroglyphic stairway has been found. It may be possible to travel this way by pick-up truck during the dry months. Two guards live at the site of Dos Pilas and it's certainly possible to **stay** here – as always, you should bring a tent or hammock and mosquito net, and enough food to share with the guards. Otherwise you can make a day-trip of it and return to Sayaxché in the evening.

The "discovery" of Cancuén

In September 2000 newspapers across the world proclaimed that an ancient Maya city, lost for 1300 years, called **Cancuén**, "place of serpents", had been found by an American–Guatemalan team of archeologists on the banks of the Río Pasión. While the actuality was very different – Cancuén had been discovered in 1907 and was even plotted on tourism-board maps of the country – the sheer size of the ruins had certainly been underestimated and new investigations revealed the site to be enigmatic in other ways. Uniquely, Cancuén seems to lack the usual religious and defensive structures so characteristic of Maya cities and appears to have existed as an essentially secular, trading city. For most of the twentieth century, the absence of soaring temple-pyramids led archeologists to assume that Cancuén was a very minor site, and it was ignored for decades. However, the vast amounts of jade, pyrite, obsidian and fine ceramics found recently indicate that this was one of the great trading centres of the Maya world, with a paved plaza (which may have been a marketplace) covering two square kilometres. Cancuén is thought to have flourished because of its strategic position between the great cities of the lowlands, like Tikal and Calakmul, and the mineral-rich highlands of southern Guatemala. The vast, almost ostentatious, **palace** complex, with 170 rooms and 11 courtyards, is Cancuén's most arresting feature and it's hoped that investigations by Guatemala's Institute of Anthropology and the National Geographic Society will help uncover much about Classic period life.

South to the Ixcán

The road south from Sayaxché skirts round the edge of the **Ceibal natural reserve**, at first slicing through a stretch of jungle, then through a flat scrubland of lone tree stumps, cattle pasture and thatched cabañas where indigenous families and their swollen-bellied children live. These Q'eqchi', many of whom are returning refugees, struggle to eke out a meagre existence from the land.

Half an hour before **Cruce del Pato**, where the road splits (see p.315), the magnificent bulk of the Cuchumatanes mountain range comes into view, with the looming, forested ridges rising abruptly from the plain. Two Del Rosío buses run daily along this road between Sayaxché and Playitas.

Twelve kilometres east of Cruce del Pato is the large Maya site of **Cancuén** (see box) where a huge Classic-period palace has been unearthed. The city had close relations with both Dos Pilas and Calakmul in the Classic period, and flourished quite late after Dos Pilas had collapsed in 761 AD. At the moment the only way to visit the site is with the specialist tour operator Maya Expeditions (see Guatemala City "Listings" p.89); don't be tempted to hike over to the ruins from the junction as you'll have to dodge past fields of grazing water buffalo, through land owned by the ex-military dictator Lucas García.

Cancuén emblem glyph

Routes to Mexico

River trade between Guatemala and Mexico is increasing rapidly, as are the number of tourists making obscure border crossings. However, travellers should bear in mind that at the time of writing, Mexican border officials were only giving **two-week visas** to travellers entering the state of Chiapas from Guatemala, due to the conflict in the region.

The most common route is now the **Bethel–Frontera Corozal** route, which is also convenient for visiting the ruins of Yaxchilán (see p.367) and Bonampak. It's also possible to travel by boat **from Sayaxché** to Benemérito, on the Mexican bank of the Río Usumacinta. Another popular route is the trip **from Flores** to El Naranjo by bus, then along the Río San Pedro to La Palma in Mexico. All are reasonably well organized and the people along the way are now used to seeing foreign faces.

Border formalities are relatively straightforward on the San Pedro route, where there's a Guatemalan immigration office in El Naranjo and a Mexican one along the river at El Pedregal. On the Río Usumacinta there are Guatemalan immigration posts at Bethel and the riverside army base in Pipiles. On the Mexican side there are immigration posts at a number of places along the Usumacinta, including Boca Lacantún, just outside Benemérito, and Frontera Corozal. Expect to have the Mexican army examine your passport anywhere in this part of Chiapas; officials are usually polite but you should bear in mind that tensions can rise because of the ongoing Zapatista uprising. Don't even think about crossing the border without getting your passport stamped: if you're caught you'll almost certainly end up in a Mexican police station for a day or so while they grill you about any Zapatista sympathies and leaf through FBI photographs trying to identify you.

From Sayaxché to Benemérito and into Mexico

Downriver from Sayaxché the **Río Pasión** snakes its way through an area of forest and swamp that is gradually being occupied by a mixture of well-organized farming co-operatives and impoverished migrants. Along the way tiny river turtles bask on exposed rocks, white herons fish in the shallows and snakes occasionally slither across the surface of the river. There are two main landmarks: a slick American mission on the left-hand bank and the army post at **Pipiles** on the right, which marks the point where the rivers Salinas and Pasión merge to form the Usumacinta. All boats have to stop at Pipiles, where passengers present their papers at the immigration post and luggage may be searched.

On the south bank of the river not far from Pipiles is the small Maya site of **Altar de los Sacrificios**, discovered by Teobert Maler in 1895. Commanding an important river junction, this is one of the oldest sites in Petén, but these days there's not much to see beyond a solitary stela. The beach below, which is exposed in the dry season, is often scattered with tiny fragments of Maya pottery, uncovered as the river eats into the base of the site, carving into ancient burials.

From Pipiles it's possible to head **up the Río Salinas**, south along the Mexican border, through an isolated area visited only by traders buying maize and selling soft drinks and aspirin. Between trips these entrepreneurial geniuses can be found in Sayaxché, loading and unloading their boats, and for a small fee they might take a passenger or two. Most boats only go part of the way up the Salinas, but if you're really determined you can travel all the way to Playitas or Playa Grande (see p.316), and there join the road east to Raxrújá and Fray Bartolomé de Las Casas, or head west across the Ixcán (p.317). This is a rough trip for which you'll need a hammock, a mosquito net, a week or two, and a great deal of patience.

Following the **Usumacinta** downstream from Pipiles you arrive at **BENEMÉRITO** in Mexico, a sprawling frontier town at the end of a dirt road from Palenque. Passengers from Sayaxché are charged US$8–10 for what is usually an eight-hour trip, although boats with business along the way can take a couple of days to get this far. Arriving by boat from Guatemala you'll be met by Mexican soldiers who'll check your passport – the **immigration office** here is not always open, so you may be sent onward to Frontera Corozal to complete the paperwork. Benemérito has a hospital, market, shops, comedores and a few desperately basic hotels – rather than stay, you're better off heading onward to Corozal (for Yaxchilán), to Lacanhá (for Bonampak) or Palenque.

By road from Benemérito to Frontera Corozal

Between Benemérito and Palenque there's a twenty kilometre branch road off the main route to the riverside village of **FRONTERA COROZAL**, the nearest settlement to Yaxchilán. There are at least five **buses** a day from Benemérito to Palenque (9hr), which pass by the junction for Corozal – otherwise, hitching is possible, though traffic is scarce. The first **immigration post** on this route is a couple of kilometres outside Benemérito at Boca Lacantún, where the road crosses the Río Lacantún – ask the bus driver to stop for you while you go in and pick up a tourist card. The last minibus colectivos leave for Palenque around 2.30pm. In Frontera Corozal itself there's very basic accommodation and if you ask around you'll be able to find somewhere to sling a hammock; you also should be able to **camp** on the football pitch once the evening game has drawn to a close. The village does have a couple of simple comedores and an **immigration post** – so if you arrive directly by boat from Sayaxché, or across the river from Bethel (see below) you can get your (currently only two-week) visa here. If you want to visit Yaxchilán you *must* register at the immigration post. For details of the river trip from Benemérito to Frontera Corozal, see below.

From Bethel to Frontera Corozal

The cheapest and most straightforward route to Mexico is along the dirt road to **BETHEL** on the Río Usumacinta, where there's a Guatemalan immigration post. Although there is officially no fee, travellers may be charged a dollar to cross the border. Three buses a day leave Flores for Bethel (5am, 8am & 1pm; 4hr 30min), passing the El Subín junction north of Sayaxché a couple of hours later. At Bethel it's relatively easy to find a lancha heading downstream to Frontera Corozal (around US$7, more if there are a shortage of passengers; 30min); however, it's usually possible to get off the bus, obtain your exit stamp in Bethel and continue on the same bus for a further 12km to the tiny settlement of **La Técnica**, a co-operative village where you can cross the Usumacinta for just US$0.70, to Corozal on the opposite bank. At the time of writing there's no accommodation, nor other facilities, in La Técnica.

Bethel itself is a pleasant village with wide grassy streets and plenty of trees to provide shade. You can **camp** above the riverbank and there are several **comedores** – try the *Café el Ranchito* for good food and useful information – and shops. In the village you can stay in **rooms** (❷) belonging to Marcelo López; his is a friendly place that's on the far side of the football field, offering simple but clean accommodation in a wooden house with shared showers. The family also provides meals.

The **Bethel ruins**, 1.5km from the village, are today little more than tall, tree-covered mounds, their existence unknown to archeologists until 1995, but there's an excellent **eco-campamento** here called the *Posada Maya* (in Flores ☎926 0525, Ⓔcentromaya@guatenet) with comfortable rooms (❹), tents (including mattresses and clean sheets) under thatched shelters (❷) or hammocks (❶) on top of a wooded cliff high above the river. Ask the owners about trips to the ruins of Yaxchilán, Piedras Negras and into the Parque Nacional Sierra del Lacandón, perhaps the remotest and best-preserved rainforest in Guatemala.

By river to Yaxchilán and Piedras Negras

As you head downriver from Benemérito, the **Río Usumacinta** marks the border between Guatemala and Mexico, passing through dense tropical rainforest, occasionally cleared to make way for pioneer villages and cattle ranches, particularly along the Mexican bank.

Below Benemérito the first place of any interest on the river is the **Planchon de Figuras**, at the mouth of the Lacantún, a river that feeds into the Usumacinta from the Mexican side. One of the least known and most unusual of all Maya sites (though hardly a site in the conventional sense), this consists of a superb collection of graffiti carved into a great slab of limestone that slopes into the river. Its origin is completely unknown, but the designs, including birds, animals, temples and eroded glyphs, are certainly Maya. A little further downriver are the **Los Chorros** waterfalls, a series of beautiful cascades some 30km before Frontera Corozal.

Yaxchilán

Boats to the Maya **ruins of Yaxchilán**, 15km beyond Frontera Corozal, can be rented in Bethel, Benemérito and Frontera Corozal. Rates are high: if you're on your own or in a small group, it's cheaper to get on a boat that's being used by a tour group, or to get a lift with one of the local boats that can sometimes be persuaded to go on to the ruins.

Yaxchilán emblem glyph

The ruins are undeniably the most spectacular on the Usumacinta, superbly positioned on the Mexican bank, spread out over several steep hills within a great loop in the river. This is an important location, and carvings at Yaxchilán, like those at the neighbouring sites of Bonampak and Piedras Negras, tell of repeated conflict with the surrounding Maya centres. By 514 AD, when its emblem glyph was used for the first time, Yaxchilán was already a place of some size, but its era of greatness was launched by the ruler Shield Jaguar II, who came to power in 682 and extended the city's sphere of influence through a campaign of conquest. At this stage it was sufficiently powerful to form a military alliance that included not only the Usumacinta centres but also Tikal and Palenque. Shield Jaguar was succeeded by his son Bird Jaguar IV, who continued the ambitious construction projects and military expansion. Less is known about the later years in Yaxchilán, although building continued well into the Late Classic period so the site was probably occupied until at least 900 AD.

What you see today is a collection of plazas, temples and ball courts strung out along the raised banks of the river, while the low hills in the centre of the site are topped with impressive palaces. The structures are all fairly low, but each of the main temples supports a massive honeycombed roof, decorated with stucco carvings. The quality of this carving is yet again exceptional, though many of the best pieces have been removed to museums around the world: one set of particularly fine lintels, depicting the bloodletting rituals of Shield Jaguar II and his wife Lady Xoc, is displayed in the British Museum in London.

More recent finds, however, including some incredibly well-preserved carving, remain on site. When the layers of vegetation are peeled back the original stonework appears unaffected by the last thousand years, with flecks of red paint still clinging to the surface. Yaxchilán's architecture focuses heavily on the river, and the remains of a built-up bank suggest that it might have been the site of a bridge or toll gate. At low water you can see a pyramid, about 8m square at the base, 6m high, with a carved altar on top. Built on the river bed and completely submerged at high water, it is believed by archeologists to be a bridge abutment.

Until fairly recently the site was still used by Lacandón Maya, who came here to burn incense, worship, and leave offerings to their gods. The whole place still has a bewitching atmosphere, with the energy of the forest, overwhelming in its fertility, threatening to consume the ruins. The forest here is relatively undisturbed and buzzes with life; toucans, spider and howler monkeys loiter in the trees, while bats are now the main inhabitants of the palaces and temples.

Arriving at the site by boat you'll be met by one of the guards who live here to ward off the ever-present threat of looting. They are happy to show you round the site, though they generally ask a small fee for their labours. You're welcome to camp too, though mosquitoes can be a problem – whether you're staying or not – particularly in the rainy season.

Piedras Negras

Forty kilometres downstream from Yaxchilán, the ruins of **Piedras Negras** loom high over the Guatemalan bank of the river. Despite being one of the most extensive ruins in Guatemala, this is one of the least accessible and least visited of Maya sites. The city was called Yokib' ("the entrance") in Maya times; the Spanish name of Piedras Negras refers to the black stones lining the river bank here.

Piedras Negras
emblem glyph

Founded around 300 AD, an unrelenting rivalry developed between the city and Yaxchilán for dominance over Usumacinta trade route, contested by bloody battles and strategic pacts with Calakmul and Tikal. Like its adversary, Piedras Negras is best known for the extraordinary quality of its **carvings**, considered by many to be the very finest to emerge from the Maya world. Several of the very best of these are on display in the Museo Nacional de Arqueología in Guatemala City, including a royal throne, some exquisitely carved stelae and panels. The most important of these panels, discovered in June 2000, has an unusually long hieroglyphic text which has allowed Mayanists to compile an excellent record of the city's Late Classic history under the ruler Itzamk'anahk K'in Ajaw (626–686 AD). However, there's still plenty to experience on site.

Upon arrival, the most immediately impressive monument is a large rock jutting over the river bank with a carving of a seated male figure presenting a bundle to a female figure. This was once surrounded by glyphs, now badly eroded and best seen at night with a torch held at a low angle. Continuing up the hill, across plazas and over the ruins of buildings you get some idea of the city's size. Several buildings are comparatively well preserved, particularly the **sweat baths**, used for ritual purification; the most imposing of all is the **Acropolis**, a huge palace complex of rooms, passages and courtyards towering 100m above the river bank. A **megalithic stairway** at one time led down to the river, doubtless a humbling sight to visitors (and captives) before the forest invaded the city. Another intriguing sight is a huge double-headed turtle glyph carved on a rock overhanging a small valley. This is a reference to the end of a *katun*; inside the main glyph is a giant representation of the day sign Ahau (also signifies Lord), recalling the myth of the birth of the maize god. During research carried out at Piedras Negras in the 1930s the artist and epigrapher Tatiana Proskouriakoff noticed that dates carved on monuments corresponded approximately to a human life span, indicating that the glyphs might refer to events in one person's lifetime, possibly the rulers of the city. Refuted for decades by the archeological establishment, the theory was later proved correct.

Traditionally, the presence of FAR guerrillas in the region protected the ruins from systematic looting – neither looters nor the army dared enter. Now the guerrillas are just a memory and access from the Mexican bank is becoming easier, it remains to be seen how long Piedras Negras can maintain its relatively untouched state. The site has been excavated since 1997, by a joint American and Guatemalan team lead by archeologists Stephen Houston and Héctor Escobedo.

Below Piedras Negras the current quickens and the river drops through two massive canyons. The first of these, **Cañon de San José**, is a narrow corridor of rock sealed in by cliffs 300m high; the second, the **Cañon de las Iguanas**, is less dramatic. Travel on this part of the river is treacherous and really only possible on white-water rafts: smaller craft have to be carried around the two canyons, and under no circumstances is it possible to travel upriver.

El Naranjo and the San Pedro river route into Mexico

The most direct route **from Flores to Mexico** takes you along the Río San Pedro, through a remote, deforested area. Twelve daily buses from Flores (5hr) run to **EL NARANJO**, a small settlement in the northwest of Petén, where the river trip starts. El Naranjo is a rough spot, consisting of little more than an army base, an immigration post and a main street leading to the ferry, with a few shops, comedores and basic hotels. Once you arrive you'll need to confirm the **boat schedule**; there's usually a service to La Palma in Mexico at around 1pm ($20 per person, min five passengers; 4hr 30min), returning at 8am the next day. The Guatemalan immigration post is next to the dock, and you'll be charged a fee (anywhere between US$1 and $5) to leave; with "regulations" often depending on the whim of the official. You can change money with the boatmen or at the tienda, but rates are poor. If you miss the boat, there's little to do here, though you could wander around the ruins near the dock; the army has machine-gun posts on top of the pyramids but the soldiers are amiable enough.

The best place **to stay** is the friendly, family-run *Posada San Pedro* across the river (☎926 1276 in Flores; ❸); the places lining the main street in town are pretty filthy. You could also try the CECON headquarters, across from the ferry 150m downstream – a boy in a canoe will take you for a couple of quetzals. This is the administrative centre for the Biotopo Laguna del Tigre, and if not in use by students and scientists there may be dorm space. They'll also let you use the kitchen.

Heading downriver, the next port of call is the Mexican immigration post, about an hour away. Beyond that another three hours bring you to **LA PALMA** in Mexico, a small riverside village with bus connections to Tenosique (the last is at 5pm) – which is a good transport hub. There's currently no bank, though there's often a moneychanger about. You can **camp** in the shelter at the restaurant *Parador Turístico* by the river bank, which has the best **food** in town; they also have a couple of basic **rooms to rent**.

If you're entering Guatemala from La Palma you'll be able to catch a bus to Flores (4–5hr) from the immigration post in El Naranjo at about 2pm.

El Perú and the Ruta Guacamaya

To the east of El Naranjo, in the upper reaches of the Río San Pedro, is **El Perú**, a seldom-visited and unreconstructed archeological site buried in some of the wildest rain forest in Petén. El Perú grew to become an important middle-ranking Petén city in the Late Classic period, and despite being the nearest place of any size west of Tikal, sided with the other great "superpower" – distant Calakmul – in the power politics of the time. Around 650 AD Yuknoom the Great of Calakmul attended the accession of El Perú's K'inich B'alam ("Great Sun Jaguar") here – the same leader later married a Calakmul princess. El Perú continued to remain under the Calakmul overlordship in the early eighth century, but would later pay for this affiliation when a resurgent Tikal overran the city in 743 AD, and there were no monuments carved here for 47 years.

The site's temple mounds are still coated in vegetation but El Perú is perhaps most famous for its many well-preserved **stelae**. The two guards welcome visitors, particularly if you bring along a little spare food. Though it's possible to get there by boat from El Naranjo, virtually everyone visits the site as part of adventure tour, best arranged in Flores (see p.336). These tours, dubbed **La Ruta Guacamaya** or "Scarlet Macaw Trail", are exciting three- to five-day trips by truck, horse and boat along rivers and through primary forest, taking in remote ruins. Close to the site, at the confluence of the Ríos San Pedro and Sacluc, a biological station has been built, where rangers monitor forests which contain the largest concentrations of scarlet macaws in northern Cental America. You've also an excellent chance of observing spider and howler monkeys, the Petén turkey and a plethora of other exotic birds around the ruins.

From Flores to Belize

The 100km from Flores to the border with Belize takes you through another sparsely inhabited section of Petén, a journey of around two and a half hours by bus down a recently paved road. Eight daily **buses** leave from the market-place. You'll need to set out early in order to get to San Ignacio or Belize City the same day: if you catch the first bus (at 5am) you can make it straight through to Chetumal, in Mexico. Along the way the bus passes through Ixlú (p.340), halfway between **Tikal** and Flores, so if you're coming directly from the site you can pick it up there. Once again you should set off as early as you can to avoid getting stranded.

Línea Dorada also operates a 5am "Mundo Maya" **express service** to Belize City (4hr 30min; US$20) and on to Chetumal (8hr; US$35), leaving from its offices on Calle Principal in Santa Elena. More than twice as expensive as the public bus, this service is quicker and smoother and also connects with services in Chetumal to Cancún. The *Hotel San Juan* mafiosi also operates a similar service.

Lagos de Mancanché, Yaxhá and around

About halfway to the border, 7km past the Ixlú junction, there's a turn-off for **Lago de Mancanché**, a wonderfully peaceful little lagoon, surrounded by thick rainforest, 2km from the main road. Delightfully situated on the banks of the lake, the *Eco Lodge El Retiro* (T & F369 8345, T204 4777, Wwww .retiro-guatemala.com; ❹–❺) is a gloriously peaceful place to stay with lovely thatched cabañas, all with shady porches, plus camping (US$5 per person) and great food. There are several good hiking trails to Lago de Salpetén and beyond, and the friendly owners also run several **tours** including jungle walks (US$10 per person) and a night boat crocodile trip (US$15).

On the south side of the road, 23km past Ixlú junction, you'll pass a sign for **Holtún**, a site with tall, unrestored temples adorned with masks, a twenty-minute walk from the road. On the roadside, look out for the sign put up by Borman Peréz, who sells good value wood and ceramic art from his house. He can guide you to the site and has a couple of budget **rooms** (❷) and space for camping; he also rents bikes and horses to visit Yaxhá.

Continuing east along the road to Belize, it's just 1500m to the junction for **Lago de Yaxhá**, a shallow limestone depression, similar but smaller than Lago de Petén Itzá, and encircled by dense jungle. The lake is home to two Maya sites, **Yaxhá** and **Topoxté**, and offers access to a third, **Nakúm**, to the north. Several Flores-based tour operators (see p.336) are now offering day-trips to Lago de Yaxhá, though Nakúm is less frequently included on tour itineraries.

Yaxhá and Topoxté

The main Flores–Belize road passes about 8km to the south of Lago de Yaxhá and neighbouring Lago de Sacnab – ask the driver to drop you at the turning, which is clearly signposted. If you're not on a tour, then you'll probably be faced with a sweltering two-hour walk to get there, though there is some traffic to and from the village of La Máquina, 2km before the lakes. Just before you reach the lakes you pass a **control post** where you may be asked to sign in. From here it's 3km to the site: head along the road between the lakes then turn left (signposted) for Yaxhá.

Yaxhá (daily 8am–5pm; currently free, a fee of US$3.20 will shortly be introduced) covering several square kilometres of a ridge overlooking the lake, is primarily a Classic period city. The early history of the site is unclear due to a lack of inscriptions, though the sheer scale of the ruins (only Tikal and El Mirador are larger in Guatemala) confirm it was undoubtedly a major player in the central Maya region.

Yaxhá emblem glyph

Recent restoration has uncovered many more buildings, some of which are almost as impressive as those at Tikal, but without the crowds. What you can also count on is real atmosphere as you try to discover the many other features still half hidden by the forest. If you're not on a guided trip then one of the guardians will show you around for a small tip. The ruins are spread out over nine plazas, and around five hundred structures have been mapped so far, including several huge pyramids and large acropolis complexes. The tallest and most impressive pyramid, Structure 216, 250m northeast of the entrance, rises in tiers to a height of over 30m. The restoration enables you to climb to the top for spectacular views over the forest and lake – particularly beautiful at sunset.

Topoxté, a much smaller site on a series of forested islands (which can become a peninsula during the dry season) close to the west shore of the lake, is best reached by boat from *El Sombrero*. There is a 4km trail to a spot opposite the island but you still have to get over to it – and large crocodiles inhabit the lake. The structures you see date mainly from the Late Postclassic era, though the site has been occupied since Preclassic times. While not on the scale of Yaxhá there are several plazas and tall temples with balustraded steps, and restoration work is in progress.

The best place to **stay** nearby is the wonderful, solar-powered *Campamento El Sombrero* (☎926 5229, ℻926 5198, ✉sombrero@guate.net; ❸/❹), 200m from the road on the south side of the lake, which has thatched rooms in wooden jungle lodges, a less expensive shared room and space for **camping**.

The thatched restaurant overlooking the lake is peaceful spot to stop for lunch even if you're not staying here. Gabriela Moretti, the friendly Italian-born owner, is a great source of archeological information as she's visited most of the remote sites in Petén and has a good library. Gabriela can arrange boat trips on the lake and horseback riding; she'll pick you up from the bus stop at the junction if you've called in advance. There's another beautiful *campamento*, run by locals on behalf of Inguat, on the far side of the lake, below the site of Yaxhá, where you can **pitch a tent** or sling a hammock on a raised wooden platform beneath a thatched shelter for free.

Fiestas

Petén may not offer Guatemala's finest fiestas, but those there are abound with typical ladino energy, featuring fireworks and heavy drinking. In some of the smaller villages you'll also see traditional dances and hear the sounds of the marimba – transported here from the highlands along with many of the inhabitants of Petén.

January
Flores has its fiesta from the 12th to 15th; the final day is the most dramatic.

March
San José has a small fiesta from the 10th to 19th with parades, fireworks and dances.

April
Poptún's fiesta, from April 27 to May 1, is held in honour of San Pedro Martír de Merona.

May
San Benito has a fiesta from the 1st to 9th, which is sure to be wild and very drunken. The border town of **Melchor de Mencos** has its fiesta from the 15th to 22nd, with the main day being the 22nd. **Dolores** has a fiesta from the 23rd to 31st, with the principal day on the 28th.

June
Sayaxché has a funfair and fiesta on the 16th, in honour of San Antonio de Padua.

July
Santa Ana's action runs from the 18th to 26th.

August
San Luis has a fiesta from the 16th to 25th, with the main day on the last day.

October
San Francisco's fiesta runs from the 1st to 4th. **San José** has a fascinating pagan fiesta (see box on p.338) on October 31, starting at 8pm with a mass in the church and continuing all night when a human skull is paraded through the town's streets.

November
San Andrés, across the lake from Flores, has a fiesta from the 21st to 30th, with the last day the main day.

December
Finally, **La Libertad** has its fiesta from the 9th to 12th.

The **ruins of Nakúm**, another large site, are about 19km north of Lago de Yaxhá, along a reasonable dirt road; if you don't have a vehicle you could walk there in about five hours or, even better, hire horses from *El Sombrero*. It's thought that Nakúm was a trading post in the Tikal empire, funnelling goods to and from the Caribbean coast, a role for which it is ideally situated at the headwaters of the Río Holmul. Once again there are a couple of guards permanently posted at the ruins and they'll be more than willing to show you around and find a spot for you to sling a hammock or pitch a tent. The most impressive structure is the residential-style palace, which has forty rooms. It's also possible to **walk to Tikal** in a day from Nakúm (around 25km), though you'll need to persuade a guard to act as a **guide**, or bring one with you – speak to the Flores tour operators (see p.336). *El Sombrero* offers a horse-riding adventure along this route, which can include a day's fishing in the lake. It's also possible to make the trip the other way round, from Tikal to Yaxhá, if you ask around amongst the guards at the site. Approached from this direction, however, the circuit is somewhat anti-climactic, as the sites get smaller and smaller.

Melchor de Mencos and the border

The nondescript but bustling border town of **MELCHOR DE MENCOS** boasts nothing of interest for the visitor, though it has a well-stocked market and some extremely basic hotels. The border itself if just past the bridge over the Río Mopan; if your bus doesn't continue to the border post get off at the Shell gas station at the bottom of the hill before the bridge and walk the last 250m. Despite the differences between Guatemala and Belize, border formalities are fairly straightforward: you'll probably be asked for a small "departure tax" of US$1 to leave Guatemala, though there is officially no fee. **Moneychangers** will pester you on either side of the border – most give a fair rate. There's also a **bank** (Mon–Fri 8.30am–6pm) just beyond the immigration building, next to the *Hotel Frontera Palace* (T & F 926 5196; ❹), which has rooms in pleasant thatched cabins, hot water and a restaurant. The owner, Marco Gross, who runs a small gift shop and travel agency, knows Petén extremely well and can organize trips to any of the Maya sites.

Buses to the border leave from the marketplace in Santa Elena eight times daily between 5am and 6pm; Rosita offer the better service in that they don't try and rip off travellers for extra cash in the way the rival Pinita company does. Línea Dorada/Mundo Maya also operates a 5am **express service**, leaving from their offices on Calle Principal in Santa Elena to Belize City (4hr 30min; US$20) and on to Chetumal (8hr; US$35), where it connects with a luxury Mexican bus to Cancún (5hr 30min; US$9). The *Hotel San Juan* operates a similar express bus service, leaving at 5am.

On the Belize side of the border, buses leave **for Belize City** every half-hour or so (3hr), usually right from the frontier. If there's no bus waiting you may have to take a shared taxi to Benque Viejo or to San Ignacio (US$2 per person; 20min) and catch a connection there.

Travel details

Buses

This is a rundown of the main scheduled bus services available: for details of other options, see the relevant accounts in the text.
Guatemala City to Flores (8–10hr). There are

around thirty daily services to Flores. The best, though most expensive, options are the three daily Línea Dorada buses which leave at 9am, 8pm and 9pm (US$16–28; 8hr) from 16 C 10–55, Zona 1

(☎926 0070, ⊕www.lineadorada.com). Fuente del Norte buses leave seven times daily (US$10–14; 8–9hr) from a clean, safe terminal at 17 C 8–46, Zona 1, Guatemala City (☎251 3817 & 253 8169). All buses pass through Poptún and past the Río Dulce bridge for Lívingston.
From Flores to Tikal (1hr 15min; US$6 return). A fleet of minibuses leaves Flores and Santa Elena approximately every 30 minutes from 4am for the ruins; book ahead from any travel agency or your hotel and they'll pick you up from where you're staying. Minibuses also leave from the airport to Tikal, connecting with planes from Guatemala City. The Pinita "chicken bus" leaves at 1pm (3hr), passing Tikal around 3pm and continues to Uaxactún; it returns from Uaxactún at 6am.
From Flores to Sayaxché (2hr). Pinita has buses at 5am, 6am, 8am, 10am, 1pm and 4pm; Del Rosío buses at 5am and noon also stop at Sayaxché en route to Cruce del Pato.
From Flores to Melchor de Mencos (2hr 30min). Pinita runs buses at 5am, 8am and 11am while Rosita buses depart at 5.30am, 7am, 9.30am, 11am, 2pm, 3pm and 6pm. From Melchor to Flores buses and minibuses run every hour or so from 3am until around 4pm.
From Flores to Belize Línea Dorada runs a daily luxury Mundo Maya bus from its terminal at Calle Principal in Santa Elena (stopping to pick up passengers in Flores from its office at C 30 de Junio) to Belize City at 5am (5hr), which continues on to the Mexican border at Chetumal (8hr) and connnects with another service up the coast to Cancún.
Flores to Carmelita (4hr) 2 daily at noon and 2pm.
Flores to El Naranjo (5hr). Pinita buses run daily at 5am (to connect with the boat) 7am, 8am, 9am, 11am, 1pm and 2pm, and Del Rosío has services at 4.30am, 8.30am, 11.30, 1pm and 1.30pm (5hr).
Poptún to Fray Bartolomé de Las Casas (5hr) 1 daily at 11.30am.

Boats

Flores to San Andrés and San José (40min and 50min). Boats from Flores and San Benito leave when full in daylight hours only.
El Naranjo to La Palma in Mexico (4hr). One boat leaves daily at 1pm.

Sayaxché to Benemérito, Mexico. A trading boat leaves most days (at least 12hr); rented speed-boats take 2hr 30min–3hr.
Sayaxché to Rancho el Caribe on the Río Petexbatun (2hr). There's a daily lancha around noon.

Planes

Guatemala City to Flores (50min). There are ten daily flights to Flores.
From Flores to Belize City (35min). Tropic Air 2 daily, Rasca 1 daily, Maya Island Air 1 daily, Island Air 1 daily.
From Flores to Chetumal (45min). 3 weekly.
From Flores to Cancún (1hr 20min). Taca 1 daily, Aerocaribe 2 daily.

From Flores to Palenque (50min). Aerocaribe 3 weekly on Mon, Wed and Fri.
From Flores to Puerto Barrios (45min). Taca, 1 daily.
You can also charter flights **from Flores** to Uaxactún, Dos Lagunas, El Naranjo, Sayaxché, Poptún, Río Dulce, Lívingston and to the Honduras border.

7

Into Honduras: Copán and the Bay Islands

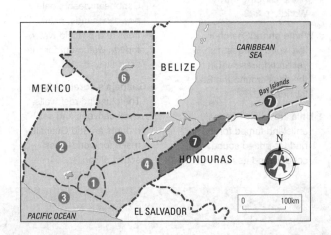

CHAPTER 7 # Highlights

Into Honduras: Copán and the Bay Islands

cross the border in **Honduras**, about five hours by road from Guatemala City, are the ruins of **Copán**, one of the most magnificent of all Maya sites. While the compact scale of the site is not initially as impressive as Tikal or Chichén Itzá, it boasts an astonishing number of decorative carvings, stelae and altars, including the longest Maya text in existence, the Hieroglyphic Stairway – some two thousand glyphs carved onto a flight of sixty stone steps. Throw in a wonderful site museum, perhaps the best in the Maya world, and the delightful and friendly village of Copán Ruinas, where most people stay, and it's not surprising that Copán now ranks as the second most-visited destination in the country. Within easy striking distance of Copán, the **Bay Islands** (Islas de la Bahía) of Utila, Roatán and Guanaja have a completely different, but equally alluring appeal: palm-fringed white-sand beaches, balmy Caribbean waters and near-pristine coral reefs which are perfect for snorkelling and scuba diving. Culturally distinct from the rest of Honduras, the islanders are the descendants of Cayman Islanders, buccaneers and shipwrecked African slaves, and most still speak a melodic, archaic-sounding English. There's little local affection for mainland Central American culture, with radios and satellite dishes tuned to North American broadcasts and reggae music dominating the dancehalls. For the visitor, **Utila** and **Roatán** offer a tremendous opportunity to visit affordable, friendly and accessible islands with none of the tourist overkill or hassle that can taint other Caribbean destinations. **Guanaja**, on the other hand, is less well set up for independent travellers, and mainly caters to scuba divers on pre-booked package trips – it's also still recovering after being badly mauled by Hurricane Mitch in 1998.

Accommodation price codes

All accommodation listed in this guide has been graded according to the following price scales. These refer to the price in US dollars of the cheapest double room in high season. For more details see p.34.

❶ Under US$5	❹ US$15–25	❼ US$60–80
❷ US$5–10	❺ US$25–40	❽ US$80–100
❸ US$10–15	❻ US$40–60	❾ Over US$100

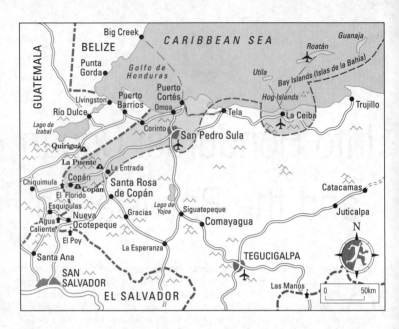

Getting to Honduras is pretty straightforward from Guatemala. Copán is connected with Guatemala City and Antigua by direct daily shuttle buses (see p.405), or you can also travel via Chiquimula (see opposite), a longer but less expensive route. From Copán you can get to the Bay Islands the same day by travelling to the city of San Pedro Sula by bus and then taking a flight to any of the three main islands. Alternatively, you could travel overland from San Pedro Sula to the coastal city of La Ceiba (3hr) and then catch one of the daily boats to Utila or Roatán, or take a flight to any of the three islands.

(Serendipity)

Copán and around

Delightfully located in a sweeping highland valley, the city-state of **Copán** was the southernmost centre of the Maya civilization. It's easy to understand what attracted the Maya to the site, on the fertile banks of the Río Copán at a pleasingly temperate altitude of 600m. Today the countryside around Copán is equally appealing and fecund, with green rolling hills of pastureland, and tobacco and coffee farms interspersed with patches of pine forest. Though the archeological site is the main attraction, there's plenty more to explore in the surrounding area, with hot springs, a new bird park and the minor site of **Las Sepulturas** just a few kilometres away. Easy-going **Copán Ruinas**, a short walk west of the ruins, is not much more than an overgrown village, but makes a great base, with attractive hotels, good restaurants and regular transport connections with Guatemala and the rest of Honduras.

Getting to Copán

Speedy, direct **shuttle buses** (US$25 one way) leave Antigua daily at 4am, pausing to pick up passengers in Guatemala City an hour later and getting to

Copán by around 10am; they return to Guatemala at around 3pm. Buses are operated by Monarcas Travel, 7 Av Nte 15A (T & F 832 4779, W www .angelfire.com/mt/monarcastravel) in Antigua. Alternatively, you can save some cash by catching a Rutas Orientales **pullman bus** from 19 C 8–18, Zona 1, in Guatemala City to the town of **Chiquimula** (every 30min between 5am and 5.30pm; 3hr 30min). From Chiquimula, local buses leave hourly (1hr 30min) until 3.30pm for the rudimentary border post at **El Florido** (open 6am–6pm), 57km to the west along an excellent, recently paved road. Border formalities are pretty straightforward, though they can be tediously slow – you may well be asked for an unofficial US$1–2 "exit tax" to leave Guatemala, and another US$1 to enter Honduras, though the official entry charge is US$0.50. Most nationalities do not need a **visa** to enter Honduras (see Basics, p.18). If you do, but you're only entering Honduras to visit Copán and intend to re-enter Guatemala almost immediately, ask the Honduran guards for a temporary entrance stamp. This is issued on a separate piece of paper, meaning that your Guatemalan visa remains valid.

The Banrural **bank** (Mon–Fri 8am–4pm, Sat 9am–1pm), a kilometre west of the border inside Guatemala, changes travellers' cheques and cashes dollars, or you can deal with the ever-present moneychangers at the border post who handle dollars, lempiras and quetzales at pretty fair rates. From El Florido, **pick-ups** run when full (about every 30min) to the town of Copán Ruinas, taking around twenty minutes; the last one leaves at around 5.45pm. Heading back into Guatemala, the last bus leaves El Florido for Chiquimula at 4pm, though it's sensible to cross as early in the day as possible to ensure onward connections in Guatemala.

If time is really tight you can **fly** to Copán from Guatemala City with Jungle Flying (see p.85), though the fare is a hefty US$220 return.

Copán Ruinas: the town

One kilometre northwest of the archeological site of Copán lies the small town of **COPÁN RUINAS**, a charming place of steep cobbled streets and red-tiled roofs, set among the lush scenery of Honduras' western highlands. Despite the weekly influx of visitors, which now generates a large part of the town's income, it has managed to remain a largely unspoilt and genuinely friendly place. Many travellers are seduced by Copán's delightfully relaxed atmosphere, clean air and rural setting, and end up spending longer here than planned, studying Spanish, eating and drinking well, or exploring the region's other minor sites, hot springs and beautiful countryside.

Arrival and information

Pick-ups and shuttle buses from the border enter town from the west, running up to the parque central. **Buses** from other destinations in Honduras enter town from the east, by the small football field. Monarcas, two blocks north of the Parque (T 651 4361), runs shuttle buses to Guatemala City and Antigua (US$25 per person). The **post office** is just behind the museum, while **Hondutel** (the national phpne company) is just south of the plaza. There's an excellent community **website** (W www.copanruinas.com) where you'll find useful hotel and restaurant listings, local news and links; you can choose between several **internet cafés**, including two branches of Maya Connections: one is just south of the plaza and the other is inside the *Hotel Los Gémelos* – rates hover around US$5 an hour.

For details of onward transport connections **to the Bay Islands** via San Pedro Sula and La Ceiba, see p.390.

Accommodation

Many of the town's **hotels** have undergone refits to attract the ever-booming organized tour market, while a swathe of new mid-range places help keep prices competitive. There's not too much choice at the budget end of the market, however, where places fill up quickly at busy times of the year.

Casa de Café B&B at the southwest edge of town, overlooking the Río Copán valley ℡651 4620, ℻651 4623, ⓦwww.todomundo.com /casadecafe. A charming place, with ten comfortable and airy rooms, all with wood panelling and nice individual touches, private bathrooms and

steaming hot water, plus a fabulous garden where you could lie in a hammock and enjoy the views all day. A huge ranch-style breakfast is included, and there's free coffee, plus a library and TV. ⑥
Hacienda San Lucas 1.8km south of the Parque ℡651 4106, ⓔsanlucas@copanruinas.com.

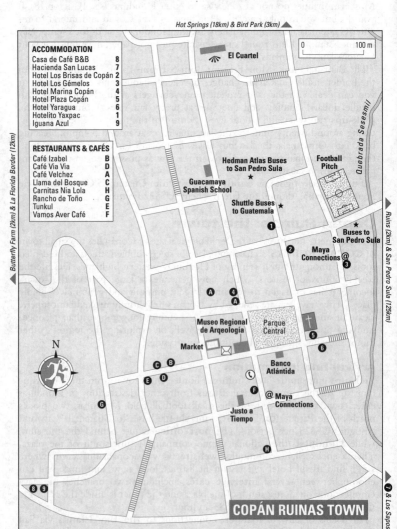

ACCOMMODATION
Casa de Café B&B	8
Hacienda San Lucas	7
Hotel Los Brisas de Copán	2
Hotel Los Gémelos	3
Hotel Marina Copán	4
Hotel Plaza Copán	5
Hotel Yaragua	6
Hotelito Yaxpac	1
Iguana Azul	9

RESTAURANTS & CAFÉS
Café Izabel	B
Café Via Via	D
Café Velchez	A
Llama del Bosque	C
Carnitas Nia Lola	H
Rancho de Toño	G
Tunkul	E
Vamos Aver Café	F

Hot Springs (18km) & Bird Park (3km)

El Cuartel

Butterfly Farm (2km) & La Florida Border (12km)

Quebrada Sesesmil

Hedman Atlas Buses to San Pedro Sula

Football Pitch

Guacamaya Spanish School

Shuttle Buses to Guatemala

Buses to San Pedro Sula

Maya Connections

Ruins (2km) & San Pedro Sula (125km)

Museo Regional de Arqeología

Parque Central

Market

Banco Atlántida

Maya Connections

Justo a Tiempo

N

COPÁN RUINAS TOWN

0   100 m

& Los Sapos

Wonderful converted farmhouse accommodation and camping set in the hills south of Copán, with startling views over the valley. There's an attached restaurant with excellent home-cooked food, plus horse-riding and hiking trails to the Los Sapos site. Breakfast included. ❻

Hotel Brisas de Copán one block north of the Parque ☎651 4118. Twenty-two very clean and good-sized, though slightly soulless, rooms, all with bath, hot water and TV. There's also parking, and a terrace bar is planned. ❹

Hotel Los Gémelos close to the bus stop ☎651 4077. Very friendly backpackers' stronghold, still going strong, with basic but spotless rooms, all with shared bath. The family provide hot water if enough people ask, and also run the adjacent Maya Communications internet café. ❷

Hotel Marina Copán just northwest of the Parque ☎651 4070, ℱ651 4477, ℮hmarina@netsys.hn. The most luxurious place in town by a long shot. The stylish rooms all have a/c and TV, and there's also a small pool, sauna, gym and bar. ❽

Hotel Plaza Copán on the east side of the Parque ☎651 4508, ℱ651 4039, ℮placopan@netsys.hn. Twenty-one good-value rooms, some overlooking the square and all with a/c and cable TV; there's also a small kidney-shaped pool. ❻

Hotel Yaragua half a block east of the Parque ☎651 4050. Smallish but comfortable and excellent-value rooms, set around a verdant little courtyard, with good-quality double beds and cable TV. ❹

Hotelito Yaxpac a block north of the Parque ☎651 4025. Run by a friendly family, with four good-value, simple, clean rooms – all have private bath, and some also have little balconies. ❷

Iguana Azul next to the Casa de Café B&B and under the same ownership ☎651 4620, ℱ651 4623, ℠www.todomundo.com /iguanaazul/index .html. Copán's definitive budget choice, with three private double rooms (❷–❸) and two very pleasant dormitories (❶), all with shared bath and decent mattresses. There's also a pretty garden, communal area and laundry facilities, plus great travel information.

The Town

Half a day is enough to take in virtually all the town's attractions. The main plaza, the **Parque Central** – lined with banks, municipal structures and an attractive, whitewashed Baroque-style church – was originally designed and built by visiting archeologists Tatiana Proskouriakoff and Gustav Stromsvik. Unfortunately, the simple elegance of the original layout, which followed classical Spanish lines, has been somewhat spoilt by grandiose remodelling initiatives, including a series of sweeping pillars and arches, which have been unleashed by a local mayor in the last few years. It does remain a popular place to kill time, however, its benches filled with cowboy-booted farmhands and camera-touting visitors. A number of new **souvenir shops** on or close to the Parque Central sell ceramics, wood and leather crafts from the region and elsewhere in the country; all are broadly similar in terms of price and range. Tabacos y Recuerdos, next to the La Posada hotel, has a wide selection of Honduran cigars.

On the west side of the plaza, and somewhat eclipsed by the new sculpture museum at the site itself, is the **Museo Regional de Arqueología** (Mon–Sat 8am–4pm; US$2). Inside are some impressive Maya carvings collected from the Copán region, including the glyph-covered Altars T and U; Stela B, depicting the ruler Waxaklajuun Ub'aah K'awiil (Eighteen Rabbit); and some remarkable and intricately detailed flints – ornamental oddities with seven interlocking heads carved from obsidian. There are also two remarkable **tombs**. The first contains the remains of a female shaman, complete with jade jewellery and the skulls of a puma, deer, and two human sacrificial victims. The other (10J-45), discovered in 1999 during road-building work, was created for an Early Classic period ruler of Copán during the sixth century and comprises a vaulted burial chamber where the as yet unidentified ruler was buried with numerous ceramics and two large, carved jade, pectoral pieces.

Just behind the museum (turn right beyond the post office), the tiny **municipal market** is worth a browse. For a wonderful view over the town and surrounding countryside, walk north from the Parque Central for about five blocks to **El Cuartel**, the old military barracks up the hill.

On the outskirts of town, a twenty-minute walk from the plaza along the road to Guatemala, is a small **butterfly park**, Enchanted Wings (daily 8.30am–5pm; US$5), owned by an English enthusiast and his Honduran wife. Unfortunately, Copán's cool winter nights periodically wipe out some of the forty or so specimens – many of which are collected from the steamier tropical environs of the north coast – so you may not find an abundance of butterflies, though look out for the speckled brown "giant owl" and the scarlet-and-yellow "helicopter", two of the hardier species. It's best to visit the park in the morning, when the butterflies hatch. On the other side of town, 3km north of the plaza, a new **bird park** with macaws and toucans is set to open in late 2001.

Eating and drinking

Copán has a wide range of places to **eat and drink**, many of them catering specifically to the tourist market, and standards are usually very high, with generous portions and good service. Virtually all restaurants stop serving at 10pm.

Café Izabel one block west of the Parque. Unpretentious comedor serving a range of well-prepared local dishes; the vegetable soup is particularly good.

Café Velchez northwest corner of the Parque. Pleasant European-style café, serving good but fairly pricey coffees, juices and licuados, alcoholic drinks (including wine by the glass), cakes and light meals. There's a cigar bar upstairs – good for people-watching.

Café Via Via two blocks west of the Parque. Belgian-owned establishment with a nice little streetside terrace and magazines to browse through. Good sandwiches, breakfasts, pancakes and omelettes.

Carnitas Nia Lola two blocks south of the Parque. The most atmospheric place in town, this highly popular restaurant–bar serves large portions of delicious grilled and barbecued meats, plus vegetarian dishes, at reasonable prices. It's

equally popular as a drinking venue, with an early evening happy hour and a good mix of locals and visitors.

Llama del Bosque two blocks west of the Parque. Slightly old-fashioned restaurant with a big menu including local breakfasts, meat and chicken dishes, *baleadas* and snacks.

Rancho de Toño two blocks west of the Parque. Vast new *palapa*-style restaurant specializing in fresh fish, with huge, reasonably priced portions and friendly service.

Tunkul Bar and Restaurant across from the *Llama del Bosque*. Busy garden restaurant–bar with good food, including burritos, vegetarian dishes and the near-legendary garlic chicken, plus lively music and a happy hour (8–9pm).

Vamos a Ver Café one block south of the Parque. Busy Dutch-owned garden café, popular with travellers, with delicious homemade soups, sandwiches and snacks.

Listings

Banks Banco Atlántida on the Parque changes travellers' cheques, dollars and quetzales (at poor rates) and gives cash advances on Visa cards.

Book exchange Justo a Tiempo, two blocks southwest of the Parque (Mon–Sat 7.30am–5.30pm); the friendly American owner also offers great cakes and coffee.

Immigration office The *migración* is on the west side of the Parque next to the museum (Mon–Fri 7am–4pm).

Language schools Copán is an excellent place to study Spanish, with two schools to choose between, though it's more expensive than Guatemala – four hours of classes plus full family-based accommodation and meals costs US$175 a week. Of the two schools, Guacamaya (T & F 651 4360, W www.guacamaya.com), three blocks north of the Parque, has the better reputation,

though Ixbalanque (T & F 651 4432, E ixbalan @hn2.com), a block and a half west of the Parque, is also worth considering.

Laundry Justo a Tiempo, two blocks southwest of the Parque (Mon–Sat 7.30am–5.30pm).

Tour operators Go Native Tours (T 651 4432, E ixbalanqu@hn2.com), a block and a half west of the Parque, and Yaragua Tours (T & F 651 4050, E yaraguatours@hotmail.com), half a block east of the Parque, both offer similarly priced tours. Trips include visits to the hot springs (see p.390; US$10 per person), horse riding (from US$15 for 3hr), the Finca El Cisne coffee farm (US$30), El Rubi waterfall (US$15), and a spectacular local cave, the Cueva el Boquerón (US$70). Xukpi Tours (T 651 4435) is an excellent specialist bird-watching outfit run by the very knowledgeable guide Jorge Barraza.

Copán ruins

COPÁN RUINS lie 1.5km east of town, a pleasant fifteen-minute walk along a raised footpath that runs parallel to the highway. Entrance to the site (daily 8am–4pm; US$10 including the Las Sepulturas ruins, though access to the archeological tunnels costs an extra US$12) is through the **visitor centre** on the left-hand side of the car park, where a small exhibition explains Copán's place in the Maya world. Inside the visitor centre there's a ticket office and a desk where you can hire a registered site **guide** (US$10 for 2hr) – an excellent investment if you really want to get the most out of Copán. On the other side of the car park is a **cafeteria**, serving drinks and reasonable meals, and a small souvenir shop.

Opposite the visitor centre is the terrific **Museum of Mayan Sculpture** (daily 8am–4pm; US$5), arguably the finest in the entire Maya region, with a tremendous collection of stelae, altars, panels and well-labelled explanations in English. You enter through a dramatic entrance doorway, resembling the jaws of a serpent, and pass through a tunnel (signifying the passage into *xibalba*, or the underworld). Dominating the museum is a full-scale, flamboyantly painted replica of the magnificent **Rosalila Temple**, built by Moon Jaguar in 571 and discovered intact under Temple 16. A vast crimson- and jade-coloured mask of the Sun God, depicted with wings outstretched, forms the main facade of the temple. Other ground-floor exhibits concentrate on aspects of Maya beliefs and cosmology, while the upper floor houses many of the finest original sculptures from the Copán valley, comprehensively displaying the skill of the Maya craftsmen.

From the museum it's a 200m walk east to the **warden's gate**, the entrance to the site proper, where your ticket will be checked and where there are usually several squabbling macaws to greet your arrival – these are tame and sleep in cages by the gate at night.

A brief history of Copán

Once the most important **city-state** on the southern fringes of the Maya world, Copán was largely cut off from all other Maya cities except **Quiriguá**, 64km to the north (see p.259). Archeologists now believe that settlers began moving into the Río Copán valley from around 1400 BC, taking advantage of the area's rich agricultural potential, although construction of the city is not thought to have begun until around 100 AD.

Copán remained a small, isolated settlement until the arrival in 426 AD of an outsider, **Yax K'uk Mo'** (Great Sun First Quetzal Macaw), the warrior–shaman who established the basic layout of the city and founded a royal dynasty which lasted for 400 years. It's unclear whether he was from Teotihuacán, the Mesoamerican superpower, or Tikal (which was under strong Teotihuacán influence at the time), but Yax K'uk Mo' became the object of an intense cult of veneration, first established by his son **Popol Hol** and continued by subsequent members of the dynasty over fifteen generations.

Little is known about the next seven kings who followed Popol Hol, but in 553 AD the **golden era** of Copán began with the accession to the throne of **Moon Jaguar**, who constructed the magnificent Rosalila Temple, now buried beneath Temple 16. The city thrived through the reigns of **Smoke Serpent** (578–628 AD), **Smoke Jaguar** (628–695 AD) and **Eighteen Rabbit** (695–738 AD), as the great fertility of the Copán region was exploited and wealth amassed from control of the jade trade along the Río Motagua. These resources and periods of stable government allowed for unprecedented political

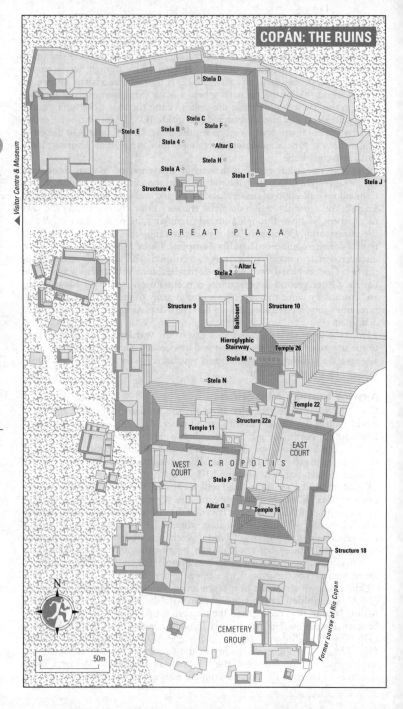

COPÁN: THE RUINS

▲ Visitor Centre & Museum

Stela D

Stela C

Stela B   Stela F

Stela E

Stela 4   Altar G

Stela H

Stela A   Stela I

Stela J

Structure 4

GREAT PLAZA

Altar L

Stela 2

Structure 9   Structure 10

Ballcourt

Hieroglyphic
Stairway   Temple 26

Stela M

Stela N

Temple 22

Temple 11   Structure 22a

EAST
COURT

WEST   A C R O P O L I S
COURT

Stela P

Altar Q   Temple 16

Structure 18

Former course of Rio Copan

CEMETERY
GROUP

N

0   50m

and social growth, as the population boomed to around 28,000 by 760 AD, the highest urban density in the entire Maya region.

Ambitious rebuilding continued throughout this era, using local andesite, a fine-grained, even-textured volcanic rock that was easily quarried and particularly suited to detailed carving, as well as the substantial local limestone beds, which were ideal for stucco production. The highly artistic carved relief style for which Copán is famous reached a pinnacle during the reign of Eighteen Rabbit – whose image is depicted on many of the site's magnificent stelae and who also oversaw the construction of the Great Plaza, the final version of the ball court and Temple 22 in the East Court.

Following the audacious capture and decapitation of Eighteen Rabbit by Quiriguá's Cauac Sky, construction at Copán came to a complete halt for seventeen years, possibly indicating a period of subjugation by its former vassal state. The royal dynasty subsequently managed to regroup, however, flourishing gloriously, albeit briefly, once more. **Smoke Shell** (749–763 AD) completed the **Hieroglyphic Stairway**, one of the most impressive of all Maya constructions, in an effort designed to symbolize this revival. Optimism continued during the early years of the reign of **Yax Pasah** (763–820 AD), Smoke Shell's son, who commissioned **Altar Q**, which illustrates the entire dynasty from its beginning, and completed the final version of **Temple 16**, which towers over the site, around 776 AD. Towards the end of his rule, however, the rot set in: skeletal remains indicate that the decline was provoked by inadequate food resources created by population pressure, resulting in subsequent environmental collapse. The seventeenth and final ruler, **Ukit Took'**, assumed the throne in 822 AD, but his reign proved miserably inauspicious. Poignantly, the only monument to his reign, Altar L, was never completed, as if the sculptor had downed his tools and walked out on the job.

The site was known to the Spanish, although they took little interest in it. A court official, Don Diego de Palacios, in a letter written in March 1576, mentions city ruins "constructed with such skill that it seems that they could never have been made by people as coarse as the inhabitants of this province". Not until the nineteenth century and the publication of *Incidents of Travel in Central America, Chiapas and Yucatán* by **John Lloyd Stephens** and **Frederick Catherwood** did Copán become known to the wider world. Stephens, the then acting US ambassador, succeeded in buying the ruins in 1839 and, accompanied by Catherwood, a British architect and artist, spent several weeks clearing the site and mapping the buildings. The instant success of the book and the interest it sparked in Mesoamerican culture ensured that Copán became a magnet for archeologists.

British archeologist **Alfred Maudsley** began a full-scale mapping, excavation and reconstruction of the site in 1891 under the sponsorship of the Peabody Museum, Harvard. A second major investigation was begun in 1935 by the Washington Carnegie Institute, during which the Río Copán was diverted to prevent it carving into the site. A breakthrough in the understanding not only of Copán but of the whole Maya world came in 1959–60, when archeologists Heinrich Berlin and Tatiana Proskouriakoff first began to decipher Maya **glyphs**, leading to the realization that they record the history of the cities and their dynasties.

Since 1977, the Instituto Hondureño de Antropología e Historia has been running a series of projects with the help of archeologists from around the world. Copán is now perhaps the best understood of all Maya cities, and a series of **tunnelling projects** beneath the Acropolis has unearthed remarkable discoveries including, in 1989, the Rosalila Temple, which is now open to the public. In 1993 the Papagayo Temple, built by Popol Hol and dedicated to his father Yax K'uk Mo', was uncovered, and in 1998 further burrowing revealed the tomb of the founder himself.

The Great Plaza

Straight ahead through the avenue of trees lies the **Great Plaza**, a large rectangular arena strewn with the magnificently carved and exceptionally well-preserved stelae that are Copán's outstanding features. Initially, however, the visual impact of this grassy expanse may seem a little underwhelming: the first structure you see is **Stucture 4**, a modestly sized pyramid-temple, while the stepped buildings bordering the northern end of the plaza are low and unremarkable. This part of the Great Plaza was once a public place, the stepped sides bordered by a densely populated residential area. The grandest buildings are confined to the monumental temples that border the southern section of the plaza, rising to form the Acropolis, the domain of the ruling and religious elite.

Copán emblem glyph

Dotted all around are Copán's famed **stelae** and altars, made from the local andesite. Most of the stelae represent **Eighteen Rabbit**, Copán's "King of the Arts" (Stelae A, B, C, D, F, H and 4). **Stela A**, dating from 731 AD, has incredibly deep carving, although the faces are now eroded; its sides include a total of 52 glyphs, translating into a famous inscription that includes the emblem glyphs of the four great cities of Copán, Palenque, Tikal and Calakmul – a text designed to show that Eighteen Rabbit saw his city as a pivotal power in the Maya world. **Stela B** depicts a slightly oriental-looking Eighteen Rabbit, wearing a turban-like headdress intertwined with twin macaws, while his hands support a bar motif, a symbol designed to show the ruler holding up the sky. **Stela C** (730 AD) is one of the earliest stones to have faces on both sides and, like many of the central stelae, has an altar at its base, carved in the shape of a turtle. Two rulers are represented here: facing the turtle (a symbol of longevity) is Eighteen Rabbit's father, Smoke Jaguar, who lived well into his eighties, while on other side is Eighteen Rabbit himself. **Stela H**, perhaps the most impressively executed of all the sculptures, shows Eighteen Rabbit wearing the latticed skirt of the Maize God, his wrists weighed down with jewellery, while his face is crowned with a stunning headdress.

The Ball Court and Hieroglyphic Stairway

South of Structure 4, towards the Acropolis, is the I-shaped **Ball Court**, one of largest and most elaborate of the Classic period, and one the few Maya courts still to have a paved floor. It was completed in 738 AD, just four months before Eighteen Rabbit's demise at the hands of Quiriguá; two previous versions lie beneath it. Like its predecessors, the court was dedicated to the great macaw deity, and both sloping sides of the court are lined with three sculpted macaw heads. The rooms that line the sides of the court, overlooking the playing area, were probably used by priests and members of the elite as they watched the game.

Pressed up against the Ball Court and protected by a vast canvas cover is the famed **Hieroglyphic Stairway**, perhaps Copán's most astonishing monument. The stairway, which takes up the entire western face of the Temple 26 pyramid, is made up of some 72 stone steps; every block is carved to form part of the glyphic sequence – around 2200 glyph blocks in all. It forms the longest known Maya hieroglyphic text, but, unfortunately, attempted reconstruction by early archeologists left the sequence so jumbled that a complete interpretation is still some way off. What is known is that the stairway was initiated to record the dynastic history of the city: some of the lower steps were first put in place by Eighteen Rabbit in 710 AD, while Smoke Shell rearranged and completed most of the sequences in 755 AD as part of his efforts to reassert the city's dignity and strength. At the base of the stairway the badly weathered **Stela M** depicts Smoke Shell and records a solar eclipse in 756 AD.

Adjacent to the Hieroglyphic Stairway, and towering over the extreme southern end of the plaza, are the vertiginous steps of **Temple 11** (also known as the Temple of the Inscriptions). The temple was constructed by Smoke Shell, who is thought to be buried beneath it, though no tomb has yet been found. At its base is another classic piece of Copán carving, **Stela N** (761 AD), representing Smoke Shell, with portraits on the two main faces of the stela and glyphs down the sides. The depth of the relief has protected the nooks and crannies, some of which still bear traces of paint – originally the carvings and buildings would have been painted in a whole range of bright colours, but for some reason only the red has survived.

The Acropolis

From the southwestern corner of the plaza, a trail runs past some original drainage ducts beyond which stone steps climb steeply up the side of Temple 11 to a soaring cluster of temples, dubbed the **Acropolis**. This lofty inner sanctum was the preserve of royalty, nobles and priests; it was the political and ceremonial core where religious rituals were enacted, sacrifices performed and rulers entombed. The whole structure grew in size over four hundred years, the temples growing higher and higher as new structures were built over the remains of earlier buildings. A warren of excavated tunnels, some open to the public, bores through the vast bulk of the Acropolis to the Rosalila Temple and several tombs. From the summit of Temple 11, beside a giant ceiba tree (a tree held sacred to the Maya), there's a panoramic view of the site below, over the Ball Court and Great Plaza to the green hills beyond.

A few metres east of Temple 11 are the **Mat House** (Structure 22A), a governmental building distinguished by its interlocking weave-like patterns, and **Temple 22**, which boasts some superbly intricate stonework around the door frames. Constructed by Eighteen Rabbit, Temple 22 functioned as a "sacred mountain" where the elite performed religious blood-letting ceremonies. Above the door is the body of a double-headed snake, its heads resting on two figures, which are in turn supported by skulls. The decoration here is unique in the southern Maya region – only Yucatán sites such as Kabáh and Chicanna have carvings of comparable quality.

The East Court

Below Temple 22 are the stepped sides of the **East Court**, a graceful plaza which also bears elaborate carvings, including life-sized jaguar heads with hollow eyes which would have once held pieces of jade or polished obsidian. In the middle of the western staircase, flanked by the jaguars, is a rectangular Venus mask, carved in superb deep relief. Rising over the court and dominating the Acropolis is the tallest structure in Copán, **Temple 16**, a thirty-metre pyramid completed by the city's sixteenth ruler, Yax Pasaj, in 776 AD. In order to build Temple 16 Yax Pasaj had to build on top of the **Rosalila Temple**, though the temple was built with extraordinary – and atypical – care so as not to destroy the earlier temple; generally, it was Maya custom to ritually deface or destroy obsolete temples or stelae. The temple served as a centre for worship during the reign of Smoke Serpent, or Butz' Chan (578–628 AD), Copán's eleventh ruler, a period that marked the apogee of the city's political, social and artistic growth – so the discovery of the Rosalila has been one of the most exciting finds of recent years. You can now view the brilliant original facade of the buried temple by entering through a short **tunnel** – an unforgettable, if costly (US$12), experience, as it may be sealed again in future years. The admission price does at least include access to two further tunnels, which extend below the East Plaza past some early cosmological stucco carvings – including a huge macaw mask – more buried temple facades and crypts including the Galindo tomb.

At the southern end of the East Court is **Structure 18**, a small square building with four carved panels in which Yax Pasaj was buried in 821 AD. The diminutive scale of the structure reveals how quickly decline set in, with the militaristic nature of the panels symptomatic of the troubled times. The tomb was empty when excavated by archeologists and is thought to have been looted on a number of occasions. From Structure 18 there's a terrific view of the valley, over the Río Copán, which eroded the eastern buildings of the Acropolis over the centuries until its path was diverted by early archeologists. South of Structure 18, the **Cemetery Group** was once thought to have been a burial site, though it's now known to have been a residential complex and home to the ruling elite. To date, however, little work has been done on this part of the ruins.

The West Court

The second plaza of the Acropolis, the **West Court**, is confined by the south side of Temple 11, which has eight small doorways, and Temple 16. **Altar Q**, at the base of Temple 16, is the court's most famous feature and an astonishing example of ancestral symbolism. Carved in 776 AD, it celebrates Yax Pasaj's accession to the throne on July 2, 763. The top of the altar is carved with six hieroglyphic blocks, while the sides are decorated with sixteen cross-legged figures, all seated on cushions, who represent previous rulers of Copán. All are pointing towards a portrait of Yax Pasaj which shows him receiving a ceremonial staff from the city's first ruler Yax K'uk Mo', thereby endorsing Yax Pasaj's right to rule. Behind the altar is a small crypt, discovered to contain the remains of a macaw and fifteen big cats, sacrificed in honour of his ancestors when the altar was inaugurated.

Las Sepultras

Two kilometres east of Copán along the highway is the smaller site of **Las Sepultras** (daily 8am–4pm; entrance with the same ticket as for Copán), the focus of much archeological interest in recent years because of the information it provides on daily domestic life in Maya times. Eighteen of the forty-odd residential compounds at the site have been excavated, comprising one hundred buildings that would have been inhabited by the elite. Smaller compounds on the edge of the site are thought to have housed young princes, as well as concubines and servants. It was customary to bury the nobility close to their residences, and more than 250 tombs have been excavated around the compounds – given the number of women found in the tombs it seems likely that the local Maya practised polygamy. One of the most interesting finds – the tomb of a priest or shaman, dating from around 450 AD – is on display in the museum in Copan Ruinas town (see p.381).

Around Copán

There are a couple of places within easy reach of Copán that make an extra day or two's stay here worthwhile. Closest is the small Maya site of **Los Sapos**, a delightful walk south from town. Ten kilometres or so in the opposite

△ Carving at Copán, Honduras

direction, the picturesque waterfall of **El Rubí** is the perfect spot for a picnic, while the **hot springs** fifteen kilometres north of town are a pleasant place to soak away your cares. Copán is also a convenient spot to cross over into Guatemala, with the **El Florido** border crossing just 12km to the west.

Los Sapos, dating from the same era as Copán, is set in the hills to the south of town, less than an hour's gentle walk away. The site, whose name derives from a rock carved in the shape of a frog, is thought to have been a place where Maya women came to bear children, though unfortunately time and weather have eroded much of the carving. To get there, follow the main road south out of town, turn left onto a dirt track just past the river bridge and follow this as it begins to climb gently into the hills, past the *Hacienda San Lucas* farmhouse hotel (see below). The views across the tobacco fields of the river valley are beautiful, and there are plenty of spots for swimming along the way.

Pick-ups leave Copán regularly throughout the day for the peaceful town of **Santa Rita**, 9km northeast. At the river bridge, just before entering the town, a path leads up to **El Rubí**, a pretty double waterfall on the Río Copán, about 2km away. Surrounded by shady woods, this is an ideal spot for a swim in the clear, cold water, followed by a picnic. Follow the path as it climbs along and above the right-hand bank of the river for about twenty minutes; just past a steep stretch and small bend to the right, a narrow path runs down through the pasture on the left to a pool and high rock, on the other side of which is El Rubí.

Around 15km north of Copán are some **hot springs** (*aguas termales*; US$0.75), set in lush highland scenery dotted with coffee fincas and patches of pine forests. Here you can either wallow around in man-made pools or make the short walk to the waters' source, where cool river water and near-boiling hot springs combine. The cheapest way to get to the *aguas termales* is to hitch a ride on a pick-up – they pass the *Hotel Paty* in Copán reasonably frequently. Expect to pay around a US$1 for the ride, which takes about fifty minutes, but don't leave it any later than 3.30pm if you're planning to hitch back to Copán. Alternatively, speak to one of Copán's tour operators (see "Listings" on p.382) – Yaragua Tours can arrange a half-day trip to the springs for US$10 per person for a minimum of four people.

Leaving Copán: on to San Pedro Sula and La Ceiba

To reach other destinations within Honduras, including the Bay Islands, you'll have to travel on to the large industrial city of **San Pedro Sula**, from where there are regular flights to the Bay Islands, or press on to the coastal city of **La Ceiba**, which has daily boat connections to Roatán and Utila, and several daily flights to all three islands.

Direct air-conditioned Hedman Atlas **luxury buses** (☏651 4106) leave Copán for San Pedro Sula daily at 2pm (2hr 45min) from their terminal two blocks north of the Parque in the *Hacienda San Lucas* information centre; the company is also planning to run two additional daily departures at some point in the future. Two other bus companies, Gama and Casarola, offer less expensive services, both direct and non-direct, to San Pedro Sula; while slower **local buses** run every two hours or so to the junction of La Entrada, from where there are plenty of connections to San Pedro Sula.

San Pedro Sula

Though it's Honduras's second city and the country's driving economic force, **SAN PEDRO SULA** presents a flat and uninspiring appearance, and is also uncomfortably hot and humid for most of the year. This is a place for business rather than sightseeing, so if you can it's best to press on for La Ceiba or catch a flight from here to the Bay Islands. Unhelpfully, there's no central **bus terminal**, though all buses from Copán (except Hedman Atlas services; see below) arrive at a private terminal at 6 Calle SO, between 6 and 7 Avenidas, some six blocks south of the main parque central. If you're looking to get out quickly, **taxis** are plentiful and pretty cheap: expect to pay around US$2 per journey in the central area, or around US$7 to the airport, 12km southeast of town.

If you do decide to stay there's a wide range of accommodation, restaurants and shops. Of the **hotels**, the basic but clean *Hotel Palmira* at 6 C, 6–7 Av SO (T 557 6522; ❷–❸) couldn't be more convenient if you've arrived on a Casarola or Gama bus from Copán, since it's right next to their shared terminal on 6 Calle SO; all the rooms come with private bathroom; some also have a/c. Alternatively, the *Gran Hotel San Pedro*, a block east of the main Parque at 3 C, 1–2 Av SO (T 553 1513, F 553 1655; ❷–❹), is a perennial favourite with travellers and has a good choice of rooms. The best mid-range hotel in town is the *Hotel Ejecutivo* at 10 Av, 2 C SO (T 552 4289, F 552 5868; ❺–❻), which has large and comfortable rooms with a/c and TV.

Moving on from San Pedro Sula, three companies operate frequent buses for **La Ceiba** (3hr), the gateway city to the Bay Islands. **Catisa–Tupsa**, located six blocks east of the Copán bus terminal at 2 Av 5–6 C SO (T 552 1042), runs twelve standard daily buses. There are also two luxury bus companies: **Viana**, at Av Circunvalación, 200m from *Wendy's* (T 556 9261), with two daily departures, and **Hedman Atlas**, at 3 C & 8 Av NO (T 553 1361), who have three daily departures. Two internal airlines, Isleña (T 552 8335) and Sosa (T 550 6545), fly from San Pedro to La Ceiba for connections to the Bay Islands; the price (US$30) is officially fixed by the Honduran government.

La Ceiba

Some 190km east along the coast from San Pedro Sula, steamy **LA CEIBA**, is one of the more approachable Honduran cities. Though there are no sights in the town itself and its beaches are pretty filthy, the city is bustling and self-assured by day, with a cosmopolitan mix of inhabitants including a large Garífuna (see p.398) community. However, it's the night that's really celebrated in La Ceiba – the city is unquestionably the **party capital** of the country, with a vibrant dancehall scene and a legendary May carnival.

All Catisa-Tupsa buses arrive at the bus terminal, 2km west of the main parque central; Viana and Hedman Atlas buses use private terminals close by. Local buses and shared taxis run very frequently to the centre. La Ceiba's airport is 9km south of town; a taxi to the centre costs US$4.50. If you want to sample La Ceiba's club scene, the action is concentrated in the string of **bars and dance venues** along the seafront. Most of the **hotels** are between the seafront and the central parque, which is about 800m inland. Of these, *Hotel San Carlos*, Av San Isidro, 5–6 C (T 443 0330; ❷), is a popular budget stronghold: a basic but safe place with a selection of fairly clean rooms, all with fans. Just south of here the *Hotel Iberia*, Av San Isidro, 5–6 C (T 443 0401; ❺) is considerably more expensive, though the spacious rooms all have two double beds, bath, a/c and TV. Better value and just a little more pricey, the refurbished *Gran Hotel Paris* on the parque central (T 443 2391, F 443 1614, W www.granhotelparis.com; ❻) has an excellent location and large, comfortable rooms (all with a/c, phone and TV), plus a pool and a quiet bar, restaurant and cybercafé.

Moving on from La Ceiba, an excellent **ferry service** leaves daily for Utila at 9.30am (1hr; US$12 one way) and for Roatán daily at 3pm (2hr;

US$13 one way). Ferries leave from the Muralla de Cabotaje municipal dock, about 5km to the east of the city; there's no bus service, so you'll need to take a taxi (US$5 from the centre; US$8 from the airport). **Flying** to the islands is also uncomplicated, with fifteen flights daily to Roatán (30min; US$20), four daily to Utila (20min; US$17) and five daily to Guanaja (40min; US$33). Availability is very rarely a problem, and you can usually buy your tickets on the spot at the airport, though it's best to book ahead in the peak holiday seasons (Christmas–Easter and August). The domestic airlines Isleña (☎443 0179), Taca (☎443 1912) and Sosa (☎443 2519) have offices on the parque central in La Ceiba and at the airport; another internal carrier, Rollins Air (☎441 2177), has an office at the airport only.

The Bay Islands

Strung along the southern fringes of the world's second largest barrier reef, the **Bay Islands** (Islas de la Bahía) are Honduras's major tourist attraction. With their clear, calm waters and abundant marine life, the islands are the ideal destination for cheap diving, sailing and fishing, while less active types can sling a hammock on one of the many palm-fringed, sandy beaches and snooze in the shade, watching the magnificent sunsets that paint the broad skies with colours as vibrant as the coral below.

Composed of three main islands and some 65 smaller cayes, this sweeping 125-kilometre island chain lies on the Bonacca Ridge, an underwater extension of the Sierra de Omoa mountain range that disappears into the sea near Puerto Cortés on the coast. **Utila**, the island closest to the mainland, attracts budget travellers from all over the world, while **Roatán** is the largest and most developed. **Guanaja**, to the east, is a more upmarket and exclusive resort destination. All three islands offer superb diving and snorkelling.

Even old hands get excited about **diving** the waters around the Bay Islands, where lizard fish and toadfish dart by, scarcely distinguishable from the coral; eagle rays glide through the water like huge birds flying through the air; parrotfish chomp steadily away at the coral; and barracuda and harmless nurse sharks circle the waters, checking you out from a distance. In addition, the world's largest fish, the **whale shark** (which can reach up to 16m in length) is a resident of the Cayman Trench, which plummets to profound depths just north of the islands. It's most frequently spotted in October and November, when dive boats run trips to look for it, but can be encountered close to Utilan waters year round.

The best **time to visit** the islands is from March to September, when the water visibility is good and the weather is clear and sunny. The rains start in October, while November and December are usually very wet, with squally showers continuing until late February. Daytime temperatures range between 25°C and 29°C year round, though the heat is rarely oppressive, thanks to almost constant east–southeast trade winds. Mosquitoes and sandflies are endemic on all the islands, and at their worst when the wind dies down; lavish coatings of baby oil help to keep the latter away.

Some history

The Bay Islands' history of conquest, pirate raids and constant immigration has resulted in a society that's unique in Honduras. The islands' original inhabitants are thought to have been the **Pech**, described by Columbus on his fourth

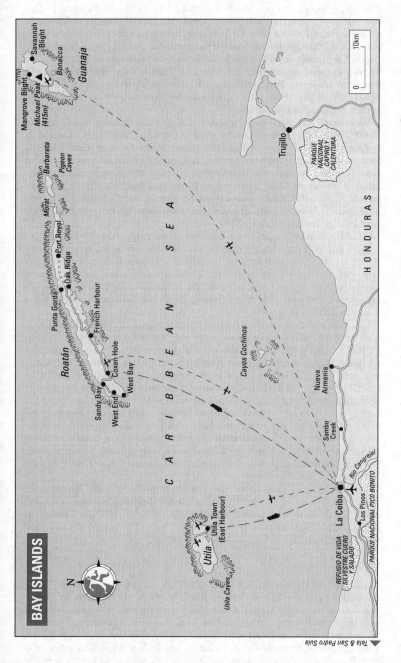

BAY ISLANDS

N

Mangrove Blight

Savannah Blight

Michael Peak (415m)

Bonacca

Guanaja

Barbareta

Pigeon Cayes

Morat

Port Royal

Oak Ridge

Punta Gorda

French Harbour

Roatán

Coxen Hole

Sandy Bay

West End

West Bay

C A R I B B E A N   S E A

Cayos Cochinos

Trujillo

PARQUE NACIONAL CAPIRO Y CALENTURA

H O N D U R A S

Nueva Armenia

Sambo Creek

Rio Canarejal

La Ceiba

Los Pinos

PARQUE NACIONAL PICO BONITO

REFUGIO DE VIDA SILVESTRE CUERO Y SALADO

Utila

Utila Town (East Harbour)

Utila Cayes

0   10km

393

voyage in 1502 as being a "robust people who adore idols and live mostly from a certain white grain from which they make fine bread and the most perfect beer". Post-conquest, the indigenous population declined rapidly as a result of enslavement and forced labour. The islands' strategic location as a provisioning point for the Europe-bound Spanish fleets ensured that they soon became the targets for **pirates**, initially Dutch and French, and subsequently English. The Spanish decision to evacuate the islands in 1650 left the way open for the pirates to move in. Port Royal, Roatán, became their base until the mid-eighteenth century, from where they launched sporadic attacks on ships and against the mainland settlements.

After the pirates left, Roatán was deserted until the arrival of the **Garífuna** in 1797. Forcibly expelled from the British-controlled island of St Vincent following a rebellion, most of the 3000-strong group were persuaded by the Spanish to settle in Trujillo on the mainland, leaving a small settlement at Punta Gorda on the island's north coast. Further waves of settlers came after the abolition of slavery in 1830, when white **Cayman Islanders** and freed **slaves** arrived first on Utila, later moving on to Roatán and Guanaja. These new inhabitants fished and built up a very successful fruit industry – until a hurricane levelled the plantations in 1877.

Honduras acquired rights to the islands following independence in 1821, yet many – not least the islanders themselves – still considered the territory to be British. In 1852, Britain declared the islands a Crown Colony, breaking the terms of the 1850 Clayton–Bulwer Treaty, an agreement not to exercise dominion over any part of Central America. Forced to back down under US pressure, Britain finally conceded sovereignty to Honduras in the Wyke–Cruz Treaty of 1859.

Today, the islands retain their cultural separation from the mainland, although with both Spanish-speaking Hondurans and North American and European ex-pats settling in growing numbers, the island's ethnic make-up continues to change. A unique form of **Creole English** is still spoken on the street, but due to the increasing number of mainlanders migrating here, Spanish – always the official language – is becoming almost as common. This government-encouraged migration has sparked tensions between English-speaking locals and the Latino newcomers, especially in Roatán, where many islanders feel they are being swamped by land-hungry outsiders with whom they have little in common. The huge growth in **tourism** since the early 1990s, a trend that shows no signs of abating, has also been controversial, with growing concerns about the environmental impact of the industry and the question of who, exactly, benefits most from the boom.

For full details of **getting to the islands** from the rest of Honduras, see pp.390–391. There are also several **international flights** to Roatán: Taca operates a direct flight once weekly from Houston, Miami and New Orleans, as well as a daily flight from Belize – call their office in Roatán (☎445 1387) for the latest schedules.

Utila

Smallest of the three main Bay Islands, **UTILA** is a key destination for budget travellers, and one of the cheapest places in the world to **learn to dive** – and even if you don't want to don tanks, the superb waters around the island offer great swimming and snorkelling. Utila is still the cheapest of the Bay Islands, with a cost of living only slightly higher than that on the mainland, although prices are gradually rising. Life is laid-back and people are generally friendly, while crimes against tourists are very rare, watch out for the periodic dancehall brawl. As elsewhere, respect local customs in dress and don't walk around in your bathing suit. Note also that drinking from glass bottles on the street is prohibited.

Arrival and information

All **boats** dock in the centre of **Utila Town** (also known as East Harbour), a large, curved harbour that's the island's only settlement and home to the vast majority of its 2000-strong population. The island's principal road, a twenty-minute walk end to end, runs along the seafront from The Point in the east to Sandy Bay in the west. A new airport is currently being hacked out of the jungle 3km north of Utila Town, at the end of the island's other main road, Cola de Mico Road, which heads inland from the dock; until it opens (which will be sometime in 2002, if the necessary finances materialize), all planes land at a dirt **airstrip** in The Point.

Wherever you arrive, you'll be met by representatives from the **dive schools** laden with maps and information on special offers. Many schools offer free accommodation during their courses, but it's worth checking out the various options before signing up. For more objective information, the Utila branch of BICA (Bay Islands' Conservation Association) has a **visitor and information office** on the main street east of the dock, though its opening hours are erratic (usually Mon–Fri 9am–noon and a couple of hours in the afternoon).

It takes just twenty minutes to stroll from the airstrip to the far western end of town. **Bikes** can be rented from Delco, next to Henderson's grocery store just west of the dock, as well as the *Mango Café* (see p.398) and other places around town – rates start at US$2 a day for an old bike, and around US$5 for a decent mountain bike (not that you'll need it). Some locals use four-wheeled motorbikes to get around and occasionally pick up hitchers.

Accommodation

Utila has more than 25 affordable **guest houses and hotels**, and a profusion of rooms for rent; there's always somewhere available, even at Christmas and Easter. Most of the dive schools have links with a hostel, so that enrolling on a scuba course gets you a few free or discounted nights' accommodation. Everywhere is within walking distance of the dock and airstrip, and the accommodation listed below is in the order that you come to it, walking west along the road from the airstrip. There are no designated places to camp except on the cayes.

From the airstrip to the main dock

Sharkey's Reef Hotel behind *Sharkey's Reef Restaurant*, near the airstrip ☏ 425 3212, ✉ hjackson@hondutel.hn. Set in a peaceful garden, the rooms here all have a/c, private bathrooms and cable TV (some also have kitchens), and there's a terrace with great views over the lagoon. ➎–➏

Trudy's two minutes' walk from the airstrip ☏ 425 3103. A popular place with large, clean rooms, and you can swim from the dock at the back. ➊

Cooper's Inn three minutes' walk from the airstrip ☏ 425 3184. One of the best budget places on the island, with clean, basic rooms and friendly management. ➊

Rubi's Inn two minutes' walk from the dock ☏ 425 3240. Very clean, with airy rooms and views over the water; kitchen facilities are available. ➊

Cola de Mico Road

Blueberry Hill just beyond Thompson's bakery, on the opposite side of the road ☏ 425 3141. Characterful cabins with basic cooking facilities, run by friendly owners, though ear plugs are essential at weekends when the *Bucket o' Blood* bar opposite fires up. ➊

Mango Inn five minutes' walk up the road from *Blueberry Hill* ☏ 425 3335, ⊛ www.mango-inn .com. Beautiful, well-run place, timber-built in Caribbean style, set in shady gardens and offering a range of rooms, from thatched a/c bungalows to pleasant dorms. Also has a book exchange and laundry service, and the attached *Mango Café* is a lively spot serving good food. Dorms ➊ (exact price varies according to package booked), rooms ➌, bungalows ➍; rates drop by at least fifty percent if you dive with the associated Utila Dive Center.

Sandy Bay

Tropical Hotel opposite the Hondutel telephone office (no phone). Very popular backpackers' stronghold; the small functional rooms all have fans and there's a communal kitchen. ❶

Utila Lodge behind the Hondutel telephone office Ⓣ425 3143, Ⓔulodge@hondutel.hn. Comfortable a/c rooms, though they're almost exclusively occupied by divers signed up on weekly packages (US$735 per person including all meals). It also has its own dock, and the owners can arrange fishing trips. ❾

Seaside Inn opposite Gunter's Dive Shop Ⓣ425 3150. A reasonable place, with plain but clean rooms (some with private bath), plus small apartments. ❶–❷

Margaritaville Beach Hotel ten minutes' walk west of the dock Ⓣ425 3266. Tranquil seafront location well away from the main dock, with large, airy rooms, all with private bath. ❷

Diving

Most visitors come to Utila specifically for the **diving**, attracted by the low prices, clear water and abundant marine life. Even in winter, the water is generally calm and common sightings include nurse and hammerhead sharks, turtles, parrot fish, stingrays, porcupine fish and an increasing number of dolphins. On the north coast of the island, Blackish Point and Duppy Waters are both good sites; on the south coast the best spots are Black Coral Wall and Pretty Bush. The good schools will be happy to spend time talking to you about the merits of the various sites.

Rather than signing up with the first dive school representative who approaches you, it's worth spending a morning walking around checking out all the schools. **Price** is not really a consideration, with the dozen or so dive shops all charging around US$140 for a three- to five-day PADI course; advanced and divemaster courses are also on offer, as are fun dives, from US$12. **Safety** is a more pertinent issue: for peace of mind, you should make sure that you understand – and get along with – the instructors, many of whom speak a number of languages. Before signing up, also check that classes have no more than six people, that the equipment is well maintained and that all boats have working oxygen and a first-aid kit. Anyone with asthma or ear problems should not be allowed to dive. The diving **insurance** sold by BICA is also a worthwhile investment: US$3 a day covers you for medical treatment in the event of an emergency.

Recommended **schools** include the Utila Dive Centre (Ⓣ425 3326, Ⓦwww.utiladivecentre.com), on the road between the dock and the dirt airstrip; Gunter's Dive Shop (425 3350, Ⓔecomar@hondutel.hn), two minutes' walk west of the dock, which also rents out sea kayaks; Alton's (Ⓣ425 3108, Ⓔaltons@hondutel.hn), two minutes' walk west of the airstrip; and Underwater Vision (Ⓣ425 3103, Ⓔtamara@psi.net.hn), opposite *Trudy's* hotel. Salty Dog's (Ⓣ425 3363, Ⓔsaltydog@hondutel.hn), a minute's walk west of the dock, has underwater photography equipment for rent, and many of the dive shops also rent out snorkelling equipment for around US$10 a day.

It's important to bear in mind that the coral reef dies when it is touched. BICA has installed buoys at each of the sites to prevent boats anchoring on the reef, and all the reputable schools will use these.

Swimming, snorkelling and walking

The best swimming near town is at the **Blue Bayou**, a twenty-minute walk west of the centre, where you can bathe in chest-deep water and snorkel further out; there's a US$1 charge to use the area, which also boasts a small sandy beach and a rickety wooden pier where you can sunbathe in peace away from the sandflies, plus a food stand selling snacks and beers. There are also hammocks slung in the shade of coconut trees and snorkelling gear available for rent (US$1.50 per hour). Blue Bayou is also the site of the **Utila Sea Turtle**

Conservation Project, a privately run scheme set up with support from BICA, where hawksbill and loggerhead turtle eggs are incubated, and the hatchlings released; visitors are welcome.

East of town, **Airport Beach**, at the end of the dirt airstrip, offers good snorkelling just offshore (though access is more difficult), as does the little reef beyond the lighthouse. The path from the end of the airstrip up the east coast of the island leads to a couple of small coves – the second is good for swimming and sunbathing. Five minutes beyond the coves, you'll come to the **Ironshores**, a mile-long stretch of low volcanic cliffs with lava tunnels cutting down to the water.

Another pleasant five-kilometre walk or cycle ride is along the Cola de Mico Road across the northern tip of the island to **Pumpkin Hill and beach**, passing the site of the new airport. The 82-metre hill, the eroded crest of an extinct volcano, gives good views over the island and across to the mainland and the dark bulk of Pico Bonito. Down on the beach, lava rocks cascade into the sea, forming underwater caves – there's good snorkelling here when the water is calm, though it's not safe to free dive down into the caves.

The Cayes

Utila Cayes – eleven tiny outcrops strung along the southwestern edge of the island – were designated a wildlife refuge in 1992. **Pigeon Caye** and **Suc Suc Caye** (also called Jewel Caye), connected by a narrow causeway, are both inhabited, and the pace of life here is even slower than that on Utila. Small launches regularly shuttle between Suc Suc and Utila (US$1), or can be rented to take you across for a day's snorkelling, if you have your own equipment. *Vicky's Rooms* on Suc Suc (❶) offers basic accommodation, and there are a couple of reasonable restaurants and a good fish market.

Water Caye, a blissful stretch of white sand, coconut palms, pellucid water and a small coral reef, is even more idyllic, given its absence of sandflies. You can **camp** here, but you'll need to bring all your own food, fuel and water; a caretaker turns up every day to collect the US$1 fee for use of the island, and hammocks can be rented for an extra US$1. Water Caye is also the venue for occasional **full-moon parties** and a spectacular annual two-day rave in July, with European house and techno DJs, organized by Sunjam and the *Mango Inn* (see ⓦ www.sunjam.com for information). **Transport** to the caye is organized during such events; at other times, dive boats will often drop you off on their way to the north coast for a small fee, or you can ask the owner of the *Bundu Café* (see below) in Utila Town.

Eating

Lobster and fish are staples on the islands, along with the usual rice, beans and chicken, while the tourist boom has brought with it European and American foods like pasta, pizza, burgers, pancakes and granola. Since most things have to be brought in by boat, prices are higher than on the mainland: main courses start at around US$4, and beers cost at least US$1. For eating on the cheap, head for the evening stalls on the road by the dock, which do a thriving trade in *baleadas*. Note that many restaurants stop serving at around 10pm.

Bundu Café on the main street, east of the dock. Serves European-style breakfasts and lunches and lassi-style milkshakes. Also has a book exchange.

Captain Jack's five minutes' walk west of the dock. Dutch–Utilan owned café–restaurant serving excellent-value lunches, including burritos and sandwiches, freshly squeezed orange juice, and delicious dinners such as fish cakes and grilled kingfish steaks.

Cross Creek at The Point. Superb Caribbean cooking from one of Utila's best chefs, served in a quiet spot beside the lagoon and majoring in flavoursome pan-fried fish and seafood. It's fairly expensive though: expect to pay around US$10 a head for a meal plus drink.

Delaney's Island Kitchen three minutes east of the dock. Simple, well-executed island cooking, plus a few Western dishes like pasta.

Golden Rose two minutes west of the dock. Good-value Caribbean and Honduran dishes, popular with dive instructors and locals.

Jade Seahorse on Cola de Mico Road. Serves great breakfasts and licuados, and good seafood.

Mango Café in the *Mango Inn*. A popular place with an interesting selection of tasty and well-presented European food, espresso and cappucci-

no, and a lively bar. Closed Mon.

Mermaid's Corner at *Rubi's Inn*. Popular pasta and pizza restaurant with a great atmosphere, though service can be very slow.

RJs at The Point, beside the bridge. Popular with dive crews and students, with a gregarious atmosphere and famously excellent meat and fish barbecues.

Thompson's Bakery Cola de Mico Road. A near-legendary place to hang out, read, drink coffee and meet other travellers while sampling the good-value breakfasts or the range of daily baked offerings – try the johnny cakes.

Nightlife

Despite its tiny population, Utila is a fearsomely hedonistic party island. The hottest place in town for travellers is the *Coco Loco Bar,* just west of the dock, which draws a lively bunch of party heads with its extended happy hour and regular house, techno and reggae parties. *Casino*, by the dock, attracts a more local crowd with thundering reggae and a dash of salsa and merengue. During the rest of the week, the *Mango Café* is a popular spot for cheap beer and a quiet drink, while the *Bucket o' Blood*, very close by on Cola de Mico Road, boasts a bombastic sound system but fewer drinkers. Further along the Cola de Mico road towards the new airport, the huge open-air *Bar in da Bush* can get very lively at weekends.

Listings

Airlines Tickets for Sosa and Rollins, covering domestic routes in Honduras, can be purchased in the captain's office by the dock.

Banks Banco Atlántida and Bancahsa, both close to the dock, change money and offer cash advances on Visa cards (Mon–Fri 8–11.30am & 1.30–4pm, Sat 8–11.30am); at other times try Henderson's store, just to the west.

Bicycles can be rented for around US$5 a day from Delco, just west of the dock, or from the *Mango Café.*

Books The *Bundu Café*, on the main street, east of the dock, has a book exchange.

Doctor The Community Medical Center is two minutes west of the dock (Mon–Fri 8am–noon).

Immigration office Next to Hondutel in Sandy Bay (Mon–Fri 9am–noon & 2–4.30pm).

Internet access Two minutes west of the dock,

Bay Island Computer Services offers internet access for US$12 an hour, plus discounted international calls.

Port office In the large building at the main dock (Mon–Fri 8.30am–noon & 2–5pm, Sat 8.30am–noon).

Post office In the large building at the main dock (Mon–Fri 9am–noon & 2–4.30pm, Sat 9–11.30am).

Telephones The best rates for international calls are at Bay Island Computer Services (see "Internet access", above) and the Reef Cinema. Avoid the Hondutel office, next to the *migración*, where the rates are extortionate.

Travel agents Tropical Travel and Utila Tour Travel Center, both east of the dock on the airstrip road, can confirm and book flights to La Ceiba and elsewhere in Central America.

Roatán

Some 50km from La Ceiba, **ROATÁN** is the largest of the Bay Islands, a curving ridged hump almost 50km long and 5km across at its widest point. Geared towards upmarket tourists, the island's accommodation mostly comes in the form of all-in luxury resort packages, although there are some good deals to be found. Like Utila, Roatán is a suberb **diving** destination, but also offers some great hiking, as well as the chance to do nothing except laze on a beach.

Coxen Hole is the island's commercial centre, while **West End** is the place to head for absolute relaxation.

Arrival and getting around

Regular **flights** from La Ceiba (and Belize and the US) land at the airport, on the road to French Harbour, 3km from Coxen Hole. A taxi to West End from here costs US$10, or you could walk to the road and wait for one of the public minibuses which head to Coxen Hole every 20 minutes or so (US$0.70) and change there. There's an information desk, a hotel reservation desk, car rental agencies and a bank at the airport. **Ferries** to the island dock in the centre of Coxen Hole.

A paved road runs west–east along the island, connecting the major communities. **Minibuses** leave regularly from Main Street in Coxen Hole, heading west to Sandy Bay and West End (every 20min until late afternoon) and east to Brick Bay, French Harbour, Oak Ridge and Punta Gorda (every 30min or so until late afternoon); fares are US$0.70–1. However, if you really want to explore, you'll need to rent a **car** or **motorbike**: in addition to the agencies at the airport, Sandy Bay Rent-a-Car (☎445 1710, ℱ445 1711) has offices at Sandy Bay and West End, and also rents out jeeps (US$45 per day) and motorbikes (US$25 per day).

Coxen Hole

COXEN HOLE (also known as Roatán Town) is dusty and run-down, and most visitors come here only to change money or shop. All the town's practical facilities and most shops are on a hundred-metre stretch of **Main Street**, near where the buses stop. For **information** about the island and its events, pick up a copy of the *Coconut Telegraph* magazine from the Cooper Building; you'll find the headquarters of BICA (Mon–Fri 9am–noon & 2–5pm) here as well, if you want to learn more about Roatán's flora and fauna.

To change **travellers' cheques** or dollars or get a Visa cash advance, try Bancahsa, or Credomatic, both on Main Street. The **migración** and **post office** are both near the small square on Main Street, while Hondutel is behind Bancahsa. HB Warren is the largest **supermarket** on the island, and there's a small and not too impressive general market just behind Main Street. The island's best set-up **internet** café, Paradise Computers (Mon–Fri 9am–5pm, Sat 9am–1pm), is a five-minute walk from the centre of town on the road to West End, and though rates are very high (around US$12 an hour), the epic cappuccinos and delicious carrot cake help compensate a little. Librería Casi Todo, in the same building as the *Qué Tal Cafe* (see below), sells secondhand **books**.

It's unlikely you'll want **to stay** in Coxen Hole unless you have a very early flight. If you do, the *Hotel Cayview*, on Main Street (☎445 1222; ❺), has comfortable rooms with a/c and private bath, while the *Hotel El Paso* (☎445 1367; ❹), nearby on the same street, has clean rooms, but with communal bathrooms only. There are a number of cheap **comedores**, serving standard Honduran food, while the *Qué Tal Cafe*, on Thicket Street just past Paradise Computers, serves European-style breakfasts and snacks.

Sandy Bay

Midway between Coxen Hole and West End, **SANDY BAY** is an unassuming community with a number of interesting attractions. The **Institute for Marine Sciences** (Sun–Tues & Thurs–Sat 9am–5pm; US$3), based at *Antony's Key Resort* (see below), has exhibitions on the marine life and geology of the islands and a museum with useful information on local history and archeology. There are also bottle-nosed **dolphin shows** (Mon, Tues, Thurs & Fri 10am & 4pm, Sat & Sun 10am, 1pm & 4pm; US$4), and you can dive or snorkel with the dolphins (US$100 and US$75 respectively; must be booked in advance on ☎445 1327). Across the road from the institute, several short nature trails weave through the jungle at the **Carambola Botanical Gardens** (daily 8am–5pm; US$3), a riot of beautiful flowers, lush ferns and tropical trees. Twenty minutes' walk from the gardens up Monte Carambola, the **Iguana Wall** is a section of cliff that's a breeding ground for iguanas and parrots. From the top of the mountain you can see across to Utila on clear days. Bordering the gardens, Sandy Bay's newest attraction is the **Tropical Treasures Bird Park** (Mon–Sat 10am–5pm; US$5, including guided tour), with toucans, parrots and scarlet macaws.

There are several places **to stay** in the Sandy Bay area, all clearly signposted, including the attractive *Beth's Hostel* (☎445 1266; ❹); the *Oceanside Inn* (☎445 1552; ❻), with large rooms and a good restaurant; and three **dive resorts**, the best of which is *Anthony's Key Resort* (☎445 1003, ℉445 1140, ⓦwww.anthonys-key.com; weekly packages from US$600), one of the smartest places on the island, with cabins set among the trees and on a small caye. Popular places **to eat** include *Rick's American Café*, set on the hillside above the road and serving giant US-style burgers, and *Monkey Lala*, next door, offering superb seafood.

West End

With its calm waters and incredible white beaches, **WEST END**, 14km from Coxen Hole, makes the most of its ideal setting, gearing itself mainly towards independent travellers on all budgets, with a good selection of attractive accommodation. Set in the southwest corner of the island, round a shallow bay, the village has retained a laid-back charm, and the gathering pace of tourist development has done little to dent the locals' friendliness.

The paved road from Coxen Hole finishes at the northern end of the village, not far from **Half Moon Bay**, a beautifully sheltered sandy

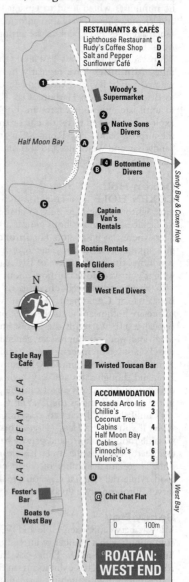

RESTAURANTS & CAFÉS
Lighthouse Restaurant	C
Rudy's Coffee Shop	D
Salt and Pepper	B
Sunflower Café	A

Woody's Supermarket

Native Sons Divers

Half Moon Bay

Bottomtime Divers

Captain Van's Rentals

Roatán Rentals

Reef Gliders

West End Divers

Eagle Ray Café

Twisted Toucan Bar

ACCOMMODATION
Posada Arco Iris	2
Chillie's	3
Coconut Tree Cabins	4
Half Moon Bay Cabins	1
Pinnochio's	6
Valerie's	5

Foster's Bar

@ Chit Chat Flat

Boats to West End

CARIBBEAN SEA

0   100m

ROATÁN: WEST END

Sandy Bay & Coxen Hole

West Bay

beach ringed with hotels. Turning to the south at the end of the paved road from Coxen Hole, a sandy track runs alongside the water's edge through the heart of West End, passing a merry bunch of guest houses, bars and restaurants set between patches of coconut palms. You can rent **cars** from Roatán Rentals, at the north of West End, or Sandy Bay Rent-a-Car close by; Captain Van's rents out bicycles, mopeds and motorbikes (though their rates are pricey). The sole **internet** café, *Chit Chat Flat*, towards the southern end of West End, charges US$12 an hour for pretty lethargic connections.

Accommodation

Most of the **accommodation** in West End and Half Moon Bay is charmingly individualistic, and heavy discounts are available during low season (April–July & Sept to mid-Dec), particularly for longer stays.

Chillie's Half Moon Bay ⓣ445 1214, ⓔmermaid@globalnet.hn. Very well set-up, English–Honduran-owned backpackers' stronghold, with dorm beds and private rooms, a kitchen and camping space. Also home to Native Sons Divers. ❸

Coconut Tree Cabins at the entrance to the village ⓣ445 1648, ⓦwww.coconuttree.com. Comfortable, spacious cabins all with covered porches, fridges and hot water. ❺–❻

Half Moon Bay Cabins Half Moon Bay ⓣ445 1075. Upmarket place with secluded cabins scattered around wooded grounds close to the water's edge; all have fan or a/c. There's also a lively restaurant and bar. ❺

Pinocchio's 200m along the seafront in West End ⓣ445 1481, ⓕ445 1008, ⓔpinocchio69@bigfoot.com. Occupies a wooden building set on a small hill above the village, with clean, airy rooms with bath. The owners are very friendly and there's a good restaurant downstairs (see below). ❺

Posada Arco Iris Half Moon Bay ⓣ445 1264, ⓦhttp.//roatanet.com/scuba/posada.htm. Set in attractive gardens just off the beach, with excellent, imaginatively furnished and spacious rooms, studios and apartments, all with fridge and hammocks, and some with a/c. ❹–❻

Valerie's about 100m along West End, then up a signposted dirt track (no phone). Venerable love-it-or-hate-it, chaotic bohemian set-up with a profusion of quirky accommodation, including two trailer-style rooms and a large dorm (US$5 per person). The North American owner is very friendly, and guests can also use the kitchen. ❷–❸

Eating and Drinking

There's a more than adequate range of **places to eat** in West End, with fish, seafood and pasta featuring heavily on many menus. **Drinking** can drain your

Watersports in and around West End

Diving courses for all levels are available in West End. Prices are officially standardized, with a four-day PADI open-water course costing around US$250, but it's worth asking around as some schools include basic accommodation, and sporadic price wars break out between the schools. Fun dives are set at US$30 a dive, though again substantial discounts are often on offer, with ten-dive packages set at US$200 or below. Recommended West End-based **schools** include Ocean Divers (ⓣ445 1925, ⓔoceandivers@global.hn), West End Divers (ⓣ445 1531, ⓦwww.roantan.com/wed), Reef Gliders (no phone, ⓔparadise@global.hn) and Bottom-Time Divers (ⓣ445 1648, ⓦwww.coconuttree.com). There's another good school, Native Sons (ⓣ445 1214, ⓔmermaid@global.hn), at *Chillie's* hotel in Half Moon Bay, as well as two decent dive schools in West Bay (see p.402).

The reef lying just offshore provides some superb **snorkelling**, with the best spots being at the mouth of Half Moon Bay and at the Blue Channel, which can be accessed from the beach 100m south of *Foster's* bar. You can also rent **sea kayaks** from the *Sea Breeze Inn*, close to the entrance road; expect to pay around US$12 for a half day or US$20 for a full day. Underwater Paradise, based in the Half Moon Bay Resort, runs popular underwater **reef tours** in a mini submarine for US$30 per person.

pocket fast, however, and it's best to seek out the half-price happy hours at many of the restaurants and bars – they start at around 4.30pm, and many of them last until 10pm. The *Twisted Toucan*, halfway along the seafront, is the liveliest place in town most nights, except Fridays, when everyone heads to *Foster's* for the weekly reggae jump up.

Lighthouse Restaurant close to the seafront between West End and Half Moon Bay. Big portions of reasonably priced Caribbean food served up in friendly, diner-like surrounds.

Pinocchio's in the hotel of the same name. One of the finest restaurants in West End, with an eclectic range of creative, but fairly pricey, European meat and fish dishes. Closed Wed.

Rudy's Coffee Stop Top-notch breakfasts of banana pancakes, omelettes, fresh coffee and juices. Closed Sun.

Salt and Pepper at the entrance to the village. Wide-ranging gourmet menu including French, Japanese and Thai dishes. Expect to pay upwards of US$10 a head with wine, though the relaxed atmosphere and excellent cooking make it worth the money.

Sunflower Café close to the centre of Half Moon Bay. Cheerful North American-owned café serving delicious omelettes, bagels and muffins. Open 7am–3pm only.

West Bay

Two kilometres southwest of West End, towards the extreme western tip of Roatán, is the stunning white-sand beach of **WEST BAY**, fringed by coconut palms and washed by crystal-clear waters. The beach's tranquillity has been mildly disrupted by a rash of cabaña and hotel construction, but provided you avoid the sandflies by sunbathing on the jetties, it's still a sublime place to relax and enjoy the Caribbean. There's decent **snorkelling** at the southern end of the beach too, though the once pristine reef has suffered in recent years from increasing river run-off and the close attentions of unsupervised day-trippers.

From West End, it's a pleasant 45-minute stroll south along the beach and over a few rock outcrops; alternatively you can take one of the small **launches** that leave *Foster's Restaurant* regularly – the last one returns around 7pm (9pm in high season). A dirt road also runs here: from West End, head up the road to Coxen Hole and take the first turning on the right. If you want **to stay**, the Swiss-owned *Bananarama* (☎992 9679, ⓦwww.roatanet.com /bananarama; ❺) has comfortable little wood cabins with mosquito nets and 24-hour hot water, while for something really luxurious, head for the Canadian-owned *Island Pearl Resort* (☎991 1858, ⓦwww.roatanpearl.com; ❾), which boasts stunning two-storey houses equipped with kitchens and hot tubs plus a gourmet restaurant set in a spacious beachside plot. Both hotels have good in-house **dive schools**.

Northern Roatán

Leaving Coxen Hole, the paved road runs northeast past the small secluded cove of Brick Bay to **FRENCH HARBOUR**, a busy fishing port and the island's second largest town. Less run-down than Coxen Hole, it's a lively place to stay for a couple of days. All the accommodation is right in the centre: the *Harbour View Hotel* (☎455 5390; ❹) has reasonable rooms with bath and hot water, while the more upmarket *Buccaneer Hotel* (☎455 5032; ❺) has a pool and a large wooden deck overlooking the water. The best place to eat is *Gio's*, by the Credomatic building on the waterfront, where you can dine on excellent but pricey seafood; for more local fare, try *Pat's Place*, 50m further on.

From French Harbour the road cuts inland along a central ridge to give superb views of both the north and south coasts of the island. After about 14km it reaches **OAK RIDGE**, an attractive fishing port with wooden houses strung along its harbour. There are some nice unspoiled beaches to the east of town, accessible by launches from the main dock. The best place to stay is the clean and pleasant *Hotel San José* (☎435 2328; ❸–❹), on a small caye a short distance across the water from the dock. Launches run from the main dock to the caye on demand (US$0.50).

About 5km from Oak Ridge on the northern coast of the island is the village of **PUNTA GORDA**, the oldest Garífuna community in Honduras. The best time to visit is for the anniversary of the founding of the settlement (April 6–12), when Garífuna from all over the country attend the celebrations. At other times it's a quiet and slightly dilapidated little port with no historical buildings. The very basic *Los Cincos Hermanos* (❷) offers fairly clean rooms and has an attached comedor.

From the end of the paved road at Punta Gorda you can continue driving along the dirt track which runs east along the island, passing the turn-off for the secluded **Paya Beach** after around 1.5km, where there's a new dive hotel, the pleasant little *Paya Beach Resort* (☎924 2220, ⓦwww.payabay.com; ❼ including all meals). A further 5km or so along is **Camp Bay Beach**, an idyllic, undeveloped stretch of white sand and coconut palms, though there are plots of land for sale here, so things may change soon. The road ends at the village of **PORT ROYAL**, on the southern edge of the island, where the faint remains of a fort built by the English can be seen on a caye offshore. The village lies in the **Port Royal Park and Wildlife Reserve**, the largest refuge on the island, set up in 1978 in an attempt to protect endangered species such as the yellow-naped parrot, as well as the watershed for eastern Roatán.

The eastern tip of Roatán is made up of mangrove swamps, with the small island of **Morat** just offshore. Beyond is **Barbareta Caye**, which has retained much of its virgin forest cover. The *Barbareta Beach Resort* runs inclusive packages (in the US ☎888/450 3483; packages from US$220 for three nights), with diving, windsurfing, hiking, mountain biking and fishing tours available. The reef around Barbareta and the nearby Pigeon Cayes offers good snorkelling; launches can be hired to reach these islands from Oak Ridge for around US$35 for a return trip.

Guanaja

The easternmost Bay Island, **GUANAJA** was the most beautiful, densely forested and undeveloped of them all until Hurricane Mitch laid siege to it for over two days during October 1998, lashing the land with winds of up to 300kph – though buildings have been patched up and reforestation projects have been implemented, it's expected that the landscape will take decades to recover. The island is some 25km long and up to four kilometres wide, and is divided into two unequal parts by a narrow canal – the only way to get between the two sections of the island is by water taxi, which adds both to the atmosphere and to the cost of living. The island is very thinly populated – most of Guanaja's 12,000 inhabitants live in **Bonacca** (also know as Guanaja Town), a crowded settlement that sits on a small caye a few hundred metres offshore. It's here that you'll find the island's shops, as well as the bulk of the reasonably priced accommodation. The only other settlements of any substance are **Savannah Bight** (on the east coast) and **Mangrove Bight** (on the north coast).

Arrival and information

Guanaja **airstrip** is on the larger section of the island, next to the canal. Aside from a couple of dirt tracks there are no roads, and the main form of transport is in small launches. **Boats** from the main dock in Bonacca meet all flights and rides can be hitched on private boats to Mangrove Bight for a nominal fee. There are no scheduled boat services to Guanaja from the mainland, but regular cargo ships sail to the island from La Ceiba and other ports in Honduras.

Virtually all the houses in Bonacca are built on stilts – vestiges of early settlement by the Cayman islanders – the buildings clinging to wooden causeways over the canals, many of which have now been filled in. The main causeway, running for about 500m east–west along the caye, with a maze of small passages branching off it, is where you'll find all the shops, banks and businesses. You can **change dollars**, travellers' cheques and get cash advances at Bancahsa, to the right of the dock (Mon–Fri 8–11.30am & 1.30–4pm, Sat 8–11.30am).

Accommodation

The biggest news to hit the island in years is that Hollywood actor Christopher Lambert and other investors are building a luxury resort on the north side of the island, though it's not projected to open until at least 2003. For now, most of the hotels on Guanaja are all-inclusive luxury **dive resorts** offering weekly packages. You'll also find a small number of mid-range **hotels** in Bonacca – though none are particularly good value for money.

Bonacca

Hotel Miller halfway along the main causeway (☎453 4327). In a slightly rundown building, though the rooms are in reasonable condition; most have hot water and, for a little extra, a/c and cable TV. ❹

Hotel Nights Inn at the extreme western end of the causeway (☎453 4465). New family-run place with clean, comfortable and fairly spacious rooms, all with cable TV and a/c. ❺

Hotel Rosario opposite the *Hotel Miller* (☎453 4240). Modern building with comfortable rooms, all with private bath, a/c and TV. ❹

The rest of the island

Bayman Bay Club on the north side of the island (☎991 0281, ✉bayman@caribe.hn). Large and pleasantly furnished cabins set in plenty of space on a wooded hillside above a small beach. Packages including dives and all meals cost US$700–750 per person per week.

Island House Resort on the north side of the island (☎ & ⓕ453 4146). Pleasant accommodation in a large house run by a friendly local dive instructor, close to several expanses of beautiful beach. Rooms with full board ❻, with full board and diving. ❼

Posada del Sol on the south side of the island (☎ & ⓕ453 4186, ✉posadadelsol@aol.com). Stylish cabins scattered around sixty acres of ground, with amenities including a pool, tennis courts, sea kayaks and snorkelling equipment. All-inclusive dive packages from US$775 per person.

Around the island

Though Guanaja's Caribbean pine forests were flattened by Mitch, there's still some decent **hiking** across the island. A wonderful trail leads from Mangrove Bight up to **Michael's Peak** (412m), the highest point of the entire Bay Islands, and down to Sandy Bay on the south coast, affording stunning views of Guanaja, Bonacca and the surrounding reef. Fit walkers can do the trail in a day, or you can camp at the summit, provided you bring your own provisions.

Some of the island's finest white-sand **beaches** lie around the rocky headland of **Michael's Rock**, near the *Island House Resort* on the north coast, with good snorkelling close to the shore. **Diving** is excellent all around the main island, but particularly off the small cayes to the east, and at **Black Rocks**, off the northern tip of the main island, where there's an underwater coral canyon. To get to these sites you'll have to contact one of the hotel-based dive schools: the *Island House Resort* usually has the best rates at around US$70 for two dives including equipment. **Fishing** and **snorkelling** can be arranged with local boatmen, who charge US$10–15 for an hour and a half on the reef. In many areas, however, the reef is close enough to swim to if you have your own snorkel gear.

Eating and drinking

There are several **restaurants** in Bonacca, though none is particularly cheap, as most of the supplies have to be shipped in from the mainland; note too that many of them close on Sundays. Try *Bonacca's Garden*, halfway along the main causeway, or the *Best Stop*, next to the basketball court, for snacks, cakes and yummy sticky buns. The funkiest **bar** in town is *Nit's Bar*, just east of the main dock, where the clapboard walls shake to classic reggae sounds, while you'll find Guanaja's best margaritas at the air-conditioned *The End of the World* bar on the main causeway.

Cayos Cochinos

Lying 17km offshore from the mainland, the **CAYOS COCHINOS** (Hog Islands) comprise two thickly wooded main islands – **Cochino Grande** and **Cochino Pequeño** – and thirteen **cayes**, all of them privately owned. The small amount of effort it takes to get there is well worth it for a few days' utter tranquillity. Fringed by a reef, the whole area has been designated a marine reserve, with anchoring on the reef and commercial fishing both strictly prohibited. The US Smithsonian Institute, which manages the reserve, has a research station on Cochino Pequeño. On land, the island's hills are studded with hardwood forests, palms and cactus, while Cochino Grande has a number of trails across its interior, and a small peak rising to 145m.

Organized accommodation on the islands is limited to the *Plantation Beach Resort* on Cochino Grande (☎442 0974, ⊛www.plantationbeachresort.com), which does weekly dive packages for around US$800, including all meals and three dives a day; they collect guests by launch from the Muralla de Cabotaje dock in La Ceiba on Saturdays (US$75 return). It can be more rewarding, however, to stay in the traditional Garífuna fishing village of **CHACHAUATE** on Lower Monitor Caye, south of Cochino Grande. The villagers have allocated a hut for visitors to sling their hammocks in for a minimal charge, and will cook meals for you. Basic groceries are available in the village, though you should bring water and your main food supplies with you from the mainland.

Unless you're staying at the *Plantation Beach*, the only way to the Cayos is to charter a boat from the Muralla de Cabotaje dock at La Ceiba (US$60–80 return for up to six people, but be sure to bargain hard).

Travel details

Buses

Chiquimula to: La Florida border (9 daily; 1hr 30min).

Copán to: San Pedro Sula (6–8 daily; 3hr).
San Pedro Sula to: La Ceiba (17 daily; 3hr).

Shuttle buses

Antigua to: Copán (1 daily at 4am; 6hr).

Guatemala City to: Copán (1 daily at 5am; 5hr).

Boats

La Ceiba to: Roatán (1 daily; 2hr); Utila (1 daily; 1hr).

Flights

La Ceiba to: Guanajá (5 daily, 40min); Roatán (15 daily, 30min); Utila (4 daily, 20min).

Belize City to: Roatán (1 daily, 1hr).
Houston to: Roatán (1 weekly, 3hr 30min).

INTO HONDURAS: COPÁN AND THE BAY ISLANDS

contexts

contexts

History

Prior to the advent of the Maya civilization little is known about the area that is now called Guatemala, and even the early origins of the Maya remains fairly mysterious. Set out here is a brief overview of the main theories, none of which can claim to dominate the academic debate. Over the last few years the situation has, if anything, become even more confused, as excavations of important new sites throw up information that casts doubt on many accepted notions. The Maya region is currently one of the hottest areas of archeology in the world, and though the historical records (including the names of rulers) are becoming much clearer, knowledge is evolving at a very fast pace with many events still prone to furious academic polemic.

Prehistory

Opinions differ as to when the first people arrived in the Americas, but the most widely accepted theory is that **Stone Age hunter-gatherers** crossed the Bering land bridge from Siberia to Alaska in several waves beginning 25,000 years ago. Travelling along an ice-free corridor (and possibly in small boats along the coastline) they migrated south into Central America. The first recognizable culture, known as **Clovis**, had emerged by at least 11,000 BC, and worked stone tools, including spearpoints, blades and scrapers, dating from 9000 BC have been found in the Guatemalan highlands.

In **Mesoamerica**, an area defined as stretching from north central Mexico through Central America to Panamá, the first settled pattern of development took place around 8000 BC, as a warming climate forced the hunter-gatherers to adapt to a different way of life. The glaciers were in retreat and the big game, which the hunters depended upon, became scarce due to the warmer, drier climate and possibly over-hunting. This period, in which the hunters turned to more intensive use of plant foods, is known as the **Archaic** period and lasted until about 1800 BC. During this time the food plants vital to the subsequent development of agriculture, such as corn, beans, peppers, squash and probably maize, were domesticated, and research on ancient pollen samples indicates that the Petén region was an area of savannahs and broad-leaved woodlands. Current theory suggests that tropical forest did not appear until the Classic period, by which time the Maya could more easily control its profuse growth.

The early Maya

Somewhere between 2000 and 1500 BC we move into the **Preclassic** (or **Formative**) era, a name used by archeologists to describe the earliest developments in the history of the **Maya**, marking the first phase on a long road of evolution and increasing sophistication which culminates with the Classic (250 –900 AD) period.

The names given to archeological periods are often confusing. Current excavations seem to be pushing back the dates when the earliest breakthroughs were made, and the dates of each period vary according to what you read; but in general terms the tail end of the Archaic era becomes **Early Preclassic** (1800–1000 BC, during which time the early Maya settled in villages throughout the region, as the foragers became farmers and began making pottery. By 1100 BC the **Olmec**, often called Mesoamerica's "mother culture", were constructing pyramid-like ceremonial platforms and carving colossal stone heads just to the northwest of the Maya region. Their artistic, polytheistic religious (and almost certainly political) influence spread throughout Maya lands, and Olmec-style carvings have been found at numerous sites along Guatemala's Pacific coast, in El Salvador and at Copán, in Honduras. The Olmec also developed an early writing system and a calendar known as the "Long Count", which was later adopted by the Maya (see opposite).

During the **Middle Preclassic** period (1000 –300 BC) there was a substantial increase in population across the Maya area. In the northern Petén, **Nakbé** had, by 500 AD, grown to become perhaps the first Maya city, complete with imposing temples and stucco sculptures – evidence that the Maya had progressed far beyond a simple peasant society. At the same time, other settlements – including Tikal and El Mirador – were building their first ceremonial structures, though they still remained little more than village-sized agricultural centres until the Late Classic era. It is thought that a common language was spoken throughout the Maya area, and that a universal belief system, practised from a very early date, may have provided the stimulus and social cohesion to build bigger towns and religious temples. Materials including obsidian and jade from the Guatemalan highlands and granite from Belize were widely traded. Pottery, including red and orange jars and dishes of the *Mamon* style, has been found at a number of settlements, indicating increasing pan-Maya communication. At the same time, food surpluses and rising prosperity levels gradually enabled some inhabitants to eschew farming duties and become seers, priests and astronomers.

Much greater advances in architecture were achieved in the **Late Preclassic** (300 BC–250 AD) era as other cities prospered in the Petén. At the start of the Late Preclassic, Nakbé was the dominant city – its ceremonial core rebuilt with a soaring cluster of temples and its plazas studded with carved stelae. But the focus quickly shifted to **El Mirador**, 12km to the north, which expanded to become a massive city, spread over twenty square kilometres, with a population of around 100,000. Almost nothing is known about the power politics of these times, but the sheer size of El Mirador indicates that the city must have acquired "superstate" status by around 100 BC. Positioned at the heart of a vast trading network, one of its gargantuan temple complexes was constructed to a height of 70m – the highest building ever to have been built by any pre-Columbian culture in the Americas.

El Mirador's only serious rival during the Late Classic era was located several hundred kilometres to the south in the highlands, on the site of the modern capital of Guatemala City. **Kaminaljuyú** had established a formidable commercial empire based on the supply of obsidian and jade, and held sway over a string of settlements along the Pacific coast including Abaj Takalik. It's clear that the southern Maya area was much more influenced by Olmec advances at the time, and that Mesoamerican writing and calendar systems first developed in this region before being introduced to the Petén.

From 1 AD pyramids and temple platforms were emerging at Tikal, Uaxactún, Calakmul and many other sites in Petén in what amounted to an explosion of Maya culture. The famous Maya corbelled arch (which was not a true arch, with a keystone, but consisted of two sides, each with stones overlapping until they eventually met, and thus could only span a relatively narrow gap) was also developed in this period, and architectural styles became more ambitious. A stratified **Maya society** was also becoming established, the nascent states led by rulers and shamanic priests who presided over religious ceremonies dictated by astronomical and calendrical events. There were specialist craftsmen, architects, scribes and traders and intensive agriculture was practised using irrigation from vast reservoirs via extensive canal networks.

But towards the end of the Late Preclassic period, during the second and third centuries AD, environmental disasters, and possibly protracted warfare, plagued the region. The greatest city in the Maya world, El Mirador, was abruptly abandoned in 150 AD, during a long dry climatic period which would have severely cut agricultural production. In the southern region, the eruption of the **Ilopango volcano** in central El Salvador smothered a vast area in ash, provoking mass migration from cities as far away as Kaminaljuyú, which was abandoned around 250 AD. Temple building and stelae carving ceased. Pacific trade routes between the southern Maya region and Mexico were disrupted, and much of the trade was rerouted to the north, bringing prosperity (but also Central Mexican influence; see below) to the cities of Petén.

The Classic Maya

The development that separates the Late Preclassic from the early **Classic period** (250–900 AD) is the introduction of the Long Count calendar and a recognizably Maya form of writing. This had occurred by the end of the third century AD and marks the beginning of the greatest phase of Maya achievement.

During the Classic period all the cities we now know as ruined or restored sites were built, almost always over earlier structures. Elaborately carved **stelae**, bearing dates and emblem-glyphs, were erected at regular intervals. These tell of actual rulers and of historical events in their lives – battles, marriages, dynastic succession and so on. As these dates have come to be deciphered they have provided confirmation (or otherwise) of archeological evidence and offered a major insight into the nature of Maya dynastic rule.

Developments in the Maya area during the Early Classic period were still powerfully influenced by a giant power to the north – **Teotihuacán**, which dominated Central Mexico, a metropolis which grew to around 250,000 during this period. Its **armed merchants**, called *pochteca*, spread the authority of Teotihuacán as far as Petén, the Yucatán and Copán. It's unlikely that Teotihuacán launched an outright military invasion of Maya territory, but the city's influence was strong enough to precipitate fundamental changes in the region. In 378 AD, an armed merchant called Siyak K'ak' ushered in a takeover of Tikal, establishing a new dynasty, while at Copán, Yax K'uk Mo' (who was almost certainly from Teotihuacán) founded that city's royal lineage in 426 AD. These Mexicans also brought alternative religious beliefs, and new styles of ceramics, art and architecture – Kaminaljuyú was rebuilt in Teotihuacán style, and Tikal and Copán temples and stelae from the era depict Central Mexican gods.

Yet while Tikal was positioning itself within the Teotihuacán sphere of influence and dominating the Petén region, an increasingly precocious rival Maya state was emerging to the north in Campeche: **Calakmul**, "the kingdom of the snake". From the fifth century, these two states grew to eclipse all other cities in the Maya world, establishing dominion over huge swathes of the region. Each controlling sophisticated trade networks, they jostled for power and influence, a struggle which eventually erupted into open warfare once Teotihuacán influence faded in the sixth century. Calakmul formed an alliance with **Caracol** (today located in Belize) and defeated Tikal in 562 AD – detailed carvings depict elaborately costumed lords trampling on bound captives. This victory caused a 130-year hiatus, during which there was no new construction at Tikal or the smaller centres under its patronage.

The prosperity and grandeur of the **Late Classic** period (600–850 AD) reached all across the Maya lands: from Bonampak and Palenque in the west, to Labná, Sayil, Calakmul and Uxmal in the north, Cerros and Altun Ha in the east, and Copán and Quiriguá in the south, as well as hundreds of smaller centres. Bound together by a coherent religion and culture, Maya architecture, astronomy and art reached degrees of sophistication unequalled by any other pre-Columbian society. Trade prospered and populations grew – by 750 AD it's estimated that the region's people numbered around ten million. Many Maya states were larger than contemporary Western European cities, then in their "Dark Ages". Masterpieces of painted pottery and carved jade (their most precious material) were created, often to be used as funerary offerings. Shell, bone and, occasionally, marble were also exquisitely carved; temples were painted in brilliant colours, inside and out. Most of the pigments have faded long ago, but vestiges remain, enabling experts to reconstruct vivid images of the appearance of the ancient cities.

In the power politics of the era, Tikal avenged its earlier bitter defeat by overrunning Calakmul in 695 AD and reasserting its influence over its former vassal states of Río Azul and El Perú. In a furious epoch of monument building, all the six great temples that define the ceremonial heart of the city were built between 670 and 810 AD. Elsewhere across Maya lands, emergent cities including Piedras Negras, Yaxhá, Yaxchilán and Dos Pilas flourished as never before, giving rise to more and more imposing temples and palaces.

The Maya in decline

The glory days were not to last very long, however. By 750 AD political and social changes were beginning to be felt; alliances and trade links broke down, wars increased and stelae recording periods of time were carved less frequently. Cities gradually became depopulated and new construction ceased in the central area after about 830 AD. Bonampak was abandoned before its famous murals could be completed, while many of the great sites along the Usumacinta river (now part of the border between Guatemala and Mexico) were occupied by militaristic outsiders.

The reason for the decline of the Maya is not (and may never be) known, though it was probably a result of several factors. It's known that the Maya lands were already under severe pressure from deforestation by the late ninth century, when the region was struck by a terrible drought. An incredibly high population density put great strains on food production, possibly exhausting the fertility of the soil, and epidemics may have combined to cause the abandonment of city life. Some Mayanists speculate that there may have been a peasant revolt caused by mass hunger and the demands of an unproductive elite.

Whatever the causes, by the end of the Classic period there appears to have been strife and disorder throughout Mesoamerica. In the Maya heartland, virtually all the key cities were abandoned and those few that remained were reduced to a fairly primitive state. Some survived on the periphery, however, particularly in northern Belize, with Lamanai and other cities remaining occupied throughout the **Postclassic** period (900 AD to the Spanish Conquest). The settlements in the Yucatán peninsula also struggled on, and though the region escaped the worst of the depopulation, it was conquered by the militaristic Toltecs from central Mexico in 987 AD, creating a hybrid of Classic Maya culture.

The decline of Maya civilization in the Petén lowlands undoubtedly prompted an influx of population into Belize, Yucatán, and also the Guatemalan highlands to the south. These areas, formerly marginal regions of relatively little development, now contained the last vestiges of Maya culture, and it's at this time that the Guatemala area began to take on some of the local characteristics which are still in evidence today. By the end of the Classic period there were small settlements throughout the highlands, usually built on open valley floors and supporting large populations with the use of terraced farming and irrigation. Little was to change in this basic village structure for several hundred years.

Pre-conquest: the highland tribes

Towards the end of the thirteenth century, however, the great cities of the Yucatán, such as Chichén Itzá and Uxmal, which were now inhabited by groups of Toltec–Maya from the gulf coast of Mexico, were also abandoned. At around the same time there was an invasion of the central Guatemalan highlands, also by a group of **Toltec–Maya**, although whether they came from the Yucatán or from the Gulf of Mexico remains uncertain. Some argue that they travelled due south into the highlands along the Usumacinta and Chixoy river valleys, while others claim that they came from further west and entered the area via the Pacific coast, which has always been a popular route for invading armies. Their numbers were probably small but their impact was profound, and following their arrival life in the highlands was radically altered.

What once had been a relatively settled, peaceful and religious society became, under the influence of the Toltecs, fundamentally secular, aggressive and militaristic. The Toltec invaders were ruthlessly well organized and in no time at all they established themselves as a ruling elite, founding a series of competing empires. The greatest of these were the **K'iche'**, who dominated the central area and had their capital, **Utatlán**, to the west of the modern town of Santa Cruz del Quiché. Next in line were the **Kaqchikel**, who were originally based to the south of the K'iche', around the modern town of Chichicastenango, but later moved their capital to **Iximché**. On the southern shores of Lago de Atitlán the **Tz'utujil** had their capital on the lower slopes of the San Pedro volcano. To the west the **Mam** occupied the area around the modern town of Huehuetenango, with their capital at **Zaculeu**, while the northern slopes of the Cuchumatanes were home to a collection of smaller groups such as the **Chuj**, the **Q'anjob'al**, and further to the east the **Awakateko** and the **Ixil**. The eastern highlands, around the modern city of Cobán, were home to the notoriously fierce **Achi** nation, with the **Q'eqchi'** to their north, while around the modern site of Guatemala City the land was controlled by the **Poqomam**, with their capital at **Mixco Viejo**. Finally, along the Pacific coast the **Pipil**, a tribe that had also migrated from the north, occupied the lowlands.

The sheer numbers of these tribes give an impression of the extent to which the area was fragmented, and it's these same divisions, now surviving on the basis of language alone, that still shape the highlands today (see map on p.445).

The Toltec rulers probably controlled only the dominant tribes – the K'iche', the Tz'utujil, the Mam and the Kaqchikel – while their lesser neighbours were still made up entirely of people indigenous to the area. Arriving in the later part of the thirteenth century, the Toltecs must have terrorized the local K'iche'–Kaqchikel highlanders and gradually established themselves in a new, rigidly hierarchical society. They brought with them many northern traditions – elements of a Nahua-based language, new gods and an array of military skills – and fused these with local ideas. Many of the rulers' names are similar to those used in the Toltec heartland to the north, and they claimed to trace their ancestry to Quetzalcoatl, a mythical ruling dynasty from the Toltec city of Tula. Shortly after the Spanish Conquest the K'iche' wrote an account of their history, the *Popol Vuh*, in which they lay claim to a Toltec pedigree, as do the Kaqchikel in their account, *The Annals of the Kaqchikel*.

The Toltec invaders were not content with overpowering just a tribe or two, so under the direction of their new rulers the K'iche' began to expand their empire by conquering neighbouring tribes. Between 1400 and 1475 they embarked on a campaign of conquest that brought the Kaqchikel, the Mam and several other tribes under their control. At the height of their power around a million highlanders bowed to the word of the K'iche' king. But in 1475 the man who had masterminded their expansion, the great K'iche' ruler **Quicab**, died, and the empire lost much of its authority. The Kaqchikel were the first to break from the fold, anticipating the death of Quicab and moving south to a new and fortified capital, Iximché, in around 1470. Shortly afterwards the other tribes managed to escape the grip of K'iche' control and assert their independence. For the next fifty years or so the tribes were in a state of almost perpetual conflict, fighting for access to the inadequate supplies of farmland. All the archeological remains from this era give evidence of this instability; gone are the valley-floor centres of pre-Toltec times, and in their place are fortified hilltop sites, surrounded by ravines and man-made ditches.

When the Spanish arrived, the highlands were in crisis. The population had grown so fast that it had outstripped the food supply, forcing the tribes to fight for any available land in order to increase their agricultural capacity. With a growing sense of urgency both the K'iche' and the Kaqchikel had begun to encroach on the lowlands of the Pacific coast. The situation could hardly have been more favourable to the Spanish, who fostered this intertribal friction, playing one group off against another.

The Spanish conquest

While the tribes of highland Guatemala were fighting it out amongst themselves, their northern neighbours, in what is now Mexico, were confronting a new and ruthless enemy. In 1521 the Spanish conquistadors had captured the Aztec capital at Tenochtitlán and were starting to cast their net further afield.

Amidst the horrors of the Conquest there was one man, **Pedro de Alvarado**, whose evilness stood out above the rest. He could hardly have been better suited to the job – ambitious, cunning, intelligent, ingenious, dashingly handsome and ruthlessly cruel.

In 1523 Cortés despatched Alvarado to Guatemala, entreating him to use the minimum of force "and to preach matters concerning our Holy Faith". His army included 120 horsemen, 173 horses, 300 soldiers and 200 Mexican warriors, largely Tlaxcalans who had allied themselves with Cortés in the conquest of Mexico. Marching south they entered Guatemala along the Pacific coast, where they met with the first wave of resistance, a small army of K'iche' warriors. These were no match for the Spaniards, who cut through their ranks with ease. From here Alvarado turned north, taking his troops up into the highlands and through a narrow mountain pass to the Quetzaltenango valley, where they came upon the deserted city of **Xelajú**, a K'iche' outpost.

Warned of the impending arrival of the Spanish, the K'iche' had struggled to build an alliance with the other tribes, but old rivalries proved too strong and the **K'iche'** army stood alone. Three days later, on a nearby plain, they met the Spaniards in open warfare. It's said that the invading army was confronted by some 30,000 K'iche' warriors, led by **Tecún Umán** in a headdress of quetzal feathers. Despite the huge disparity in numbers, sling-shot and foot soldiers were no match for cavalry and gunpowder, and the Spaniards were once again able to wade through the Maya ranks. Legend has it that the battle was brought to a close when Alvarado met Tecún Umán in hand-to-hand conflict – and cut him down.

Accepting this temporary setback, the K'iche' decided to opt for a more diplomatic solution and invited the Spaniards to their capital **Utatlán**, where they planned to trap and destroy them. But when Alvarado saw their city he grew suspicious and took several K'iche' lords as prisoners. When hostilities erupted once again he killed the captives and had the city burnt to the ground.

Having dealt with the K'iche', Alvarado turned his attention to the other tribal groups. The **Kaqchikel**, recognizing the military superiority of the Spanish, decided to form some kind of alliance with them and as a result of this the Spaniards established their first headquarters, in 1523, alongside the Kaqchikel capital of **Iximché**. From here they ranged far and wide, overpowering the countless smaller tribes. Travelling east, Alvarado's army met the **Tz'utujil** on the shores of Lake Atitlán. Here the first battle took place at a site near the modern village of Panajachel, and the second beneath the Tz'utujil capital, at the base of the San Pedro volcano, where the Spaniards were helped by a force of Kaqchikel warriors who arrived on the scene in some 300 canoes. Moving on, the Spanish travelled south to the Pacific coast, where they overcame the **Pipil** before making their way back to Iximché.

In 1524 Alvarado sent his brother Gonzalo on an expedition against the **Mam**, who were conquered after a month-long siege during which they holed up in their fortified capital **Zaculeu**. In 1525 Alvarado himself set out to take on the **Poqomam**, at their capital **Mixco Viejo**, where he came up against another army of some 3000 warriors. Once again they proved no match for the well-disciplined Spanish ranks.

Despite this string of relatively easy gains it wasn't until well into the 1530s that Alvarado managed to assert control over the more remote parts of the highlands. Moving into the Cuchumatanes his forces were beaten back by the **Uspanteko** and met fierce opposition in the **Ixil**. And while Alvarado's soldiers were struggling to contain resistance in these isolated mountainous areas, problems also arose at the very heart of the campaign. In 1526 the Kaqchikel rose up against their Spanish allies, in response to demands for tribute; abandoning their capital the Kaqchikel moved into the mountains, from where they waged a guerrilla war against their former partners. As a result of this the Spanish were forced to abandon their base at Iximché, and moved instead to a site near the modern town of Antigua.

Here, on St Cecilia's Day, November 22, 1527, they established their first permanent capital, the city of **Santiago de los Caballeros**. For ten years indigenous labourers toiled in the construction of the new city, neatly sited at the base of the Agua volcano, putting together a cathedral, a town hall, and a palace for Alvarado. The land within the city was given out to those who had fought alongside him, and plots on the edge of town were allocated to his remaining Maya allies.

Meanwhile, one particularly thorny problem for the Spanish was presented by the **Achi** and **Q'eqchi'** Maya, who occupied what are now the Verapaz highlands. Despite all his efforts Alvarado was unable to conquer either of these tribes, who fought fiercely against the invading armies. In the end he gave up on the area, naming it *Tierra de Guerra* and abandoning all hopes of controlling it. The situation was eventually resolved by the Church. In 1537 **Fray Bartolomé de Las Casas**, the "protector of the Indians", travelled into the area in a bid to persuade the locals to accept both Christianity and Spanish authority. Within three years the priests had succeeded where Alvarado's armies had failed, and the last of the highland tribes was brought under colonial control in 1540. Thus did the area earn its name of *Verapaz*, true peace.

Alvarado himself grew tired of the Conquest, disappointed by the lack of plunder, and his reputation for brutality began to spread. He was forced to return to Spain to face charges of treason, but returned a free man with a young wife at his side. Life in the New World soon sent his bride to an early grave and Alvarado set out once again, in search of the great mineral wealth that had eluded him in Guatemala. First he travelled south to Peru, where it's said that Pizarro paid him to leave South America. He then returned to Spain once again, where he married **Beatriz de la Cueva**, his first wife's sister, and the two of them made their way back to Guatemala, where he dropped off his new bride before setting sail for the Spice Islands. Along the way he stopped in Mexico, to put down an uprising, and was crushed to death beneath a rolling horse.

From 1524 until his death in 1541 Alvarado had ruled Guatemala as a personal fiefdom, desperately seeking adventure and wealth and enslaving and abusing the local population in order to finance his urge to explore. By the time of his death all the Maya tribes had been overcome, although local uprisings, which have persisted to this day, had already started to take place.

Colonial rule

The early years of colonial rule were marked by a turmoil of uprisings and political wrangling, and while the death of Alvarado might have been expected to bring a degree of calm, it was in fact followed by fresh disaster. When Alvarado's wife, Beatriz de la Cueva, heard of his death she plunged the capital into a period of prolonged mourning. She had the entire palace painted black, inside and out, and ordered the city authorities to appoint her as the new governor. Meanwhile, the area was swept by a series of storms, and on the night of September 10, 1541, it was shaken by a massive earthquake. The sides of the Agua volcano shuddered, undermining the walls of the cone and releasing its contents. A great wall of mud and water swept down the side of the cone, and the city of Santiago was buried beneath it.

The surviving colonial authorities moved up the valley to a new site, where a second **Santiago de los Caballeros** was founded in the following year. This new city served as the administrative headquarters of the **Audiencia de Guatemala**, which was made up of six provinces: Costa Rica, Nicaragua, San Salvador, Honduras, Guatemala and Chiapas (now part of Mexico). With Alvarado out of the way the authorities began to build a new society, re-creating the splendours of the homeland. Santiago was never endowed with the same wealth or freedom as Mexico City and Lima, but it was nevertheless the centre of political and religious power for two hundred years, accumulating a superb array of arts and architecture. By the mid-eighteenth century its population had reached some 80,000. Here colonial society was at its most developed, rigidly structured along racial lines with pure-blood Spaniards at the top, indigenous slaves at the bottom, and a host of carefully defined racial strata in between. The city was regularly shaken by scandal, intrigue and earthquakes, and it was eventually destroyed in 1773 by the last of these, after which the capital was moved to its modern site.

Perhaps the greatest power in colonial Central America was the **Church**. The first religious order to reach Guatemala was the **Franciscans**, who arrived with Alvarado himself, and by 1532 the **Mercedarians** and **Dominicans** had followed suit, with the **Jesuits** arriving shortly after. **Francisco Marroquín**, the country's first bishop, rewarded these early arrivals with huge concessions, including land and indigenous people, which later enabled them to earn fortunes from sugar, wheat and indigo, income boosted by the fact that they were exempt from tax. In later years a whole range of other orders arrived in Santiago, and religious rivalry became an important shaping force in the colony. The wealth and power of the Church fostered the splendour of the colonial capital while ruthlessly exploiting the native people and their land. In Santiago alone there were some eighty churches, and alongside these were schools, convents, hospitals, hermitages, craft centres and colleges. The religious orders became the main benefactors of the arts, amassing a wealth of tapestry, jewels, sculpture and painting, and staging concerts, fiestas and endless religious processions. Religious persecution was at its worst between 1572 and 1580, when the office of the **Inquisition** set up in Santiago, seeking out those who had failed to receive the faith and dealing with them harshly. Not much is known about the precise nature of the Guatemalan inquisition, however, as no written records have survived.

By the eighteenth century the power of the Church had started to get out of control, and the Spanish kings began to impose taxes on the religious orders and to limit their power and freedom. The conflict between Church and State came to a head in 1767, when Carlos III banished the Jesuits from the Spanish colonies.

The Spanish must have been disappointed with their conquest of Central America as it offered none of the instant plunder that had been found in Mexico and Peru. They found small amounts of silver around the modern town of Huehuetenango and a few grains of gold in the rivers of Honduras, but nothing that could compare with the vast resources of Potosí (a huge silver mine in Bolivia) or highland Mexico. In Central America the **colonial economy** was based on agriculture. The coastal area produced cacao, tobacco, cotton and, most valuable of all, indigo; the highlands were grazed with sheep and goats; and cattle, specially imported from Spain, were raised on coastal ranches. In the low-lands of Petén and the jungles of the lower Motagua valley, the mosquitoes and forests remained unchallenged, although here and there certain aspects of the forest were developed; chicle, the raw material of chewing gum, was bled from the sapodilla trees, as was sarsaparilla, used to treat syphilis.

At the heart of the colonial economy was the system of *repartamientos*, where-by the ruling classes were granted the right to extract labour from the indige-nous population. It was this that established the system whereby the Maya pop-ulation was transported to the Pacific coast to work the plantations, a pattern that is still a tremendous burden today (see box on p.231).

Meanwhile, in the capital it was graft and corruption that controlled the movement of money, with titles and appointments sold to the highest bidder. All of the colony's wealth was funnelled through the city, and it was only here that the monetary economy really developed.

The impact of the Conquest was perhaps at its most serious in the highlands, where the **Maya population** had their lives totally restructured. The first stage in this process was the *reducción*, whereby scattered native communities were combined into new Spanish-style towns and villages. Between 1543 and 1600 some 700 new settlements were created, each based around a Catholic church. Ostensibly, the purpose of this was to enable the Church to work on its new-found converts, but it also had the effect of pooling the available labour and making its exploitation that much easier. The highland villages were still bound up in an ancient system of subsistence farming, although its pattern was now disturbed by demands for tribute.

Maya **social structures** were also profoundly altered by post-conquest changes. The great central authorities that had previously dominated were now eradicated, replaced by local structures based in the new villages. *Caciques* (local chiefs) and *alcaldes* (mayors) now held the bulk of local power, which was bestowed on them by the Church. In the distant corners of the highlands, how-ever, priests were few and far between, only visiting the villages from time to time. Those that they left in charge developed not only their own power struc-tures but also their own religion, mixing the new with the old. By the start of the nineteenth century the Maya population had largely recovered from the initial impact of the Conquest, and in many places these local structures became increasingly important. In each village *cofradías* (brotherhood groups) were entrusted with the care of saints, while *principales* (village elders) held the bulk of traditional authority, a situation that still persists today. Throughout the highlands, village uprisings became increasingly commonplace as the new indigenous culture became stronger and stronger.

Perhaps even more serious for the indigenous population than any social changes were the **diseases** that arrived with the conquistadors. Waves of plague, typhoid and fever swept through a population without any natural resistance to them. In the worst-hit areas the native population was cut by some ninety percent, and in many parts of the country their numbers were halved.

Two centuries of colonial rule totally reshaped the structure of Guatemalan society, giving it new cities, a new religion, a transformed economy and a racist hierarchy. Nevertheless, the impact of colonial rule was perhaps less marked than in many other parts of Latin America. Only two sizeable cities had emerged and the outlying areas had received little attention from the colonial authorities. While the indigenous population had been ruthlessly exploited and suffered enormous losses at the hands of foreign weapons and imported diseases, its cul-ture was never eradicated. It simply absorbed the symbols and ideas of the new Spanish ideology, creating a dynamic synthesis that is neither Maya nor Catholic.

Independence

The racist nature of colonial rule had given birth to deep dissatisfaction amongst many groups in Central America. Spain's policy was to keep wealth and power in the hands of those born in Spain (*chapetones*), a policy that left growing numbers of Creoles (including those of Spanish blood born in Guatemala) and Mestizos (of mixed blood) resentful and hungry for power and change. (For the majority of the indigenous people, both power and wealth were way beyond their reach.) As the Spanish departed, Guatemalan politics was dominated by a struggle between **conservatives**, who sided with the Church and the Crown, and **liberals**, who advocated a secular and more egalitarian state. One result of the split was that independence was not a clean break, but was declared several times.

The spark, as throughout Spanish America, was Napoleon's invasion of Spain and the abdication of King Fernando VII. In the chaos that followed a liberal constitution was imposed on Spain in 1812 and a mood of reform swept through the colonies. At the time Central America was under the control of **Brigadier Don Gabino Gainza**, the last of the Captains General. His one concern was to maintain the status quo, in which he was strongly backed by the wealthy landowners and the church hierarchy. Bowing to demands for independence, but still hoping to preserve the power structure, Gainza signed a formal **Act of Independence** on September 15, 1821, enshrining the authority of the Church and seeking to preserve the old order under new leadership. Augustín de Iturbide, the short-lived emperor of newly independent Mexico, promptly sent troops to annex Guatemala to the Mexican empire, a union which was to last less than a year.

A second Declaration of Independence, in 1823, joined the Central American states in a loose **federation**, adopting a constitution modelled on that of the United States, abolishing slavery and advocating liberal reforms. The federation, however, was doomed by the struggle between and within each of the countries. The first president of the federation was **General Manuel José Acre**, a Salvadorean, who fought bitterly with his party and then founded a government of his own. This prompted others to do the same and the liberals of Salvador, Honduras and Guatemala united under the leadership of **Francisco Morazán**, a Honduran general. Under his rule **Mariano Gálvez** became the chief of state in Guatemala: religious orders were abolished, the death penalty done away with, and trial by jury, a general school system, civil marriage and the Lívingston law code were all instituted.

The liberal era, however, lasted little longer than the Mexican empire, and the reforming government was overthrown by a revolt from the mountains. Throughout the turmoil of independence, life in the highlands remained harsh, with the indigenous population still bearing the burdens imposed on them by two centuries of colonial rule. In 1823 a cholera epidemic swept through the entire country, killing thousands and only adding to the misery of life in the mountains. Seething with discontent, the Maya were united behind an illiterate but charismatic leader, the 23-year-old **Rafael Carrera**, under whose command they marched on Guatemala City.

Carrera respected no authority other than that of the Church, and his immediate reforms swept aside the changes instituted by the liberal government. The religious orders were restored to their former position and traditional Spanish titles were reinstated. The conservatives had little in common with Carrera but they could see that he offered to uphold their position with a tremendous weight of popular support, and hence they sided with him. Under Carrera Guatemala fought a bitter war against Morazán and the federation, eventually establishing itself as an independent republic in 1847. Carrera's other great challenge came from the state of **Los Altos**, which included much of the western highlands and proclaimed itself an independent republic in defiance of him: it was a short-lived threat, however, and the state was soon brought back into the republic.

In 1865 Carrera died, at the age of fifty, leaving the country ravaged by the chaos of his tyranny and inefficiency. He was succeeded by **Vicente Cerna**, another conservative, who was to rule for the next six years.

Meanwhile, the liberal opposition was gathering momentum yet again and 1867 saw the first **liberal uprising**, led by **Serpio Cruz**. His bid for power was unsuccessful but it inspired two young liberals, Justo Rufino Barrios and Francisco Cruz, to follow suit. In the next few years they mounted several other unsuccessful revolts, and in 1870 Serpio Cruz was captured and hanged.

Ruffino Barrios and the coffee boom

1871 marked a major turning point in Guatemalan politics. In that year Rufino Barrios and Miguel García Granados set out from Mexico with an army of just 45 men, entering Guatemala via the small border town of Cuilco. The **liberal revolution** thus set in motion was an astounding success, the army growing by the day as it approached the capital, which was finally taken on June 30, 1871. Granados took the helm of the new liberal administration but held the presidency for just a few years, surrounding himself with ageing comrades and offering only very limited reforms.

Meanwhile, out in the district of Los Altos, **Rufino Barrios**, now a local military commander, was infuriated by the lack of action. In 1872 he marched his troops to the capital and installed them in the San José barracks, demanding immediate elections. These were granted and he won with ease. Barrios was a charismatic leader with tyrannical tendencies (monuments throughout the country testify to his sense of his own importance) who regarded himself as the great reformer and was intent on making sweeping changes. Above all he was a man of action. His most immediate acts were classic liberal gestures: the restructuring of the education system and an attack on the Church. The University of San Carlos was secularized and modernized, while clerics were forbidden to wear the cloth and public religious processions were banned. The Church was outraged and excommunicated Barrios, which prompted him to expel the archbishop in retaliation.

The new liberal perspective, though, was instilled with a deep arrogance and Barrios would tolerate no opposition, regarding his own racial and economic outlook as absolute. In order to ensure the success of his reforms he developed an effective network of secret police and struggled to make the army increasingly professional. In later years he founded the *politecnica*, an academy for young officers, and the army became an essential part of his political power base.

Alongside all this Barrios set about reforming agriculture, in which he presided over a boom period, largely as a result of the cultivation of **coffee**. It was this more than anything else that distinguished the era and was to fundamentally reshape the country. When the liberals came to power coffee already accounted for half the value of the country's exports, and by 1884 the volume of output had increased five times. To foster this expansion Barrios founded a Ministry of Development, which extended the railway network (begun in 1880), established a national bank, and developed the ports of Champerico, San José and Iztapa to handle the growth in exports. Between 1870 and 1900 the volume of foreign trade increased twenty times.

All this had an enormous impact on Guatemalan **society**. Many of the new plantations were owned and run by German immigrants, and indeed the majority of the coffee eventually found its way to Germany. The newcomers soon formed a powerful elite and, although most of the Germans were later forced out of Guatemala (during World War II), their impact can still be felt, directly in the Verapaz highlands, and more subtly in the continuing presence of an extremely powerful clique. Their wealth based on the income from plantation farming, and they are still central to political life in Guatemala. The new liberal perspective maintained that foreign ideas were superior to indigenous ones, and while immigrants were welcomed with open arms the Maya population was still regarded as hopelessly inferior.

Indigenous society was also deeply affected by the needs of the coffee boom, and it was here that the new crop had the most damaging and lasting effect. Under the previous regime landowners had complained that the native population was reluctant to work on the plantations and that this endangered the coffee crop. Barrios was quick to respond to their needs and instituted a system of **forced labour**. In 1876 he ordered local political chiefs to make the necessary workers available: up to one-quarter of the male population could be despatched to work on the fincas; in addition to this the landowners continued to employ their old methods and debt peonage spread throughout the highlands. Conditions on the fincas were appalling and the workforce was treated with utter contempt.

As a result of the coffee boom many Maya lost not only their freedom but also their land. From 1873 onwards the government began confiscating land that was either unused or communally owned, and selling it to the highest bidder. In some instances villages were given small tracts of land taken from unproductive fincas, but in the vast majority of cases it was the Maya who lost their land to large coffee plantations. Huge amounts of the country were seized, and land that had been communally owned for centuries was gobbled up by the new wave of agribusiness. In many areas the villagers rose up in defiance, and there were significant **revolts** throughout the western highlands. In Momostenango some 500 armed men faced the authorities, only to find their village overrun by troops and their homes burnt to the ground. In Cantel troops shot all of the village officials, who were campaigning against plans to build a textile factory on their land. Throughout the latter years of the nineteenth and the early ones of the twentieth century, villages continued to rise up in defiance of demands on their land and labour. At the same time the loss of their most productive land forced the Maya to become dependent on seasonal labour, while attacks on their communities drove them to increasing introspection.

Jorge Ubico and the banana empire

Rufino Barrios was eventually killed in 1885 while fighting to re-create a unified Central America, and was succeeded by a string of short-lived, like-minded presidents. The next to hold power for any time was **Manuel Estrada Cabrera**, a stern authoritarian who restricted union organization and supported the interests of big business. He ruled from 1898 until he was overthrown in 1920, by which time he was on the verge of insanity.

Meanwhile, a new and exceptionally powerful player was becoming involved: the **United Fruit Company**, whose influence asserted itself over much of Central America in the early decades of the twentieth century and which was to exercise tremendous power over the next fifty years. The story of the United Fruit Company starts in Costa Rica, where a man named Minor Keith was contracted to build a railway from San José to the Pacific coast. Running short of money he was forced to plant bananas on land granted as part of the railway contract. The business proved so profitable that Keith merged his own Tropical Trading and Transport Company with his main rival The Boston Fruit company, to form the United Fruit Company.

The Company first moved into Guatemala in 1901, when it bought a small tract of land on which to grow bananas, and in 1904 it was awarded a contract to complete the railway from Guatemala City to Puerto Barrios. The company was also granted 100ft on either side of the track, exempted from paying any tax for the next 99 years, and assured that the government wouldn't interfere with its activities. In 1912 ownership of the Pacific railway network fell to the company and, as it already controlled the main Caribbean port, this gave it a virtual monopoly over transport. It was around this time that large-scale banana cultivation really took off, and by 1934 United Fruit controlled a massive amount of land, exporting around 3.5 million bunches of bananas annually and reaping vast profits. In 1941 some 25,000 Guatemalans were employed in the banana industry.

The power of the United Fruit Company was by no means restricted to agriculture, and its influence was so pervasive that the company earned itself the nickname *El Pulpo*, "the octopus". Control of the transport network brought with it control of the coffee trade: by 1930 28 percent of the country's coffee output was handled by the company's Caribbean port, Puerto Barrios. During the 1930s it cost as much to ship coffee from Guatemala to New Orleans as it did from Río de Janeiro to New Orleans.

Against this background the power of the Guatemalan government was severely limited, with the influence of the United States increasing alongside that of the United Fruit Company. In 1919 Guatemala faced a financial crisis and President Cabrera was ousted by a coup the following year. He was replaced by **Carlos Herrera**, who represented the Union Party, a rare compromise between liberal and conservative politicians. Herrera refused to use the traditional weapons of tyranny and his reforms threatened to terminate United Fruit Company contracts. As a result of this Herrera was to last barely more than a year, replaced by **General José María Orellano** in December 1921. Orellano had no qualms about repressive measures and his minister of war, Jorge Ubico, killed some 290 opponents in 1926, the year in which Orellano died of a heart attack. His death prompted a bitter power struggle between

Jorge Ubico, a fierce radical, and **Lazaro Chacón** who won the day and was elected as the new liberal president. In the next few years indigenous farmers began to express their anger at the United Fruit Company monopoly, while the company demanded the renewal of longstanding contracts, squeezing Chacon from both sides. His rule came to an end in 1930, when he suffered a stroke.

The way was now clear for **Jorge Ubico**, a charismatic leader who was well connected with the ruling and land-owning elite. Ubico had risen fast through the ranks of local government as *jefe político* in Alta Verapaz and Retalhuleu (greatly assisted by the patronage of his godfather Rufino Barrios), earning a reputation for efficiency and honesty. As president, however, he inherited financial disaster. Guatemala had been badly hit by the Depression, accumulating debts of some US$5 million: in response Ubico fought hard to expand the export market for Guatemalan produce, managing to sign trade agreements that exempted local coffee and bananas from import duties in the United States. But increased trade with the great American power was only possible at the expense of traditional links with Europe.

Within Guatemala Ubico steadfastly supported the United Fruit Company and the interests of US business. This relationship was of such importance that by 1940 ninety percent of all Guatemalan exports was being sold in the United States. Trade and diplomacy drew Guatemala ever closer to the United States, a relationship exemplified when Ubico, against his will, was forced to bow to US pressure for the expulsion of German landowners in the run-up to World War II.

Internally, Ubico embarked on a radical programme of reform, including a sweeping drive against corruption and a massive road-building effort, which bought him great popularity in the provinces. Despite his liberal pretensions, however, Ubico sided firmly with big business when the chips were down, always offering his assistance to the United Fruit Company and other sections of the landowning elite. The system of debt peonage was replaced by the **vagrancy law**, under which all landless peasants were forced to work 150 days a year. If they weren't needed by the fincas then their labour was used in the road-building programme or some other public works scheme. The power of landowners was further reinforced by a 1943 law that gave them the power to shoot poachers and vandals, and in effect landowners were given total authority over their workforce. Throughout his period of office Ubico ignored the rights and needs of the peasant population, who were still regarded as ignorant and backward, and as a result of this there were continued uprisings in the late 1930s and early 1940s.

Internal security was another obsession that was to dominate Ubico's years in office, as he became increasingly paranoid. He maintained that he was a reincarnation of Napoleon and was fascinated by all aspects of the military: he operated a network of spies and informers whom he regularly used to unleash waves of repression, particularly in the run-up to elections. In 1934, when he discovered an assassination plan, three hundred people were killed in just two days. To prevent any further opposition he registered all printing presses in the country and made discipline the cornerstone of state education.

But while Ubico tightened his grip on every aspect of government, the rumblings of opposition grew louder. In 1944 discontent erupted in a wave of student violence, and Ubico was finally forced to resign after fourteen years of tyrannical rule. Power was transferred to **Juan Frederico Ponce Viades**, who attempted to continue in the same style, but by the end of the year he was also faced with open revolt, and finally the pair of them were driven into exile.

Ten years of "spiritual socialism"

The overthrow of Jorge Ubico released a wave of opposition that had been bottled up throughout his rule. Students, professionals and young military officers demanded democracy and freedom. It was a mood that was to transform Guatemalan politics and was so extreme a contrast to previous governments that the handover was dubbed **the 1944 revolution**.

Power was initially passed to a joint military and civilian junta, elections were planned, and in March 1945 a new constitution was instituted, extending suffrage to include all adults and prohibiting the president from standing for a second term of office. In the elections **Juan José Arévalo**, a teacher, won the presidency with 85 percent of the vote. His political doctrine was dubbed "spiritual socialism", and he immediately set about effecting much-needed structural reforms. Under a new budget, a third of the government's income was allocated to social welfare, to be spent on the construction of schools and hospitals, a programme of immunization, and a far-reaching literacy campaign. The vagrancy laws were abolished, a national development agency was founded, and in 1947 a labour code was adopted, granting workers the right to strike and union representation.

The expulsion of German plantation owners during World War II had placed several large fincas in the hands of the state, and under Arévalo some of these were turned into co-operatives, while new laws protected tenant farmers from eviction. Other policies were intended to promote industrial and agricultural development: technical assistance and credit were made available to peasant farmers and there was some attempt to colonize Petén.

In Arévalo's final years the pace of reform slackened somewhat as he concentrated on consolidating the gains made in early years and evading various attempts to overthrow him. Despite his popularity Arévalo was still wary of the traditional elite: church leaders, old-school army officers and wealthy landowners all resented the new wave of legislation, and there were repeated coup attempts.

Elections were scheduled for 1950 and during the run-up the two main candidates were **Colonel Francisco Arana** and **Colonel Jacobo Arbenz**, both military members of the junta that had taken over at the end of the Ubico era. But in 1949 Arana, who was favoured by the right, was assassinated. Suspicion fell on Arbenz, who was backed by the peasant organizations and unions, but there was no hard proof. For the actual vote Arana was replaced by **Brigadier Ydígoras Fuentes**, an army officer from the Ubico years.

Arbenz won the election with ease, taking 65 percent of the vote, and declared that he would transform the country into an independent capitalist nation and raise the standard of living. But the process of "overthrowing feudal society and ending economic dependency" was to lead to a direct confrontation between the new government and the American corporations that still dominated the economy.

Aware of the size of the task that faced him, Arbenz enlisted the support of the masses, encouraging the participation of peasants in the programme of agrarian reform and inciting the militancy of students and unions. He also attempted to break the great monopolies, building a state-run hydroelectric plant to rival the American-owned generating company and a highway to compete with the railway to the Caribbean, and planning a new port alongside Puerto Barrios, which was still owned by the United Fruit Company. At the same time Arbenz began a series of suits against foreign corporations, seeking unpaid taxes. Internally, these measures aroused a mood of national pride, but they were strongly resented by the American companies whose empires were under attack.

Che Guevara in Guatemala

Ernesto "Che" Guevara arrived in Guatemala on New Year's Eve 1953, broke and with no place to stay. He had graduated as a doctor in his native Argentina five months previously, and immediately left to explore Latin America – hitching rides, sleeping rough and cadging meals along the way.

The future *comandante* spent eight months in Guatemala City, living in Zona 1, the historic heart of the capital in a number of cheap hospedajes. Most of his days were spent in a fruitless search for work as a doctor, surviving on the generosity of the people he met and scratching a meagre income from a series of casual jobs: teaching a few Spanish classes, doing some translation work and peddling encyclopedias and images of the black Christ of Esquipulas in the capital's streets.

But Guevara had not just come to Guatemala to look for work. In the early 1950s, Guatemala City was a mecca for political idealists, communists and budding revolutionaries from Latin America, all attracted to the country by the reformist president Arbenz (see opposite) and his party's doctrine of "spiritual socialism". In a letter to his aunt, Guevara wrote of his travels through the region, and avowed his intentions to challenge American hegemony:

Along the way, I had the opportunity to pass through the dominions of the United Fruit ... I have sworn before a picture of the old and mourned comrade Stalin that I won't rest until I see these capitalist octopuses annihilated. In Guatemala I will perfect myself and achieve what I need to be an authentic revolutionary.

One of the first people he met in Guatemala was Hildea Gadea, a well-connected young Peruvian who was to become his first wife. Hildea was an exiled member of Peru's ARPA rebels, and introduced Che to a number of other young political activists, including Rolando Morán who was to become the leader of the Guatemalan EGP guerrillas (see p.148). Guevara was to form his political consciousness in Guatemala City, his beliefs shaped by hours reading Marx, Trotsky and Mao, an instinctive hatred of USA imperialism, and marathon theological debates. Of all the myriad Latino leftist groups in the city, it was the Cubans who most impressed Che, for they alone had actually launched an armed uprising against a dictatorship (the failed Moncada assault after Batista had cancelled the 1952 Cuban elections). Guevara met the Cuban Ñico López who would later introduce him to Fidel and Raúl Castro, and with whom he would later regroup in Mexico, set sail for Cuba in 1956 and initiate the revolution.

Guevara remained in Guatemala City throughout the attacks on the capital in June 1954. The young radical wrote to his family denouncing the indecisiveness of the Arbenz government and its inability to organize local militias to defend the country. He swore allegiance to the Soviet Union, and joined the Communist Party while holed up in the Argentine embassy, awaiting deportation after Arbenz had been humiliatingly deposed.

Many of the young Guatemala-based comrades later reassembled in Mexico City where they digested the downfall of Arbenz. Perhaps the biggest lesson Guevara learned was that rather than attempt to negotiate with Washington, it was essential to combat American interference with armed resistance. He was convinced that Guatemala had been betrayed "*inside and out*", and argued that future revolutionaries must be prepared to establish their internal authority by force, and eliminate enemies using repression and firing squads if necessary – "*victory will be conquered with blood and fire, there can be no pardon for the traitors*".

The situation became even more serious with the **law of agrarian reform** passed in July 1952, which stated that idle and state-owned land would be distributed to the landless. Some of this land was to be rented out for a lifetime lease, but the bulk of it was handed over outright to the new owners, who were to pay a small percentage of its market value. The former owners of the land were to be compensated with government bonds, but the value of the land was calculated on the basis of the tax they had been paying, usually a fraction of its true value.

The new laws outraged landowners, despite the fact that they were given the right to appeal. Between 1953 and 1954 around 884,000 hectares were redistributed to the benefit of some 100,000 peasant families. It was the first time since the arrival of the Spanish that the government had responded to the needs of the indigenous population, although some studies suggest that the whole issue confused them, and they were unsure how to respond. The landowner most seriously affected by the reforms was the United Fruit Company, which only farmed around fifteen percent of its land holdings, and lost about half of its property.

As the pace of reform gathered, Arbenz began to take an increasingly radical stance. In 1951 the Communist Party was granted legal status, and in the next election four party members were elected to the legislature. But the Arbenz government was by no means a communist government, although it remained staunchly anti-American.

In the United States the press repeatedly accused the new Guatemalan government of being a communist beachhead in Central America, and the US government attempted to intervene on behalf of the United Fruit Company. Tellingly, Allen Dulles, the new director of the CIA, also happened to be a member of the fruit company's board.

In 1953 President Eisenhower finally approved plans to overthrow the government. The CIA set up a small military invasion of Guatemala to depose Arbenz and install an alternative administration more suited to their tastes. A ragtag army of exiles and mercenaries was put together in Honduras, and on June 18, 1954, Guatemala City was bombed with leaflets demanding the resignation of Arbenz. Aware that the army would never support him, Arbenz had bought a boatload of Czechoslovakian arms, hoping to arm the people, but the guns were intercepted by the CIA before they reached Puerto Barrios. On the night of June 18, Guatemala was strafed with machine-gun fire while the invading army, described by Arbenz as "a heterogeneous Fruit Company expeditionary force", was getting closer to the city by the hour.

On June 27 Arbenz declared that he was relinquishing the presidency to **Colonel Carlos Enrique Díaz**, the army chief of staff. And on July 3 John Peurifoy, the American Ambassador to Guatemala, flew the new government to Guatemala aboard a US Air Force plane. Guatemala's attempt to escape the clutches of outside intervention and bring about social change had been brought to an abrupt end.

Counter-revolution and military rule

Following the overthrow of Arbenz it was the army that rose to fill the power vacuum, and it was to dominate politics for the next thirty years, sending the country into a spiral of violence and economic decline. Since the time of Jorge Ubico the army had become increasingly professional and political, and now it began to receive increasing amounts of US aid, expanding its influence to include a wide range of public works and infrastructure projects.

In 1954 the American ambassador had persuaded a provisional government to accept **Castillo Armas** as the new president, and the gains of the previous ten years were immediately swept away. Hardest hit was the indigenous population, who had enjoyed the greatest benefits under the Arbenz administration, as ladino rule was firmly reinstated. The constitution of 1945 was revoked and replaced by a more restrictive version; illiterates were disenfranchised, left-wing parties were outlawed, and large numbers of unionists and agrarian reformers were simply executed. Restrictions placed on foreign investment were lifted and all the land that had been confiscated was returned to its previous owners. Meanwhile, Armas surrounded himself with old-style Ubico supporters, attempting to reinstate the traditional elite and drawing heavily on US assistance in order to develop the economy.

To lend a degree of legitimacy to the administration Armas held a referendum in which voters were given the chance to support his rule (though what else was on offer was never made clear). With or without popular support, however, the new government had only limited backing from the armed forces, and coup rumblings continued throughout his period of office, which was brought to a close in 1957, when he was shot by his own bodyguard.

The assassination was followed by several months of political turmoil, out of which **Ydígoras** (who had stood against Arbenz in 1954, but declined an offer to lead the CIA invasion) emerged as the next president, representing the National Democratic Renovation Party. Ydigoras was to rule for five years, a period that was marked by corruption, incompetence, outrageous patronage and economic decline caused by a fall in coffee prices, although as some compensation the formation of the Central American Common Market helped to boost light industry. The government was so disastrous that it prompted opposition even from within the ranks of the elite. In 1960 a group of young military officers, led by **Marco Yon Sosa** and **Turcios Lima**, attempted, without success, to take control, while in 1962 a large section of the Congress withdrew its support from the government.

Ydígoras was eventually overthrown when Arévalo threatened to return to Guatemala and contest the 1963 elections, which he might well have won. The possibility of another socialist government sent shock waves through the establishment in both Guatemala and the United States, and John F. Kennedy gave the go-ahead for another coup. In 1963 the army once more took control, under the leadership of **Peralta Azurdia**.

Peralta was president for just three years, during which he fiddled with the constitution and took his time in restoring the electoral process. Meanwhile, the authoritarian nature of his government came up against the first wave of armed resistance. Two failed coupsters from 1960, Turcios Lima and Marco Yon Sosa, both army officers, took to the eastern highlands and waged a **guerrilla war** against the army. Trained in counterinsurgency by the US army in Panamá and both in their early twenties, they began to attack local army posts. A second organization, FAR, emerged later that year, and the Guatemalan Labour Party (PGT) formed a shaky alliance with the guerrillas, attempting to represent their grievances in the political arena and advocating a return to Arévalo's rule.

Peralta finally lost control in the 1966 elections, which were won by **Julio Cesar Montenegro** of the centre-left Partido Revolucionario. Before taking office, however, Montenegro was forced to sign a pact with the military, obliging him to obey their instructions and giving the army a totally free hand in all affairs of national security. Montenegro was elected on July 1, and his first act was to offer an amnesty to the guerrillas; when this was rejected a ruthless counterinsurgency campaign swung into action (a pattern of events that was repeated in the early 1980s under Ríos Montt).

Under the command of Colonel Arana Osorio, "the Jackal of Zacapa", specially trained units, backed by US advisers, undermined peasant support for the guerrillas by terrorizing the local population. The guerrillas were soon forced to spend much of their time on the move, and further damage was done to the movement by the death of Turcios Lima, in a car crash. By the end of the decade the guerrilla movement had been virtually eradicated in the eastern highlands, and its activities, greatly reduced, shifted to Guatemala City, where the US ambassador was assassinated by FAR rebels in 1968.

Meanwhile, Montenegro declared his government to be "the third government of the revolution", aligning it with the socialist administrations of Arévalo and Arbenz. But despite the support of reformers, students, professionals and a large section of the middle classes, his hands were tied by the influence of the army. Above all else the administration was marked by the rise of political violence and the increasing power of an alliance between the army and the MLN, a right-wing political party. Political assassination became commonplace as "**death squads**" such as the *Mano Blanco* and *Ojo por Ojo* operated with impunity, killing peasant leaders, students, unionists and academics.

Economic decline and political violence

The history of Guatemala between 1970 and the early 1990s was dominated by electoral fraud and political violence. At the heart of the crisis was the injustice and inequality of Guatemalan society: while the country remained fairly prosperous the benefits of its success never reached the poor, who were denied access to land, education or health care, with many of their number forced instead to work in the coastal plantations that fuelled the capital's affluence. The victims of this system had little to lose, while the ruling elite refused to concede any ground.

In the 1970 elections the power of the military and the far right (represented by the MLN and PID) was confirmed, and **Colonel Arana Osorio**, who had directed the counterinsurgency campaign in the east, was elected president. The turnout was under fifty percent, of which Arana polled just under half, giving him the votes of around four percent of the population (bearing in mind that only a small percentage was enfranchised).

Once in power he set about eradicating armed opposition, declaring that "if it is necessary to turn the country into a cemetery in order to pacify it, I will not hesitate to do so". The reign of terror, conducted by both the armed forces and the "death squads", reached unprecedented levels. Once again the violence was to claim the lives of students, academics, opposition politicians, union leaders and agrarian reformers. According to one estimate there were 15,000 political killings during the first three years of Arana's rule.

The next round of presidential elections was held in 1974, and was contended by a broad coalition of centre-left parties under the banner of the National

Opposition Front (FNO), headed by General Efraín Ríos Montt. The campaign was marked by manipulation and fraud on the part of the right, who pronounced their candidate, **Kjell Laugerud**, as the winner. The result caused uproar, and for several days the situation was extremely tense. Ríos Montt was eventually persuaded to accept defeat and packed off to a diplomatic post in Spain, although many had hoped that reforming elements within the armed forces would secure his right to the presidency.

Meanwhile, the feared severity of the Laugerud regime never materialized and instead he began to offer limited reforms, incorporating Christian Democrats into his government. Greater tolerance was shown towards union organizations and the co-operative movement, and the government launched a plan for the colonization of Petén and the Northern Transversal Strip in an attempt to provide more land. The army, though, continued as ever to consolidate its authority, spreading its influence across a wider range of business and commercial interests and challenging Laugerud's moderation.

All of this was interrupted by a massive **earthquake** on February 4, 1976. The quake left around 23,000 dead, 77,000 injured and a million homeless. For the most part it was the homes of the poor, built from makeshift materials and on unstable ground, that suffered the most, while subsistence farmers were caught out just as they were about to plant their corn. On the Caribbean coast Puerto Barrios was almost totally destroyed and remained cut off from the capital for several months.

In the wake of the earthquake, during the process of reconstruction, fresh centres of regional control emerged on both sides of the political spectrum. The electoral process seemed to offer no respite from the injustice that was at the heart of Guatemalan society, and many of the victims felt the time had come to take action. A revived trade union organization championed the cause of the majority, while a new guerrilla organization, the Guerrilla Army of the Poor (EGP), emerged in the Ixil area, and army operations became increasingly ferocious. In 1977 President Carter suspended all military aid to Guatemala because of the country's appalling human rights record.

In the following year, 1978, Guatemala's elections were once again dominated by the army, who engineered a victory for **Brigadier General Fernando Lucas García**, who had served as defence minister in the Laugerud administration. The run-up to the elections was marred by serious disturbances in Guatemala City, after bus fares were doubled. Lucas García promised to bring the situation under control, and things took a significant turn for the worse as the new administration unleashed a fresh wave of violence. All opposition groups met with severe repression, as did journalists, trade unionists and academics. Conditions throughout the country were deteriorating rapidly, and the economy was badly affected by a fall in commodity prices, while several guerrilla armies were developing strongholds in the highlands.

As chaos threatened, the army resorted to extreme measures, and within a month there was a major massacre. In the village of **Panzós**, Alta Verapaz, a group of local people arriving for a meeting were cut down by soldiers, leaving a hundred of them dead (see p.315). In Guatemala City the situation became so dangerous that political parties were driven underground. Two leading members of the Social Democrats, who were expected to win the next election, lost their lives in 1979. Once they were out of the way the government turned on the Christian Democrats, killing more than a hundred of their members and forcing Vinicio Cerezo, the party's leader, into hiding.

Throughout the Lucas administration the **army** became increasingly powerful and the death toll rose steadily. In rural areas the war against the guerrillas was reaching new heights as army casualties rose to 250 a month, and the demand for conscripts grew rapidly. The four main guerrilla groups had an estimated 6000 combatants and some 250,000 unarmed collaborators. Under the Lucas administration the horrors of **repression** were at their most intense, both in the highlands and in the cities. The victims again included students, journalists, academics, politicians, priests, lawyers, teachers, unionists, and above all peasant farmers, massacred in their hundreds. Accurate figures are impossible to calculate but it's estimated that around 25,000 Guatemalans were killed during the four years of the Lucas regime.

But while high-ranking officers became more and more involved in big business and political wrangling, the officers in the field began to feel deserted. Here there was growing discontent as a result of repeated military failures, inefficiency and a shortage of supplies, despite increased military aid from Israel.

Ríos Montt

The 1982 elections were again manipulated by the far right, who ensured a victory for **Aníbal Guevara**. However, on March 23 a group of young military officers led a successful coup, which installed **General Efraín Ríos Montt** (who had been denied the post in 1974) as the head of a three-member junta. The coup leaders argued that they had been left with no option as the ruling elite had overridden the electoral process three times in the last eight years, and the takeover was supported by the majority of the opposition parties.

Ríos Montt was a committed Christian, a member of the Iglesia del Verbo, and throughout his rule Sunday-night television was dominated by presidential sermons. Above all he was determined to restore law and order, eradicate corruption, and defeat the guerrillas, with the ultimate aim of restoring "authentic democracy". Government officials were issued with identity cards inscribed with the words "I do not steal. I do not lie."

In the immediate aftermath of the coup things improved dramatically. Repression dropped overnight in the cities, a welcome relief after the turmoil of the Lucas regime. Corrupt police and army officers were forced to resign, and trade and tourism began to return.

However, in the highlands the war intensified, as Ríos Montt declared that he would defeat the guerrillas by Christmas. Throughout June they were offered **amnesty** if they turned themselves in to the authorities, but once the month had passed (and only a handful had accepted) the army descended on the highlands with renewed vigour. Montt had instituted a new "code of conduct" for the army, binding soldiers not to "take a pin from the villagers". The army set about destroying the guerrillas' infrastructure by undermining their support within the community. In those villages that had been "pacified" the local men were forcibly organized into Civil Defence Patrols (PACs), armed with ancient rifles, and told to patrol the countryside. Those who refused were denounced as "subversives". Thus the people of the villages were forced to take sides, caught between the attraction of guerrilla propaganda and the sheer brutality of the armed forces.

Ríos Montt's bizarre blend of stern morality and ruthlessness was as successful as it was murderous, and the army was soon making significant gains against the guerrillas. In late 1982 President Reagan, deciding that Guatemala had been given a "bum rap", restored American military aid. Meanwhile, the "state of siege" became a "state of alarm", under which special tribunals were given the power to try and execute suspects. By the middle of 1983 Ríos Montt was facing growing pressure from all sides. Leaders of the Catholic Church were outraged by the influx of evangelical preachers, while politicians, business people, farmers and professionals were angered by the lack of progress towards democratic rule, and landowners were frightened by rumours of land reform.

In August 1983 Ríos Montt was overthrown by yet another military coup, this one backed by a US government keen to see Guatemala set on the road to democracy. The new president was **General Mejía Víctores** and although the death squads and disappearances continued, elections were held for an 88-member Constituent Assembly, which was given the task of drawing up a new constitution in preparation for presidential elections.

Under Víctores there was an upturn in the level of rural repression, though the process of reconstruction initiated by Ríos Montt continued. Internal refugees were rehoused in "model villages", where they were under the control of the army. Scarcely any money was available for rebuilding the devastated communities, and it was often widows and orphans who were left to construct their own homes. In the Ixil Triangle alone the war had displaced 60,000 people (72 percent of the population), and nine model villages were built to replace 49 that had been destroyed. Nationwide a total of 440 villages had been destroyed and around 100,000 had lost their lives.

In 1985 presidential elections were held, the first free vote in Guatemala for thirty years.

Cerezo and the return to democratic rule

The elections were won by **Vinicio Cerezo**, a Christian Democrat whose father had served in the Arbenz administration. Cerezo was by no means associated with the traditional ruling elite and had himself been the intended victim of several assassination attempts. His election victory was the result of a sweeping wave of popular support, and in the run-up to the election he offered a programme of reform that he claimed would rid the country of repression.

Once in office, however, Cerezo was aware that his room for manoeuvre was subject to severe limitations, and he declared that the army still held 75 percent of the power. From the outset he could promise little: "I'm a politician not a magician. Why promise what I cannot deliver? All I commit myself to doing is opening up the political space, giving democracy a chance."

Throughout his six-year rule Cerezo offered a **non-confrontational approach**, seeking above all else to avoid upsetting the powerful alliance of business interests, landowners and generals. To protect himself, he courted the support of a group of sympathetic officers, and with their aid survived several coup attempts. But the administration remained trapped in the middle; the right accused Cerezo of communist leanings, while the left claimed that he was evading his commitment to reform.

Political killings dropped off a great deal under civilian rule, although they by no means stopped. Murder was still a daily event in Guatemala in the late 1980s and the war between the army and the guerrillas still raged in remote corners of the highlands. In Guatemala City the death squads continued to operate freely. No one accused Cerezo of involvement in the killings but it was clear that they were often carried out by policemen or soldiers as the right continued to use violent repression to direct and control the political situation.

In many ways the Cerezo administration was a bitter disappointment to the Guatemalan people. Although these early years of civilian rule did create a breathing space, by the time the decade drew to a close it was clear that the army was still actively controlling political opposition. Having forsaken the role of government, the generals allowed Cerezo to take office, presenting an acceptable face to the world, but the army continued to control the countryside and the economy continued to serve a small but potent elite. Rural and urban killings and "**disappearances**" also increased in the final years of Cerezo's rule – in February 1989 there were 220 killings, of which 82 were politically motivated.

The country's leading **human rights organization**, the Mutual Support Group (GAM), hoped that civilian rule would present them with a chance to investigate the fate of the "disappeared" and to face up to the country's horrific recent history. Cerezo, however, chose to forget the past, and ongoing abuses went largely uninvestigated and unpunished. GAM's leaders, meanwhile, became victims of the death squads.

Nevertheless, the promise of civilian rule created a general thaw in the political climate, fostering the growth of numerous pressure groups and fresh demands for reform, making protests and strikes a regular feature of Guatemalan life. Real change, however, never materialized. Despite the fact that at least 65 percent of the population were still living below the official poverty line, little was done to meet their needs in terms of education, health care or employment. The thirst for **land reform** reared its head once again, and under the leadership of Padre Andrés Girón some 35,000 peasants demanded action. Girón's approach was direct – he accused business interests of "exploiting and killing our people. We want the south coast, that's where the wealth of Guatemala lies." Cerezo avoided the issue and in a bid to appease conservative military and business interests steered clear of any significant tax reform or privatization policy, antagonizing most Guatemalans further and prompting waves of strikes. Acknowledging that his greatest achievement had been to survive, Cerezo organized the country's first civilian transfer of power for thirty years in 1990.

The Serrano and de León administrations

The **1990 elections** were dogged by controversy. The constitution prevented Cerezo from standing for re-election, while another former president, General Ríos Montt, was barred from running for office since he had previously come to power as the result of a military coup. In the end, the election was won by a former minister in the Ríos Montt government: **Jorge Serrano**. However, with a third of the population not registered to vote and an abstention rate of 56 percent, Serrano had the support of less than a quarter of the people. An engineer and evangelical with a centre-right economic position, Serrano once again proved both uninterested and incapable of effecting any real reform or bringing to an end the civil war. The level of human rights abuse remained high, death squad activity continued, the economy remained weak and the army was still a powerful force, using intimidation and murder to stamp out opposition. Economic activity was still controlled by a tiny elite: less than two percent of landowners owned more than 65 percent of the land, leaving some 85 percent of the population living in poverty.

Nevertheless, Guatemala's dispossessed and poor continued to clamour for change. Maya peasants became increasingly organized and influential, denouncing the continued bombardment of villages and rejecting the presence of the army and the system of civil patrols. Matters were brought into sharp focus in 1992 when **Rigoberta Menchú** was awarded the Nobel Peace Prize for her campaigning work on behalf of Guatemala's indigenous population. In spite of the efforts of the Serrano administration, the country's civil war still rumbled on and three main guerrilla armies, united as the **URNG**, continued to confront the government's army.

Small groups of refugees began to return from exile in Mexico and start civil communities, though an estimated 45,000 still remained. The territorial dispute with **Belize** was officially resolved when the two countries established full diplomatic relations in 1991; but the decision to recognize Belize as an independent country provoked hostility with ultra-nationalists and the Guatemalan military.

By early 1993 Serrano's reputation had plummeted following a series of **scandals** involving corruption and his backing of a casino and racetrack development that had suspected links with Colombian drug cartels. Despite his membership of no fewer than four evangelical churches, Serrano had supported a venture dependent on gambling and alcohol consumption that was probably financed by cocaine barons.

In May 1993 Serrano responded to the wave of popular protest with a **self-coup**, declaring he would rule by decree because the country was endangered by civil disorder and corruption. He also argued that the drug mafia planned to take over Guatemala; few were convinced and the US responded by suspending its annual US$67 million of aid. Basically he wanted to hang onto power and talked the generals into supporting him. Protests from the left and right got Serrano removed after just two days and another army appointee was also rejected through popular protest. The whole sorry affair revealed much about Guatemala: that the army (backed by big business and landowners) allowed civilians to run the government so that they could get on with the more serious business of running the country. Guatemala still retained its hopelessly unbalanced structure but the army was now susceptible to the force of popular protest.

Congress finally appointed **Ramiro de León Carpio**, the country's human rights ombudsman, as the new president. One of his first moves was a reshuffle of the senior military command, although he rejected calls for revenge, declaring that stability was the main goal. There was great early optimism at de León's appointment but public frustration quickly grew as the new government failed to address fundamental issues: crime and land ownership, tax and constitutional reform. Some progress was made in peace negotiations with the URNG guerrilla leadership, however, and the Indigenous Rights Act, passed in 1995, allowed greater constitutional freedom for Guatemala's *indígenas* and legal provision for state education in Maya languages.

Arzú and the peace accords

In January 1996, polls to elect a new president demonstrated the country's increasing lack of faith in the electoral process, which had failed to bring any real change after the much-heralded return to civilian rule in 1986. Some 63 percent of registered voters stayed at home and it was only a strong showing in Guatemala City that ensured the success of **Álvaro Arzú**, a former mayor of the capital. Blond, blue-eyed and somewhat bland, Arzú represented Guatemala's so-called modernizing right. His party, the PAN or National Advancement Party, had strong oligarchic roots, and was committed to private-sector-led growth and the free market, though Arzú's early adoption of a relatively progressive stance, appointing new defence, foreign and economic ministers and shaking up the armed forces' power structure, surprised many.

Arzú moved quickly to bring an end to the 36-year civil war, meeting the URNG guerrilla leaders, and working towards a final settlement. The **Peace Accords**, signed on December 29, 1996, concluded almost a decade of talks and terminated a conflict that had claimed 150,000 lives and left another 50,000 "disappeared". The core purpose of the Peace Accords was to investigate previous human rights violations through a Truth Commission overseen by MINUGUA (the UN mission to Guatemala), to recognize the identity of indigenous people and to eliminate discrimination and promote socio-economic development for all Guatemalans. Though the aims of the Peace Accords were undeniably ambitious, progress was laboriously slow during the Arzú years. In one of the biggest setbacks, the electorate narrowly turned down a proposal to amend the constitution to allow for greater Maya rights in May 1999. Turnout was woeful – around eighteen percent – with most of the indigenous community failing to vote, a collective rejection that underlined the deep-rooted animosity felt by most indigenous people towards a political system that had exploited them for centuries.

Though Arzú presided over a token reduction in armed forces numbers, the army's influence and position as the nation's real power broker remained unchallenged throughout his term. Though blamed for eighty percent of the atrocities of the civil war, army officers implicated in orchestrating massacres successfully avoided prosecution – Arzú simply dared not touch them. Then in April 1998, two days after publishing a long-awaited human rights investigation into wartime slaughters (see p.467), **Bishop Juan Geradi** was bludgeoned to death in his own garage. The murder stunned the nation; though most Guatemalans had long been accustomed to horrific levels of political violence, most thought the days of disappearances and death squads were over, and as one newspaper put it, "This wasn't supposed to happen. Not any more."

The acute fragility of the nascent Guatemalan democracy was revealed – most observers immediately recognizing Geradi's assassination as an act sanctioned by a vengeful military intent on preserving its dominant power base. Despite international and domestic outrage – hundreds of thousands attended a silent protest in the capital days after the killing – the Arzú government seemed paralysed, incapable of reigning in the real perpetrators of the murder. The investigation descended to near-farcical levels at times (a priest's dog was implicated at one stage) as terrified judges, prosecutors and key witnesses fled abroad following death threats. As Arzú departed the presidential palace in December 1999, Geradi's murderers remained at large and the investigation unsolved.

Despite this horrific killing, levels of political violence fell in the Arzú years, though there was an alarming upsurge in the **crime rate**. Petty theft, muggings, robberies, drug- and gang-related incidents and murders soared. In 1997, despite its relatively small population, Guatemala had the fourth-highest incidence of kidnapping in the world, with over 1000 people abducted. A new police force, the PNC, trained by experts from Spain, Chile and the USA, quickly gained a reputation as bad as its predecessor for endemic corruption and ineffectualness. Not surprisingly, law and order became the key issue of the 1999 election campaign.

President Portillo

Former lawyer and professor **Alfonso Portillo** won Guatemala's 1999 presidential elections, the first peacetime vote in nearly forty years, with a mandate to implement the Peace Accords, and tackle impunity and the criminal gangs. In the grossest of ironies, Portillo sought to boost his ratings during the presidential campaign by confessing to killing two men during a brawl in Mexico in 1982, declaring, "a man who defends his life will defend the lives of his people". He claimed that he had acted in self-defence, then fled the country because he had no chance of a fair trial. The tactic paid off handsomely, as Portillo, leader of the right-wing FRG (Guatemalan Republican Front) won by a landslide after a second round of voting. Portillo campaigned on a populist platform to cut poverty by tackling corruption and tax evasion, though perhaps the conclusive factor was the support of his political mentor, the former general and founder of the FRG Ríos Montt. Montt, Guatemala's most controversial politician, who had been ruled illegible to stand for the presidency because of his role in an earlier coup, was widely perceived to be really in control, pulling all the strings behind the scenes.

Initially, there was a positive groundswell of optimism as Portillo unveiled a diverse cabinet which included academics, indigenous activists and human rights advocates. Nevertheless, many of the key institutions – including the Bank of Guatemala and the Ministries of the Economy, Communications and Interior – were placed under the control of right wing FRG politicians and pro-business monetarists. In a bold move, Portillo severed the military chain of command by appointing a moderate colonel, Juan de Dios Estrada, instead of a general as Minister of Defence, an action which infuriated the army top brass. Portillo also moved quickly to solve the Geradi murder – another key campaign pledge – as prosecutors arrested three senior military personnel who would later be tried with the murder within weeks of his inauguration. Credibly, the military suspects (an intelligence chief and two members of the elite presidential guard) and a priest (who was found guilty of acting as an accomplice) were eventually brought to trial, and found guilty of plotting Geradi's murder in June 2001 – over three years after the bishop was killed. Despite intense pressure on the prosecution, and a bomb exploding outside the home of one judge on the first day of the trial, justice had prevailed, breaking the historically almost complete impunity of the armed forces.

The Geradi case aside, Portillo's brief honeymoon period quickly subsided as a series of corruption scandals was unearthed, crime rates continued to soar and immunity from punishment persisted elsewhere. The new president even dispatched his family to Canada in June 2000 after threats from a kidnapping gang, a savage indictment of the security situation. By early 2001, barely a week seemed to pass without an armed bank robbery or a public lynching as rural Guatemalans frustrated with the country's bankrupt justice system administered mob rule, killing suspected criminals. In March 2001, a judge was hacked to death by a crowd in the isolated town of Senahú, after he had freed an accused rapist because of a lack of evidence (see p.314). Confidence in Portillo plummeted to an all-time low in June 2001 following a mass breakout from Guatemala's main maximum security prison. Seventy of the country's most notorious criminals – murderers, rapists, kidnappers and gang lords – blasted their way out of jail, armed with a smuggled arsenal of sub-machine-guns and grenade launchers, with obvious internal connivance. Many media figures expressed doubt that Portillo would be permitted to finish his presidential term, as persistent rumours of a military-backed coup swept through the country.

Guatemala under Portillo has also suffered from a faltering **economy**, as traditional exports (principally coffee, sugar and bananas) have been hit by low commodity prices, droughts, and the nation's high interest rates affected investment. The quetzal remained weak against international currencies, prompting the government to introduce dollarization in May 2001, and to sign up for customs union with Honduras, El Salvador and Nicaragua by 2003 in an effort to boost the economy. Efforts to improve income tax collection, a key part of the Peace Accords, failed to materialize. According to MINUGUA, the United Nations mission, only 36 percent of the government's commitments had been met by 2001. Income retribution remained woefully skewed, with only Sierra Leone and Brazil having less unequal tax structures according to World Development Report figures. Guatemala also has little **industry** of its own, and much of the work available to unskilled Guatemalans is in foreign-owned textile factories where garments are assembled for export to the US and Korea. These factories operate in special tax-exempt zones, free from any import or export duties where workers earn a typical daily wage of around US$3–4. In 2001, over 100,000 Guatemalans (mainly women) were working in these factories.

Away from mainstream politics, a **Maya cultural revival** has matured as Guatemala's indigenous people pursue the freedom of organization, protest and participation denied them for centuries. Hundreds of schools have been founded to educate Maya children in their own tongue, increasing numbers of indigenous writers and journalists have emerged, more and more Maya books and magazines are being published and *indígena* radio stations have been set up. The shifting mood has even influenced youth culture, with Maya shamanic courses becoming popular and ladino university students asserting their mixed-race identity and proclaiming a Maya heritage. Yet despite these changes Guatemala remains a seismically divided country. Racism is endemic and most Maya, still subject to institutionalized discrimination, live in extreme poverty (over eighty percent, according to the government's own figures).

In many ways, the years since the Peace Accords have been a bitter disappointment to many Guatemalans. Though the peace has held, political violence has been replaced by random acts of criminal thuggery and the unreformed justice system is seemingly moribund. The economic outlook remains weak, with low living standards and substandard health care and educational opportunities for the vast majority of people. With the highest population growth rate in the hemisphere (almost three percent per annum) and land reform untackled, more and more poor Guatemalans have fled to the USA as illegal migrants, in a desperate search for opportunities denied them at home. Increasingly, more and more marginal plots are being farmed and campesinos, loggers and cattle ranchers continue to butcher rapidly diminishing forests and threaten protected reserves and national parks. Though there is ground for optimism in some areas, it remains to be seen how Guatemala's previously vibrant **tourism industry** will be affected following the attacks on the World Trade Center and Pentagon in September 2001. Many key points of the Peace Accords also have not been tackled, and the country's immediate future looks unstable, as Guatemala seemingly faces many more difficult years ahead.

Chronology of the Maya

c.20,000–10,000 BC ▶ **Paleo-Indian culture (also called Lithic or Early Hunter periods).** Waves of hunter-gatherers from Asia cross the Bering land bridge (and possibly also use a maritime route) to the American continent.

c.10,000 BC ▶ **Clovis culture.** Worked stone projectile points – first identified at Clovis, New Mexico – used to hunt large herbivores, including mammoths, found at many sites in North and Central America.

c.6000–1800 BC ▶ **Archaic (Proto-Maya) period.** General warming of the climate following the retreat of northern ice sheets. The Pacific littoral region in Guatemala is the most intensely inhabited area of the Maya world, though there are well-established villages and trade routes throughout the region. Villagers farm maize and beans, catch fish and make pottery. Clay figures discovered from this period may be the first religious artefacts. A Proto-Maya language is thought to have been spoken.

August 13 3114 BC ▶ The mythical starting date of the Maya Calendar (13.0.0.0.0. 4 Ahau 8 Kumk'u) marks the beginning of the current "Great Cycle", the creation of the present world; due to end on December 21, 2012.

1800 BC–250 AD ▶ **Preclassic (or Formative) period.** The **Olmec** culture, the first emergent civilization of Mesoamerica, brings an early calendar and new gods. Trade in jade, salt and cacao increases between villages in Guatemala, and the first Maya great cities, Nakbé and El Mirador, emerge towards the end of the period.

1700 BC ▶ Olmec civilization emerges on Gulf coast of Mexico, just outside the Maya region.

1400 BC ▶ First settlement in Copán valley.

c.1000 BC ▶ Earliest confirmed settlement at Nakbé.

1000–300 BC ▶ **Middle Preclassic period.** Relatively sophisticated building construction at Nakbé in northern Petén. Many of the earliest foundations of the central region's sites established. Olmec, then Izapa cultures, dominate the Pacific coast.

750 BC ▶ **Nakbé** is flourishing. Possibly the very first Maya "city", it is dominated by eighteen-metre-high temples. Maya culture eclipses Olmec influence in Petén.

500 BC ▶ First evidence of ceremonial buildings at **Tikal**.

300 BC–250 AD ▶ **Late Preclassic.** Early development of the foundations of Maya civilization: calendar, writing, architectural design and sophisticated artistic style. Monumental temple cities emerge. Causeways (*sacbes*) are built and trade links flourish.

300 BC ▶ Nakbé temples rebuilt to 45-metre height and colossal stucco masks constructed. Early building work at **El Mirador**.

200 BC ▶ **Miraflores culture** thrives on Pacific coast and Guatemalan highlands, centred at

Kaminaljuyú; elaborate stelae carved. First ceremonial structures built at **Tikal**, **Uaxactún** and possibly **Calakmul** (in Mexico).

150 BC ▶ The first great Maya city-state, **El Mirador**, emerges; seventy-metre-high temples are built, their soaring stone staircases framed by giant masks.

36 BC ▶ First known Long Count date, corresponding to December 7, 36 BC inscribed on Stela 2 at **Chiapa de Corzo**, Chiapas.

c.1 AD ▶ Major pyramids, platforms and giant stucco masks constructed at Uaxactún, Tikal and Cerros, but the region is dominated by El Mirador with a population that peaks at around 100,000. Emergence of **Teotihuacán** in Mexico.

36 AD ▶ First known Maya Long Count date, on Stela 1 at **El Baúl** on Pacific coast.

c.150 AD ▶ **El Mirador** abandoned, possibly due to disease or environmental collapse; Yax Ehb' Xok establishes the first ruling dynasty at Tikal. **Calakmul** emerges as a major power.

199 AD ▶ Earliest recorded use of Long Count date in central region.

250 AD ▶ **Kaminaljuyú** all but abandoned.

250–600 AD ▶ Early Classic period. Maya region and much of Mexico influenced, or even dominated by, the great metropolis of Teotihuacán, north of modern-day Mexico City until around 450 AD. Calakmul later emerges as the regional superpower, challenging and defeating Tikal. Dated inscriptions emerge in the lowlands. Elaborate carved stelae erected

throughout central region after 435 AD. Extensive trade network along Caribbean coast between Yucatán and Honduras.

292 AD ▶ Stela 29 carved at **Tikal**, with Long Count calendar date.

c.359 AD ▶ Yoaat B'alam I (Progenitor Jaguar) becomes first king of **Yaxchilán**.

378 AD ▶ Siyaj K'ak' (Lord Fire-Born), probably from **Teotihuacán**, ejects (and almost certainly kills) **Tikal's** ruler Chak Tok Ich'aak (Great Jaguar Claw I) and defeats **Uaxactœn**.

400 AD ▶ Guatemalan highlands under strong Teotihuacán influence; **Kaminaljuyú** rebuilt in its style.

426 AD ▶ Yax K'uk Mo' (Great Sun First Quetzal Macaw), probably from Teotihuacán, founds dynasty at **Copán**.

435 AD ▶ Completion of Baktun 8 (9.0.0.0.0). Population of **Copán** rises and building work accelerates.

c.514 AD ▶ Warriors from **Piedras Negras** return home with prisoners from Yaxchilán, including the king, Knot-eye Jaguar I.

556 AD ▶ Wak Chan K'awil (Double Bird) of **Tikal** (537–562 AD) enacts an "axe war" against **Caracol**.

562 AD ▶ Yajaw Te' K'inich II (Lord Water) of **Caracol** retaliates in concert with Sky Witness of **Calakmul** and overruns the city; no new monuments are raised at Tikal for 130 years. Calakmul becomes regional superpower.

534–593 AD ▶ Middle Classic hiatus: dearth of stelae carving and building throughout region previously under Tikal control.

c.600 AD ▶ Population density in core Maya region reaches an estimated 965 people per square kilometre.

600–800 AD ▶ **Late Classic period.** Golden age of the Maya, as civilization reaches intellectual and artistic peak and numerous powerful city-states emerge in central region, though the mighty superpowers of **Calakmul** and a re-emergent **Tikal** dominate. Monumental construction of temples, plazas, pyramids and palaces. Puuc, Río Bec and Chenes cities all flourish in northern area; spectacular construction throughout the Maya world.

611 AD ▶ Scroll Serpent of **Calakmul** attacks Palenque and destroys the city centre.

615 AD ▶ K'inich Hanaab Pakal (Great Sun Shield) begins 68-year reign at **Palenque**.

628 AD ▶ Smoke Imix's (Ruler 12) 67-year reign begins at **Copán**.

645 AD ▶ B'alaj Chan K'awil (Lightening Sky) founds city of **Dos Pilas**.

657 AD ▶ Yuknoom the Great of **Calakmul** attacks Tikal, whose ruler Nuun Ujol Chaak (Shield Skull) takes refuge in Palenque.

659 AD ▶ Nuun Ujol Chaak of **Tikal** wins battle against Yaxchilán, probably launched from his exile.

672 AD ▶ Nuun Ujol Chaak of **Tikal** returns from exile and launches a "star war" against **Dos Pilas**. B'alaj Chan K'awil takes refuge (probably in Calakmul). In 677 AD he returns to Dos Pilas, and in 679 AD successfully repels Tikal.

682 AD ▶ Hasaw Chan K'awill (Heavenly Standard Bearer) begins 52-year reign at **Tikal** and achieves its resurgence in a series of successful military campaigns against Calakmul and vast construction projects. Lightening Sky of **Dos Pilas** sends his daughter Lady Six Sky to **Naranjo** to re-establish the royal house there. Itzamnaaj B'alam II (Shield Jaguar) begins reign at **Yaxchilán**.

693 AD ▶ K'ak Tilaw Chan Chaak (Smoking Squirrel), new ruler of **Naranjo** retaliates against **Caracol** by repeatedly attacking its allies, Ucanal (693 AD and 698 AD), Yaxhá (710 AD) and Sacnab (711 AD).

695 AD ▶ Smoke Imix of Copán dies; succeeded by Waxaklajuun Ub'aah K'awil ("Eighteen Rabbit"). Hasaw Chan K'awil of **Tikal** captures Yich'aak K'ak (Fiery Claw) of **Calakmul**, breaking its power in the central Petén.

c.700 AD ▶ **Yaxchilán** dominates the Usumacinta region. Population of Caracol estimated at over 100,000.

734 AD ▶ Hasaw Chan K'awil of **Tikal** dies; succeeded by his son, Yik'in Chan K'awil (Divine Sunset Lord). He organizes Tikal's attacks on **El Perú** (743 AD) and on **Naranjo** (in 744 AD). These are the last recorded "star war events" in Petén.

735 AD ▶ Ruler 3 of **Dos Pilas** captures Yich'aak B'alam (Jaguar Claw) of **Ceibal**, and reduces Ceibal to subjugation for the next sixty years.

738 AD ▶ **Copán's** Waxaklajuun Ub'aah K'awil killed by Cauac Sky of **Quiriguá**, a subordinate city.

No monuments are built at Copán for seventeen years.

c.750 AD ▶ Population peaks in central region, total Maya numbers estimated to be around ten million.

790 AD ▶ Bonampak murals painted, but site abandoned shortly afterwards. **Dos Pilas** overrun. End of the *katun* celebrated across the Maya world with carved stelae.

800–910 AD ▶ Terminal Classic period. Overpopulation and intense agricultural cultivation in region, and an epochal drought, leads to environmental collapse. **Ceibal** flourishes briefly in isolation. Most main cities almost abandoned by 900 AD except in the northern area (Mexico) and in Belize, where trade continues along the rivers and coast.

808 AD ▶ Skull Mahk'ina III of **Yaxchilán** captures ruler 7 of **Piedras Negras** ending Classic Maya culture in the upper Usumacinta region.

810 AD ▶ Dark Sun builds Temple III, the last of **Tikal's** temple pyramids. Last dated inscription at **Quiriguá**.

830 AD ▶ Completion of Baktun 9.

849 AD ▶ Ceibal erects five stelae to commemorate the katun (10.1.0.0.0).

c.860 AD ▶ Population of central region down to a third of previous level.

869 AD ▶ Last recorded date at **Tikal**.

c.900 AD ▶ Uxmal and **Chichén Itzá** abandoned.

909 AD ▶ Erection of the last stela in Maya region at **Toniná** (to commemorate the katun ending 10.4.0.0.0.0).

910–c.1530 AD ▶ Postclassic period

910–1200 AD ▶ Early Postclassic period. Maya collapse sees cities abandoned throughout the region. The **Toltec** from Central Mexico invade Yucatán, bringing a new religious cult and architectural styles such as the *Chacmool*. Itza influence replaces Toltec.

1200 AD ▶ Chichén Itzá reoccupied by Toltec; new construction begins. Itza driven from Campeche coast.

c.1250 AD ▶ Toltec enter Guatemala. **Utatlán** founded.

c.1450 AD ▶ Itza establish **Tayasal** (also called Noh Petén) on Lago Petén Itzá.

1450 AD ▶ K'iche' state dominates warring highlands.

1470 AD ▶ Kaqchikel throw off K'iche' control and found their capital at **Iximché**.

1500 AD ▶ Continual conflict in Guatemalan highlands between the main tribal groups.

1519 AD ▶ Cortés lands in Cozumel.

1521 AD ▶ Aztec capital of **Tenochtitlán** falls to Spanish under Cortés.

Chronology of Guatemala

1523 ▶ Alvarado arrives in Guatemala. Establishes capital at Tecpán next to Iximché in 1524.

1523–40 ▶ **Spanish Conquest** of Guatemala proceeds: first Spanish capital founded 1527.

1541 ▶ Alvarado dies; new capital founded at **Antigua**.

17th c. ▶ **Colonial rule** is gradually established throughout the country. Antigua is the capital of the whole of Central America, and the power of the Church grows.

1697 ▶ Conquest of the Itza at Tayasal on Lago de Petén Itzá: the last of the independent Maya.

1773 ▶ Earthquake destroys Antigua.

1776 ▶ Guatemala City becomes capital.

18th c. ▶ Colonial Guatemala remains a backwater, with no great riches for the Spanish.

1821 ▶ Mexico and Central America gain **independence** from Spain; Guatemala annexed by Mexico, then joins Central American Federation.

1847 ▶ Guatemala becomes republic, independent of Central America under **Rafael Carrera**.

1850 ▶ Guatemala and Britain continue to squabble over Belize.

1862 ▶ Belize becomes part of the British empire.

1867 ▶ First **liberal uprising** under Serpio Cruz.

1871 ▶ Liberal revolution; **Rufino Barrios** becomes president. Start of coffee boom.

1906 ▶ Railway between Pacific and Caribbean coasts completed.

1930 ▶ **Jorge Ubico** president – banana boom and height of **United Fruit Company** power.

1944–54 ▶ "Spiritual Socialism" presidencies of **Arévalo** and **Arbenz**; ended by CIA-backed military coup.

1954 ▶ **Castillo Armas** president: the start of **military rule** and a series of military-backed dictators.

1960s ▶ First **guerrilla** actions, rapidly followed by repressive clampdowns and rise of **death squads** under **Colonel Carlos Arana**.

1968 ▶ US ambassador John Gordon Mein killed by FAR guerrillas in Guatemala City; Guatemalan writer Miguel Ángel Asturias wins Nobel Prize for Literature.

1970 ▶ **Colonel Arana Osorio** president.

1974 ▶ Electoral fraud wins presidency for **Kjell Laugerud**.

1976 ▶ **Earthquake** leaves 23,000 dead, a million homeless.

1978 ▶ **Lucas García** president; thousands die through repression. US bans arms sales to Guatemala. Intense fighting in the highlands between army and guerrillas.

1982 ▶ **Ríos Montt** seizes presidency. Army begins scorched earth campaign in the highlands. Belize becomes independent.

1986 ▶ **Vinicio Cerezo** elected: return to civilian rule though power of military remains great.

1990 ▶ **Jorge Serrano** elected on less than 25 percent of vote.

1991 ▶ Guatemala recognizes Belizean independence. Peace talks between guerrillas and government.

1992 ▶ Rigoberta Menchú wins Nobel Peace Prize.

1993 ▶ Serrano ousted by generals – **Ramiro de León Carpio** appointed.

1996 ▶ **Álvaro Arzú** and the PAN elected. Peace Accords signed.

1998 ▶ **Hurricane Mitch** devastates much of Central America and kills hundreds in Guatemala; Bishop Juan Geradi assassinated.

2000 ▶ FRG's **Alfonso Portillo** sworn in as president, backed by Ríos Montt.

2001 ▶ Growing instability: crime wave and riots against VAT tax increase; severe drought hits eastern highlands.

The Maya achievement

For some three thousand years before the arrival of the Spanish, Maya civilization dominated Mesoamerica, leaving behind some of the most impressive architecture in the entire continent. The scale and grandeur of some Maya cities, such as El Mirador, built around 100 BC, was greater than anything that existed in Europe at the time, and the artistry and splendour of Maya civilization at the height of the Classic era arguably eclipsed that of its Old World contemporaries. The Maya culture was complex and sophisticated, fostering the highest standards of engineering, astronomy, stone carving and mathematics, as well as an intricate writing system.

To appreciate all this you have to see for yourself the remains of the great centres. Despite centuries of neglect, abuse and encroaching jungle, they are still astounding – the biggest temple–pyramids tower up to 70m above the forest floor, well above the jungle canopy. Stone monuments, however, leave much of the story untold, and there is still a great deal that we have to learn about Maya civilization. What follows is the briefest of introductions to the subject, hopefully just enough to whet your appetite for the immense volumes that have been written on it; some of these are listed in "Books" on pp.480–490.

The Maya society

By the Early Classic period, the Maya cities had become organized into a hierarchy of power, with cities such as Kaminaljuyú, Tikal and Calakmul dominating vast areas and controlling the smaller sites through a complex structure of **alliances**. The cities jostled for power and influence, occasionally erupting into open warfare, which was also partly fuelled by the need for sacrificial victims. The distance between the larger sites averaged around 30km, and between these were myriad smaller settlements, religious centres and residential groups. The structure of the alliances can be traced through the use of **emblem glyphs**. Only the glyphs of the main centres are used in isolation, while the names of smaller sites are used in conjunction with those of their larger patrons. Of all the myriad Classic cities, the dominant ones were clearly Tikal and Calakmul, with Palenque, Copán, Caracol, Piedras Negras and Yaxchilán accepting secondary status until the early eighth century when the hierarchy began to dismantle. Cancuén, Yaxhá, Dos Pilas, Naranjo, and Quiriguá were other key cities, each lording it over, and probably extracting tribute from, many more minor settlements. Trade, marriages and warfare between the large centres were commonplace as the cities were bound up in an endless round of competition and conflict.

By the Late Classic period, **population densities** across a broad swathe of territory in the central area were as high as 965 people per square kilometre – an extraordinarily high figure, equivalent to densities in rural China or Java today – and as many as ten million people lived in the wider Maya region. It's thought there were strict divisions between the classes, with perhaps eighty percent being preoccupied with intensive cultivation to feed these vast numbers. The peasant farmers, who were at the bottom of the social scale, also

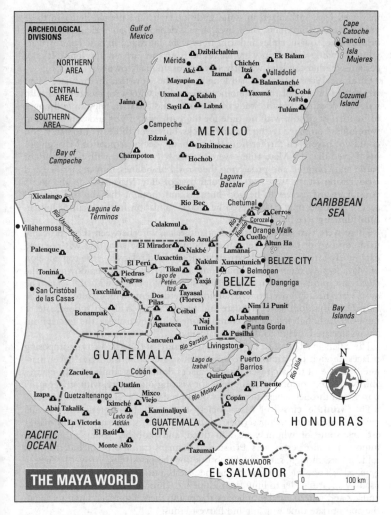

ARCHEOLOGICAL
DIVISIONS

NORTHERN
AREA

CENTRAL
AREA

SOUTHERN
AREA

Gulf of
Mexico

Cape
Catoche
Cancún
Isla
Mujeres

Dzibilchaltún
Mérida
Aké Izamal
Mayapán
Uxmal Kabáh
Jaina
Sayil Labná

Chichén
Itzá Valladolid
Balankanché
Yaxuná

Ek Balam

Cobá
Xelhá
Tulúm

Cozumel
Island

Campeche MEXICO
Edzná
Champoton
Dzibilnocac
Hochob

Bay of
Campeche

Laguna
Bacalar

Becán
Río Bec
Chetumal
Cerros
Corozal
Orange Walk
Cuello
Altun Ha
Lamanai
Xunantunich BELIZE CITY
Belmopan
Dangriga
Caracol

CARIBBEAN
SEA

Xicalango
Villahermosa
Palenque
Toniná
San Cristóbal
de las Casas
Yaxchilán

Laguna de
Términos

Calakmul
Río Azul
El Mirador Nakbé
El Perú Uaxactún
Piedras Tikal
Negras
Dos
Pilas
Bonampak
Aguateca
Cancuén

Lago de
Petén
Itzá
Tayasal
(Flores)
Yaxjá
Ceibal
Naj
Tunich

Nakúm

Nim Li Punit
Lubaantun
Punta Gorda
Pusilhá

BELIZE

Bay
Islands

GUATEMALA
Zaculeu
Izapa Utatlán
Abaj Takalik Iximché
La Victoria
El Baúl
Monte Alto
Quetzaltenango
Cobán
Mixco
Viejo
Kaminaljuyú
Lado de
Atitlán
GUATEMALA
CITY

Lívingston
Lago de
Izabal
Río Sarstún
Puerto
Barrios
Quiriguá
Río Motagua
Copán
El Puente

Tazumal

HONDURAS

PACIFIC
OCEAN

SAN SALVADOR EL SALVADOR

THE MAYA WORLD

0   100 km

N

provided the labour necessary to construct the monumental temples that decorate the centre of every city (the Maya did not have the wheel) as well as perform regular "military service" duties. Even in the suburbs where the peasants lived, there are complexes of religious structures with simple, small-scale temples where ceremonies took place.

While the remains of the great Maya sites are a testament to the scale and sophistication of Maya civilization, they offer little insight into daily life in Maya times. To reconstruct the lives of the **ordinary Maya** archeologists have turned to the smaller residential groups that surround the main sites, littered with the remains of household utensils, pottery, bones and farming tools. These groups are made up of simple structures made of poles and wattle-and-daub, each of which was home to a single family. The groups as a whole probably housed an extended family, who would have farmed and hunted together and may well have specialized in some trade or craft. The people living in these groups were commoners, their lives largely dependent on agriculture. Maize, beans, cacao, squash, chiles and fruit trees were cultivated in raised and irrigated fields, while wild fruits were harvested from the surrounding forest. It's not certain whether the land was privately or communally owned.

Until the 1960s, Mayanists had long shared the view that the ordinary Maya were ruled by a scholarly astronomer–priest elite, who were preoccupied with religious devotion and the study of calendrics and the stars. They were thought to be men of reason, with no time for the barbarity of war and conquest, and were often compared to the ancient Greeks. However, this early utopian vision could not have been further from the truth: the decipherment of Maya glyphs has proved that the Maya rulers were primarily concerned with the glories of battle and conquest and preserving their royal bloodlines; human sacrifice and bloodletting rituals were also a pivotal part of elite Maya society. The rulers considered themselves to be god–humans and thought that the line of royal accession could only be achieved by sacred validation in the form of human **bloodletting** (see box on p.450).

There were two **elite classes**: *ahau* and *cahal*, who between them probably made up two or three percent of the population. The *ahau* title was reserved exclusively for the ruler and extremely close blood relatives – the top echelon of Maya society; membership could only be inherited. One step down was the *cahal* class, most of whom would have shared bloodlines with the *ahau*. The *cahal* were mainly governors of subsidiary settlements which were under the control of the dominant city-state and their status was always subordinate to the *ahau*. Although *cahal* lords commissioned their own stelae, the inscriptions always declared loyalty to the regional ruler.

The rulers lived close to the ceremonial centre of the Maya city, in imposing palaces, though the rooms were limited in size because the Maya never mastered the use of the arch (see p.500). Palaces doubled as administrative centres and were used for official receptions for visiting dignitaries, with strategically positioned thrones where the ruler would preside over religious ceremonies.

The "**middle class**" of Maya society consisted of a professional class (*ah na:ab*) of architects, senior scribes (*ah tz'ib*), sculptors, bureaucrats and master artisans, some of whom were also titled, and probably young princes and important court performers. Priests and shamans can also be included in this middle class though, surprisingly, no title for the priesthood has yet been recognized. It's possible that not giving the priests a title may have been a method used by a fearful ruler to limit their influence. Through their knowledge of calendrics and supernatural prophecies, the priests were also relied upon to divine the appropriate time to plant and harvest crops.

There's no doubt that **women** played an influential role in Maya society, and in the Late Classic period there were even some women rulers – Lady Ahpo Katun at Piedras Negras, Lady Ahpo-Hel at Palenque and a Lady Six Sky at Naranjo. Women also presided at court and were given prestigious titles – Lady Cahal of Bonampak, for example. More frequently, however, as in Europe, dynasties were allied and enhanced by the marriage of royal women between cities. One of the best documented strategic marriages occurred after the great southern city of Copán had suffered the humiliation of having its leader captured and sacrificed by upstart local rival Quiriguá in 738 AD – a royal marriage was arranged with a noblewoman from Palenque over 500km away.

Maya **agriculture** was continually adapting to the needs of the developing society, and the early practice of slash-and-burn was soon replaced by more intensive and sophisticated methods to meet the needs of a growing population.

Some of the land was terraced, drained or irrigated in order to improve its fertility and ensure that fields didn't have to lie fallow for long periods, and the capture of water became crucial to the success of a site.

The large lowland cities, today hemmed in by the forest, were once surrounded by open fields, canals and residential compounds, while slash-and-burn agriculture probably continued in marginal and outlying areas. Agriculture became a preoccupation, with the ordinary Maya trading at least some of their food in markets, although all households still had a kitchen garden where they grew herbs and fruit.

Maize has always been the basis of the Maya **diet**, in ancient times as much as it is today. Once harvested it was made into *saka*, a corn-meal gruel, which was eaten with chile as the first meal of the day. During the day labourers ate a mixture of corn dough and water, and we know that tamales were also a popular speciality. The main meal, eaten in the evenings, would have been similarly maize-based, although it may well have included meat and vegetables. As a supplement to this simple diet, deer, peccary, wild turkeys, duck, pigeons and quail were all hunted with bows and arrows or blowguns. The Maya also made use of dogs, both for hunting and the dinner table. Fish were also eaten, and the remains of fish hooks and nets have been found in some sites, while there is evidence that those living on the coast traded dried fish far inland. As well as food, the forest provided firewood, and cotton was cultivated to be dyed with natural colours and then spun into cloth.

The Maya calendar

One of the cornerstones of Maya thinking was an obsession with **time**. For both practical and mystical reasons the Maya developed a highly sophisticated understanding of arithmetics, calendrics and astronomy, all of which they believed gave them the power to understand and predict events. All great occasions were interpreted on the basis of the Maya calendar, and it was this precise understanding of time that gave the ruling elite its authority. The majority of the carvings, on temples and stelae, record the exact date at which rulers were born, ascended to power, and died.

The basis of all Maya **calculation** was the vigesimal counting system, which used multiples of twenty. All figures were written using a combination of three symbols – a shell to denote zero, a dot for one and a bar for five – which you can still see on many stelae. When calculating calendrical systems the Maya used a slightly different notation known as the head-variant system, in which each number from one to twenty was represented by a deity, whose head was used to represent the number.

When it comes to the Maya **calendar** things start to get a little more complicated as a number of different counting systems were used, depending on the reason the date was being calculated. The basic unit of the Maya calendar was the day, or *kin*, followed by the *uinal*, a group of twenty days roughly equivalent to our month; but at the next level things start to get even more complex as the Maya marked the passing of time in three distinct ways. The **260–day almanac** (16 *uinals*) was used to calculate the timing of ceremonial events. Each day was associated with a particular deity that had strong influence over those born on that particular day. This calendar wasn't divided into months but had 260 distinct day names – a system still in use among some Kaqchikel and

Mam Maya who name their children according to its structure and celebrate fiestas according to its dictates. A second calendar, the so-called "**vague year**" or *haab*, was made up of eighteen *uinals* and five *kins*, a total of 365 days, making it a close approximation of the solar year. These two calendars weren't used in isolation but operated in parallel so that once every 52 years the new day of the solar year coincided with the same day in the 260-day almanac, a meeting that was regarded as very powerful and marked the start of a new era.

Finally the Maya had another system for marking the passing of history, which is used on dedicatory monuments. The system, known as the **long count**, is based on the great cycle of thirteen *baktuns* (a period of 5128 years). The current period dates from August 13, 3114 BC, and is destined to come to an end on December 10, 2012. The dates in this system simply record the number of days that have elapsed since the start of the current great cycle, a task that calls for ten different numbers – recording the equivalent of years, decades, centuries, and so on. In later years the Maya sculptors obviously tired of this exhaustive process and opted instead for the short count, an abbreviated version.

Astronomy

Alongside their fascination with time, the Maya were obsessed with the sky and devoted much time and energy to unravelling its patterns. Several large sites such as Copán, Uaxactún and Chichén Itzá have **observatories** carefully aligned with solar and lunar sequences.

The Maya showed a great understanding of **astronomy** and with their 365-day "vague year" were just a quarter of a day out in their calculations of the solar year, while at Copán, towards the end of the seventh century AD, Maya astronomers had calculated the lunar cycle at 29.53020 days, not too far off our current estimate of 29.53059. In the Dresden Codex their calculations extend to the 405 lunations over a period of 11,960 days, as part of a pattern that set out to predict eclipses. At the same time they had calculated with astonishing accuracy the movements of Venus, Mars and perhaps Mercury. Venus was of particular importance to the Maya as they linked its presence with success in war, and there are several stelae that record the appearance of Venus prompting the decision to strike at an enemy – an attack known as a "**star war**".

Maya time: the units

1 *kin* = 24 hours
20 *kins* = 1 *uinal*, or 20 days
18 *uinals* = 1 *tun*, or 360 days
20 *tuns* = 1 *katun*, or 7200 days
20 *katuns* = 1 *baktun*, or 144,000 days
20 *baktuns* = 1 *pictun*, or 2,880,000 days
20 *pictuns* = 1 *calabtun*, or 57,600,000 days
20 *calabtuns* = 1 *kinchiltun*, or 1,152,000,000 days
20 *kinchiltuns* = 1 *alautun*, or 23,040,000,000 days

Religion

Maya **cosmology** is far from straightforward as at every stage an idea is balanced by its opposite and each part of the universe is made up of many layers. To the Maya this is the third version of the earth, the previous two having been destroyed by deluges. The current version is a flat surface, with four corners, each associated with a certain colour: white for north, red for east, yellow for south and black for west, with green at the centre. Above this the sky is supported by four trees, each a different colour and species, which are also sometimes depicted as gods, known as *Bacabs*. At its centre the sky is supported by a ceiba tree. Above the sky is a heaven of thirteen layers, each of which has its own god, while the very top layer is overseen by an owl. Other attested models of the world include that of a turtle (the land) floating on the sea. However, it was the underworld, *Xibalbá*, the "Place of Fright", which was of greater importance to most Maya, as it was in this direction that they passed after death, on their way to the place of rest. The nine layers of hell were guarded by the "Lords of the Night", and deep caves were thought to connect with the underworld.

Woven into this universe the Maya recognized an incredible array of **gods**. Every divinity had four manifestations based upon colour and direction and many also had counterparts in the underworld and consorts of the opposite sex. In addition to this there was an extensive array of patron deities, each associated with a particular trade or particular class. Every activity from suicide to sex had its representative in the Maya pantheon.

Religious ritual

The combined complexity of the Maya pantheon and calendar gave every day a particular significance, and the ancient Maya were bound up in a demanding **cycle of religious ritual**. The main purpose of ritual was the procurement of success by appealing to the right god at the right time and in the right way. As every event, from planting to childbirth, was associated with a particular divinity, all of the main events in daily life demanded some kind of religious ritual and for the most important of these the Maya staged elaborate ceremonies.

While each ceremony had its own format there's a certain pattern that binds them all. The correct day was carefully chosen by priestly divination, and for several days beforehand the participants fasted and remained abstinent. The main ceremony was dominated by the expulsion of all evil spirits, the burning of incense before the idols, a sacrifice (either animal or human), and bloodletting.

In divination rituals, used to foretell the pattern of future events or account for the cause of past events, the elite used various **drugs** to achieve altered states of consciousness. Perhaps the most obvious of these was alcohol, either made from fermented maize or a combination of honey and the bark of the balnche tree. Wild tobacco, which is considerably stronger than the modern domesticated version, was also smoked. The Maya also used a range of hallucinogenic mushrooms, all of which were appropriately named, but none more so than the *xibalbaj obox*, "underworld mushroom", and the *k'aizalah obox*, "lost judgement mushroom".

Ritual bloodletting was a fundamental part of Maya religious life, practised by all strata of society. It took many forms, from cursory self-inflicted blood offerings to elaborate ceremonies involving the mass sacrifice of captive kings and enemy warriors. The Maya modelled their lives according to a vision of the cosmos, and within this arena, human actions could affect the future, auspiciously or otherwise. Pivotal to this vision was the concept that blood-spilling helped repay man's debt to the gods, who had endowed the gift of life.

The K'iche' Maya creation story, the **Popol Vuh**, tells of the creation, destruction and recreation of previous imperfect worlds before their own was made. Earlier races had been conceived and then destroyed for failing to praise their creators. Finally the Maya people were made by mixing ground maize, the region's food staple, with the sacrificial blood of the gods. Consumed by the omnipresent fear that the world could again be destroyed, the Maya sought to appease the gods and ensure continued prosperity through bloodletting.

First practised by the **Olmec**, Mesoamerica's "mother culture", more than 3000 years ago, bloodletting continued until the arrival of the conquistadors. Among the early Maya, ritual blood offerings were primarily concerned with renewal and agricultural fertility, closely linked to creation mythology. Later, in the Classic period, with increasing social complexity and proven agricultural reliability, bloodletting may have become more related to the shifting concerns of the day, including warfare and political alliances. The practice later grew to apocalyptic degrees of carnage among the **Aztecs**, horrifying the Spanish, whose chronicler Diego Duran describes the sacrifice of 80,000 victims at the rededication of the Templo Mayor in their capital.

As well as direct representations of the sacrificial act, the Maya developed a symbolic iconography of bloodletting, so that the smallest motif, such as three knotted bands or smoke scrolls, could express blood sacrifice. Maya bloodletting iconography had its roots in Olmec art, including the elaborate vision quest serpent, depicted in the eighth century Yaxchilán lintels, which grew from the corpus of Olmec serpentine motifs. Through their wealth and control of resources, the Maya nobility recorded their actions by using non-perishable artistic mediums – the fact that depictions of bloodletting were chosen for preservation on **stone**, a costly and laborious medium, confirms its religious, social and political significance.

A common bloodletting ritual may have consisted of cutting earlobes, cheeks, thighs or other fleshy parts of the body and collecting the blood to burn, or sprinkling it directly on a shrine or idol. Undertaken for numerous reasons – to bless a journey, the planting of crops, or the passing of a family member – these rites may have been performed individually or by an entire community, accompanied by prayers, the sacrifice of animals and the burning of copal incense.

Elite bloodletting rituals often took place at important or auspicious occasions: during accession ceremonies, at the birth of an heir, to mark the passing of a calendar round, in times of war, drought or disease, and to ensure regeneration and prosperity. Bloodletting also served as a rite of passage, or the individual quest for a prophetic vision and communication with the gods, providing access to the spiritual world.

There seem to have been two main **auto-sacrificial rituals** practised by the Maya elite. These were not undertaken lightly and carried severe physical and psychological repercussions. As part of a larger ceremony, the actual act of letting blood may have been preceded by days of preparation, meditation, fasting, sexual abstinence and bodily purification with sweat baths. A male rite was to draw blood by pricking the penis with either a stingray spine, obsidian lancet or flint knife. The second rite, piercing the tongue, was probably practised by both sexes although is most famously illustrated by Lady Xoc in the **Yaxchilán lintels**, now housed in the British Museum. The blood offering was then soaked into bark paper and collected in ceremonial bowls to be burnt as a presentation and petition to the Gods.

The Maya also practised bloodletting in the form of **captive sacrifice**, a highly ceremonial affair in which prolonged death and torture were features – gruesomely depicted in the Bonampak murals. Prisoners then either faced death by decapitation, or by having their heart removed. Hearts were then burnt as an offering to the gods, while decapitated heads might be displayed on a skull-rack.

Maya **warfare** often reflected the need for ritual bloodletting, as warriors frequently sought to capture alive rulers of rival cities, who would then be imprisoned and sacrificed at a later date. The soaring temples of the city centre then served as ceremonial theatres for elaborate religious rituals, allowing victories to be proclaimed to the entire community. Sacrificial victims would have been especially important to mark the accession of a new ruler, the bloodletting adding legitimacy to the king and affirming his power.

Blood offerings were integral to ancient Amerindian life, a tradition passed on from the Olmec, to the Maya and then on to the Aztec. Bloodletting developed from culture to culture through material and ideological exchange but always retained its central elements – links to the supernatural, mythical origins and a vital connection with the continued prosperity of mankind and mother earth.

Simone Clifford-Jaeger

Indigenous Guatemala

A vital indigenous culture is perhaps Guatemala's most unique feature. It's a strange blend of contradictions, and while the Maya people may appear quiet and humble, their costumes, fiestas and markets are a riot of colour, creativity and celebration. In many ways the Maya live in a world of their own, responding to local traditions and values and regarding themselves as *indígenas* first and Guatemalans second.

The indigenous Maya, the vast majority of whom live in the western highlands, make up just over half of Guatemala's population, although it's extremely hard to define exactly who is Maya. For the sake of the national census, people who consider themselves indigenous are classed as such, regardless of their parentage. And when it comes to defining Maya as a group, culture is more

important than pedigree, as the Maya define themselves through their relationships with their land, gods, villages and families. Holding aloof from the melting pot of modern Guatemalan society, Maya people adhere instead to their traditional *costumbres*, codes of practice that govern every aspect of life.

As a result of this the only way to define Maya culture is by describing its main characteristics, acknowledging that all indigenous Guatemalans will be a part of some of them, and accepting that many are neither *indígena* nor ladino, but combine elements of both.

Indigenous culture

When the Spanish set about destroying the Maya tribes of Guatemala they altered every aspect of life for the indigenous people, uprooting their social structures and reshaping their communities. Before the Conquest the bulk of the population had lived scattered in the hills, paying tribute to a tribal elite, and surviving through subsistence farming and hunting. Under Spanish rule they were moved into new **villages**, known as *reducciones* where their homes were clustered around a church and a marketplace. Horizons shrank rapidly as allegiances became very localized and tribal structures were replaced by the village hierarchies that still dominate the highlands today.

For the last 450 years the Maya population has suffered repeated **abuse**, as the predominantly white elite have exploited indigenous land and labour, regarding the Maya as an expendable commodity. But within their own communities indigenous Guatemalans were left pretty much to themselves and developed an astoundingly introspective culture that is continually adapting to new threats, reshaping itself for the future. **Village life** has been insulated from the outside world and in many areas only a handful of the population speak fluent Spanish, the remainder speaking one of the 28 indigenous languages and dialects (see map on p.445). Today's indigenous culture is a complex synthesis including elements of Maya, Spanish and modern American cultures.

The vast majority of the indigenous population still live by **subsistence farming**, their homes either spread across the hills or gathered in small villages. The land is farmed using the *milpa* system to produce beans, chilles, maize and squash – which have been the staple diet for thousands of years. To the Maya, land is sacred and the need to own and farm it is central to their culture, despite the fact that few can survive by farming alone. Many have been forced to migrate to the coast for several months a year, where they often work in appalling conditions on the **plantations**, in order to supplement their income. However huge numbers are now choosing to head north to the USA to work illegally instead, their remittances now forming a crucial part of the highland economy in remote Cuchumatán mountain villages. In the central highland region, where transport and communications are better, the prosperity of many villages is boosted by a local **craft**: in Momostenango they produce wool and blankets, around Lago de Atitlán the villagers make reed mats, in Cotzal and San Pablo la Laguna they make rope, while other villages specialize in market gardening, pottery, flowers or textiles. **Tourism** dollars are also beginning to make a financial impact in some regions, not just around Lago de Atitlán (to which visitors have always been drawn) but also in the Ixil, Todos Santos and Quetzaltenango areas too.

Family life is rigidly traditional with large families very much a part of the indigenous culture. Marriage customs vary from place to place but in general the groom is expected to pay the bride's parents, and the couple may well live with their in-laws. Authority within the village is usually given to men, although in the Ixil area women are involved in all decision making. Customs are slowly changing, but generally men spend most of the day tending the *milpas* (cornfields) and vegetable plots, while woman are based in the family home, concentrating on looking after the children, cooking and weaving. However Maya women are by no means confined to the house and frequently

Evangelism in Guatemala

One of the greatest surprises awaiting first-time travellers in Guatemala is the number of evangelical churches in the country, with fundamentalist, Pentecostal or neo-Pentecostal services taking place in most towns and villages. Although early Protestant missions came to Guatemala as far back as 1882, the impact of US-based churches remained marginal and largely unnoticed until the 1950s, when **state repression** and the subsequent **guerrilla war** began to weaken the power of the Catholic church. Up until this time, more than 95 percent of the population was officially Catholic, though the rural Maya had their own hybrid forms of worship which mixed Catholic ceremony with pagan rites.

While the hierarchy of the Catholic church remained fervently anti-Communist and closely aligned with the economic, political and military elite, during the early 1960s many rural Catholic priests became increasingly active in supporting peasant leagues and development projects, with some even joining the guerrillas. Consequently, the generals, politicians and big landowners began to consider the Catholic church as being riddled with Communist sympathizers, and targeted troublemakers accordingly. By the early 1980s, so many priests had been murdered by the state-sponsored death squads that the Catholic church pulled out of the entire department of El Quiché in protest. In contrast, most of the evangelical missionaries preached the importance of an army victory over the guerrillas and, with their pro-business, anti-Communist rhetoric, attracted many converts anxious to avoid suspicion and survive. In addition, the early evangelicals had made it a priority to learn the native Maya languages, and had the Bible translated into K'iche', Mam, Kaqchikel and other tongues.

However, the devastating **1976 earthquake** was the catalyst for the tidal wave of US evangelism which has swept through Guatemala. Church-backed disaster relief programmes brought in millions of dollars of medicine, food and toys to those prepared to convert, and shattered villages were rebuilt with new schools and health centres. In the eyes of the impoverished rural villagers, Protestantism became linked with prosperity, and its lively church services, where dancing, music and singing were the norm, quickly gained huge popularity.

The movement received another boost in 1982, when **General Ríos Montt** seized power in a military coup to become Guatemala's first evangelical leader. The population was treated to Montt's maniacal, marathon Sunday sermons, and a new flood of mission teams entered the country from the USA. For many Guatemalans, Ríos Montt represented the best and worst of evangelism: he was frenzied and fanatical on one hand, but honest and strict on the other (despite widespread human rights violations under his brief tenure). Ríos Montt was ousted after just seventeen months in power, though he remains Guatemala's most powerful political figure – leader of the ruling RFG, and the real force behind his protégé, the current president Alfonso Portillo.

Guatemala is today the least Catholic country in Latin America, with around sixty percent of the population looking to the Vatican for guidance and about forty percent supporting the evangelicals. However, as some denominations have been promising miracles, such as bumper harvests, which have failed to materialize, it remains to be seen whether the latter can retain this level of worship.

travel to distant markets to sell excess fruit, vegetables and textiles and to buy, or barter for, thread and supplies. In some places particularly noted for their weavings, such as Nebaj or Chajul, whole families decamp to Antigua or Panajachel for three or four days to sell their crafts to tourists.

Indigenous religion

Every aspect of Maya life – from the birth of a child to the planting of corn – is loaded with religious significance, based on a complicated **fusion of the Maya pantheon and the Catholic religion**. Christ and the saints have taken their place alongside *Dios Mundo*, the God of the World, and *Hurakan*, the Heart of Heaven. The two religions have merged to form a hybrid, in which the outward forms of Catholicism are used to worship the ancient pantheon, a compromise that was probably fostered by Spanish priests. The symbol of the cross, for example, was well known to the Maya, as used to signify the four winds of heaven, the four directions, and everlasting life. Today many of the deities have both Maya and Hispanic names, and are usually associated with a particular saint. All the deities remain subordinate to a mighty and remote supreme being, and Christ takes a place in the upper echelons of the hierarchy.

For the Maya, **God** is everywhere, bound up in the seasons, the mountains, the crops, the soil, the air and the sky. Every important event is marked by prayer and offerings, with disasters often attributed to divine intervention. Even more numerous than the gods are the **spirits** that are to be found in every imaginable object, binding together the universe. Each individual is born with a *nahaul*, or spiritual counterpart, in the animal world, and his or her destiny is bound up with that particular animal. The spirits of dead ancestors are also ever-present and have to be looked after by each successive generation.

Traditionally, **worship** is organized by the community's religious hierarchy. All office-holders are male and throughout their lives they progress through the system, moving from post to post. The various posts are grouped into *cofradías*, ritual brotherhoods, each of which is responsible for a particular saint. Throughout the year the saint is kept in the home of an elder member, and on the appointed date, in the midst of a fiesta, it's paraded through the streets, to spend the next year somewhere else. The elder responsible for the saint will have to pay for much of the fiesta, including costumes, alcohol and assorted offerings, but it's a responsibility, or *cargo*, that's considered a great honour. In the traditional village hierarchy it's these duties that give the elders a prominent role in village life and through which they exercise their authority. Spending money on **fiestas** is really the only way that wealthy villagers can use their money in an acceptable way. (In some villages, such as Chichicastenango and Sololá, a *municipalidad indígena*, or indigenous council, operates alongside the *cofradías*, and is similarly hierarchical. As men work their way up through the system they may well alternate between the civil and religious hierarchies.) The *cofradías* don't necessarily confine themselves to the traditional list of saints, and have been known to foster "evil" saints, such as San Simón or **Maximón**, a drinking, smoking ladino figure, sometimes referred to as Judas or Pedro de Alvarado.

On a more superstitious level, personal religious needs are catered for by *brujos*, native priests who communicate with the gods and spirits. This is usually done on behalf of an individual client who's in search of a blessing, and often takes place at shrines and caves in the mountains, with offerings of *copal*, a type of incense, and alcohol. They also make extensive use of old Maya sites, and small burnt patches of grass litter many of the ruins in the highlands. *Brujos* are also credited with the ability to cast spells, predict the future and communicate with the dead. For specific medical problems, the Maya appeal to *zahorines* who practise traditional medicine with a combination of invocation and herbs, and are closely associated with the *brujo* tradition.

Until the 1950s, when Catholic **missionaries** became active in the highlands, many indigenous Guatemalans had no idea that there was a gulf between their own religion and orthodox Catholicism. To start with the missionaries drew most of their support from the younger generation, many of whom were frustrated by the rigidity of the village hierarchy. Gradually, this has eroded the authority of the traditional religious system, undermining the *cofradías*, disapproving of traditional fiestas, and scorning the work of the *brujos*. As a part of this the reforming movement Catholic Action, combining the drive for orthodoxy with an involvement in social issues, has also had a profound impact.

After the 1976 earthquake, waves of Protestant missionaries, known as *evangélicos* arrived in Guatemala, and their presence has also accelerated the decline of traditional religion (see box on p.454). In the 1980s their numbers were greatly boosted by the influence of Ríos Montt, at a time when the Catholic Church was suffering severe repression. These days there are at least three hundred different sects in operation, backed by a huge injection of money from the USA, and offering all sorts of incentives to fresh converts. But indigenous religion is no stranger to oppression and despite the efforts of outsiders the *brujos* and *cofradías* are still in business, and fiestas remain drunken and vaguely pagan.

Markets and fiestas

At the heart of the indigenous economy is the **weekly market**, which remains central to life in the highlands and provides one of the best opportunities to see Maya life at close quarters. The majority of the indigenous population still lives by subsistence farming but spares a single day to gather together in the nearest village and trade its surplus produce. The market is as much a social occasion as an economic one and people come to talk, eat, drink, gossip and have a good time. In some places the action starts the night before with marimba music and heavy drinking.

On market day itself the village is filled by a steady flow of people, arriving by pick-up or bus, on foot, or by donkey. In no time at all trading gets under way, and the plaza is soon buzzing with activity and humming with conversation, although raised voices are a rarity, with bargains struck after long and tortuous negotiations. Markets certainly don't operate in the way that "westerners" might expect and rival traders will happily set up alongside one another, seemingly more concerned about the day's conversation than the volume of trade.

The scale and atmosphere of markets varies from place to place. The country's largest is in **San Francisco el Alto**, on Fridays, and draws traders from throughout the country. Other famous ones are the Friday market in Sololá, and the Thursday and Sunday markets in Chichicastenango, but almost every village has its day. Some of the very best are in tiny, isolated hamlets, high in the mountains, like Chajul or Santa Eulalia.

Once a year every village, however small, indulges in an orgy of celebration in honour of its patron saint – you'll find a list of them at the end of each chapter. These **fiestas** are a great swirl of dance, music, religion, endless firecrackers, eating and outrageous drinking, and express the vitality of indigenous culture. They usually centre on religious processions, in which the image of the local patron saint is paraded through the streets, accompanied by the elders of the *cofradía*, who dress in full regalia. (All members of a *cofradía* usually have special ceremonial costumes, superbly woven and beautifully decorated.) The larger fiestas also involve funfairs and week-long markets. Traditional music is played with marimbas, drums and flutes; or professional bands may be hired, blasting out popular tunes through crackling PA systems.

Dance, too, is very much a part of fiestas, and incorporates routines and ideas that date from ancient Maya times. Dance costumes are incredibly elaborate, covered in mirrors and sequins, and have to be rented for the occasion. Despite the cost, which is high by highland standards, the dancers see their role both as an obligation – to tradition and the community – and an honour. Most of the dances form an extension of some vague dramatic tradition where local history was retold in dance dramas, and are loosely based on historical events. The *Dance of the Conquistadors* is one of the most popular, modelled on the *Dance of the Moors* and introduced by the Spanish as a re-enactment of the Conquest, although in some cases it's been instilled with a significance that can never have been intended by the Spanish. The dancers often see no connection with the Conquest, but dance instead to release the spirits of the dead, a function perhaps closer to Maya religion than Catholicism. The *Palo Volador*, a dramatic dance in which men swing perilously to the ground from a twenty-metre pole, certainly dates from the pre-Columbian era (these days you'll only see it in Cubulco, Chichicastenango and Joyabaj), as does the *Dance of the Deer*, while the *Dance of the Bullfight* and the *Dance of the Volcano* relate incidents from the Conquest itself. Most of the dances do have steps to them, but the dancers are usually blind drunk and sway around as best they can in time to the music, sometimes tumbling over each other or even passing out – so don't expect to see anything too dainty.

Maya costume

To outsiders the most obvious and impressive feature of indigenous culture is the **hand-woven cloth** that's worn by the majority of the women and some of the men. This, like so much else in the Maya world, is not simply a relic of the past but a living skill, responding to new ideas and impulses and re-created by each generation.

Nevertheless, **weaving** is one of the oldest of Maya crafts, and was practised for centuries before the arrival of the Spanish. We know that it was a highly valued talent, and the Maya goddess Ix Chel, "she of the rainbow", who presided over childbirth, divination and healing, is often depicted at her loom. In pre-Columbian times the majority of the population probably wore long white cotton tunics, similar to those worn by the Lacandón Maya today. In the highlands it's a style that has been largely superseded, although in some villages, such as Soloma and San Mateo Ixtatán, the basic format is still the same, now embellished with magnificent embroidery. We also know, from Maya tombs and sculptures, that the nobility wore elaborate headdresses and heavily decorated cloth, using blues and reds created with vegetable dyes. Here it seems that tunics and robes were also the fashion of the day.

After the Conquest, the indigenous nobility was virtually eradicated and the focus was shifted from large regional centres to small village communities. Meanwhile, silk and wool were introduced by the Spanish, as were a whole range of new dyes. Not much is known about the development of Maya costume in colonial times, and it's impossible to say when or why each village developed a distinctive style of dress. Some argue that the styles were introduced by the Spanish as a means of control, rather like the branding of sheep, while others claim that they developed naturally from the introspective nature of village culture. The truth is probably to be found somewhere between the two: we know that Spanish symbols were introduced into traditional costume designs, but that at times the Spanish had little influence over life in the villages.

Women's clothing

Today there are around 150 villages where women still wear **traditional costume**, each with its own patterns, designs and colours. What little we know of their development shows that designs are constantly changing, adopting new patterns and ideas. The advent of literacy, a recent development in most areas, means that modern *huipiles* might include the word *escuela* (school), the name of the village, or even the words *Coca Cola*. Synthetic thread, including garish silvers and golds, has also been absorbed into many of the patterns, and as village society starts to open up, some designs, once specific to a single village, are coming to be used throughout the country.

Nevertheless, the basic style of the clothing worn by women has changed little since Maya times. The most significant development is simply that the *huipil*, which once hung loose, is now tucked into the skirt. Only in one or two places have the women added sleeves, or gathered their skirts, although in recent times young women have responded to outside influences and the latest generation of costumes tends to emphasize the shape of the body. But in defiance of modern fashion Maya women still wear their hair in an assortment of bizarre styles, ranging from the halos of Santiago Atitlán to the pompoms of Aguacatán and Nebaj. Ceremonial *huipiles*, which are always the most spectacular, are still worn loose, in classic Maya style.

The basic element of a Maya woman's costume is the *huipil*, a loose-fitting blouse, normally woven by the women themselves on a **back-strap loom**. All *huipiles* are intricately decorated, either as a part of the woven pattern or with complex embroidery, and these designs are specific to each village. To protect the embroidery some women wear their *huipiles* inside out, saving the full splendour for market days. Longer ceremonial *huipiles*, reserved for fiestas, are usually more extravagant, often hanging low in the most traditional style. Under the *huipil* a skirt, or *corte*, is worn, and these are becoming increasingly standardized. Usually woven on a foot loom, it is a simple piece of cloth, up to five metres long, joined to form a tube into which the women step. Most common are the *jaspeado cortes* woven on looms in Salcajá, San Francisco Totonicapán and Cobán by commercial weavers, and tie-dyed in universally worn patterns. In some cases there are distinct styles, but these tend to be used in a general region rather than in specific villages: the brilliant reds of Nebaj and Chajul, the yellows of San Pedro and San Marcos, and the blues of the Huehuetenango area, for example. To add individuality to their skirts the women decorate them with thin strips of coloured embroidery, known as *randa*. And to hold them up they use elaborate **sashes**, woven in superb colours and intricate patterns, and often including decorative tassels. Perhaps the most outlandish part of women's costume is the headdress, which varies widely and seems to have no connection with modern styles. The most famous of these are the halos of Santiago Atitlán – twelve-metre strips of cloth – while the turbans of Nebaj and Aguacatán are some of the finest. In addition to the cloth that they wear the women also weave *tzutes*, used to carry babies or food, and shawls that ward off the highland chill.

Men's clothing

Highland men have always had greater contact with the outside world that the women, and as a result have been more susceptible to change. From the outset their costume was influenced to a greater extent by the arrival of the Spanish, and today **men's traditional costume** is worn in only a few villages. The more traditional styles are generally reflected in ceremonial costume, while everyday clothes are heavily influenced by non-traditional "western" styles. If you're around for a fiesta you'll probably see some fantastic costumes worn by men who wear jeans every other day of the year.

On the whole even "traditional costumes" now have more in common with shirt and trousers than the ancient loose-hanging tunic. Nevertheless, men's costumes do include superb weaving and spectacular designs. Their jackets are particularly unusual, ranging from the superb reds of Nebaj, modelled on those worn by Spanish officers, to the ornate tuxedo style of Sololá. (Those worn in Sololá seem to undergo regular changes, and the greys of late have now been superseded by a very ornate white version.) In the Cuchumatanes the men wear *capixays*, small ponchos made from wool, and in San Juan Atitán these bear a remarkable similarity to monks' habits. Other particularly unusual features are *rodilleras* (or *delanteras*) short woollen skirts, worn in Nahualá and San Antonio Palopó, the superbly embroidered shorts of Santiago Atitlán and Santa Catarina Palopó, and the astounding cowboy-style shirts of Todos Santos and Sololá.

Although fewer men wear traditional costume the styles that remain are astonishingly diverse, their scarcity making them appear all the more outlandish. The *tzute*, a piece of cloth worn either on the head or folded on the shoulder, is of particular significance, often marking out an important member of the *cofradía*. In some villages the mayor, dressed in jeans and a T-shirt, will still wear a woven *tzute* on his shoulder as a symbol of office.

Designs

The **designs** used in the traditional costume of both men and women are as diverse as the costumes themselves, an amazing collection of sophisticated patterns, using superb combinations of colour and shape. They include a range of animals, plants and people, as well as abstract designs, words and names. Many of them probably date from long before the Conquest: we know that the double-headed eagle or *k'ot* was emblematic in San Juan Cotzal, and the sun, moon and snake were commonly used in classic Maya design, while the peacock, horse and chicken can only have been introduced after the arrival of the Spanish. The **quetzal** is perhaps the most universal feature and is certain to date from pre-conquest times, when the bird was seen as the spiritual protector of K'iche' kings. The significance of the designs is as imprecise as their origins, although according to Lily de Jongh Osborne, an expert on Maya culture, designs once expressed the weaver's position within the social hierarchy, and could also indicate marital status. One particularly interesting design is the bat on the back of the jackets of Sololá, which dates back to the bat dynasty, among the last Kaqchikel rulers. In days gone by each level of the village hierarchy wore a different style of jacket, although today fashion is the prime consideration, and each generation is simply more outrageous than the last.

Human rights in Guatemala

Since the arrival of the Spanish, Guatemalan history has been characterized by political repression and economic exploitation, involving the denial of the most basic human rights. A horrifying catalogue of events stretches across the last 480 years, but reached levels as barbaric as any previously seen in the late 1970s and the early 1980s. The chief victims have always been the indigenous Maya, generally regarded as backward, ignorant and dispensable. Today the story of Guatemalan repression is very much an unfinished history, although the level of violence has declined significantly in the last few years.

The early years

When **Pedro de Alvarado** arrived in Guatemala in 1523 he brought with him the notions of violent conquest and racist exploitation that have dominated the country to the present day. In the early years of the Conquest towns were burnt to the ground and huge numbers of indigenous people were massacred and enslaved. At the same time they had to contend with repeated epidemics that were to halve their numbers. Once the initial Conquest was over the survivors were systematically herded into villages, deprived of their land, and forced to work in the new plantations: a pattern that seems all too familiar in modern Guatemala.

Equally familiar is the response of the indigenous population, who rose in defiance. It took almost two centuries for their numbers to recover from the devastation of the Conquest, but by the start of the eighteenth century uprisings were common. There were **revolts** in 1708, 1743, 1760, 1764, 1770, 1803, 1817, 1818, 1820, 1838, 1839, 1898 and 1905, all of which met with severe repression.

Independence brought little change. Under **Rufino Barrios** (1873–85) the demands of the coffee industry put fresh strains on the indigenous population, as their land and labour were once again exploited for the benefit of foreign investors and the ruling elite. Under **Jorge Ubico** (1931–44) laws were introduced that obliged Maya men to work on the plantations, and for the first time the government developed a network of spies and informers, giving it the capacity to deal directly with dissenting voices: a capacity it demonstrated in 1934, when Ubico discovered a plot to assassinate him and had some 300 people killed in just two days.

The most significant developments, at least in terms of human rights, came during the socialist governments of **Arévalo** and **Arbenz** (1945–55), which for the first time sought to meet the needs of the indigenous population. Local organizations such as unions and co-operatives were free to operate, suffrage was extended to include all adults, health and schooling were expanded, and land was redistributed to the dispossessed. For the first time in the country's history the issues of inequality and injustice were seriously addressed.

However, in 1954 the government was overthrown by a CIA-backed coup, which cleared the stage for military rule and ushered in the modern era of repression.

Military rule

After 1954 the army dominated the government, operating in alliance with the landowning elite and foreign business interests to consolidate the power of the right. Large-scale repression wasn't to begin until the mid-1960s, but directly after the takeover the army began gathering the names of those who had been active under the socialist administration. In association with the CIA they put together a list of some 70,000 people – a much-used reference source once the killing began.

The **guerrilla** movement, which developed out of an army revolt in 1960, was first active in the eastern highlands. Throughout the 1960s political violence was on the increase, aimed not just at the guerrillas, but at all political opponents and left-wing sympathizers. In the war against the guerrillas the army was unable to strike directly at its enemy and opted instead to eradicate their support in the community. Between 1966 and 1977 some 10,000 non-combatants were killed in a bid to destroy a guerrilla force that numbered no more than 500; and by the early 1970s the guerrillas were on the run, unable to mount attacks or add to their numbers.

In other parts of the country there was a brutal clampdown on a range of "suspect" organizations. In Guatemala City this campaign gave birth to the "**death squads**", put together by the right-wing MLN (National Liberation Movement) and the army. The first to emerge was *Mano Blanco*, who swore "to eradicate national renegades and traitors to the fatherland". Death squads became a permanent feature of Guatemalan politics during military rule – assassinating unionists, left-wing politicians and students. Victims were usually abducted by men in unmarked cars, and later their bodies were found, dumped by the roadside, mutilated and tortured.

By 1975 the guerrilla movement was once again on the rise, as were peasant organizations, co-operatives and unions, all inspired by the move towards **liberation theology**, under which the Catholic Church began to campaign on social issues. The experience of 1954 proved to the Guatemalan people that their political options were severely restricted, and in the 1970s and 1980s many directed their energies towards grass-roots organization, forming groups such as the CUC (Committee for Campesino Unity). But in response to this the repression continued, and in 1976 Amnesty International stated that a total of 20,000 Guatemalans had been killed in the previous decade.

The closing years of the 1970s saw a rapid polarization of the situation that gave birth to a fresh wave of violence. The **guerrilla movements** were by now well established in many different parts of the country, as repression in the highlands drove increasing numbers to seek refuge in their ranks. At this stage there were four main organizations: the PGT (Guatemalan Workers Party), who operated in Guatemala City and on the Pacific coast; FAR (the Rebel Armed Forces), who fought throughout Petén; EGP (the Guerrilla Army of the Poor), who had several fronts in northern Quiché; and ORPA (Organization of People in Arms), who functioned in San Marcos and Atitlán.

The election of **General Lucas García** in 1978 marked the onset of unprecedented mass repression. Once again the list of victims included left-wing politicians, labour leaders, lawyers, priests, nuns, teachers, unionists, academics and students, all of whom were regarded as subversive. In the highlands the war against the guerrillas also reached a new intensity, as selective killings were replaced by outright massacres. Once again the army found itself pitched against an elusive enemy and resorted to indiscriminate killings in a bid to undermine peasant support for the guerrillas.

Repression was so widespread that human rights organizations found it almost impossible to keep track of the situation, although certain incidents still came to light. In April 1981 Oxfam estimated that 1500 had been killed in Chimaltenango in the previous two months. Precise numbers are impossible to calculate, but according to some estimates 25,000 died during the first four years of the Lucas administration, the vast majority killed either by the security forces or by death squads, which were often operated by off-duty soldiers or policemen and directed by the G-2 intelligence agency from an annexe of the Palacio Nacional.

Ríos Montt

In March 1982 Lucas was replaced by **General Efrían Ríos Montt**, and the state's tactics changed considerably. The guerrillas were offered amnesty, death squad activity dropped off, and an office was set up to investigate the fate of the disappeared. But Ríos Montt had vowed to defeat the guerrillas by Christmas and in rural areas the level of violence increased as the army began to make big gains in the fight against the rebels. In the early months of Ríos Montt's rule massacres were still commonplace as it took him some time to reshape the armed forces and provide an alternative to the brutal approach they had adopted under Lucas García. The campaign still claimed a heavy death toll, despite the downturn in indiscriminate slaughter. According to Amnesty International there were 2186 killings in the first four months of the new administration, and by now some 200,000 refugees had fled the country. Amnesty's report on the Ríos Montt administration (see box on p.464) is a catalogue of horror, though in many ways the events described were more typical of the Lucas García regime. However, its eyewitness accounts of army campaigns capture the full extent of repression in the highlands.

Under Ríos Montt the army campaign was much more successful, utilizing CIA strategies and intelligence, and the guerrillas were driven into the remote corners of the highlands. Soldiers swept through the mountains, rounding up those who had fled from previous campaigns and herding them into refugee camps, while villagers were forced to defend their own communities in Civil Defence Patrols. Those who returned from the mountains were put to work by the army, who fed and "re-educated" them. Accounts of the army campaign under Ríos Montt are deeply divided. Some commentators see him as a significant reformer, who saved the rural population by transforming the approach of the army. On the other hand most liberal Guatemalans regard him as the most brutal of all the country's rulers. Interestingly, Ríos Montt (who is now leader of the FRG party) remains particularly popular in the highlands. Most Ixil Maya (see p.430), who suffered more than any other in the civil war years, speak highly of him, saying that when he came to power he managed to put a stop to the indiscriminate violence which had plagued the country.

Ríos Montt was replaced by **Mejía Víctores** in August 1983, and under the new administration there was a significant drop in the level of rural repression, although selective killings were still everyday events. In 1984, however, the number of urban disappearances rose once again, with around fifty people abducted each month, many victims picked out by the CIA, which had a huge

Eyewitness testimony

The following account of a massacre in San Francisco Nentón that took place on July 17, 1982, was related to a priest in a Mexican refugee camp by survivors; the account is taken from an Amnesty International report.

At 11am on Saturday 17 July the army arrived in San Francisco having passed through the nearby villages of Bulej and Yalambojoch. The army had previously visited the village on 24 June and had told the inhabitants that they could be killed if they were found not to be peacefully working in their homes and their fields. Soldiers had also said, however, that the villagers should not run away from the army, as it was there to defend them. On 17 July some 600 soldiers arrived on foot. A helicopter circled nearby and eventually landed. The military were accompanied by an ex-guerrilla, now in military uniform, who was apparently acting as the army's informer. The people were told to assemble for a discussion with the colonel. It was the first day on which the village's new civil defense patrol was to have begun its duties. Some of the survivors said that the patrol, of 21, was taken away shortly after the arrival of the army and had not been seen since. They are presumed dead.

According to testimonies collected by priests, the villagers first sensed they were in danger when a man who survivors said had been "tied up like a pig" was brought before them by the soldiers. They knew he had not been involved in anything, and yet saw that he was being "punished". They also saw how "angry" the commander appeared to be and began to fear for themselves. They were first asked to unload the soldiers' supplies from the helicopter, which they did. The men were then shut up in the courthouse to begin praying "to make peace with God", as they were about to suffer. A survivor described how: "We pray, 11 o'clock, 12 o'clock passes. By now, everyone has come into town and been shut up. At 1 o'clock, it began: a blast of gunfire at the women, there in the church. It makes so much noise. All the little children are crying."

This witness went on to tell how the women who survived the initial gunfire were taken off in small groups to different houses by soldiers where they were killed, many apparently with machetes. After they had been killed, the houses were set on fire. This witness and the others interviewed described a particularly atrocious killing they had seen, the murder of a child of about three. The child was disembowelled, as were several others, but kept screaming, until a soldier smashed his head with a

presence in Guatemala at the time in the name of "fighting Communism". In the highlands the process of reconstruction began. Guerrilla forces had dropped to around 1500, and although military campaigns continued, "model villages" were now being built to replace those that had been destroyed. Even so the conditions for refugees and survivors were still highly restricted and many large and impoverished communities are now made up entirely of widows and orphans. Important grassroots **human rights organizations** began to spring up in this period, including GAM (Mutual Support Group), from the families of the disappeared, and CONAVIGUA (National Commission of Guatemalan Widows), a very significant and largely indigenous group. Though the members of these groups faced routine intimidation and frequent death threats, they marked the emergence of a new period of Maya political activism, galvanizing support in indigenous communities throughout the country.

Towards the end of 1985 the country faced its first free elections in thirty years, after a period that had seen eighteen different administrations and cost the lives of 120,000 people. Another 39,000 had "disappeared", 440 villages had been destroyed, and 150,000 Guatemalans had fled to Mexico.

pole, then swung him by his feet and threw him into a burning house. "Yes", said the witness, "yes, I saw it. Yes, I saw how they threw him away, threw him into the house."

The witness continued: "At 2 o'clock, they began with all the men. They ordered them out of the courthouse in small groups, and then blasted them with gunfire. It went on and on. They tied up the men's hands and then 'bang, bang'. We couldn't see, we could only hear the noise of the guns. The killing took place in the courtyard outside the courthouse, then they'd throw the bodies into the church. They killed the three old people with a blunt machete, the way you would kill sheep."

Another witness described how the old were killed: "The old people said, 'What have we done, no, we are tired and old. We're not thinking of doing anything. We're not strong. We can't do anything any more.' But they said, 'You're not worth anything any more, even if you're tired, get out of there.' They dragged them out, and knifed them. They stabbed and cut them as if they were animals and they were laughing when they killed them. They killed them with a machete that had no teeth. They put one man on the table and cut open his chest, the poor man, and he was still alive, and so they started to cut his throat. They cut his throat slowly. He was suffering a lot. They were cutting people under the ribs, and blood came rushing out and they were laughing." Another survivor continued: "When they got to the end, they killed six people in the courthouse. One was a military commissioner. They didn't care. They killed him there at his table with his three policemen."

"By now it was 6.30pm. It was getting dark outside. They threw a bomb into the corner of the courthouse. It was bloody, two were killed. How the blood ran! It ran all over me. Then they fired at the remaining bodies in the courthouse. Then they threw all the bodies in a heap. They dragged people by the feet, as if they were animals. They threw me on top of the dead bodies."

One witness ended his testimony: "Father my heart is so heavy with pain for the dead, because of what I have seen. I saw how my brothers died. All of them: friends, godparents, everyone, as we are all brothers. My heart will cry for them the rest of my life. But they had committed no crime. Nobody said: 'This is your crime. Here is the proof.' They just killed them, that's all. That's how death came."

A list of the dead was compiled in Mexico on September 5. It included 302 people, 92 of whom were under twelve, and the youngest less than two months old.

Civilian rule

In 1986 the election of **Vinicio Cerezo** as Guatemala's first civilian president for almost thirty years was widely regarded as a major opportunity to improve the human rights situation within the country. Cerezo himself had on several occasions come close to assassination, and members of his party, the Christian Democrats, were always a favourite target of the death squads.

Following Cerezo's inauguration there was a marked decrease in the quantity of human rights violations although in a matter of months things started to deteriorate once again. Abductions, killings and intimidation remained widespread, with the victims drawn from the same groups as before. Between February 1986 and January 1987 there were at least one thousand killings, the vast majority attributable to "death squads". No one accused Cerezo of involvement in the murders, but it does seem that they were carried out by members of the security forces, which was a measure of his inability to control them.

In rural areas the level of violence dropped off significantly. With guerrilla forces estimated at 1000 to 3000, the army had little need to use the same heavy-handed tactics it had employed in the past. Many observers felt that the reduction in human rights abuse was simply a reflection of a more refined strategy by the army, who had already established control and could now use a more subtle but no less effective form of repression – killing selective targets rather than destroying entire communities. Abuses of the indigenous population remained common however. In many areas they were forced to participate in **civil patrols** (despite assurances that they would have the option not to), which themselves became important in the system of repression and were responsible for intimidation, murder and abduction.

In 1988, just two years after the return to civilian rule, the level of violence began to increase sharply. Many people's worst fears were confirmed in November of that year when 22 bodies were found in a shallow grave near El Aguacate, a small village in the department of Chimaltenango. The killings continued throughout Cerezo's term in office and there was no real effort either to find the bodies of the disappeared – despite the pleas of their relatives – or to bring the guilty to trial. Cerezo himself remained preoccupied with holding onto power, fending off several coup attempts and trying to build some kind of power base. As president he adopted a nonconfrontational approach which not only ensured a reprieve for the guilty but also allowed for the continued abuse of human rights. In his more candid moments Cerezo admitted that the continuing power of the army restricted his room for manoeuvre and argued that any investigation of past abuses would be impossible as he would have to put the entire army on trial.

The Peace Accords and military impunity

In 1990 Cerezo handed the reins of power to **President Serrano**, but the situation remained bleak, with abductions, torture, intimidation and extrajudicial executions still commonplace. According to several US human rights groups, five hundred Guatemalans either "disappeared" or were killed in extrajudicial executions in 1992 alone. That said, the administration was forced to tackle several high-profile cases, including the murder of street children and the assassinations of US citizen Michael Devine and the anthropologist Myrna Mack Chang, and for the first time members of the armed forces were convicted of human rights violations. A number of defiant local groups continued to denounce violations, particularly GAM, many of whose members and leaders were kidnapped and murdered. By contrast the government's Human Rights Commission received over one thousand complaints of human rights violations and acted on none of them.

Meanwhile out **in the highlands** a number of new factors emerged. In December 1990 the people of Santiago Atitlán expelled the army from their village, after troops shot and killed thirteen people (see p.168). In the wake of this incident a number of other villages called for army bases to be closed. The confidence of the Maya population was further boosted in 1992, when the Nobel Peace Prize was awarded to Rigoberta Menchú (see p.469), briefly focusing world attention on the plight of Guatemala's indigenous population.

In early 1993 the first **refugees** began returning from Mexico, many settling in the Ixcán region of northern El Quiché and Alta Verapaz. Their return provoked a fresh crisis in the countryside and the army bombarded nearby villages and resorted to familiar tactics to terrorize those returning. As more refugees have come home, the shortage of land and the uncertainty surrounding their future provided additional tension and resulted in further human rights abuses by the armed forces. The most serious case was the massacre of eleven people (and the wounding of thirty more) by soldiers in the village of **Xamán** in Alta Verapaz on October 5, 1995 (see p.317). Since then thousands more have returned from exile, including ex-guerrillas, and relations have generally been good with other established communities, though unemployment is very high amongst the returning refugees.

The **Indigenous Rights Accords of 1995** (see p.433) sought to tackle these outstanding issues, with commitments to educate Maya children in their native tongue, to promote the use of indigenous languages at national and local level, to encourage greater political participation for the Maya, and to preserve their sacred areas. However, only limited progress has been made to date. The Arzú government delayed the imposition of a Children's Code to ensure that schools teach Maya and Garífuna children in their native languages and, in a major setback, the Guatmemalan electorate narrowly voted against a proposed constitutional change in 1999 that would have added inherent indigenous rights to the state's body of laws. It look increasingly likely that other central commitments will take decades to implement, even if the will is still there.

One of the most crucial strands of the **Peace Accords of December 1996** was the establishment of a Truth Commission, overseen by **MINUGUA** (the UN mission to Guatemala), to investigate human rights abuses committed during the civil war. However, the Commission's lack of legal teeth, its short lifespan, and a stipulation that only abuses "linked to the armed conflict" should be investigated meant that its powers were limited from the outset and no names were named. Despite this, military forces (including the army, civil patrols, police and death squads) were held culpable for 93 percent of the killings. The Catholic Church also set up a research team, REMHI, to document painstakingly the civil war atrocities, a three-year project compiled with 5465 individual testimonies. The investigation concentrating on the wave of violence at the height of the repression between 1980 and 1983, and the findings, published in April 1998, were unequivocal: government military forces were accountable for ninety percent of the killings, while the guerrillas and paramilitary groups were responsible for remainder.

Two days after the report was presented, **Bishop Juan Geradi**, who was in charge of the REMHI project, was found beaten to death at his home in Guatemala City. The assassination of one of Guatemala's most prominent human rights campaigners outraged the nation, bringing thousands on to the streets in protest. For three years, as the murder investigation dragged on, a succession of prosecutors and witnesses received death threats and it seemed the perpetrators would escape justice. However, in 2000, the incoming Portillo government moved quickly to solve the crime, bringing charges against three elite military chiefs and a priest, who were all found guilty in June 2001.

The Geradi case confirmed in the starkest terms the weakness of the nation's justice system and the extreme obstacles to obtaining prosecutions in Guatemala. Though levels of political violence have undoubtedly dropped since the early 1990s, a climate of fear persists and those who dare to challenge the interests of the elite and the criminal gangs face intimidation and violence. Victims have included journalists, like Jorge Alegría, gunned down in Puerto

Barrios in September 2001, environmentalists, lawyers, union leaders and human rights activists.

Human rights groups also express severe concern about the plight of several thousand **street children** (see box p.65) mainly living in the capital, who are frequently targeted by vigilantes, security guards and policemen. Child kidnapping rings also operate in Guatemala, stealing babies to sell to North America and Europe.

Guatemala's **Maya population** also remain severely discriminated against, largely living in extreme poverty (81 percent, according to government estimates), suffering appalling health care and education (75 percent are illiterate), and with some of the lowest life expectancies of any ethnic group in the world. A Maya man will live on average to around 47 years of age, a woman to 48, up to seventeen years less than their mestizo compatriots. Non-Spanish speakers rarely get court translators or bilingual state defence lawyers and, despite forming over fifty percent of the population, only a handful of the eighty Congressional deputies are indigenous.

In its 2001 report on Guatemala, Amnesty International rated the continuing **impunity of the armed forces** against prosecution for directing the campaign of terror during the civil war as the nation's most pressing human rights issue:

There has been little or no justice for those who suffered abuses in the context of Guatemala's civil conflict and few of those responsible for past violations have been brought to justice. Instead, witnesses and others involved in the few legal proceedings initiated in order to seek justice for gross violations of human rights have suffered intimidation and attacks.

Despite these threats, Guatemalan human rights groups are attempting to prosecute ex-military leaders through the international and national courts. The Rigoberta Menchú Foundation (see p.470) has filed suits abroad against the former generals Lucas García and Ríos Montt, using the Pinochet and Milosevic cases as references. Other organizations have successfully obtained compensation from the Guatemalan government through the Inter-American justice system for the families of victims of violence. In Guatemala, all prosecutions are fraught with difficulty, but the CALDH (Centre for Legal Action on Human Rights) has aided indigenous massacre survivors to file suits against the military high command from the Lucas García administration for killings in their villages. It has been essential to organize international accompaniment for the communities who have presented the legal actions, in order to prevent reprisals against them.

Amnesty sees the progress and outcome of these actions as a vital test of Guatemalan democracy. This is the first time that victims of massive human rights violations have brought charges against the intellectual authors of these crimes, and a positive outcome could lead to genuine reconciliation in the country and break the impunity of the army forces. It would also show that Guatemala is subscribing to international standards of human rights and demonstrate that the nation's legal system can be used to obtain justice and seek redress for offences.

For more information on **human rights in Guatemala** contact either the Guatemalan Human Rights Commission – USA (ⓦwww.ghrc-usa.org), Amnesty International (ⓦwww.amnesty.org) or Human Rights Watch (ⓦwww.hrw.org). All these organizations publish regular bulletins on the current situation in Guatemala and produce annual reports.

Rigoberta Menchú and the Nobel Peace Prize

Five hundred years after Columbus reached the Americas the Nobel committee awarded their peace prize to Rigoberta Menchú, a 33-year-old K'iche' Maya woman who had campaigned tirelessly for peace in Guatemala, and for the advancement of indigenous people across the world. In their official statement the Nobel institute described Menchú as "a vivid symbol of peace and reconciliation across ethnic, cultural and social dividing lines."

Within Guatemala, however, the honour provoked controversy. Few doubted that Menchú had firm connections and deep sympathies with Guatemala's guerrillas, although after she was awarded the prize she distanced herself from the armed struggle. Nevertheless, many people argued that her support for armed uprising made her an inappropriate winner of a peace prize. A couple of days before the announcement the army's chief spokesman Captain Julio Yon Rivera said she had "defamed the fatherland", although once the prize was awarded he claimed to have been expressing a personal opinion that was not the official view of the Guatemalan army. Others feared that the prize would be interpreted as a vindication of the guerrillas and only serve to perpetuate the civil war.

Menchú's own words in the first volume of her autobiography *I, Rigoberta Menchú*, however, show her to be essentially a pacifist and suggest that her unspoken support for the guerrillas was very much a last resort. "For us, killing is something monstrous. And that's why we feel so angered by all the repression... Even though the tortures and kidnappings had done our people a lot of harm, we shouldn't lose faith in change. This is when I began working in a peasant organization and went on to another stage of my life. There are other things, other ways."

Menchú's story is undeniably tragic and her account offers a harrowing insight into the darkest years of Guatemalan history and the impact on her family's village and the nation's indigenous people. However, serious doubts have recently emerged as to the accuracy of sizeable parts of her life as recounted in *I, Rigoberta Menchú*, following the publication of an iconoclastic biography of Menchú, written in 1998 by David Stoll: *Rigoberta Menchú and the Story of all Poor Guatemalans*. Stoll concluded that substantial sections of the Menchú legend had been fabricated or greatly exaggerated, and that she had "drastically revised the pre-war experience of her village to suit the needs of the revolutionary organization she had joined."

In *I, Rigoberta Menchú*, she describes how the barbaric cruelty of the Guatemalan civil war affected her family, who were political activists, and how they were branded guerrilla-sympathizers by the military. Menchú recounts the fight to protect the family farm from greedy ladinos, how they were compelled to work in the plantations of the Pacific coast to survive, and that she received no formal schooling. The deaths of her brother, mother and father at the hands of the armed forces are agonizingly retold. Expanding to cover the wider picture in Guatemala, Menchú condemns the massive disparities between the country's ladino and Maya, and rich and poor. The biography sold strongly, and Menchú was soon invited to speak at events and conferences all over the world. Tirelessly campaigning for the rights of the Guatemalan Maya and other oppressed minorities from exile in Mexico, she frequently travelled to the United Nations in Geneva and New York to press her case. This period of the Nobel laureate's life is narrated in *Crossing Borders*, the second volume of her autobiography, and an altogether less traumatic and controversial read.

Rigoberta Menchú returned to Guatemala in 1994 as an iconic but refractory figure; in the global arena, however, her reputation was unblemished until the publication of David Stoll's biography. Stoll's book provided compelling evidence that Menchú's family's land dispute was an internecine family feud rather than a racially charged indigenous–ladino altercation; that she never had toiled in the fields of Pacific coast plantations and had been educated at two private convent schools. He alleged a guerrilla past and questioned the accuracy of her account about the deaths of two of her brothers.

After the biography's publication an international furore ensued, with allegations from the *New York Times* that that she had received "a Nobel prize for lying". Menchú evaded responding directly to Stoll's charges, though admitted that she had received some formal education at a convent school in Chiantla. She has subsequently sought to distance herself somewhat from *I, Rigoberta Menchú*, and accused the editor of distorting her testimony. Geir Lunestad, director of the Nobel institute, has also supported Menchú, declaring that the decision to give Menchú the award was because of her work on behalf of indigenous people, not based on her family history.

Since 1998, as the dust had settled, Menchú's reputation has remained largely undiminished at home and abroad amongst her supporters. It is not in dispute that her mother, father and brothers died at the hands of the military (with another 200,000 Guatemalans) whose extreme brutality has been documented in two Truth Commission reports. Her success bringing global attention to the terrible suffering inflicted on (and continuing repression of) Guatemala's Maya is incontestable, and her work on behalf of the world's indigenous peoples has been unrelenting and effective. Today, Rigoberta Menchú is adored by most Guatemalan Maya and the political left, many of whom see her as a future presidential candidate, and despised by the Guatemalan oligarchy. Through her foundation (see below), she continues to press for civil and human rights in Guatemala, attempting to galvanize the indigenous electorate, few of whom have ever bothered to vote historically. Recently she has filed charges in the international courts against the former military rulers Lucas García and Ríos Montt, and fought to end the impunity of the armed forces for their civil war atrocities.

For more information on the Rigoberta Menchú Foundation, consult the website ⓦ www.rigobertamenchu.org.

Landscape and wildlife

Guatemala embraces an astonishingly diverse collection of environments, ranging from the permanently moist rainforests and mangroves of the Caribbean coast to the exposed western highlands, where the ground is often hard with frost. Its wildlife is correspondingly varied; undisturbed forests provide a home to both temperate species from the north and tropical ones from the south, as well as a number of indigenous species found nowhere else in the world.

The Pacific coast

Guatemala's **Pacific coastline** is marked by a thin strip of black volcanic sand, pounded by the surf. There are no natural harbours and boats have to take their chances in the breakers or launch from one of the piers (though the purpose-built Puerto Quetzal takes large, ocean-going ships). The sea itself provides a rich natural harvest of shrimp, tuna, snapper and mackerel, most of which go for export. The coastal waters are also ideal for sport fishing. A couple of kilometres offshore, dorado, which grow to around forty pounds, are plentiful, while further out there are marlin, sailfish, wahoo and skipjack.

The **beach** itself rises from the water to form a large sandbank, dotted with palm trees, behind which the land drops off into low-lying mangrove swamps and canals. In the east, from San José to the border, the **Chiquimulilla Canal** runs behind the beach for around 100km. For most of the way it's no more than a narrow strip of water, but here and there it fans out into swamps, creating a maze of waterways that are an ideal breeding ground for young fish, waterfowl and a range of small mammals. The sandy shoreline is an ideal nesting site for three species of **sea turtles**, including the giant leatherback (see box on p.248), which periodically emerge from the water, drag themselves up the beach and deposit a clutch of eggs before hauling their weight back into the water. At Monterrico, to the east of San José, a nature reserve protects a small section of the coastline for the benefit of the turtles, and with luck you might see one here. **The Reserva Monterrico–Hawaii** (see p.249) is in fact the best place to see wildlife on the Pacific coast as it includes a superb mangrove swamp, typical of the area directly behind the beach, which you can easily explore by boat.

The **mangroves** are mixed in with water lilies, bulrushes and tropical hardwoods, amongst which you'll see **herons**, **kingfishers** and an array of **ducks** including **muscovies** and **white whistling ducks**. In the area around Monterrico flocks of **wood stork** are common, and you might also see the **white ibis** or the occasional **great jabiru**, a massive stork that nests in the area. With real perseverance and a bit of luck you might also catch a glimpse of a **racoon**, **anteater** or **opossum**. You'll also be able to see **alligators** and **iguanas**, if not in the wild then at the reserve headquarters where they are kept on a breeding programme. Other birds that you might see almost anywhere along the coast include **plovers**, **coots** and **terns**, and a number of winter migrants including **white** and **brown pelicans**.

Between the shore and the foothills of the highlands, the **coastal plain** is an intensely fertile and heavily farmed area, where the volcanic and alluvial soils are ideal for sugar cane, cotton, palm oil, rubber plantations and cattle ranches. In recent years soya and sorghum, which require less labour, have been added to this list. Guatemala's coastal **agribusiness** is high cost and high yield: the soils are treated chemically and the crops regularly sprayed with a cocktail of pesticides, herbicides and fertilizers. There's little land that remains untouched by the hand of commercial agriculture so it's hard to imagine what this must once have looked like, but it was almost certainly very similar to Petén, a mixture of savannah and rainforest supporting a rich array of wildlife. These days it's only the swamps, steep hillsides and towering hedges that give any hint of its former glory, although beautiful flocks of white **snowy** and **cattle egrets** feed alongside the beef cattle.

Finally, one particularly interesting lowland species is the **oropendola**, a large oriole which builds a long woven nest hanging from trees and telephone wires. They tend to nest in colonies and a single tree might support fifty nests. You'll probably notice the nests more than the birds, which thrive throughout Guatemala and neighbouring countries.

The Boca Costa

Approaching the highlands, the coastal plain starts to slope up towards a string of volcanic cones, and this section of well-drained hillside is known as the **Boca Costa**. The volcanic soils, high rainfall and good drainage conspire to make it ideal for growing **coffee**, and it's here that some of Guatemala's best beans are produced with rows of olive-green bushes ranked beneath shady trees.

Where the land is unsuitable for coffee, lush tropical forest still grows, clinging to the hills. As you head up into the highlands, through deeply cleft valleys, you pass through some of this superb forest, dripping with moss-covered vines, bromeliads and orchids. The full value of this environment had remained unexplored for many years and the foundation of the **Faro Field Station**, on the southern slopes of the **Santiaguito** volcano, revealed an amazing, undisturbed ecosystem, protected by the threat of volcanic eruption. Over 120 species of bird have been sighted here, including some real rarities such as **solitary eagles**, **quetzals** and **highland guans**. The **azure-rumped tanager**, seen here in June 1988, hadn't previously been sighted in Guatemala since the mid-nineteenth century. The Guatemala Birding Resource Center (see p.188), a specialist tour operator based in Quetzaltenango, runs excellent trips to the Boca Costa region.

The highlands

The highlands proper begin with a chain of **volcanoes**. There are 37 peaks in all, the main backbone ranged in a direct line from the southwest border with Mexico, running parallel with the Pacific coastline before continuing into El Salvador. (In the eastern highlands, away from the main chain, there's another sprinkling of older, less spectacular weathered cones.) The highest of the main peaks is **Tajumulco** (4220m), which marks the Mexican border, and there are also three active cones, **Fuego**, **Pacaya** and **Santiaguito**, all of which belch sulphurous fumes, volcanic ash, and the occasional fountain of molten rock. Beneath the surface their subterranean fires heat the bedrock and there are several places where spring water emerges at near boiling point, offering the luxury of a hot bath (for the best of these see Fuentes Georginas p.192).

On this southern side of the central highlands there are two large lakes, set in superb countryside and hemmed in by volcanic peaks. Both tell a rueful tale of environmental mismanagement. **Lago de Amatitlán**, to the south of Guatemala City, is further down the road to contamination, its waters already blackened by pollution and its shores ringed with holiday homes. It remains a popular picnic spot for the capital's not so rich. Further to the west is **Lago de Atitlán**, still spectacularly beautiful, with crystal blue water, but increasing tourist development threatens to damage its delicate ecological balance. The greatest damage so far was done by the introduction of the **black bass** in 1958, in a bid to create sport fishing. The bass is a greedy, thuggish beast and in no time at all its presence had reshaped the food chain. Smaller fish became increasingly rare, as did crabs, frogs, insects and small mammals. Worst hit was the **Atitlán grebe**, a small, flightless water bird unique to the lake. Young grebes were gobbled up by the hungry bass, and by 1965 just eighty of them survived By 1984, falling water levels caused by the 1976 earthquake, combined with tourist development of the lakeshore, cut their numbers by another thirty, and today the bird is extinct. Meanwhile the beauty of Lago de Atitlán remains under threat from overdevelopment, population growth and soil erosion.

On the northern side of the volcanic ridge are the **central valleys** of the highlands, a complex mixture of sweeping bowls, steep-sided valleys, open plateaux and jagged peaks. This central area is home to the vast majority of Guatemala's population and all the available land is intensely farmed, with hillsides carved into workable terraces and portioned up into a patchwork of small fields. Here the land is farmed by campesinos using techniques that predate the arrival of the Spanish. The *milpa* is the mainstay of Maya farming practices: a field is cleared, usually by slash and burn, and is planted with maize as the main crop, with beans, chilles and squash grown beneath it at ground level. Traditionally, the land is rotated between *milpa* and pasture, and also left fallow for a while, but in some areas it's now under constant pressure, the fertility of the soil is virtually exhausted and only with the assistance of fertilizer can it still produce a worthwhile crop. The pressure on land is immense and each generation is forced to farm more marginal territory, planting on steep hillsides where exposed soil is soon washed into the valley below.

Some areas remain off limits to farmers, however, and there are still substantial tracts of the highlands that are **forested**. In the cool valleys of the central highlands pine trees dominate, intermixed with oak, cedar and fir, all of which occur naturally. To the south, on the volcanic slopes and in the warmth of deep-cut valleys, lush subtropical forest thrives in a world kept permanently moist – similar in many ways to the forest of Verapaz, where constant rain fosters the growth of cloudforest.

Heading on to the north the land rises to form several **mountain ranges**. The largest of these are the Cuchumatanes, a massive chain of granite peaks that reach a height of 3837m above the town of Huehuetenango. Further to the east there are several smaller ranges such as the Sierra de Chuacús, the Sierra de las Minas and the Sierra de Chamá. The high peaks support stunted trees and open grassland, used for grazing sheep and cattle, but are too cold for maize and most other crops.

Bird life is plentiful throughout the highlands; you'll see a variety of **hummingbirds**, flocks of screeching **parakeets**, **swifts**, **egrets** and the ever-present **vultures**. Slightly less commonplace are the **quails** and **wood partridges**, **white-tailed pigeons**, and several species of doves including the **little Inca** and the **white-winged dove**. Last but by no means least is the **quetzal**, which has been revered since Maya times. The male quetzal has fantastic green tail-feathers which snake behind it through the air as it flies: these have always been prized by hunters and even today the bird is very rare indeed. Near Copán is the **Biotopo del Quetzal**, a protected area of cloudforest in the department of Baja Verapaz where quetzals breed, but you'll have a better chance of spotting Guatemala's national bird in the more remote mountains of the **Sierra de Caquipec** to the northeast.

The highlands also support a number of small **mammals**, including foxes and small cats, although your chances of seeing these are very slim indeed.

The rainforests of Petén

To the north of the highlands the land drops away into the **rainforests** of Petén, a huge chunk of which remain miraculously undisturbed, although recent oil finds, guerrilla war and migrant settlers are all putting a terrific strain on this ecological wonderland. The forest of Petén extends across the Mexican border, where it merges with the Lacandón and Campeche rainforests, and into Belize, where it skirts around the lower slopes of the Maya Mountains, reaching to the Caribbean coast.

Around fifty percent of Petén is still covered by **primary forest**, with a canopy that towers between 30 and 50m above the forest floor, made up of hundreds of species of trees, including ceiba, mahogany, aguacate, ebony and sapodilla. The combination of a year-round growing season, plenty of moisture and millions of years of evolution have produced an environment that supports literally thousands of species of plants and trees. While temperate forests tend to be dominated by a single species – fir, oak or beech, say – it's diversity that characterizes the tropical forest. Each species is specifically adapted to fit into a particular ecological niche, where it receives a precise amount of light and moisture.

It's a biological storehouse that has yet to be fully explored although it has already yielded some astonishing **discoveries**. Steroid hormones, such as cortisone, and diosgenin, the active ingredient in birth control pills, were developed from wild yams found in these forests; and tetrodoxin, which is derived from a species of Central American frog, is an anesthetic 160,000 times stronger than cocaine.

Despite its size and diversity the forest is surprisingly **fragile**. It forms a closed system in which nutrients are continuously recycled and decaying plant matter fuels new growth. The forest floor is a spongy mass of roots, fungi, mosses, bacteria and micro-organisms, in which nutrients are stored, broken down with the assistance of insects and chemical decay, and gradually released to the waiting roots and fresh seedlings. The thick canopy prevents much light reaching the forest floor, ensuring that the soil remains damp but warm, a hotbed of chemical activity. The death of a large tree prompts a flurry of growth as new light reaches the forest floor, and in no time at all a young tree rises to fill the gap. But once the trees are removed the soil is highly vulnerable, deprived of its main source of fertility. Exposed to the harsh tropical sun and direct rainfall, an area of cleared forest soon becomes prone to flooding and drought. Recently cleared land will contain enough nutrients for four or five years of good growth, but soon afterwards its usefulness declines rapidly and within twenty years it will be almost completely barren. If the trees are stripped from a large area soil erosion will silt the rivers and parched soils disrupt local rainfall patterns.

However, **settlement** needn't mean the end of the rainforest, and in the past this area supported a huge population of Maya, who probably numbered as many as ten million in this region during the Late Classic era. (Some archeologists, however, argue that during Maya occupation Petén was a mixture of savannah and grassland, and that relatively recent climatic changes have enabled it to evolve into rainforest.) Only one small group of Maya, the Lacandones, still farm the forest using traditional methods. They allow the existing trees to point them in the right direction, avoiding areas that support mahogany, as they tend to be too wet, and searching out ceiba and ramon trees, which thrive in rich, well-drained soils. In April a patch of forest is burnt down and then, to prevent soil erosion, planted with fast-growing trees such as bananas and papaya, and with root crops to fix the soil. A few weeks later they plant their main crops: maize and a selection of others, from garlic to sweet potatoes. Every inch of the soil is covered in growth, a method that mimics the forest and thereby protects the soil. The same land is cultivated for three or four years and then allowed to return to its wild state, although they continue to harvest from the fruit-bearing plants and in due course return to the same area. The whole process is in perfect harmony with the forest, extracting only what it can afford to lose and ensuring that it remains fertile. Sadly, the Lacandón are a dying breed and the traditional farming practices are now used by very few. In their place are waves of new settlers, burning the forest and planting grass for cattle. Neither the cattle, the farmers nor the forest will survive long under such a system.

In its undisturbed state the rainforest is still superbly beautiful and is home to an incredible range of wildlife. Amongst the birds, the spectacular scarlet, blue-and-emerald green **ocellated turkey**, found only in Petén, is perhaps the most famous. But the forest is also home to three species of **toucan**, **motmots** (a type of bird of paradise), several species of **parrot** including **Aztec** and **green parakeets**, and the endangered **scarlet macaw**, which is said to live to at least fifty. As in the highlands, **hummingbirds**, **buzzards** and **hawks** are all common. A surprising number of these can be seen fairly easily in the **Parque Nacional Tikal**, particularly if you hang around until sunset.

Although **mammals** are widespread, they are almost always elusive, and your best chance of seeing them is at the bigger reserves and archeological sites, where they may have lost some of their fear of humans. At many forest sites you'll almost certainly see **monkeys**, including the acrobatically agile **spider** and the highly social **howlers**, which emit a chilling, deep-throated roar. The largest land animal in Guatemala the **tapir** (dante) weighing up to 300kg, and usually found near water. Tapirs are endangered and you're not likely to see one without a guide. Two species of **peccary** (wild pigs), the collared and the white-lipped, wander the forest floors in large groups, seeking out roots and palm nuts. The smaller herbivores include the **paca** (also known as the tepescuintle and agouti), a rodent about the size of a piglet, which is hunted everywhere for food. You'll often see **coati**, inquisitive and intelligent members of the racoon family, foraging in the leaf litter around archeological sites with their long snouts, often in family groups of several dozen. Coatis and small

grey foxes are frequently seen at Tikal, and in many places you can see **opossums** or **armadillos**.

Five species of wild **cat** are found in the region, though most are now rare outside the protected areas. **Jaguars** (called *tigres* in Guatemala) formerly ranged over the whole of the country, but today the densest population is found in the northern Petén, though they are very rarely seen. **Pumas** live in remote forest areas; less rare but still uncommon are the much smaller **ocelot** and the **margay**, which is about the size of a large domestic cat. The **jaguarundi** is the smallest and commonest of the wild cats, and as it hunts during the day you might spot one on a trail.

Take a trip along almost any river in Petén and you've a good chance of seeing **green iguanas**, **mud turtles** or **Central American river turtles** sunning themselves on logs. **Egrets** and **kingfishers** fish from overhanging branches while large rivers such as Río de la Pasión and lakes, including Lago de Petexbatún are correspondingly rich, packed with **snook**, **tarpon** and **mullet**.

Crocodiles are becoming increasingly common in Petén, after previously being hunted almost to extinction, and are now frequently spotted at Lago de Yaxhá and Laguna Perdida. They are not dangerous to humans unless they are very large – at least 3m long – but heed the warnings of locals if they advise against swimming in a particular lagoon.

Although there are at least 50 species of **snake** in the region, only a few are venomous and you're unlikely to see any snakes at all. One of the commonest is the **boa constrictor**, which is also the largest, growing up to 4m, though it poses no threat to humans. Others you might see are **coral snakes** (which are venomous) and **false coral snakes** (which are not); in theory they're easily distinguished by noting the arrangement of adjacent colours in the stripes, but it's best to admire all snakes from a distance unless you're an expert.

At night in the forest you'll hear the characteristic chorus of frog mating calls and you'll frequently find the **red-eyed tree frog** – a beautiful pale green creature about the size of the top joint of your thumb – in your shower in any rustic cabin. Less appealing perhaps are the giant **marine toads**, the largest toad in the Americas, weighing in at up to 1kg and growing to over 20cm. Like most frogs and toads it has toxic glands and the toxin of the marine toad has hallucinogenic properties – a property the ancient Maya exploited in their ceremonies by licking these glands and interpreting the resultant visions.

The Caribbean Coast and the Bay Islands

Much of Guatemala's small **Caribbean coastline** is protected as part of the Biotopo Punta del Manabique (see p.267), a rich wetland habitat, while just inland there are several additional ecologically diverse reserves around the Río Dulce and Lago de Izabal. This region offers some of the country's finest birdwatching territory, with over 300 species spotted inside the Reserva Bocas del Polochic alone. Though there are tiny coral outcrops in Guatemalan waters, there's much more to see around the exceptional reefs of the **Bay Islands**, where all the three main islands all have excellent scuba-diving schools.

Immediately inland from the Guatemalan coast, the **littoral forest** is characterized by salt-tolerant plants, often with tough, waxy leaves which help conserve water. Species include red and white **gumbo limbo**, **black poisonwood**, **zericote**, **palmetto** and of course the **coconut**, which typifies Caribbean beaches, though it's not actually a native. The littoral forest supports a very high density of fauna, especially **migrating birds** owing to the succession of fruits and seeds, yet, due to its location, it's also facing increased development pressure.

Much of the shoreline around Punta del Manabique and Lívingston is still largely covered with **mangroves**, which play an important economic role, not merely as nurseries for commercial fish species but also for their stabilization of the shoreline and their ability to absorb the force of gales and hurricanes. The dominant species of the coastal fringe is the **red mangrove**, although in due course it undermines its own environment by consolidating the sea bed until it becomes more suitable for the less salt-tolerant black and white mangroves. The basis of the shoreline food chain is the nutrient-rich mud, held in place by the mangroves, whose roots are home to **oysters** and **sponges**. In the shallows, "meadows" of **seagrass beds** provide nurseries for many fish and invertebrates, and pasture for conch and turtles. The extensive root system of seagrasses also protects beaches from erosion by holding the fragments of sand and coral together.

The coastal zone is home to sparse numbers of the **West Indian manatee**, which can reach 4m in length and weigh up to 450kg. These placid and shy creatures move between freshwater lagoons and the open sea. They were once hunted for their meat but are now protected, and the Biotopo Chacón Machaca (see p.274) has been established in the Golfete region of the Rio Dulce as a manatee sanctuary. Despite this measure, the manatee remains very rare in Guatemala, and you've a much better chance of spotting one in Belize, where their habitat has been better protected.

Over in the **Bay Islands**, the **coral reefs** are some of the best preserved in the Caribbean, forming an astoundingly beautiful world where fish and coral come in every imaginable colour. The corals look like a brilliant underwater forest, but in fact each coral is composed of colonies of individual **polyps**, feeding off plankton wafting past in the current. There are basically two types of coral: the hard, calcareous, reef-building corals, such as **lettuce coral**, **brain coral** and **elkhorn coral** (known scientifically as the **hydrocorals**; 74 species), and the soft corals such as **sea fans** and **feather plumes** (the **ococorals**; 36 species). On the reefs you'll find the **chalice sponge**, which is a garish pink, the appropriately named **fire coral**, the delicate **feather-star crinoid** and the **apartment sponge**, a tall thin tube with lots of small holes in it.

Incredibly, the extensive reefs surrounding the Bay Islands survived the ten-metre waves of **Hurricane Mitch** in 1998 almost intact. Even in Guanaja, which took a direct hit (Mitch pounded the island for over two days), the coral remains in generally excellent condition, though fish numbers have declined a little because of overfishing around the reefs, despite the island's marine reserve status. The Bay Islands' reef environment is characterized by between 500m and a kilometre or so of shallow **fringing reef**, interspersed with sandy patches, which extends from the shoreline – this area is no deeper than 12m. This fringing reef then reaches a **reef crest**, where the waves break, from where the coral plummets almost vertically off the northern coasts of Roatán, Utila and Guanaja. These steep drop-offs form dramatic **reef**

walls, spectacular topographic features for which the Bay Islands are particularly renowned. The reef walls form the edge of the **continental shelf**, which plunges down to a depth of 3000m within a few kilometres north of the islands, forming a vast underwater canyon called the Cayman Trench.

It's the Bay Islands' position between these shallow and deep-water habitats that makes for such exciting scuba-diving. When cruising the reef walls on the northern coasts of the islands, it's possible to observe the abundant coral life while keeping eye on the big blue, and perhaps spot **pelagic sealife** like tarpon or manta rays swept close to the shore. The southern coasts of all the islands are a little different: here the reef has a shallower profile with coral outcrops interspersed with channels and small cayes, and pelagic species are much less common.

The seas around the Bay Islands are rich with all the main marine species found in the Caribbean. You're pretty much guaranteed to see a wide variety of reef life including **angel-** and **parrotfish**, **tiger groupers** and small striped **sergeant-majors**, while **hawksbill turtles** are also frequently spotted. **Stingrays** and **eagle rays** are usually a little more elusive, while **reef sharks** (the harmless nurse shark is the most common species) are only occasionally encountered. Keep an eye out for **conger** and **moray eels**, **spiny lobster** and the giant **king crab** hiding in holes and crevices in the reef wall, while **great**

Conservation organizations

Alianza Verde (Green Alliance, ⓦ www .greendeal.org). Based in CINCAP, Flores (see p.331), and supported by Conservation International, this is a consortium of ecotourism operators and conservation organizations, working closely with Guatemala's National Protected Areas Commission (CONAP) and ProPetén (see below), focusing primarily on sustainable development in the Maya Biosphere Reserve. It is developing "Green Deal", a code of practice and certification for ecotourism businesses.

Bay Islands Conservation Association (BICA) (see p.395, ☎ 445 1424, in US ☎ 1-800/227-3483). A well-organized environmental group, involved with establishing and managing marine parks in the Bay Islands.

Centre for Conservation Studies (CECON). A department of Guatemala's University of San Carlos, with head offices at the Botanical Garden in Guatemala City (see p.77). CECON manages and conducts scientific research in all seven of the nations' biotopos. These are often the best-protected areas within reserves, such as El Zotz near Tikal, Monterrico on the Pacific coast and the Biotopo del Quetzal in Baja Verapaz. Others are in very remote areas and there's usually some basic accommodation for visitors.

Defensores de la Naturaleza (ⓦ www .defensores.org). Excellent group successfully-combining conservation with sustainable tourism in the Reserva Sierra de las Minas and the Bocas de Polochic Wildlife Reserve (see pp.301 & 279); currently beginning a new project in the vast Sierra de Lacandón national park in western Petén, which contains the greatest biodiversity in Guatemala.

Fundary (ⓦ www.guate.net/fundarymanabique). Working with communities in the Punta de Manabique Reserve (see. p.267) to establish sustainable tourism in this biotopo on Guatemala's Caribbean coast. Volunteers (preferably with a background in biology or ecotourism) are needed to patrol marine turtle nesting beaches, undertake manatee and dolphin observation and work in the iguana and parrot reserves.

ProPetén (see p.332). Funded largely by Conservation International (above), this is the largest NGO in Petén, working on numerous conservation and resource management projects in the Maya Biosphere Reserve.

Proyecto Eco-Quetzal, 2a C 14–36, Zona 1, Cobán (☎ 952 1047, ⓔ bidaspeq@guate.net). Long-established NGO, with a successful record in protecting the forests around Cobán by offering economic alternatives to indigenous people, including excellent ecotourism projects in remote areas led by Q'eqchi Maya guides.

barracuda can often be seen hunting on the reef crest at dawn and dusk.

It has only recently been established that the world's largest fish, the plankton-feeding **whale shark** (which can grow to over 12m) is resident to the waters around Utila, though it also visits the coasts around Roatán and Guanaja in October and November to gorge on snapper and grouper eggs. Dolphins are also sometimes seen just offshore – mostly the **Atlantic bottle-nosed dolphin**, though further out large schools of the smaller **spotted dolphin** sometimes follow ocean-going ships.

Books

In the past Guatemala has never inspired a great deal of literature, but in recent years the country's political turmoil has spawned a boom in non-fiction. Politics and Maya culture are the two main themes explored. Most travel and historical accounts deal with Central America as a whole, offering only a small slice of the country.

For less mainstream, and especially for contemporary Latin American books, there are a few useful specialist **sources**. In the US the Inter-Hemispheric Resource Center (Ⓦwww.irc-online.org) produces a wide range of publications, and some Guatemala-specific titles. The Yax Te' press (Ⓦwww.yaxte.org) publish a very interesting collection of titles, concentrating on indigenous culture and language. In the UK the Latin America Bureau (Ⓦwww.lab.org.uk) publishes books about Guatemala and the region's society, current affairs and politics. In London, Maya - The Guatemalan Indian Centre (see p.19) has a library of more than 2000 books about Guatemala, including many very rare volumes, while the Canning House Library (see p.20) has the UK's largest publicly accessible collection of books and periodicals on Latin America.

Where possible, we have given both the US and UK publishers, with the US publisher first (US; UK); o/p means a book is out of print.

Travel

Stephen Connoly Benz *Guatemalan Journey* (University of Texas Press, US). A contemporary perspective on the complexities of Guatemalan society and the impact of US culture and evangelism, with informative accounts of life in the capital and the textile factory businesses.

Fabío Bourbon *The Lost Cities of the Maya: The Life and Art of Frederick Catherwood* (Swan Hill, UK). The only complete colour reproductions available in a recent book of Catherwood's amazing paintings of Maya cities lost in the jungle as he travelled around the region 160 years ago with the diplomat John Lloyd Stephens (see below). Catherwood's eye for detail and superb artistic skill (as well as Stephens' writing) stimulated and sustained the tremendous public interest in the ancient Maya, though Catherwood's role had in many ways been neglected until this publication.

Peter Canby *Heart of the Sky – Travels Among the Maya* (HarperCollins). The author treads a familiar path through the Maya World, encountering an interesting collection of ex-pats, Mayanists, priests, Guatemala City's idle rich and a female shaman. If not as erudite as Ronald Wright's masterful account (see below), it's still an accessible and informative read.

Anthony Daniels *Sweet Waist of America* (Trafalgar Square; Arrow; both o/p). A delight to read. Daniels takes a refreshingly even-handed approach to Guatemala and comes up with a fascinating cocktail of people and politics, discarding the stereotypes that litter most books on Central America. The book also includes interesting interviews with prominent characters from Guatemala's recent history.

Thomas Gage *Travels in the New World* (University of Oklahoma Press;

UK o/p). Unusual account of a Dominican friar's travels through Mexico and Central America between 1635 and 1637, including some fascinating insights into colonial life as well as some great attacks on the greed and pomposity of the Catholic Church abroad.

★ **Aldous Huxley** *Beyond the Mexique Bay* (Flamingo, UK; o/p). Huxley's travels in 1934 took him from Belize through Guatemala to Mexico, swept on by his fascination for history and religion, and sprouting bizarre theories on the basis of everything he saw. There are some great descriptions of Maya sites and indigenous culture, with superb one-liners summing up people and places.

Patrick Marnham *So far from God* (Viking Penguin, o/p; Bloomsbury). A saddened and vaguely right-wing account of Marnham's travels through the Americas from the US to Panamá (missing out Belize). Dotted with amusing anecdotes and interesting observations, the book was researched in 1984, and its description of Guatemala is dominated by the reign of terror. The Paraxtut massacre, mentioned by Marnham, has since been unmasked as a fabrication.

Jonathan Evan Maslow *Bird of Life, Bird of Death* (Dell; Penguin; both o/p). Again travel and political comment are merged as Maslow sets out in search of the quetzal, using the bird's uncertain future as a metaphor for contemporary Guatemala and contrasting this with the success of the vulture. It's a sweeping account, very entertaining, but more concerned with impressing the reader than representing the truth.

Jeremy Paxman *Through the Volcanoes* (Paladin, UK, o/p). Similar in many ways to Patrick Marnham's book, this is another political travel account investigating the turmoil of Central America and finding solace in the calm of Costa Rica. Paxman's travels take him through all seven of the republics, and he offers a reasonable overview of the politics and history of the region.

Nigel Pride *A Butterfly Sings to Pacaya* (Constable, UK, o/p). The author, accompanied by his wife and four-year-old son, travels south from the US border in a Jeep, heading through Mexico, Guatemala and Belize. A large section of the book is set in Maya areas and illustrated by the author's drawings of landscapes, people and animals. Though the travels took place nearly twenty years ago, the pleasures and privations they experience rarely appear dated; the description of the climb of the Pacaya volcano is one of the highlights of the book.

Christopher Shaw *Sacred Monkey River: A Canoe Trip with the Gods* (W.W. Norton). Engaging account of the author's canoe journey along the Usumacinta River that divides Mexico and Guatemala. Nicely crafted prose is enlivened with erudite analysis of ancient Maya cosmology and culture, and the contemporary political and environmental issues affecting the region.

★ **John Lloyd Stephens** *Incidents of Travel in Central America, Chiapas, and Yucatán* (Dover; Prentice Hall). Stephens was a classic nineteenth-century traveller. Acting as American ambassador to Central America, he indulged his own enthusiasm for archeology; while the republics fought it out among themselves he was wading through the jungle stumbling across ancient cities. His journals, told with superb Victorian pomposity punctuated with sudden waves of enthusiasm, make great reading. Some editions include fantastic illustrations by Catherwood of the ruins overgrown with tropical rainforest.

Paul Theroux *The Old Patagonian Express* (Houghton Mifflin; Penguin). An epic train journey from Boston to Patagonia that takes in a couple of miserable train trips in Guatemala. Theroux doesn't have much time for Guatemalans, dismissing them as unhelpful and taciturn, but as usual, his way with words paints a vivid picture. See p.61 for a taster.

Marcus McPeek Villatoro *Walking to La Milpa* (Moyer Bell). Engaging but disturbing account of a lay missionary's three-year stint in the frontier settlement of Poptún in Petén,

giving an insight into the superstitions, dangers and celebrations of life in rural Guatemala.

★ **Ronald Wright** *Time Among the Maya* (Henry Holt; Abacus). A vivid and sympathetic account of travels from Belize through Guatemala, Chiapas and Yucatán, meeting the Maya of today and exploring their obsession with time. The book's twin points of interest are the ancient Maya and the recent violence. An encyclopedic bibliography offers ideas for exploration in depth, and the author's knowledge is evident in the superb historical insight he imparts through the book. Certainly one of the best travel books on the area.

Fiction, autobiography and poetry

★ **Miguel Ángel Asturias** *Hombres de Maíz* (Macmillan, o/p; Verso). Guatemala's most famous author, Asturias is deeply indebted to Guatemalan history and culture in his work. "Men of Maize" is generally regarded as his masterpiece, classically Latin American in its magic realist style, and bound up in the complexity of indigenous culture. His other works include *El Señor Presidente*, a grotesque portrayal of social chaos and dictatorial rule, based on Asturias's own experience; *El Papa Verde*, which explores the murky world of the United Fruit Company; and *Weekend en Guatemala*, describing the downfall of the Arbenz government. Asturias won the Nobel prize for literature before his death in 1974.

Paul Bowles *Up Above the World* (Ecco Press; Peter Owen). Paul Bowles is at his chilling, understated best in this novel based on experiences of Guatemala in the late 1930s.

Jane Bowles used the same visit for her fiction in *A Guatemalan Idyll* and other tales, recently republished in *Everything is Nice: Collected Stories of Jane Bowles* (Peter Owen, UK).

★ **Francisco Goldman** *The Long Night of White Chickens* (Grove-Atlantic; Faber). Drawing on the stylistic complexity of Latin American fiction, this novel tells the tale of a young Guatemalan orphan who flees to the US and works as a maid. When she finally returns home she is murdered. It's an interesting and ambitious story flavoured with all the bitterness and beauty of Guatemala's natural and political landscape. The novel inspired the film *Men With Guns*.

Gaspar Pedro Gonzáles *A Mayan Life* (Yax Te' Press, US). Absorbing story about the personal and cultural conflicts facing a Q'anjob'al Maya in the Cuchumatanes mountains as he seeks a higher education. Gonzales claims this is the first novel ever written by a Maya author, though it is obviously highly autobiographical.

Norman Lewis *The Volcano Above Us* (Penguin, UK, o/p). Vaguely historical novel published in 1957 that pulls together all the main elements of Guatemala's recent history. The image that it summons is one of depressing drudgery and eternal conflict, set against a background of repression and racism. In the light of

what's happened it has a certain prophetic quality, and remains gripping despite its miserable conclusions.

Víctor Perera *Rites: A Guatemalan Boyhood* (Mercury House; Eland). Autobiographical account of a childhood in Guatemala City's Jewish community. It may not cast much light on the country, but it's an interesting read, pulling together an unusual combination of cultures.

History, politics and human rights: Guatemala and the Bay Islands

Tom Barry *Guatemala – A Country Guide* (Interhemispheric Research Center). A comprehensive and concise account of the political, social and economic situation in Guatemala, with a mild left-wing stance. Currently the best source for a good overview of the situation.

William V. Davidson *Historical Geography of the Bay Islands, Honduras* (South University Press, US). A study of physical and cultural geographical development of the islands. Useful for pieces of interesting background information.

Edward F. Fisher and R. McKenna Brown (eds) *Maya Cultural Activism in Guatemala* (University of Texas Press, US). Effectual summary of the indigenous movement in Guatemala, with strong chapters on clothing and identity and the revival of interest in Maya language and hieroglyphic writing.

★ **Jim Handy** *Gift of the Devil* (South End Press). Superb history of Guatemala: concise and readable with a sharp focus on the Maya population and the brief period of socialist government. Though now a little out of date (it was written in

the mid-1980s), the book nevertheless manages to offer a convincing perspective on the modern Guatemalan state. By no means objective, Handy sets out to expose the development of oppression and point the finger at the oppressors.

George Lovell *A Beauty That Hurts: Life and Death in Guatemala* (Between the Lines, Canada). A good contemporary analysis enlivened by interviews with exiles and community leaders. The book also scrutinizes recent political events through newspaper articles, and reviews the historical context that has shaped twenty-first century Guatemala.

Víctor Montejo *Testimony: Death of a Guatemalan Village* (Curbstone Press). Yet another horrifying account of murder and destruction. In this case it's the personal testimony of a school teacher, describing the arrival of the army in a small highland village and the killing that follows.

★ **Trish O'Kane** *In Focus: Guatemala – A Guide to the People, Politics and Culture* (Latin American Bureau; Interlink). Excellent, very accessible introduction to Guatemala, offering a concise summary of the historical, political, economic and social situation, plus an enlightening look at modern Maya culture and activism.

Mario Payeras *Days of the Jungle* (Monthly Review Press; Casa de las Americas; o/p). A slim volume written under the auspices of the EGP, one of Guatemala's main guerrilla armies. In this sense it's unique, as the voice of the guerrillas is rarely heard. Here one of their number tells of the early days of the organization, as they enter Guatemala through the jungles of the northwest and attempt to establish contacts amongst the local population. There are, however, serious doubts about the accuracy of the story.

★ **Víctor Perera** *Unfinished Conquest* (University of California Press). Superb, extremely readable account of the civil war tragedy, plus comprehensive attention to the political, social and economic inequalities affecting the author's native country. Immaculately researched, the book's strength comes from the extensive interviews with both ordinary and influential Guatemalans and incisive analysis of recent history. The best introduction to the subject.

REMHI *Guatemala: Never Again* (Orbis; LAB; o/p). Abridged translation of the seminal report published by the Catholic Church of Guatemala into the civil war atrocities. The investigation contains an excellent historical background to the conflict, harrowing personal testimonies, incisive analysis of military and guerrilla strategies and a chapter devoted to preventing a recurrence.

Stephen Schlesinger and Stephen Kinzer *Bitter Fruit: The Untold Story of the American Coup In Guatemala* (Harvard University Press). As the title says, this book traces the American connection in the 1954 coup, delving into the murky water of United Fruit Company politics and proving that the invading army received its orders from the White House.

Jean-Marie Simon *Eternal Spring – Eternal Tyranny* (Norton). Of all the books on human rights in Guatemala, this is the one that speaks with blinding authority and the utmost clarity. Combining the highest standards in photography with crisp text, there's no attempt to persuade you – the facts are allowed to speak for themselves, which they do with amazing strength. If you want to know what happened in Guatemala during the civil war years, there is no better book, though Simon clearly takes sides, aligning herself with the revolutionary left – there's no mention of abuses committed by the guerrillas.

Central American politics

Tom Barry *Central America Inside Out* (Grove-Atlantic; Avalon). Well-informed background reading on the entire region. By the same author, *Inside Guatemala* (InterHemispheric Education Resource Center) is part of a series of guides covering the history, politics, economy and society of Central America; packed with accessible facts and analysis.

Peter Dale-Scott and Jonathan Marshall *Cocaine Politics: Drugs, Armies and the CIA in Central America* (University of California Press). Polemical but well-researched exposé of CIA involvement in cocaine trafficking and political oppression in Central America in the 1980s. Reveals the truth behind the Iran–Contra scandal and gives the lie to the rhetoric of the war on drugs.

James Dunkerley *Power in the Isthmus* (Norton; Verso Editions). Detailed account of Central American politics offering a good summary of the contemporary situation, albeit in a rather turgid academic style. His later book, *The Pacification of Central America* (Verso Editions), published in 1994, is a similarly well-compiled account with plenty of statistics. It covers more recent events, in particular the region's civil wars, up to the beginning of the peace process.

Susan C. Stonch (ed) *Endangered Peoples of Latin America* (Greenwood, US). For a book covering the whole continent there's a surprising amount of information on Central America, with a disturbing analysis of why tourism and new environmental and conservation laws can exclude local people from their own land and resources. Chapters documenting how the Maya of Mexico are overwhelmed by the explosive growth of tourism and the successful struggle of the English-speaking Bay Islanders to be recognized as an indigenous group in Honduras present just two of the contemporary problems facing the people of the region.

William Weinberg *War on the Land: Ecology and Politics in Central America* (Zed Books; Humanities Press). The author tells a story of intertwining conflicts and causes between conservation (and to a small extent ecotourism), land rights and politics in the individual Central American countries in a volume that deftly straddles the gap between academic interest and the general reader.

Ralph Lee Woodward Jr *Central America: A Nation Divided* (Oxford University Press). A good general summary of the Central American situation, despite its daft title.

Indigenous culture

Linda Asturias de Barrios *Comalapa: Native Dress and its Significance* (Ixchel Museum, Guatemala). Only available in Guatemala, this is a work of skilled academic research, investigating weaving skills and their place within modern Maya communities.

Robert Carmack *Quichean Civilization* (University of California Press). Thorough study of the K'iche' and their history, drawing on archeological evidence and accounts of the Conquest. A useful insight into the structure of highland society at the time of the Conquest.

Gareth W. Cook *Renewing the Maya World: Expressive Culture in a Highland Town* (University of Texas). Absorbing look at the annual fiesta traditions and dances that renew the cosmic order in the highland town of Momostenango, and their link to ancient Maya creation myths.

Krystyna Deuss *Indian Costumes from Guatemala* (K. Deuss, UK, o/p). A useful survey of the traditional costumes worn in Guatemala, and one of the best introductions to the subject.

Grant D. Jones *The Conquest of the Maya Kingdom* (Stanford University

Press). A massive academic tome that's also a fascinating history of the Itza Maya and a gripping tale of how the Spanish entered and finally defeated the last independent Maya kingdom, at Tayasal, site of present-day Flores.

☒ **Rigoberta Menchú** I, *Rigoberta Menchú – An Indian Woman in Guatemala* and *Crossing Borders* (Verso; Norton). Momentous story of one of Latin America's most remarkable women, Nobel Peace Prize winner Rigoberta Menchú. The first volume is a horrific account of family life in the Maya highlands, recording how Menchú's family were targeted, terrorized and murdered by the military. The book also reveals much concerning K'iche' Maya cultural traditions and the enormous gulf between ladino and indigenous society in Guatemala. The second volume is more optimistic, documenting Menchú's life in exile in Mexico, her work at the United Nations fighting for indigenous people and her return to Guatemala. Though Menchú's courage and determination are undeniable, serious doubts have since arisen concerning the accuracy of her story recounted in the first book – best read with David Stoll's biography (see below).

Mary Ellen Miller and Karl Taube *The Gods and Symbols of Ancient Mexico and the Maya: An Illustrated Dictionary of Mesoamerican Religion* (Thames & Hudson). A superb modern reference tool for studying ancient Mesoamerica, written by two leading scholars. Taube's *Aztec and Maya Myths* (University of Texas Press/British Museum Press) is perfect as a short accessible introduction to the region's mythology.

Hans Namuth *Los Todos Santeros* (Nishen, UK, o/p). Splendid book of black-and-white photographs taken in the village of Todos Santos Cuchumatán, to the north of Huehuetenango. The book was inspired by the work of anthropologist Maud Oakes (see below).

Maud Oakes *Beyond the Windy Place: The Two Crosses of Todos Santos* (Gollancz, UK, o/p). An anthropologist who spent many years in the Mam-speaking village of Todos Santos. Oakes' studies of life in the village were published in the 1940s and 1950s and still make fascinating reading.

☒ **The Popol Vuh** (Touchstone; Scribner's). The great poem of the K'iche', written shortly after the Conquest and intended to preserve the tribe's knowledge of its history. It's an amazing swirl of ancient mythological characters and their wandering through the K'iche' highlands, tracing K'iche' ancestry back to the beginning. There are several versions on offer though many of them are half-hearted, including only a few lines from the original. The best is translated by Dennis Tedlock.

☒ **James D. Sexton** (ed) *Son of Tecún Umán* (Waveland Press; University of Arizona Press); *Campesino* (University of Arizona Press); and *Ignacio* (University of Pennsylvania Press). Three excellent autobiographical accounts written by an anonymous Maya from the south side of Lago de Atitlán. The books give an impression of life inside a modern Maya village, bound up in poverty, local politics and a mixture of Catholicism and superstition, and manage to avoid the stereotyping that usually characterizes description of the indigenous population. The earliest is *Son of Tecún Umán*, which takes us from 1972 to 1977, while the second account, *Campesino*, leads up to 1982 and includes the worst years of political violence. *Ignacio* completes the tale.

David Stoll *Rigoberta Menchú and the Story of All Poor Guatemalans* (Westview Press in US and UK). Iconoclastic biography, based on painstaking research and testimony, that delivers a formidable broadside against considerable pieces of the Menchú story.

Philip Werne *The Maya of Guatemala* (Minority Rights Group, UK, o/p). A short study of repression and the Maya of Guatemala. The latest edition (published in 1994) is now a little out of date but interesting none the less.

Archeology

★ Michael Coe *The Maya* (Thames & Hudson). Now in its sixth edition, this clear and comprehensive introduction to Maya archeology is one of the best on offer. Coe has also written several more weighty, academic volumes. His *Breaking the Maya Code* (Penguin; Thames & Hudson), a very personal history of the decipherment of the glyphs, owes much to the fact that Coe was present at many of the most important meetings leading to the breakthrough. The book demonstrates that the glyphs did actually reproduce Maya speech. *The Art of the Maya Scribe* (Thames & Hudson), written with Justin Kerr, developer of "rollout" photography – a technique enabling the viewer to see the whole surface of a cylindrical vessel – is a wonderfully illustrated history of Maya writing which also takes the reader on a journey through the Maya universe and mythology via the astonishingly skillful calligraphy of the Maya artists themselves.

★ David Drew *The Lost Chronicles of the Maya Kings* (University of California Press; Weidenfeld and Nicolson). Superbly readable and engaging; Drew draws on a wealth of material including some of the very latest findings to deliver an excellent account of ancient Maya political history. The alliances and rivalries between the main cities are skillfully unravelled, and there's a particularly revealing

analysis of late Classic Maya power politics.

William L. Fash *Scribes, Warriors and Kings* (Thames & Hudson). The definitive study of the ruins of Copán, with the complete historical background, superb maps and lavishly adorned with drawings and photographs.

Charles Gallenkamp *Maya* (Viking Penguin; Penguin; both o/p). Perhaps a touch over-the-top on the sensational aspects of Maya archeology, this is none the less another reasonable introduction to the subject.

Peter D. Harrison *The Lords of Tikal* (Thames and Hudson) Outstanding study of the Petén metropolis, based on more than thirty years of research and the very latest hieroglyphic readings. There's a tremendous amount of detail about the city's monuments and artefacts and the rulers and who commissioned them.

★ Simon Martin and Nikolai Grube *Chronicle of the Maya Kings and Queens* (Thames & Hudson). Published to universal acclaim, this groundbreaking work is based on exhaustive new epigraphic studies, and the re-reading of previously translated glyphic texts. The historical records of several key Maya cities – including Tikal, Piedras Negras and Dos Pilas – complete with biographies of 152 kings and 4 queens, plus full dynastic sequences, and all the key battles and dates are included. As Micheal D Coe, author of *The Maya* (see above) says, "There's nothing else like this book. It supersedes everything else ever written on Maya history."

Linda Schele and David Freidel (et al.). The authors, in the forefront of the "new archeology", have been personally responsible for decoding many of the glyphs. While the writing style, which frequently includes "recreations" of scenes inspired by their discoveries, is controversial, it has nevertheless inspired a devoted following. *A Forest of Kings: The Untold Story of the Ancient Maya* (Quill, US), in conjunction with *The Blood of Kings* by Linda Schele and Mary Miller (Thames & Hudson) shows that, far from being governed by peaceful astronomer-priests, the ancient Maya were ruled by hereditary kings, lived in populous, aggressive city-states, and engaged in a continual entanglement of alliances and war. *The Maya Cosmos* (Quill, US), by Schele, Freidel and Joy Parker, is perhaps more difficult to read, dense with copious notes, but continues to examine Maya ritual and religion in a unique and far-reaching way. *The Code of Kings* (Scribner, US), written in collaboration with Peter Matthews and illustrated with Justin Kerr's famous "rollout" photography of Maya ceramics, examines in detail the significance of the monuments at selected Maya sites. It's her last book – Linda Schele died in April 1998 – and a classic of epigraphic interpretation.

Peter Schmidt, Mercedes de la Garza and Enrique Nalda (eds) *Maya Civilization* (Thames & Hudson). Monumental collaborative effort, with sections written by many prominent Mayanists, lusciously presented with over 600 colour images of some breathtaking Maya art. The scholarly text is also impressive, with contributions on the importance of Calakmul to the Classic Maya history and detailed essays on the highlands of Guatemala, Maya cosmology and codices.

Robert Sharer *The Ancient Maya* (Stanford University Press; Cambridge University Press). The classic, comprehensive account of Maya civilization, now in a completely revised and much more readable fifth edition, yet as authoritative as ever. Required reading for archeology students, it provides a fascinating reference for the non-expert. Also worth reading and even more accessible is his *Daily Life in Maya Civilization* (Greenwood, US).

J. Eric S. Thompson *The Rise and Fall of the Maya Civilization* (University of Oklahoma Press, US). A major authority on the ancient Maya during his lifetime, Thompson produced many academic studies, of which this is one of the more accessible. Although recent researchers have overturned many of Thompson's theories, his work provided the inspiration for the postwar surge of interest in the Maya, and he remains a respected figure.

Wildlife and the environment

Les Betelsky *Belize and Northern Guatemala* (Academic Press). Although other specialist wildlife guides may cover the subject in more detail, this is the only reasonably comprehensive single-volume guide to the mammals, birds, reptiles, amphibians and marine life of the region. Helpfully, the illustration of each creature is given opposite its description, avoiding confusing page-flicking.

Louise H. Emmons *Neotropical Rainforest Mammals* (University of Chicago in Press, US). Supported by François Feer's colour illustrations, this highly informative book is written by experts for non-scientists. Local and scientific names are given, along with plenty of interesting snippets.

Steve Howe and Sophie Webb *The Birds of Mexico and Northern Central America* (Oxford University Press). A tremendous work, the result of years of research, this is the definitive book on the region's birds. Essential for all serious ornithologists.

★ **Thor Janson** *In the Land of Green Lightning* (Pomegranate, US) Exquisite photographic collection, concentrating on the diverse wildlife and environment of the Maya region. Includes some astounding images of an exploding Volcán Pacaya.

C. Kaplan *Coral Reefs of the Caribbean and Florida* (Houghton Mifflin, US). Useful handbook on the abundant undersea wildlife of the Atlantic coasts of Guatemala and Honduras.

John C. Kricher *A Neotropical Companion* (Princeton University Press). Subtitled "An Introduction to the Animals, Plants and Ecosystems of the New World Tropics", this contains an amazing amount of valuable information for nature lovers. Researched mainly in Central America, so there's plenty that's directly relevant.

Don Moser *The Jungles of Central America* (Time-Life Books, US, o/p). Glossy trip through the wildernesses of Central America. By no means a comprehensive account of the region's wildlife but a good read nonetheless, with several informative sections on Guatemala.

Frank B. Smythe *The Birds of Tikal* (Natural History Press, US). This is sadly all that's on offer for budding ornithologists in Guatemala, but we should be thankful for small mercies. The book can usually be bought in Tikal.

Guides

Elizabeth Bell *Antigua Guatemala: The City and its Heritage.* The best guide to Antigua, written by a long-term resident and prominent historian, and available from several shops in Antigua.

Simon Calder *The Panamericana* (Vacation Work). Prolific writer, broadcaster and veteran backpackper, Calder travels the entire Carretera Panamericana – the Pan-American Highway – from the Texas border to Yaviza in Panamá. An up-to-date,

enormously funny and candid guide to the route and places just off it, it's also packed with practical information and wry observation; the diagrams of border crossings are particularly useful.

William Coe *Tikal: A Handbook to the Ancient Maya Ruins* (University of Pennsylvania Press, US). Superbly detailed account of the site, usually available at the ruins. The detailed map of the main area is essential for in-depth exploration.

Sharon Collins *Diving and Snorkeling Roatán and Honduras' Bay Islands* (Lonely Planet). Covers many of the main dive sites in Utila and Roatán, though the Guanaja content is sketchy.

★ Joyce Kelly *Archaeological Guide to Northern Central America* (University of Oklahoma Press). Detailed and practical guide to dozens of sites, from the crowded to the remote. All have excellent photographs and accurate maps. The "star ratings" – based on a site's archeological importance, degree of restoration and accessibility – may affront purists, but they do offer a valuable opinion on how worthwhile a particular visit might be. This volume covers 38 Maya sites and 25 museums in Guatemala, Belize, Honduras and El Salvador, and is an indispensable companion for anyone travelling in the region.

Barbara Balchin de Koose *Antigua for You* (Watson, Guatemala).

The latest in a line of guides focusing on Guatemala's most popular tourist city, this book gives a very good and comprehensive account of the colonial architectural wonders, but not much else.

Lily de Jongh Osborne *Four Keys to Guatemala* (Mayflower Publishing, UK, o/p). One of the best guides to Guatemala ever written, including a short piece on every aspect of the country's history and culture. Osborne also wrote a good book on indigenous arts and crafts in Guatemala. Sadly, both books are now out of print.

Carlos E. Prahl Redondo *Guia de los Volcanes de Guatemala* (Club Andino Guatemalteco). A very comprehensive and systematic account of the nation's 37 volcanoes and how to get to the top of them, put together by a local teacher. Only available in Spanish.

Cookbooks

Copeland Marks *False Tongues and Sunday Bread: A Guatemalan and Maya Cookbook* (Donald I. Fine, US). Having travelled in Guatemala and suffered the endless onslaught of beans and tortillas, you may be surprised to find that the country has an established culinary tradition.

Copeland Marks, an American food writer, has spent years unearthing the finest Guatemalan recipes, from hen in chocolate sauce to the standard black beans. A beautifully bound celebration of Guatemalan food as it should be.

language

language

Language

Guatemala takes in a bewildering collection of languages, but fortunately for the traveller Spanish will get you by in all but the most remote areas. Some middle-class Guatemalans speak English, but it's essential to learn at least a few Spanish phrases or you're in for a frustrating time.

The **Spanish** spoken in Guatemala has a strong Latin American flavour to it, and if you're used to the dainty intonation of Madrid then this may come as something of a surprise. If you're new to Spanish it's a lot easier to pick up than the Castilian version. Everywhere you'll find people willing to make an effort to understand you, eager to speak to passing gringos.

The rules of **pronunciation** are pretty straightforward and, once you get to know them, strictly observed. Unless there's an accent, words ending in d, l, r and z are **stressed** on the last syllable, all others on the second last. All **vowels** are pure and short.

A somewhere between the A sound of back and that of father.

E as in get.

I as in police.

O as in hot.

U as in rule.

C is soft before E and I, hard otherwise: *cerca* is pronounced serka.

G works the same way, a guttural H sound (like the *ch* in loch) before E or I, a hard G elsewhere – *gigante* becomes higante.

H is always silent.

J is the same sound as a guttural G: *jamón* is pronounced hamON.

LL sounds like an English Y: *tortilla* is pronounced torteeya.

N is as in English unless it has a tilde (accent) over it, when it becomes NY: *mañana* sounds like manyana.

QU is pronounced like an English K.

R is rolled, RR doubly so.

V sounds more like B, *vino* becoming beano.

X is slightly softer than in English – sometimes almost SH – *Xela* is pronounced shela.

Z is the same as a soft C, so *cerveza* becomes servesa.

Below is a list of a few essential words and phrases, though if you're travelling for any length of time a **dictionary** or **phrase book** is obviously a worthwhile investment. Any good Spanish phrasebook or dictionary should see you through in Guatemala, but specific Latin American ones are the most useful. The *University of Chicago Dictionary of Latin-American Spanish* is a good allrounder, while *Mexican Spanish: A Rough Guide Phrasebook* has a menu reader, rundown of colloquialisms and a number of cultural tips that are relevant to many Latin American countries, including Guatemala. If you're using a dictionary, remember that in Spanish CH, LL, and Ñ count as separate letters and are listed after the Cs, Ls, and Ns respectively. If you really want to get to grips with Guatemalan slang, swear words and expressions look out for *¿Qué Onda Vos?* by Juan Carlos Martínez López and Mark Brazaitis, which includes a superb round-up of *guatemaltequismos*. It's available from several bookshops and the La Unión language school in Antigua (see p.110).

Maya languages

After years of state-backed *castellanización* programmes when Spanish was the only language of tuition and Maya schoolchildren were left virtual classroom spectators, a network of Maya schools has now been established, with hundreds alone in Q'eqchi' areas of Guatemala. A strong indigenous cultural movement has now developed in the country, intent on preserving the dozens of different Maya languages still spoken (for a comprehensive map, see p.452). Because the Maya birthrate is much higher than the ladino, there is now every chance that the main languages like K'iche', Kaqchikel and Mam will survive, though the fate of the more isolated tongues is far from secure.

If you're planning an extended stay in a remote indigenous region to do development work, it's extremely helpful to learn a little of the local language first. There are a number of language schools (see p.47) where you go can **study a Maya language** and pick up the essentials. The Yax Te' Foundation (Ⓦwww.yaxte.org), devoted to promoting and supporting Maya culture and language, has some excellent study material and dictionaries.

Maya words do not easily translate into Spanish (or English) so you may see the same place spelt in different ways: *K'umarkaaj* can be spelt *K'umarcaah* or even *Gumarcaj*. Nearly all Maya words are pronounced stressing the final syllable, which is often accented: Atitlán is A-tit-LAN, Wakná is wak-NA.

C is always hard like a K, unlike Spanish.
J is a guttural H, as in Spanish.
U like a W at the beginning of a word and like an OO in the middle or at the end of a word – Uaxactún is pronounced wash-ak-TOON.
X sounds like SH – *Ixcún* is pronounced ish-KOON.

Spanish words and phrases

Basics

Yes, No – **Sí, No**	Open, Closed – **Abierto/a, Cerrado/a**
Please, Thank you – **Por favor, Gracias**	With, Without – **Con, Sin**
Where?, When? – **¿Dónde?, ¿Cuándo?**	Good, Bad – **Buen(o)/a, Mal(o)/a**
What?, How much? – **¿Qué?, ¿Cuánto?**	Big, Small – **Gran(de), Pequeño/a**
Here, There – **Aquí, Allí**	More, Less – **Más, Menos**
This, That – **Este, Eso**	Today, Tomorrow – **Hoy, Mañana**
Now, Later – **Ahora, Más tarde**	Yesterday – **Ayer**

Greetings and responses

Hello, Goodbye – **Hola, Adiós**	Could you speak more slowly? – **¿Podría hablar más lento?**
Good morning – **Buenos días**	
Good afternoon/night – **Buenas tardes/ noches**	Not at all/You're welcome – **De nada**
	Do you speak English? – **¿Habla (usted) inglés?**
See you later – **Hasta luego**	
Sorry – **Lo siento/discúlpeme**	I don't speak Spanish – **No hablo español**
Excuse me – **Con permiso/perdón**	What (did you say)? – **¿Mande?**
How are you? – **¿Cómo está (usted)?**	My name is... – **Me llamo...**
I (don't) understand – **(No) Entiendo**	What's your name? – **¿Cómo se llama usted?**

I am English - **Soy inglés(a)**
 American - **americano (a)**
 Australian - **australiano(a)**
 British - **británico(a)**
 Canadian - **canadiense**
 Dutch - **holandés(a)**

Irish - **irlandés(a)**
New Zealander - **neocelandés(a)**
Scottish - **escosés(a)**
South African - **sudafricano(a)**
Welsh - **galés(a)**

Needs – hotels and transport

I want - **Quiero**
I'd like - **Quisiera**
Do you know…? - **¿Sabe…?**
I don't know - **No sé**
There is (is there)? - **(¿)Hay(?)**
Give me…(one like that) - **Deme…(uno así)**
Do you have…? - **¿Tiene…?**
…the time - **…la hora**
…a room - **…un cuarto**
…with two beds/double bed - **…con dos camas/cama matrimonial**
It's for one person (two people) - **Es para una persona (dos personas)**
…for one night (one week) - **…para una noche (una semana)**
It's fine, how much is it? - **¿Está bien, cuánto es?**
It's too expensive - **Es demasiado caro**
Don't you have anything cheaper? - **¿No tiene algo más barato?**
Can one…? - **¿Se puede…?**
…camp (near) here? - **¿…acampar aquí (cerca)?**
Is there a hotel nearby? - **¿Hay un hotel aquí cerca?**

How do I get to…? - **¿Por dónde se va a…?**
Left, right, straight on - **Izquierda, derecha, derecho**
Where is…? - **¿Dónde está…?**
…the bus station - **…el terminal de camionetas**
…the nearest bank - **…el banco más cercano**
…the post office - **…el correo/la oficina de correos**
…the toilet - **…el baño/sanitario**
Where does the bus to…leave from? - **¿De dónde sale la camioneta para…?**
I'd like a (return) ticket to… - **Quisiera un boleto (de ida y vuelta) para…**
What time does it leave (arrive in…)? - **¿A qué hora sale (llega en…)?**
What is there to eat? - **¿Qué hay para comer?**
What's that? - **¿Qué es eso?**
What's this called in Spanish? - **¿Cómo se llama este en español?**

Numbers and days

0 - **cero**	21 - **veintiuno**	first - **primero/a**
1 - **un/uno/una**	22 - **veintidós**	second - **segundo/a**
2 - **dos**	30 - **treinta**	third - **tercero/a**
3 - **tres**	31 - **treinta y uno**	fourth - **cuarto/a**
4 - **cuatro**	40 - **cuarenta**	fifth - **quinto/a**
5 - **cinco**	50 - **cincuenta**	sixth - **sexto/a**
6 - **seis**	60 - **sesenta**	seventh - **séptimo/a**
7 - **siete**	70 - **setenta**	eighth - **octavo/a**
8 - **ocho**	80 - **ochenta**	ninth - **noveno/a**
9 - **nueve**	90 - **noventa**	tenth - **décimo/a**
10 - **diez**	100 - **cien**	
11 - **once**	101 - **ciento uno**	Monday - **lunes**
12 - **doce**	200 - **doscientos**	Tuesday - **martes**
13 - **trece**	201 - **doscientos uno**	Wednesday - **miércoles**
14 - **catorce**	500 - **quinientos**	Thursday - **jueves**
15 - **quince**	1000 - **mil**	Friday - **viernes**
16 - **dieciséis**	2000 - **dos mil**	Saturday - **sábado**
20 - **veinte**	1,000,000 - **un millión**	Sunday - **domingo**

Spanish food and dishes

Basics

Azúcar – Sugar
Carne – Meat
Ensalada – Salad
Huevos – Eggs
Mantequilla – Butter
Pan – Bread

Pescado – Fish
Pimienta – Pepper
Queso – Cheese
Sal – Salt
Salsa – Sauce
Verduras/Legumbres – Vegetables

Soups (*sopas*) and starters

Sopa – Soup
　de arroz – with rice
　de fideos – with noodles
　de lentejas – Lentil
　de verduras – Vegetable

Consome – Consomme
Caldo – Broth (usually with meat)
Ceviche – Raw fish salad, marinated in lime juice
Entremeses – Hors d'oeuvres

Meat (*carne*) and poultry (*aves*)

Alambre – Kebab
Bistec – Steak
Cabrito – Kid goat
Carne (de res) – Beef
Carnitas – Stewed chunks of meat
Cerdo – Pork
Chorizo – Sausage
Chuleta – Chop
Codorniz – Quail
Conejo – Rabbit
Cordero – Lamb
Costilla – Rib

Guisado – Stew
Higado – Liver
Lengua – Tongue
Milanesa – Breaded escalope
Pato – Duck
Pavo/Guajalote – Turkey
Pechuga – Breast
Pierna – Leg
Pollo – Chicken
Salchicha – Hot dog or salami
Ternera – Veal
Venado – Venison

Specialities

Chile relleno – Stuffed pepper
Chuchitos – Stuffed maize dumplings
Enchilada – Flat, crisp tortilla piled with salad or meat
Mosh – Porridge
Pan de banana – Banana bread

Pan de coco – Coconut bread
Quesadilla – Cheese-flavoured sponge
Taco – Rolled and stuffed tortilla
Tamale – Boiled and stuffed maize pudding
Tapado – Fish stew with plantain and vegetables, served on Caribbean coast

Vegetables (*legumbres, verduras*)

Aguacate – Avocado
Ajo – Garlic
Casava/Yuca – Potato-like root vegetable
Cebolla – Onion
Col – Cabbage
Elote – Corn on the cob
Frijoles – Beans
Hongos – Mushrooms

Lechuga – Lettuce
Pacaya – Bitter-tasting local vegetable
Papas – Potatoes
Pepino – Cucumber
Plátanos – Plantain
Tomate – Tomato
Zanahoria – Carrot

Fruit (fruta)

Banana – Banana
Ciruelas – Greengages
Coco – Coconut
Frambuesas – Raspberries
Fresas – Strawberries
Guanabana – Pear-like cactus fruit
Guayaba – Guava
Higos – Figs
Limon – Lime
Mamey – Pink, sweet, full of pips
Mango – Mango

Melocoton – Peach
Melon – Melon
Naranja – Orange
Papaya – Papaya
Piña – Pineapple
Pitahaya – Sweet, purple fruit
Sandia – Watermelon
Toronja – Grapefruit
Tuna – Cactus fruit
Uvas – Grapes

Eggs (huevos)

a la Mexicana – Scrambled with mild tomato,
  onion and chilli sauce
con Jamon – with ham
con Tocino – with bacon
Fritos – Fried

Motuleños – Fried, served on a tortilla with
  ham, cheese and sauce
Rancheros – Cheese-fried and smothered in
  hot chilli sauce
Revueltos – Scrambled
Tibios – Lightly boiled

Common terms

a la Parilla – Grilled
al Horno – Baked
al Mojo de ajo – Fried in garlic and butter
Asado/a – Roast

Empanado/a – Breaded
Picante – Hot and spicy
Recado – A sauce for meat made from garlic,
  tomato and spices

Sweets

Crepas – Pancakes
Ensalada de Frutas – Fruit salad
Flan – Crème caramel
Helado – Ice cream

Plátanos al Horno – Baked plantains
Plátanos en Mole – Plantains in chocolate
  sauce

Glossary

Aguardiente - Raw alcohol made from sugar cane.

Aguas - Bottled fizzy drinks such as **Coca-Cola** or **Pepsi**.

Alcalde - Mayor.

Aldea - Small settlement.

Altiplano - The highlands of western Guatemala.

Atol - Drink usually made from maize dough, cooked with water, salt, sugar and milk. Can also be made from rice.

Ayuntamiento - Town hall.

Baleada - Stuffed tortilla street snack (Honduras only).

Barranca - Steep-sided ravine.

Barrio - Residential district.

Biotopo - Protected area of ecological interest, usually with limited tourist access.

Boca Costa - Western volcanic slopes of the Guatemalan highlands, prime coffee-growing country.

Brujo - Maya priest (or shaman) who can communicate with the spirit world.

Caldh - (Centre for Legal Action on Human Rights). Pressure group campaigning for justice on behalf of the victims of the civil war violence.

Calvario - Church, often with pagan religious traditions, always located on the western outskirts of a town; also known as the house of the ancestors.

Camioneta - Second-class, or "chicken" bus. In other parts of Latin America the same word means a small truck or van.

Campesino - Pressure group.

Cantina - Local hard-drinking bar.

Cayuco - Canoe.

Chapín - Nickname for a citizen of Guatemala.

Chicle - Sapodilla tree sap from which chewing gum is made.

Classic - Period during which ancient Maya civilization was at its height, usually given as 300–900 AD.

Codex - Maya manuscript made from the bark of the fig tree and written in hieroglyphs. Most were destroyed by the Spanish, but a copy of the Dresden Codex can be found in the Popol Vuh museum in Guatemala City (see p.79).

Cofradía - Religious brotherhood dedicated to the protection of a particular saint. These groups form the basis of religious and civil hierarchy in traditional highland society and combine Catholic and pagan practices.

Comedor - Basic Guatemalan restaurant, usually with just one or two things on the menu, and always the cheapest places to eat.

Conavigua - (National Coordination of Guatemalan Widows). Influencial, mainly indigenous pressure group.

Copal - Pine resin incense burned at religious ceremonies.

Corriente - Another name for a second-class bus.

Corte - Traditional Guatemalan skirt.

Costumbre - Guatemalan word for traditional customs of the highland Maya, usually of religious and cultural significance. The word often refers to traditions which owe more to paganism than to Catholicism; practitioners are called **costumbristas**.

Creole - Guatemalan of mixed Afro-Caribbean descent.

Cuadra - Street block.

CUC - (Committee of Peasant Unity).

Cusha - Home-brewed liquor.

Don/Doña - Sir/Madam. A term of respect mostly used to address a professional person or employer.

Efectivo - Cash.

EGP (Ejército Guerrillero de los Pobres) - (Guerrilla Army of the Poor). A Guatemalan guerrilla group that operated in the Ixil triangle and Ixcán areas.

Evangélico - Christian evangelist or fundamentalist, often missionaries. Name given to numerous Protestant sects seeking converts in Central America.

FAR (Fuerzas Armadas Rebeldes) - (Rebel Armed Forces). Guatemalan guerrilla group that was mainly active in Petén.

FDNG (Frente Democrático Nueva Guatemala) - (New Guatemalan Democratic Front). Left-wing political party set up by ex-guerrilla groups.

Finca - Plantation-style farm.

FRG (Frente Republicano Guatemalteco) - (Guatemalan Republican Front). Right-wing political party of Ríos Montt and Alfonso Portillo, currently in power.

GAM - (Mutual Support Group). Pressure group campaigning for justice for the families of the "disappeared".

Garífuna - Black Carib with a unique language and strong African heritage living in Lívingston and villages along the Caribbean coast between Belize and Nicaragua. See p.398.

Gringo/gringa - Any white-skinned foreigner, not necessarily a term of abuse.

Hospedaje - Another name for a small basic hotel.

Huipil - Woman's traditional blouse, usually woven or embroidered.

Indígena - Indigenous person of Maya descent.

Indio - Racially abusive term to describe someone of Maya descent. The word indito is equally offensive.

Inguat - Guatemalan tourist board.

I.V.A. - Guatemalan sales tax of twelve percent.

Ixil - Highland tribe grouped around the three towns of the Ixil triangle – Nebaj, Chajul and San Juan Cotzal.

Kaqchikel - (Also spelt "Cakchiquel"). Indigenous highland tribe occupying an area between Guatemala City and Lake Atitlán.

K'iche' - (Also spelt "Quiché"). Largest of the highland Maya tribes, centred on the town of Santa Cruz del Quiché.

Ladino - A vague term – at its most specific defining someone of mixed Spanish and Maya blood, but more commonly used to describe a person of "Western" culture, or one who dresses in "Western" style, be they pure Maya or of mixed blood.

Legua - The distance walked in an hour, used extensively in the highlands.

Leng - Slang for centavo.

Mam - Maya tribe occupying the west of the western highlands, the area around Huehuetenango.

Mariachi - Mexican musical style popular in Guatemala.

Marimba - Xylophone-like instrument used in traditional Guatemalan music.

Maya - General term for the large tribal group who inhabited Guatemala, southern Mexico, Belize, western Honduras and a slice of El Salvador since the earliest times, and still do.

Mestizo - Person of mixed native and Spanish blood, more commonly used in Mexico.

Metate - Flat stone for grinding maize into flour.

Milpa - Maize field, usually cleared by slash-and-burn.

Minugua - United Nations mission, in Guatemala to oversee the peace process.

MLN (Movimiento de Liberacion Nacional) - (National Liberation Movement). Right-wing political party in Guatemala.

Natural - Another term for an indigenous person.

Palapa - Thatched palm-leaf hut.

PAN (Partido Avanzada Nacional) - (National Advancement Party). Right wing neo-liberal political party, currently in opposition.

Parque - Town's central plaza; or a park.

Pensión - Simple hotel.

PGT (Partido Guatemalteco de Trabajadores) - (Guatemalan Labour Party), also known as the Guatemalan Communist Party.

Pipil - Indigenous tribal group which occupied much of the Guatemalan Pacific coast at the time of the Conquest. Only their art survives, around the town of Santa Lucía Cotzumalguapa.

Pisto - Slang for cash.

Pullman - Fast and comfortable bus, usually an old Greyhound.

Punta rock - The music of the Garífuna.

Q'eqchi' - (Also spelt "Kekchi"). Maya tribal group based around Cobán, the Verapaz highlands, Lake Izabal and the Petén.

Remhi - The Catholic Church's Truth Commission, set up to investigate the civil war atrocities.

Sierra - Mountain range.

Tecún Umán - Last king of the K'iche' tribe, defeated in battle by Alvarado.

Telgua - Formerly state-owned, recently privatized national telecom company.

Tienda - Shop.

Típica - Clothes woven from multicoloured textiles, usually geared towards the Western customer.

Traje - Traditional Maya costume.

Tzute - Headcloth or scarf worn as a part of traditional Mayan costume.

Tz'utujil - Indigenous tribal group occupying the land to the south of Lake Atitlán.

URNG (Unidad Revolucionaria Nacional Guatemalteca) - (Guatemalan National

Revolutionary Unity); umbrella organization of the four former guerrilla groups, now disbanded.

USAC (Universidad de San Carlos) – (University of San Carlos). Guatemala's national university, formerly a hotbed of political activism.

Xate – Decorative palm leaves harvested in Petén for export to the US, to be used in flower arrangements.

Xela – Another name for the city of Quetzaltenango.

Maya architectural terms

Altar – Elaborately carved altars, often of a cylindrical design, were grouped round the fringes of the main plaza. Used to record historical events, they could have also functioned as sacrificial stones. See also **zoomorphs**.

Ball court – Narrow, stone-flagged rectangular court with banked sides where the Maya ball game was played. The courts symbolized a stage between the real and supernatural worlds and for the ball players it could be a game of life and death – losers were sometimes sacrificed.

Corbel arch – "False arch" where each stone slightly overlaps the one below. A relatively primitive technique which severely limits the width of doorways and interiors.

Glyph – Element in Maya writing, roughly the equivalent of a letter or phrase; used to record historical events. Some glyphs are phonetic, while others represent an entire description or concept as in Chinese characters. Dominant Classic and Postclassic sites had unique emblem glyphs; some like Copán and Tikal used several.

Lintel – Top block of stone or wood above a doorway or window, often carved to record important events and dates. Those from Yaxchilán (see p.367) are especially well executed.

Palace – Maya palaces occupied prominent locations near the ceremonial heart of the city, usually resting on low platforms, and almost certainly housed the royal elite. There are particularly striking palaces at Tikal and Cancuén.

Postclassic – Period between the decline of Maya civilization and the arrival of the Spanish, 900–1530 AD.

Preclassic – Archeological era preceding the blooming of Maya civilization, usually given as 1500 BC–300 AD.

Putún – Style dominant at Ceibal in central Petén (see p.359), exhibiting strong Mexican characteristics.

Roof comb – Decorative top crest on stone temples, possibly intended to enhance verticality. Originally painted in arresting colours and often framed by giant stucco figures.

Sacbé – Paved Maya road or raised causeway near the centre of Maya cities. Probably designed for ceremonial processions and to save rulers from sloshing through the lowland marshes. Sacbés were also trade routes and there are hundreds of kilometres still evident in northern Petén today.

Stela – Freestanding, often exquisitely carved, stone monument. Decorating major Maya sites, stelae fulfilled a sacred and political role commemorating historical events. Among the largest and most impressive are the ones at Quiriguá (see p.259) and Copán (see p.383).

Temple – Monumental stone structure of pivotal religious significance built in the ceremonial heart of a city, usually with a pyramid-shaped base and topped with a narrow room or two used for secretive ceremonies and bloody sacrifices. Those at Tikal (see p.340) and El Mirador (see p.356) reach over 60m.

Toltec – Style of the central Mexican tribal group who invaded parts of the Maya region.

Zoomorph – Spectacular stone altar intricately carved with animal images and glyphs; there are spectacular examples at Quiriguá (see p.259).

index

and small print

Index

Map entries are in colour

I

INDEX

Twenty Years of Rough Guides

In the summer of 1981, Mark Ellingham, Rough Guides' founder, knocked out the first guide on a typewriter, with a group of friends. Mark had been travelling in Greece after university, and couldn't find a guidebook that really answered his needs.There were heavyweight cultural guides on the one hand – good on museums and classical sites but not on beaches and tavernas – and on the other hand student manuals that were so caught up with how to save money that they lost sight of the country's significance beyond its role as a place for a cool vacation. None of the guides began to address Greece as a country, with its natural and human environment, its politics and its contemporary life.

Having no urgent reason to return home, Mark decided to write his own guide. It was a guide to Greece that tried to combine some erudition and insight with a thoroughly practical approach to travellers' needs. Scrupulously researched listings of places to stay, eat and drink were matched by careful attention to detail on everything from Homer to Greek music, from classical sites to national parks and from nude beaches to monasteries. Back in London, Mark and his friends got their Rough Guide accepted by a far-sighted commissioning editor at the publisher Routledge and it came out in 1982.

The Rough Guide to Greece was a student scheme that became a publishing phenomenon. The immediate success of the book – shortlisted for the Thomas Cook award – spawned a series that rapidly covered dozens of countries. The Rough Guides found a ready market among backpackers and budget travellers, but soon acquired a much broader readership that included older and less impecunious visitors. Readers relished the guides' wit and inquisitiveness as much as the enthusiastic, critical approach that acknowledges everyone wants value for money – but not at any price.

Rough Guides soon began supplementing the "rougher" information – the hostel and low-budget listings – with the kind of detail that independent-minded travellers on any budget might expect. These days, the guides – distributed worldwide by the Penguin group – include recommendations spanning the range from shoestring to luxury, and cover more than 200 destinations around the globe. Our growing team of authors, many of whom come to Rough Guides initially as outstandingly good letter-writers telling us about their travels, are spread all over the world, particularly in Europe, the USA and Australia. As well as the travel guides, Rough Guides publishes a series of dictionary phrasebooks covering two dozen major languages, an acclaimed series of music guides running the gamut from Classical to World Music, a series of music CDs in association with World Music Network, and a range of reference books on topics as diverse as the Internet, Pregnancy and Unexplained Phenomena. Visit **www.roughguides.com** to see what's cooking.

Rough Guide Credits

Text editors: Olivia Eccleshill and Ann-Marie Shaw
Series editor: Mark Ellingham
Editorial: Martin Dunford, Jonathan Buckley, Jo Mead, Kate Berens, Helena Smith, Judith Bamber, Orla Duane, Ruth Blackmore, Geoff Howard, Claire Saunders, Gavin Thomas, Alexander Mark Rogers, Polly Thomas, Joe Staines, Richard Lim, Duncan Clark, Peter Buckley, Lucy Ratcliffe, Clifton Wilkinson, Alison Murchie, Matthew Teller, Andrew Dickson (UK); Andrew Rosenberg, Stephen Timblin, Yuki Takagaki, Richard Koss, Hunter Slaton (US)
Production: Susanne Hillen, Andy Hilliard, Link Hall, Helen Prior, Julia Bovis, Michelle Draycott, Katie Pringle, Mike Hancock, Zoë

Nobes, Rachel Holmes, Andy Turner
Cartography: Melissa Baker, Maxine Repath, Ed Wright, Katie Lloyd-Jones
Picture research: Louise Boulton, Sharon Martins, Mark Thomas
Online: Kelly Cross, Anja Mutic-Blessing, Jennifer Gold, Audra Epstein, Suzanne Welles, Cree Lawson (US)
Finance: John Fisher, Gary Singh, Edward Downey, Mark Hall, Tim Bill
Marketing & Publicity: Richard Trillo, Niki Smith, David Wearn, Chloë Roberts, Demelza Dallow, Claire Southern (UK); Simon Carloss, David Wechsler, Kathleen Rushforth (US)
Administration: Tania Hummel, Julie Sanderson

Publishing Information

This second edition published January 2002 by **Rough Guides Ltd**,
62–70 Shorts Gardens, London WC2H 9AH
Penguin Putnam, Inc. 375 Hudson Street, NY 10014, USA
Distributed by the Penguin Group
Penguin Books Ltd,
80 Strand, London WC2R ORL
Penguin Putnam, Inc.
375 Hudson Street, NY 10014, USA
Penguin Books Australia Ltd,
487 Maroondah Highway, PO Box 257, Ringwood, Victoria 3134, Australia
Penguin Books Canada Ltd,
10 Alcorn Avenue, Toronto, Ontario, Canada M4V 1E4
Penguin Books (NZ) Ltd,
182–190 Wairau Road, Auckland 10, New Zealand
Typeset in Bembo and Helvetica to an original design by Henry Iles.

Printed in Italy by LegoPrint S.p.A

© Iain Stewart 2002

552pp includes index
A catalogue record for this book is available from the British Library

ISBN 1-85828-523-2

The publishers and authors have done their best to ensure the accuracy and currency of all the information in **The Rough Guide to Guatemala**, however, they can accept no responsibility for any loss, injury, or inconvenience sustained by any traveller as a result of information or advice contained in the guide.

Help us update

We've gone to a lot of effort to ensure that the second edition of **The Rough Guide to Guatemala** is accurate and up to date. However, things change – places get "discovered", opening hours are notoriously fickle, restaurants and rooms raise prices or lower standards. If you feel we've got it wrong or left something out, we'd like to know, and if you can remember the address, the price, the time, the phone number, so much the better.

We'll credit all contributions, and send a copy of the next edition (or any other Rough Guide if you prefer) for the best letters. Everyone who writes to us and isn't already a subscriber will receive a copy of our full-colour thrice-yearly newsletter. Please mark letters: **"Rough Guide Guatemala Update"** and send to: Rough Guides, 62–70 Shorts Gardens, London WC2H 9AH, or Rough Guides, 4th Floor, 345 Hudson St, New York, NY 10014. Or send an email to:
mail@roughguides.co.uk or
mail@roughguides.com

Acknowledgements

In **Guatemala**: thanks to Lorena Artola, all at Inguat (especially Sandra Monterroso and Migdalia), Tom Lingenfelter and Xelapages, Geo Mendoza at Monarcas, José and Lucky, Villa Sumaya, Defensores de la Naturaleza, the Proyecto Eco-Quetzal in Cobán, Phillipa Myers and the Rainbow team, Ileana, Deedle and Dave, and Fiona and Bruce for coming along for the ride.

In **Honduras**: Howard Rosenzweig and his family in Copán, the Posada Arco Iris, all at the Mango Inn and UDC, Don Pearly and all the Baymen crew in Guanaja and all at Honduras Tips and Honduras This Week.

In the **UK**: thanks to Olivia and Annie for a superb job, Peter Eltringham for his support and expertise, Kate Berens, all the Rough Guides production team, especially Andy Turner for typesetting, Mark Thomas for picture research, Maxine Repath and Katie Lloyd-Jones for cartography, and Susannah Wight for proofreading, Jamie Marshall and Maya in London, Casa Alianza, Amnesty International and all at the Guatemalan and Honduran embassies in London. Special thanks to Mark Whatmore for all his input on previous editions of this guide.

Readers' letters

Thanks to all the readers who took the trouble to write in with their comments and suggestions (and apologies to anyone whose name we've misspelt or omitted):

Karin Amna and Emil Olssen for the good cross border information, Kathleen Bennett, Martine Bruin, Roland Bueth, J Clark, Francis and Maite Coke, Jodi Coleman, S Crossland, Nancy Cushwa, Mark Danter, Niels de Greef, Alison and Dana Doncaster, Daniel Dreux, Frank Ebling, J W Flatt, Andrew Fleckner, Nathan Garneau, Ross and Anne Gelbspan, Mike Goss, John K Graham, Meredith Grant, Laura Hamilton, Matt Hartell, J Healy, Jean-François Héroux for the superb backroad detail, Alan Hickey, Camilla Hinde, Sunny Ho, Tahirah Johnson, Kristi L. Kilbourne and Jerónimo Villalta, Denise Koch, David Kuhn, Joanne Mixco, Toby Nortcliffe, Marc Overas, Zenia Paz, Monique Peeters, Dauphinot Piper, David Ponsford, Barbara Raunig and Alex Burdiak, Greg Rec, Sue Reinhart, Tammy Ridenour, Jeffrey Rollins, Louise Rothwell, Cathy and John Schieffelin, Terry Scott, Pietro Scozzari, Andrew Sheng, Donald Smith, Tony Smith, Jim Syms, Richard Thompson, Yolande Walschap, Andreas Wangsmo, Martin Wielens, Maria Yule, Kristen Zecchi, Sophie Zonnis, Arjan Zutt.

SMALL PRINT

Photo Credits

The ideas expressed in this code were developed by and for independent travellers.

Learn About The Country You're Visiting

Start enjoying your travels before you leave by tapping into as many sources of information as you can.

The Cost Of Your Holiday

Think about where your money goes - be fair and realistic about how cheaply you travel. Try and put money into local peoples' hands; drink local beer or fruit juice rather than imported brands and stay in locally owned accommodation. Haggle with humour and not aggressively. Pay what something is worth to you and remember how wealthy you are compared to local people.

Embrace The Local Culture

Open your mind to new cultures and traditions - it will transform your experience. Think carefully about what's appropriate in terms of your clothes and the way you behave. You'll earn respect and be more readily welcomed by local people. Respect local laws and attitudes towards drugs and alcohol that vary in different countries and communities. Think about the impact you could have on them.

Exploring The World – The Travellers' Code

Being sensitive to these ideas means getting more out of your travels - and giving more back to the people you meet and the places you visit.

Minimise Your Environmental Impact

Think about what happens to your rubbish - take biodegradable products and a water filter bottle. Be sensitive to limited resources like water, fuel and electricity. Help preserve local wildlife and habitats by respecting local rules and regulations, such as sticking to footpaths and not standing on coral.

Don't Rely On Guidebooks

Use your guidebook as a starting point, not the only source of information. Talk to local people, then discover your own adventure!

Be Discreet With Photography

Don't treat people as part of the landscape, they may not want their picture taken. Ask first and respect their wishes.

We work with people the world over to promote tourism that benefits their communities, but we can only carry on our work with the support of people like you. For membership details or to find out how to make your travels work for local people and the environment, visit our website.

www.tourismconcern.org.uk

TourismConcern
Campaigning for Ethical and Fairly Traded Tourism

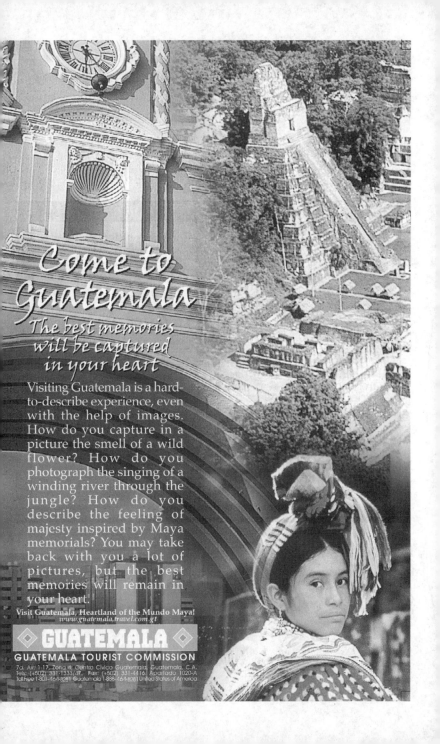

dramatically different
Mexico & Central America

Guatemala Mexico Honduras Belize
Costa Rica Panama Nicaragua El Salvador